Human Rights and the WTO

The Case of Patents and Access to Medicines

Human Rights and the WTO

The Case of Patents and Access to Medicines

The Case of Patents and Access to Medicines

HOLGER HESTERMEYER

OXFORD

UNIVERSITY PRESS

OXFORD
UNIVERSITY PRESS

Great Clarendon Street, Oxford OX2 6DP

Oxford University Press is a department of the University of Oxford.
It furthers the University's objective of excellence in research, scholarship,
and education by publishing worldwide in

Oxford New York

Auckland Cape Town Dar es Salaam Hong Kong Karachi
Kuala Lumpur Madrid Melbourne Mexico City Nairobi
New Delhi Shanghai Taipei Toronto

With offices in

Argentina Austria Brazil Chile Czech Republic France Greece
Guatemala Hungary Italy Japan Poland Portugal Singapore
South Korea Switzerland Thailand Turkey Ukraine Vietnam

Oxford is a registered trade mark of Oxford University Press
in the UK and in certain other countries

Published in the United States
by Oxford University Press Inc., New York

British Library Cataloguing in Publication Data

Data available

Library of Congress Cataloging in Publication Data

Hestermeyer, Holger.
Human rights and the WTO: the case of patents and access to
medicines / Holger Hestermeyer.
    p. cm.
Includes bibliographical references and index.
ISBN 978–0–19–921520–1
1. Human rights—Economic aspects.   2. World Trade Organization.
3. Patents (International law)   4. Drugs—Prices.   5. International trade—
Social aspects.   6. Social responsibility of business.   7. Right to health care.
I. Title.
K3240.H475 2007
346.04'86—dc22   2007015384

Typeset by Newgen Imaging Systems (P) Ltd., Chennai, India
Printed in Great Britain
on acid-free paper by
Biddles Ltd., King's Lynn

ISBN 978–0–19–921520–1

1 3 5 7 9 10 8 6 4 2

Meinen Eltern
In Dankbarkeit

Acknowledgements

This book has both enriched and challenged my life during the last few years. It has accompanied me from my first steps at Heidelberg's Max Planck Institute for Comparative Public Law and International Law, throughout a visiting scholarship at UC Berkeley and throughout my clerkships in Hamburg and Berlin. In February 2006 it was accepted as a doctoral thesis at the University of Hamburg. Since then the book has been updated to include more recent developments, most importantly the December 2005 decision to amend the TRIPS Agreement that could not be included in the doctoral thesis, as it was handed in before that date.

It is a time-honored tradition to take this opportunity to thank those people who have assisted the work with their advice, their kind words, their support, and their patience. First and foremost I would like to thank my parents and my brother who over the years have given me an unparalleled amount of love, patience, and encouragement. I owe a special thanks to my mother who supported me and my work on the thesis in a myriad of ways.

At every step of the way I had the pleasure, honour and privilege of meeting people who have had a considerable influence on both this work and my way of thinking. Prof Dr Wolfrum supervised the thesis, granting me both the freedom I needed to develop my thoughts and the prodding I needed to put them on paper. For this and for the years of support and trust in me he deserves my heartfelt thanks. I would also like to thank Prof Dr Oeter for acting as a second reviewer. Prof Mark Lemley and Prof Jim Gordley introduced me to American thinking on the law and American patent law and discussed issues selflessly both during my year as an LL.M. student and two years later as a visiting scholar at UC Berkeley.

Many scholars and friends allowed me to benefit from their comments and advice. Prof Dr Eibe Riedel, the German member of the Committee on Economic, Social and Cultural Rights, shared his insights into the right to health. Prof Paul Volberding of UCSF let me benefit from his unparalleled knowledge on AIDS and its treatment. Maria Pogisho of the Patents, Trade Marks, Companies and Close Corporation Registration office of the Namibian Ministry of Trade and Industry gave me a better understanding of the situation of patent offices in developing countries. Andy Grotto, Prof Dr Anne van Aaken, Dr Christiane Philipp, Dr Karen Kaiser, Dr Nicola Wenzel, Prof Paul Volberding, Stan Karas, and Prof Dr Stefan Voigt as well as anonymous reviewers read parts of the draft and suggested improvements. Another invaluable interlocutor in numerous legal discussions was Christoph Baum.

I could not have tackled an endeavour like this one without the support of wonderful friends who were there for me when I needed them and tolerated stretches of silence that were far too long. To them I extend a cordial thank you.

The work also owes great debt to several institutions. The German National Merit Foundation (Studienstiftung des deutschen Volkes) supported my research both in Germany and in the United States with a doctoral fellowship that gave me financial independence. The Max Planck Institute for Intellectual Property, Competition and Tax Law in Munich, the Max Planck Institute for Comparative and International Private Law in Hamburg, UC Berkeley, Stanford and, most of all, Heidelberg's Max Planck Institute for Comparative Public Law and International Law allowed me to use their libraries. The latter institution in particular has become an intellectual home.

Finally, I would like to thank the people at Oxford University Press, in particular John Louth, Cheryl Prophett, Rebecca Smith, and Fiona Stables for their kind and efficient help. They guided a young author safely through the shallows of publishing his first book.

Summary Contents

Table of Cases (Selection)	xvii
Table of Laws and Treaties (Selection)	xxii
List of Abbreviations	xxvii
Introduction	xxxiii
1. Background of the Debate	1
2. Patent Law	18
3. Access to Medicine as a Human Right	76
4. Conflict between Patents and Access to Medicine	137
5. Access to Medicine as a Human Right in the WTO Order	207
Annex 1: Summary of Arguments	293
Annex 2: States and their Membership in Relevant Organizations and Agreements	303
Annex 3: WTO Disputes on the TRIPS Agreement	308
Bibliography	312
Index	361

Detailed Contents

Table of Cases (Selection)	xvii
Table of Laws and Treaties (Selection)	xxii
List of Abbreviations	xxvii
Introduction	xxxiii

1.	**Background of the Debate**	1
I	Finding a Cure for a New Disease	2
II	BW's Decision on AZT Pricing Causes Outrage	5
III	The HIV/AIDS Pandemic Today	6
IV	The TRIPS Agreement and Access to Medicine: The South African Medicines Act	11
V	Beyond AIDS Drugs: Anthrax and Cipro	15
2.	**Patent Law**	18
I	A Short Primer on Patents	19
II	The History of Patent Law	20
	1 Patent Privileges	21
	2 The First Patent Acts	22
	3 The 19th Century	27
	4 The Patentability of Pharmaceutical Products	28
III	Rationales of Patent Law	29
	1 Natural Law Rationale	29
	2 Contract Rationale	30
	3 Reward Rationale	31
	4 Incentive Rationale	31
	5 Prospect Theory	32
IV	International Patent Law	33
	1 International Patent Law before the TRIPS Agreement	34
	2 Shortcomings of the Traditional System	36
	3 The North-South Divide: Arguments for and against Stronger Patent Protection	37
	4 Unilateral Pressure on Developing Countries	39
	5 The WTO/GATT setting	41
	A Background: The GATT	41
	B Intellectual Property in the GATT	43
	C The Uruguay Round	44
	D Validity of the TRIPS Agreement	48

V TRIPS Agreement Patent Standards   49
  1 Interpretation in Light of the Object and Purpose of the
    TRIPS Agreement   50
  2 Basic Principles of the TRIPS Agreement   51
  3 Conditions of Patentability   53
    A Patentable Subject Matter   53
      a Inventions   54
      b All Fields of Technology, Exceptions, Non-Discrimination   55
        aa All Fields of Technology   55
        bb Exceptions for Pharmaceuticals?   56
        cc Non-Discrimination   59
        dd The Drug Approval Process: Patent Law Implications   60
      c Product and Process Patents   64
    B Novelty   65
    C Inventive Step   66
    D Capability of Industrial Application   66
    E Disclosure   67
  4 Rights Conferred   67
  5 Transitional Arrangements   70
  6 Conclusion on Patent Law   75

3. Access to Medicine as a Human Right   76

  I Background   79
    1 International Human Rights   79
    2 Health and Human Rights   83
    3 Intellectual Property and Human Rights   84
  II The Interpretation of Human Rights Conventions   85
  III Justiciability   86
    1 Terminology   87
    2 Economic, Social, and Cultural Rights as Justiciable Rights   89
  IV Who is Bound by International Human Rights Law?   94
    1 Human Rights Obligations of Corporations   94
    2 Human Rights Obligations of International Organizations   99
  V Conventions   102
    1 ICESCR   102
      A Access to Medicine as Part of the Right to Health   102
        a Content of the Right   103
        b Duties imposed on States Parties   107
          aa Obligation to Respect   108
          bb Obligation to Protect   109
          cc Obligation to Fulfil   110
          dd Justifying Non-Compliance with Lack of
              Financial Means   110
      B Enjoyment of the Benefits of Scientific Progress   112
    2 The WHO   112
    3 ICCPR   115

A Content of the Right   115
B Duties Imposed on States Parties   118
4 Universal Declaration of Human Rights   119
5 Other Agreements   121
VI General International Law   121
1 Customary International Law   122
A Treaties and Customary International Law   122
B State Practice   123
C *Opinio juris*   133
2 General Principles   134
VII Conclusion on Human Rights   136

4. **Conflict between Patents and Access to Medicine**   137

I   Interference of Patents with Access to Medicine due to Price Effects   138
1 Microeconomic Theory   138
A Competitive Market   138
B Monopoly Pricing   142
C Patents as Monopolies—other Pricing Factors   144
D Pricing in Developing Countries   146
2 Empirical Studies and Extrapolations   148
3 Severity of the Access Impact   150
II   Justification of the Interference   152
1 Protection of the Inventor's Material Interests   153
A Author—Scope *ratione personae*   154
B Interests of Inventors—Scope *ratione materiae*   155
C Moral and Material Interests   157
D The Right in the Conflict with Access to Medicine   157
2 Justification as an Incentive for Future Research   158
III Effects on Third Parties: Duty to Cooperate   166
IV   A Conflict between the Patent and the Human Rights Regime?   169
1 Conflict of International Legal Regimes: Terminology   170
A Fragmentation of International Law   170
B International Legal Regimes   172
C Conflict   173
a Definition of Conflict   174
b Typologies of Conflicts   179
2 Conflict of International Legal Regimes: Towards Hierarchy?   182
A Law of Coexistence and Reciprocity—A Law without Hierarchy   182
B Law of Cooperation and Community Interests—Hierarchy in
International Law   185
a *Erga Omnes* Obligations—Integral Treaties   187
b *Jus cogens*   190
c Non-consenting States and Community Interests   192
C Institutionalization, Factual Hierarchy   193
D 'Soft-enforced' Human Rights Meet 'Hard-enforced' WTO   197

	a The WTO Regime	197
	aa Normative Hierarchy: An Instrumental Order of the Bilateral or Integral Type?	197
	bb The WTO in the Factual Hierarchy of Regimes: A Powerhouse	199
	cc The WTO and Regime Conflict	200
	b The Human Rights Regime	203
	aa Normative Hierarchy: Law of Values	203
	bb Factual Hierarchy: Soft Enforcement	205
	cc Human Rights and Regime Conflict	205
	c Perplexity	206

5. Access to Medicine as a Human Right in the WTO Order   207

I   Access to Medicine as a Human Right within WTO Dispute Settlement   208

   1 Five Models for the Use of Non-WTO Law in WTO Dispute Settlement   209

   2 The WTO: A Self-contained Regime?   210

   3 Jurisdiction   212

    A Violation Complaints   213

    B Non-Violation Complaints   213

    C *De Lege Ferenda*   214

   4 Applicable Law   215

    A Examples of Provisions   215

    B Article 7 of the DSU   216

    C Article 11 of the DSU   218

    D Article 3.2 of the DSU   218

     a The Function of Article 3.2 of the DSU   218

     b The Approach Prescribed by the DSU: Use of International Law for Interpretation   219

     c Interpretation in Light of the Object and Purpose   222

   5 Jurisprudence on Non-WTO Law in WTO Dispute Settlement   223

    A Treaties   223

    B General International Law   226

   6 Access to Medicine as *jus cogens* within WTO Dispute Settlement?   229

II   TRIPS Agreement Flexibilities in the Light of Human Rights   229

   1 Parallel Imports   230

    A No International Exhaustion   232

    B Mandatory International Exhaustion   232

    C The Choice is Left to Members   233

   2 Limited Exceptions   234

    A Limited   235

    B Conflict with Normal Exploitation   236

    C Prejudice Legitimate Interests   236

    D Article 27 of the TRIPS Agreement and Its Scope   237

    E Examples of Measures under Article 30 of the TRIPS Agreement   238

3 Compulsory Licences 239
A Grounds for Granting Compulsory Licences 241
  a Local Working Requirements and Article 27 of the
    TRIPS Agreement 242
  b Commonly Suggested Grounds 244
B Procedure of the Grant 245
  a Authorization on Individual Merits 245
  b Prior Negotiations 245
    aa The Requirement of Prior Negotiations 246
    bb Waiver of the Requirement 246
  c Adequate Remuneration 247
  d Review of the Decisions 249
C Scope of the Rights under Compulsory Licences 249
  a Limited by the Purpose 250
  b Non-exclusive, Non-assignable 250
  c Territoriality 250
    aa Interpretation of the Provision 251
    bb Options for Members Lacking Pharmaceutical
      Manufacturing Capacity 251
D Conclusion as to Compulsory Licences 253
4 Revocation of Patents 253
5 Conclusion 255
III WTO Decisions to Remedy Insufficiencies 255
1 The Doha Declaration 256
A Negotiating History 256
B Content of the Decision 257
C Evaluation 261
2 The Decision of 30 August 2003 261
A Negotiating History 262
B Content of the Decision 264
  a Product Scope of the Decision 265
  b Country Scope 265
  c Waiver of Article 31(f) of the TRIPS Agreement 266
    aa Notification by Importing Member 267
    bb Conditions of Compulsory Licence Granted by
      Exporting Member 267
    cc Notification by Exporting Member 268
  d Waiver of Article 31(f) of the TRIPS Agreement within
    Regional Trade Agreements 268
  e Waiver of Article 31(h) of the TRIPS Agreement 269
  f Further Safeguards against Trade Diversion 269
  g Technicalities 270
C Implementation 270
D Evaluation 271
3 Amendment of the TRIPS Agreement 272
A Negotiating History 272

B   Content of the Decision   274
C   Evaluation   275
4 The Legal Status of the Decisions: Flexibility in Decision-Making   276
A   Background: Decision-Making in the WTO   276
B   The Doha Declaration   279
C   The Decision of 30 August 2003   282
D   The Amendment of the TRIPS Agreement   286
5 Conclusion   286
IV Towards Solving the Conflict   287
1 Possible Solutions   287
2 Challenges Ahead: FTAs and BITs   289
A   Free Trade Agreements   289
B   Bilateral Investment Treaties   291
C   Conclusion   292

Annex 1: Summary of Arguments   293
Annex 2: States and their Membership in Relevant Organizations
           and Agreements   303
Annex 3: WTO Disputes on the TRIPS Agreement   308

Bibliography   312
Index   361

Table of Cases (Selection)

PCIJ / ICJ

The SS 'Wimbledon', PCIJ Rep 1923, Ser A, No 1 211

The Case of the SS 'Lotus', PCIJ Rep 1927, Ser A, No 10 .... 122, 133

Jurisdiction of the Courts of Danzig, Advisory Opinion, PCIJ Rep 1928, Ser B, No 15 80

Customs Régime between Germany and Austria, Advisory Opinion, PCIJ Rep 1931,
Ser A/B, No 41 189

Lighthouse Case between France and Greece, PCIJ Rep 1934, Ser A/B, No 62 175–6

The Oscar Chinn Case, PCIJ Rep 1934, Ser A/B, No 63 189

Corfu Channel Case, Judgment of 9 April 1949, ICJ Rep 1949, 4......................... 135

Reparation for Injuries Suffered in the Service of the United Nations, Advisory Opinion,
ICJ Rep 1949, 174 100

Interpretation of Peace Treaties, Advisory Opinion, ICJ Rep 1950, 65 135

Colombian-Peruvian Asylum Case, Judgment of 20 November 1950, ICJ Rep 1950, 266...... 121

Reservations to the Convention on Genocide, Advisory Opinion, ICJ Rep 1951, 15 ...... 135, 189

Fisheries Case, Judgment of 18 December 1951, ICJ Rep 1951, 116 121

Case Concerning Rights of Nationals of the United States of America in Morocco,
Judgment of 27 August 1952, ICJ Rep 1952, 176 .... 113, 123

Case Concerning Right of Passage over Indian Territory (Preliminary Objections),
Judgment of 26 November 1957, ICJ Rep 1957, 125.............................. 178

Case Concerning the Temple of Preah Vihear (Cambodia v Thailand), Merits,
Judgment of 15 June 1962, ICJ Rep 1962, 6 122

South West Africa, Second Phase, Judgment, ICJ Rep 1966, 6........................... 123

North Sea Continental Shelf, Judgment, ICJ Rep 1969, 3 .... 122–3, 125, 133, 191

Barcelona Traction, Light and Power Company, Limited, Judgment, ICJ Rep 1970, 3 187–8

Legal Consequences for States of the Continued Presence of South Africa in Namibia
(South West Africa) notwithstanding Security Council Resolution 276 (1970),
Advisory Opinion, ICJ Rep 1971, 16 .... 122, 175–6, 277

Aegean Sea Continental Shelf, Judgment, ICJ Rep 1978, 3.............................. 175

United States Diplomatic and Consular Staff in Tehran, Judgment,
ICJ Rep 1980, 3.. 37, 120, 122, 211

Military and Paramilitary Activities in and against Nicaragua (Nicaragua v United States of
America), Merits, Judgment, ICJ Rep 1986, 14 .... 37, 122, 127, 191, 194

Territorial Dispute (Libyan Arab Jamahiriya/Chad), Judgment, ICJ Rep 1994, 6.......... 85, 175

East Timor (Portugal v Australia), Judgment, ICJ Rep 1995, 90.......................... 188

Legality of the Use by a State of Nuclear Weapons in Armed Conflict, Advisory Opinion,
ICJ Rep 1996, 66 114

Legality of the Threat or Use of Nuclear Weapons, Advisory Opinion, ICJ Rep 1996, 226...... 191

Gabčíkovo-Nagymaros Project (Hungary/Slovakia), Judgment, ICJ Rep 1997, 7.......... 85, 277

LaGrand (Germany v United States of America), Judgment, ICJ Rep 2001, 466............... 88

Avena and Other Mexican Nationals (Mexico v United States of America), Judgment,
ICJ Rep 2004, 12... 88

Legal Consequences of the Construction of a Wall in the Occupied Palestinian Territory, Advisory
Opinion, ICJ Rep 2004, 136 93

WTO APPELLATE BODY

US—Gasoline, WT/DS2/AB/R (1996) 175–6, 201, 212, 223, 227
Japan—Alcoholic Beverages, WT/DS8, 10, 11/AB/R (1996) 175–6, 220
Australia—Salmon, WT/DS18/AB/R (1998) 202
Brazil—Desiccated Coconut, WT/DS22/AB/R (1997) 225
EC—Hormones, WT/DS26, 48/AB/R (1998) 225–7, 236
EC—Bananas, WT/DS27/AB/R (1997) 224, 227
Canada—Periodicals, WT/DS31/AB/R (1997) 178
US—Shirts and Blouses, WT/DS33/AB/R (1997) 228
India—Mailbox, WT/DS50/AB/R (1997) 56, 73–4
Argentina—Textiles and Apparel, WT/DS56/AB/R (1998) 225
US—Shrimp, WT/DS58/AB/R (1998) 202, 224
Guatemala—Cement (I), WT/DS60/AB/R (1998) 177–8
EC—Computer Equipment, WT/DS62, 67, 68/AB/R (1998) 223–4
EC—Poultry, WT/DS69/AB/R (1998) 225–6
Korea—Dairy Safeguards, WT/DS98/AB/R (1999) 175–6, 178, 227
Canada—Milk/Dairy, WT/DS103, 113/AB/R (1999) 175–6, 227
US—FSCs, WT/DS108/AB/R (2000) 227
Argentina—Footwear, WT/DS121/AB/R (1999) 175–6, 178
Mexico –HFCS (21.5), WT/DS132/AB/RW (2001) 227
EC—Asbestos, WT/DS135/AB/R (2001) 56–7, 175–6, 202, 214, 227
Canada—Patent Term, WT/DS170/AB/R (2000) 54, 69, 225–6
US—Japan Hot-Rolled Steel, WT/DS184/AB/R (2001) 227
US—Cotton Yarn, WT/DS192/AB/R (2001) 227
US—Line Pipe Safeguards, WT/DS202/AB/R (2002) 227
EC—Sardines, WT/DS231/AB/R (2002) 225–6
EC—Tariff Preferences, WT/DS246/AB/R (2004) 227
US—Steel Safeguards, WT/DS248, 249, 251, 252, 253, 254, 258, 259/AB/R (2003) 178
US—Softwood Lumber IV, WT/DS257/AB/R (2004) 220
US—Softwood Lumber V, WT/DS264/AB/R (2004) 220
US—Upland Cotton Subsidies, WT/DS267/AB/R (2005) 177
Dominican Republic—Cigarettes, WT/DS302/AB/R (2005) 56

WTO PANELS

EC—Bananas, WT/DS27/R/USA (1997) 177–8
Turkey—Textiles, WT/DS34/R (1999) 177
Japan—Film, WT/DS44/R (1998) 226
India—Mailbox, WT/DS50/R (1997) 56, 73–4
Indonesia—Automobiles, WT/DS54, 55, 59, 64/R (1998) 71, 177, 219
Canada—Aircraft, WT/DS70/R (1999) 225–6
India—Patents (EC), WT/DS79/R (1998) 74
Canada—Patent, WT/DS114/R (2000) 51, 59–60, 235–9, 243, 252
Argentina—Footwear, WT/DS121/R (1999) 219–20, 227
US—Anti-Dumping Act of 1916, WT/DS136/R (2000) 227
India—Autos, WT/DS146, 175/R (2001) 219–20
US—Sections 301, WT/DS152/R (1999) 41
Guatemala—Cement (II), WT/DS156/R (2000) 227–8
US—Copyright Act, WT/DS160/R (2000) 178, 226, 235

US—Anti-Dumpting Act of 1916 (complaint by Japan), WT/DS162/R (2000)..............178
Korea—Government Procurement, WT/DS163/R (2000)......................214, 216, 228
Canada—Patent Term, WT/DS170/R (2000) 178, 219–20
US—Lamb Safeguards, WT/DS177, 178/R (2000) 227
Argentina—Poultry, WT/DS241/R (2003) 195
EC—Sugar Subsidies. Complaint by Thailand, WT/DS283/R (2004).....................224
Dominican Republic—Cigarettes, WT/DS302/R (2004) 225
EC—Biotech, WT/DS291/R (2006) 220, 224–5, 227

WTO ARBITRATION (ART 22.6 DSU / 4.11 SCM AGREEMENT)

EC –Hormones, WT/DS26/ARB (1999)..226
EC—Bananas, WT/DS27/ARB/ECU (2000) 45
Brazil—Export Financing Programme for Aircraft, WT/DS46/ARB (2000) 227

GATT

US—Section 337 of the Tariff Act of 1930, L/6439—36S/345 (1989) 41, 43, 56, 202
Thailand—Cigarettes, DS10/R—37S/200 (1990)................................56, 201–2
Canada—EC—Article XXVIII Rights, DS12/R (1990)..................................213
US—Tuna I, DS21/R—39S/155 (1991) (not adopted) 201
US—Tuna II, DS29/R (1994) (not adopted) 201, 223–4
EC—Imposition of Anti-Dumping Duties on Imports of Cotton Yarn from Brazil,
    ADP/137 (1995)...226

ECJ

C-16/74, Centrafarm BV v Winthrop BV [1974] ECR 1183.............................233
C-10/89, SA CNL-Sucal NV v HAG GF AG [1990] ECR I-3711 233
C-9/93, IHT Internationale Heiztechnik v Ideal-Standard [1994] ECR I-2789 233
C-267/95, C-268/95, Merck & Co Inc v Primecrown Ltd [1996] ECR I-6285...............233
C-355/96, Silhouette International Schmied GmbH & Co KG v Hartlauer
    Handelsgesellschaft mbH [1998] ECR I-4799 234
C-173/98, Sebago Inc v G-B Unic SA [1999] ECR I-4103.............................234
C-459/03, Commission v Ireland, [2006] ECR I-4635................................195

HUMAN RIGHTS COMMITTEE

Guillermo Ignacio Dermit Barbato and Hugo Haroldo Dermit Barbato v Uruguay,
    Communication No 84/1981, UN Doc A/38/40 (1983), in Yearbook of the
    Human Rights Committee 1983–1984. Volume I, 419, 488 118–119
Herrera Rubio v Colombia, Communication No 161/1983, in Yearbook of the
    Human Rights Committee 1987–1988. Volume II, 430.......................118–119
W Delgado Páez v Colombia, Communication No 195/1985, in Yearbook of the
    Human Rights Committee 1989–1990. Volume II, 396 118
Nydia Bautista de Arellana v Colombia, Communication No 563/1993, in UN GAOR,
    51st Sess, Supp No 40, at 132, UN Doc A/51/40, at para 8.3 (1997)...................119
Dimitry L Gridin v Russian Federation, Communication No 770, UN Doc
    CCPR/C/69/D/770/1997 at para 8.2 (2000) 90

EUROPEAN COURT OF HUMAN RIGHTS

Marckx v Belgium, 31 Eur CtHR (ser A) (13 June 1979) 90
Airey v Ireland, 32 Eur CtHR (ser A) (9 October 1979) 90
Loizidou v Turkey, Preliminary Objections, 310 Eur CtHR (ser A) (23 March 1995) 194
D v United Kingdom, 24 EHRR 423 (1997) (2 May 1997) 129

EUROPEAN COMMISSION OF HUMAN RIGHTS

X v Ireland, Application N° 6839/74, 7 DR 78 (1976) 117
X v United Kingdom, Application N° 7154/75, 14 DR 31 (1978) 117
Smith Kline and French Laboratories Ltd v Netherlands, Application N° 12633/87,
    66 DR 70, 79 (1990) 158
Lenzing AG v United Kingdom, Application N° 38817/97, 94-A DR 136 (1998) 100

OTHER INTERNATIONAL COURTS AND TRIBUNALS

African Commission on Human and Peoples' Rights, Social and Economic Rights Action Centre
    and the Centre for Economic and Social Rights v Nigeria, Communication No 155/1996,
    ACHPR/COMM/A044/1, paras 53 f (27 May 2002)..................... 93–5, 108, 117
Communidad Andina, Tribunal de Justicia, Proceso 89-AI-2000 (2001) 65
ICTY, Prosecutor v Duško Tadić, Appeals Chamber, Judgment, Case No IT-94-1-A
    (15 July 1999) 194
Inter-American Commission on Human Rights, Jorge Odir Miranda Cortez et al v El Salvador,
    Inter-American Commission on Human Rights Report N° 29/01. Case 12.249
    (7 March 2001)... 105, 117
Inter-American Court of Human Rights, Villagrán Morales v Guatemala (Caso de los
    'niños de la calle'), 1999 Inter-Am CtHR (Ser C) No 63 (19 November 1999) 117
ITLOS, Case concerning the Conservation and Sustainable Exploitation of Swordfish Stocks in the
    South-Eastern Pacific Ocean (Chile v EC), Case No 7 195
ITLOS, The MOX Plant Case (Ireland v UK), Case No 10 195
MERCOSUR, Laudo IV—Pollos—de Brasil a Argentina (2001) 195
MERCOSUR, Tribunal Permanente de Revisión, Laudo N° 1/2005 215
Permanent Court of Arbitration, The MOX Plant Case (Ireland v United Kingdom) 195
Permanent Court of Arbitration, Dispute Concerning Access to Information under Article 9 of the
    OSPAR Convention (Ireland v United Kingdom) 195

DOMESTIC: SOUTH AFRICA

Certification of the Constitution of the Republic of South Africa, 1996 (4) SA 744 (CC); 1996 (10)
    BCLR 1253 (CC) (Constitutional Court, 1996)...................................... 92
Soobramoney v Minister of Health, KwaZulu-Natal, 1998 (1) SA 765 (CC); 1997 (12)
    BCLR 1696 (CC) (Constitutional Court, 1997)..................................... 111
Government of the Republic of South Africa and Others v Grootboom and Others 2001 (1)
    SA 46 (CC); 2000 (11) BCLR 1169 (CC) (Constitutional Court, 2000)......... 92, 94, 107
Minister of Health et al v Treatment Action Campaign et al 2002 (5) SA 721 (CC); 2002
    (10 BCLR 1033 (CC) (Constitutional Court, 2002) 92, 104, 111–12
Pharmaceutical Manufacturers' Association of South Africa et al v President of the
    Republic of South Africa, Case No 4183/98 (High Court of South Africa
    (Transvaal Provincial Division)) 11–15, 232, 255–6, 286

DOMESTIC: UNITED STATES OF AMERICA

Grant v Raymond, 31 US 218 (1832) 26
Funk Bros Seed v Kalo Inoculant Co, 333 US 127 (1948) 54
Shelley v Kraemer, 334 US 1 (1948) 98
Graham v John Deere Co, 383 US 1 (1966) 66
Brenner v Manson, 383 US 519 (1966) 31, 67
Kewanee Oil Co v Bicron Corp et al, 416 US 370 (1974) 30
Diamond v Chakrabarty, 447 US 303 (1980).. 54
Nixon v United States, 506 US 224 (1993).. 87
Novopharm, Inc v Burroughs Wellcome Co, 516 US 1071 (1996) 6
JEM AG Supply, Inc v Pioneer Hi-Bred Int'l, Inc, 534 US 124 (2001) 30
Sosa v Alvarez-Machain et al, 542 US 692 (2004) 97
Parke-Davis & Co v HK Mulford Co, 196 F 496 (2nd Cir 1912) 54
Filartiga v Pena-Irala, 630 F 2d 876 (2nd Cir 1980) 98, 129
Roche Products, Inc v Bolar Pharmaceutical Co, Inc, 733 F2d 858 (Fed Cir 1984) 61–62
Institut Pasteur v United States, 814 F2d 624 (Fed Cir 1987)............................. 3
Amgen Inc v Chugai Pharmaceutical Co, 927 F2d 1200 (Fed Cir 1991)..................... 55
Hilao et al v Estate of Marcos (In re Estate of Ferdinand Marcos, Human Rights Litigation),
    25 F3d 1467 (9th Cir 1994) 129
Burroughs Wellcome Co v Barr Laboratories, Inc et al, 40 F3d 1223 (Fed Cir 1994).......... 4, 6
Kadic v Karadzic, 70 F3d 232 (2nd Cir 1995) 97
Juicy Whip, Inc v Orange Bang, Inc, 185 F3rd 1364 (Fed Cir 1999)........................ 67
John Doe v Unocal Corporation, 2002 WL 31063976 (9th Cir 2002) 97
Flores et al v Southern Peru Copper Corporation, 343 F3d 140 (2nd Cir 2003) 127, 132

Table of Laws and Treaties (Selection)

African Charter on Human and Peoples' Rights
  (Banjul Charter)
  Art 4 . . . . 117, 121, 128
  Art 16 . . . . 94, 121
Agreement between the Government of the
  United States of America and the
  Government of the Kingdom of
  Bahrain on the Establishment of a Free
  Trade Area (US–Bahrain FTA)
  Art 14.9.1 290
Agreement between the United States of
  America and the Hashemite Kingdom
  of Jordan on the Establishment of a Free
  Trade Area (US–Jordan FTA)
  Art 4.20 290
Agreement Establishing the World Trade
  Organization (WTO Agreement)
  General 48, 78, 101
  Preamble 101
  Art III:2 281
  Art III:5 225
  Art IV:1 . . . . 276, 281
  Art IV:2 . . . . 276, 284
  Art IV:3 276
  Art IV:4 276
  Art IV:5 276
  Art IV:6 276
  Art IV:7 276
  Art IV:8 276
  Art V 288
  Art IX 279
  Art IX:1 . . . . 277–8, 280–2, 285
  Art IX:2 . . . . 218, 277, 279–81
  Art IX:3 . . . . 218, 278–9, 282–3
  Art IX:4 . . . . 270, 275, 278, 282–4
  Art X 218, 277, 282
  Art X:1 . . . . 278, 286
  Art X:2 278
  Art X:3 . . . . 274, 278, 286
  Art X:4 278
  Art X:6 278
  Art XI:2 72
  General Interpretative Note to
    Annex 1A 176

Agreement on Trade-Related Aspects of
  Intellectual Property Rights (TRIPS
  Agreement)
  Preamble 50, 78, 244
  Art 1.1 . . . . 48, 52
  Art 1.3 . . . . 198, 212
  Art 2.1 . . . . 52, 232, 241
  Art 2.2 52
  Art 3 . . . . 70, 72, 232
  Art 3.1 52
  Art 4 . . . . 52, 70, 72, 232, 259, 278
  Art 5 . . . . 70, 72
  Art 6 . . . . 8, 232–4, 259
  Art 7 . . . . 50–1, 57–8, 60, 101, 169,
                                            235–7, 244
  Art 8 . . . . 60, 235–7, 241
  Art 8.1 . . . . . 50–1, 57–8, 101, 169, 241, 258
  Art 8.2 . . . . 50–1, 58, 230
  Art 13 235
  Art 27 . . . . 13, 19, 53, 59–60,
                                     237–8, 243, 254
  Art 27.1 . . . . 54, 59, 64–6, 237–8, 242–3
  Art 27.2 . . . . 56, 64, 203
  Art 27.3 . . . . 57, 203
  Art 28 . . . . 67, 233, 235, 238, 249, 254
  Art 28.1 . . . . 59, 68, 232, 234, 249
  Art 28.2 67
  Art 29 254
  Art 29.1 67
  Art 30 . . . . 59, 229, 234–5, 237–40,
                                     243, 252, 263, 266
  Art 31 . . . . 229, 234, 237, 240–1, 243–4,
                                  249, 253, 273–4
  Art 31(a) 245
  Art 31(b) 244–6, 252
  Art 31(c) 241, 244, 250
  Art 31(d) 248, 250
  Art 31(e) 250
  Art 31(f) 132, 252, 262, 264, 266–8,
                                          274–5, 282–3
  Art 31(g) 250
  Art 31(h) 247, 269, 274–5, 282–3
  Art 31(i) 249
  Art 31(j) 249

Art 31(k) 244, 246, 250, 252
Art 31(l) 244
Art 31*bis* (not in force) 274
Art 31*bis* 1 (not in force) 274
Art 31*bis* 2 (not in force) 274
Art 31*bis* 3 (not in force) 274–5
Art 31*bis* 4 (not in force) 275
Art 31*bis* 5 (not in force) 275
Art 32 . . . . 229, 253–4
Art 33 . . . . 69, 73, 254
Art 34 . . . . 20, 68
Art 39.3 62
Art 40 230
Art 41 69
Art 42 . . . . 69, 245
Art 44 69
Art 44.2 247
Art 45 69
Art 50 69
Art 60 239
Art 62 245
Art 64 213
Art 65.1 . . . . 70, 72
Art 65.2 70
Art 65.3 70
Art 65.4 70
Art 65.5 70–2
Art 66.1 71–2
Art 66.2 . . . . 73, 244, 259
Art 70.6 243
Art 70.8 73–4
Art 70.9 73–5
Art 71.2 . . . . 276, 278
Art 73 . . . . 58–9, 203, 274, 289
Annex (not in force) 274
Annex para 1 (not in force) 275
Annex para 2 (not in force) 274
Annex para 3 (not in force) 275
Annex para 4 (not in force) 275
Annex para 5 (not in force) 275
Annex para 6 (not in force) 275
Annex para 7 (not in force) 275
Appendix to the Annex
   (not in force) 275
Doha Declaration 255–61, 263–5,
                        279–82, 286–7, 290
Decision of 30 August
   2003 . . . . 261–75, 282–6, 290
Amendment 272–6, 286, 290
American Convention on Human Rights

Art 4 . . . . 117, 121, 128
Art 26 105
Additional Protocol to the American
   Convention on Human Rights in
   the Area of Economic, Social
   and Cultural Rights 'Protocol
   of San Salvador',
   Art 10 . . . . 105, 121
American Declaration of the Rights and Duties
   of Man
   Art I 121, 128
   Art XIII 155, 158
Brazil
   Constituição Federal de 1988 (Constitution)
      Art 5 128
   Lei da Propriedade Industrial N 9.279 de 14
      de Maio de 1996
      Art 10 55
      Art 68 243
Charter of Fundamental Rights of the
   European Union (not in force)
   Art 2 . . . . 121, 128
   Art 17 158
   Art 35 121
Charter of the United Nations
   Preamble 81
   Art 1 . . . . 81, 167
   Art 2 184
   Art 10 120
   Art 11 120
   Art 12 120
   Art 13 . . . . 81, 120
   Art 14 120
   Art 55 . . . . 81, 120, 167, 204
   Art 56 . . . . 81, 120, 167, 204
   Art 57 84
   Art 62 81
   Art 68 . . . . 77, 81
   Art 94 37
   Art 96 114
   Art 103 . . . . 190, 204
Chile–United States Free Trade Agreement
   (US–Chile FTA)
   Art 17.1.5 291
   Art 17.10.2 290
Comunidad Andina (Andean Community)
   Decisión 486 Régimen Común sobre
      Propiedad Industrial
      Art 15 55
      Art 21 65

Constitution of the World Health Organization
(WHO Constitution)
   Preamble 84, 113–15
   Art 8 113
   Art 19 114
   Art 20 114
   Art 21 114
   Art 22 114
   Art 23 114–15
Convention (No 169) concerning Indigenous
and Tribal Peoples in Independent
Countries
   Art 25 121
Convention for the Protection of Human
Rights and Fundamental Freedoms
(European Convention on Human
Rights, ECHR)
   Art 2 . . . . 117, 121, 128
   Protocol to the Convention for the
   Protection of Human Rights and
   Fundamental Freedoms (Protocol 1),
   Art 1 158
Convention on the Elimination of All Forms of
Discrimination against Women
(CEDAW)
   Art 12 121
Convention on the Grant of European
Patents (European Patent
Convention, EPC)
   Art 52 . . . . 29, 54, 57
   Art 54 65
   Art 64 36
Convention on the Rights of the Child
   Art 6 128
   Art 24 121
The Dominican Republic–Central
America–United States Free Trade
Agreement (CAFTA-DR)
   Art 15.9.6 290
   Art 15.10.1 290
   Understanding regarding certain Public
   Health Measures 290
European Social Charter
   Art 11 121
France
   Code de la Propriété Intellectuelle
   Art L 611-10 29
   Art L 611-16 29
   Art L 613-16 245
The General Agreement on Tariffs and Trade
(GATT)

General 40, 42–9, 52, 201, 213, 221,
                223–5, 277–9, 284
   Art I 42, 238
   Art III. 42, 232, 238
   Art IX 43
   Art XI. 42, 197, 232
   Art XII. 43
   Art XV. 225
   Art XVIII 43, 71
   Art XIX 178
   Art XX. . . 43, 56, 201–3, 224, 232, 238, 258
   Art XXI 201
   Art XXII 213
   Art XXIII 42, 197, 213, 227, 266
   Art XXVIII 225
Germany
   Grundgesetz für die Bundesrepublik
     Deutschland (Constitution)
     Art 2 128
     Art 19 154–5
   Patentgesetz (Patent Act)
     § 1 54
     § 3 65
     § 5 . . . . 29, 57
     § 6 154
     § 24 244
India
   Constitution of India
     Art 21 128
International Convention on the
     Elimination of All Forms of Racial
     Discrimination
   Art 5 121
International Covenant on Civil and Political
     Rights (ICCPR)
   General. 82–3, 87, 89–93,
             115–19, 125–6, 153, 192
   Preamble 96
   Art 1 181
   Art 2 . . . . 96, 115
   Art 2(1) 115, 118
   Art 2(2) 115, 118
   Art 2(3). 97, 115
   Art 4 . . . . 116, 152–3
   Art 5(1). 96–7
   Art 6(1) 95, 115–19, 128, 152, 222
   Art 7 98
   Art 8(1) 95
   Art 11 92
   Art 12(1) 95
   Art 16 92

Optional Protocol to the International
Covenant on Civil and Political
Rights, Art 1 . . . . 87, 115
International Covenant on Economic, Social
and Cultural Rights (ICESCR)
General 82–4, 86–93, 102–12,
125–6, 153–5, 192–3
Preamble 96
Art 1 181
Art 2 . . . . 96, 103
Art 2(1) 89, 91, 102, 107–8, 167
Art 2(2) 108
Art 4 . . . . 138, 152–3
Art 6 93
Art 7 93
Art 10 93
Art 11 . . . . 93, 181
Art 12 . . . . . 93, 102–12, 113, 131, 167, 222
Art 12(1) 107
Art 12(2) 103–4
Art 13 . . . . 90, 93, 181
Art 14 . . . . 90, 93
Art 15(1)(a) 156, 158
Art 15(1)(b) 112, 156, 158
Art 15(1)(c) 84, 153–8
Art 15(2) 112, 153, 156, 158
Art 17 87
The International Law Commission's Draft
Articles on Responsibility of States
for Internationally Wrongful Acts
(not in force)
Art 48 188
Art 55 212
Paris Convention for the Protection of
Industrial Property
General 34, 36–7, 212–13
Art 1 35
Art 2 35
Art 3 35
Art 4 35
Art 4 *bis* 35, 232
Art 4 *ter* 35
Art 4 *quater* 35
Art 5A(1) 36
Art 5A(2) 35, 241–4
Art 5A(3) 35, 254
Art 5A(4) 35, 242
Art 5 *bis* 35
Art 15 35
Art 19 52
Art 28 37

South Africa
Constitution of South Africa
§ 11 128
Medicines and Related Substances Control Act
s 15 C 12–15, 232, 255–6
Statute of the International Court of Justice
Art 38 . . . . 79, 102, 121–2, 134, 215
Understanding on Rules and Procedures
Governing the Settlement of Disputes
(Dispute Settlement Understanding,
DSU)
Art 1 . . . . 213, 226
Art 1.1 213
Art 1.2 176–7
Art 2 226
Art 3.2 . . . . 209, 212, 218–23, 226, 228
Art 6 216
Art 6.2 178
Art 7 . . . . 217–9, 225–6
Art 7.1 216–17
Art 7.2 216
Art 7.3 . . . . 213, 216–17
Art 11 218
Art 13.1 288
Art 13.2 288
Art 19.2 . . . . 209, 218
Art 22 . . . . 45, 197, 199
Art 23.1 213
Appendix 1 213
United States of America
Alien Tort Statute
28 USC § 1350 97
Constitution of the United States of America
Art 1, section 8 cl 8 24
XIVth Amendment, section 1 128
Federal Food, Drug, and Cosmetic Act
21 USC § 321 61
21 USC § 355 61–3
21 USC § 360 63
Omnibus Trade and Competitiveness
Act of 1988 (Special 301) . . . 13, 15, 40
Patent Act
35 USC § 100 65
35 USC § 101 . . . . 28, 66–7
35 USC § 102 . . . . 66, 154
35 USC § 103 66
35 USC § 156 61–2
35 USC § 271 . . . . 62, 69
35 USC § 287 . . . . 29, 57
Tariff Act of 1930
Section 337 41

United States of America (*cont.*):
  Trade Act of 1974
    Section 301 . . . . 13, 15, 40, 49
United States–Australia Free Trade Agreement
  Art 17.9.1 290
  Art 17.9.4 290
United States–Morocco Free Trade Agreement
  Art 15.9.2 290
  Art 15.9.4 290
  Side Letter on Public Health 290
Universal Declaration of Human Rights
    (UDHR)
  General 81, 83, 96, 119–20,
                                          125–6, 156
  Preamble 96
  Art 3 . . . . 119, 128
  Art 22 119
  Art 25(1) 119
  Art 27(1) 119
  Art 27(2) 84, 153
  Art 29(1) 96
  Art 30 96
Vienna Convention on the Law of Treaties
  Art 2(1) 221
  Art 18 102
  Art 28 225–7
  Art 30 . . . . 185, 226

Art 30(2) 185
Art 30(3) 185, 226
Art 30(4) 179, 185
Art 31 . . . . 85, 220, 224, 226, 280, 285
Art 31(1) 50, 85, 91, 220–5
Art 31(2) 220–1, 264, 285–6
Art 31(3) 50, 86, 92, 220–2,
                                          224–5, 266, 281
Art 32 . . . . 85–6, 98, 220, 225–6,
                                          238, 280, 285
Art 33 85
Art 33(3) 85
Art 33(4) 85
Art 35 125
Art 38 123
Art 41 185
Art 41(1) 189
Art 43 122
Art 52 49
Art 53 . . . . 116, 190–1, 229
Art 59 185
Art 59(1) 226
Art 60 227
Art 65 191
Art 66 191
Art 67 191
Art 68 191

List of Abbreviations

ABC	American Broadcasting Company
ACT UP	AIDS Coalition to Unleash Power
AFDI	Annuaire français de droit international
AIDS	Acquired Immunodeficiency Syndrome
AIPLA QJ	American Intellectual Property Law Association Quarterly Journal
AJIL	American Journal of International Law
Am Bus L J	American Business Law Journal
Am Econ Rev	American Economic Review
Am J L & Medicine	American Journal of Law & Medicine
Am J of Bioethics	American Journal of Bioethics
Am U L Rev	American University Law Review
ANDA	Abbreviated new drug application
AÖR	Archiv des öffentlichen Rechts
APEC	Asia Pacific Economic Co-operation
ARIPO	African Regional Industrial Property Organization
ARSP	Archiv für Rechts- und Sozialphilosophie
Art	Article
ASEAN	Association of South-East Asian Nations
ASIL	American Society of International Law
Australian Y B Int'l L	Australian Yearbook of International Law
AVR	Archiv des Völkerrechts
AZT	azidothymidine
B U J Sci & Tech L	Boston University Journal of Science & Technology Law
BU Int'l L J	Boston University International Law Journal
BB	Betriebs-Berater
BBC	British Broadcasting Corporation
Berkeley Tech L J	Berkeley Technology Law Journal
BITs	bilateral investment treaties
Brook J Int'l L	Brooklyn Journal of International Law
Bull of Hum Rts	Bulletin of Human Rights
BW	Burroughs Wellcome
BYIL	British Yearbook of International Law
Cardozo J Int'l & Comp L	Cardozo Journal of International and Comparative Law
CDC	Centres for Disease Control
CEPR	Centre for Economic Policy Research
Chicago J Int'l L	Chicago Journal of International Law
CIA	Central Intelligence Agency
CITES	Convention on International Trade in Endangered Species of Wild Fauna and Flora
CMH	Commission on Macroeconomics and Health

Colum J Transnat'l L	Columbia Journal of Transnational Law
Conn J Int'l L	Connecticut Journal of International Law
Cornell Int'l L J	Cornell International Law Journal
DNA	deoxyribonucleic acid
DSU	Dispute Settlement Understanding
DVBl	Deutsches Verwaltungsblatt
E Afr J Peace & Hum. Rts.	East African Journal of Peace & Human Rights
eg	*exempli gratia* (for example)
EHRLR	European Human Rights Law Review
EC	European Community
ECHR	European Court of Human Rights
ECOSOC	Economic and Social Council
ed(s)	editor(s)
EEA	European Economic Area
EFTA	European Free Trade Association
EIPR	European Intellectual Property Review
EJIL	European Journal of International Law
Emory L J	Emory Law Journal
EPC	Convention on the Grant of European Patents
EPO	European Patent Office
et al	*et alii* (and others)
EU	European Union
EuGRZ	Europäische Grundrechte-Zeitschrift
EuZW	Europäische Zeitschrift für Wirtschaftsrecht
f	and the following one
FDA	Food and Drug Administration
FDCA	Federal Food, Drug, and Cosmetic Act
Fed Circuit BJ	Federal Circuit Bar Journal
Fed Reg	Federal Register
ff	and the following ones
Fla J Int'l L	Florida Journal of International Law
Fla L Rev	Florida Law Review
Food & Drug L J	Food and Drug Law Journal
Food Drug Cosm L J	Food Drug Cosmetic Law Journal
Fordham Intell Prop Media & Ent L J	Fordham Intellectual Property, Media & Entertainment Law Journal
FTA	free trade agreement
GATS	General Agreement on Trade in Services
GATT	General Agreement on Tariffs and Trade
Geo Wash Int'l L Rev	George Washington International Law Review
GRUR	Gewerblicher Rechtsschutz und Urheberrecht
GRUR Int	Gewerblicher Rechtsschutz und Urheberrecht, Internationaler Teil
GYIL	German Yearbook of International Law
Harv Int'l L J	Harvard International Law Journal

Harv J L & Tech	Harvard Journal of Law & Technology
Harv J on Legis	Harvard Journal on Legislation
Hastings Int'l & Comp L Rev	Hastings International and Comparative Law Review
HHS	United States Department of Health and Human Services
HIV	Human Immunodeficiency Virus
Hum Rts Brief	Human Rights Brief
Hum Rts Q	Human Rights Quarterly
ie	*id est* (that is)
ICCPR	International Covenant on Civil and Political Rights
ICESCR	International Covenant on Economic, Social, and Cultural Rights
ICJ	International Court of Justice
ICLQ	International and Comparative Law Quarterly
ICTSD	International Centre for Trade and Sustainable Development
ibid	*ibidem* (in the same place)
IDEA	IDEA: The Journal of Law and Technology
IFPMA	International Federation of Pharmaceutical Manufacturers Associations
IIC	International Review of Intellectual Property and Competition Law
ILC	International Law Commission
IMF	International Monetary Fund
Ind L Rev	Indiana Law Review
Indian J Int'l L	Indian Journal of International Law
Int'l Affairs	International Affairs
Int'l J of Indus Org	International Journal of Industrial Organization
Int'l Org	International Organization
IRS	Internal Revenue Service
ITLOS	International Tribunal for the Law of the Sea
ITO	International Trade Organization
J Health Econ	Journal of Health Economics
J L & Econ	Journal of Law and Economics
J Marshall L Rev	John Marshall Law Review
J Org Chem	Journal of Organic Chemistry
J Pat & Trademark Off Soc'y	Journal of the Patent and Trademark Office Society
J World Intell Prop	Journal of World Intellectual Property
JCP	Juris-Classeur Périodique
JAMA	Journal of the American Medical Association
JIEL	Journal of International Economic Law
JPO	Japan Patent Office
JWT	Journal of World Trade
LDCs	Least-developed countries
LJIL	Leiden Journal of International Law
Loy LA L Rev	Loyola of Los Angeles Law Review
Loy U Chi L J	Loyola University of Chicago Law Journal

Melb J Int'l L	Melbourne Journal of International Law
MERCOSUR	Mercado Común del Sur (Common Market of the South)
Mich L Rev	Michigan Law Review
Michigan J Int'l L	Michigan Journal of International Law
Minn J Global Trade	Minnesota Journal of Global Trade
MIPR	Minnesota Intellectual Property Review
N Y L Sch J Int'l & Comp L	New York Law School Journal of International and Comparative Law
NY City L Rev	New York City Law Review
NY Times	New York Times
NYU J. Int'l L & Pol	New York University Journal of International Law and Politics
NAID	National Institute of Allergy and Infectious Diseases
NBC	National Broadcasting Company
NCI	National Cancer Institute
NDA	new drug application
Netherlands Q of Hum Rts	Netherlands Quarterly of Human Rights
New Eng J Med	New England Journal of Medicine
NGO	nongovernmental organization
NIH	National Institutes of Health
NILR	Netherlands International Law Review
NJW	Neue Juristische Wochenschrift
Nordic J Int'l L	Nordic Journal of International Law
NVwZ	Neue Zeitschrift für Verwaltungsrecht
OAPI	Organisation Africaine de la Propriété Intellectuelle
OECD	Organization for Economic Co-operation and Development
OJ	Official Journal
Osgoode Hall L J	Osgoode Hall Law Journal
OSPAR Convention	Convention for the Protection of the Marine Environment of the North-East Atlantic
OTCs	over-the-counter drugs
PTO	Patent and Trademark Office
Pace Int'l L Rev	Pace International Law Review
para	Paragraph
PCP	*Pneumocystis carinii pneumonia*
PCT	Patent Cooperation Treaty
PhRMA	Pharmaceutical Research and Manufacturers of America
Proc Nat Acad Sci	Proceedings of the National Academy of Sciences of the United States of America
RIDE	Revue Internationale de Droit Économique
RdC	Recueil des Cours de l'Académie de droit international de la Haye
Res in L & Econ	Research in Law and Economics
Rev of Econ & Statistics	Review of Economics and Statistics
RGDIP	Revue générale de droit international public
RNA	ribonucleic acid

SUL Rev	Southern University Law Review
SAJHR	South African Journal on Human Rights
SARS	Severe Acute Respiratory Syndrome
Seton Hall L Rev	Seton Hall Law Review
Sw J L & Trade Am	Southwestern Journal of Law and Trade in the Americas
SPG Law & Contemp Probs	SPG Law and Contemporary Problems
Stud Transnat'l Legal Pol'y	Studies in Transnational Legal Policy
Suffolk Transnat'l L Rev	Suffolk Transnational Law Review
TB	Tuberculosis
Tenn L Rev	Tennessee Law Review
Tex Int'l L J	Texas International Law Journal
transl	translator
TRIPS Agreement	Agreement on Trade-related Aspects of Intellectual Property Rights
Tul L Rev	Tulane Law Review
Tulsa J Comp & Int'l L	Tulsa Journal of Comparative & International Law
U Chi L Rev	University of Chicago Law Review
U Ill L Rev	University of Illinois Law Review
U Pa J Int'l Econ L	University of Pennsylvania Journal of International Economic Law
UC Davis J Int'l L & Pol'y	University of California, Davis Journal of International Law and Policy
UK	United Kingdom
UN	United Nations
US	United States
UCLA J Int'l L & Foreign Aff	UCLA Journal of International Law and Foreign Affairs
UDHR	Universal Declaration of Human Rights
UNAIDS	Joint United Nations Programme on HIV/AIDS
UNCLOS	United Nations Convention on the Law of the Sea
UNCTAD	United Nations Conference on Trade and Development
UNDP	United Nations Development Programme
UNESCO	United Nations Educational, Scientific and Cultural Organization
UNYB	Yearbook of the United Nations
USTR	United States Trade Representative
Va J Int'l L	Virginia Journal of International Law
Vand J of Transnat'l L	Vanderbilt Journal of Transnational Law
Vienna Convention	Vienna Convention on the Law of Treaties
Villanova L R	Villanova Law Review
VRÜ	Verfassung und Recht in Übersee
Wash L Rev	Washington Law Review
WCO	World Customs Organization

WHO	World Health Organization
Widener L Symp J	Widener Law Symposium Journal
WIPO	World Intellectual Property Organization
Wis Int'l L J	Wisconsin International Law Journal
Wis L Rev	Wisconsin Law Review
WTO	World Trade Organization
Yale J Health Pol'y, L & Ethics	Yale Journal of Health Policy, Law, and Ethics
Yale J Int'l L	Yale Journal of International Law
Yale L J	Yale Law Journal
YBILC	Yearbook of the International Law Commission
ZaöRV	Zeitschrift für ausländisches öffentliches Recht und Völkerrecht
ZeuS	Zeitschrift für europarechtliche Studien

Introduction

> I swear to fulfill, to the best of my ability and judgment, this covenant: (...)
> I will apply, for the benefit of the sick, all measures which are required,
> avoiding those twin traps of overtreatment and therapeutic nihilism.
>
> L Lasagna, Hippocratic Oath—Modern Version

Pharmaceuticals have become an indispensable weapon in man's fight against disease. The synthesization of aspirin at the end of the 19th Century, that of penicillin in the middle of the 20th Century,[1] and the invention of the first HIV/AIDS medication in the 1980s constitute milestones in our struggle for better health. But while the developed world is making progress towards a longer, healthier life, people in developing countries threaten to be left on the sidelines as life expectancy in many African countries actually drops due to the AIDS pandemic. To them, access to the medicines of the rich remains largely utopian—they cannot afford the prices that pharmaceutical companies charge for their latest achievements.

This study treats the conflict between patent law obligations under the Agreement on Trade-related Aspects of Intellectual Property Rights (TRIPS Agreement) and access to medicine, a conflict that is, at its core, a conflict between the law of the World Trade Organization (WTO) and human rights law. In its focus the study fills a gap between the voluminous literature on international patent law and pharmaceuticals on the one hand and the much more sparse human rights literature on access to medicine on the other. Beyond the contribution to the on-going scholarly debate on how to accommodate human rights within the WTO system and how to progress towards a solution of the conflict between the TRIPS Agreement and access to medicine my intention is to provide a comprehensive introduction to the debate for non-specialists, a debate that increasingly connects different legal fields from patent law and food and drug law to public international law and international human rights law.

The core of the predicament can be described as follows: as science progresses the development of new drugs has become more and more expensive—current data puts the price tag for the development of one new drug at between $115m and $802m.[2] The pharmaceutical industry pays a large part of that cost. Globally, the pharmaceutical industry is estimated to have invested more than $45b in research and development for new drugs in 2002.[3] It goes without saying that in a

---

[1] H Wußing (ed), *Geschichte der Naturwissenschaft* (1987) 403, 472–73.   [2] cf chapter 4.
[3] IFPMA, *Research & Development*, at <http://www.ifpma.org/Issues/issues_research.aspx>.

market economy in which pharmaceutical manufacturers are in the business to make money these investments will only be undertaken by the industry if they ultimately pay off. If any competitor could freely copy an invention that has cost millions in its development, nobody would invest in inventive activity. Hence, countries (through the national patent offices) grant patents, basically the right to exclude others from making or selling the invention in the territory for which they are granted and thus a quasi-monopoly in that territory for the duration of the patent term. The quasi-monopoly enables the patentee to set higher prices for the product and collect monopoly rents, thus possibly recouping research and development costs and making a profit on top. The innovative pharmaceutical industry has used the system successfully, returning between 14% and 25% of its revenue in profits.[4]

Before the coming into force of the TRIPS Agreement, countries were largely at liberty in deciding whether they wanted to grant patents and how to construct their patent system. Many countries had chosen not to grant patents for pharmaceutical products. On the one hand, they feared that most of the patents would be granted to foreign, multi-national corporations, and wanted to enable their often infant industries to freely copy the products and produce them in an off-patent, competitive environment (non- or no longer patented drugs are called 'generics'). On the other hand, they were afraid that the higher prices a patentee can demand as a monopolist would render pharmaceutical products unaffordable for large parts of their population and preferred a competitive setting that would drive the prices down. With the adoption of the TRIPS Agreement as part of the WTO Agreements in 1994 and the expiration of most of its transitional periods, all major WTO Members will have to adopt patent laws that provide for the grant of pharmaceutical patents. The new patenting situation allows inventors to obtain patents for a newly invented pharmaceutical product in most countries that can produce the product and hence prevent competitors from making generic versions of the drug for the duration of the patent term.

The danger of this situation lies in the fact that generics—produced and priced in a competitive environment—are usually sold at much lower prices than the original brand-name patented drug. If prices are raised by switching from generic to patented drugs, consumers in the developing world who do not benefit from comprehensive health-insurance schemes can no longer afford the medicines. Since the 1950s, however, a right to health, in reality a right to health care, has been developing in public international law. Access to medicine is an essential component of this right. It is with this right to access to medicine that the TRIPS Agreement comes into conflict.

The discussion about pharmaceutical patents under the TRIPS Agreement and the flexibilities the TRIPS Agreement provides for WTO Members wishing to weaken patent standards, such as compulsory licenses, parallel imports, and

---

[4] cf chapter 4.

'limited exceptions' under Art 30 of the TRIPS Agreement, has become one of the dominating debates within the WTO. In the course of this discussion many of the propositions just made have been and are the subject of much controversy. The discussions have resulted in the decision to amend a core WTO agreement for the first time. These controversies will have to be discussed in the following chapters.

Chapter 1 discusses the facts that have brought the conflict between the TRIPS Agreement and access to medicine into the limelight. The public discussion was initially triggered by the pricing decision of the patent holder of the first AIDS medicine AZT. It took on global proportions when the pharmaceutical industry sued the South African government that wanted to break patents on pharmaceuticals to provide its population with cheap AIDS medication. The chapter will also recount the events surrounding the anthrax attacks in the United States, when the Canadian and US governments threatened to break Bayer's patent on *Cipro*.

Chapter 2 describes the patent component of the conflict between the TRIPS Agreement and access to medicine. It will provide the reader with the necessary background in patent law, its history, and rationales and then describes the obligations the TRIPS Agreement imposes on WTO Members. It will show that the lack of jurisprudence leaves many of the details of the obligations imprecise. However, Members clearly have to provide for 20-year product patents in the pharmaceutical area.

Chapter 3 turns to the human rights law part of the conflict. The relevant background in human rights law will be presented and it will be shown that access to medicine is a human right guaranteed both under treaty law and under general international law.

Chapter 4 first demonstrates in economic terms that pharmaceutical patents result in higher prices in developing countries, thus constituting a barrier to access to medicine in those countries. It will then show that this barrier is not justified under human rights law. Neither a human rights protection of inventors, nor the incentive function of patents for encouraging future research can justify patents in the developing world. The chapter then defines the term 'conflict' between international regimes and will show that such a conflict exists between the TRIPS Agreement and access to medicine, as an instance of a larger conflict between the WTO Agreements and human rights. What makes this conflict particularly problematic is that human rights, while not in general legally on a higher normative level, at least have a higher normative appeal than WTO law. However, its strong enforcement system puts WTO law on a higher level in a factual hierarchy of regimes, so that ultimately state behaviour will largely be determined by the solution found within the WTO regime.

Chapter 5 first discusses to what extent human rights can be applied in WTO dispute settlement, finding that they can only be used as an aid to interpreting the 'covered agreements'. The chapter then takes up that approach and interprets the 'TRIPS flexibilities' using the right to access to medicine. It demonstrates that the right serves as a helpful argument for a broad interpretation of the flexibilities, but suffers from the defect that it is merely one argument amongst many and cannot provide developing countries with legal security as to the interpretation of the flexibilities. It is this lack of legal security that discourages developing countries from making use of the flexibilities, particularly in the face of pressure for greater intellectual property protection by the developed world. The WTO decisions taken in the area of TRIPS and access to medicine to improve the situation will be presented and discussed, including the amendment to the agreement, which is not yet in force. The first decision made some progress towards accommodating developing countries' concerns by authoritatively interpreting some of the flexibilities, in particular concerning parallel imports, and by strengthening access to medicine as an argument in the interpretation. The second and third decisions effectively amended the agreement to provide for a mechanism to give compulsory licenses some effect to help countries without pharmaceutical production facilities. However, the decisions fall short of resolving the conflict. Of particular interest besides the substance of the decisions is the procedure with respect to the first two decisions. While they are valid and binding, the disregard of the WTO towards its procedural rules shows that, where WTO law conflicts with human rights law, a sloppy approach to procedural rules emerges as an additional flexibility. I submit that further progress needs to be made and such progress can only be made by importing human rights considerations into WTO law. Rather than hoping for treaty amendments in that respect the study places its faith in the Appellate Body and suggests the security exception of Art. 73 of the TRIPS Agreement as a convenient hook for hanging a human rights exception within the TRIPS Agreement on. Mention is also made of further difficulties on the road ahead, namely Free Trade Agreements and Bilateral Investment Treaties containing so-called 'TRIPS-plus' obligations.

1

Background of the Debate

The conflict between the Agreement on Trade-related Aspects of Intellectual Property Rights (TRIPS Agreement) and access to medicine—the subject of this study—sounds exceedingly dry: patents are commonly deemed to be an abstract topic accessible only to those skilled in sciences—even by lawyers. What is worse, the TRIPS Agreement belongs to the World Trade Organization (WTO) Agreements and thus additionally suffers from the stigma of technicality attached to that particular area of international law. And yet, the conflict between international patent law and access to medicine has garnered an astonishing amount of public attention in recent years. Before examining the legal questions raised in detail, it is worthwhile presenting some of the events that have caused the issue to stand at the forefront of the international debate surrounding globalization. These events are not only essential to understand the legal arguments made, they also explain the rancour with which activists and the pharmaceutical industry exchange arguments and accusations. But the historic account comes with a caveat: most of the events presented focus on the HIV/AIDS pandemic and even though no presentation of the conflict between the TRIPS Agreement and access to medicine would be complete without them, the solutions appropriate for the pandemic might differ from what is appropriate for other cases.

The first part of this chapter treats the appearance of the HIV/AIDS pandemic and the invention of the first medication targeting HIV itself, a scientific success that can largely be credited to publicly funded research institutions (I). Nevertheless, a private company obtained a patent on the use of the drug against AIDS in several countries and priced the drug in such a way that many people could not afford it, causing an outcry by AIDS activists (II). Part III will bring us up to date on the AIDS pandemic, its extent, currently available treatment, and the accessibility of that treatment. Part IV will then recount the South African pharmaceutical trial that brought the issue of patents and access to drugs to the attention of a wider public. Contrary to a common perception, the issue of the TRIPS Agreement and access to medicine is not limited to HIV/AIDS drugs. To illustrate this point, part V will tell the story of *Cipro*, a patented antibiotic that gained sudden prominence as the only approved treatment for anthrax and the patent on which Canada and the United States threatened to break to drive down the price.

I Finding a Cure for a New Disease

The beginnings in the developed world[1] of what proved to be the most severe pandemic of our times went almost unnoticed: in 1981 in New York several young gay men were identified with an unusually aggressive case of a rare skin disease called *Karposi's sarcoma*,[2] while at roughly the same time the US Centers for Disease Control (CDC) observed a significant increase in cases of another rare disease by the name *Pneumocystis carinii pneumonia* (PCP).[3] The *New York Times* reported a 'rare cancer seen in homosexuals',[4] but over time members of other groups, too, were acknowledged as falling victim to the disease: drug addicts, recipients of blood transfers and, later, heterosexuals in general. The early connection of the Acquired Immunodeficiency Syndrome (AIDS)[5] with marginalized groups and sex attached a powerful stigma to the disease and those affected that endures to this day, hampering the public health response to the pandemic.[6] Maybe it was partly for this reason that the realization that AIDS was a worldwide pandemic did not emerge until 1984 with the publication of a CDC-sponsored study in Zaire finding the disease already rampant there.[7]

Before researchers could consider finding a cure for the new disease they had to track down the agent responsible for it. Two publicly funded institutions staked a claim to scientific victory, illustrating the importance of public sector research for medical science. A group of researchers headed by Montagnier at the *Institut Pasteur* isolated the new virus—later to be called 'Human Immunodeficiency Virus' (HIV)[8]—in May 1983 and subsequently developed a test for the new disease.[9] Researchers under Gallo, head of the Tumour Cell Biology lab at the National

---

[1] Much later studies showed that HIV/AIDS had already been prevalent in Africa before these events.

[2] KB Hymes *et al*, 'Kaposi's sarcoma in homosexual men: A report of eight cases' (1981) 2 Lancet 598.

[3] PS Arno and KL Feiden, *Against the Odds. The Story of AIDS Drug Development, Politics and Profits*, (1992) 86; MD Grmek, *History of AIDS. Emergence and Origin of a Modern Pandemic*, 6 (RC Maulitz and J Duffin trans 1990).

[4] L Altman, 'Rare Cancer Seen in 41 Homosexuals', *NY Times* (3 July 1981).

[5] CDC, 'Update on acquired immune deficiency syndrome (AIDS)' (1982) 31 Morbidity and Mortality Weekly Rep 507.

[6] Behrman describes how the Reagan administration engaged in denial of the imminent pandemic. It was Congress that pushed through funding: By the end of Reagan's second term AIDS research funding had jumped to $500m a year. G Behrman, *The Invisible People. How the US Has Slept through the Global AIDS Pandemic, the Greatest Humanitarian Catastrophe of Our Time* (2004) 1 ff; M Goozner, *The $800 Million Pill. The Truth Behind the Cost of New Drugs* (2004) 95, 102.

[7] The study went unpublished for almost a year before it was accepted by the Lancet. In 1983 the Word Health Organization saw no necessity to get involved as 'AIDS is being well taken care of by some of the richest countries in the world (. . .) where most of the patients are to be found' (memo cited by Behrman). Behrman (n 6 above) 10, 14.

[8] JL Marx, 'Aids Virus Has New Name—Perhaps' (1986) 232 Science 699.

[9] F Barre-Sinoussi *et al*, 'Isolation of a T-Lymphotropic Retrovirus from a Patient at Risk for Acquired Immune Deficiency Syndrome (AIDS)' (1983) 220 Science 868.

Cancer Institute (NCI), part of the US National Institutes of Health (NIH), isolated a virus, too, mass-produced it and developed a test for antibodies.[10] Besides the scientific honours what was at stake in the race were patents on an antibody test kit. The first US patent was awarded to the United States naming Gallo as inventor,[11] prompting the *Institut Pasteur* to initiate an interference proceeding at the US Patent and Trademark Office and a lawsuit against the United States before the US Claims Court.[12] It took an agreement between President Reagan and Prime Minister Chirac to settle the issue, declaring Gallo and Montagnier joint inventors of the test kit and splitting the royalties based on sales in each country.[13] The Agreement was revised in 1994 in favour of France, when US health officials conceded that Gallo had actually identified a virus provided under a cooperation contract by the *Institut Pasteur* and not, as he had claimed and as had been assumed during the patenting of the test kit, a different virus.[14]

With the virus identified, progress towards an AIDS medication could be made. Again, public institutions were very much at the forefront of the research. Indeed, one public institution had already achieved a breakthrough before HIV was even discovered: funded by the NCI Horwitz, a researcher at the Detroit Institute for Cancer Research, synthesized a chemical entity called *azidothymidine* (AZT) to stop malignant cells in 1964.[15] The compound proved a failure and had no appreciable anti-tumour activity.[16] Horwitz never patented AZT, which thus fell into the public domain. Ten years later Ostertag of the *Max Planck Institut für Experimentelle Medizin*, a publicly funded German research institute, experimented with AZT, finding that '[i]n some instances azidothymidine might favourably replace [Bromodeoxyuridine] BrdUrd for medical treatment of diseases caused by

[10] Arno and Feiden (n 3 above) 12.

[11] US Patent No 4,520,113, Serological detection of antibodies to HTLV-III in sera of patients with AIDS and pre-AIDS conditions. A similar application by the *Institut Pasteur* had been made in Europe in September 1983 and in the United States in December 1983. The US patent was granted one year after Gallo's test was on the market. C Norman, 'Patent Dispute Divides AIDS Researchers. The War on AIDS, Pt 2' (1985) 230 Science 640; C Norman, 'FDA Approves Pasteur's AIDS Test Kit' (1986) 213 Science 1063.

[12] *Institut Pasteur v United States*, 10 Cl Ct 304 (Cl Ct, 1986). The lawsuit was an action for breach of contract, alleging that the virus used by Gallo had been provided by the *Institut Pasteur* solely for study purposes—a claim that Gallo denied, arguing he had extracted a different virus. The suit was dismissed on jurisdictional grounds, but the decision was reversed on appeal. *Institut Pasteur v United States*, 814 F2d 624 (Fed Cir, 1987). DM Barnes, 'AIDS Case Dismissed on Legal Technicality' (1986) 233 Science 414.

[13] Arno and Feiden (n 3 above) 13; DM Barnes 'AIDS patent dispute settled' (1987) 236 Science 17. On the whole issue RI Gordon, 'Facilitating the Transnational Exchange of Scientific Information: Institut Pasteur v United States' (1988) 6 BU Int'l LJ 179.

[14] L Garrett, 'French First to Isolate HIV', *Newsday* (12 July 1994); E Chen, 'US Admits French Role in HIV Test Kit', *Los Angeles Times* (12 July 1994); J Cohen and E Marshall, 'NIH-Pasteur: A Final Rapprochement?' (1994) 265 Science 313; J Cohen, 'Pasteur Wants More HIV Blood Test Royalties' (1992) 255 Science 792; J Cohen, 'HHS: Gallo Guilty of Misconduct' (1993) 259 Science 168; J Cohen, 'US-French Patent Dispute Heads for a Showdown' (1994) 265 Science 23.

[15] JP Horwitz, J Chua, and M Noel, 'The Monomesylates of 1-(2'-Deoxy-β-D-lyxofuranosyl) thymine' (1964) 29 J Org Chem 2076.   [16] Arno and Feiden (n 3 above) 40 ff.

DNA viruses',[17] in other words: AZT showed promise in the treatment of retro-viruses. Not until a decade later, with the advent of AIDS, would the combined findings of Horwitz and Ostertag prove their significance. In its quest for a cure for AIDS, the NCI created a special task force, a member of which developed a method to screen compounds for effectiveness against HIV. Lacking adequate facilities, the NCI attempted to make the private sector run the tests in their labs, but the corporations recoiled. The potential market for an AIDS drug appeared to be too small and the prospect of a dangerous virus escaping from a company's lab was a liability nightmare. Finally, the NCI ran the tests in its own lab, with the drug companies providing the compounds. The samples sent by the companies were coded to protect the identity of the compounds.[18] In 1985 the Institute's researchers found what they had been looking for: one of the compounds showed activity against HIV. The compound turned out to be AZT, sent in by the British pharmaceutical company Burroughs Wellcome (BW), which had chosen AZT for testing at the NCI lab after screening compounds using two mouse retroviruses. BW had already drafted a patent application for the United Kingdom before send-ing the compound to NCI. After the NCI tests were successful, BW filed the patent application and, soon after, filed for a patent in the United States (granted in 1988), claiming amongst others '[a] method of treating a human having acquired immunodeficiency syndrome comprising the oral administration of' AZT.[19] It also initiated the course towards approval of AZT by the US Food and Drug Administration (FDA).[20] With the clinical studies successful[21] the FDA approved AZT in 1987 and BW, which before had given away free AZT priced at $10m to some 4,500 patients,[22] began to market the drug under the trademark *retrovir*.[23] BW also obtained special beneficial treatment in the United States available for 'orphan drugs', drugs for diseases affecting only a few patients, because the patient population eligible for AZT under the original indication of the drug was small.[24] For many years AZT was to remain the only drug available in HIV treatment.

---

[17] W Ostertag et al, 'Induction of Endogenous Virus and of Thymidine Kinase by Bromo-deoxyuridine in Cell Cultures Transformed by Friend Virus' (1974) 71 Proc Nat Acad Sci USA 4980, 4984.   [18] Arno and Feiden (n 3 above) 39 ff.
[19] US Patent No 4,724,232, Treatment of human viral infections (note that several patents with similar claims were granted, which will be treated as one for the purposes of this study). BW could not claim the compound itself, as that had been invented much earlier by Horwitz. *Burroughs Wellcome Co v Barr Laboratories, Inc et al*, 828 FSupp 1208, 1211 (E D North Carolina, 1993); *Burroughs Wellcome Co v Barr Laboratories, Inc et al*, 40 F3d 1223, 1225 f (Fed Cir, 1994); Arno and Feiden (n 3 above) 41 ff.   [20] Arno and Feiden (n 3 above) 42.
[21] Phase I: R Yarchoan et al, 'Administration of 3'-Azido-3'Deoxythymidine, an Inhibitor of HTLV-III/LAV Replication, to Patients with AIDS or AIDS-Related Complex' (1986) 1 Lancet 575; phase II: MA Fischl et al, 'The Efficacy of Azidothymidine (AZT) in the Treatment of Patients with AIDS and AIDS-Related Complex' (1987) 317 New Eng J Med 185.
[22] Arno and Feiden (n 3 above) 43.
[23] *Burroughs Wellcome Co v Barr Laboratories, Inc et al*, 40 F3d 1223, 1226 (Fed Cir, 1994).
[24] Arno and Feiden (n 3 above) 56.

II BW's Decision on AZT Pricing Causes Outrage

The patent on the use of AZT to treat AIDS put BW in the favourable position of being able to set the price for a drug that promised to be the only available life-saving therapy for a desperate patient population. The decision the company took became one of the causes around which activists were to rally and illustrates the claim that pharmaceutical patents result in higher prices thus reducing the accessibility of drugs: BW set the retail price for a year's supply of AZT for one patient at $10,000. The tab was staggering for HIV/AIDS patients, who also had to grapple with the reluctant government response to the disease. They began to set up highly effective activist groups. The AIDS Coalition to Unleash Power (ACT UP) was particularly rambunctious. In later years, some of their activists went so far as to barricade themselves in BW's offices.[25] Many other groups have taken up the cause, as well, such as Médecins sans Frontières, the Consumer Project on Technology, OXFAM, or the Treatment Action Campaign. The outcry of those affected by the disease led to Congressional hearings scrutinizing the pricing decision. BW argued that the high price was justified by the cost of research, development, synthesizing, and marketing of the drug as well as the need to generate revenues, particularly in light of the fact that better therapies could be introduced soon.[26] The argument did not convince Congressional critics. BW's research and development costs were far below the average drug development costs given the extent of government involvement in the research.[27] At the same time sales of AZT were booming due to a large trial conducted under Volberding of the San Francisco General Hospital and funded by the National Institute of Allergy and Infectious Diseases (NAID)[28] showing that AZT could slow the progression of AIDS if administered to HIV-positive patients without symptoms and not just to patients with fully developed AIDS.[29] By the end of 1991, cumulative sales exceeded $1b.[30] The pressure that Congressman Waxman put on BW attained a 20 per cent cut in the AZT price in 1987,[31] but the cut was not sufficiently steep to silence activists. BW continued to refer to its own research efforts to justify the price level of AZT. This justification, however, began to enrage US government researchers, who responded with a letter published in the *New York Times* pointing out the government's significant contribution to the development of AZT and lambasting BW's reluctance to work with live HIV.[32] The NIH began to insert a reasonable pricing clause in the cooperative research and development agreements it signed with the industry for federally funded research. However, the clause was

---

[25] ACT UP, *ACT UP Capsule History 1989*, at <http://www.actupny.org/documents/cron-89.html>.

[26] Arno and Feiden (n 3 above) 55 ff.   [27] Arno and Feiden (n 3 above) 58.

[28] Phone interview with Volberding.   [29] Arno and Feiden (n 3 above) 113, 130 ff.

[30] Arno and Feiden (n 3 above) 59.

[31] M Chase, 'Wellcome Unit Cuts Price of AIDS Drug 20%', *Wall Street Journal* (15 December 1987).   [32] Arno and Feiden (n 3 above) 136 ff.

later eliminated for fear that it would discourage the industry from collaborating with the public sector.[33]

The fact that BW could obtain a patent on the use of AZT in AIDS treatment seems surprising considering that the compound was synthesized by Horwitz with US public funding, tested for antiretroviral activity by Ostertag with German public funding and tested for activity against HIV by the NCI, again with US public funding. Two companies, Barr Laboratories and Novopharm, questioned the validity of the patent and filed Abbreviated New Drug Applications[34] for generic versions of AZT, ie copies of the drug using the same active ingredient. In the ensuing suit for patent infringement filed by BW they stated that NCI scientists should have been named as coinventors of AZT. Novopharm argued that the failure to do so with deceptive intent rendered the patent unenforceable for inequitable conduct. Barr Laboratories relied on a licence to manufacture and sell AZT it had obtained from the US government, the owner of the alleged interests of the NCI scientists. In a 1994 decision, the Federal Circuit sided with BW. It reasoned that conception, the 'formation in the mind of the inventor, of a definite and permanent idea of the complete and operative invention, as it is hereafter to be applied in practice', is the touchstone of inventorship.[35] As evidenced by the draft UK patent application, BW inventors had such a definite and permanent idea before they sent AZT to the NCI and thus the NCI scientists were not joint inventors.[36] Nevertheless, litigation over the validity of the AZT patent continued throughout the patent's life span. The non-profit organization 'AIDS Healthcare Foundation' raised both antitrust and patent invalidity claims before the US District Court for the Central District of California in a suit that was refiled in 2003.[37] The US AZT patent expired in 2005.[38]

III The HIV/AIDS Pandemic Today

Since the early days of the HIV/AIDS pandemic our knowledge about the pandemic has grown enormously. AIDS is characterized by a range of symptoms that

---

[33] Goozner (n 6 above) 127, 148; PS Arno and MH Davis, 'Why Don't We Enforce Existing Drug Price Controls? The Unrecognized and Unenforced Reasonable Pricing Requirements Imposed upon Patents Deriving in Whole or in Part from Federally Funded Research' (2001) 75 Tul L Rev 631.

[34] See chapter 2 for a description of the drug approval process.

[35] *Burroughs Wellcome Co v Barr Laboratories, Inc et al*, 40 F3d 1223, 1228 (Fed Cir, 1994).

[36] *Burroughs Wellcome Co v Barr Laboratories, Inc et al*, 40 F3d 1223, 1227 ff (Fed Cir, 1994). Writ of *certiorari* denied: *Novopharm, Inc v Burroughs Wellcome Co*, 516 US 1071 (1996). Similar litigation took place in other countries, cf Supreme Court of Canada, *Apotex Inc v Wellcome Foundation Ltd*, 2002 SCC 77 (2002); Cour d'Appel de Paris, *Wellcome Foundation Limited v Apotex France and Apotex Inc* (2003) 34 IIC 297.

[37] The Attorney General of the State of California submitted an amicus brief in support of the NGO: *AIDS Healthcare Foundation v GlaxoSmithKline PLC* (US District Court Central District of CA), CV 03-2792 *Brief of Amicus Curiae State of California in Support of AIDS Healthcare Foundation's Opposition to GlaxoSmithKline's Motion for Partial Summary Judgment* (2004).

[38] Aids Healthcare Foundation, 'Glaxo Loses Patent on First AIDS Drug, AZT; AHF Blasts Glaxo's & Drug Industry's Greed' Press Release, 17 September 2005.

differ from case to case. The disease is caused by HIV—a retrovirus, ie a virus having a core consisting of RNA and replicating as DNA inside the host cells by means of the enzyme reverse transcriptase. HIV attaches itself to the body's T4 lymphocyte cells and reprograms them to produce new viruses which are later released to infect new cells. The T4 lymphocytes are part of the body's immune defence, so the infection with HIV leaves the body defenceless against a number of opportunistic infections, which can cause the death of the patient. Two strains of the virus are widespread: HIV1, which was the first discovered virus, and HIV2, a virus that has been detected in West Africa. HIV is transmitted by blood, sexual intercourse or from mother to child.[39]

The scope of the pandemic facing the world defies the imagination. The Joint United Nations Programme on HIV/AIDS (UNAIDS), which brings together ten United Nations agencies in a common effort to fight the pandemic, estimates that as of 2005 there were 38.6 million people living with HIV. The brunt of the disease's burden is carried by the developing world: 24.5 million of the affected people live in Sub-Saharan Africa, compared to 720,000 in Western Europe and 1,300,000 in North America.[40] 25 million people have already died of the disease.[41] In some countries HIV/AIDS has reached an extent that threatens the very foundations of society: in Swaziland more than 30 per cent of all adults are infected, three other Sub-Saharan African countries have infection rates of more than 20 per cent, South Africa is struck severely with an infection rate of 18.8 per cent.[42] In many countries life expectancy has dropped due to AIDS, eg in Cambodia it is estimated to be four years lower than it would have been without the disease.[43] The devastating effects are felt in every sector of society: staggering numbers of AIDS orphans have to be supported, teachers to pupil ratios are reduced due to high infection rates among teaching staff, household income declines significantly where AIDS affects a working family member, economic growth suffers, health systems are overstretched, and so on.[44] Tragically, many of the countries affected already belonged to the poorest countries in the world before the advent of the pandemic. But even though Africa is hardest hit, other regions should not be lost from sight: the pandemic is spreading in Asia and Eastern Europe, too.[45] The threat that AIDS poses to the world can hardly be overestimated. In 2004 the UN Secretary-General's High-level Panel on Threats, Challenges and Change listed AIDS as a threat to international peace and security and gave the world a failing

---

[39] J Hubley, *The AIDS Handbook. A Guide to the Prevention of AIDS and HIV* (3rd edn, 2002) 13 ff; Goozner (n 6 above) 95.

[40] UNAIDS, *2006 Report on the Global AIDS Epidemic* (2006) 6, 505 ff.

[41] UNAIDS (n 40 above) 17.   [42] UNAIDS (n 40 above) 506.

[43] UNAIDS (n 40 above) 83.

[44] KR Hope, 'Africa's HIV/AIDS Crisis in a Development Context' (2001) 15 International Relations 15, 21 ff; M Rabbow, 'From Awareness to Behavioural Change—Challenges in HIV/AIDS Control in Southern Africa/Namibia' (2001) 36 afrika spectrum 17.

[45] UNAIDS (n 40 above) 8 ff; R Guyonnet, 'Alerte en Asie', *Jeune Afrique/L'Intelligent* (25 December 2001).

grade for its response: 'International response to HIV/AIDS was shockingly slow and remains shamefully ill-resourced.'[46]

Treatment is an essential element of any strategy to fight AIDS.[47] For years AZT was the only available medication attacking HIV itself. As a so-called nucleoside reverse transcriptase inhibitor AZT inhibits the reverse transcriptase HIV needs to reproduce.[48] But the one-drug treatment was defective, not just because of the toxicity of the drug, but mainly because HIV reproduces quickly and mutates around the drug. Today, three other classes of antiretroviral drugs are available: protease inhibitors, non-nucleoside reverse transcriptase inhibitors, and fusion inhibitors. As of October 2003, 20 antiretroviral agents belonging to these four classes have been approved in the United States.[49] The World Health Organization (WHO) currently recommends a therapy with two nucleoside reverse transcriptase inhibitors and one non-nucleoside reverse transcriptase inhibitor or a protease inhibitor.[50] These modern therapies have changed the prospect for HIV-positive patients drastically. If several drugs aiming at different targets are administered simultaneously, the chances of the virus mutating around the drugs is basically zero.[51] Experts hope that a patient receiving proper treatment can live through a normal life span.[52] Initially, the combination drug regime was difficult to follow. Patients had to take several drugs at different times of the day, some with food, some on a fasting stomach, some of the medication even requiring refrigeration.[53] This gave some justification to the claim that treatment in the third world is not feasible and should only be administered carefully as it might lead to an increase in resistances. However, in the area of AIDS there is no more justification to this claim: the WHO-recommended three-drug combination is available as a generic fixed-dose combination with the three components in one pill that has to be taken once or twice a day. It can therefore be administered in countries with extremely poor infrastructure with an adequate adherence to the therapy—anywhere in the third world.[54] The Indian drug manufacturer Cipla, the best-known developing country generic manufacturer, offers such a combination under the name of *triomune*, consisting of *nevirapine* (patents for which are owned by Boehringer Ingelheim), *stavudine* (patents for which are owned by Bristol-Myers Squibb), and *lamivudine* (patents for which are owned by GlaxoSmithKline), requiring one pill to be taken twice a day.[55] Cipla was granted a patent on the combination in

[46] High-level Panel on Threats, Challenges and Change, *A More Secure World: Our Shared Responsibilty* (2004) 24.

[47] UNAIDS, *Report on the Global HIV/AIDS Epidemic 2002* (2002) 16.

[48] Arno and Feiden (n 3 above) 40 ff.

[49] Panel on Clinical Practices for Treatment of HIV Infection, *Guidelines for the Use of Antiretroviral Agents in HIV-1-Infected Adults and Adolescents* (2004) 8.

[50] WHO, *Scaling up Antiretroviral Therapy in Resource-limited Settings: Treatment Guidelines for a Public Health Approach. 2003 Revision* (2003) 12 ff.   [51] Goozner (n 6 above) 142.

[52] Phone interview with Volberding.   [53] Phone interview with Volberding.

[54] The same is not necessarily true for all diseases. Where it is not the case, an appropriate solution for the access problem can only be found on a case-by-case basis.

[55] 'Generic AIDS Pill Gets Patent in Africa', *Reuters* (13 July 2004).

South Africa.[56] Since May 2002 the same combination has also been produced by Thailand's state-owned Government Pharmaceutical Organization under the name of *GPO-Vir*.[57] Fixed-dose combinations are not just convenient for the patient, they also improve adherence to drug regimes and thus reduce the risk of drug resistance.[58] However, the combination is only available where its components are not under patent or where the patent owners have granted licenses. For antitrust reasons brand-name companies, ie the companies holding patents on the components, have not yet offered such a combination themselves, as that would require the collaboration of all the companies holding patents on the components of the combination.[59] However, the first such treatment is expected to be available in the developed world soon.[60]

Sadly, the availability of treatment does not imply its accessibility. Numerous campaigns by the WHO,[61] the Global Fund to Fight AIDS, Tuberculosis and Malaria,[62] UNAIDS,[63] governments,[64] NGOs,[65] and pharmaceutical companies[66] have been mounted to increase access of HIV infected people to treatment. Particularly in the last few years, great progress has been made, but despite the efforts UNAIDS states that as of December 2005 at least 80 per cent of those in clinical need of antiretroviral drugs were not receiving them.[67]

[56] According to Smith from Cipla/Medpro in South Africa Cipla has filed for patents for *triomune* in South Africa, DRC, Namibia, and all ARIPO countries. J Love, 'CIPLA 3 in 1 ARV patent', *IP-Health* (5 July 2004); 'Generic AIDS Pill Gets Patent in Africa', *Reuters* (13 July 2004).

[57] 'Thailand Eyes Generic Versions of Two AIDS Drugs', Reuters, 10 July 2004; A Kazmin, 'Thailand's Cheap Aids Drugs Revive Patients' Hope' *Financial Times* (9 July 2004).

[58] D Sontag, 'Early Tests for US in Its Global Fight on AIDS', *NY Times* (14 July 2004).

[59] DG McNeil Jr, 'Study Finds Generic AIDS Drug Effective', *NY Times* (2 July 2004). GlaxoSmithKline offers a combination pill which combines three drugs from the same class instead of a mix of classes.

[60] A Pollack, 'New Medicine for AIDS Is One Pill, Once a Day', *NY Times* (9 July 2006).

[61] At the WHO Mann set up the United Nations' Special Programme on AIDS, later renamed as the Global Programme on AIDS, in 1986. ME Wojcik, 'On the Sudden Loss of a Human Rights Activist: A Tribute to Dr Jonathan Mann's Use of International Human Rights Law in the Global Battle against AIDS' (1998) 32 J Marshall L Rev 129. Numerous programmes were to follow, most recently the '3 by 5' initiative aiming to treat three million people by 2005. UNAIDS (n 40 above) 150 ff.

[62] *The Framework Document of the Global Fund to Fight AIDS, Tuberculosis and Malaria*, available at <http://www.theglobalfund.org/en/files/publicdoc/Framework_uk.pdf> (2002).

[63] UNAIDS, *Uniting the World Against AIDS*, at <http://www.unaids.org/en/AboutUNAIDS/default.asp>.

[64] Intense coverage was given to President Bush's 'Emergency Plan for AIDS Relief', committed to provide $15b over five years in the global fight against AIDS. Besides doubts whether the funding will really be made available in light of the Iraq war, criticism focuses on the question to what extent generic drugs will be provided under the programme and a peculiar nexus of the programme urging state recipients of HIV/AIDS help to not reject US food assistance with genetically modified food. United States Leadership Against HIV/AIDS, Tuberculosis, and Malaria Act of 2003, Pub L 108-25, 117 Stat 711 (2003) (particularly § 104A(g)(1)(C), (2) of the Act); Office of the United States Global AIDS Coordinator (ed), *The President's Emergency Plan for AIDS Relief, US Five-Year Global HIV/AIDS Strategy* (2004).

[65] Some examples are Médecins Sans Frontières' Access to Essential Medicines Campaign, Oxfam International's Cut the Cost Campaign and the Consumer Project on Technology's Health Care and Intellectual Property Campaign.

[66] International Federation of Pharmaceutical Manufacturers Associations, *Building Healthier Societies Through Partnership* (2004) 6 ff.   [67] UNAIDS (n 40 above) 155.

But the advances made should not be slighted: the price of a WHO-recommended combination antiretroviral regime for one patient and one year was at $10,000–$12,000 in 2000.[68] Generic drugs, produced where the drugs are not on patent, have brought down the prices significantly. By 2002 Cipla offered the regime at $350 a year, treatment costs in 2004 with *GPO-Vir* in Thailand have been reported at $348.[69] A deal between the Clinton Foundation and Indian generic drug manufacturers planned to bring this figure down to approximately $140.[70] The ambitious goal was achieved. In 2006 the most common three-drug combination pill reportedly cost $136 a year.[71] But the supply of cheap generics depends on a mere handful of countries in which the medicine is not patented and which have the technological capacity to manufacture the medicine. Both manufacturers of the *triomune* combination that in 2004 were prequalified by the WHO for procurement by UN Agencies are situated in India.[72] The Indian generic pharmaceutical industry, which has thrived under a national legal regime allowing it to reverse-engineer drugs on patent elsewhere and shielding it against foreign competition by regulatory controls, high tariffs, foreign equity restrictions, and price controls, is certainly the most important developing country generic industry, competing successfully with Western firms.[73] Besides India, the capacity to manufacture generic AIDS drugs exists only in a few developing countries, among them Argentina, Brazil, China, Cuba, Egypt, South Africa, and Thailand. However, many of them import the active pharmaceutical ingredients from India.[74]

Despite the difficulties, some countries have achieved remarkable success. Thus, Brazil provides free AIDS drugs to anyone who tests HIV positive and registers with the public health system. Of the 600,000 HIV-positive patients in July 2003, 250,000 received care and 130,0000 antiretrovirals. The rate of new infections has plateaued since 1996.[75] The system relies on Brazil manufacturing generic medicine itself, ie medicine not protected by patents. Such production was made possible by weak patent protection and, in 1997, certain loopholes in the Brazilian

[68] UNAIDS, *2004 Report on the Global AIDS Epidemic* (2004) 103.

[69] A Attaran and L Gillespie-White, 'Do Patents for Antiretroviral Drugs Constrain Access to AIDS Treatment in Africa?' (2001) 286 JAMA 1886, 1891; 'Thailand Eyes Generic Versions of Two AIDS Drugs', *Reuters* (10 July 2004).

[70] S Vedantam, 'AIDS Plan Would Cut Drug Costs for Poor. WHO Would Provide 3-in-1 Pill to Nations', *Washington Post* (25 October 2003); S Boseley, 'Clinton's Aids Deal Snubs Bush Plan', *The Guardian* (7 April 2004).

[71] DG McNeil Jr, 'Clinton in Deal to Cut AIDS Treatment Costs', *NY Times* (12 January 2006).

[72] WHO, *Procurement, Quality and Sourcing Project: Access to HIV/AIDS Drugs and Diagnostics of Acceptable Quality. Suppliers Whose HIV-Related Products Have Been Found Acceptable, in Principle, for Procurement by UN Agencies* (15th edn, 2004). In 2004, two drugs produced by Cipla were withdrawn from the list because of problems in a laboratory testing bioequivalence. LK Altman and DG McNeil Jr, 'UN Agency Drops 2 Drugs for AIDS Care Worldwide', *NY Times* (16 June 2004).

[73] S Banerji, *The Indian Intellectual Property Rights Regime and the TRIPs Agreement*, in C Long (ed), *Intellectual Property Rights in Emerging Markets* (2000) 47, 80 ff.

[74] A-C D'Adesky, *Moving Mountains. The Race to Treat Global AIDS* (2004) 64 ff, 383.

[75] A-C D'Adesky (n 74 above) 28 ff.

Patent Act,[76] staunchly attacked by the United States,[77] but defended by Brazil with equal force.[78] Brazil produces 15 AIDS drugs itself and buys 13 further anti-retrovirals from private corporations. Brazil's AIDS programme has reaped praise even from the US government: in 2003 Brazil and the US agreed to cooperate in advancing AIDS treatment programmes in Mozambique and Angola, with Brazil providing expertise in technology transfer for manufacturing generic antiretrovirals and overseeing their use in countries without adequate health care systems.[79]

IV The TRIPS Agreement and Access to Medicine: The South African Medicines Act

Cheap generics can only be manufactured where the medication is not protected by patents. In the past, many developing countries and some developed countries did not allow patents on pharmaceutical products. But pressure by the United States and the European Communities to provide pharmaceutical patents grew. Brazil was not the only country that felt the heat. Thailand, for example, changed its patent laws under the threat of trade sanctions.[80] In 1994 the TRIPS Agreement was signed as part of the WTO deal. It obliges all Members of the WTO to adopt a minimum standard of patent protection after a transitional period.

Even though the discussion on patents and access to medicine was already well under way in the early 1990s, it had not obtained much public interest. The topic of patents simply did not seem to lend itself to debate outside of technically interested circles. This changed with the South African Medicines and Related Substances Control Amendment Act, 1997, signed into law by President Mandela on 12 December 1997.[81] Faced with an epidemic of unprecedented proportions and the ensuing burden on its overstretched health budget, South Africa had decided

[76] The Brazilian Patent Act established a local working requirement, permitting compulsory licensing for failure to work the subject-matter of the patent in Brazil, and partly allowed parallel imports: Art 68(1), (2), (4) Lei da Propriedade Industrial N 9.279 de 14 de Maio de 1996, effective 15 May 1997. In 2005 Brazil threatened that it would issue a compulsory license for Abbott's AIDS drug Kaletra. T Benson, 'Brazil to Copy AIDS Drug Made by Abbott', *NY Times* (25 June 2005). The deal Brazil apparently negotiated with Abbott included an almost 50% price cut. P Prada, 'Brazil Near Deal with Abbott for Price Cut on AIDS Drug', *NY Times* (5 October 2005).

[77] At first the United States resorted to unilateral trade sanctions, see chapter 2. In 2000, the United States requested the establishment of a WTO panel. *Brazil—Measures Affecting Patent Protection. Request for the Establishment of a Panel by the United States*, WT/DS199/3 (2001). The dispute was resolved by a mutually agreed solution.

[78] Brazil requested WTO consultations on certain provisions in Chapter 18 of the US Patent Act that concern inventions made with federal assistance and favour substantial manufacture in the United States. *United States—US Patent Code. Request for Consultations by Brazil*, WT/DS224/1 (2001).

[79] D'Adesky (n 74 above) 31.

[80] RS Park, 'The International Drug Industry: What the Future Holds for South Africa's HIV/AIDS Patients' (2002) 11 Minn J Global Trade 125, 135.

[81] Medicines and Related Substances Control Amendment Act 1997, Republic of South Africa Government Gazette No 18505, Act No 90, 1997 (12 December 1997).

to take action to keep medication affordable, a decision that was all the more hastened by the fact that drug prices in South Africa were at times higher than in some developed countries.[82] Among the measures envisioned by the Medicines and Related Substances Control Amendment Act was a provision that gave the Minister of Health the authority to limit patent rights. The highly contested newly introduced section 15C of the Medicines and Related Substances Control Act read:

The minister may prescribe conditions for the supply of more affordable medicines in certain circumstances so as to protect the health of the public, and in particular may

(a) notwithstanding anything to the contrary contained in the Patents Act, 1978 (Act No. 57 of 1978), determine that the rights with regard to any medicine under a patent granted in the Republic shall not extend to acts in respect of such medicine which has been put onto the market by the owner of the medicine, or with his or her consent;

(b) prescribe the conditions on which any medicine which is identical in composition, meets the same quality standard and is intended to have the same proprietary name as that of another medicine already registered in the Republic, but which is imported by a person other than the person who is the holder of the registration certificate of the medicine already registered and which originates from any site of manufacture of the original manufacturer as approved by the council in the prescribed manner, may be imported;

(c) prescribe the registration procedure for, as well as the use of, the medicine referred to in paragraph (b).

The provision allows the Minister of Health to make use of two measures that have become a staple in the discussion of access to medicine and patent law: parallel imports and compulsory licences. Parallel imports of a drug, authorized by paragraphs (a) and (b) of the section,[83] are imports of a patented drug without authorization by the patentee from a country where the patentee itself placed the drug on the market at a lower price. Compulsory licences for drugs go beyond that in that the government authorizes third parties, in return for adequate remuneration for the patentee, to manufacture and sell the patented drug without the consent of the patentee, or to import the drug from a country where it has been put on the market by a third party manufacturer. The Minister of Health is authorized to grant such licences under the *chapeau* of section 15C, as paragraphs (a) and (b) only serve as examples of the Minister's authorization.[84]

[82] RL Ostergard, Jr, 'The Political Economy of the South Africa—United States Patent Dispute' (1999) 2 J World Intell Prop 875 ff; Statement by South Africa in Council for Trade-Related Aspects of Intellectual Property Rights, *Special Discussion on Intellectual Property and Access to Medicines*, IP/C/M/31 (10 July 2001).

[83] P Marc, 'Compulsory Licensing and the South African Medicine Act of 1997: Violation or Compliance of the Trade Related Aspects of Intellectual Property Rights Agreement?' (2001) 21 NYL Sch J Int'l & Comp L 109 (albeit using a broader definition of parallel imports); J Fedtke, 'Das Recht auf Leben und Gesundheit, Patentschutz und das Verfahren des High Court of South Africa zur Verfassungsmäßigkeit des südafrikanischen Medicines and Related Substances Control Amendment Act' (2001) 34 VRÜ 489, 499–500.

[84] WP Nagan, 'International Intellectual Property, Access to Health Care, and Human Rights: South Africa v United States' (2002) 14 Fla J Int'l L 155, 168; KM Bombach, 'Can South Africa

The international pharmaceutical industry, the US government and EU officials had already criticized the Act in the harshest terms before it was signed into law.[85] A swift reaction to the signature therefore had to be expected. On 18 February 1998 42 applicants, among them several big multinational pharmaceutical companies, filed suit against the South African government.[86] The industry argued that many provisions of the Act were in violation of the South African Constitution. With respect to section 15C the powers granted to the Minister of Health to prescribe conditions for the supply of more affordable medicines were regarded as too vague, particularly as the power includes the authorization to restrict patent rights.[87] The industry also argued that the provision violated its constitutionally protected property rights.[88] Finally, the provision was alleged to be inconsistent with Art 27 of the TRIPS Agreement as it purportedly discriminates against patent rights in the pharmaceutical field.[89] The US government followed the lead of the industry and put South Africa on its 'Special 301' Watch List, a list of countries that deny adequate and effective intellectual property protection,[90] reasoning that the Act granted the Minister of Health an ill-defined authority to authorize parallel imports, issue compulsory licences, and potentially otherwise abrogate patent rights.[91] In addition, the United States withheld preferential tariff treatment under the Generalized System of Preferences on four items.[92] The South African government, on the other hand, pointed out that under the South African Constitution it had an obligation to protect its citizens' right to health.[93]

Fight AIDS? Reconciling the South African Medicines and Related Substances Act with the TRIPS Agreement' (2001) 19 BU Int'l L J 273, 276–277.

[85] For a comprehensive overview of the history of the conflict cf Cptech (ed), *Appendix B. Time-line of Disputes over Compulsory Licensing and Parallel Importation in South Africa*, at <http://www.cptech .org/ip/health/sa/sa-timeline.txt>; an excellent account of the conflict is P Acconci, 'L'Accesso ai Farmaci Essenziali. Dall'Accordo TRIPS alla Dichiarazione della Quarta Conferenza Ministeriale OMC di Doha' (2001) 4 La Communitá Internazionale, 637, 646 ff.

[86] High Court of South Africa (Transvaal Provincial Division), *Pharmaceutical Manufacturers' Association of South Africa et al v President of the Republic of South Africa*, Case No 4183/98, Notice of Motion (1998).

[87] Paragraphs 2.1 ff of the Notice of Motion (n 86 above). Cf §§43, 44 of the South African Constitution; T Kongolo, 'Public Interest *versus* the Pharmaceutical Industry's Monopoly in South Africa' (2001) 4 J World Intell Prop 605, 616 ff.

[88] Paragraph 2.3 of the Notice of Motion (n 86 above). Cf §25 of the South African Constitution.

[89] Paragraph 2.4 of the Notice of Motion (n 86 above). Cf §44 (4), 231 (2), 231 (3) of the South African Constitution.

[90] Marc (n 83 above) 121. For details on the Special 301 Watch List see chapter 2.

[91] Ostergard (n 82 above) 880.

[92] Park (n 80 above) 137. Cf p 156 (Development Assistance) of the 'Act Making Omnibus Consolidated and Emergency Appropriations for the Fiscal Year Ending September 30, 1999 and for Other Purposes', Pub L 105-277 (199) (21 October 1998) ('*Provided further*, that none of the funds appropriated under this heading may be made available for assistance for the central Government of the Republic of South Africa, until the Secretary of State reports in writing to the appropriate committees of the Congress on the steps being taken by the United States Government to work with the Government of the Republic of South Africa to negotiate the repeal, suspension, or termination of section 15(c) of South Africa's Medicines and Related Substances Control Amendment Act No. 90 of 1997').

[93] Fedtke (n 83 above) 502.

The lawsuit of the pharmaceutical industry put the issue of access to medicine and the TRIPS Agreement on the international agenda—and the growing awareness of the extent of the AIDS pandemic ensured that it remained there. From a public relations point of view, the lawsuit turned into an unmitigated disaster for the pharmaceutical industry. Treatment Action Campaign, a South African NGO representing people affected by AIDS, joined the case as *amicus curiae*.[94] 300,000 individuals and 140 groups across 130 nations signed a petition demanding that the pharmaceutical industry withdraw its suit.[95] In the United States activists disrupted Vice-President Gore's campaign to draw attention to the problem. The Congressional Black Caucus started to take note and ask questions on patents and AIDS medication.[96] Articles in major newspapers such as the *New York Times* and the *Chicago Tribune* gave the cause an ever-growing audience. Soon the issue of patents and access to medicine seemed to be everywhere. Among the fora discussing the topic were the World Intellectual Property Organization (WIPO), which held a panel discussion on intellectual property and human rights in November 1998,[97] the WHO, which became the scene of heated debates on the topic during the discussion of its Revised Drug Strategy, that ultimately urged Member States to ensure that public health interests are paramount for pharmaceutical policies,[98] and the Sub-Commission on the Promotion and Protection of Human Rights, that passed a resolution on intellectual property rights and human rights.[99] Many of the numerous discussions on the AIDS pandemic and on the best way forward in the fight against the disease covered the patent question as a side issue.

Finally the pressure became too much to bear. With the Secretary-General of the United Nations mediating, the pharmaceutical industry decided to withdraw their lawsuit. In a joint statement with the South African government released on 19 April 2001 the industry declared its commitment to work together with the Republic of South Africa to further the health of the South African population. The government affirmed its commitment to the TRIPS Agreement and pledged to consult with the industry and the public about the regulations it would pass to implement Section 15C.[100] The United States, too, caved in. In September 1999 it announced that an agreement had been reached with South Africa. In the agreement the governments affirm their commitment to the TRIPS Agreement and their appreciation of the South African Government's efforts to provide affordable health care to its people. South Africa explicitly states that its implementation of

---

[94] Fedtke (n 83 above) 503.   [95] Park (n 80 above) 148.

[96] Ostergard (n 82 above) 881 ff.

[97] World Intellectual Property Organization (ed), *Intellectual Property and Human Rights. A Panel Discussion to commemorate the 50th Anniversary of the Universal Declaration of Human Rights. Geneva, November 9, 1998* (1999).   [98] *Revised Drug Strategy*, WHA Res 52.19 (24 May 1999).

[99] *Intellectual Property and Human Rights*, Sub-Commission on Human Rights Res 2000/7 (17 August 2000).

[100] *Text of Agreement in PMA et al v Republic of South Africa et al (High Court of South Africa—Transvaal Provincial Division, Case No. 4182/98)*.

the Medicines Act would be TRIPS compliant.[101] An executive order by President Clinton forbidding the United States to seek the revision of intellectual property laws of Sub-Saharan African countries that promote access to HIV/AIDS pharmaceuticals and are TRIPS compliant paved the way to halting the 'Special 301' action against South Africa.[102]

V Beyond AIDS Drugs: Anthrax and Cipro

The heated fight about HIV/AIDS drugs has gained so much coverage that it seems as though the debate about the TRIPS Agreement and access to pharmaceuticals is intrinsically limited to the question of access to AIDS drugs. Given the scale of the HIV/AIDS pandemic, there can be no doubt that the disease is currently the single most important example of the conflict between patents and access to medicine. However, it is not the only one—to name just a few examples: Novartis' cancer drug *Glivec* has caused fierce debates,[103] Myriad Genetic's patent on breast-cancer related genes has nearly quintupled prices for genetic tests for breast cancer in Canada and spawned a renewed discussion on patents in health care in Canada.[104] Another example is *oseltamivir*, better known under its trade name *Tamiflu*, the patents on which are owned by Gilead and still in force.[105] The medication marketed by Roche is WHO's recommended treatment for avian influenza or 'bird flu'.[106] Cases of the disease in humans, transmitted from infected animals, have been rare, but have raised the spectre of an influenza epidemic if the

---

[101] Department of Trade and Industry, *Joint Understanding between the Governments of South Africa and the United States of America*, at <http://www.polity.org.za/html/govdocs/pr/1999/pr0917b.html?rebookmark=1> (17 September 1999).

[102] Section 1(a) Executive Order No 13155, *Access to HIV/AIDS Pharmaceuticals and Medical Technologies* (10 May 2000). The Bush administration explicitly continued this policy. NA Bass, 'Implications of the TRIPS Agreement for Developing Countries: Pharmaceutical Patent Laws in Brazil and South Africa in the 21st Century' (2002) 34 The Geo Wash Int'l L Rev 191, 212.

[103] The Indian company Natco Pharma launched a generic version of *Glivec* under the name *VEENAT* on 26 January 2003 for 10% of the price of *Glivec*. Later the same year Novartis obtained exclusive marketing rights for the drug in India, a decision that Natco challenged in court. Meanwhile, Novartis has obtained a stay blocking six Indian companies from manufacturing generic versions of the drug. In South Korea activists unsuccessfully sought a compulsory license after a 30% price hike for *Glivec*. C Cookson and G Dyer, 'A Drugs Deal for the World's Poorest: Now the Fight over Patents and Cheap Medicine is in Middle-Income Countries', *Financial Times* (2 September 2003); 'Novartis Receives EMR for Glivec', *Express Pharma Pulse* (12 November 2003); 'Natco to Challenge Grant of Exclusive Rights to Novartis Cancer Drug', *The Hindu Business Line* (13 November 2003); J Datta, 'Exclusive Marketing Rights—Novartis Gets Stay against 6 Firms', *The Hindu Business Line* (25 January 2004); 'Government raised the Glivec Price', *IP-Health* (21 January 2003); Korea: Rejection of Glivec Compulsory License, *IP-Health* (10 March 2003).

[104] ER Gold and DK Lam, 'Balancing Trade in Patents—Public Non-Commercial Use and Compulsory Licensing' (2003) 6 J World Intell Prop 5, 7–8.

[105] Roche, *Factsheet Tamiflu* (2006).

[106] WHO, *WHO Rapid Advice Guidelines on Pharmacological Management of Humans Infected with Avian Influenza A (H5N1) Virus*, ii (2006).

virus should mutate to enable human-to-human transmission.[107] With countries scrambling to stockpile *Tamiflu*, Roche's drug turned into a blockbuster and concerns surfaced that Roche would be unable to satisfy the growing demand. In several countries there were discussions about imposing compulsory licenses, forcing Roche to issue sub-licences for the drug. As the *Tamiflu* patent had not yet been granted in India, Cipla decided to start producing the drug.[108]

Of particular interest for this study is yet another example due to its political implications: Bayer's *Cipro*. In October 2001, shortly after the tragedy of the 11 September 2001 terror attacks on the United States, mysterious letters containing anthrax were sent to a number of important personalities, including Democratic Senator Daschle, New York Governor Pataki, as well as the offices of NBC and ABC television.[109] Bayer, a large German corporation, produced the only medication approved for treating anthrax in the United States: the antibiotic *Cipro*. Whereas in Europe the patent on *Cipro* had already expired, the product was still under patent in the United States and Canada.[110]

Demand for the drug skyrocketed as individuals prepared for large-scale biological terror attacks within the United States. The US government announced that the White House wanted to purchase a sufficient quantity of antibiotics to cover 12 million people for 60 days. Despite immediate increases in Bayer's production capacity the demand significantly outpaced the growing supply. The Indian drug maker Cipla, that had been producing a generic version of the drug for more than a decade and sold it for a fraction of the cost of the brand-name drug,[111] offered to supply *Cipro* to the United States. The situation was fraught with irony: Cipla, one of the major suppliers of generic AIDS drugs and as such on the other side of the trenches in the fight about access to AIDS drugs, offered *Cipro* to the United States, even though it was still protected by Bayer's patent.[112] At first, however, it seemed that the US administration would hold on to its pro-patent position. Bayer announced it would triple *Cipro* production to 200 million tablets over three months and the US Secretary of Health and Human Services, Thompson, stated publicly that his agency would not disregard patents.[113]

But the situation changed when Canada announced that it would purchase 900,000 tablets of a generic version of *Cipro* for what was reported to be roughly

---

[107] WHO, *Avian influenza ("bird flu")—Fact sheet*, at <http://www.who.int/mediacentre/factsheets/avian_influenza/en/index.html> (2006).

[108] 'Avian Influenza. In a Flap', *The Economist* (20 October 2005); 'Tamiflu Maker Roche Agrees on Generics', *Reuters* (8 December 2005); M Binyon, 'Indian Hero's New Mission: To Bring Cheap Drug for Bird Flu to Millions', *The Times* (6 March 2006).

[109] 'Milzbrand legt Repräsentantenhaus zum Teil lahm', *Handelsblatt* (18 October 2001).

[110] 'Angst vor Milzbrand bringt Schub für Bayer-Produkt', *Handelsblatt* (17 October 2001).

[111] V Sridhar, 'Perilous Patent', *Frontline* (24 November 2001).

[112] M Peterson and R Pear, 'Anthrax Fears Send Demand for a Drug Far Beyond Output', *NY Times* (16 October 2001).

[113] M Fleischer-Black, 'The Cipro Dilemma—In the Anthrax Crisis, Tommy Thompson Distorted Patent Law to Save Public Health. Good Move?', *The American Lawyer* (January 2002); S Vedantam/T Chea, 'Drug Firm Plays Defense in Anthrax Scare', *Washington Post* (20 October 2001).

half the price that Bayer would have charged. After Bayer threatened litigation the two sides agreed that Canada would not break Bayer's patent and Bayer would deliver medication within 48 hours' notice at $1.30 per pill—much lower than its usual government price of $1.83. Secretary of Health and Human Services Thompson radically changed his position: he threatened that the United States would buy *Cipro* from generic manufacturers if Bayer would not make significant price concessions.[114] The threat was backed by an Executive Order issued by President Bush extending national defence contracting authority to the Department of Health and Human Services, an implicit threat that the Department would contract with a competitor to obtain *Cipro*.[115] Bayer felt its options were exhausted and agreed to supply 100 million tablets of *Cipro* for $0.95 per tablet. In addition, the United States obtained an option for an additional 200 million tablets.[116] The about-face in the US government's position compared to the one adopted during the South African trial was widely noted.[117] To this day the debate about access to medicine and patent law continues and the United States has remained the most ardent defender of stringent patent protection.

[114] S Vedantam and DL Brown, 'US Seeks Price Cut from Cipro Maker', *Washington Post* (24 October 2001); K Bradsher and EL Andrews, 'US Says Bayer Will Cut Cost of its Anthrax Drug', *NY Times* (24 October 2001).

[115] Executive Order No 13232, *Further Amendment to Executive Order 10789, as Amended, To Authorize the Department of Health and Human Services To Exercise Certain Contracting Authority in Connection with National Defense Functions* (20 October 2001).

[116] Bayer, *Bayer to Supply Government by Year-End with 100 Million Tablets for $95 Million* (24 October 2001) at <http://lists.essential.org/pipermail/ip-health/2001-October/002261.html>; Department of Health and Human Services, *HHS, Bayer Agree to Cipro Purchase* (24 October 2001), at <http://www.cptech.org/ip/health/cl/cipro/dhhs10242001.html>.

[117] C Lenz and T Kieser, 'Schutz vor Milzbrandangriffen durch Angriffe auf den Patentschutz?' (2002) NJW 401; E Clark, 'America's Anthrax Patent Dilemma' (BBC, 23 October 2001), at <http://news.bbc.co.uk/1/hi/business/1613410.stm>.

2

Patent Law

At the core of the alleged conflict between the TRIPS Agreement and access to medicine is the claim that patents on pharmaceuticals raise prices, thereby reducing the accessibility of drugs. Given the extent of the AIDS crisis described in the last chapter, accessibility of AIDS drugs clearly is of vital importance. A thorough background on patent law, particularly its international aspects, is indispensable in an analysis of the alleged conflict. This chapter will provide this background and describe the minimum obligations of World Trade Organization (WTO) Members with respect to patent laws. Whether these obligations conflict with human rights obligations will be analyzed in chapter 4. The flexibilities provided by the TRIPS Agreement as well as the measures taken by the WTO to enhance those flexibilities in the area of pharmaceutical patents will be described in chapter 5. The reason for describing the flexibilities after determining that there is a conflict between the two orders lies in the definition of 'conflict' under public international law, presented in chapter 4.

After a short primer on patents (I) the study will discuss the history of patent law. The historic account will demonstrate that the popular image of patents as a duly acquired, traditional, and well-deserved 'natural law' property position is inaccurate. Rather, patents for a long time were granted by national authorities as an instrument to advance national development, not as a right of the inventor. The historic survey will also show that legislators have always endeavoured to achieve a balance in patent law to preserve its positive effects as an incentive for innovation while minimizing its negative effects, such as higher prices. With respect to pharmaceutical products, many industrialized countries used to consider the arguments against granting product patents to prevail: they have not introduced product patent protection for pharmaceutical products until relatively recently (II). I will then turn to the rationales of modern day patent legislation and demonstrate that today's patents are almost universally justified by utilitarian ideas rather than natural law property arguments (III). Part IV will show the development of international patent law culminating in the TRIPS Agreement. The TRIPS Agreement requires Members of the WTO to grant patents and it imposes minimum standards for patent laws. Even under the TRIPS Agreement, however, the principle of territoriality remains valid, under which patents have no effect outside of the territory for which they are granted, usually a nation state. The minimum standards imposed by the TRIPS Agreement will be described in part V. The TRIPS Agreement also allows states to weaken patents in several respects, as by granting compulsory licences, patent law's equivalent to takings. These optional so-called 'flexibilities' will be covered in chapter 5.

I A Short Primer on Patents

Patent law is domestic law. There is quite an astonishing variety of national patent laws. Rather than presenting any one of them, this section intends to give a cursory overview over certain common features. Patents can be obtained by an inventor, or the first person to file for a patent,[1] for products or processes that are new, involve an inventive step,[2] and are capable of industrial application,[3] by disclosing the invention to the patent office in a way that a person skilled in the art will be able to carry out the invention. The application consists of a description of the invention ('specification') and of language claiming precisely the technology that was invented and that will be the subject of the patent rights—the so-called 'claims'.[4] Patent offices are, generally, a national institution.[5] They usually examine whether the requirements for patentability under their national laws are fulfilled,[6] grant the patent if that is the case, and publish the patent application.[7] Product patents confer the right to prevent third parties not having the patentee's consent from making, using, offering for sale, selling, or importing for these purposes the patented product. Process patents similarly confer the right to prevent third parties not having the patentee's consent from using the process and using, offering for sale, selling, or importing for these purposes a product obtained directly by the patented process.[8] Anyone engaging in one of these activities with respect to the subject

---

[1] Whether patents should be granted to the first to file, or the first person to invent is one of the classic patent law debates. The United States grants patents to the first person to invent, although reform might be under way. On 8 June 2005 Rep Lamar Smith introduced HR 2795, the Patent Reform Act of 2005, which would change the US system to a first-to-file system. A similar reform effort is the Patent Reform Act of 2006, introduced on 3 August 2006 by Sen Orrin G Hatch and Sen Patrick Leahy as S 3818. As the Acts have not yet been passed, they will be disregarded hereinafter. Germany switched from a first-to-file to a first-to-invent system in 1936. H Hubmann and H-P Götting, *Gewerblicher Rechtsschutz* (7th edn, 2002) 140.

[2] The US Patent Act requires inventions to be 'non-obvious'.

[3] The US Patent Act requires the invention to be useful.

[4] HF Schwartz, *Patent Law and Practice* (3rd edn, 2001) 10.

[5] There are currently three major regional patent offices that grant patents that are treated like national patents of the member states after they have been granted: the European Patent Office (EPO), the African Regional Industrial Property Organization (ARIPO), and the *Organisation Africaine de la Propriété Intellectuelle* (OAPI).

[6] Not all countries provide for such an examination. Some merely established a registration system in which the patent office only registers the patents. However, examination systems are common in most important patent systems, eg the US system, the European system, and the German Patent system. Hubmann and Götting (n 1 above) 162; M Barrett, *Intellectual Property* (3rd edn, 1999–2000) 21.

[7] Commonly, the application is published a certain time after filing, whether by that time the patent has been granted or not.   [8] Article 27 ff of the TRIPS Agreement.

matter claimed in the patent[9] faces damages and injunctive relief. Product patents are more desirable for the patentee than process patents, because product patents grant the patentee market exclusivity for the product, whereas the owner of process patents faces competition by others producing the same product by a different process.[10] At times the dichotomy can cause some perplexity with observers: the first one to invent a process to produce a product gains exclusivity for the whole product, the inventor finding a second process can merely claim the process. Some critics have argued that chemical patents should never be issued on the compound itself, but only on a specific use and on a specific process of producing the compound,[11] but whatever the merits of such a proposal—the current state of the law is different.

Patent rights are only granted for a limited term, commonly 20 years from the filing of the application. Some countries impose additional limits on patent rights. One common such limit is a 'local working requirement', obliging the patentee to actually manufacture the product or use the process within the country of the grant. Another one is the governmental grant of compulsory licences under certain circumstances. Such a licence allows a third party to use the patent without the consent of the patentee, usually in return for a 'reasonable' fee.

According to the Continental tradition, patent law is part of industrial property law (*propriété industrielle/gewerblicher Rechtsschutz*). The more and more popular Anglo-American nomenclature is somewhat broader and combines industrial property law and copyright and neighbouring rights to the area of intellectual property law.[12]

II The History of Patent Law

Much can be learned about the nature and purpose of patent law by studying its history. At times, intellectual property holders seem to be forgetful of the history of this area of law, validating what Blackstone wrote in his *Commentaries on the Laws of England* concerning property law:

There is nothing which so generally strikes the imagination, and engages the affections of mankind, as the right to property; or that sole and despotic dominion which one man

---

[9] The doctrine of equivalents broadens the patent claims beyond a mere literal reading to discount the presence of mere minor changes. AR Miller and MH Davis, *Intellectual Property in a Nutshell* (3rd edn, 2000) 131 ff.

[10] It is also far easier to prove the infringement of a product patent, as anyone selling the product is clearly infringing. Many countries resolve this difficulty for process patent holders by reversing the burden of proof, so that the defendant will have to prove it is using a different process (see Art 34 of the TRIPS Agreement). Nevertheless, patentees might be reluctant to commence a lawsuit, because they are uncertain whether the defendant makes use of the patented process.

[11] PH Eggert, 'Uses, New Uses and Chemical Patents—A Proposal' (1969) 51 J Pat Off Soc'y 768, 784 ff.

[12] RP Merges, PS Menell and MA Lemley, *Intellectual Property in the New Technology Age* (1997) 21; Hubmann and Götting (n 1 above) 1 ff. For readable introductions to the field see Barrett (n 6 above); Miller and Davis (n 9 above).

claims and exercises over the external things of the world, in total exclusion of the right of any other individual of the universe. And yet there are very few, that will give themselves the trouble to consider the origin and foundation of this right. Pleased as we are with the possession, we seem afraid to look back to the means by which it was acquired, as if fearful of some defect in our title[13]

Fearlessly opening Pandora's Box we shall see that patents, the history of which reaches back more than 500 years, were granted as a means to promote the industrial advancement of the nation. Although the natural law argument of the fairness of ownership in one's own inventions has certainly exerted an influence on the development of patent law, legislators have always tried to tailor patent laws to the goal of inducing the introduction of new knowledge within their territory with minimal disadvantages to society. The common claim that inventors traditionally (and everywhere) have a right to a patent is therefore misplaced.

1 Patent Privileges

Rulers in the middle ages often saw new arts and industries arise in foreign countries and were faced with the challenge of spurring the industrial development of their own territory. To them, it mattered little whether they did so by inducing inventions in their realm or by importing knowledge from abroad. Attracting foreigners skilled in new arts was an important tool in advancing national industries, but it proved no simple task at times when flexibility of workers was unheard of and when many an attempt to settle and work abroad was thwarted by closed societies and restrictive rules such as guild rules.[14] To induce artisans skilled in arts that were unknown in their realm to overcome such difficulties, settle in their territories, and train their subjects in these new arts rulers used their power to grant 'privileges', which were also granted to inventors.[15] In fact, at the time no distinction was made between privileges granted for inventions and privileges granted for the importation of knowledge. Both were granted for an art that was new to the realm.[16]

Privileges could take various forms. In 1331 the Flemish Weaver Kempe received sovereign protection by Edward III of England in return for training Edward's

---

[13] W Blackstone, *Commentaries on the Laws of England. Book the Second* (4th edn, 1770) 2.

[14] Guild monopolies banned non-members from competing with guild members.

[15] The power to grant privileges was not restricted to the function of introducing new knowledge. Thus, for example, Wenceslas II of Bohemia granted exclusive exploitation rights as an incentive for the investment necessary for the exploitation of mines—another commonly mentioned ancestor of modern day intellectual property law. Y Plasseraud and F Savignon, *L'Etat et l'Invention. Histoire des Brevets* (1986) 29; Hubmann and Götting (n 1 above) 15. Earlier precedents are cited in M Vukmir, 'The Roots of Anglo-American Intellectual Property Law in Roman Law' (1992) 32 IDEA 123; RP Merges and JF Duffy, *Patent Law and Policy: Cases and Materials* (3rd edn, 2002) 1 ff; F Pollaud-Dulian, *Droit de la Propriété industrielle* (1999) 61; W Weiß and C Herrmann, *Welthandelsrecht* (2003) 41.

[16] EC Walterscheid, 'The Early Evolution of the United States Patent Law: Antecedents (Pt 1)' (1994) 76 J Pat & Trademark Off Soc'y 697, 706–707.

subjects in his trade[17] and in 1404 the Duke of Silesia exempted Michael Bod from guild rules[18] for inventing a means to draw water artificially out of a mine without horses.[19] Maybe the first time a privilege took the form of a limited monopoly, ie a time-limited exclusive right to exercise the art in question in the territory of the sovereign granting the privilege, was 1105.[20] Bestowing the beneficiary with such a monopoly later became common,[21] with one of the best-known examples being a monopoly granted to Brunelleschi in 1421 for a machine for transporting merchandise on the Arno.[22] The person introducing the new art did not have a right to such privileges: rulers granted them at their discretion in open letters, '*litterae patentes*'—hence the term patent.[23]

2 The First Patent Acts

Patents continued to be granted at the discretion of the ruler as an incentive not just for invention, but also for the importation of knowledge well into the 18th century. 1474 saw the enactment of the world's first patent statute in Venice,[24] channelling the somewhat haphazard practice into legislation. It protected 'new and ingenious device[s]' not previously made in Venice, ie also the importation of knowledge, upon notice to the *Provveditori di Comun* of the reduction of the invention to perfection. Others were forbidden to make the same or similar devices without the consent of the patentee for ten years. The protection was justified in the preamble of the statute by arguing that it would induce more people to invent devices for the common good. The legislator tried to achieve a balance by allowing the government to take and use the device on the condition that no one but the patentee should operate it.[25]

---

[17] A Mossoff, 'Rethinking the Development of Patents: An Intellectual History, 1550–1800' (2001) 52 Hastings LJ 1255, 1259.

[18] Exemption from guild rules was a common feature of privileges granted for the introduction of knowledge. FD Prager, 'A History of Intellectual Property from 1545 to 1787' (1994) 26 J Pat & Trademark Off Soc'y 711, 714; EC Walterscheid, 'The Early Evolution of the United States Patent Law: Antecedents (Pt 2)' (1994) 76 J Pat & Trademark Off Soc'y 849, 851; G Mandich, 'Venetian Patents (1450–1550)' (1948) 30 J Pat & Trademark Off Soc'y 166, 167 (trans FD Prager).

[19] Hubmann and Götting (n 1 above) 16–17.

[20] Granted by de Mortagne in the Normandy to an abbot for windmills. S Lapointe, 'L'Histoire des brevets' (2000) 12 Les Cahiers de Propriété Intellectuelle 633, 636.

[21] Walterscheid (n 16 above), 707, TM Meshbesher, 'The Role of History in Comparative Patent Law' (1996) 78 J Pat & Trademark Off Soc'y 594, 601.

[22] Granted by the city of Florence. A translation of the grant was published as FD Prager, 'Brunelleschi's Patent', (1946) 28 J Pat & Trademark Off Soc'y 109. Brunelleschi's shipping adventure was a commercial failure and he remains known to the world for the *cupola* of the *Duomo* in Florence.

[23] W Blackstone, *Commentaries on the Laws of England. Book the Second* (4th edn, 1770) 346, who noted that the king's grants were a matter of public record and that these grants, whether of lands, honours, liberties, franchises, or something else were contained in charters or letters patent, open letters which were not sealed up, addressed to the subjects at large, and recorded in the patent-rolls. On the term 'privilege', see H Mohnhaupt, 'Die Unendlichkeit des Privilegienbegriffs' in B Dölemeyer and H Mohnhaupt (eds), *Das Privileg im europäischen Vergleich. Bd. 1* (1997) 1.

[24] E Berkenfeld, 'Das älteste Patentgesetz der Welt' (1949) GRUR 139.

[25] Walterscheid (n 16 above) 708.

The patent practice of England, like that of most countries,[26] strove to make sure that the new industry was actually introduced into the realm. It required the patentee to work the patent, ie to manufacture the invented product in England and threatened revocation of the patent for failure to do so. The patent could also be revoked for failure to teach the new art to an Englishman where the patent was granted to a foreigner, for lack of novelty, ie if the invention had already been previously known within England, or simply for 'inconveniency', which basically meant a the discretion of the Crown.[27] Despite these safeguards, the reign of Elizabeth I experienced a growing and damaging abuse of the patent practice. Monopolies were granted to favourites of the court even for industries well-established within England, such as the salt industry. It was in this context that the King's Bench held in *Darcy v Allen*[28] that patent monopolies should only be granted where the product was previously unknown within England,[29] noting amongst others that patent monopolies posed the danger of the patentee demanding unreasonably high prices for the product.[30] Despite the ruling, the abuse of patent monopolies continued under the reign of James I, until in 1623 Parliament felt obliged to pass the Statute of Monopolies[31] to curb the use of monopolies. The statute reflects a general scepticism about the merits of monopolies that also spread to the British colonies. Thus, Jefferson was long convinced that the risk of abuse from patents outweighed their benefits.[32] The Statute of Monopolies was to remain the only statutory basis for granting patents in England for 200 years.[33] It allows the grant of patent monopolies only

> for the term of fourteen years or under (. . .) of the sole working or making of any manner of new manufactures, within this realm, [to] (. . .) the true and first inventor and inventors of such manufactures.[34]

---

[26] Walterscheid (n 18 above) 854. Germany's flourishing patent custom featured monopoly patents balanced by a local working requirement or by permitting others to manufacture the invented product for a fee. Germany's patent custom withered away in the 30-years war. Hubmann and Götting (n 1 above) 17; H Pohlmann, 'Neue Materialien zur Frühentwicklung des deutschen Erfinderschutzes im 16. Jahrhundert' (1960) GRUR 272, 274 translated as H Pohlmann, 'The Inventor's Right in Early German Law. Materials of the Time from 1531 to 1700' (1961) 43 J Pat & Trademark Off Soc'y 121, 125 (trans FD Prager). [27] Walterscheid (n 18 above) 857, 871.

[28] King's Bench, *Darcy v Allen* (1603) 72 Eng Rep 830; 74 Eng Rep 1131, 77 Eng Rep 1260.

[29] *Darcy v Allen* (1603) 74 Eng Rep 1131, 1139.

[30] '[C]eo done power al Darcy sole a vender cards, sans limiter ascu price, per que il poit vender al unreasonable prices, quel srôit grand oppssion', *Darcy v Allen* (1603) 72 Eng Rep 830, 831. Curiously, the products at issue in this landmark case were playing cards.

[31] VII Statutes at Large 255 (1763). The statute is quoted in full by AW Deller, *Deller's Walker on Patents. Volume One* (2nd edn, 1964) 31.

[32] In a 1787 letter to a French inventor Jefferson wrote that although government intervention in matters of invention 'has its use, yet it is in practice so inseparable from abuse, that [the United States] think it better not to meddle with it'. T Jefferson, 'Letter to Jeudy de L'Hommande (Aug 9, 1787)' in JP Boyd (ed), *The Papers of Thomas Jefferson. Volume 12. 7 August 1787 to 31 March 1788* (1955) 11; he was even more explicit in a letter to Madison: 'but the benefit even of limited monopolies is too doubtful to be opposed to that of their general suppression', T Jefferson, 'Letter to James Madison (July 31, 1788)', in JP Boyd (ed), *The Papers of Thomas Jefferson. Volume 13. March to 7 October 1788* (1956) 440, 443. [33] Walterscheid (n 18 above) 874.

[34] Section VI of the Statute.

It has been speculated that the 14-year term was chosen because it represented the length of two consecutive apprenticeships, the assumption allegedly being that by the end of the term two generations of apprentices had mastered the art and it was therefore securely introduced into the realm.[35] Sometimes the grant was explicitly conditioned on training apprentices in the art.[36]

In the decades after the passage of the Statute of Monopolies the mode of introduction of new knowledge into a country shifted away from teaching apprentices face-to-face. In the 17th and 18th century it became common to require the patentee to submit a written specification enabling someone of ordinary skill in the art to practice the invention.[37] Given that artisans could now learn the new art from reading the public documents, the obligation to train apprentices became superfluous.[38] The requirement to deliver specifications was included in the first US Patent Act, the Patent Act of 1790,[39] passage of which was based on the power the US Constitution had granted to Congress to 'promote the progress of science and useful arts, by securing for limited times to authors and inventors the exclusive right to their respective writings and discoveries'.[40] Specifications have since become a standard feature of patent law. The 1790 Act is remarkable for yet another reason: it abolished patents for the importation of knowledge. Washington had argued in favour of incentives for the introduction of new inventions from abroad[41] and Congress had provided in the Patent Bill that patents were available 'for matters not before known or used within the United States'. The bill would thus have allowed importation patents, ie patents for matters known abroad, but not within the United States—it even explicitly provided that first importers of knowledge were to be treated like inventors.[42] But importation patents faced criticism, as they would have prevented Americans from freely copying British inventions.[43]

---

[35] EC Walterscheid, 'Defining the Patent and Copyright Term: Term Limits and the Intellectual Property Clause' (2000) 7 J Intell Prop L 315, 325 (expressing doubts about this theory).

[36] Deller (n 31 above) 35.

[37] EC Walterscheid, 'The Early Evolution of the United States Patent Law: Antecedents (Pt 3)' (1995) 77 J Pat & Trademark Off Soc'y 771, 777 ff.   [38] Walterscheid (n 37 above) 777.

[39] 1 Stat 109–112 (10 April 1790).

[40] US Const, Art 1, §8, cl 8. On the clause: TT Ochoa and M Rose, 'The Anti-Monopoly Origins of the Patent and Copyright Clause' (2002) 84 J Pat & Trademark Off Soc'y 909; EC Walterscheid, 'To Promote the Progress of Science and Useful Arts: The Background and Origin of the Intellectual Property Clause of the United States Constitution' (1994) 2 J Intell Prop L 1. In colonial times patents were theoretically granted by authority of the royal prerogative or by the powers vested in the royal governors. In practice, however, most patents were granted on a case-by-case basis by colonial legislatures. EC Walterscheid, 'The Early Evolution of the United States Patent Law: Antecedents (5 Pt I)' (1996) 78 J Pat & Trademark Off Soc'y 615, 623–631.

[41] LG de Pauw, CB Bickford, and LS Hauptman (eds), *Documentary History of the First Federal Congress of the United States of America. March 4, 1789–March 3, 1791. Volume III. House of Representatives Journal* (1977) 253. After the 1790 US Patent Act Hamilton envisaged pecuniary rewards for the importation of knowledge. A Hamilton, 'Report on the Subject of Manufactures' in HC Syrett (ed), *The Papers of Alexander Hamilton, vol. X. December 1791–January 1792*, 230, 308, 338 (1966). The first draft of the same report by Coxe suggested land grants. T Coxe, *Draft of the Report on the Subject of Manufactures*, in HC Syrett (ed), *The Papers of Alexander Hamilton, vol. X. December 1791–January 1792* (1996) 15, 18–19.

[42] EC Walterscheid, *To Promote the Progress of Useful Arts: American Patent Law and Administration, 1798–1836* (1998) 121.   [43] Walterscheid (n 42 above), 123.

The critics prevailed and importation patents were abolished in the House and Senate debates, allowing patents only 'for matters not before known or used'. Thus, knowledge or use of the invention anywhere could defeat novelty.[44] Later commentators argued that a federal law allowing the grant of patents for importation of knowledge would be unconstitutional.[45] Over time,[46] importation patents in other countries, too, faded out of existence and laws required the invention to be new and not just unknown in the country granting the patent.

However, even under the US Patent Act of 1790 the grant of patents largely remained a discretionary affair.[47] Petitions for patents had to be directed to the patent board, which could grant the patent if it deemed the invention sufficiently useful and important.[48] Under English law, too, patents continued to be granted solely at the discretion of the Crown, as the Lord Chancellor pointed out in 1790.[49] Not surprisingly, inventors everywhere had long come to embrace a different view in that respect. They stressed that the grant of patents was only fair and even that it had become a custom.[50] The Industrial Revolution and the growing importance of inventors in its wake gave their argument the necessary edge. James Watt 'feared that an engineer's life without patent was not worthwhile'.[51] The teachings of philosophers like Locke supported their position. Locke argued that every man has a natural right to the fruits of his work, rooting patent protection in natural law.[52] The theory of a property right of the inventor in his or her invention obtained its most decisive victory in the French Revolution. The French Patent Act passed in

---

[44] Walterscheid (n 42 above), 137. The foreign inventor was prevented from obtaining a patent both abroad and in the US by the US Patent Act of 1793, which allowed the grant of patents solely to US citizens.

[45] Among them the influential voice of Justice Story. J Story, *Commentaries on the Constitution of the United States with a Preliminary Review of the Constitutional History of the Colonies and States, Before the Adoption of the Constitution. Volume II*, 89 (3rd edn, 1858). *Livingston & Fulton v Van Ingen et al* (Court for the Correction of Errors of NY, 1812) 9 Johns 507, 560–561.

[46] France continued to grant such patents under Art 3 of its 1791 Act and has not abolished them until 1844 (Art 31 of the 1844 Act), as it became apparent that the provision resulted in a race to patent goods invented abroad. E Pouillet, *Traité Théorique et Pratique des Brevets d'Invention et de la Contrefaçon* (3rd edn, 1889) 320.

[47] The act states 'it shall be lawful' to grant a patent, not that it has to be granted. The language alone is sufficiently persuasive on this point, Walterscheid (n 42 above) 168 ff; *contra* DW Banner, 'An Unanticipated, Nonobvious, Enabling Portion of the Constitution: The Patent Provision—The Best Mode' (1987) 69 J Pat & Trademark Off Soc'y 631, 638.

[48] Paragraph 1 of the Patent Act of 1790. The patent board consisted of the Secretary of State, the Secretary for the Department of War, and the Attorney General. Walterscheid (n 42 above) 136.

[49] Walterscheid (n 18 above) 879. C MacLead, *Inventing the Industrial Revolution. The English Patent System, 1660–1800* (1988) 22–23.

[50] Andreas Schulz wrote in his 1551 petition that the grant of the privilege was an 'old laudable custom'. Pohlmann GRUR (n 26 above), 272, 274. Galileo's petition for a patent to the Doge of Venice in 1594 mentioned that it would not be proper if the fruit of his labour would become common property. Deller (n 31 above) 38.

[51] EC Walterscheid, 'The Early Evolution of the United States Patent Law: Antecedents (Pt 4)' (1996) 78 J Pat & Trademark Off Soc'y 77, 81. J Madison, 'The Federalist No. 43', in A Hamilton, J Jay, and J Madison, *The Federalist. A Commentary on the Constitution of the United States* (1888).

[52] J Locke, 'An Essay Concerning the True Original Extent and End of Civil Government' in RM Hutchins (ed), *Great Books of the Western World. 35 Locke Berkeley Hume* (1952) 25, 30.

1791[53] and completed by a Regulation dated 25 May 1791[54] stated explicitly that '*[t]oute découverte ou nouvelle invention dans tous les genres d'industrie, est la propriété de son auteur*'.[55] The grant of the patent was regarded as merely declaratory. Despite this paradigm shift, patents remained limited in time—with a patent term of 5, 10, or 15 years at the choice of the patentee.[56] The Act even included further safeguards, among them an obligation to work the patent within France. If without justification the patentee did not work his or her patent in France within two years of the grant, it could be revoked.[57]

The revolutionary act proved very influential in many respects.[58] Even though its natural law rationale did not withstand the test of time, patents began to be granted as of right. Although the language of the new US Patent Act of 1793[59] did not explicitly grant the inventor a right to a patent, it was interpreted to do so by the US Supreme Court.[60] The 1844 French Patent Act,[61] notwithstanding the fact that it scrapped the language of the 1791 Act, retained the right to a patent,[62] which has been with us ever since. The safeguards of the old Act were also retained, indeed, they were built upon by adding that the patent could be revoked if the inventor did not exploit the invention in France within two years or ceased the exploitation for two consecutive years without justification.[63] This provision was not abolished until 1953.[64] Many other countries included similar working requirements in their patent legislation.[65] The United States, however, consciously rejected such an approach.[66]

---

[53] 'Loi relative aux découvertes utiles, et aux moyens d'en assurer la propriété à ceux qui seront en être les auteurs', in T Regnault, *De la Législation et de la Jurisprudence concernant les Brevets d'Invention, et Perfectionnement et d'Importation* (1825) 135.

[54] 'Décret portant réglement sur la propriété des auteurs d'inventions et découvertes en tout genre' (25 Mai 1791), in JB Duvergier (ed), *Collection Complète des Lois, Decrets, Ordonnances, Règlemens et Avis du Conseil D'État. Tome Deuxième* (1834) 360.

[55] 'Any discovery or new invention, in any kind of industry, is the property of its author.' (trans Walterscheid (n 51 above) footnote 143). Note that the same rights are granted for the importation of an invention in Art 3 of the Act.   [56] Article 8 of the Act.

[57] Article 16 No 4 of the Act.

[58] P Roubier, *Le Droit de la Propriété Industrielle. Partie Générale I.—Les Droits Privatifs (Histoire et nature juridique, régime intérieur et international). II.—Les Actions en Justice (Action en contrefaçon et action en concurrence déloyale)* (1952) 70–71.

[59] 1 Stat 318 (21 February 1793). The new Act had become necessary because the high government officials sitting on the patent board (among them Secretary of State Jefferson) did not have the time to fulfil their tasks competently. Walterscheid (n 42 above) 195.

[60] *Grant v Raymond* (1832) 31 US 218, 241; Walterscheid (n 42 above) 236, 260 ff.

[61] 'Loi sur les brevets d'invention (5 July 1844)', in JB Duvergier (ed), *Collection Complète des Lois, Decrets, Ordonnances, Règlemens et Avis du Conseil D'État. Tome 44* (1844) 553.

[62] C Couhin, *La Propriété Industrielle, Artistique & Littéraire. Tome Premier* (1894) 265 ff.

[63] Article 32 No 2 of the Act.

[64] Décret no 53-970 du 30 septembre 1953 modifiant et complétant la loi du 5 juillet 1844 sur les brevets d'invention et instituant des licences dites obligatoires, JO 1953, 8630. The decree provides, however, that if the patent, without justification, is not worked within three years a compulsory license may be granted.

[65] A list of working requirements in different national patent statutes was maintained in the 1930s by K Schroeter and R Poschenrieder, *Der Ausübungszwang in der Patentgesetzgebung aller Länder* (loose-leaf 2 volumes, 1934 *et seq*).   [66] Walterscheid (n 42 above) 141, footnote 107.

3 The 19th Century

The developments in England, the United States, and France served as examples to other countries.[67] Austria announced the establishment of a patent system in a *Hofdekret* (royal decree) in 1794 and enacted a patent law in 1810. Russia followed in 1812, Prussia in 1815, Belgium and the Netherlands in 1817, Spain in 1820, Bavaria in 1825, Sardinia in 1826, the Vatican State in 1833, Sweden in 1834, Württemberg in 1836, Portugal in 1837, and Saxonia in 1843.[68] However, in the second half of the 19th century the further spread of patent laws succumbed to a growing anti-patent mood connected to the free-trade movement of the 19th century. Patents, with their ability to exclude others from a country's market, were regarded as an impediment to free trade and therefore as harmful.[69] This attitude is perhaps most visible in the German *Zollverein*, a customs union between German states established in 1833, that soon had to find a compromise between free trade within the union and patent rights granted by states. It decided that the patentee could not oppose the import of goods where the goods were produced in another member of the union.[70] But the debate was far more widespread: Britain re-evaluated its patent system; the North German Federation decided not to adopt such a system and in Switzerland proposals for a patent system repeatedly failed. In the Netherlands opposition to patent laws was so fierce that the Dutch Patent Act was repealed in 1869.[71] Switzerland and the Netherlands both industrialized without a patent system.[72]

With the end of the free-trade movement in the 1870s the spread of patent laws could continue: Germany introduced a Patent Act in 1877, Japan in 1885,[73] Switzerland in 1907, and the Netherlands in 1910.[74] But not every country decided to adopt patent laws and some countries carved out large exceptions to patentability, at times such action was purposely taken as an approach to development. Thus, East Asian countries, such as Japan, South Korea, and Taiwan probably owe a lot of their economic success to their ability to imitate foreign inventions due to weak intellectual property laws during the early phases of their development.[75]

---

[67] BZ Khan, 'Intellectual Property and Economic Development: Lessons from American and European History' Commission on Intellectual Property Rights Study Paper 1a (2002) 9.

[68] F Machlup, *An Economic Review of the Patent System, Study of the Subcommittee on Patents, Trademarks, and Copyrights of the Committee on the Judiciary, United States Senate, Eighty-Fifth Congress, Second Session* (1958) 3–4.

[69] HI Dutton, *The Patent System and Inventive Activity During the Industrial Revolution 1750– 1852* (1984) 24.

[70] World Intellectual Property Organization, *Introduction to Intellectual Property. Theory and Practice* (1997) 19. For this reason the *Zollverein* has been called 'anti-patent', E Stringham, 'Patents and Gebrauchsmuster in International Law' in GB Dinwoodie, WO Hennesey, and S Perlmutter (eds), *International Intellectual Property Law and Policy* (2001) 376.

[71] E Schiff, *Industrialization without National Patents* (1971) 21.

[72] The standard work on this issue is Schiff (n 71 above).

[73] An earlier act was in force for one year only.   [74] Machlup (n 68 above) 4–5.

[75] N Kumar, 'Intellectual Property Rights, Technology and Economic Development: Experiences of Asian Countries' Commission on Intellectual Property Rights Study Paper 1b (2002) 4 ff.

4 The Patentability of Pharmaceutical Products

The availability of patents does not necessarily imply the availability of patents on pharmaceutical products or processes for the production of such products, which are of particular relevance to the study.

Originally, privileges were granted for a rather incoherent assortment of different subject matters at the discretion of the ruler. The first statutes, however, defined the subject matter eligible for patent protection. The broad language of the Statute of Monopolies, for example, allowed patents for 'the sole working or making of any matter of new manufacture'.[76] The term was interpreted by the courts to include patents on 'substances (such as medicines) formed by chemical and other processes'[77] and, after some initial doubt, it was extended to the processes themselves.[78] In the United States, the 1790 Act had allowed patents for the invention of 'any useful Art, Manufacture, Engine, Machine, or Device, or any improvement therein not before known or used'.[79] The terminology changed in the Patent Act of 1793 to 'any new and useful art, machine, manufacture, or composition of matter, or any new and useful improvement (...)'[80]—quite similar to modern US patent law that allows patents on 'any new and useful process, machine, manufacture, or composition of matter, or any new and useful improvement thereof'.[81] Pharmaceutical substances—which are chemical compounds—fall squarely under the term 'composition of matter'.

Other countries feared the public health effects of patents on pharmaceuticals. Thus, the French Patent Act of 1844 explicitly excluded '*[l]es compositions pharmaceutiques ou remèdes de toute espèce*'[82] from patent protection. The exception was included in the Act both to combat the practice of quacks to advertise for their medication with the fact that it was patented[83] and out of fear of the appropriation of medicines necessary for the public health by inventors.[84] It passed despite arguments that it would prevent fair compensation for important inventions. Like similar exceptions in many other countries, the act banned patents on the product itself, the pharmaceutical composition, but not on the process of fabrication of a pharmaceutical substance.[85] Pharmaceutical products remained unpatentable in France until 1959, when an *ordonnance* imposed that special patents would be

---

[76] Section VI of the Statute of Monopolies.

[77] *Boulton v Bull* (Court of Common Pleas and Exchequer Chamber, 1795) 126 Eng Rep 651, 660.

[78] Initially courts argued that a known manufacture made by a new process was a new manufacture. L Edmunds, *The Law and Practice of Letters Patent for Inventions with the Patents Acts and Rules Annotated, and the International Convention, a Full Collection of Statutes, Forms and Precedents, and an Outline of Foreign and Colonial Patent Laws* (1890) 17 ff.   [79] § 1 of the Patent Act 1790.

[80] § 1 of the Patent Act 1793.   [81] 35 USC § 101.

[82] 'Pharmaceutical compositions or medicines of all kinds' (translation by author) (Art 3). See also Art 30 No 2 of the Act, declaring a patent obtained on subject matter enumerated in Art 3 null and void. This provision was necessary as the French Act established a registration and not an examination system. Pouillet (n 46 above) 430.   [83] Couhin (n 62 above) 277.

[84] Pouillet (n 46 above) 103.

[85] Roubier (n 58 above) 98. Patents were not granted where there was only one process to produce the good and product and process patents were therefore de facto virtually indistinguishable.

granted for pharmaceutical products, with the possibility of a compulsory license if the product is produced in insufficient quality or quantity or if the price is abnormally high.[86] However, France continues to exclude methods of surgical or therapeutic treatment and diagnostic methods from patentability as not being susceptible to industrial application.[87] It is far from alone in this respect: the Convention on the Grant of European Patents (EPC) contains a similar exception in Article 52(4) and the German *Patentgesetz* in § 5(2).[88]

France was also far from an exception when it came to excluding pharmaceutical products form patentability. Many developed countries have not adopted patent protection for pharmaceutical products until the second half of the 20th century, eg Germany (1968), Japan (1976), Switzerland (1977), Italy (1978), Spain (1992), Portugal (1992), Norway (1992).[89] Another approach that countries took to safeguard public health was to grant compulsory licences in the area of pharmaceuticals. Thus, eg, the United Kingdom and Canada used to single out the pharmaceutical field (with a few others) for granting compulsory licences and maintained these rules into the early 1990s.[90]

III Rationales of Patent Law

The historical account shows clearly that states regarded and used patents as a tool for enhancing their development and public welfare. This section will show that the finding is in line with the current philosophy of patent law. Even though the rationales of patent law are commonly used cumulatively, nowadays national patent laws are largely justified by utilitarian ideas.

1 Natural Law Rationale

Propelled by philosophers like Locke, the assumption that individuals have an automatic property right in their ideas started to gain ground in the late 18th century.

---

[86] Ordonnance no 59-250 du 4 février 1959 relative à la réforme du régime de la fabrication des produits pharmaceutiques et à diverses modifications du Code de las Santé publique, JCP 1959, III, 24201. The details were fixed by decrees in 1960 and in 1968 the provisions were included in the Patent Act. R Plaisant, 'Les Brevets Spéciaux de Médicaments' (1961) I JCP 1616; J Schmidt-Szalewski and J-L Pierre, *Droit de la Propriété Industrielle* (1996) 34.

[87] Article L 611-16 and Art L 611-10 para 1 Code de la Propriété Intellectuelle.

[88] The US Patent Act does not exclude the patentability of such methods. However, after a 1996 amendment it excludes infringement remedies with respect to 'a medical practitioner's performance of a medical activity that constitutes an infringement (...)' (for details see 35 USC § 287 (c)).

[89] P Challú, 'The Consequences of Pharmaceutical Product Patenting' (1991) 15-2 World Competition 65, 75; JO Lanjouw and IM Cockburn, 'New Pills for Poor People? Empirical Evidence after GATT' (2001) 29 World Development, 265, 288; M Scuffi, 'Die Erfindungen auf dem Pharmasektor— Stand der Mailänder und Turiner Rechtsprechung' (1991) GRUR Int 481. Britain, too, at one point constrained the patentability of chemical substances: between 1919 and 1949 a claim to a substance had to be for a 'substance-by-process' WR Cornish, *Intellectual Property: Patents, Copyright, Trademarks and Allied Rights* (1981) 133 f.

[90] S Koshy, '*The Effect of TRIPs on Indian Patent Law: A Pharmaceutical Industry Perspective*' (1995) 1 BUJ Sci & Tech L 4.

Locke argued that men have a natural right in the fruits of their labour, property arises from the mixing of labour with objects.[91] Intellectual property has to be treated just like other property. After garnering significant support particularly during the French Revolution and mostly in Continental Europe,[92] the theory today remains most prominent in copyright law. In the patent law field, as a German scholar remarked, it merely 'cannot be neglected totally'.[93] Too many aspects of patent law contradict natural law notions: the fact that inventors have to go through an administrative procedure to obtain a patent rather than having an automatic right in their invention, the loss of all rights of parallel inventors if someone else obtains a patent,[94] and, most prominently, its time-limited character. Particularly among national Anglo-American patent lawyers the theory is almost universally rejected.[95] Recently, however, natural law arguments have reappeared in the debate in the international context, at times under the guise of human rights law. Chapter 4 will show that it is not modern-day patents, but rather the inventors' moral and material interests that are protected under human rights law.

2 Contract Rationale

Patents are sometimes conceptualized as a contract between the inventor and society:[96] the inventor agrees to disclose an invention to the public in a way that enables any person skilled in the art to which it pertains to reproduce it, although he could also keep it a secret. In return, society grants a monopoly patent. It is along these lines the US Supreme Court calls disclosure the '*quid pro quo* of the right to exclude'.[97]

Although the contract rationale is commonly cited, it is not entirely convincing. Many inventions can be reproduced by engineers simply by studying the product in question (reverse engineering). In these cases society does not need to grant patents to learn about the invention.[98] Where reverse engineering is impossible and society has a reason to offer patents, inventors have but little incentive to apply for them, as they can keep the invention secret perpetually and thus do not need patent protection.[99]

---

[91] Locke (n 52 above). On the philosophical background in-depth see D Stengel, 'Intellectual Property in Philosophy' (2004) 90 ARSP 20.   [92] Dutton (n 69 above) 18.

[93] Hubmann and Götting (n 1 above) 49; See Fiscal and Financial Branch of the Department of Economic and Social Affairs, *The Role of Patents in the Transfer of Technology to Developing Countries. Report of the Secretary-General* UN Doc E/3861/Rev 1, 9 (1964) ('Patent legislation has never been based solely on the concept of the patent as the confirmation of an inherent, rather than the creation of a statutory, property right').   [94] R Kraßer, *Patentrecht* (5th edn, 2004) 35–36.

[95] Dutton (n 69 above) 18; Schiff (n 71 above) 3.

[96] Walterscheid (n 42 above) 211; Dutton (n 69 above) 22.

[97] (Emphasis in original) *Kewanee Oil Co v Bicron Corp et al* (1974) 416 US 370, 484; *JEM AG Supply, Inc v Pioneer Hi-Bred Int'l, Inc* (2001) 534 US 124, 142.   [98] Schiff (n 71 above) 4.

[99] But note that patents also protect against the danger of independent rediscovery by someone else. V Denicolò and LA Franzoni, 'The Contract Theory of Patents' (2004) 23 Int'l Rev L & Econ 365.

The rationale has also been criticized by the US Supreme Court, which wondered whether disclosure is still of value in the light of the highly developed art of drafting patents, which tries to disclose as little information as possible.[100] This criticism, however, is misplaced. Where the disclosure is not enabling, the law does not allow the grant of a patent. Patents granted in spite of this are not valid.[101]

3 Reward Rationale

The great economists Smith and Mill regarded patents as a reward awarded to the inventor for contributing a new art to society.[102] This rationale, too, has now been discredited. First of all, inventions do not happen in a vacuum. They draw on the groundwork laid by others and are sometimes even made by several people almost simultaneously. Only the first inventor, however, obtains the patent. It seems doubtful to endow this patent with any moral claim as a just reward.[103] Secondly, the reward a patent offers is rarely proportional to the social value of the invention. Many factors influence the profit that can be reaped from a patent, not least of all the amount of time that is lost in between obtaining a patent and having a marketable product that is accepted by consumers. This time gap can be particularly long for inventions of great social value.[104]

4 Incentive Rationale

The incentive rationale is easily the single most influential rationale of modern day patent law. It argues that patents are justified as an incentive for research and development. Without patents, others are free to copy an invention and compete with the inventor. But the competition is unfair: the inventor has had to invest time and money in research and development, the competitor did not incur such costs. Who would commit resources to research and development in such a system? Patents correct this market failure and allow inventors to offset their costs for research and development, making invention a profitable business.[105] In today's

---

100 *Brenner v Manson* 383 US 519 (1966) 533 f.

101 I Cooper, 'Patent Problems for Chemical Researchers—the Utility Requirement After *Brenner v Manson*' (1976) 18 IDEA 23, 28.

102 A Smith, *An Inquiry into the Nature and Causes of the Wealth of Nations, volume III* (11th edn, 1805) 141; JS Mill, 'Principles of Political Economy with Some of Their Applications to Social Philosophy' in *Collected Works of John Stuart Mill. Volume III* (1965) book V, ch X, § 4.

103 ET Penrose, *The Economics of the International Patent System* (1951) 26 ff.

104 Machlup (n 68 above) 30.

105 F List, *Das Nationale System der politischen Ökonomie* (1841) 425; Merges, Menell, and Lemley (n 12 above), 12 ff; MJ Trebilcock and R Howse, *The Regulation of International Trade* (2nd edn, 1999) 309. Lincoln, too, embraced this rationale when he stated that the patent system 'added the fuel of *interest* to the *fire* of genius' (emphasis in original); A Lincoln, 'Second Lecture on Discoveries and Inventions (Feb 11, 1859)', in RP Basler, MD Pratt, and LA Dunlap (eds), *The Collected Works of Abraham Lincoln. Volume III* (1953) 356, 363.

economy, patents additionally signal to investors a firm's innovative capacity and thus give an incentive for even greater investment.[106]

This rationale, too, has not gone uncriticized. The arguments advanced are legion: invention is a natural occupation of men; honour and prizes are a sufficient motivation for invention; the head start of the innovator over the competitor is a sufficient incentive for invention; patents channel resources into invention from more socially useful activities; the advantages of patents do not justify their social costs.[107] The reality of the patent system proves to be exceedingly complex: whereas patents for the inventor are an incentive for research, patents for third parties raise the cost of invention and serve as a disincentive, providing ammunition for advocates of the 'inventive commons'. Proffering conclusive economic evidence has proven so arduous a task that in a study for the US Congress in the 1950s Machlup concluded that on the economic facts it would be irresponsible to introduce a patent system if none were in place and it would be irresponsible to abolish a system that is in place.[108] Since then, however, the costs necessary for research and development in some areas have continued to rocket. The German pharmaceutical industry alone has invested €3.82b in research and development in 2003,[109] the German car industry even €14.5b.[110] The estimated worldwide research and development expenditure of pharmaceutical companies in 2002 exceeded $45b.[111] In light of these figures even scholars with a critical attitude towards the patent system generally concur that patents in some areas are necessary as an incentive for innovation. However, criticism about many aspects of the system prevails, such as the grant of patents of doubtful innovative quality, the grant of overly broad patents, excessive patenting by companies to boost patent portfolios, or the abuse of patents to stifle research.[112] I will return to the merits of patents as an incentive in pharmaceutical research in chapter 4.

5 Prospect Theory

More recently, Kitch has advanced the 'prospect function' of patents as a further rationale of the patent system. He argues that patents are usually obtained before the patentee has developed clear ideas about the exploitation of the patent. Patents

---

[106] Commission on Intellectual Property Rights, Innovation and Public Health, *Public Health. Innovation and Intellectual Property Rights* (2006) 33.

[107] A detailed overview is given by Machlup (n 68 above) 24.

[108] Machlup (n 68 above) 80.

[109] Verband Forschender Arzneimittelhersteller eV, *Statistics 2004. Die Arzneimittelindustrie in Deutschland* (2004) 2.

[110] Verband der Automobilindustrie, *Auto Jahresbericht 2004* (2004) 12.

[111] International Federation of Pharmaceutical Manufacturers Associations, *Research & Development*, at <http://www.ifpma.org/Issues/issues_research.aspx> (2004).

[112] Federal Trade Commission, *The Proper Balance of Competition and Patent Law and Policy* (2003); Committee on Intellectual Property Rights in the Knowledge-Based Economy, National Research Council, *A Patent System for the 21st Century* (2004).

provide the patentee with the necessary legal security to investigate market opportunities and search for venture capital.[113] The patentee can also organize further
research in a way that prevents the wasteful duplication of similar efforts by others:
many patents are merely the starting point of research leading to commercially more
important inventions. Anyone interested in doing such research will now know
who to turn to for a licence. The patent also constitutes an important incentive for
the patent holder himself to make further investments to maximize the value of
the patent.[114]

Kitch's theory can be credited with emphasizing the oft-neglected importance
of the exploitation of patents. It is particularly meritorious as to the search and
exploitation for market opportunities. However, the theory is incorrect as to the
organization of further research. Research is an inherently chaotic progress, often
driven by the fact that several researchers are competing on similar projects and
contributing different ideas, a necessary component of research that Kitch's theory
wrongly regards as a waste of resources. Organizing research would require the foresight of knowing which way to venture—a foresight that is all the more improbable
the larger the field of research is.[115] Many scholars have therefore argued against
patents where an area is particularly research-sensitive, favouring a non-proprietary
'innovation commons', eg for software research[116] or in the area of biotechnology,
particularly with respect to gene fragments that can be used as research tools.[117]
The Wrights' airplane patent illustrates the problems involved in allowing patentees to organize research. In their quest to monopolize the airplane market, the
Wright brothers used their patent on a feature of airplanes that is no longer in use to
impede, as much as possible, the efforts of inventors such as Curtiss to improve
planes, almost driving Curtiss into bankruptcy. The development led one inventor
to comment: 'A man has to have ten years in law school before he has a chance of
becoming an aviator'.[118]

IV International Patent Law

By the 19th century cross-border trade had become a common occurrence and
inventors were seeking to patent their inventions abroad. In the face of the rich
variety of different national patent laws of the 18th and 19th century such attempts

---

[113] NP de Carvalho, *The TRIPS Regime of Patent Rights* (2002) 2.

[114] EW Kitch, 'The Nature and Function of the Patent System' (1977) 20 JL & Econ 265, 275 ff.

[115] L Lessig, *The Future of Ideas. The Fate of the Commons in a Connected World* (2001) 209.

[116] Lessig (n 115 above) 17 ff, 207 ff; V Grassmuck, *Freie Software. Zwischen Privat- und Gemeineigentum* (2002).

[117] R Wolfrum, P-T Stoll, and S Franck, *Die Gewährleistung freier Forschung an und mit Genen und das Interesse an der wirtschaftlichen Nutzung ihrere Ergebnisse* (2002); MA Heller and RS Eisenberg, 'Can Patents Deter Innovation? The Anticommons in Biomedical Research' (1998) 280 Science 698.

[118] S Shulman, *Unlocking the Sky. Glenn Hammond Curtiss and the Race to Invent the Airplane* (2002) 57.

were often futile. Some laws denied patent protection to foreigners outright or prevented the patenting of subject matter already patented abroad, others imposed stringent local working requirements within a short period of time and threatened the revocation of the patent where the patentee imported the patented goods from abroad. But even where such fundamental problems did not exist, patenting an invention in several countries proved a daunting task: inventors had to draft applications in the national languages complying with each country's different laws and rules within the relevant time limits. If they lived up to that improbable challenge, success was nevertheless unlikely, as in some countries the publication of a foreign patent granted to the inventor himself defeated novelty.[119] This section will describe the solutions the international system offered for these problems before the TRIPS Agreement (1), the perceived shortcomings of those solutions (2), the arguments in the fierce debate between the developed and the developing world whether remedying the alleged shortcomings is desirable (3), the attempt to solve the problems within the traditional setting for intellectual property negotiations and by unilateral measures (4), and the negotiations leading up to the TRIPS Agreement (5).

1 International Patent Law before the TRIPS Agreement

At first, international attempts at remedying the confused state of patent law were limited to a small number of bilateral treaties. The tide began to turn when US inventors considered not attending an international exposition held in Vienna in 1873 for fear that their inventions might not be adequately protected and could be copied. Subsequent negotiations not only led to changes in the Austrian patent law, but also to an international conference on patent rights in Vienna in 1873. The conferences marked the end of the anti-patent movement connected with free trade and a decisive victory for the pro-patent side. It is noteworthy that, during the conference, the United States advocated regarding patents as property rights rather than instruments of public policy, a natural law position.[120] The Vienna Conference was followed up by a conference in Paris in 1878 and ultimately resulted in the adoption of the Paris Convention for the Protection of Industrial Property (Paris Convention) in 1883. By the time the TRIPS Agreement came into effect (1 January 1995) the Convention, which also covers other industrial property such as trademarks, had been ratified by 129 states and substantially revised a number of times.[121]

---

[119] On the whole issue GB Dinwoodie, WO Hennesey and S Perlmutter, *International Intellectual Property Law and Policy* (2001) 377; P-T Stoll, *Technologietransfer. Internationalisierungs- und Nationalisierungstendenzen. Die Gestaltung zwischenstaatlicher Wirtschaftsbeziehungen, privater Verfügungsrechte und Transaktionen durch die Vereinten Nationen, die UNCTAD, die WIPO und die Uruguay-Runde des GATT* (1994) 215 ff.

[120] H Kronstein and I Till, 'A Reevaluation of the International Patent Convention' in GB Dinwoodie, WO Hennesey and S Perlmutter, *International Intellectual Property Law and Policy* (2001) 378, 382 ff. Kronstein and Till erroneously consider this US position to be novel—as stated above it was most ardently embraced during the French Revolution.

[121] Penrose (n 103 above); M Plaisant, *Traité de Droit Conventionnel International concernant la Propriété Industrielle* (1949); L Donzel, *Commentaire de la Convention Internationale Signée à Paris le*

The Paris Convention set up a Union for the protection of industrial property[122] with a secretariat to carry out the administrative tasks of the Union.[123] Today this task is carried out by the World Intellectual Property Organization (WIPO), a specialized agency of the United Nations set up in 1970,[124] which administers 23 other intellectual property conventions besides the Paris Convention and boasts 183 member states.[125] Substantively, the Convention mainly brought about a number of important improvements in cross-border patenting. Thus, it contains an obligation of national treatment forcing member states to grant nationals of all member states of the Union the same advantages in the area of industrial property law that they grant their own citizens.[126] The Convention also simplifies obtaining patents in several countries a lot by granting a patentee who filed a first patent application in a member state a 12-month priority period for filing for patents in other member states. During this period intervening acts cannot invalidate the filings, nor can third parties obtain a patent on the invention.[127] However, national patents remain independent from each other both concerning their grant and their validity[128] and the Convention did not venture much into harmonizing national patent laws. Besides the right of the inventor to be mentioned in the patent[129] and the obligation not to refuse or invalidate patents on the grounds of domestic legal restrictions on the sale of the patented product,[130] the Convention contains substantive rules on compulsory licences and the revocation of patents. Article 5A(2) of the Paris Convention explicitly allows member states to impose non-exclusive compulsory licences to prevent abuses of the exercise of the patent right, 'for example, failure to work'. But such licences for failure to work or insufficient working of the patent can only be applied for after a period fixed in the Convention. They cannot be granted if the inaction is justified by legitimate reasons.[131] Forfeiture of a patent can only be provided for where a compulsory licence would not be sufficient[132]

---

20 Mars 1883 pour la Protection de la Propriété Industrielle (1891); P Katzenberger and A Kur, 'TRIPs and Intellectual Property' in F-K Beier and G Schricker (eds), *From GATT to TRIPs—The Agreement on Trade-Related Aspects of Intellectual Property Rights* (1996) 1, 10; On the revisions: Stoll (n 119 above).

[122] Article 1 (1) of the Paris Convention (originally Art 1).

[123] Article 15 of the Paris Convention (originally Art 13). The secretariat was called the *Bureau international de l'Union pour la protection de la propriété industrielle*. In 1893 it merged with the secretariat of the Berne Convention for the Protection of Literary and Artistic Works to form the *Bureaux Internationaux Réunis pour la Protection de la Propriété Intellectuelle* (BIRPI).

[124] Convention Establishing the World Intellectual Property Organization.

[125] World Intellectual Property Organization, *General Information*, at <http://www.wipo.int/about-wipo/en/gib.htm#P29_4637>.

[126] Article 2 of the Paris Convention. The same benefits must also be granted to nationals of non-member states domiciled or having real and effective industrial or commercial establishments in the territory of a member state. Article 3 of the Paris Convention.

[127] Article 4 of the Paris Convention. G Schricker, 'Problems of Convention Priority for Patent Applications' in F Abbott, T Cottier, and F Gurry (eds), *The International Intellectual Property System. Commentary and Materials Pt One* (1999) 678. In addition, Art 5*bis*(1) of the Paris Convention grants a six-month grace period for the payment of maintenance fees for the patent.

[128] Article 4*bis* of the Paris Convention.   [129] Article 4*ter* of the Paris Convention.

[130] Article 4*quater* of the Paris Convention.   [131] Article 5A(4) of the Paris Convention.

[132] Article 5A(3) of the Paris Convention.

and may not be the consequence of the mere importation by the patentee of the patented good into the country of the patent grant.[133]

The other major universal patent treaty, the Patent Cooperation Treaty (PCT) signed in 1970, does not tackle harmonization of patent laws, either. Instead, it facilitates obtaining national patents from national and regional patent offices under their laws by offering inventors the possibility to file one 'international patent application' designating the State Parties in which they seek patent protection. The term international patent application is somewhat misleading, as the PCT does not provide for the grant of an international patent.[134]

The harmonization and integration of patent laws on a regional level is further advanced. Thus the EPC, that established the European Patent Office (EPO) in 1973, contains detailed provisions on substantive patent law. The EPO applies these standards when granting European patents. However, European patents are not international patents. They are granted for the countries designated by the patentee and, once granted, are treated like national patents.[135] The African Regional Industrial Property Organization (ARIPO) and the *Organisation Africaine de la Propriété Intellectuelle* (OAPI) also grant 'bundles of national patents'.[136]

2 Shortcomings of the Traditional System

In the second half of the 20th century developed countries' economies began to enter an era that became known as that of the 'knowledge-based economy'. Patents were fast becoming one of the most essential assets of the industry and developed countries perceived the international system for their protection to be inadequate mainly in four respects:

(1) Even though the Paris Convention enjoyed wide support, membership was far from universal. Developing countries in particular were reluctant to sign the agreement.[137]

---

[133] Article 5A(1) of the Paris Convention. On the whole Convention see World Intellectual Property Organization, 'International Protection of Industrial Property Paris Convention for the Protection of Industrial Property (1883)' in F Abbott, T Cottier, and F Gurry (eds), *The International Intellectual Property System. Commentary and Materials Pt One* (1999) 647.

[134] Inventors can also order an international search report or an international preliminary examination under the PCT. For details, see F Abbott, T Cottier, and F Gurry (eds), *The International Intellectual Property System. Commentary and Materials Pt Two* (1999) 1430 ff; World Intellectual Property Organization, 'Basic Facts about the Patent Cooperation Treaty' in F Abbott, T Cottier, and F Gurry (eds), *The International Intellectual Property System. Commentary and Materials Pt Two* (1999) 1433; J Straus, 'Implications of the TRIPs Agreement in the Field of Patent Law' in F-K Beier and G Schricker (eds), *From GATT to TRIPs—The Agreement on Trade-Related Aspects of Intellectual Property Rights* (1996) 160, 174. Another Treaty, the Patent Law Treaty adopted at Geneva on 1 June 2000 seeks to harmonize formal procedures in respect of patent applications. Its territorial scope is currently quite limited. It came into force on 28 April 2005 and currently has 14 Contracting Parties.   [135] See Art 64 of the EPC.

[136] F Abbott, T Cottier, and F Gurry (eds), *The International Intellectual Property System: Commentary and Materials. Pt One* (1999) 461 ff; Abbott, Cottier, and Gurry (n 134 above) 1468 ff; Stoll (n 119 above) 225.

[137] D Matthews, *Globalising Intellectual Property Rights. The TRIPs Agreement* (2002) 10 ff. Stoll (n 119 above) 325–326; P-T Stoll and K Raible, 'Schutz geistigen Eigentums und das TRIPS-Abkommen' in H-J Prieß, GM Berrisch, and C Pitschas (eds), *WTO-Handbuch* (2003) 565, 569–570.

(2) The international obligations incurred by states with respect to patent laws were not effectively enforced. Disputes about the interpretation and application of the Paris Convention could be brought to the International Court of Justice (ICJ) under Article 28 of the Paris Convention, but critics regarded the ICJ procedure as lacking bite, not to mention the fact that not all member states were bound by Article 28 that was only introduced during the Stockholm revision of the Paris Convention, which had not been ratified by all member states.[138]

(3) The international patent system was largely silent on the enforcement of patents by national judicial authorities.[139]

(4) There was a lack of harmonization of all aspects of national patent laws leading to a lack of protection: no minimum patent term was set, the regulation of compulsory licenses was too liberal,[140] countries were free to exclude areas from patentability. The result was that in 1988 pharmaceutical products were not patentable in 49 member states, methods for the treatment of the human or animal body not patentable in 44 member states, chemical products not patentable in 22 member states, and pharmaceutical processes not patentable in 10 member states.[141]

3 The North-South Divide: Arguments for and against Stronger Patent Protection

With most of the patents owned by companies from developed countries it did not take much foresight to predict that developing countries would be reluctant to embrace stronger international standards on patent law. What ensued was a bitter debate pitting the developed world favouring strong universal minimum patent standards against the developing world that rejected (and often still rejects) such standards. Two main lines of argument are discernable.

The first line of argument by developed countries is that countries with strong patent protection defray the cost of innovation, whereas countries without such protection free-ride on the innovation, profiting from the knowledge without

---

[138] D Gervais, *The TRIPS Agreement: Drafting History and Analysis* (2nd edn, 2003) 9–10. FM Abbott, 'Protecting First World Assets in the Third World: Intellectual Property Negotiations in the GATT Multilateral Framework' (1989) 22 Vand J of Transnat'l L 689, 703. The UN Charter obliges parties to ICJ proceedings to comply with the ICJ decision and provides for recourse to the Security Council in case of non-compliance (Art 94 of the UN Charter). So far the Security Council has never taken enforcement action under this provision, it merely threatened Chapter VII action in the *Tehran Hostages* case and fell short of adopting a resolution in the *Nicaragua* case, when Art 94 of the UN Charter was invoked. Despite the weak enforcement mechanism compliance with ICJ judgments has been good. TD Gill, *Rosenne's The World Court. What It Is and How It Works* (6th edn, 2003) 33 ff; C Paulson, 'Compliance with Final Judgments of the International Court of Justice Since 1987' (2004) 98 AJIL 434.

[139] T Dreier, 'TRIPS und die Durchsetzung von Rechten des geistigen Eigentums' (1996) GRUR Int 205.   [140] Abbott (n 138 above) 703–704.

[141] Straus (n 134 above) 174.

contributing to the costs of its development.[142] The industry complains of significant losses due to piracy in developing countries. An influential report prepared
by the US International Trade Commission estimated the losses suffered by US
companies alone from misappropriation of intellectual property at $43b to $61b in
1986.[143] The argument is a moral rather than a legal one, however: the principle of
territoriality prevents patents from having an effect in countries other than the
country for which they have been granted. Copying a product in a country where
it is not protected due to weak patent laws is legal, irrespective of whether the
product is patented elsewhere. Because of their limited territorial scope patents do
not give rise to any justified expectations of an enhanced market position for sales
in other countries. To speak of 'losses' suffered by the industry or 'piracy' is hence
misplaced. Such an argument relies on natural law property notions[144] or notions
of fairness. Given that the natural law rationale of patent law is now almost universally rejected at the national level,[145] it is somewhat of a surprise to see it reappear
so forcefully in the international debate.[146] Developing countries are correct to
point out that during their own development industrialized countries have used
patent laws merely as a tool for their development.

The second line of argument regards strong intellectual property protection in
developing countries as being in the informed self-interest of those states. It would
foster local creativity and research in products adapted to local needs, encourage
foreign direct investment and technology transfer as companies would be more
willing to invest in and transfer knowledge to countries where their intellectual
assets are well protected.[147] Many scholars came down hard against this view. In
his book, *In Defense of Globalization*, Columbia economist Bhagwati quipped that
the notion that poor countries benefit from paying for patents they hitherto had
been accessing freely sounds 'as implausible as the Mafia telling its victims that
the protection money would keep them safe from arson'.[148] Weak domestic
intellectual property protection, these scholars submit, enables developing country

---

[142] JH Reichman, 'Intellectual Property in International Trade: Opportunities and Risks of a
GATT Connection' (1989) 22 Vand J Transnat'l L 747, 756, 770 ff.

[143] Abbott (n 138 above) 699 ff.

[144] Reichman (n 142 above) 806 ff who argues that intellectual property should be treated just
like any other property.   [145] S Templeman, 'Intellectual Property' (1998) 1 JIEL 603.

[146] There seems to be a noticeable disconnection between national and international patent scholars, eg in the United States: international patent scholars have eagerly embraced natural law notions
for patent law, whereas in the domestic debate the natural law rationale is universally rejected.

[147] CA Primo Braga, 'The Economics of Intellectual Property Rights and the GATT: A View
From the South' (1989) 22 Vand J Transnat'l L 243, 251 ff, 260–261; T Cottier, 'The Prospects for
Intellectual Property in GATT' (1991) 28 Common Market Law Review 383, 390 ff; C Heath,
'Bedeutet TRIPS wirklich eine Schlechterstellung von Entwicklungsländern?' (1996) GRUR Int
1169. Overviews of studies can be found in CM Correa, *Intellectual Property Rights, the WTO and
Developing Countries. The TRIPS Agreement and Policy Options* (2000) 23–24, 26 ff; WE Siebeck *et al*,
'Strengthening Protection of Intellectual Property in Developing Countries: A Survey of the Literature'
(1990) World Bank Discussion Paper No 112.

[148] J Bhagwati, *In Defense of Globalization* (2004) 183. J Stiglitz, *Globalization and Its Discontents*,
(2002) 245–246.

industries to copy technology from abroad without having to license it and thus fosters technology transfer.[149] Given the weak empirical evidence of a correlation of higher standards of intellectual property protection and foreign direct investment they fear that if developing countries adopt strong patent protection, patented goods would only be imported into developing countries rather than produced there,[150] entailing a wealth transfer from the developing to the developed world[151] and entrenching the technological and industrial lead of the developed world that started to be challenged by the increasing technological savvy of some developing nations.[152]

The fight over stronger intellectual property protection continues to this day.[153] It is a key to understanding the further developments in international patent law. I will come back to the economic discussion in chapter 4, focusing on the pharmaceutical field.

4 Unilateral Pressure on Developing Countries

Efforts by industrialized countries to achieve the desired changes within the WIPO setting time and again failed. Progress in that setting was limited to new technologies.[154] With multilateral negotiations failing to achieve the desired result industrialized nations resorted increasingly to unilateral pressure. Both the United States and the European Communities withdrew trade benefits granted to individual developing countries under the Generalized System of Preferences for failure

---

[149] Correa (n 147 above) 18–19; G Rahn, 'Die Bedeutung des gewerblichen Rechtsschutzes für die wirtschaftliche Entwicklung: Die japanischen Erfahrungen' (1982) GRUR Int 577, 581; Commission on Intellectual Property Rights, *Integrating Intellectual Property Rights and Development Policy* (2002) 22.

[150] FM Abbott, 'Commentary: The International Intellectual Property Order Enters the 21st Century' (1996) 29 Vand J Transnat'l L 471, 473–474; CM Correa, *Intellectual Property Rights and Foreign Direct Investment* (1993) UN Doc ST/CTC/SER.A/24, 33–34.

[151] Primo Braga (n 147 above) 256. Commission on Intellectual Property Rights (n 149 above) 21.

[152] J Foyer, 'Problèmes Internationaux Contemporains des Brevets d'Invention' (1981–II) 171 RdC 341 378 ff; Reichman (n 142 above) 754. Statements by the US industry arguing that intellectual property protection is necessary to maintain US competitiveness in the face of increasing competition from newly industrializing countries indicate that the aspiration to entrench its industrial lead constitutes at least one of a number of motives of the developed world. RM Gadbaw, 'Intellectual Property and International Trade: Merger or Marriage of Convenience?' (1989) 22 Vand J Transnat'l L 223, 226; J Straus, 'Bedeutung des TRIPS für das Patentrecht' (1996) GRUR Int 179, 181.

[153] 'WIPO Development Agenda Meeting Breaks Down over Chair's Text' 10 *Bridges Weekly Trade News Digest* 24 (5 July 2006); WIPO, *Proposal by Argentina and Brazil for the Establishment of a Development Agenda for WIPO*, WO/GA/31/11 (27 August 2004); KE Maskus and JH Reichman, 'The Globalization of Private Knowledge Goods and the Privatization of Global Public Goods' (2004) 7 JIEL 279. On the whole discussion see AM Pacón, 'What Will TRIPs Do for Developing Countries?' in F-K Beier and G Schricker (eds), *From GATT to TRIPs—The Agreement on Trade-Related Aspects of Intellectual Property Rights* (1996) 329.

[154] Eg the Treaty on Intellectual Property in Respect of Integrated Circuits; A Schäfers and D Schennen, 'Der erste Teil der Diplomatischen Konferenz zum Abschluß eines Vertrages zur Harmonisierung des Patentrechts' (1991) GRUR Int 849, 852; T Bodewig, 'Aktuelle Informationen, Internationales—Tagung der Leitenden Organe der WIPO; PVÜ-Revision; Harmonisierung des Patentrechts; GATT' (1988) GRUR Int 81.

to grant intellectual property protection.[155] Even more notorious became the United States' use of section 301 of the US Trade Act of 1974,[156] which permits the United States to impose unilateral trade sanctions against foreign countries with trade practices it perceives as unjustifiable, unreasonable, discriminatory, or inconsistent with trade agreements. In the field of intellectual property law the provision is strengthened by 'Special 301' proceedings:[157] each year the US Trade Representative (USTR) has to identify countries that deny 'adequate and effective' intellectual property protection, designating as priority countries those whose practices are perceived as the most egregious and damaging for US commerce and that are unflinching in negotiations. That status normally triggers an automatic investigation under section 301 of the Trade Act of 1974 and can ultimately result in 'retaliatory' trade sanctions.[158] Pharmaceutical patent protection has played an important role in these so-called 'Special 301' proceedings with the US innovative pharmaceutical industry raising its concerns about foreign countries' intellectual property protection in submissions it prepares for the USTR. The USTR regularly follows up on these concerns.[159]

Section 301 proved an effective tool in promoting US interests, as most countries gave in to the pressure before the threat of trade sanctions materialized.[160] One case in which sanctions actually were imposed occurred in 1988, when the USTR imposed 100 per cent 'retaliatory' tariffs on Brazilian imports worth $39m after a section 301 investigation initiated by pharmaceutical manufacturers because of Brazil's refusal to grant patent protection to pharmaceuticals. Brazil regarded the tariffs as a breach of US obligations under the General Agreement on Tariffs and Trade (GATT), as Brazil had no obligation under international law to grant such patent protection.[161] A GATT Panel was established in 1989, but the proceedings were suspended when Brazil gave in to the pressure announcing that it

---

[155] MCEJ Bronckers, 'The Impact of TRIPS: Intellectual Property Protection in Developing Countries' in MCEJ Bronckers, *A Cross-Section of WTO Law* (2000) 185, 188.

[156] 19 USC § 2411. Section 301 of the Trade Act was amended in 1994 to bring it into conformity with WTO law.

[157] 'Special 301' was introduced by the Omnibus Trade and Competitiveness Act of 1988, 102 Stat 1107 (23 August 1988).

[158] Abbott (n 138 above) 708 ff; HS Shapiro, 'Section 301 of the Trade Act of 1974' in WK Ince and LA Glick (eds), *Manual for the Practice of US International Trade Law* (2001) 1275, 1287–1288, 1332 ff. The USTR is the principle trade adviser of the US President and in charge of international trade negotiations, USTR, *Mission of the USTR*, at <http://www.ustr.gov/Who_We_Are/Mission_of_the_USTR.html>.

[159] Examples include Canada's and Germany's drug pricing scheme (2004); Argentina's protection of test data (2003, 2002, 2001); Brazil's local working requirement (2002, 2001); Hungary's protection of test data (2002, 2001); Canada's patent term (2001); Argentina's failure to provide a system of exclusive marketing rights for pharmaceutical products (2001). USTR, *2001 Special 301 Report* (2001); USTR, *2002 Special 301 Report* (2002); USTR, *2003 Special 301 Report* (2003); USTR, *2004 Special 301 Report* (2004).

[160] Stoll (n 119 above) 330–331. Examples include Argentina, Korea, Taiwan, and Singapore—the Argentinian example concerns pharmaceutical patents. Gadbaw (n 152 above) 229.

[161] Abbott (n 138 above) 710.

would change its patent law. The US withdrew its retaliatory sanctions.[162] Section 301 has remained a divisive issue and its WTO-consistency was challenged before a WTO Panel in 1999.[163]

5 The WTO/GATT setting

The developed world continued to strive for a multilateral intellectual property agreement remedying the perceived shortcomings of the international intellectual property system, but the failure to make progress within WIPO made another forum step into the limelight: the GATT.

A Background: The GATT

The 1947 GATT was the instrument to prevent the world from falling back into protectionism. In the first half of the 19th century Ricardo's 'theory of comparative advantage' demonstrated that free trade benefits even a nation that cannot produce any good more efficiently than its trading partner.[164] Ever since, most economists have considered free trade to be of benefit for all nations.[165] But economic theory did not prevent nations from resorting to exorbitant protectionist measures to preserve their own industries in the late 1920s, a disastrous economic policy that experts in the United States regarded as one link in the chain of events leading up to World War II.[166] Three institutions were meant to safeguard the post-war economic world order from such mishaps: the International Monetary

---

[162] RE Hudec, *Enforcing International Trade Law. The Evolution of the Modern GATT Legal System* (1993) 571; M Getlan, 'TRIPs and the Future of Section 301: A Comparative Study in Trade Dispute Resolution' (1995) 34 Colum J Transnat'l L 173, 188.

[163] *United States—Sections 301–310 of the Trade Act of 1974*, WT/DS/152/R (1999) (upholding the challenged provisions of §§ 301–310 of the US Trade Act, partly because of statements by the US Administration not to use its discretion in a way violating WTO obligations). The US Tariff Act of 1930 (19 USC § 1337) offers an additional tool relevant for intellectual property concerns: Its § 337 enables the United States International Trade Commission to exclude articles infringing US intellectual property rights from entry into the United States after a trial-type hearing. LA Glick, 'Section 337 of the Tariff Act of 1930 (Unfair Trade Practices and Methods of Competition in Importation of Products into the United States)' in WK Ince and LA Glick (eds), *Manual for the Practice of U.S. International Trade Law* (2001) 1. The provision was held to be inconsistent with US GATT obligations *United States—Section 337 of the Tariff Act of 1930*, L/6439—36S/345 (1989) and the amended version has also been challenged: *United States—Section 337 of the Tariff Act of 1930 and Amendments Thereto, Request for Consultations by the European Communities and their Member States*, WT/DS186/1 (2000).

[164] The theory hypothesizes as follows: suppose England produces a unit of cloth with the labour of 100 men and a unit of wine with the labour of 120 men. Portugal can produce cloth with the labour of 90 and wine with the labour of 80 men. In absolute terms Portugal can produce both products more cheaply and there does not seem any reason to engage in trade. Nevertheless, both countries will benefit from trade: if England exports cloth and imports wine, England can save the additional labour it would have taken to produce wine whereas Portugal saves the additional labour involved in producing cloth. The comparative advantage that England enjoys in making cloth and Portugal in wine is sufficient to justify trade. Trebilcock and Howse (n 105 above) 3 ff.

[165] For a recent discussion see Bhagwati (n 148 above) 52 ff.

[166] Trebilcock and Howse (n 105 above) 17 ff.

Fund and the International Bank for Reconstruction and Development both set up during the Bretton Woods Conference in 1944, and the International Trade Organization (ITO), a comprehensive trade organization.[167] But the ITO never came to pass because of resistance in US Congress.[168] Only GATT, an agreement on the trade of goods originally meant to be part of the ITO order, entered into force on the basis of the Protocol of Provisional Application of the General Agreement on Tariffs and Trade.[169] Under the 1934 Reciprocal Trade Agreement Act[170] the US President had the authority to sign this mere trade agreement without having to go to Congress.[171]

The GATT contains Members' tariff concessions and general obligations of Members, most important of which are the most-favoured nation clause,[172] the obligation to grant products imported from other Members' territories the same treatment as like domestic products with respect to internal taxation and regulation,[173] and the ban on prohibitions or restrictions other than duties, taxes, or other charges (eg quotas, import licences).[174] An important feature of the GATT system was its dispute resolution mechanism as it had evolved based on the treaty provisions. The procedure could be invoked for 'nullification or impairment' of benefits expected under the agreement, whether stemming from a breach of the agreement or not. Disputes were referred to a panel of experts, the reports of which had to be adopted by a consensus of the contracting parties, so that the losing party could block the adoption of the report. The loser of a dispute was faced with the possibility of the contracting parties allowing the winner to suspend obligations or concession owed to the loser under GATT.[175] Hudec lucidly described the procedure as 'A Diplomat's Jurisprudence': as indicated by the concept of nullification or impairment the procedure, at the mid-point between negotiation and adjudication, served to preserve the balance of the concessions negotiated rather than to enforce legal rules. Given the consensus requirement, panels had to refrain from hard-and-fast rulings and adopt soft suggestions instead to achieve the adoption of the report. The ruling could then be used to strengthen the argument of the free-trade interest groups not only in the international debate, but also in the internal debate about the challenged measures of the Member against which the

---

[167] On the ITO: C Wilcox, *A Charter for World Trade* (1949) (including the text of the Havana Charter); RE Hudec, *The GATT Legal System and World Trade Diplomacy* (1975) 9 ff.

[168] TW Zeiler, *Free Trade Free World. The Advent of GATT* (1999) 147 ff.

[169] To simplify national ratification procedures the Protocol ensured that existing legislation did not have to be changed ('grandfather rights'). Under the Protocol Part II of GATT (Article III–XXIII) applies only to the extent not inconsistent with existing legislation.

[170] 48 Stat 943 (12 June 1934). The president's authority was extended by An Act to Extend the Authority of the President under section 350 of the Tariff Act of 1930 as amended, and for other purposes, 59 Stat 410 (5 July 1945).

[171] JH Jackson, *Restructuring the GATT System* (1990) 13–14.   [172] Article I of the GATT.

[173] Article III of the GATT.   [174] Article XI of the GATT.

[175] Article XXIII of the GATT. On the dispute resolution mechanism JH Jackson, *The World Trading System. Law and Policy of International Economic Relations* (2nd edn, 1997) 112 ff.

complaint was lodged.[176] This character of GATT dispute settlement explains why trade diplomats have repeatedly questioned the relevance of law within the GATT setting, even though their argument must be held as moot since the creation of the WTO.[177]

B Intellectual Property in the GATT

The GATT contains only few provisions on intellectual property rights. Article XX(d) of the GATT is the most important of these. It exempts contracting parties from GATT obligations and under certain circumstances allows them to restrict trade in goods to protect intellectual property.[178] Negotiators thus regarded intellectual property as a (permissible) impediment to trade and rightly so:[179] national intellectual property rights commonly grant the right to block imports of infringing goods. Apart from two minor references to intellectual property in Article XII:3(c)(iii) of the GATT and Article XVIII:10 of the GATT the only other noteworthy provision on intellectual property is Article IX of the GATT that covers marks of origin. With the limited exception of Article IX:6 of the GATT the Agreement does not impose any obligation to grant intellectual property rights.[180]

Within the GATT setting contracting parties negotiated tariff reductions in trade negotiating rounds, giving GATT the appearance of a quasi-international organization. The seventh round, the 1973–1979 Tokyo Round, also addressed non-tariff measures. In a first effort to include intellectual property protection in the GATT framework the United States proposed an anti-counterfeiting code, but it could not obtain the support necessary for such a code.[181] Four understandings as well as nine agreements were ultimately adopted during the round, covering, eg, technical barriers to trade and government procurement. GATT Members were largely free to pick and choose which of those agreements they wanted to adhere to, the so-called *à la carte* approach.[182]

---

[176] RE Hudec, 'The GATT Legal System: A Diplomat's Jurisprudence' in RE Hudec, *Essays on the Nature of International Trade Law* (1999) 17.

[177] RE Hudec, 'GATT or GABB? The Future Design of the General Agreement on Tariffs and Trade' in RE Hudec, *Essays on the Nature of International Trade Law* (1999) 77.

[178] *United States—Section 337 of the Tariff Act of 1930* (n 163 above).

[179] The difficult relationship between free trade and intellectual property is already evinced by the historic fact that the free-trade movement halted the spread of patent laws. For an in-depth study of the conflict between trade liberalization and the protection of intellectual property see VN Geisel, *Das TRIPS-Übereinkommen in der WTO-Rechtsordnung. Eine Untersuchung zum Spannungsverhältnis zwischen dem Schutz von geistigen Eigentumsrechten und der WTO-Zielsetzung der Handelsliberalisierung* (2003) 59 ff; M Michaelis and T Bender in M Hilf and S Oeter (eds), *WTO-Recht. Rechtsordnung des Welthandels* (2005) § 24 para 6 ff.

[180] Primo Braga (n 147 above) 245 ff; Negotiating Group on Trade-Related Aspects of Intellectual Property Rights, Including Trade in Counterfeit Goods, *GATT Provisions Bearing on Trade-Related Aspects of Intellectual Property Rights. Note by the Secretariat*, MTN.GNG/NG11/W/6 (22 May 1987).

[181] Abbott (n 138 above) 712–713.

[182] On the history of the GATT and world trade see Jackson (n 175 above) 31 ff; R Wolfrum, 'Das Internationale Recht für den Austausch von Waren und Dienstleistungen' in R Schmidt (ed),

C The Uruguay Round

The 1970s and 1980s saw the emergence of serious competition for the developed world from Japan and East Asia. US policymakers started to worry about the growing US trade deficit. The US industry, which had long been involved in promoting intellectual property rights in trade relations, was requested in 1984 to provide input on the question of including intellectual property in the upcoming GATT round. The industry favoured the inclusion of intellectual property in the GATT setting and the CEOs of a few large companies formed a high-level interest group, the 'Intellectual Property Committee'. The committee consulted with foreign industry groups, drafted proposals, and did lobbying work to promote its view.[183] Developing countries strongly objected to the negotiation of substantive intellectual property standards in the GATT setting. They argued that WIPO was the sole appropriate forum for such negotiations.[184] However, the United States, the European Communities, Japan, and other industrialized countries prevailed. The 1986 Punta del Este Ministerial Declaration initiating the Uruguay Round contained a negotiation mandate on 'Trade related aspects of intellectual property rights, including trade in counterfeit goods':

In order to reduce the distortions and impediments to international trade, and taking into account the need to promote effective and adequate protection of intellectual property rights, and to ensure that measures and procedures to enforce intellectual property rights do not themselves become barriers to legitimate trade the negotiations shall aim to clarify GATT provisions and elaborate as appropriate new rules and disciplines.[185]

When the Uruguay Round came to an end on 15 April 1994 it had ushered in a new era for world trade. The Members signed a wholly new agreement, the Final Act of the Uruguay Round and the Marrakesh Agreement Establishing the World Trade Organization (hereinafter: the WTO Agreement), rather than just an amendment to the GATT. The Agreement set up an international organization, the World Trade Organization (WTO), which by the time of the writing of this study has grown to 149 Members, and includes not just rules on trade in goods (the GATT 1994, which includes the GATT 1947), but also on trade in services (General Agreement on Trade in Services (GATS)), intellectual property rights (TRIPS Agreement), dispute settlement (Dispute Settlement Understanding (DSU)), and a Trade Policy Review Mechanism. Members had to adopt all of these and a few more 'multilateral

---

Öffentliches Wirtschaftsrecht (1996) 535, 562 ff; P Picone and A Ligustro, *Diritto dell'Organizzazione Mondiale del Commercio* (2002) 3 ff; Weiß and Herrmann (n 15 above) 38 ff; HG Krenzler, 'Die Nachkriegsentwicklung des Welthandelssystems—von der Havanna-Charta zur WTO' in H-J Prieß and G Berrisch and C Pitschas (eds), *WTO-Handbuch* (2003) 1.

[183] SK Sell, 'Industry Strategies for Intellectual Property and Trade: The Quest for TRIPS, and Post-TRIPS Strategies' (2002) 10 Cardozo J Int'l & Comp L 79; SK Sell, *Private Power, Public Law. The Globalization of Intellectual Property Rights* (2003).   [184] Primo Braga (n 147 above) 250–251.

[185] 'GATT Ministerial Declaration on the Uruguay Round of Multilateral Trade Negotiations', (1986) 25 ILM 1623 (20 September 1986).

trade agreements' in a 'single-package' approach.[186] All of these agreements, including the TRIPS Agreement, can be enforced by a unified dispute settlement procedure that is considerably stronger than the old system: the complainant has a right to the creation of a panel and panel reports can only be rejected by a consensus against adoption; appeals against a panel report can be filed with a standing Appellate Body. The linkage of several agreements also widens enforcement options. If the suspension of concessions or obligations within the same sector or under the same agreement is not practicable or effective and the circumstances are serious enough, a country may seek the suspension of concessions or other obligations under another WTO agreement (so-called 'cross-retaliation').[187] For developing countries this opens the door to retaliate for GATT or GATS violations by suspending obligations under the TRIPS Agreement, enhancing their power to induce compliance from economically stronger countries.[188]

The negotiation process of the TRIPS Agreement had been particularly arduous. The mandate had not resolved the different views of developed and developing countries, it had only changed the terminology: the industrialized countries, particularly the United States and Japan, wanted to negotiate a comprehensive agreement on intellectual property standards,[189] whereas developing countries time and again emphasized the limitation of the mandate to 'trade-related' aspects of intellectual property rights, referring to WIPO as the proper forum for comprehensive intellectual property agreements.[190] Developed countries argued that in a knowledge-based economy differing intellectual property standards had come to

---

[186] In contrast, Members can freely choose to adopt or reject the 'plurilateral trade agreements' in Annex 4 of the WTO Agreement.

[187] Article 22.3 (c) of the DSU. Note the definition of 'agreement' in Art 22.3 (g) of the DSU.

[188] *European Communities—Regime for the Importation, Sale and Distribution of Bananas—Recourse to Arbitration by the European Communities under Article 22.6 of the DSU* WT/DS27/ARB/ECU (2000). It is more common for developed countries to threaten retaliation by suspending GATT obligations for a violation of TRIPS obligations by other Members. On the Marrakesh Agreement results for dispute settlement see Jackson (n 175 above) 44 ff, 124 ff; B Lal Das, *The World Trade Organisation. A Guide to the Framework for International Trade* (1999) 397 ff; P-T Stoll, 'Die WTO: Neue Welthandelsorganisation, neue Welthandelsordnung. Ergebnisse der Uruguay-Runde des GATT' (1994) 54 ZaöRV 241, 269 ff.

[189] F Kretschmer, 'Aktuelle Informationen. Internationales—GATT und gewerblicher Rechtsschutz' (1988) GRUR Int 186.

[190] C Bail, 'Das Profil einer neuen Welthandelsordnung: Was bringt die Uruguay Runde?—Teil 2' (1990) EuZW 465, 468–469. For examples from the TRIPS Agreement negotiations in the Negotiating Group on Trade-Related Aspects of Intellectual Property Rights, including Trade in Counterfeit Goods see *Meeting of 25 March 1987*, MTN.GNG/NG11/1 (10 April 1987) paras 6 ff; *Meeting of the Negotiating Group of 10 June 1987*, MTN.GNG/NG11/2 (23 June 1987) paras 4–5; *Meeting of the Negotiating Group of 23 September 1987*, MTN.GNG/NG11/3 (8 October 1987) paras 5 ff, 9; *Meeting of the Negotiating Group of 28 October 1987*, MTN.GNG/NG11/4 (17 November 1987) paras 11 ff; *Meeting of the Negotiating Group of 23–24 November 1987*, MTN.GNG/NG11/5 (14 December 1987) paras 12 ff, 27; *Meeting of the Negotiating Group of 29 February–3 March 1988*, MTN.GNG/NG11/6 (8 April 1988) paras 7, 12, 23. The legal competence of GATT to deal with the issue also was subject to debate. Pacón (n 153 above) 330–331; Cottier (n 147 above) 392 ff; HP Kunz-Hallstein, 'The United States Proposal for a GATT Agreement on Intellectual Property and the Paris Convention for the Protection of Industrial Property' (1989) 22 Vand J Transnat'l L 265, 268 ff.

constitute a third generation of trade distortions, displacing legitimate goods by unauthorized copies that are possibly even finding their way into other countries and thus destroying the incentive to invent provided by patent law. In this changed environment, they claimed, lack of intellectual property protection threatened to nullify the benefits bargained for in the GATT. The United States even regarded minimum intellectual property protection as a prerequisite for free trade.[191] The developed countries' argument suggested a 'trade-related' character of all of intellectual property law. The argument was inherently weak, not because of a lack of trade effects of intellectual property law—intellectual property law affects the competitive environment and thus ultimately also trade,[192] but because many national regulations can claim similar effects[193] and the argument did not explain why intellectual property law, which traditionally had been regarded as separate from international trade law,[194] was singled out for inclusion in the WTO. Ultimately, it was most likely strategic reasons rather than 'substantive linkage' claims based on a factual link between trade and intellectual property[195] that made developed countries advance intellectual property within the WTO setting. Thus, negotiations within the WTO accorded developed countries the possibility to offer developing countries concessions in the trade arena in return for obtaining an agreement on intellectual property protection. Such concessions could not be offered in the

[191] Negotiating Group on Trade-Related Aspects of Intellectual Property Rights, including Trade in Counterfeit Goods, *Meeting of 25 March 1987*, MTN.GNG/NG11/1 (10 April 1987) paras 4–5; Cottier (n 147 above) 383–384; Reichman (n 142 above) 806; Gadbaw (n 152 above) 226.

[192] For a study of the trade effects of intellectual property rights see A Ting Goh and J Olivier, 'Free Trade and Protection of Intellectual Property Rights: Can We Have One Without the Other' CEPR Discussion Paper No 3127 (2002).

[193] Negotiating Group on Trade-Related Aspects of Intellectual Property Rights, including Trade in Counterfeit Goods, *Meeting of the Negotiating Group of 23 September 1987*, MTN.GNG/NG11/3 (8 October 1987) para 5 ('if the GATT were to deal with all issues having trade effects, there would be virtually no limit to the scope of its activities.'); M Spence, 'Which Intellectual Property Rights are Trade-Related?' in F Francioni (ed), *Environment, Human Rights and International Trade* (2001) 263.

[194] Thus, the two areas of law were practiced by entirely distinct groups of specialists. At a conference bringing together the two groups of scholars the trade expert Jackson avowed: 'Of course we trade lawyers would hope to leave many of these issues to the intellectual property lawyers. I feel very much outside of my territory in this area and I do not claim any intellectual property expertise, merely some interest.' (JH Jackson, 'Remarks of Professor John H. Jackson' (1989) 22 Vand J Transnat'l L 343). Conversely, the patent scholar Chisum stated: 'I speak really from the perspective of a scholar in intellectual property law, particularly patents. I am a total novice when it comes to GATT matters and international trade.' (DS Chisum, 'Remarks of Professor Donald S. Chisum' (1989) 22 Vand J Transnat'l L 341). A WTO Panel held a similar view and wrote that the TRIPS Agreement 'occupies a relatively self-contained, *sui generis* status in the WTO Agreement' (emphasis in original) (*India—Patent Protection for Pharmaceutical and Agricultural Chemical Products*, WT/DS/50/R (1997) para 7.19).

[195] For this dichotomy see DW Leebron, 'Linkages' (2002) 96 AJIL 5. Note that generally there is no reason to regard strategic linkage claims as inferior to substantive ones. For a more thorough treatment of these questions see HP Hestermeyer, 'The Language of Trade Linkage. Lessons for the Singapore Issues Learned from TRIPS' in A Steinmann, F Höhne, and P-T Stoll (eds), *Die WTO vor neuen Herausforderungen. Tagungsband des 5. Graduiertentreffen im Internationalen Wirtschaftsrecht in Göttingen 2004* (2005) 139 ff.

specialized WIPO forum.[196] Concessions included increased market access, special attention to developing countries' concerns, eg by transition arrangements, concessions on agricultural export subsidies from Europe, and promises to refrain from unilateral trade measures from the United States.[197] A second reason for choosing the GATT setting was that developed countries enjoyed an extraordinary negotiating power within the GATT regime: not only had developing countries shown that they could not cooperate effectively in that setting, because other trade interests posed an obstacle to their forming an alliance,[198] but the market size of 65 per cent of the combined gross domestic product of WTO Members of the United States and the European Union allowed them to set the agenda and made it prohibitive for developing countries to stay outside the Uruguay Round's single undertaking and lose access to these markets.[199] Finally, inclusion of the TRIPS Agreement in the GATT/WTO system remedied one of the perceived defects of the international intellectual property system by making the strong WTO dispute settlement mechanism available for the enforcement of international intellectual property law obligations.

But even after the developing countries had dropped their fundamental resistance to an intellectual property agreement, the negotiations progressed slowly, as substantive questions ranging from patentable subject-matter, non-discrimination, patent term, burden of proof to compulsory licensing were subject to discussion.[200] Pharmaceutical patents were discussed, too. Developing countries demanded their exclusion from patent protection for public health reasons. They supported their argument by the fact that many industrialized countries have not introduced pharmaceutical product patent protection until late in their development.[201] Many industrialized countries rejected this demand as unacceptable.[202] A similar conflict took place about the question of local working requirements. Developing countries and Canada wanted to impose an obligation on patentees to work the patent

[196] Gadbaw (n 152 above) 228; J Reinbothe, 'Der Schutz des Urheberrechts und der Leistungsschutzrechte im Abkommensentwurf GATT/TRIPs' (1992) GRUR Int 707, 708; B Boval, 'L'Accord sur les Droits de Propriété Intellectuelle quit Touchent au Commerce (ADPIC ou TRIPS)' in Société Française pour le Droit International (ed), *La Réorganisation Mondiale des Échanges. Colloque de Nice* (1996) 131, 137.
[197] Abbott (n 150 above) 472; R Hudec, 'Remarks of Professor Robert Hudec' (1989) 22 Vand J Transnat'l L 321; Michaelis and Bender (n 179 above) § 24 para 14. But see Correa (n 147 above) 3 who asserts that developing countries did not obtain any concessions.
[198] Pacón (n 153 above) 330. Cottier observed 'flexible alliance'-building within the TRIPS negotiations. Cottier (n 147 above) 388.
[199] Steinberg showed that the consensus-based decision-making process did not stand in the way, but rather disguised power-based decision-making within the GATT, concluding that the decision-making rules based on sovereign equality of states were 'organized hypocrisy'. RH Steinberg, 'In the Shadow of Law or Power? Consensus-Based Bargaining and Outcomes in the GATT/WTO' (2002) 56 Int'l Org 339; P Drahos, 'Developing Countries and International Intellectual Property Standard-Setting' UK Commission on Intellectual Property Rights Study Paper 8, 10 ff; G Curzon and V Curzon, 'GATT: Traders' Club' in RW Cox and HK Jacobson (eds), *The Anatomy of Influence, Decision Making in International Organization* (1973) 298, 326, 330.　　[200] Cottier (n 147 above) 405 ff.
[201] See this chapter above.　　[202] Cottier (n 147 above) 406–407.

locally, the other developed countries favoured a provision according to which a requirement to work the patent in a country could be satisfied by imports.[203] Not all the disputes about substantive intellectual property rights pitted developing countries against developed ones, at times the fault line ran through the developed world, eg in the question of moral rights in copyright law.[204] Despite all of these difficulties agreement was reached and the TRIPS Agreement entered into force on 1 January 1995 as Annex 1C to the WTO Agreement.

D   Validity of the TRIPS Agreement

In the years after the coming into force of the TRIPS Agreement as the full extent of the consequences of the Agreement started to become clear, discontent with the Agreement began to grow massively in many developing countries, particularly in India and Brazil, and in activist circles. At times the discontent is explicitly or implicitly voiced as a challenge to the validity of the TRIPS Agreement, more often than not appealing to notions of fairness rather than to any concrete legal grounds for invalidity.[205] The criticism should not be discarded lightly as hyperbole by a few radical activists. Writing in the preface to a study on the TRIPS Agreement and its impact on pharmaceuticals and health for all even the former Indian Supreme Court judge Iyer states that:

Some pensive scholars and discerning intellectuals, with a Cassandra touch, predicted for the Third World the fatal fate of 'GATTastrophe', yet others, with sober, but convincing submissions, cautioned that these GATT treaties and the WTO may well spell re-colonisation of the newly freed nations (. . .) To genuflect before Big Powers and consent by legislative action, to pollute our salutary patent law and policy ony (*sic*) to placate the drug multi-nationals and GATT-WTO treaty commands is a kind of dependencia syndrome which we must resist.[206]

---

[203] Cottier (n 147 above) 407. Bail (n 190 above) 469.   [204] Cottier (n 147 above) 389.

[205] Eg Shanker points out that the PhRMA, the US interest group of innovative pharmaceutical manufacturers, often wrongly reads US patent standards into the TRIPS Agreement and that developed countries have at times opposed practices that they themselves used not so long ago as inconsistent with the TRIPS Agreement. He then argues that Art 1.1 of the TRIPS Agreement allowing WTO Members to implement more extensive intellectual property protection than prescribed by the TRIPS Agreement and failing to impose an upper ceiling on such protection removes any certainty from the TRIPS Agreement, which should therefore be held void for violating *jus cogens*. The argument has no merit, as the permissibility of higher intellectual property standards, whether wise or not, is not connected to the certainty of the minimum levels of intellectual property protection, and thus the obligations imposed on states by the TRIPS Agreement. However, Shanker is correct to criticize the practice of lobby groups and developed countries to read ever higher standards of intellectual property protection into the minimum standards imposed by the TRIPS Agreement. Of course, these interpretations are not dispositive for the WTO system and it is the most common occurrence that interested parties interpret legal provisions to advance their own interests. What raises concern in the context of the TRIPS Agreement is that many developing countries do not have the expertise or the market power to challenge developed countries' interpretations. Ultimately, thus, the argument is one about power and fairness. D Shanker, 'India, the Pharmaceutical Industry and the Validity of TRIPS' (2002) 5 J World Intell Prop 315, 356 ff; D Shanker, 'Legitimacy and the TRIPS Agreement' (2003) 6 J World Intell Prop 155.

[206] VR Krishna Iyer, 'A Prolegomenon' in BK Keayla, *Conquest by Patents. TRIPs Agreement on Patent Laws: Impact on Pharmaceuticals and Health for All* (1999) 1, 8.

Given these strong words, a few remarks on the validity of the TRIPS Agreement are in order. The legal ground that the critical arguments could best be subsumed under is the invalidity of the treaty for coercion of the developing countries. Recourse by the United States to its section 301 of the Trade Act of 1974 before and during the negotiations of the TRIPS Agreement could buttress such an argument. The provision allowed the threat and use of trade sanctions, most probably in violation of GATT, aimed at pressuring countries to change their laws in the absence of any obligation to do so. The offer to suspend such unilateral action in return for obtaining consent to the TRIPS Agreement was awkward, as it seemed to offer compliance with international law in return for obtaining the desired agreement.[207] But even though this certainly deserves criticism, it does not lead to the invalidity of the Agreement. While the Vienna Convention on the Laws of Treaties (Vienna Convention) explicitly voids treaties procured by the threat or use of force in violation of the UN Charter,[208] states did not agree to include economic or political pressure in the provision and only condemned such pressure in a declaration in the Final Act of the Conference.[209] Even assuming, *arguendo*, that economic duress voids an agreement the TRIPS Agreement is valid. Its adoption was achieved in a complex negotiation process for several multifaceted Agreements involving numerous trade-offs, several of them for the benefit of developing countries.[210] The process cannot be reduced to a sufficiently clear-cut case of economic duress.

V TRIPS Agreement Patent Standards

Against this background we can now examine which obligations the TRIPS Agreement imposes on WTO Members with respect to pharmaceutical patents. The section will show that the wording of the agreement leaves much room for Members to manoeuvre, particularly in the area of pharmaceuticals, as the provisions on object and purpose demand an interpretation of the agreement respecting public health. However, Members are under a clear obligation to grant pharmaceutical product patents.

Given that there is little WTO case law interpreting the language of the TRIPS Agreement,[211] I will often draw on national patent laws to illustrate the meaning

---

[207] Jackson (n 194 above) 350.   [208] Article 52 of the Vienna Convention.

[209] W Heintschel von Heinegg, in K Ipsen (ed), *Völkerrecht* (4th edn, 1999) 155 ff; H Fischer, in Ipsen, ibid 936–937; I Brownlie, *Principles of Public International Law* (6th edn, 2003) 590–591; United Nations Conference on the Law of Treaties, 'Declaration on the Prohibition of Military, Political or Economic Coercion in the Conclusion of Treaties' (1969) 29 ZaöRV 693.

[210] Eg the Agreement on Textiles and Clothing, leading to the elimination of quantitative restrictions in the sector. WTO Secretariat, *Guide to the Uruguay Round Agreements* (1999) 65.

[211] In 25 cases consultations have been requested, in 13 of these a mutually agreed solution was reached, nine resulted in Panel Reports, in three of the latter cases Appellate Body Reports were adopted. Eleven of the cases were filed in patent law matters. Overall, 16 cases were initiated by the

of the TRIPS provisions. The reader should bear in mind, however, that national examples are not dispositive for interpreting an international agreement unless they constitute subsequent practice in the application of the treaty which establishes the agreement of the parties regarding its interpretation.[212]

1 Interpretation in Light of the Object and Purpose of the TRIPS Agreement

Before undertaking the task of interpreting the TRIPS Agreement obligations, a note on the act of interpretation itself is in order. It is common knowledge that an international treaty has to be interpreted 'in good faith in accordance with the ordinary meaning to be given to the terms of the treaty in their context and in the light of its object and purpose'.[213] 'Interpretation' is a limited exercise—any interpretation of an agreement has to remain within the metes and bounds of the wording of the agreement. The act of interpretation consists of choosing the pertinent meaning of the words in the given situation from the variety of meanings those words can have.

The object and purpose of the TRIPS Agreement can be found in its preamble and in its Articles 7–8 The preamble lists a whole number of goals: Members desire to 'reduce distortions and impediments to international trade', taking into account both the need for intellectual property protection and the need to prevent that protection from itself becoming an impediment to trade. Furthermore, Members recognize that intellectual property rights are private rights. They also acknowledge that intellectual property rights' underlying public policy objectives include developmental and technological objectives.[214] The developmental concerns are further attested to by the recognition that least-developed country Members have special needs requiring maximum flexibility in the implementation of the agreement. Article 7 of the TRIPS Agreement puts down the objectives of the Agreement more narrowly as follows:

The protection and enforcement of intellectual property rights should contribute to the promotion of technological innovation and to the transfer and dissemination of technology, to the mutual advantage of producers and users of technological knowledge and in a manner conducive to social and economic welfare, and to a balance of rights and obligations.

United States, six by the European Communities, one each by Canada, Brazil, Australia. The opponents were Pakistan, Portugal, India (2), Indonesia, Canada (2), European Communities (5), Argentina (2), Brazil, United States (4), Ireland, Japan (2), Sweden, Greece, Denmark. See Annex 3 for a list of cases.

[212] Article 31(3) of the Vienna Convention on the Law of Treaties (Vienna Convention).

[213] Article 31(1) of the Vienna Convention. On the applicability of the Vienna Convention see chapter 5.

[214] N Ayse Odman, 'Using TRIPS to Make the Innovation Process Work' (2000) 3 J World Intell Prop 343, 344 ff.

Even though the provision is merely a 'should' provision, it authoritatively states the objectives of the agreement. Besides putting down a utilitarian public policy rationale for granting patents,[215] namely promoting technological innovation and technology transfer and dissemination,[216] the provision expresses the idea that the TRIPS Agreement seeks to strike a balance between the rights of the patent holder and the interests of the users.[217] The Agreement clearly does not intend to solely further the interests of the inventor, but also imposes limits on those interests for reasons of social and economic welfare.[218] Accessibility of medicine is one of the interests of society that have to be brought into balance with the TRIPS Agreement, as is stated in Article 8 of the TRIPS Agreement:

(1) Members may, in formulating or amending their laws and regulations, adopt measures necessary to protect public health and nutrition, and to promote the public interest in sectors of vital importance to their socio-economic and technological development, provided that such measures are consistent with the provisions of this Agreement.

(2) Appropriate measures, provided that they are consistent with the provisions of this Agreement, may be needed to prevent the abuse of intellectual property rights by rights holders or the resort to practices which unreasonably restrain trade or adversely affect the international transfer of technology.

Any interpretation of the TRIPS Agreement therefore has to take account of public health interests.[219] Whether Articles 7–8 of the TRIPS Agreement can serve as a basis for an exception from patentability will be discussed below.

2 Basic Principles of the TRIPS Agreement

Even though the TRIPS Agreement is often regarded as the most successful attempt to date at harmonizing intellectual property laws, it does not contain an obligation

---

[215] Stoll and Raible (n 137 above) 571–572.

[216] This includes both international technology transfer as well as the diffusion of the knowledge within a country. F Höhne in J Busche and P-T Stoll (eds), *TRIPs*, Art 7, para 5 (2007).

[217] The original proposal for what is now Arts 7–8 contained detailed provisions outlining both the rights and obligations of patent owners. Negotiating Group on Trade-Related Aspects of Intellectual Property Rights Including Trade in Counterfeit Goods, *Communication from Argentina, Brazil Chile, China, Colombia, Cuba, Egypt, India, Nigeria, Peru, Tanzania, Uruguay and Pakistan,* MTN.GNG/NG11/W/71 (14 May 1990).

[218] P Rott, *Patentrecht und Sozialpolitik unter dem TRIPS-Abkommen* (2002) 114; Gervais (n 138 above) 2.76; ICTSD and UNCTAD, *Resource Book on TRIPS and Development*, Part I, 115 (2002); JT Gathii, 'Construing Intellectual Property Rights and Competition Policy Consistently with Facilitating Access to Affordable AIDS Drugs to Low-end Consumers' (2001) 53 Fla L Rev 727, 763 ff; JT Gathii, 'Rights, Patents, Markets and the Global AIDS Pandemic' (2002) 14 Fla J Int'l L 261, 307 ff; but see AA Yusuf, 'TRIPs: Background, Principles and General Provisions' in CM Correa and AA Yusuf (eds), *Intellectual Property and International Trade: The TRIPs Agreement* (1998) 3, 11–12, who assumes that Art 7 of the TRIPS Agreement prefers community interests over the interests of individuals.

[219] In *Canada—Patent* the European Communities argued that the final text of the TRIPS Agreement reflected the balancing required by Arts 7–8 of the TRIPS Agreement and that interpreting the TRIPS Agreement with a view to Arts 7–8 would therefore amount to 'double counting'. The Panel correctly rejected this claim. *Canada—Patent Protection of Pharmaceutical Products,* WT/DS114/R (2000) paras 7.25–7.26 (*Canada—Patent*); C Correa, *Acuerdo TRIPs* (1996) 31.

to adopt harmonized national laws:[220] it imposes minimum standards for intellectual property protection. As Article 1.1 of the TRIPS Agreement explicitly states, Members may 'but shall not be obliged to, implement in their law more extensive protection than is required by this Agreement, provided that such protection does not contravene the provisions of this Agreement'. Also, Members undertook the obligation to accord the treatment provided for in the TRIPS Agreement to the nationals of other Members only.[221] They are under no obligation in respect of their own citizens. In practice, however, it is highly unlikely that any state will adopt laws granting TRIPS compliant intellectual property rights to foreigners, but not to its own citizens.[222]

The relationship between the TRIPS Agreement and the Paris Convention is clarified in Article 2 of the TRIPS Agreement. Article 2.1 of the TRIPS Agreement requires Members to comply with the substantive provisions of the Paris Convention,[223] thus extending those obligations to Members not party to the Paris Convention.[224] Article 2.2 of the TRIPS Agreement provides that Parts I to IV of the TRIPS Agreement shall not derogate from obligations under the Paris Convention. The latter provision enabled State Parties to the Paris Convention to comply with their obligation to conclude separate agreements for the protection of industrial property only insofar as they do not contravene the provisions of the Paris Convention.[225] The approach taken by the TRIPS Agreement has been described as a 'Paris-Plus' approach, incorporating the relevant provisions of the Paris Convention and adding additional obligations on top of it.

Much like the GATT the TRIPS Agreement also contains obligations of national treatment and most-favoured nation treatment, although it does not impose such an obligation with respect to like products. Rather, it obliges Members to 'accord to the nationals of other Members treatment no less favourable than that it accords to its own nationals with regard to the protection of intellectual property (. . .)'[226] and to accord any 'advantage, favour, privilege or immunity' with regard to the protection of intellectual property granted to the nationals of any other country immediately to the nationals of all other Members.[227] The Agreement does, however, make some exceptions to the most-favoured nation obligation.[228]

---

[220] A Otten and H Wagner, 'Compliance with TRIPS: The Emerging World View' in F Abbott, T Cottier, and F Gurry (eds), *The International Intellectual Property System. Commentary and Materials Pt One* (1999) 697, 698–699.

[221] To define 'nationals' the Agreement refers to the relevant intellectual property conventions, ie for patent law to the Paris Convention, and thus also includes, eg, persons with a commercial establishment on the territory of a WTO Member. Gervais (n 138 above) 2.20, and n 126 above.

[222] A Staehelin, *Das TRIPs-Abkommen. Immateralgüterrechte im Licht der globalisierten Handelspolitik* (2nd edn, 1999) 53.

[223] Articles 1–12, 19 of the Paris Convention in the Stockholm revision. Gervais (n 138 above) 2.32. Some of these provisions will be discussed in detail in chapter 5.

[224] The same can be said for states not parties to the Stockholm revision of the Paris Convention.

[225] Article 19 of the Paris Convention.   [226] Article 3.1 of the TRIPS Agreement.

[227] Article 4 of the TRIPS Agreement.   [228] Article 4 of the TRIPS Agreement.

3 Conditions of Patentability

The key obligation of the TRIPS Agreement with respect to patents is contained in Article 27 ff of the TRIPS Agreement, which oblige Members to make patents available when the conditions of patentability under the TRIPS Agreement are fulfilled. The language of these provisions closely mirrors the terminology common in many national patent laws, but it lacks the clarification that those provisions have undergone in decades of litigation. Some scholars seem to take it for granted that their own national standards have been adopted lock, stock, and barrel in the TRIPS Agreement. Such an approach is clearly erroneous. The principle *in dubio mitius* has to be applied, according to which in case of any doubt about the meaning of a provision, the interpretation imposing fewer obligations on Members has to be adopted. Additionally, it has already been shown that the interpretation has to take account of public health concerns. Following these principles, vaguely worded provisions of the TRIPS Agreement admit a number of possible implementations.[229] The following sections will illustrate some of these possibilities. They will show that Members have some flexibility in structuring their patent system for pharmaceutical patents. However, they will also illustrate that Members are clearly obliged to provide for product patent protection for drugs.

Much like national patent laws the TRIPS Agreement covers the requirements of patentable subject matter (A), novelty (B), inventive step (C),[230] capability of industrial application (D),[231] and disclosure (E). Significantly, the TRIPS Agreement also contains an obligation of non-discrimination, which will be treated in part A.

A Patentable Subject Matter

Article 27 of the TRIPS Agreement, the central provision on patent protection, prescribes that

1. Subject to the provisions of paragraphs 2 and 3, patents shall be available for any inventions, whether products or processes, in all fields of technology, provided that they are new, involve an inventive step and are capable of industrial application. Subject to paragraph 4 of Article 65, paragraph 8 of Article 70 and paragraph 3 of this Article, patents shall be available and patent rights enjoyable without discrimination as to the place of invention, the field of technology and whether products are imported or locally produced.

2. Members may exclude from patentability inventions, the prevention within their territory of the commercial exploitation of which is necessary to protect *ordre public* or morality, including to protect human, animal or plant life or health or to avoid serious prejudice

---

[229] Granting a higher level of intellectual property protection is permissible as the TRIPS Agreement only imposes minimum standards.

[230] According to a footnote this term is deemed to be synonymous with the term 'non-obvious'.

[231] This term is synonymous with the 'utility' requirement.

to the environment, provided that such exclusion is not made merely because the exploitation is prohibited by their law.

3. Members may also exclude from patentability:

(a) diagnostic, therapeutic and surgical methods for the treatment of humans or animals;

(b) plants and animals other than micro-organisms, and essentially biological processes for the production of plants or animals other than non-biological and microbiological processes. However, Members shall provide for the protection of plant varieties either by patents or by an effective *sui generis* system or by any combination thereof. The provisions of this subparagraph shall be reviewed four years after the date of entry into force of the WTO Agreement.[232]

The subject matter eligible for patent protection is vast: Article 27.1 of the TRIPS Agreement makes patents available for any inventions, whether products or processes, in all fields of technology. Clearly pharmaceutical products and processes are thus within the scope of patentability.

a Inventions

Nevertheless, the scope of eligible subject matter is not unlimited and the restriction is highly relevant in the field of pharmaceuticals: patents only have to be available for inventions.[233] The TRIPS Agreement does not define the term, opting to remain flexible in light of the inherently open character of technological change.[234] It has become commonplace, however, to distinguish inventions, which are patentable, from discoveries, which are not.[235] Under this distinction everything already existing in nature, such as ideas, laws of nature, and materials discovered in nature, is not patentable.[236] This excludes substances with medicinal properties found in nature from patentability.

Many developed countries have adopted a narrow definition of 'discovery'. Thus, in the United States a discovered substance is not patentable, but a purified substance that does not occur naturally in that form and possesses a therapeutic value that the original non-purified product does not possess is patentable.[237] Similar

---

[232] Emphasis in original, footnote deleted.

[233] *Canada—Term of Patent Protection*, WT/DS170/AB/R (2000) paras 65–66.

[234] Some national laws contain definitions of invention, eg the Vietnamese Patent Act. C Heath, 'Industrial Property Protection in Vietnam' (1999) 30 IIC 419, 426.

[235] Eg § 1(2) Patentgesetz 1981 (Germany); Art 52(2) of the EPC; Correa (n 147 above) 51–52. Generally, discoveries also fail the test of novelty.

[236] Correa (n 147 above) 52. For US law see Miller and Davis (n 9 above) 21 ff; AL Durham, *Patent Law Essentials. A Concise Guide* (1999) 24. The same rule was applied by the US Supreme Court when it allowed a patent on a genetically engineered microorganism. *Diamond v Chakrabarty* 447 US 303 (1980), cf *Funk Bros Seed v Kalo Inoculant Co* 333 US 127 (1948).

[237] *Parke-Davis & Co v HK Mulford Co* 189 F 95 (CCSDNY, 1911) (adrenaline); *Parke-Davis & Co v HK Mulford Co* 196 F 496 (2nd Cir, 1912). DS Chisum, *Chisum on Patents. A Treatise on the Law of Patentability, Validity and Infringement. Volume 1* (loose-leaf, last updated 2003) 1–75 ff.

rules are followed, eg under the EPC and German patent law.[238] Applying the same
principle, US Courts allowed patents on DNA sequences as patents on chemical
compounds in their 'purified and isolated' form.[239] There is, however, nothing
in the TRIPS Agreement forcing countries to adopt a narrow definition of discovery.[240] Several developing countries do not allow a substance to escape the
verdict of having been discovered by mere purification of the substance.[241] Such
an approach is permitted by the TRIPS Agreement.[242]

b All Fields of Technology, Exceptions, Non-Discrimination
aa All Fields of Technology The extension of patents to all fields of technology
by the TRIPS Agreement was regarded as one of the greatest achievements of the
Agreement in the eyes of the intellectual property community.[243] Although the
Agreement fails to define the term 'technology', it is undisputed that the pharmaceutical field is included and patents have to be made available in that field. In
fact, the availability of patents for pharmaceuticals was one of the main focuses of
the debate and had been fought for intensively by the pharmaceutical industry
lobby.[244] The change from prior practice was significant: 49 states parties to the
Paris Convention had exempted pharmaceutical products from patentability and
ten states parties to the Paris Convention excluded pharmaceutical processes.[245]

---

[238] BPatG (1978) GRUR 238, 239 ('Naturstoffe'); Correa (n 147 above) 53; Hubmann and
Götting (n 1 above) 120.

[239] *Amgen Inc v Chugai Pharmaeutical Co Ltd* 13 USPQ2d 1737, 1759 (D Mass, 1989); *Amgen
Inc v Chugai Pharmaceutical Co* 927 F2d 1200 (Fed Cir, 1991). Such patents pose many difficult
questions, particularly with respect to the inventive step required. K Bozicevic, 'Patenting DNA-
Obviousness Rejections' (1992) 74 J Pat & Trademark, Off Soc'y 750; DL Burk and MA Lemley, 'Is
Patent Law Technology-Specific?' (2002) 17 Berkeley Tech LJ 1155, 1156. For criticism based on the
growing ease with which DNA is sequenced: RS Eisenberg, 'Re-Examining the Role of Patents in
Appropriating the Value of DNA Sequences' (2000) 49 Emory LJ 783, 786, RS Eisenberg, 'Patenting
the Human Genome' (1990) 39 Emory LJ 721.

[240] Schiuma disagrees. He asserts that all members have to provide patent protection in an area of
technology to reduce trade distortions if some important WTO members provide patent protection
for that area of technology, because the objective of the TRIPS Agreement is to reduce trade distortions. This approach is flawed, as it leaves some WTO members with the power of defining the terminology of the agreement. D Schiuma, 'TRIPS and Exclusion of Software "as Such" from Patentability'
(2000) 31 IIC 36, 37 ff.

[241] See Art 10 (IX) Lei da Propriedade Industrial N 9.279 de 14 de Maio de 1996 (Brazil), Art 15 (b)
of Decision 486 (Andean Community); for a less clear position Arts 16 II, 19 II Ley de la Propiedad
Industrial (Mexico). On the issue: Correa (n 147 above) 53–54.

[242] CM Correa, 'Implementing the TRIPS Agreement in the Patents Field—Options for Developing Countries' (1998) 1 J World Intell Prop 75, 77–78; Straus (n 152 above) 191; K Timmermans
and T Hutadjulu, *The TRIPS Agreement and Pharmaceuticals. Report of an ASEAN Workshop on the
TRIPs Agreement and its Impact on Pharmaceuticals. Jakarta 2–4 May 2000* (2000) 30–31.

[243] Straus (n 152 above) 188.   [244] See n 183 above.

[245] See n 141 above; Negotiating Group on Trade-Related Aspects of Intellectual Property Rights,
including Trade in Counterfeit Goods, *Existence, Scope and Form of Generally Internationally Accepted
and Applied Standards/Norms for the Protection of Intellectual Property. Note Prepared by the International
Bureau of WIPO*, MTN.GNG/NG11/W/24/Rev.1 at Annex II (15 September 1988).

It is therefore no surprise that patent protection for pharmaceuticals has also featured prominently in the cases in which consultations have been requested so far. Thus, the United States requested consultations with Pakistan,[246] Argentina,[247] and India[248] alleging lack of patent protection or the equivalent transitional protection for pharmaceuticals.

bb Exceptions for Pharmaceuticals?   Several scholars have tried to argue that pharmaceuticals or at least essential pharmaceuticals can be excluded from patentability under one of the exceptions that the TRIPS Agreement contains, allowing Members to exclude certain areas from patentability. At first glance some of the exceptions seem to be pertinent.

Article 27.2 of the TRIPS Agreement allows the exemption of 'inventions, the prevention within their territory of the commercial exploitation of which is necessary to protect *ordre public* or morality, including to protect human, animal or plant life or health (. . .)'[249] from patentability. Assuming, *arguendo*, that patents impede access to medicine by raising the price level, could it not be argued that excluding the patentability of pharmaceuticals is necessary for the protection of human health?[250] Such an argument misreads Article 27.2 of the TRIPS Agreement. While human health is explicitly included in the concept of *ordre public*, the provision requires the prevention of the *commercial exploitation* of the invention to be necessary to protect the *ordre public*. The commercial exploitation of the invention is the marketing of the invention for profit.[251] The determination whether the prevention of the commercial exploitation is 'necessary', following WTO jurisprudence on Article XX of the GATT, involves 'in every case a process of weighing and balancing a series of factors'—but the measure cannot be necessary if 'an alternative measure which [the Member] could reasonably be expected to employ and which is not inconsistent with other GATT provisions is available to it'.[252] The risk to public health in the case of patents and access to medicine,

---

[246] *Pakistan—Patent Protection for Pharmaceutical and Agricultural Chemical Products. Notification of a Mutually-Agreed Solution*, WT/DS36/4 (1997).

[247] *Argentina—Patent Protection for Pharmaceuticals and Test Data Protection for Agricultural Chemicals. Notification of Mutually Agreed Solution*, WT/DS/171/3 (2002).

[248] *India—Patent Protection for Pharmaceutical and Agricultural Chemical Products*, WT/DS50/R (1997) and *India—Patent Protection for Pharmaceutical and Agricultural Chemical Products*, WT/DS50/AB/R (1997) (*India—Mailbox*).   [249] Emphasis in original.

[250] PL Wojahn, 'A Conflict of Rights: Intellectual Property Under TRIPS, the Right to Health and AIDS Drugs' (2001–2002) 6 UCLA J Int'l L & Foreign Aff 463, 480; SM Ford, 'Compulsory Licensing Provisions Under the TRIPs Agreement: Balancing Pills and Patents' (2000) 15 Am U Int'l L Rev 941, 965; P Marc, 'Compulsory Licensing and the South African Medicine Act of 1997: Violation or Compliance of the Trade Related Aspects of Intellectual Property Rights Agreement?' (2001) 21 NYL Sch J Int'l & Comp L 109, 122.

[251] In-depth: Rott (n 218 above) 220 ff.

[252] *Dominican Republic—Measures Affecting the Importation and Internal Sale of Cigarettes*, WT/DS302/AB/R (2005) paras 66 ff; *Thailand—Restrictions on Importation of and Internal Taxes on Cigarettes*, DS10/R—37S/200 (1990) para 75 (*Thailand—Cigarettes*); *United States—Section 337 of the Tariff Act of 1930*, L/6439—36S/345 (1989), para 5.26, both cited with approval in *European Communities—Measures Affecting Asbestos and Asbestos-containing Products*, WT/DS135/AB/R (2001)

however, does not stem from the commercial exploitation of pharmaceutical inventions, but rather from the alleged patent rents, ie from the patentability of these inventions.[253] Preventing the sale of pharmaceuticals for profit is neither necessary to achieve the intended public health goals nor does it even further those goals. States intend to open their market for the (for profit) sale of generics rather than prevent their sale.[254] This distinction is at times overlooked by authors hoping to find a general exception from patentability for pharmaceuticals.[255]

Members can also exclude diagnostic, therapeutic, and surgical methods for the treatment of humans or animals from patentability under Article 27.3(a) of the TRIPS Agreement. The provision was inspired by a similar (but more narrow) exception in the EPC[256] and has widely been used by as diverse countries as Mexico[257] and Germany.[258] The United States has enacted narrower provisions with a similar effect.[259] But here, too, pharmaceuticals are not covered by the exception. The plain wording of Article 27.3(a) of the TRIPS Agreement does not allow Members to also exclude from patentability devices or products used to apply the methods, such as test kits or pharmaceuticals.[260] Patents for these have to be granted, even though the reason for excluding one category, but not the other from patentability is elusive.[261]

Some authors regard Articles 7 and 8.1 of the TRIPS Agreement as a basis for excluding pharmaceuticals from patentability either entirely or at least to the extent

---

paras 170–171 (*EC—Asbestos*). On the applicability of this definition to Art 27: Gervais (n 138 above) 2.262; R Weissmann, 'A Long, Strange TRIPS: The Pharmaceutical Industry Drive to Harmonize Global Intellectual Property Rules, and the Remaining WTO Legal Alternatives Available to Third World Countries' (1996) 17 U Pa J Int'l Econ L 1069, 1101 ff; Rott (n 218 above) 230.

[253] Rott (n 218 above) 236; Straus (n 152 above) 189; AO Sykes, 'TRIPs, Pharmaceuticals, Developing Countries and the Doha "Solution"' John M Olin Law & Economics Working Paper No 140 (2nd Series), (University of Chicago Law School, 2002) 6 (also published as AO Sykes, 'TRIPS, Pharmaceuticals, Developing Countries, and the Doha "Solution"' (2002) 3 Chicago J Int'l L 47).

[254] Some authors argue that only a complete ban of any and all distribution of the invention can be upheld under the provision, others would permit not-for profit distribution. Correa (n 147 above) 62–63; TG Ackermann, 'Diso'ordre'ly Loopholes: TRIPS Patent Protection, GATT and the ECJ' (1997) 32 Tex Int'l L J 489, 508–509.

[255] R Elliott, *TRIPS and Rights: International Human Rights Law, Access to Medicines and the Interpretation of the WTO Agreement on Trade-Related Aspects of Intellectual Property Rights, Canadian HIV/AIDS Legal Network & AIDS Law Project, South Africa* (2001) 46 ff.

[256] Article 52(4) of the EPC, see Straus (n 152 above) 189.

[257] Article 19 VII Ley de la Propiedad Industrial.

[258] § 5 (2) Patentgesetz 1981. Dogmatically this provision is an unrebuttable presumption against the capability of industrial application, Stoll and Raible (n 137 above) 591.

[259] 35 USC § 287(c) provides that remedies against patent violations shall not apply to medical practitioners or a related health care entity for the performance of a medical or surgical procedure. It was enacted for fear that patents in the area 'restrict access to patented procedures, increase costs of medical care, and interfere with patient confidentiality'. Patents do, however, remain available. Chisum (n 237 above) 1–93 ff, see, eg US Patent No 5,601,557, Anchoring and manipulating tissue, claiming a method for anchoring in bone a member and attached suture.

[260] Straus (n 152 above) 189–190; Correa (n 147 above) 67.

[261] For doubts about the justification of the distinction see also Federal Court of Australia, *Anaesthetic Supplies Pty Limited v Rescare Limited*, 26 IIC 399 (1995) (1994).

that the pharmaceuticals are essential.[262] As stated above, these two provisions contain the objectives and principles of the Agreement, eg that the protection of intellectual property rights should contribute to the dissemination of technology, to the mutual advantage of producers and users of technological knowledge, and in a manner conducive to social and economic welfare (Art 7) and that Members may adopt measures necessary to protect public health, provided that such measures are consistent with the provisions of the Agreement (Art 8.1). As is indicated by its title, Article 7 of the TRIPS Agreement puts down the objectives of the Agreement, the goals its provisions are intended to serve. It is not meant as an exception to those provisions. The abstract goals worded in a 'should' format do not subtract from the concrete 'shall' obligations imposed in the Agreement.[263] Nevertheless, the provision plays a vital role in the interpretation of the Agreement. Articles 8.1 and 8.2 of the TRIPS Agreement cannot serve as exceptions to the obligations of the Agreement, either, as they allow measures only insofar as they are consistent with the provisions of the TRIPS Agreement. Yusuf has argued that this caveat in Article 8 of the TRIPS Agreement tests a measure's 'overall consistency' with the agreement, which can at times be affirmed even where a measure may be inconsistent with some of the specific standards of the Agreement.[264] It is, however, difficult to imagine how a measure that is in violation of a provision of the TRIPS Agreement can 'overall' be consistent with the Agreement, as such 'overall' compliance can only be measured according to the compliance with single provisions. Articles 7 and 8 of the TRIPS Agreement can therefore not serve as exceptions to the obligations imposed by the TRIPS Agreement.[265]

Finally, a country could try to invoke the national security exception contained in Article 73 of the TRIPS Agreement. The provision states that:

Nothing in this Agreement shall be construed:

(...)

(b) to prevent a Member from taking any action which it considers necessary for the protection of its essential security interests;

(...)

(iii) taken in time of war or other emergency in international relations; (...)

The term 'security', once clearly reserved for the domain of war and peace, has been used more broadly recently, including other areas, such as diseases.[266] Under

---

[262] AM von Hase, 'The Application and Interpretation of the Agreement on Trade-Related Aspects of Intellectual Property Rights' in CM Correa and AA Yusuf (eds), *Intellectual Property and International Trade: The TRIPs Agreement* (1998) 93, 133; Yusuf (n 218 above) 13–14 (1998); JH Reichman, 'From Free Riders to Fair Followers: Global Competition under the TRIPS Agreement' (1996–1997) 29 NYU J Int'l L & Pol, 11, 35; Geisel (n 179 above) 139.

[263] Gervais (n 138 above) 2.75; K Gamharter, *Access to Affordable Medicines. Developing Responses under the TRIPS Agreement and EC Law* (2004) 71.   [264] Yusuf (n 262 above) 13.

[265] Most authors now agree on this point, eg Rott (n 218 above) 119.

[266] In chapter 1 it was already stated that the Secretary-General's High-level Panel on Threats, Challenges and Change listed AIDS as a threat to international peace and security.

such an interpretation, a Member would not be prevented from taking actions it considers necessary against a disease that threatens its essential security interests in time of war or other emergency in international relations. Even though there are good reasons to adopt a broad view on the definition of security and it can be argued that at least the AIDS pandemic constitutes an emergency in international relations and (for many states) a threat to national security, this broad view of 'security' is still only emerging. Consequently, no state has invoked the provision so far and cannot safely do so, yet. Apart from this exception, neither a complete exclusion of pharmaceutical products nor an exclusion of essential pharmaceutical products from patentability is thus permissible under the TRIPS Agreement.

cc Non-Discrimination   The impermissibility of excluding pharmaceutical products from patentability is reinforced by one of the most hotly contested provisions of the TRIPS Agreement: the obligation of non-discrimination contained in Article 27.1 of the TRIPS Agreement, that demands that 'patents shall be available and patent rights enjoyable without discrimination as to the place of invention, the field of technology and whether products are imported or locally produced'. The scope of application of the provision explicitly covers both the question of the availability of patent rights, ie questions of patentability, and the rights conferred by patents according to Article 28.1 of the TRIPS Agreement.[267] Three types of discrimination are banned: discrimination as to the place of invention, the field of technology, and the local production or production abroad.[268] Thus, discriminating against pharmaceuticals would constitute an impermissible discrimination as to the field of technology. But what is discrimination under the Agreement? Differences between fields of technology indubitably require responses tailored to the field of technology.[269] Therefore Australia argued in the *Canada—Patent* case that '[i]t was not inconsistent with the TRIPS Agreement to provide for distinct patent rules that respond to practical consequences of differences between fields of technology (. . .)'.[270] The Panel responded to this need and pointed out that discrimination 'is a normative term, pejorative in connotation, referring to results of the unjustified imposition of differentially disadvantageous treatment'.[271] 'Article 27 does not prohibit bona fide exceptions to deal with problems that may exist only in certain product areas.'[272] The Panel went on to distinguish *de iure* and *de facto* discrimination.[273] With regard to the latter type of discrimination it held that not all

---

[267] Chapter 5 will show that it is debatable whether the provision also applies to the so-called flexibilities of the TRIPS Agreement contained, eg in Art 30 of the TRIPS Agreement.

[268] The ramifications of the provision on non-discrimination as to importation or local production will be discussed in chapter 5.

[269] Burk and Lemley have demonstrated convincingly that the US patent system, while on the face of it is 'a unified patent system that provides technology-neutral protection to all kinds of technologies' is 'technology-specific in application' stemming from significant differences in the interpretation of the patentability requirements in different fields of technology. Burk and Lemley (n 239 above).

[270] *Canada—Patent* (n 219 above) para 5.9.   [271] *Canada—Patent* (n 219 above) para 7.94.

[272] *Canada—Patent* (n 219 above) para 7.92.

[273] *Canada—Patent* (n 219 above) para 7.94.

differential treatment is discrimination and inquired into the de facto discriminatory effect and into the discriminatory purpose, albeit it considered this latter inquiry not to focus on subjective purposes of officials, but on the objective characteristics of the measures at issue.[274] Scholars have noted that the distinction between (permissible) differential treatment and (impermissible) discrimination allows for an interpretation respecting the objectives and purposes of the TRIPS Agreement, ie Articles 7–8 of the TRIPS Agreement. Members therefore have more latitude when legislating to preserve public health than in other fields.[275] Ultimately, the threshold between differential treatment and discrimination will have to be determined on a case-by-case basis, adding to the legal insecurity for developing countries wishing to take measures in the area of public health. The fact that Members enjoy some latitude to pass industry-specific patent laws is also illustrated by states' actions to fine-tune their patent laws with respect to the effects of the drug approval process that many countries have established.

dd The Drug Approval Process: Patent Law Implications One of the specifics that distinguish pharmaceuticals from other products is that in most countries pharmaceuticals have to be approved by an administrative agency before they can be marketed, a procedure commonly conducted by national authorities. Not only does this approval process have a significant impact on patents, interplaying with several aspects of patent laws, but where generics are not approved the innovator drug enjoys a market exclusivity that is strikingly similar to the exclusivity a patent holder enjoys. Many countries have passed industry-specific patent laws to fine-tune patent laws with respect to the effects of such a review process. It is therefore necessary to have a basic understanding of the review procedure. This section will present some common features of the process by using the US approval process as an example.[276]

---

[274] *Canada—Patent* (n 219 above) paras 7.100 ff; Rott (n 218 above) 189 ff.

[275] Rott (n 218 above) 191; P Rott, 'TRIPS-Abkommen, Menschenrechte, Sozialpolitik und Entwicklungsländer' (2003) GRUR Int 103, 110; ICTSD and UNCTAD (n 218 above) Part Two, 35; FM Abbott, 'WTO TRIPS Agreement and Its Implications for Access to Medicines in Developing Countries' UK Commission on Intellectual Property Rights Study Paper 2a (2002) 38; R Howse, 'The Canadian Generic Medicines Panel. A Dangerous Precedent in Dangerous Times' (2000) 3 J World Intell Prop 493, 505. The Panel itself seems critical of such an approach, stating that the rule of non-discrimination may well constitute a deliberate limitation of Members' ability to pursue the policies mentioned in Arts 7–8 of the TRIPS Agreement (*Canada—Patent* (n 219 above) para 7.92); this, however, is besides the point—Arts 7–8 remain relevant for the purpose of interpreting Art 27 of the TRIPS Agreement. D Shanker, 'The Vienna Convention on the Law of Treaties, the Dispute Settlement System of the WTO and the Doha Declaration on the TRIPS Agreement' (2002) 36 JWT 721, 738, 742.

[276] In the EU, Council Regulation (EEC) 2309/93 of 22 July 1993 Laying down Community Procedures for the Authorization and Supervision of Medicinal Products for Human and Veterinary Use and Establishing a European Agency for the Evaluation of Medicinal Products, as amended [1993] OJ L214/1 (24 August 1993) created a centralized Community procedure for the authorization of medicinal products, see also Council Directive (EEC) 65/65 of 26 January 1965 on the Approximation of Provisions Laid down by Law, Regulation or Administrative Action Relating to Medicinal Products, as amended [1965] OJ L22/369 (9 February 1965).

In the United States new drugs[277] have to be approved by the Food and Drug Administration (FDA) under the Federal Food, Drug, and Cosmetic Act (FDCA)[278] before they can be marketed in interstate commerce.[279] The drug approval process proceeds through several stages:[280] preclinical investigations determine whether the drug is sufficiently safe for trials in humans, phase 1 studies examine the drug in a small number of test subjects, phase 2 studies involve an expanded group of patients afflicted with the disease being studied, and phase 3 studies involve up to several thousand test subjects. After phase 3 studies the applicant prepares a new drug application (NDA), containing amongst others a description of the investigations, of the composition of the drug, of the manufacturing processes, and a list of the patents claiming the drug or methods of use, and submits it to the FDA.[281] The FDA approves the drug upon finding that it is safe and effective, that adequate manufacturing controls are in place and that the labelling meets the applicable standards.[282]

The impact of the approval process on the enjoyment of pharmaceutical patent rights is twofold: the patentee loses the commercial value of the part of the patent term during which the clinical studies are conducted, because the pharmaceutical cannot be marketed until the drug is approved. On the other hand, it enjoys some exclusivity beyond the patent term, as the manufacturers of competing generic drugs, too, need to obtain FDA approval before they can market the generics[283] and they cannot conduct the studies necessary for approval during the patent term as such activities were held to infringe the patent on the drug in the *Bolar* case.[284] The Drug Price Competition and Patent Term Restoration Act of 1984, also known as the Hatch-Waxman Act was intended to remove both distortions of the patent term.[285] The Act restores the time of the patent term lost due to the approval process by extending the patent 'by the time equal to the regulatory review period for the approved product which period occurs after the date the patent is issued',[286]

---

[277] 'Drug' is defined in 21 USC § 321(g)(1); 'new drug' in 21 USC § 321(p). Biologic drugs and over-the-counter drugs (OTCs) are subject to different rules that will not be discussed here. DO Beers, *Generic and Innovator Drugs. A Guide to FDA Approval Requirements* (5th edn, 1999) 1–2 ff.

[278] 21 USC §§ 301 ff.   [279] 21 USC § 355 (a).

[280] For a description of the FDA process see GM Levitt, JN Czaban, and AS Paterson, 'Human Drug Regulation' in DG Adams, RM Cooper and JS Kahan (eds), *Fundamentals of Law and Regulation. Volume II. An In-depth Look at Therapeutic Products* (1997) 159.   [281] 21 USC § 355(b)(1).

[282] The determination involves weighing the benefits against the risks. Levitt, Czaban and Paterson (n 280 above) 171, 194. The patents the drug company asserts are published without any FDA examination in the 'Orange Book', which is available on the Internet: Food and Drug Administration, *Electronic Orange Book. Approved Drug Products with Therapeutic Equivalence Evaluations*, at <http://www.fda.gov/cder/ob/default.htm>. EH Dickinson, 'FDA's Role in Making Exclusivity Determinations' (1999) 54 Food & Drug LJ 195, 196.   [283] Beers (n 277 above) 1–23.

[284] *Roche Products, Inc v Bolar Pharmaceutical Co Inc* 733 F2d 858, 863 (Fed Cir, 1984).

[285] Pub L No 98-417, 98 Stat 1585 (1984). Congress tried to reach a comprehensive deal in discussions between generic drug makers and innovative pharmaceutical companies. AB Engelberg, 'Special Patent Provisions for Pharmaceuticals: Have they Outlived their Usefulness? A Political, Legislative and Legal History of U.S. Law and Observations for the Future' (1999) 39 IDEA 389.

[286] 35 USC § 156 (c).

albeit limiting the total patent term for this extended patent to 14 years.[287] On the other hand the Act overrode the Federal Circuit decision in *Bolar* and explicitly allowed making, using, offering for sale, selling, or importing a patented invention for the purpose of submitting an FDA application (the so-called 'Bolar exemption'), thus promoting generic competition.[288] To further facilitate the market entry of generics the Act simplified the FDA application process for generic medicine, allowing abbreviated new drug applications (ANDAs) that solely require a showing of bioequivalence of the generic drug to the listed reference drug.[289]

It is at this intersection that another provision of the TRIPS Agreement comes into play: the applicant of an NDA invested significant resources into the studies necessary to compile the application and wants these to be protected.[290] The TRIPS Agreement requires that:

Members, when requiring, as a condition of approving the marketing of pharmaceutical or of agricultural chemical products which utilize new chemical entities, the submission of undisclosed test or other data, the origination of which involves a considerable effort, shall protect such data against unfair commercial use. (. . .)[291]

Thus, the TRIPS Agreement requires protection of the test data in an application for approval of a new drug. Whether this prevents an administrative agency from approving a generic upon a showing of bioequivalence at least for a period of time is a contested issue, which turns on whether such action has to be regarded as 'unfair commercial use' of the submitted test data.[292] The US, in which no ANDA can be accepted for five years for drugs 'no active ingredient' of which has been approved before,[293] and the EU, which applies a similar rule with a six-to ten-year

---

[287] 35 USC § 156 (c)(3). For further details see 35 USC § 156.   [288] 35 USC § 271 (e).

[289] 21 USC § 355 (j). Levitt, Czaban and Paterson (n 280 above) 186 ff. The generic manufacturer also has to state the relationship of the generic with patents on the reference drug listed in the NDA. If the manufacturer claims that the patents will not be infringed or are invalid, the ANDA can result in a patent infringement suit in an intricate procedure that is connected with a 30-month delay of the approval of the generic and a 180-day market exclusivity for the first generic competitor, opening the door to abuse of the complex provisions. For details read 21 USC § 355(j); 35 USC § 271(e)(2); E Powell-Bullock, 'Gaming the Hatch-Waxman System: How Pioneer Drug Makers Exploit the Law to Maintain Monopoly Power in the Prescription Drug Market' (2002) 29 J Legis 21, 30 ff; DO Beers, *Generic and Innovator Drugs. A Guide to FDA Approval Requirements. 2003 Supplement* (5th edn, 2003) 21 ff; Federal Trade Commission, *Generic Drug Entry Prior to Patent Expiration: An FTC Study* (2002).

[290] JT O'Reilly, *Food and Drug Administration. Volume One* (2nd edn loose-leaf, last updated 2002) § 13.15.   [291] Article 39.3 of the TRIPS Agreement.

[292] For a thorough discussion of these questions, see CM Correa, *Protection of Data Submitted for the Registration of Pharmaceuticals: Implementing the Standards of the TRIPS Agreement* (2002). Note that requiring the unnecessary repetition of tests poses questions with regard to the protection of animals involved in tests and, of course, with regard to the protection of human test subjects. R Wolfrum, 'Verfassungsrechtliche Fragen der Zweitanmeldung von Arzneimitteln, Pflanzenbehandlungsmitteln und Chemikalien—Zugleich ein Beitrag zum Schutz technischer Innovationen' (1986) GRUR 512, 516.

[293] 21 USC § 355(j)(5)(D)(ii). TS Coleman, 'Waxman-Hatch Exclusivity Provisions Not Related to Patent Status' (1991) 46 Food Drug Cosm LJ 345, 353. There is also some lesser protection for data of 'new clinical investigations (other than bioavailability studies) essential to the approval', 21 USC § 355(j)(5)(D)(iii), 21 USC § 355(c)(3)(D)(iii). Dickinson (n 282 above) 201. Note that an NDA can be accepted.

period,[294] answer in the affirmative.[295] The United States has urged, eg, Argentina[296] and Israel[297] to adopt more stringent standards. However, it is doubtful whether the approval procedure of an administrative agency can be viewed as *commercial use*. A closer look at the approval process reveals that there is even no *use* of the data submitted in the NDA: the subject of the examination is bioequivalence of the generic to the original drug—the examiners will not look at the original data submitted.[298]

Regulators have used the approval process to grant incentives closely reminiscent of patents by providing for exclusivity periods in which no other marketing approval will be granted—whether an NDA or ANDA was filed. Thus, manufacturers of 'orphan drugs', drugs treating rare diseases or conditions, profit from a seven-year exclusivity period in the United States independent of patent protection,[299] a manufacturer conducting paediatric tests requested by the FDA benefits from a six months exclusivity.[300] It is questionable whether all of these industry-specific rules, insofar as they provide market exclusivity, comply with the obligation of non-discrimination as to the field of technology. Canada has taken up the

---

[294] Article 4(2) No 8 (a)(iii) of Council Directive (EEC) 65/65, as amended, requires a six-year period (ten years for high-technology medicinal products) and allows Member States to choose a ten-year period instead. The centralized European procedure grants a ten-year period. Article 13(4) of Council Regulation (EC) 2309/93, as amended.

[295] J Gorlin, 'Encouragement of New Clinical Drug Development: The Role of Data Exclusivity' (2000) IFPMA 5.

[296] *Argentina—Certain Measures on the Protection of Patents and Test Date. Request for Consultations by the United States*, WT/DS196/1 (2000).

[297] M Wagner, 'Intellectual property bill risks US censure' *Jerusalem Post* (9 September 2004).

[298] This argument was advanced by the Canadian Federal Court of Appeal in *Bayer Inc. v The Attorney General of Canada et al*, Docket: A-679-98 (19 May 1999).

[299] 21 USC § 360cc. The rationale is that market incentives for research in this area are too low. Orphan Drug Act, Pub L No 97-414, 96 Stat 2049 (1983). Diseases qualify for orphan drug protection if they affect less than 200,000 persons in the United States or if there is no reasonable expectation of recovering developing costs from US sales; L-H Rin-Laures and D Janofsky, 'Recent Development Concerning the Orphan Drug Act' (1991) 4 Harvard J L & Tech 269, 275; RA Bohrer and JT Prince, 'A Tale of Two Proteins: The FDA's Uncertain Interpretation of the Orphan Drug Act' (1999) 12 Harvard J L & Tech 365. Similar incentives are granted in Europe under Regulation (EC) 141/2000 of the European Parliament and of the Council of 16 December 1999 on orphan medicinal products [2000] OJ L18/1 (22 January 2000).

[300] 21 USC § 355a. The term is available as a tag-on to a market exclusivity the manufacturer already enjoys (eg a patent or an orphan drug exclusivity). Market incentives for these tests were insufficient to such an extent that drugs began carrying disclaimers discouraging their use in children. C-P Milne, 'Exploring the Frontiers of Law and Science: FDAMA's Pediatric Studies Incentive' (2002) 57 Food & Drug LJ 491. The Food and Drug Administration Modernization Act of 1997, Pub L No 105-115, 111 Stat 2296 (1997) and the Best Pharmaceuticals for Children Act of 2002, Pub L No 107-109, 115 Stat 1408 (2002) were enacted to extend relevant provisions of the old Act that were to sunset on 1 January 2002. NR Allen, 'When Does the Clock Begin Ticking? Interaction of the Hatch-Waxman Act 180-Day Generic Abbreviated New Drug Application and Food and Drug Administration Modernization Act Pediatric Exclusivity Provisions—A Significant Issue in Eli Lilly & Co. v Barr Laboratories, Inc' (2002) 30 AIPLA QJ 1; LH Breslow, 'The Best Pharmaceuticals for Children Act of 2002: The Rise of the Voluntary Incentive Structure and Congressional Refusal to Require Pediatric Testing' (2003) 40 Harv J on Legis 133, 176 ff.

question and requested consultations challenging Europe's supplementary protection for pharmaceuticals as a discrimination of other fields of technology.[301] However, many of the rules are likely to be upheld as legal differentiation rather than illegal discrimination.

c Product and Process Patents

Article 27.1 distinguishes product and process patents. Product patents are patents on the product itself, in the case of pharmaceuticals, eg compound substances or new molecules, regardless of the process for producing them.[302] The holder of a product patent can prevent others from making the product even by a process unknown to the patent holder.

Process patents are somewhat less tangible than product patents. A process is a way to produce a result.[303] Under this heading patents are available for processes to produce a pharmaceutical product, eg chemical processes to produce a compound. Such a process can be patented even where the product has been patented by someone else, in which case the second inventor may not make the product without the licence of the inventor of the product, and the inventor of the product cannot use the new process without a licence of the patentee of the process.[304]

A third category of patents of major importance in the pharmaceutical field are patents on uses of a product ('new use patent'). Thus, if a known glue turns out to be an effective cancer treatment, a patent could be granted on a 'method of fighting cancer which comprises administering to a patient substance X'.[305] Whether states have to provide such patents depends on the interpretation of Article 27.1 of the TRIPS Agreement. It could be argued that a medical use is a way to produce a result (namely healing or improvement of the medical condition treated) and therefore states have to make process patents available for such uses. But this interpretative claim is rather weak and a number of arguments militate against it: new uses are arguably not 'inventions', but merely the discovery of an existing but unknown property of an existing material. Even if they should be considered 'inventions', the mere use of a pharmaceutical is a therapeutic method for the treatment of humans and therefore subject to the exception of Article 27.2 of the TRIPS Agreement. State practice, too, does not support the claim that new use patents are covered by Article 27.1, because Members' positions on new use patents are

---

[301] At issue are Council Regulation (EEC) 1768/92 of 18 June 1992 Concerning the Creation of a Supplementary Protection Certificate for Medicinal Products [1992] OJ L182/1 (2 July 1992) and Regulation (EC) 1610/96 of 23 July 1996 Concerning the Creation of a Supplementary Protection Certificate for Plant Protection Products [1996] OJ L193/30 (8 August 1996); European Communities—Patent Protection for Pharmaceutical and Agricultural Chemical Products. Request for Consultations by Canada, WT/DS153/1 (1998).

[302] For US law: Chisum (n 237 above) 1–13 ff. Note that it is the chemical substance not the chemical formula that is patentable.   [303] Schwartz (n 4 above) 62.

[304] The constellation is called one of 'blocking patents'. Chisum (n 237 above) 1–72.

[305] US Patent No 4,988,690, 1-aryloxy-2,3,4,5-tetrahydro-3-benzazepines and anti-depressant use thereof, claim 140 is an example of such a claim.

highly inconsistent: in the United States such claims are explicitly allowed by the Patent Act.[306] The German Patent Act allows patents on first medicinal indications and courts have permitted patents on further indications.[307] In the United Kingdom a known substance can only be claimed for use in a method of medical treatment the first time such a use is disclosed—patents are not available for further medicinal uses, even in treating a different disease.[308] Article 54(5) of the EPC allows patents on a product for the identification of the first medical indication, which then covers all therapeutic uses. Patents on a second medical indication could be regarded as methods of therapeutic treatment and therefore not be patentable; however, since 1984 the EPO grants such claims if they are formulated according to the 'Swiss formula'.[309] The new industrial property regime of the Andean Community explicitly does not allow new use patents.[310] The Andean Court confirmed that new uses are discoveries rather than inventions.[311] The goal of the TRIPS Agreement of achieving a balance between intellectual property protection and other socio-economic concerns and the principle *in dubio mitius* favour leaving the choice to the sole competencies of Members. Under a proper interpretation new use patents are therefore not mandated by Article 27.1 of the TRIPS Agreement.[312]

B Novelty

According to Article 27.1 of the TRIPS Agreement the invention must be 'new' to be patentable. An invention is no longer new if it is part of the prior art, ie if it has already been available to the public anywhere in the world.[313] Members show some minor differences in how they approach the concept of novelty. The United States applies a somewhat limited concept, according to which novelty is defeated by disclosure in US or foreign printed publications before the invention by the

---

[306] 35 USC § 100(b). Such a patent covers only the new use and not the product. A manufacturer might be liable for contributory infringement, but such liability must be rejected if the product is capable of substantial non-infringing use. Chisum (n 237 above) 1–290 ff.

[307] § 3(3) Patentgesetz 1981; BGH (1983) GRUR 729 ('Hydropiridin'); Hubmann and Götting (n 1 above) 131.

[308] UK Patent Office, *Manual of Patent Practice* (5th edn, 2003) para 2.44.

[309] 'Use of X for the manufacture of a medicine to treat Y', Enlarged Board of Appeal of the EPO, *EISAI/Second Medical Indication*, G5/83, OJ EPO 1985, 64; ICTSD and UNCTAD (n 218 above) Part Two, 17–18.

[310] Article 21 of Decision 486. On the regime: ID Mogollón-Rojas, 'The New Andean Pact Decision No 486 on the Common Industrial Rights Regime. Complying with TRIPS Regulations' (2001) 4 J World Intell Prop 549; M Ruiz, *The Andean Community's New Industrial Property Regime: Creating Synergies between the CBD and Intellectual Property Rights*, Bridges November–December 2000, 11; Alexia Perez, 'The Implementation of the GATT/WTO TRIPS Agreement in Venezuela. An Overview in 1998' (1998) 1 J World Intell Prop 747.

[311] Tribunal de Justicia de la Comunidad Andina, *Proceso 89-AI-2000* (2001); the case was litigated under similar provisions of the old Andean intellectual property regime (Decision 344).

[312] ICTSD and UNCTAD (n 218 above) Part Two, 18.

[313] ICTSD and UNCTAD (n 218 above) Part Two, 20; Correa (n 147 above) 57 ff.

applicant but only by knowledge or use of others in the United States.[314] Other countries accept anything that has been made available to the public in writing or orally anywhere in the world as prior art.[315] Commentators have generally held such variations to be consistent with the TRIPS Agreement, as the wording of the provision does not regulate these details.[316]

C *Inventive Step*

The benefits granted by patent law should not be granted too easily. An invention can be new and yet it constitutes only a minor change over the prior art. Therefore the TRIPS Agreement demands that the invention involve an 'inventive step', the terminology of non-obviousness used in the United States is regarded as identical according to a footnote. Most countries apply an abstract definition of the requirement resembling the one contained in 35 USC § 103, that negates non-obviousness 'if the differences between the subject matter sought to be patented and the prior art are such that the subject matter as a whole would have been obvious at the time the invention was made to a person having ordinary skill in the art to which said subject matter pertains'.[317] Nevertheless, state practice in the application of such a definition differs significantly from country to country. The definition shows that the inventive step is judged by establishing the differences between the scope and content of the prior art and the patent claims and evaluating them in light of the ordinary skill in the art.[318] The United States benchmark for this step has been criticized repeatedly as too low, allowing for a large number of trivial patents that impede legitimate competition.[319] States are free to opt for higher standards for the inventive step requirement.[320]

D *Capability of Industrial Application*

Finally, Article 27.1 of the TRIPS Agreement requires that the invention be capable of an industrial application, recognizing the US requirement of 'utility' in 35 USC

---

[314] For details see 35 USC § 102(a). Note that § 102 creates statutory bars to protection. Thus, for example, an inventor is barred from obtaining a patent if the invention was described in a printed publication more than one year prior to the application. In general, whereas novelty relates to events performed by others, events giving rise to a statutory bar can also be performed by the inventor himself. The provision has the effect of creating a grace period of 12 months in which the inventor has to file an application after he published the invention himself. For details see Miller and Davis (note 9 above) 40 ff.   [315] Eg Germany, Hubmann and Götting (n 1 above) 127.

[316] Correa (n 147 above) 57 ff.

[317] Hubmann and Götting (n 1 above) 123 put the German requirement as follows: '[Die gefundene Lösung] muss einen Schritt hinausgehen über das, was einem Durchschnittsfachmann, dem der Stand der Technik bekannt ist, nahe liegt'. (The solution has to go a step further than what would have been obvious to an average expert aware of the current state of the art (translation by author).)

[318] *Graham v John Deere Co* 383 US 1 (1966); PS Canelias, *Patent Practice Handbook* (loose-leaf, last updated 2002) s 6.03.

[319] ICTSD and UNCTAD (n 218 above) Part Two, 21; criticism is particularly intense concerning the lax handling of the obviousness requirement for patents on DNA, Burk and Lemley (n 239 above) 1178 ff; For details J Rosenstock, *The Law of Chemical and Pharmaceutical Invention* (2nd edn, loose-leaf, 2003) § 5.01.   [320] ICTSD and UNCTAD (n 218 above) Part Two, 21.

§ 101 as equivalent. The European tradition, in which the requirement of industrial applicability originated, regards the requirement as fulfilled if the invention can be used in any field of industry, including agriculture.[321] The bar of utility in the US is lower, requiring only that the invention accomplishes an intended purpose (ie it works) that is not immoral, illegal, or solely detrimental and that it is capable of some beneficial use in society.[322] The question of utility has regained importance in the chemical field where patents are often sought for compounds with no known use. The Supreme Court allows patents on compounds only if they have a specific known benefit in the currently available form.[323]

E Disclosure

Article 29.1 of the TRIPS Agreement provides that:

Members shall require that an applicant for a patent shall disclose the invention in a manner sufficiently clear and complete for the invention to be carried out by a person skilled in the art and may require the applicant to indicate the best mode for carrying out the invention known to the inventor at the filing date (. . .).

The disclosure requirement is one of the fundamental principles of patent law and, as shown above, one of the justification of patents. Patents can fulfill their social purpose only if Members ensure that the disclosure is really enabling and do not grant patents where this is not the case.

4 Rights Conferred

If the conditions of patentability are fulfilled, the national patent offices have to grant a patent. According to Article 28.2 of the TRIPS Agreement a patent can be assigned, transferred by succession, or licensed to others. Article 28 also puts down the minimum content of the rights that are conferred by patents[324] and distinguishes for this purpose between product and process patents. The former

---

[321] ICTSD and UNCTAD (n 218 above) Part Two, 21; Hubmann and Götting (n 1 above) 132.

[322] Schwartz (n 4 above) 64, MA Epstein, *Epstein on Intellectual Property* (loose-leaf, last updated 2003) § 5.02[B]. The latter two requirements are no longer strictly adhered to. *Juicy Whip, Inc v Orange Bang, Inc* 185 F 3rd 1364, 1368 (Fed Cir, 1999), allowing a patent the purpose of which is to deceive customers about the nature of drinks they buy.

[323] *Brenner v Manson* 383 US 519, 534 f (1966); Chisum (n 237 above) 4–30 ff. The requirement is of considerable importance for the patentability of cDNA sequences ('complementary DNA'), sequences matching the messenger RNA sequences (Merges and Duffy (n 15 above) 250). The PTO's Utility Examination Guidelines state that a DNA sequence 'may meet the statutory utility requirement if, eg it can be used to produce a useful protein or it hybridizes near and serves as a marker for a disease gene'. United States Patent and Trademark Office, *Utility Examination Guidelines* 66 Fed Reg 1092, 1094 (2001); RS Eisenberg and RP Merges, 'Opinion Letter as to the Patentability of Certain Inventions Associated with the Identification of Partial cDNA Sequences' (1995) 23 AIPLA QJ 1, 7 ff; John H Barton, 'The Human Genome Patent Applications' (1993) 354 PLI/Pat 681; AK Rai and RS Eisenberg, 'Bayh-Dole Reform and the Progress of Biomedicine' (2003) 66-SPG Law & Contemp Probs 289, 295–296.

[324] ICTSD and UNCTAD (n 218 above) Part Two, 79.

confer on the patentee the exclusive rights 'to prevent third parties not having the owner's consent from the act of: making, using, offering for sale, selling, or import- ing for these purposes that product'.[325] Patents thus do not grant a positive right to use or market the invention, rather they confer negative rights, the right to exclude others from certain actions. Patentees of pharmaceutical products have no automatic right to market the products, they can only exclude others from mak- ing, using, selling, etc. the product. The right to exclude others from competing with him allows the patent holder to fully exploit the value of the invention. However, the right is not meant to give the patentee control over a product after he has placed it on the market himself—it can then be sold, used, or offered for sale freely and without the patentee's permission, the patent right has been 'exhausted' once the product was placed on the market. This doctrine has come to be known as the doctrine of exhaustion, or the first sale doctrine.[326] Article 6 of the TRIPS Agreement refers to the doctrine and provides that '[f]or the purposes of dispute settlement under this Agreement, subject to the provisions of Articles 3 and 4 nothing in this Agreement shall be used to address the issue of the exhaustion of intellectual property rights'. The concept of exhaustion has raised little controversy where the patent holder places the product on the national market and thereby exhausts his rights in the same market (national exhaustion). Whether the same also applies in an international context is one of the most controversial issues in international intellectual property law. After all, the patent also grants the right to exclude others from importing the product for the purpose of using, offering for sale or selling it,[327] albeit a footnote provides that the right, like all other rights conferred under the TRIPS Agreement in respect of the use, sale, importation, or other distribution of goods is subject to Article 6. This difficult question will be deferred and discussed in chapter 5.

Process patents confer on their owner the exclusive rights 'to prevent third parties not having the owner's consent from the act of using the process, and from the acts of: using, offering for sale, selling, or importing for these purposes at least the product obtained directly by that process'.[328] As it is often impossible for the patentee to prove that an alleged infringer used the patented process and not another process without access to the manufacturing plants, the TRIPS Agreement also provides for a reversal of the burden of proof in this respect in civil litigation under certain circumstances.[329]

To prevent the rights from ringing hollow, the TRIPS Agreement puts down obligations on Members with respect to the enforcement of patent rights. Thus, Members have to make available civil judicial procedures in which the patentee

---

[325] Article 28.1(a) of the TRIPS Agreement (footnote deleted).
[326] The principle stems from decisions of the German *Reichsgericht* in the first decade of the 20th Century, HC Jehoram, 'International Exhaustion versus Importation Right: a Murky Area of Intellectual Property Law' (1996) GRUR Int 280; MM Slotboom, 'The Exhaustion of Intellectual Property Rights, Different Approaches in EC and WTO Law' (2003) 6 J World Intell Prop 421, 422.
[327] ICTSD and UNCTAD (n 218 above) Part Two, 80.
[328] Article 28.1(b) of the TRIPS Agreement.
[329] For details see Art 34 of the TRIPS Agreement.

can demand injunctive relief or damages from a third party not having the owner's consent that engages in one of the enumerated activities with respect to the patented invention and thus infringes the patent.[330]

The minimum term of protection that Members have to provide for patents is 20 years counted from the filing date.[331] Patentees can rarely profit economically from the totality of the patent term. Often, the invention is patented before the market opportunities have been surveyed or the product requires administrative approval before it can be brought to the market, as is the case with pharmaceuticals. The period necessary for these actions can eat up a substantial part of the patent term.[332] This raises the question whether the term of protection of the TRIPS Agreement is meant to be an effective term of protection or a formal term running from the filing date. A similar question was before the Appellate Body in *Canada—Term of Patent Protection*,[333] in which Canada defended its 17-year patent term from the grant of the patent for patents granted within a certain time period against a complaint by the United States arguing, amongst others, that because of the duration of the patent examination in other countries its 17-year term from the grant of the patent was equivalent to a 20-year term from filing. The Appellate Body forcibly rejected the Canadian argument stating that Article 33 imposes a clear minimum standard of 20 years from the date of filing.[334] It rightly interpreted the patent term to be, just as stated, 20 years from the filing date. Consequently, Members also cannot be forced to go beyond this standard and compensate for time eaten up by administrative approval processes.

The precise duration of the patent term is of enormous practical importance. Each day a pharmaceutical company delays the entry of competitors for a blockbuster drug adds a significant amount of money to its profits. Not surprisingly, companies have used numerous techniques to try to delay the market entry of generic competitors. Some of these techniques, like filing a new use patent or a patent on a new formulation of the drug, do not, legally speaking, prevent competitors from entering the market by producing the old drug and pursuing the old use. However, they raise the risk of lawsuits and the cost of entry for the competitor. Companies have also filed patents on intermediate products in the production of the drug and on 'metabolites', chemical compounds into which a patient's body converts the drug. In the latter case, the patient would infringe the patent and the generic competitor would be liable for inducing infringement.[335] In most of these

---

[330] Articles 41, 42, 44, 45, 50 of the TRIPS Agreement. The determination of when a patent is infringed is handled differently from country to country and involves issues such as claim construction; C Correa, *Integrating Public Health Concerns into Patent Legislation in Developing Countries*, (2000) 34–35. Some countries also prohibit inducement of infringement and contributory infringement, eg the United States in 35 USC § 271(b) and (c). There is nothing in the TRIPS Agreement requiring such a prohibition.   [331] Article 33 of the TRIPS Agreement.

[332] A Otten, 'Les Brevets Couvrant les Produits Pharmaceutiques et l'Accord sur les Adpic' (2000) RIDE 161, 162–163.   [333] *Canada—Term of Patent Protection* (n 233 above).

[334] *Canada—Term of Patent Protection* (n 233 above) paras 93 ff.

[335] For a description of many of these doubtful techniques see Federal Trade Commission (n 289 above) A-39 ff.

cases, the new patents with which companies effectively try to prolong their old patents do not withstand scrutiny and are invalid. Countries should strive to prevent such abuse by stringently examining patents before the grant and allowing post- and pre-grant opposition proceedings.

5 Transitional Arrangements

The changes brought about by the TRIPS Agreement were vast for many WTO Members: they had to grant patents in areas where they had traditionally not done so—particularly in the pharmaceutical field—and establish an efficient enforcement system. There was wide agreement that transition periods beyond the entry into force of the TRIPS Agreement on 1 January 1995 were necessary to allow Members some time to comply with their obligations.[336] Both the general one-year transition period for all Members[337] and an additional four-year period[338] for developing country Members and Members in the process of transformation from a centrally-planned into a market, free-enterprise economy,[339] have expired. Two transition periods, however, remain relevant—particularly in the area of pharmaceuticals. The recent expiry of the first of these two periods is cause for grave concern in the area of pharmaceuticals.

The first of these transition periods is Article 65.4 of the TRIPS Agreement which provides that where:

a developing country Member is obliged by this Agreement to extend product patent protection to areas of technology not so protectable in its territory on the general date of application of this Agreement for that Member, as defined in paragraph 2, it may delay the application of the provisions on product patents of Section 5 of Part II to such areas of technology for an additional period of five years.

The provision grants a transition period until 1 January 2005 solely for product patents in areas of technology in which a Member did not provide for product patent protection on 1 January 2000 and has thus expired only recently.[340] It has already been said that many countries have not granted pharmaceutical product patents before the TRIPS Agreement was negotiated so that the provision was of tremendous importance in this area. If a developing country chose to grant pharmaceutical product patents earlier than 1 January 2005, it could no longer abolish or

---

[336] B Anzellotti in Busche and Stoll (n 216 above) Art 65, paras 1–2.

[337] Article 65.1 of the TRIPS Agreement.

[338] The transition period did not apply to Arts 3, 4, 5 of the TRIPS Agreement. Article 65.2 of TRIPS Agreement.

[339] These Members were only eligible for the additional transition period under certain conditions, Art 65.3 of the TRIPS Agreement.

[340] The provision refers to the 'general date of application of this Agreement for that Member, as defined in paragraph 2', which is the end of the transition period mentioned in this paragraph. ICTSD and UNCTAD (n 218 above) Part 6.1, 13 wrongly regard 1 January 1996 as the relevant date. Because of Art 65.5 of the TRIPS Agreement the interpretation does not lead to a different result.

diminish such protection. Article 65.5 of the TRIPS Agreement prevented any such roll-back by providing that a 'Member availing itself of a transition period under paragraphs 1, 2, 3 or 4 shall ensure that any changes in its laws, regulations and practice made during that period do not result in a lesser degree of consistency with the provisions of this Agreement'.[341] Only developing countries could profit from the transition period. WTO law does not define 'developing country', but Article XVIII:1 of the GATT mentions two relevant criteria: Members, the economies of which can only support low standards of living and are in the early stages of development.[342] Members themselves decide whether they fall into this category.[343] Even though self-identification has inevitably led to some quarrels, eg during China's accession to the WTO,[344] it is largely uncontested that two thirds of the WTO Members are developing countries, with India, Brazil, South Africa, Thailand, and Egypt all falling into this category.[345] It was these countries that had emerged as the most important producers of generic medicine for the time during which the medicine was still under patent in the developed world, belonging to the few countries with respective production facilities. Hence, the expiration of this transition period is of particular relevance: with this transition period expired, there will be no more sources for generic medicine while the medicine is still under patent in the developed—and now in the developing—world. The second transition period does little to remedy this situation.

This second period is a general transition period for least-developed Members, which, according to Article 66.1 of the TRIPS Agreement, benefit from a ten-year

---

[341] The United States relied on this provision when it challenged Argentina's change from a ten-year period of protection of test data submitted for marketing approval for agricultural chemical products to no such protection in *Argentina—Patent Protection for Pharmaceuticals and Test Data Protection for Agricultural Chemicals. Request for Consultations by the United States*, WT/DS171/1 (1999). It also raised claims under the provision in *Indonesia—Certain Measures Affecting the Automobile Industry*, WT/DS54/R, WT/DS55/R, WT/DS59/R, WT/DS64/R (1998) paras 14.280 ff.

[342] The WTO Agreements do contain a definition of developing country members for the purposes of subsidies and countervailing measures in Annex VII of the Agreement on Subsidies and Countervailing Measures. G Verdirame, 'The Definition of Developing Countries under GATT and other International Law' (1996) 39 GYIL 164, 174 ff; Guy Feuer, 'L'Uruguay Round, les Pays en Développement et le Droit International du Développement' (1994) 40 AFDI 758, 773. To obtain a basic overview of which countries could fall into the category the reader should consult the European Union's scheme of generalized tariff preferences for developing countries, excluding countries if during three consecutive years they have been classified by the World Bank as high-income countries and their mathematically defined development index is higher than −1. Article 3(1), (2) of Council Regulation (EC) 2501/2001 of 10 December 2001 Applying a Scheme of Generalised Tariff Preferences for the Period from 1 January 2002 to 31 December 2004 [2001] OJ L346/1 (31 December 2001); prolonged by Council Regulation (EC) 2211/2003 of 15 December 2003 Amending Regulation (EC) No 2501/2001 Applying a Scheme of Generalised Tariff Preferences for the Period from 1 January 2002 to 31 December 2004 and Extending it to 31 December 2005 [2003] OJ L332/1 (19 December 2003).

[343] P Gallagher, *Guide to the WTO and Developing Countries* (2000) xxiv.

[344] WM Morrison, *China—U.S. Trade Issues*, CRS Issue Brief for Congress, 5, at <http://fpc.state.gov/documents/organization/21120.pdf>; 'Accessions Update: China and Others in the Pipeline' (1991) 3 *Bridges Weekly Trade News Digest* 37 (20 September 1999). Weiß and Herrmann (n 15 above) 421–422.

[345] WTO, *Understanding the WTO: Developing Countries. Overview*, at <http://www.wto.org/english/thewto_e/whatis_e/tif_e/dev1_e.htm>.

transition period from the date of application as defined under Article 65.1, ie 1 January 1996, for all obligations under the TRIPS Agreement, except for Articles 3, 4, and 5 of the TRIPS Agreement. Unlike developing countries, least-developed countries are free to roll back their current level of protection of intellectual property and use their transition period to the fullest, as Article 65.5 does not apply to Article 66.1. The category of least-developed country Members is well defined: according to Article XI:2 of the WTO Agreement the WTO recognizes as least-developed countries the countries designated as such by the United Nations. To be added to the United Nations list of least-developed countries a country has to have a low per capita income (currently a gross domestic product per capita of under $750 based on a three-year average estimate), a low level of human resource development, and a high degree of economic vulnerability.[346] As of the time of writing of this study, 32 of the WTO Members were least-developed countries.[347] Article 66.1 of the TRIPS Agreement recognizes that a transition period until 1 January 2006 might not suffice for least-developed country Members and therefore explicitly provides for the possibility of the Council for TRIPS extending this period upon duly motivated request by a least-developed country Member. Members made use of this provision in 2002 to extend the transition period with respect to pharmaceutical products for obligations under Sections 5 and 7 of Part II of the TRIPS Agreement, ie obligations concerning patents and protection of undisclosed information, to 1 January 2016.[348] In November 2005 WTO Members extended the transition period for least-developed country Members until 1 July 2013.[349]

In practice, the generous transition periods for least-developed country Members are of little relevance with respect to pharmaceuticals. This is not just due to the insignificant market size of these Members, but mostly to practical considerations. The most effective strategy for a multi-national corporation to shield itself from competition in respect of innovative drugs is to obtain patents in all countries in which factories capable of manufacturing the drug are located. Enforcing the patents in those countries will block all competing manufacturers and thus

---

[346] The criteria were established by the Committee for Development Planning in 1971 and improved by the Committee for Development Policy. Committee for Development Policy, *Advance, Unedited Copy of the Report of the Committee for Development Policy on its Sixth Session* (29 March–2 April 2004), UN Doc E/2004/33, at paras 14 ff (2004); Office of the High Representative for the Least Developed Countries, Landlocked Developing Countries and Small Island Developing States, *The Criteria for the Identification of the LDCs*, at <http://www.un.org/special-rep/ohrlls/ldc/ldc%20criteria.htm>.

[347] A list of these countries is available at WTO, *Understanding the WTO: The Organization. Least-developed countries*, at <http://www.wto.org/english/thewto_e/whatis_e/tif_e/org7_e.htm>.

[348] Council for TRIPS, *Extension of the Transition Period under Article 66.1 of the TRIPS Agreement for Least-Developed Country Members for Certain Obligations with Respect to Pharmaceutical Products*, IP/C/25 (1 July 2002).

[349] Council for TRIPS, *Extension of the Transition Period under Article 66.1 for Least-Developed Country Members*, IP/C/40 (30 November 2005).

eliminate competition worldwide. Obtaining patents in countries without manu-facturing capacity is not necessary.[350] Needless to say, most least-developed coun-tries lack the capacity to manufacture drugs. Despite the TRIPS Agreement obligation of developed countries to provide incentives for technology transfer to least-developed countries[351] and, lately, the monitoring of this obligation by the Council for TRIPS via a state reporting mechanism,[352] this situation is unlikely to change in the near future.

Moreover, all transition periods in the area of pharmaceutical product patents[353] have been put into question by additional obligations the TRIPS Agreement imposes on Members making use of the transition periods: as an exception to the transitional arrangements[354] Article 70.8 of the TRIPS Agreement requires such Members to put in place what has come to be known as a 'mailbox' system and Article 70.9 obliges them to grant five-year exclusive marketing rights for pharma-ceutical products. Both of these obligations were the subject of the *India—Patent Protection for Pharmaceutical and Agricultural Chemical Products* cases,[355] in which two panels and the Appellate Body ruled that India had not implemented the obligations correctly.

The mailbox system requirement obliges Members to:

(a) (...) provide as from the date of entry into force of the WTO Agreement a means by which applications for patents for such inventions can be filed;

(b) apply to these applications, as of the date of application of this Agreement, the criteria for patentability as laid down in this Agreement as if those criteria were being applied on the date of filing in that Member or, where priority is available and claimed, the pri-ority date of the application; and

(c) provide patent protection in accordance with this Agreement as from the grant of the patent and for the remainder of the patent term, counted from the filing date in accord-ance with Article 33 of this Agreement, for those of these applications that meet the criteria for protection referred to in subparagraph (b).[356]

---

[350] This fact is at times overlooked, R Kampf, 'Patents versus Patients?' (2002) 40 AVR 90, 91.

[351] Article 66.2 of the TRIPS Agreement.

[352] Ministerial Conference, *Implementation-related Issues and Concerns, Decision of 14 November 2001*, WT/MIN(01)/17 (20 November 2001) para 11.2; Council for TRIPS, *Implementation of Article 66.2 of the TRIPS Agreement. Decision of the Council for TRIPS*, IP/C/28 (20 February 2003); Council for TRIPS, *Report on the Implementation of Article 66.2 of the TRIPS Agreement*, IP/C/W/412 (10 November 2003) and addenda, Council for TRIPS, *Report on the Implementation of Article 66.2 of the TRIPS Agreement*, IP/C/W/431 (16 November 2004) and addenda.

[353] The same is true for agricultural chemical product patents.

[354] *India—Patent Protection for Pharmaceutical and Agricultural Chemical Products*, WT/DS50/R (1997) para 7.25; *India—Patent Protection for Pharmaceutical and Agricultural Chemical Products*, WT/DS50/AB/R (1997) para 53 (*India—Mailbox*).

[355] On the cases, see J Werner, 'The TRIPS Agreement under the Scrutiny of the WTO Dispute Settlement System—The Case of Patent Protection for Pharmaceutical and Agricultural Chemical Products in India' (1998) 1 J World Intell Prop 309.

[356] Article 70.8 of the TRIPS Agreement.

During the transition period the only obligation on the Member making use of the period is subparagraph (a).[357] The subparagraph has to be interpreted against the background of subparagraphs (b) and (c), which constitute part of its context.[358] It requires Members to put in place a system that allows the filing of applications for patents for pharmaceutical products from 1 January 1995 and that provides a sound legal basis[359] to preserve the filing and priority dates of these applications. Only when the transition period has ended does the Member have to apply the criteria for patentability using the preserved filing and priority dates.[360]

For products subject to a patent application under Article 70.8(a) of the TRIPS Agreement the Member has to grant exclusive marketing rights:

notwithstanding the provisions of Part VI, for a period of five years after obtaining marketing approval in that Member or until a product patent is granted or rejected in that Member, whichever period is shorter, provided that, subsequent to the entry into force of the WTO Agreement, a patent application has been filed and a patent granted for that product in another Member and marketing approval obtained in such other Member.[361]

India had argued that it was under no obligation to establish a system for the grant of exclusive marketing rights before all the conditions for the grant of the rights stipulated in the provision had been met by a specific product,[362] any other interpretation would have the effect that developing country Members could postpone legislative changes in all fields of technology except the most sensitive ones.[363] However, Article 70.9 of the TRIPS Agreement explicitly applies *notwithstanding* the transition periods contained in Part VI of the TRIPS Agreement and therefore, just like Article 70.8(a), became effective as of the entry into force of the TRIPS Agreement.[364] Members making use of the transition periods therefore had to maintain a mechanism that would grant the exclusive marketing rights during the transition periods. As the word exclusive, meaning 'excluding or having power to exclude' or 'limiting or limited to possession, control, or use by a single individual or group',[365] suggests, exclusive marketing rights grant the power to exclude others from bringing the product to the market and therefore resemble patents. In light of this it is highly doubtful whether making use of the transition period in the area of

[357] *India—Patent Protection for Pharmaceutical and Agricultural Chemical Products* (n 354 above) para 7.23. *India—Patent Protection for Pharmaceutical and Agricultural Chemical Products. Complaint by the European Communities and their Member States*, WT/DS79/R (1998) para 7.32.

[358] *India—Mailbox* (n 354 above) para 56; *India—Patent Protection for Pharmaceutical and Agricultural Chemical Products* (n 357 above) para 7.37.

[359] *India—Mailbox* (n 354 above) para 69 ff. *India—Patent Protection for Pharmaceutical and Agricultural Chemical Products* (n 357 above) paras 7.43 ff.

[360] *India—Mailbox* (n 354 above) paras 56 ff.   [361] Article 70.9 of the TRIPS Agreement.

[362] *India—Patent Protection for Pharmaceutical and Agricultural Chemical Products* (n 354 above) para 7.7.   [363] *India—Mailbox* (n 354 above) para 78.

[364] *India—Mailbox* (n 354 above) para 82. The wording of the provision according to which the rights shall be 'granted' (and not 'shall be available') does not imply the contrary. *India—Patent Protection for Pharmaceutical and Agricultural Chemical Products* (n 357 above) para 7.65.

[365] FC Mish *et al* (eds), *Merriam-Webster's Collegiate Dictionary* (10th edn, 1998).

pharmaceutical product patents was beneficial at all. WTO Members have seen the defect of these obligations and taken action to prevent the provision from nullifying the value of the transition period for the most vulnerable states. They waived the obligations under Article 70.9 for least-developed country Members until 1 January 2016.[366]

6 Conclusion on Patent Law

As demonstrated above, patent law is an instrumental legal order that is meant to provide the necessary incentives for further research and development, a rationale that is largely supported by the history of patents. Throughout history countries have tried to tailor patent laws to their developmental agenda, often deciding not to grant patents for pharmaceutical products. With the advent of the WTO, however, a paradigm change took place and minimum standards were imposed with respect to intellectual property laws by the TRIPS Agreement.

In that Agreement WTO Members have undertaken significant obligations in the area of patent law: they are obliged to grant patents for all inventions, in particular also for pharmaceutical products and processes. None of the exceptions contained in the Agreement allow Members to exclude pharmaceuticals or essential pharmaceuticals from patentability, with the possible exception of the provision on national security. While Members have some latitude as to how they draft their patent laws, in particular with more or less stringent requirements for patentability, the TRIPS Agreement obliges them to grant pharmaceutical patents conferring certain rights.

The TRIPS Agreement also provides for transition periods. On 1 January 2005 the most significant of these in the area of pharmaceuticals expired, obliging developing country Members (with the exception of LDCs) such as India and Brazil, to grant pharmaceutical patents. Now all Members with real pharmaceutical manufacturing capacity have to grant patents, so that the innovator can effectively prevent the manufacture of generics worldwide until the expiration of the patent term, raising the question of whether patent laws in the developing world are compatible with human rights standards with renewed urgency.

---

[366] General Council, *Least-Developed Country Members—Obligations under Article 70.9 of the TRIPS Agreement with Respect to Pharmaceutical Products, Decision of 8 July 2002*, WT/L/478 (12 July 2002). Note, however, that many least-developed countries—at times due to political pressure—already provide patent protection for pharmaceutical products. P Thorpe, 'Study on the Implementation of the TRIPS Agreement by Developing Countries' UK Commission on Intellectual Property Rights Study Paper 7.

3

Access to Medicine as a Human Right

The imposition of WTO-wide minimum standards for patent protection in the pharmaceutical field has not gone uncontested. Time and again during the negotiations of the TRIPS Agreement developing countries especially voiced public health concerns to argue for weaker or more flexible patent protection in the pharmaceutical field.[1] What had been essentially policy-based objections against minimum patent standards for pharmaceuticals during the negotiations started to be coined in human rights terminology after the TRIPS Agreement came into force. With NGOs[2] and scholars[3] taking the lead soon the World

[1] Negotiating Group on Trade-Related Aspects of Intellectual Property Rights, including Trade in Counterfeit Goods, *Meeting of the Negotiating Group of 23–24 November 1987*, MTN.GNG/NG11/5 (14 December 1987) para 7 (stating that rules should be sensitive to national objectives with respect to health), Negotiating Group on Trade-Related Aspects of Intellectual Property Rights, including Trade in Counterfeit Goods, *Meeting of the Negotiating Group of 11–12 May 1989*, MTN.GNG/NG11/12 (13 June 1989) para 5 (arguing that patents are part of a national economic policy to further technological development and that therefore public concerns like the provision of health care have to be taken into account to achieve a balanced solution guaranteeing that technologies to meet basic health needs are made available to developing countries on fair and reasonable terms); Negotiating Group on Trade-Related Aspects of Intellectual Property Rights, including Trade in Counterfeit Goods, *Meeting of the Negotiating Group of 12–14 July 1989*, MTN.GNG/NG11/14 (12 September 1989) para 79.1 (suggestion to allow developing countries to exclude the area of health care from patentable subject matter); Negotiating Group on Trade-Related Aspects of Intellectual Property Rights, including Trade in Counterfeit Goods, *Meeting of the Negotiating Group of 2, 4 and 5 April 1990*, MTN.GNG/NG11/20 (24 April 1990) paras 22, 34 (proposing to allow the exclusion of subject matter from patentability or the grant of compulsory licences on health care grounds); Negotiating Group on Trade-Related Aspects of Intellectual Property Rights, including Trade in Counterfeit Goods, *Meeting of the Negotiating Group of 14–16 May 1990*, MTN.GNG/NG11/21 (22 June 1990) para 52 (mentioning a Japanese proposal relating to compulsory licences which might apply to pharmaceuticals without which the life of the public as a whole would be endangered, for example in the event of a serious epidemic); Negotiating Group on Trade-Related Aspects of Intellectual Property Rights, including Trade in Counterfeit Goods, *Meeting of the Negotiating Group of 1 November 1990*, MTN.GNG/NG11/27 (14 November 1990) para 4 (mentioning a developing country representative reaffirming the vital importance of the possibility of exclusion of certain products and processes from patentability on grounds of public interest, health, or nutrition for developing countries); but see Negotiating Group on Trade-Related Aspects of Intellectual Property Rights, including Trade in Counterfeit Goods, *Meeting of the Negotiating Group of 16–19 May 1988*, MTN.GNG/NG11/7 (21 June 1988) (criticizing compulsory licences in the interest of public health as penalizing pharmaceutical inventions).

[2] Most relevant are the lobbying work of Médecins Sans Frontières' Access to Essential Medicines Campaign (eg MSF, *AccessNews* (February 2002)); Oxfam International's Cut the Cost Campaign (eg Oxfam, 'TRIPS and Public Health. The next battle' Oxfam Briefing Paper 15 (2002)); CPTech's Health Care and Intellectual Property Campaign (CPTech, *Health Care and Intellectual Property*, at <http://www.cptech.org/ip/health>); other very active NGOs in the area include Health Action International, Act Up, Treatment Action Campaign, HealthGAP; N Geffen, 'Pharmaceutical Patents, Human Rights and the HIV/AIDS Epidemic', TAC discussion document (2001).

[3] Eg WP Nagan, 'International Intellectual Property, Access to Health Care, and Human Rights: South Africa v United States' (2002) 14 Fla J Int'l L 155; S Ghosh, 'Pills, Patents, and Power: State

Health Organization,[4] the UN General Assembly,[5] the Commission on Human Rights,[6] the Sub-Commission on the Promotion and Protection of Human Rights,[7] the Committee on Economic, Social and Cultural Rights,[8] the UN High Commissioner for Human Rights,[9] and the Special Rapporteurs on

Creation of Gray Markets as a Limit on Patent Rights' (2001) 53 Fla L Rev 789, (2002) 14 Fla. J Int'l L 217.

[4] Eg *Intellectual Property Rights, Innovation and Public Health*, WHA Res 56.27 (28 May 2003) (initiating the establishment of a body to study intellectual property rights and their effect on public health); Commission on Intellectual Property Rights, Innovation and Public Health, *Public Health. Innovation and Intellectual Property Rights* (2006) (the report of that body), *Ensuring Accessibility of Essential Medicines*, WHA Res 55.14 (18 May 2002); World Health Organization, *Globalization, TRIPS and Access to Pharmaceuticals*, WHO Policy Perspectives on Medicines, No 3 (March 2001); World Health Organization, *Network for Monitoring the Impact of Globalization and TRIPS on Access to Medicines. Meeting Report, 19–21 February 2001 Chulalongkorn University Bangkok, Thailand* (2002) 20 ff.

[5] Eg *Access to Medication in the Context of Pandemics such as HIV/AIDS, Tuberculosis and Malaria*, GA Res, UN Doc A/RES/58/179 (22 December 2003); *The Right of Everyone to the Enjoyment of the Highest Attainable Standard of Physical and Mental Health*, GA Res, UN Doc A/RES/58/173 (22 December 2003).

[6] Eg *Access to Medication in the Context of Pandemics such as HIV/AIDS*, Commission on Human Rights Res 2002/32, para 7 (22 April 2002), less obvious: *Access to Medication in the Context of Pandemics such as HIV/AIDS*, Commission on Human Rights Res 2001/33, para 3b (23 April 2001); *Access to Medication in the Context of Pandemics such as HIV/AIDS, Tuberculosis and Malaria*, Commission on Human Rights Res 2003/29, para 5b (22 April 2003); *Access to Medication in the Context of Pandemics such as HIV/AIDS, Tuberculosis and Malaria*, Commission on Human Rights Res 2004/26, paras 6b, 7, 11 (16 April 2004); *The Right of Everyone to the Enjoyment of the Highest Attainable Standard of Physical and Mental Health*, Commission on Human Rights Res 2004/27, chapeau (16 April 2004). The Commission on Human Rights was a subsidiary organ of ECOSOC (Article 68 of the UN-Charter) established in 1946 by an ECOSOC Resolution: ECOSOC Res 5 (I) (16 February 1946), in ESCOR 1st year 1st sess 1946, at 163; ECOSOC Res 9 (II) (21 June 1946), in ESCOR 1st year 2nd sess 1946, at 400. It was active, eg in the area of standard-setting for human rights, cf E Riedel, in B Simma *et al* (eds), *The Charter of the United Nations. A Commentary. Volume II*, (2nd edn, 2002) Art 68, paras 84 ff; RKM Smith, *Textbook on International Human Rights* (2003) 61–62. In 2006 the Commission on Human Rights was replaced by the UN Human Rights Council: *Human Rights Council*, GA Res, UN Doc A/RES/60/251 (3 April 2006); SR Lyons, 'The New United Nations Human Rights Council' (2006) 10 ASIL Insight 7.

[7] Eg *Intellectual Property and Human Rights*, Sub-Commission on Human Rights Res 2001/21 (16 August 2001); *Intellectual Property and Human Rights*, Sub-Commission on Human Rights Res 2000/7 (17 August 2000). The sub-commission was set up in 1946 as the Sub-Commission on Prevention of Discrimination and Protection of Minorities, a sub-commission of the Commission on Human Rights, ECOSOC Res 9 (II) (n 6 above) paras 9–10. It was renamed in 1999 by ECOSOC Dec 1999/256, in ESCOR 1999 Supp 1, at 127. It is mostly charged with undertaking studies and making recommendations to the Commission. Smith (n 6 above) 63. In 2006 the Human Rights Council assumed the mandates and responsibilities of the Commission. In June 2006 the Council decided to extend the mandates and mandate-holders of the Sub-Commission exceptionally for one year.

[8] *Substantive Issues Arising in the Implementation of the International Covenant on Economic, Social and Cultural Rights. Follow-up to the day of general discussion on article 15.1 (c), Monday, 26 November 2001. Human Rights and Intellectual Property. Statement by the Committee on Economic Social and Cultural Rights*, UN Doc E/C12/2001/15 (14 December 2001); *General Comment 17* (2005). Although charged with monitoring the International Covenant for Economic, Social and Cultural Rights (ICESCR) the Committee was not set up by the ICESCR itself, but in 1985 by ECOSOC Res 1985/17 to help ECOSOC in its monitoring task, ECOSOC Res 1985/17 in ESCOR 1985 Supp 1, 15; Smith (n 6 above) 69–70.

[9] *Economic, Social and Cultural Rights. The Impact of the Agreement on Trade-Related Aspects of Intellectual Property Rights on Human rights. Report of the High Commissioner*, UN Doc E/CN4/Sub2/2001/13 (27 June 2001). The office of the High Commissioner was created in 1993 by a General

Globalization[10] alleged that the TRIPS Agreement touches on human rights standards that guarantee the accessibility of medicine.

Analytically their claim is three-pronged. Firstly, it alleges the existence of a legal right to access to medicine. The right is not mentioned explicitly in any agreement, but commonly based on the right to health and the right to life. Secondly, it asserts that the adoption of patent legislation, now mandatory under the TRIPS Agreement, leads to inventors' (or rather corporations' to whom they assigned their patents) charging higher prices because of their ability to patent new pharmaceuticals, rendering those pharmaceuticals unaffordable for parts of the population, particularly in developing countries—a question of fact rather than of law. Thirdly, it maintains that this price effect can infringe the right to access to medicine, even though the prices are set by private parties and that this infringement is not justified by other considerations, such as the necessity of patents to enable research and development.

Many scholars have replied to the challenge that patents are necessary to stimulate research for new medicine. The legal implications of this argument will be discussed in the next chapter. More recently, other scholars have added that intellectual property, too, is protected as a human right. Some have even ventured so far as to imply that the TRIPS Agreement itself is a human rights agreement.[11] Even though the latter claim is far-fetched given that the TRIPS Agreement, as an Annex to the Marrakesh Agreement Establishing the World Trade Organization (hereinafter: WTO Agreement), is a negotiated trade agreement based—as described in chapter 2 and as indicated by its preamble[12]—on an economic rationale and neither meant to be a human rights agreement nor fulfilling

Assembly Resolution. *High Commissioner for the Promotion and Protection of All Human Rights*, GA Res 48/141 (20 December 1993), UN GAOR, 48th Sess, Supp No 49, at 261, UN Doc A/48/49 (Vol I). The High Commissioner has the primary responsibility for the United Nations human rights activities under the direction of the Secretary General of the United Nations. Smith (n 6 above) 63–64.

[10] J Oloka-Onyango and D Udagama, *Economic Social and Cultural Rights. Globalization and its Impact on the Full Enjoyment of Human Rights*, UN Doc E/CN.4/Sub.2/2001/10 (2 August 2001) paras 19–34.

[11] S Kreibich, *Das TRIPs-Abkommen in der Gemeinschaftsordnung. Aspekte der Kompetenzverteilung zwischen WTO, Europäischer Gemeinschaft und ihren Mitgliedstaaten* (2002) 200–201 (discussing 'human rights content' of the TRIPS-Agreement); J Pauwelyn, *Conflict of Norms in Public International Law. How WTO Law Relates to other Rules of International Law* (2003) 73 (stating that the TRIPS Agreement might protect a value in itself rather than being merely instrumental); J Neumann, *Die Koordination des WTO-Rechts mit anderen völkerrechtlichen Ordnungen. Konflikte des materiellen Rechts und Konkurrenzen der Streitbeilegung* (2001) 292 ('Das TRIPS formt also den Schutzauftrag dieser Menschenrechtsnormen aus'); A Blüthner, *Welthandel und Menschenrechte in der Arbeit* (2004) 444 (concluding that the TRIPS Agreement at least has human rights connections).

[12] The beginning of the preamble reads: '*Desiring* to reduce distortions and impediments to international trade' (emphasis in original). See on this issue F Höhne in J Busche and P-T Stoll (eds), *TRIPs* (2007) Präambel, paras 7, 24; ICTSD and UNCTAD, *Resource Book on TRIPS and Development*, part I 113–114 (2002). (Note, however, para 4 of the preamble: '*Recognizing* that intellectual property rights are private rights' (emphasis in original).)

such a function,[13] the claim of human rights protection for intellectual property as such deserves further discussion.

This chapter will first provide a background note on international human rights law in general and the right to health, the most commonly mentioned basis for a right to access to medicine, as well as the right to intellectual property in particular (I). It will then discuss the interpretation of human rights conventions (II). The rights at issue are closely connected to the notion of economic, social, and cultural rights. Some authors argue that this category of human rights is of doubtful legal relevance at best, an objection that is treated under the heading of 'justiciability' (III). In a third step, I examine who is bound by the rights, namely whether private parties—pharmaceutical companies—are directly bound by them and whether the WTO is bound by human rights law (IV). Finally, the right to access to medicine will be discussed in detail, proceeding in the order of the sources recognized by international law as stated in Article 38 of the Statute of the International Court of Justice (ICJ) (V):[14] international conventions, customary international law, and general principles of law. The analyses of the right conducted so far commonly determine its content and scope and point to several treaties as its legal basis. Not all states, however, have signed all of the treaties on which the right is founded. The scope of the obligation incurred by state parties to only some of the treaties differs from the obligations undertaken by state parties to other or all treaties. The obligations imposed by each of the legal sources will therefore be determined separately. This approach is of particular importance for the ensuing analysis of the interaction between the human rights obligations and the obligations under the TRIPS Agreement. The questions whether the ability to patent pharmaceuticals really leads to higher prices and whether the interference with the right to access caused by higher prices can be justified because of human rights protection for intellectual property or the necessity of patents to foster research and development will be left for the next chapter.

I Background

1 International Human Rights

Originally, public international law was conceived as the body of law regulating the relationship between states. As Oppenheim wrote in his treatise on International Law in 1912: 'Subjects of the rights and duties arising from the Law of Nations are States solely and exclusively.'[15] International law did provide rules

---

[13] K Kaiser, *Geistiges Eigentum und Gemeinschaftsrecht. Die Verteilung der Kompetenzen und ihr Einfluss auf die Durchsetzbarkeit der völkerrechtlichen Verträge* (2004) 410 ff; LR Helfer, 'Adjudicating Copyright Claims under the TRIPS Agreement: The Case for a European Human Rights Analogy' (1998) 39 Harv Int'l L J 357, 397–398. [14] 55 UNYB 1449 (2001).
[15] L Oppenheim, *International Law. A Treatise. Vol. I. Peace* (2nd edn, 1912) 19. See also D Anzilotti, *Corso di Diritto Internazionale (Ad uso degli studenti dell'Università di Roma), Volume*

for the treatment of foreigners (the 'law of aliens'), but only the foreigners' home countries and not the individuals themselves could appeal to these rules.[16] Treatment of individuals by their own home state was regarded as an internal matter of that state. But little[17] presaged the sweeping change that international law would undergo after World War II—a truly 'constitutional moment'.[18] After the genocidal rule of the Nazi regime international law could no longer stand idly by when a state abused and killed its own citizens. Protecting the individual from its own government by granting rights to individuals became a moral imperative.[19] International law had come to see the person behind the state.[20]

President Roosevelt set the stage for the development of modern human rights law when he called for a world founded upon four essential human freedoms, among them civil and political freedoms as well as 'freedom from want'.[21] The UN Conference on International Organizations made good on that promise by including several references to human rights in the Charter of the UN,[22] though

Primo: Introduzione—Teorie Generali (3rd edn, 1928) 112 ff (somewhat critical, though not from a human rights standpoint, but because of empirical observations); J Delbrück and R Wolfrum, *Völkerrecht. Begründet von Georg Dahm. Band I/1 Die Grundlagen. Die Völkerrechtssubjekte* (2nd edn, 1989) 125.

[16] L Henkin, *The Age of Rights* (1990) 14; K Ipsen, in K Ipsen (ed), *Völkerrecht* (4th edn, 1999) 704 ff. In-depth: J Delbrück and R Wolfrum, *Völkerrecht. Begründet von Georg Dahm. Band I/2 Der Staat und andere Völkerrechtssubjekte; Räume unter internationaler Verwaltung*, (2nd edn, 2002) 104 ff; K Doehring, *Völkerrecht* (2nd edn, 2004) 374 ff; A Bleckmann, *Völkerrecht* (2001) 281 ff. The law of aliens does not just prohibit the discrimination of foreigners—as many developing countries argued under the Calvo Doctrine, but also establishes minimum standards for their treatment. FV García-Amador, 'Calvo Doctrine, Calvo Clause' in R Bernhardt (ed), *Encyclopedia of Public International Law, I* (1992) 521.

[17] Commonly named progenitors of international human rights law (besides the law of aliens) include the doctrine of humanitarian intervention, international humanitarian law, documents banning slave trade, and the protection of minority rights within the League of Nations system. T Buergenthal, *International Human Rights in a Nutshell* (2nd edn, 1995) 3 ff; Smith (n 6 above) 7 ff; A Verdross and B Simma, *Universelles Völkerrecht. Theorie und Praxis* (3rd edn, 1984) 797; I Brownlie, *Principles of Public International Law* (6th edn, 2003) 530–531.

[18] The term 'constitutional moment' is closely tied to Ackerman's writing: B Ackerman, *We the People. 1 Foundations* (1991) 266 ff. Here it is meant to imply that the historical crisis led to a radical change in the structure of international law.

[19] H Lauterpacht, *International Law and Human Rights* (1950) 3 ff (linking rights and duties of individuals); The International Military Tribunal explicitly rejected the argument that international law is concerned only with actions of sovereign states: International Military Tribunal, *Trial of The Major War Criminals Before the International Military Tribunal. Nuremberg 14 November 1945–1 October 1946. Volume XII. Proceedings 27 August 1946–1 October 1946* (1948, reprint 1995) 465–466; for earlier precedence: *Jurisdiction of the Courts of Danzig*, PCIJ, Ser B, No 15, 17–18 (judgment of 3 March 1928).

[20] For a clear and outright rejection of the traditional tenet that only states are subjects of international law see, eg, H Kelsen, *Principles of International Law* (1952) 114 ff; *Contra*: A Verdross, *Völkerrecht* (2nd edn, 1950) 101 ff. In-depth: Delbrück and Wolfrum (n 16 above) 259 ff.

[21] Buergenthal (n 17 above) 21–22; AN Holcombe, *Human Rights in the Modern World* (1948) 4. As a Democratic presidential candidate campaigning at a time of economic crisis Roosevelt had already stated that '[e]very man has a right to life, and this means that he also has a right to make a comfortable living'. M Gilbert, *History of the Twentieth Century* (2001) 212. The same language was also used by Annan in his Report of the Secretary-General: K Annan, In Larger Freedom: Towards Development, Security and Human Rights for All. Report of the Secretary-General, UN Doc A/59/2005 (2005).   [22] Hereinafter UN Charter.

falling short of including a declaration of human rights.[23] Besides being mentioned in the preamble of the UN Charter, the promotion of human rights is one of the purposes of the organization, as stated by Article 1(3) of the UN Charter, which reads in the relevant part:

[The Purposes of the United Nations are:] To achieve international co-operation in solving international problems of an economic, social, cultural, or humanitarian character, and in promoting and encouraging respect for human rights and for fundamental freedoms for all (...).

To achieve these purposes both the UN (Article 55 of the UN Charter) and its members (Article 56 of the UN Charter) commit themselves to promote higher living standards, solutions of international economic, social and health problems, and universal respect for, and observance of, human rights. Even though states are only obliged to 'promote' rather than to 'abide by' human rights, UN involvement in human rights law became a success story, partly because it succeeded in internationalizing human rights concerns and partly because it provided a forum for further developments.[24] The UN Charter endows both the General Assembly[25] and the Economic and Social Council (ECOSOC)[26] with competencies in the human rights field. Additionally, ECOSOC is required to set up commissions in economic and social fields and for the promotion of human rights.[27] It was the Commission on Human Rights that prepared the Universal Declaration of Human Rights (UDHR), which was adopted by the UN General Assembly in 1948[28] as a description of the 'common standard of achievement' in the human rights field. As a General Assembly Resolution the UDHR is not binding.[29] The UN continued to strive for a legally binding document on human rights, but the road towards this goal proved cumbersome. It had become commonplace to distinguish two categories of rights: civil and political rights, the heritage of the French Revolution and of the US Bill of Rights, protect the individual from undue interference from the state. Economic, social, and cultural rights, stemming from socialist ideas born during the Industrial Revolution, require states to promote the economic, social, and cultural well-being of the individual.[30]

---

[23] Proposals for such a declaration had been made by the Netherlands (in case an alternative proposal fails), Panama, Cuba (proposing to bind member states to a General Assembly Resolution in the Charter). United States Department of State, *The United Nations Conference on International Organization. San Francisco, California April 25 to June 26, 1945. Selected Documents* (1946) 97, 103 ff.

[24] R Wolfrum, 'The Progressive Development of Human Rights: A Critical Appraisal of Recent UN Efforts' in J Jekewitz *et al* (eds), *Des Menschen Recht zwischen Freiheit und Verantwortung, Festschrift für Karl Josef Partsch zum 75. Geburtstag* (1989) 67 ff.

[25] Article 13(1)(b) of the UN Charter.   [26] Article 62 of the UN Charter.

[27] Article 68 of the UN Charter.   [28] UNGA res 217A (III), 10 December 1948.

[29] Over time, however, it achieved a significant legal status as discussed below. A Eide *et al* (eds), *The Universal Declaration of Human Rights: A Commentary* (1992).

[30] This distinction is advanced by TC Van Boven, 'Les Critères de Distinction des Droits de l'Homme' in K Vasak (ed), *Les Dimensions Internationales des Droits de l'Homme* (1978) 45, 53. It is submitted that the two categories cannot be neatly distinguished, nor can they be properly defined, as it is unclear whether the definition of the categories hinges on the subject matter of the right as implied

At times the former rights are referred to as 'first generation rights', whereas the latter are called 'second generation rights'.[31] The discussions exposed an ideological rift. Socialist countries saw both categories on an equal footing—if they preferred any category, it was the economic and social rights as they regarded them as a prerequisite for the exercise of civil and political rights. They therefore wanted both categories to be included in a comprehensive human rights document.[32] Western liberal democracies gave clear preference to civil and political rights, arguing that (1) only those rights were justiciable, (2) only civil and political rights could be implemented immediately, whereas the implementation of economic and social rights had to be progressive, and (3) political rights were guaranteeing freedom from state action whereas generally speaking economic and social rights required states to take action to protect and promote those rights. According to Western countries, only two separate instruments could adequately account for the fundamental differences between the two categories.[33] The latter position ultimately prevailed and two treaties were drafted: the International Covenant on Civil and Political Rights (ICCPR) and the International Covenant on Economic, Social, and Cultural Rights (ICESCR). Despite numerous resolutions, proclamations, and declarations affirming that the two sets of rights are indivisible and interdependent,[34] symbolized also by them having been opened for signature

by their names or on the distinction between positive and negative duties. MCR Craven, *The International Covenant on Economic, Social, and Cultural Rights. A Perspective on its Development* (1995) 7 ff; A Eide and A Rosas, 'Economic, Social and Cultural Rights: A Universal Challenge' in A Eide, C Krause and A Rosas (eds), *Economic, Social and Cultural Rights. A Textbook* (2nd edn, 2001) 3 ff.

[31] This terminology appears, eg, in K Drzewicki, 'The Right to Work and Rights in Work' in A Eide, C Krause and A Rosas (eds), *Economic, Social and Cultural Rights. A Textbook* (2nd edn, 2001) 223, 227; M Nowak, 'The Right to Education' in A Eide, C Krause and A Rosas (eds), *Economic, Social and Cultural Rights. A Textbook* (2nd edn, 2001) 245, 252–253; K Hailbronner, 'Der Staat und der Einzelne als Völkerrechtssubjekte' in W Graf Vitzthum (ed), *Völkerrecht* (2nd edn, 2001) 161, 237. It was criticized forcefully by Eide and Rosas (n 30 above) 4; it is commonly credited to K Vasak, 'A 30-year Struggle. The Sustained Efforts to Give Force of Law to the Universal Declaration of Human Rights' *The UNESCO Courier* (29 November 1977). Riedel uses the term 'dimension' rather than 'generation': E Riedel, 'Menschenrechte der dritten Dimension' in E Riedel, *Die Universalität der Menschenrechte. Philosophische Grundlagen Nationale Gewährleistungen Internationale Garantien* (2003) 329.

[32] *Draft International Covenants on Human Rights. Annotation prepared by the Secretary General,* 23 at para 9, UN Doc A/2929 (1 July 1955); I Szabo, 'Fondements historiques et développement des droits de l'homme' in K Vasak (ed), *Les dimensions internationales des droits de l'homme. Manuel destiné à l'enseignement des droits de l'homme dans les universités* (1978) 11, 20–21; P Daillier and A Pellet, *Droit International Public. Nguyen Quoc Dinh* (6th edn, 1999) 641–642.

[33] K Arambulo, *Strengthening the Supervision of the International Covenant on Economic, Social and Cultural Rights. Theoretical and Procedural Aspects* (1999) 17; HJ Steiner and P Alston, *International Human Rights in Context. Law, Politics, Morals* (1996) 256.

[34] *Alternative Approaches and Ways and Means within the United Nations System for Improving the Effective Enjoyment of Human Rights and Fundamental Freedoms,* GA Res 32/130 (16 December 1977), UN GAOR, 32nd Sess, Supp No 45, at 150, 151 para 1(a), UN Doc A/32/45; *Declaration on the Right to Development,* GA Res 41/128 (4 December 1986), UN GAOR, 41st Sess, Supp No 53, at 186, 187 Art 6 (2), UN Doc A/41/53; *Question of the Realization in All Countries of the Economic, Social and Cultural Rights Contained in the UDHR and in the ICESCR, and Study of Special Problems Which the Developing Countries Face in their Efforts to Achieve these Human Rights,* Commission on Human

simultaneously on 16 December 1966,[35] the distinction between them endures. Economic, social, and cultural rights have long been neglected and only recently started to attract more interest.[36]

Since the coming into force of the two Covenants many new additional human rights instruments have been created, but the UDHR and the two Covenants remain the centrepiece of universal human rights protection, the 'International Bill of Human Rights', the commitment to which states have reaffirmed in numerous declarations.[37] Nevertheless, they still pose difficult and largely unresolved conceptual questions, such as whether the obligations they impose are owed *erga omens partes*, ie whether all parties can complain of a breach.

2 Health and Human Rights

The ancestor of a human rights approach to health is the mere exercise of governmental functions in health care. The remnants of the ancient Roman sewage system are eloquent testimony to the fact that governments have striven to improve sanitation and thus public health since ancient times.[38] By the 18th century German monarchs had come to regard the protection of public health as part of their duties, their task to build a *gute policey*, a good order.[39] Public health became an international concern as international transportation became more common and knowledge about infectious diseases spread. Several international conferences were held in the 19th century to prevent the spread of alien diseases to Europe and International Sanitary Conventions were signed for the same purpose.[40] In the

Rights Res 2004/29, para 8 (19 April 2004); *Proclamation of Teheran, Final Act of the International Conference on Human Rights. Teheran, 22 April to 13 May 1968*, UN Doc A/CONF32/41, 3 para 13 (1968); *Vienna Declaration and Program of Action*, UN Doc A/CONF157/23, I para 5 (12 July 1993).

[35] *International Covenant on Economic, Social and Cultural Rights, International Covenant on Civil and Political Rights and Optional Protocol to the International Covenant on Civil and Political Rights*, GA Res 2200 (XXI) (16 December 1966), UN GAOR, 21st Sess, Supp No 16, at 49, UN Doc A/6316.

[36] Eide and Rosas (n 30 above) 3. On the reasons for the neglect of economic, social, and cultural rights see the discussion between van Hoof and Vierdag: F van Hoof, 'Explanatory Note on the Utrecht Draft Optional Protocol' in F Coomans and F van Hoof (eds), *The Right to Complain about Economic, Social and Cultural Rights* (1995) 147, 159; EW Vierdag, 'Comments on the Utrecht and Committee Draft Optional Protocols' in F Coomans and F van Hoof (eds), *The Right to Complain about Economic, Social and Cultural Rights* (1995) 199, 200. See also B Simma, 'Der Schutz wirtschaftlicher und sozialer Rechte durch die Vereinten Nationen' in S Vassilouni (ed), *Aspects of the Protection of Individual and Social Rights* (1995) 75.

[37] Eg *Proclamation of Teheran* (n 34 above) para 3; *Vienna Declaration and Programme of Action* (n 34 above); *Status of the International Covenants on Human Rights*, Commission on Human Rights Res 2004/69, para 4 (21 April 2004); 'Final Act of the Conference on Security and Co-operation in Europe of 1 August 1975 (Helsinki)' (1975) 14 ILM 1292.

[38] BCA Toebes, *The Right to Health as a Human Right in International Law* (1999) 8.

[39] M Stolleis, *Geschichte des öffentlichen Rechts in Deutschland. Erster Band, Reichspublizistik und Policeywissenschaft 1600–1800* (1988) 345; Toebes (n 38 above) 12–13.

[40] Toebes (n 38 above) 12, HK Nielsen, *The World Health Organisation. Implementing the Right to Health* (2nd edn, 2001) 12.

first half of the 20th century two international organizations were set up to supervise these conventions and to fulfil the League of Nations members' commitment to 'take steps in matters of international concern for the prevention and control of disease'.[41] The concept of a human right to health, however, has not developed until after World War II, when the World Health Organization (WHO), a specialized agency of the UN,[42] replaced the two old organizations at the helm of global health policy. Going beyond the mere concern for health expressed in the UN Charter,[43] the Constitution of the WHO, which came into force on 7 April 1948,[44] became the first international legal document to contain an explicit right to the 'enjoyment of the highest attainable standard of health', albeit only in its preamble. Health was defined as 'a state of complete physical, mental and social well-being'. Despite its potential of exposing normal states of life, such as sadness after the death of a relative, to treatment as a disease, the definition became very influential.[45] The right to health was taken up in numerous legal instruments, most significantly in the ICESCR.

3 Intellectual Property and Human Rights

The last chapter illustrated how the development of national and international intellectual property law has largely been driven by utilitarian considerations. It also described the 'natural law' rationale, according to which the ideas of an individual, its labour, should belong to it. This idea was particularly popular during the French Revolution.[46] Even though the notion is now largely discredited as a rationale for modern-day patent law[47] (other than the debate about 'moral rights', protecting a special bond between an author and her work in copyright law),[48] it became the ancestor for another concept: the protection of the moral and material interests of the author of a scientific, literary, or artistic production, which found its way into the UDHR[49] and, later, into the ICESCR.[50] Until very recently these provisions have stirred next to no interest.[51]

---

[41] Article 23(f) of the Covenant of the League of Nations. The two organizations were the Office International d'Hygiène Publique and the Health Organization of the League of Nations. Nielsen (n 40 above) 13.   [42] Article 57 of the UN Charter.

[43] The concern had been included after the Brazilian delegation had submitted a statement that '[m]edicine is one of the pillars of peace'. Toebes (n 38 above) 15.

[44] Nielsen (n 40 above) 14–15. On the history of the WHO, see S Sze, *The Origins of the World Health Organization. A Personal Memoir 1945–1948* (1982); World Health Organization, *The First Ten Years of the World Health Organization* (1958).

[45] This potential should not be underestimated, given that pharmaceutical companies have an incentive to market and sell their products to as broad a customer base as possible. R Moynihan and R Smith, 'Too much medicine? Almost certainly' (2002) 324 British Medical Journal 859.

[46] See chapter 2.

[47] For criticism of the natural law rationale, eg R Nozick, *Anarchy, State, and Utopia* (1974) 174 ff.

[48] Note Art 6*bis* of the Berne Convention for the Protection of Literary and Artistic Works. C Doutrelepont, 'Das droit moral in der Europäischen Union' (1997) GRUR Int 293; A Lucas-Schloetter, 'Die Rechtsnatur des Droit Moral' (2002) GRUR Int 809.

[49] Article 27(2) of the UDHR.   [50] Article 15(1)(c) of the ICESCR.

[51] LR Helfer, 'Human Rights and Intellectual Property' (2004) 22 Netherlands Q of Hum Rts 167, 169.

They were rediscovered, however, in the debate about the protection of indigenous knowledge.[52] In the human rights discourse, which is still in its infancy, some voices have alleged that intellectual property law itself is protected by the human rights norms—resuscitating the natural law rationale. Other commentators have objected to the notion of human rights protection of intellectual property. They have argued that the need to balance consumer and right holder interests and the priority of the well-being of consumers militates against any human rights protection of intellectual property.[53] Additionally, they have submitted that intellectual property rights are different from fundamental human rights in that the latter protect values as such, whereas the former are instrumental, ie they serve the advancement of other fundamental values that have to be identified.[54] The next chapter will show that intellectual property as protected by modern-day intellectual property law and the moral and material interests of the inventor as protected by international human rights law are different notions and not co-extensive, a view that has also been adopted by the Committee on Economic, Social, and Cultural Rights.[55]

II The Interpretation of Human Rights Conventions

Before delving into the material legal problems and, amongst other, interpreting the Human Rights Covenants, a few words on the methodology of interpreting the Covenants seem warranted.[56] The rules of treaty interpretation are laid down in Articles 31–33 of the Vienna Convention on the Law of Treaties (Vienna Convention), which are not just applicable for its State Parties, but for every state, as the rules are deemed to be rules of customary international law.[57] According to Article 31(1) a treaty has to be interpreted 'in good faith in accordance with the ordinary meaning to be given to the terms of the treaty in their context and in the light of its object and purpose'. A treaty authenticated in two or more languages is presumed to have the same meaning in all languages.[58]

---

[52] Helfer (n 51 above) 171 ff; D Weissbrodt and K Schoff, 'The Sub-Commission's Initiative on Human Rights and Intellectual Property' (2004) 22 Netherlands Q of Hum Rts 181, 191 ff.

[53] RL Ostergard, Jr, 'Intellectual Property: A Universal Human Rights?' (1999) 21 Hum Rts Q 156.

[54] P Drahos, 'The Universality of Intellectual Property Rights: Origins and Development' in World Intellectual Property Organization (ed), *Intellectual Property and Human Rights. A Panel Discussion to commemorate the 50th Anniversary of the Universal Declaration of Human Rights. Geneva, November 9, 1998* (1999) 13.

[55] Committee on Economic, Social and Cultural Rights, *General Comment No 17* (2005), para 3.

[56] On the comparable issue of the methodology of interpretation of the TRIPS Agreement see chapters 2 and 5

[57] *Territorial Dispute (Libyan Arab Jamahiriya/Chad)*, ICJ Reports 1994, 4, para 41 (3 February 1994); *Gabčíkovo-Nagymaros Project (Hungary/Slovakia)*, Judgment, ICJ Reports 1997, 7, paras 42–6 and 99 (25 September 1997) (on other provisions of the Vienna Convention); A Aust, *Modern Treaty Law and Practice* (2000) 10–11, 184 ff; A Watts, 'The International Court and the Continuing Customary International Law of Treaties' in N Ando, E McWhinney and R Wolfrum (eds), *Liber Amicorum Judge Shigeru Oda. Volume I* (2002) 251.

[58] Article 33(3), (4) of the Vienna Convention.

Together with the context any subsequent practice in the application of the treaty which establishes the agreement of the parties regarding its interpretation as well as any relevant rules of international law applicable in the relations between the parties and any subsequent agreement between the parties regarding the interpretation of the treaty or the application of its provision has to be taken into account.[59] Article 32 of the Vienna Convention permits recourse to supplementary means of interpretation, particularly the *travaux préparatoires*, only to confirm the result of an interpretation or to determine the meaning of a norm where the interpretation leads to an absurd or unreasonable result or leaves the meaning ambiguous or obscure. Human rights treaties differ from other treaties in that they move beyond the traditional reciprocal international order. They call for an interpretation that provides an effective protection of the rights granted rather than one following the principle *in dubio mitius* (choosing the interpretation that imposes the least restriction on state sovereignty).[60] An evolutive approach to interpretation has to be adopted, interpreting the norms of the treaty in the light of modern-day thinking, thus taking changes in society into account.[61] Interpretations of other human rights instruments and national human rights provisions are frequently used as persuasive arguments.[62] Human rights instruments thus cross-fertilize each other.

III Justiciability

Both access to medicine and the protection of the moral and material interests of authors demand more than just inaction, ie simply abstaining from interfering with those rights. They impose the obligation to take positive measures, eg to protect the rights from interference by third parties. Some commentators regard the imposition of positive obligations as a special feature of rights granted by the ICESCR and have argued that the rights in that Covenant are not 'justiciable'.

---

[59] Article 31(3) of the Vienna Convention.

[60] F Reindel, *Auslegung menschenrechtlicher Verträge am Beispiel der Spruchpraxis des UN-Menschenrechtsausschusses, des Europäischen und des Interamerikanischen Gerichtshofs für Menschenrechte* (1995) 82, 113, 139 ff; V Pechota, 'The Development of the Covenant on Civil and Political Rights' in L Henkin (ed), *The International Bill of Rights. The Covenant on Civil and Political Rights* (1981) 32, 69–70; J Kokott, *Beweislastverteilung und Prognoseentscheidungen bei der Inanspruchnahme von Grund- und Menschenrechten* (1993) 408–409; P-M Dupuy, 'L'Unité de l'Ordre Juridique International. Cours Général de Droit International Public' (2002) 297 RdC 9, 31.

[61] R Bernhardt, 'Thoughts on the Interpretation of Human-Rights Treaties' in F Matscher and H Petzold (eds), *Protecting Human Rights: The European Dimension, Studies in honor of Gérard J. Wiarda* (1988) 65, 69; R Bernhardt, 'Evolutive Treaty Interpretation, Especially of the European Convention on Human Rights' (1999) 42 GYIL 11, 12; G Letsas, 'The Truth in Autonomous Concepts: How to Interpret the ECHR' (2004) 15 EJIL 279, 301–302.

[62] A-M Slaughter, *A New World Order* (2004) 79 ff.

The debate is fraught with misunderstandings stemming from the vagueness of the concept of 'justiciability'[63] and from inappropriate analogies to national law.[64]

1 Terminology

Commonly, justiciability is defined as '1. appropriate for or subject to court trial (. . .) 2. That can be settled by law or a court of law (. . .)'[65] Some commentators[66] use the notion to state that the ICESCR, unlike the ICCPR through its Optional Protocol,[67] is not implemented by way of an individual communication procedure but by a reporting procedure, in which member states submit reports on their progress in the implementation of the agreement[68] and those reports are examined by the Committee on Economic, Social and Cultural Rights, a Committee of 18 independent experts established by ECOSOC for this purpose and which reports back to ECOSOC.[69] The procedure has been described as one

---

[63] Justiciability has rightly been called a 'fluid concept', C Scott, 'The Interdependence and Permeability of Human Rights Norms: Towards a Partial Fusion of the International Covenants on Human Rights' (1989) 27 Osgoode Hall LJ 769, 839; F Coomans, 'Clarifying the Core Elements of the Right to Education' in F Coomans and F van Hoof (eds), *The Right to Complain about Economic, Social and Cultural Rights* (1995) 11, 19; M Ssenyonjo, 'Justiciability of Economic and Social Rights in Africa: General Overview, Evaluation and Prospects' (2003) 9 East African Journal of Peace & Human Rights 1, 7.

[64] For debates on economic, social, and cultural rights in national law see JP Müller, 'Soziale Grundrechte in der Verfassung?' (1973) 92 Zeitschrift für Schweizerisches Recht, Neue Folge 687; E Grisel, 'Les droits sociaux' (1973) 92 Zeitschrift für Schweizerisches Recht, Neue Folge 1; EW Vierdag, 'The Legal Nature of the Rights Granted by the International Covenant on Economic, Social and Cultural Rights' (1978) 9 NYIL 69, 80.

[65] JP Picket *et al* (eds), *The American Heritage Dictionary of the English Language* (4th edn, 2000); RL Bledsoe and BA Boczek, *The International Law Dictionary* (1987); G Evans and J Newnham, *Dictionary of International Relations* (1998); *Nixon v United States* 506 US 224 (1993).

[66] Vierdag (n 64 above) 73. P Alston, 'Economic and Social Rights' (1994) 26 Stud Transnat'l Legal Pol'y 137, 157. See also H Kelsen, *Reine Rechtslehre. Einleitung in die rechtswissenschaftliche Problematik* (1934) 47 f (stating that a right requires the power of enforcement, if necessary by a lawsuit).

[67] Article 1 of the Optional Protocol allows individuals claiming a violation of their rights under the ICCPR to submit written communications to the Human Rights Committee.

[68] Article 17 ff of the ICESCR.

[69] ECOSOC Res 1985/17 (n 8 above). B Simma and S von Bennigsen, 'Wirtschaftliche, soziale und kulturelle Rechte im Völkerrecht' in JF Baur, KJ Hopt, KP Mailänder (eds), *Festschrift für Ernst Steindorff zum 70. Geburtstag am 13. März 1990* (1990) 1477, 1492 ff; B Simma, 'The Implementation of the International Covenant on Economic, Social and Cultural Rights' in F Matscher (ed), *Die Durchsetzung wirtschaftlicher und sozialer Grundrechte* (1991) 75; E Riedel, 'New Bearings to the State Reporting Procedure: Practical Ways to Operationalize Economic, Social and Cultural Rights—The Example of the Right to Health' in S von Schorlemer (ed), *Praxishandbuch UNO. Die Vereinten Nationen im Lichte globaler Herausforderungen* (2003) 345. Efforts to introduce an individual communication procedure are underway, but have so far not succeeded. The Committee itself first contemplated the adoption of an optional protocol in its fifth session. The idea was taken up in reports by Türk and Alston (D Türk, *The Realization of Economic, Social and Cultural Rights*, UN Doc E/CN.4/Sub.2/1992/16 (1992) para 210; P Alston, *Draft Optional Protocol Providing for the Consideration of Communications*, UN Doc E/C.12/1994/12 (1994)) and encouraged by the Vienna Declaration and Programme of Action (n 34 above) at Part II, para 75. The Committee finally submitted

of 'constructive dialogue'.[70] The observation that there is no judicial enforcement mechanism is both true and applicable to much of public international law as very few areas of international law are subject to automatic enforcement by an international court or tribunal.[71]

Others assert that economic, social, and cultural rights are inherently different from civil and political rights and not amenable to be applied by judicial bodies as such. They regard the provisions as stating goals, imposing a 'programme', rather than creating concrete rights and obligations.[72] The distinction between this and the former notion of 'justiciable' might seem forced to a national lawyer, but in international law the notion of legal rights that exist, but are not enforceable in judicial proceedings is rather common[73] and different from the notion that a right cannot even theoretically be enforced by courts. It is the latter notion that will have to be discussed in more detail.

a draft to the Commission on Human Rights: *Draft Optional Protocol to the International Covenant on Economic, Social and Cultural Rights. Annex*, UN Doc E/CN.4/1997/105 (1997). K Arambulo, 'Drafting an Optional Protocol to the International Covenant on Economic, Social and Cultural Rights: Can an Ideal Become Reality' (1996) 2 UC Davis J Int'l L & Pol'y 111; Alternative suggestions include, eg a proposal to merge human rights treaty bodies: R Wolfrum, 'International Convention on the Elimination of All Forms of Racial Discrimination' in E Klein (ed), *The Monitoring System of Human Rights Treaty Obligations* (1998) 49, 69; against a complaint mechanism for the ICESCR MJ Dennis and DP Stewart, 'Justiciability of Economic, Social, and Cultural Rights: Should There Be an International Complaints Mechanism to Adjudicate the Rights to Food, Water, Housing, and Health?' (2004) 98 AJIL 462.

   [70] Simma (n 36 above) 82; E Riedel, 'Verhandlungslösungen im Rahmen des Sozialpakts der Vereinten Nationen' (2000) Arbeitspapiere—Mannheimer Zentrum für Europäische Sozialforschung Nr 28.
   [71] On the different notions of justiciability MK Addo, 'Justiciability Re-examined' in R Beddard and DM Hill (eds), *Economic, Social and Cultural Rights. Progress and Achievement* (1992) 93, 96. The question whether international law itself is law need not be discussed here. On that question see Kelsen (n 20 above) 18 ff, note especially viii.
   [72] Others regard the provisions as imposing 'programmatic' obligations on states, but not as creating rights. Vierdag (n 64 above) 83, 95; M Bothe, 'Les concepts fondamentaux du droit à la santé: Le point de vue juridique' in R-J Dupuy (ed), *Le droit à la santé en tant que droit de l'homme. The Right to Health as a Human Right* (1979) RdC 1978 Colloque 14, 21. See the discussion in a UN University Workshop: R-J Dupuy (ed), 'Résumé des débats—Summing up' in R-J Dupuy (ed), *Le droit à la santé en tant que droit de l'homme. The Right to Health as a Human Right* (1979) RdC 1978 Colloque 124, 130 ff. Minow argues that the individualism of rights rhetoric is unhelpful for allocating resources, nevertheless she sees the value of using a rights rhetoric. Harvard Law School Human Rights Program (ed), *Economic and Social Rights and the Right to Health. An Interdisciplinary Discussion Held at Harvard Law School in September, 1993* (1995) 3.
   [73] Support for the position that this is also true for individual rights can be found in the *LaGrand Case (Germany/United States of America)*, Judgment, ICJ Reports 2001, 466, paras 77, 128 (3) (27 June 2001) (concerning the rights of the individual under Art 36(1) of the Vienna Convention on Consular Relations, which can only be enforced by the home state as the enforcement procedure of the optional protocol is only available to the state); note Separate Opinion of Vice-President Shi (considering the view that Art 36(1) creates individual rights for the detained person in addition to rights of the sending state at least questionable). The court affirmed its finding in *Case Concerning Avena and other Mexican Nationals (Mexico/United States of America)*, ICJ Judgment, at para 61, 153 (31 March 2004). K Oellers-Frahm, 'Die Entscheidung des IGH im Fall LaGrand—Eine Stärkung der internationalen Gerichtsbarkeit und der Rolle des Individuums im Völkerrecht', (2001) EuGRZ 265, 267–268.

2 Economic, Social, and Cultural Rights as Justiciable Rights

Traditionally, the main distinction between civil and political and economic, social, and cultural rights is seen in that the former protect individuals from government interference by granting them a right to demand abstention from the state (negative right). Implementing this pledge of abstention does not require the state to commit financial resources. In contrast the latter category of rights demands action on the part of the state (positive rights) and thus also the commital of resources.[74] From these budgetary implications many authors have inferred the non-justiciable character of economic, social, and cultural rights: at the most radical it is alleged that because of their limited resources states are simply unable to fulfil economic, social, and cultural rights.[75] Invoking the old Roman maxim that *impossibilium nulla obligatio est*[76]—there is no duty to do the impossible—it is argued that these rights cannot be legal in character, but merely 'utopian'[77] or 'moral'.[78] A less radical proposition is that the budgetary implications of economic, social, and cultural rights make them mere relative rights, as opposed to the absolute civil and political rights rooted in human dignity:[79] whereas the content of the latter is fixed and they can be implemented immediately, the content of the former varies according to a state's financial resources and they are to be implemented progressively only.[80] Progressive implementation, however, implies that some parts of the rights are implemented before others, requiring a choice of which parts to implement first (and thus a choice among possible beneficiaries). These choices are not necessary in the domain of civil and political rights, as those have to be applied to everybody immediately.[81] It is now argued that the necessity of choices in the implementation of economic, social, and cultural rights demonstrates that they are too vague to be enforced in court.[82] Courts are ill-equipped (and lack the legitimacy) to take the necessary decisions on the priorities in the implementation of the rights. They should be left to the administration.[83] Also,

[74] M Bossuyt, 'La Distinction Juridique entre les Droits Civils et Politiques et les Droits Économiques, Sociaux et Culturels' (1975) Revue des Droits de l'Homme, Human Rights Journal 783, 788, 790, 796; T Tomandl, *Der Einbau sozialer Grundrechte in das positive Recht* (1967) 6; M Scalabrino-Spadea, 'Le Droit à la Santé. Inventaire de Normes et Principes de Droit International' in Institut International d'Études des Droits de l'Homme (ed), *Le Médecin face aux Droits de l'Homme* (1990) 95.

[75] M Cranston, *What are Human Rights?* (1973) 66; C Tomuschat, 'International Standards and Cultural Diversity' (1985) Bulletin of Human Rights. Special Issue. Human Rights Day 24, 34; Vierdag (n 64 above) 93; C Tomuschat, 'Die Bundesrepublik Deutschland und die Menschenrechtspakte der Vereinten Nationen' (1978) 26 Vereinte Nationen 1, 2; J Isensee, 'Verfassung ohne soziale Grundrechte. Ein Wesenszug des Grundgesetzes' (1980) 19 Der Staat 367, 376–377 (pointing out the importance of the interpretation of the rights).

[76] Dig 50, 17, 185 (Celsus), printed in P Krueger and T Mommsen (eds), *Corpus Iuris Civilis. Volumen Primum. Institutiones Digesta* (7th edn, 1895) 873.   [77] Cranston (n 75 above) 68.

[78] Harvard Law School Human Rights Program (n 72 above) 1 (question asked by H Steiner).

[79] Bossuyt (n 74 above) 790 f; Vierdag (n 64 above) 82.   [80] Article 2(1) of the ICESCR.

[81] Bossuyt (n 74 above) 791–792; Vierdag (n 64 above) 82.

[82] Vierdag (n 64 above) 93–94; SB Shah, 'Illuminating the Possible in the Developing World: Guaranteeing the Human Right to Health in India' (1999) 32 Vand J Transnat L 435, 446–447.

[83] Bossuyt (n 74 above) 793–794, 806.

given how all-encompassing these 'programmatic'[84] rights are, court enforcement of them would deal a death-blow to the separation of powers.[85]

The classical distinction between civil and political rights on the one hand and economic, social, and cultural rights on the other hand cannot be maintained. Not only does it fly in the face of numerous documents claiming the indivisibility and interdependence of all human rights,[86] but the conceptual distinction between the rights itself is not valid. The dichotomy of negative and positive state obligations cannot serve as its basis, as nowadays civil and political rights contained in most legal documents, such as the ICCPR,[87] the European Convention on Human Rights (ECHR),[88] and many national constitutions,[89] have been recognized to contain a positive component. Conversely, economic, social, and cultural rights include a negative component, requiring state abstention, eg the right to education[90] includes the freedom to teach and to establish schools and not just the duty of the state to establish schools.[91] As Eide has stated, all human rights analytically entail an obligation to respect, protect, and fulfil the right,[92] albeit the centre of gravity might be on a different obligation for different rights. The budgetary implications of economic, social, and cultural rights cannot serve as a distinguishing factor for the categories of rights, either. Some classic civil and political rights evidently require state expenditure, eg periodic elections.[93]

---

[84] *General Debate on the Draft International Covenant on Human Rights and Measures of Implementation*, UN GAOR, 6th Session, 3rd Committee, 368th meeting (13 December 1951), at 127, UN Doc A/C.3/SR.368 (1951) para 20 ff; Brownlie (n 17 above) 539. Note that the notion of programmatic ('programme rights') implies a state obligation to establish a programme for taking measures, but not an enforceable right. Vierdag (n 64 above) 83.

[85] Vierdag (n 64 above) 92–93.

[86] N 34 above. For a thorough discussion of the notion of indivisibility see IE Koch, 'Social Rights as Components in the Civil Right to Personal Liberty: Another Step Forward in the Integrated Human Rights Approach?' (2002) 20 Netherlands Q of Hum Rts 29. The drafters of the Covenants themselves seemed to have a hard time deciding which right falls into which category, eg including the freedom to form trade unions in both Covenants.

[87] Human Rights Committee, *General Comment 31 [80]* (2004), paras 6, 8; replacing Human Rights Committee, *General Comment 3/13* (1981), para 1. *Dimitry L Gridin v Russian Federation*, Communication No 770, UN Doc CCPR/C/69/D/770/1997 at para 8.2 (2000) (holding that the failure by a trial court to control the hostile atmosphere and pressure created by the public in the court room making it impossible for defence counsel to properly cross-examine and present a defence constitutes a violation of the right to a fair trial).

[88] European Court of Human Rights, *Marckx v Belgium*, Application 6833/74 (1979) 31 ECHR 15; European Court of Human Rights, *Airey v Ireland*, Application 6289/73 (1979) 32 ECHR 14; C Dröge, *Positive Verpflichtungen der Staaten in der Europäischen Menschenrechtskonvention* (2003) 284 ff.

[89] A notable exception is the United States Constitution, DP Currie, 'Positive und negative Grundrechte' (1986) 111 AÖR 230, 238, 249–250; T Giegerich, *Privatwirkung der Grundrechte in den USA* (1992) 46–47.   [90] Articles 13–14 of the ICESCR.

[91] Vierdag (n 64 above) 86.

[92] A Eide, *The New International Economic Order and the Promotion of Human Rights. Report on the Right to Adequate Food as a Human Right*, UN Doc E/CN.4/Sub.2/1987/23 (1987) paras 66 ff, 115.

[93] Vierdag (n 86 above) 82; Koch (n 86 above) 32. Holmes and Sunstein show that *all* rights require public spending, as national enforcement by courts, police, etc are costly. S Holmes and CR Sunstein, *The Cost of Rights. Why Liberty Depends on Taxes* (2000) 43 ff.

Given that the distinction of the two traditional groups of rights is flawed, it is unconvincing to argue that economic, social, and cultural rights are impossible to fulfil. At times such an argument seems to be based on a literal reading of the name of the rights such as 'the right to health'. The establishment of such a right would, of course, be absurd, as no one can provide good health where nature and human frailty take their toll. But the term 'right to health' is a misnomer as the right is actually more of a right to health care. It is conceded that the immediate full realization of a right to health care or of the right to food and other such rights is impossible. Human misery cannot be ended in a day. If the ICESCR imposed such an obligation, it would have to be read as merely hortatory even though it is contained in a binding international treaty.[94] But the Covenant does not demand the immediate full implementation of its rights and instead commits State Parties to undertake:

to take steps, individually and through international assistance and co-operation, especially economic and technical, to the maximum of [their] available resources, with a view to achieving progressively the full realization of the rights recognized in the present Convention by all appropriate means, including particularly the adoption of legislative measures.[95]

This provision shows convincingly that the Covenant is not utopian—it does not demand the immediate full realization of the rights of the ICESCR.[96]

The argument that the ICESCR is not justiciable because of the intricacies involved in progressive implementation is somewhat more convincing, but it, too, ultimately fails. The notion of progressive realization of rights does not imply that there are no immediate state obligations.[97] The Covenant itself makes clear that State Parties undertake 'to take steps' towards the realization of the rights.[98] This obligation is, according to a good faith interpretation of its wording in light of the objective of realizing the rights in the ICESCR,[99] an obligation to take concrete steps within a reasonable time, as well as a duty to use reasonable care in trying to achieve the goals.[100] The interpretation is affirmed by the even stronger Spanish and French wording (*adoptar medidas, agir*). The Committee on Economic, Social and Cultural Rights adopted a similar interpretation in its General Comment No 3, stating that the Covenant imposes various obligations with immediate effect, in particular the undertaking to take steps and the duty of non-discrimination.[101] General Comments are non-binding interpretations adopted to assist states in their interpretation of the Covenant. In drafting them the Committee draws on

[94] Cf generally P Weil, 'Towards Relative Normativity in International Law' (1983) 77 AJIL 413.
[95] Article 2(1) of the ICESCR.
[96] Simma and von Bennigsen (n 69 above) 1488 (arguing that the ICESCR is justiciable, but does not grant individual rights).   [97] Simma (n 36 above) 78–79.
[98] Article 2(1) of the ICESCR.
[99] Cf Art 31(1) of the Vienna Convention on the Law of Treaties.
[100] Simma (n 36 above) 80.
[101] Committee on Economic, Social and Cultural Rights, *General Comment No 3* (1990), paras 1–2.

its expert knowledge of state practice in the application of the Covenant, which is relevant for the interpretation together with the context according to Article 31(3)(b) of the Vienna Convention.[102]

The argument that obligations imposed by the ICESCR are too vague to be justiciable overlooks the fact that vague legal obligations are rather common. Some of the civil and political rights, too, are formulated in a very imprecise manner,[103] not to mention that international and national judicial bodies are regularly called upon to apply such vague notions as 'good faith'.

Courts enjoy much leeway in the interpretation of vague terms, which gives credence to the next claim by critics, however doubtful it may be under international law, that justiciable economic, social, and cultural rights violate the separation of powers, particularly as judicial decisions in this area would have a stark impact on the budget. The argument was before the Constitutional Court of South Africa in *Certification of the Constitution of the Republic of South Africa*. The Court rightly dismissed it, arguing that the budget is often also implicated in civil and political rights and the tasks conferred on the courts in the area of socio-economic rights is not different enough from the normal tasks of a court to warrant a different treatment of the rights.[104] Courts should, of course, tread carefully in these waters, but in other areas of the law, too, courts have properly recognized that political organs are better situated to analyze and weigh the relevant factors and granted deference to those bodies. A correct interpretation of economic, social, and cultural rights has to give some deference to the executive and the legislature.[105] The Constitutional Court of South Africa acknowledged this in *Minister of Health et al v Treatment Action Campaign et al*, in which the court had to address the scope of the socio-economic obligations under the South African Constitution:

Courts are ill-suited to adjudicate upon issues where court orders could have multiple social and economic consequences for the community. The Constitution contemplates rather a restrained and focused role for the courts, namely, to require the state to take measures to meet its constitutional obligations and to subject the reasonableness of these measures to evaluation.[106]

---

[102] Rule 65, Rules of Procedure of the Committee on Economic, Social and Cultural Rights. Provisional Rules of Procedure Adopted by the Committee at its third session (1989), as amended 1993, Compilation of Rules of Procedure Adopted by Human Rights Treaty Bodies, UN Doc HRI/GEN/3/Rev 1 (28 April 2003). Note that some authors claim that General Comments are (binding) authoritative interpretations. However, there is little to support such a claim. Weissbrodt and Schoff (n 52 above) 183.

[103] Addo (n 71 above) 101 (mentioning Arts 11, 16 of the ICCPR).

[104] *Ex Parte Chairperson of the Constitutional Assembly: In re Certification of the Constitution of the Republic of South Africa*, 1996 (4) SA 744 (CC); 1996 (10) BCLR 1253 (CC) para 77 f (6 September 1996).

[105] *Government of the Republic of South Africa and Others v Grootboom and Others* 2001 (1) SA 46 (CC); 2000 (11) BCLR 1169 (CC) at para 32 (4 October 2000) (rejecting the notion of minimum core obligations in the South African context with the argument that the court does not possess the information necessary to determine such obligations).

[106] *Minister of Health et al v Treatment Action Campaign et al* 2002 (5) SA 721 (CC); 2002 (10) BCLR 1033 (CC) at para 38 (5 July 2002). See I Hare, '*Minister of Health v Treatment Action*

An entirely different attack on economic, social, and cultural rights, which must be seen in the context of the Cold War, purports that these rights are inferior to civil and political rights[107] and the attempt to endow them with human rights status would result in weakening traditional human rights.[108] The attempt to illustrate this argument by examples (the right to life is more important than a right to holidays with pay)[109] shows its fallacy, as such a comparison can cut both ways: a person who is denied her right to food or to health will care very little for her freedom to form trade unions. The juxtaposition merely illustrates the indivisibility of human rights: only where basic needs and basic freedoms are fulfilled at the same time can human beings live in dignity.

Arguably, much of the opposition to justiciable economic, social, and cultural rights can be explained with the justified fear that socialist countries would try and deflect criticism from their human rights violations by pointing to their guarantee of a workplace, inconceivable in a market economy.[110] With the end of the Cold War, however, this fear is no longer warranted. States have ratified the ICESCR, a binding international treaty, and are therefore bound by it.[111] Any argument that these rights are not of a legal nature has to overcome the simple truism that a legally binding document is legally binding. It hence has to be concluded that the rights contained in the ICESCR are justiciable. This position was confirmed by the ICJ in its advisory opinion on the *Legal Consequences of the Construction of a Wall in the Occupied Palestinian Territory*. It ruled that the ICESCR was applicable and relevant in assessing the legality of the measures taken by Israel and found possible violations of Articles 6, 7, 10, 11, 12, 13, and 14 of the ICESCR, notably including the right to health.[112] Equally, the African Commission on Human and Peoples' Rights has applied social and economic rights granted under the Banjul Charter.[113] In *Social and Economic Rights Action Centre and the Centre for Economic*

Campaign: The South African AIDS Pandemic and the Constitutional Right to Healthcare' (2002) 5 EHRLR 624, 629–630.

[107] Bossuyt explicitly rejects the thought that civil and political rights might be more important. Bossuyt (n 74 above) 805.

[108] Cranston (n 75 above) 68. The supposed danger of economic, social, and cultural rights being used to justify violations of civil and political rights has been stressed by the US State Department. DP Forsythe, 'Socioeconomic Human Rights: The United Nations, the United States, and Beyond' (1982) 4 Human Rights Quarterly 433, 436.   [109] Cranston (n 75 above) 71.

[110] See Vierdag (n 64 above) 85.

[111] GJH van Hoof, 'The Legal Nature of Economic, Social and Cultural Rights: a Rebuttal of Some Traditional Views' in P Alston and K Tomaševski (eds), *The Right to Food* (1984) 97, 101.

[112] *Legal Consequences of the Construction of a Wall in the Occupied Palestinian Territory*, ICJ Judgment (9 July 2004) paras 112, 130.

[113] African Charter on Human and Peoples' Rights (Banjul Charter). The Charter allows for individual communications to the African Commission on Human and Peoples' Rights. The system is completed by an African Court on Human and People's Rights, a key organ of the African Union according to the Protocol to the African Charter on Human and People's Rights on the Establishment of an African Court on Human and People's Rights that entered into force on 25 January 2004. S Lyons, 'The African Court on Human and Peoples' Rights' (2006) 10 ASIL Insight 24. On the African Union HP Hestermeyer, 'African Union replaces Organization of African Unity' (2002) 3 German Law Journal 8.

and Social Rights v Nigeria it found that Nigeria had violated the right to health and the right to a clean environment by not requiring environmental impact studies prior to allowing an oil consortium to exploit oil reserves in Ogoniland and by not monitoring the project.[114] Several other regional and universal human rights treaties allow complaints for violations of (at least some) economic, social, and cultural rights[115] and many national courts have either applied those rights or extended civil and political rights to include economic, social, and cultural issues,[116] thus demonstrating that these rights can be applied by courts. The crux of economic, social, and cultural rights is in determining their content,[117] or in the words of the Constitutional Court of South Africa: 'The question is (...) not whether socio-economic rights are justiciable under our Constitution, but how to enforce them in a given case.'[118]

IV Who Is Bound by International Human Rights Law?

Having determined that economic, social, and cultural rights are of a legal nature it is now time to ask who is bound by them. The answer is obvious for states: if they have signed the relevant treaty, they are bound by it and all states are bound by general international law.[119] But are pharmaceutical companies, responsible for the pricing of pharmaceuticals, and the WTO, the international organization administrating the TRIPS Agreement, also bound by international human rights law?

1 Human Rights Obligations of Corporations

Traditionally, human rights were conceived as limits on state power, they were not directly binding on individuals.[120] Recent developments, however, assail this proposition. States have privatized many of the obligations that used to be considered as being among their core tasks—from the provision of basic services to warfare.[121] Corporate power has grown to rival that of states: in 2002 the corporation

---

[114] *Social and Economic Rights Action Centre and the Centre for Economic and Social Rights v Nigeria*, Communication No 155/1996, ACHPR/COMM/A044/1 (27 May 2002) para 53 f.

[115] Eg a protocol to the European Social Charter establishes a collective complaints system, RR Churchill and U Khaliq, 'The Collective Complaints System of the European Social Charter: An Effective Mechanism for Ensuring Compliance with Economic and Social Rights?' (2004) 15 EJIL 417, 421.   [116] See the cases mentioned below.

[117] Committee on Economic, Social and Cultural Rights, *General Comment No 14* (2000), para 1; Toebes (n 38 above) 170; P Rott, *Patentrecht und Sozialpolitik unter dem TRIPS-Abkommen* (2002) 94.

[118] *Government of the Republic of South Africa and Others v Grootboom and Others* 2001 (1) SA 46 (CC); 2000 (11) BCLR 1169 (CC) at para 20 (4 October 2000).

[119] BE Carter and PR Trimble, *International Law* (3rd edn, 1999) 134 ff.

[120] For the US Constitution see JE Nowak and RD Rotunda, *Constitutional Law* (5th edn, 1995) 343–344; For Spain see L López Guerra *et al*, *Derecho Constitucional. Volumen I* (3rd edn, 1997) 142 ff; For Germany see A Bleckmann, *Staatsrecht II—Die Grundrechte* (4th edn, 1997) 219 ff.

[121] PW Singer, *Corporate Warriors. The Rise of the Privatized Military Industry* (2004).

with the largest sales figure, Wal-Mart at $217,799m,[122] outdid Austria's 2002
GDP, the twentieth biggest national GDP of the world, and was not that much
smaller than the GDP of all of Sub-Saharan Africa ($319,288m).[123] As with
state power, corporate power can be abused to violate the rights of individuals.
Abundant examples of such abuse can be found in the news.[124] Responding to the
fact that individuals are increasingly as powerless towards big corporations as they
are towards states and that human rights can be violated by both states and corporations some countries imposed human rights obligations directly on corporations.
Thus, the Portuguese Constitution of 2 April 1976 binds public and private 'institutions' by its rights, freedoms, and guarantees.[125] Other states have passed legislation for that purpose.[126] This study has to inquire whether international human
rights obligations are directly binding on corporations. If that is the case, which is
supported by strong arguments at least *de lege ferenda*,[127] pharmaceutical companies would be bound directly by the right to access to medicine (should such a
right exist) and thus could be held accountable where their pricing violates the
obligations imposed under the right.

The ordinary meaning of international human rights norms seems to support
the proposition that corporations, too, are directly bound by them. Wordings
such as 'No one shall be held in slavery'[128] or 'Every human being has the inherent
right to life'[129] impose the respect of the right as such and do not address states
only. Where states are the sole addressees a different wording seems to have been
chosen as illustrated by the right to health: 'The States Parties to the present
Covenant recognize the right of everyone to the enjoyment of the highest attainable standard of physical and mental health.'[130] The argument is not entirely convincing, though: given that international law traditionally has been the legal order

---

[122] Wal-Mart (ed), *Annual Report 2002.*

[123] World Bank (ed), *Total GDP 2002, World Development Indicators database.*

[124] M Monshipouri, CE Welch, Jr, and ET Kennedy, 'Multinational Corporations and the Ethics
of Global Responsibility: Problems and Possibilities' (2003) 25 Hum Rts Q 965, 971 ff. On Nike's
use of child labour and poor health standards in factories: S Greenhouse, 'Nike Shoe Plant in
Vietnam is Called Unsafe for Workers' *NYTimes* (8 November 1997); JH Cushman Jr, 'Nike Pledges
to End Child Labor and Increase Safety' *NY Times* (13 May 1998). On Shell's involvement in violations of the rights of the Ogoni people, see *Social and Economic Rights Action Centre and the Centre for
Economic and Social Rights v Nigeria, supra* n 114. On the involvement of private contractors in
torture in US prisons in Iraq: D Jehl and K Zernike, 'Greater Urgency on Prison Interrogation Led to
Use of Untrained Workers' *NY Times* (28 May 2004).

[125] Article 18(1) of the Constitution. JJ Gomes Canotilho and V Moreira, *Constituição da
República Portuguesa Anotada* (3rd edn, 1993) Art 18 IV. Several African Constitutions explicitly rec-
ognize the horizontal applicability of their Bills of Rights, DM Chirwa, 'The Right to Health in
International Law: Its Implications for the Obligations of State and Non-State Actors in Ensuring
Access to Essential Medicine' (2003) 19 SAJHR 541, 564.

[126] Eg US Civil Rights Act of 1964, Pub L 88–353, 78 Stat 241 (2 July 1964); German
Allgemeines Gleichbehandlungsgesetz, BGBl I 2006, 1897 (14 August 2006).

[127] SR Ratner, 'Corporations and Human Rights: A Theory of Legal Responsibility' (2001) 111
Yale L J 443; A Clapham, *Human Rights in the Private Sphere* (1993) 89 ff.

[128] Article 8(1) of the ICCPR.   [129] Article 6(1) of the ICCPR.

[130] Article 12(1) of the ICESCR.

between states and did not reach individuals at all, a departure from this doctrine would have to be made in explicit terms, as it has been made in the case of international criminal law.[131] The fact that not all rights mention that they bind only states is simply based on the fact that such a limitation is self-understood in international law.

The purpose of human rights instruments supports a broad interpretation. Many of the rights protected by the Covenants, such as the right to life, can also be violated by private parties.[132] The purpose of the conventions, the protection of the rights, would thus be furthered if the Covenants would be held to also directly bind private parties.

The preambles of the ICCPR and the ICESCR, which serve as context for the purpose of interpreting the human rights norms, seem to extend the binding effect of the Covenants to private parties, too: 'the individual, having duties to other individuals and to the community to which he belongs, is under a responsibility to strive for the promotion and observance of the rights recognized in the present Covenant'. A similar provision is contained in the preamble of the UDHR, which in addition states in its Article 29(1) that '[e]veryone has duties to the community in which alone the free and full development of his personality is possible'. But the preambles provide only weak support for private party obligations: preambles do not create legal obligations by themselves; their legal value is limited to aiding in the interpretation of the agreement.[133] The UDHR is equally unhelpful: even assuming that it is legally binding[134] it refrains from listing specific obligations of individuals.

In contrast, Article 2 of the ICCPR and Article 2 of the ICESCR indicate that only states are bound by the rights of the Covenants. These provisions define the obligations that State Parties incur. They do, however, not impose obligations on individuals.[135] This clear wording is a strong argument against the Covenants' imposing direct obligations on private parties and, thus, on corporations. Some authors attempt to rebut this argument by pointing to Article 5(1) of the ICCPR (and similarly Article 30 of the UDHR). The provision states that:

[n]othing in the present Covenant may be interpreted as implying for any State, group or person any right to engage in any activity of perform any act aimed at the destruction of any of the rights and freedoms recognized herein (...).

---

[131] NS Rodley, 'Can Armed Opposition Groups Violate Human Rights?' in KE Mahoney and P Mahoney (eds), *Human Rights in the Twenty-first Century. A Global Challenge* (1993) 297.

[132] K Wiesbrock, *Internationaler Schutz der Menschenrechte vor Verletzungen durch Private* (1999) 19; F Matscher, 'Menschenrechte in Europa: Gedanken zur Weiterentwicklung des Grundrechtsschutzes in Europa' in W Schuhmacher (ed), *Perspektiven des europäischen Rechts* (1994) 305, 316 ff.

[133] H-D Treviranus, 'Preamble' in R Bernhardt (ed), *Encyclopedia of Public International Law, III* (1997) 1097, 1098.   [134] See this chapter below.

[135] E Klein, 'The Duty to Protect and to Ensure Human Rights Under the International Covenant on Civil and Political Rights' in E Klein (ed), *The Duty to Protect and to Ensure Human Rights. Colloquium. Potsdam, 1–3 July 1999* (2000) 296–297. Rodley (n 131 above) 308. But see M Nowak, *U.N. Covenant on Civil and Political Rights. CCPR Commentary* (1993) Art 2 para 20

They reason that this provision only makes sense if groups and persons are bound by the Covenant directly: if they were not bound, their right to engage in any activity aiming at the destruction of the protected rights would be unaffected by the Covenant.[136] But this reasoning is based on a misreading of Article 5(1) of the ICCPR. The provision merely states that the agreement cannot be interpreted to grant individuals a right to engage in infringing activities and thus ensures that the agreement does not inadvertently retrogress in the protection of human rights.[137]

State practice in the application of the Covenants does not support direct human rights obligations for corporations, either. Paust has argued the contrary, relying on US precedents holding a company liable for violations of international human rights law under the Alien Tort Statute, which provides for district court jurisdiction for actions by aliens for a tort committed in violation of the law of nations or a treaty of the United States.[138] However, his evaluation of the case law is overly optimistic given that US courts explicitly recognized only a handful of crimes, including slave trade, to give rise to individual liability without state action.[139] The 2004 US Supreme Court ruling in *Sosa v Alvarez-Machain* further limits the Alien Tort Statute, holding that it recognizes claims only for international law norms with as definite a content as those admitted under the Statute when it was enacted (violation of safe conducts, infringement of the rights of ambassadors, piracy)[140] and explicitly extending this standard of definiteness also to the question whether human rights violations by private parties are recognized. This makes it highly unlikely that the Court would acknowledge sweeping corporate human rights obligations. The German *Bundesverfassungsgericht* (Federal Constitutional Court) agrees, holding that 'outside the area of minimum human rights standards current general international law contains only few norms that

(pointing out that the wording that a remedy shall be available 'notwithstanding' that the violation has been committed by persons acting in an official capacity in Art 2(3) can be read to mean that the rights are not only protected from violations by the state. However, the provision can also be read to emphasize the responsibility of states for official acts).

[136] On the equivalent provision in the ECHR: M-A Eissen, 'The European Convention on Human Rights and the Duties of the Individual' (1962) 32 Nordisk Tidsskrift for International Ret 230, 234–235; B Moser, *Die Europäische Menschenrechtskonvention und das bürgerliche Recht. Zum Problem der Drittwirkung von Grundrechten* (1972) 106; D Spielmann, *L'Effet Potentiel de la Convention Européenne des Droits de l'Homme entre Personnes Privées* (1995) 36.

[137] Pechota (n 60 above) 68.

[138] 28 USC § 1350. *John Doe v Unocal Corporation* 2002 WL 31063976 (9th Cir, 2002). The case was settled in 2004 days before the arguments in the scheduled rehearing en banc: Order *John Doe v Unocal Corporation*, filed 13 April 2005 Case No: CV-96–06112-RSWL.

[139] *Kadic v Karadzic* 70 F3d 232, 241 ff (2nd Cir, 1995); *John Doe v Unocal Corporation*, 2002 WL 31063976 (9th Cir, 2002). See also *Iwanowa v Ford Motor Co* 67 FSupp2d 424 (DNJ, 1999) 443 ff (stating *obiter* that it agrees with the *Kadic* Court and finds individuals bound by the prohibition of the deportation of civilian populations to slave labour as a war crime); *Eastman Kodak Co v Kavlin* 978 FSupp 1078 (S D Fla, 1997) 1091 ff (holding that conspiring with state actors to violate the law of nations can constitute a claim under the Alien Tort Statute).

[140] *Sosa v Alvarez-Machain et al* 124 S Ct 2739 (2004) footnote 20.

create rights or duties of private individuals'.[141] A thorough reading of the Covenants in their context hence does not support direct human rights obligations of private parties and corporations under the Covenants.

Some authors have drawn on the *travaux préparatoires* to argue that the Covenants impose obligations on private parties. The US proposal that the future Article 7 of the ICCPR should impose that 'no State' could subject any person to torture was changed to 'no-one shall be subjected to torture (...)' to include possible violations committed by individuals.[142] However, as the interpretation of the human rights instruments in their context (and against the backdrop of the structure of international law) yielded that human rights provisions do not bind private parties,[143] the Vienna Convention does not allow recourse to the *travaux préparatoires*.

The fact that private parties are not directly bound by international human rights law does not imply that international human rights have no effect whatsoever in the private sphere. As demonstrated by national legal systems, human rights law can exert a considerable indirect influence on the dealings of private parties. Courts have applied a number of approaches to justify such an indirect influence.[144] At times they have attributed human rights violations by individuals to the state by focusing on the legal enforcement of a private deal. Thus, in *Shelley v Kraemer*, the ratio of which has fallen into disuse because of its excessive breadth,[145] the US Supreme Court refused to enforce a discriminatory agreement between private parties, holding that the enforcement of the agreement by a court would constitute an action of the state and would thus deny equal protection of the law.[146] Another increasingly popular construction for the indirect influence of human rights law is the doctrine of indirect third-party applicability (*mittelbare Drittwirkung*). The *Bundesverfassungsgericht* held that the human rights provisions of the German *Grundgesetz* constitute an objective order based on values (*objektive Wertordnung*),[147] permeating the whole legal system and hence influencing its interpretation. The influence is particularly pronounced in the interpretation

---

[141] BVerfGE 46, 342, 362 (translation by author). This is the German case cited by *Memorandum for the United States as Amicus Curiae in Filartiga v Pena-Irala*, at 21, 630 F2d 876 (2nd Cir, 1980) that Paust refers to in support of private party human rights obligations.

[142] Eissen (n 136 above) 237–238.

[143] S Joseph, 'Pharmaceutical Corporations and Access to Drugs: The "Fourth Wave" of Corporate Human Rights Scrutiny' (2003) 25 Hum Rts Q 425, 437; Y Dinstein, 'The Right to Life, Physical Integrity and Liberty' in L Henkin (ed), *The International Bill of Rights. The Covenant on Civil and Political Rights* (1981) 119; A Seibert-Fohr, 'Die Deliktshaftung von Unternehmen für die Beteiligung an im Ausland begangenen Völkerrechtsverletzungen. Anmerkungen zum Urteil Doe I v Unocal Corp. des US Court of Appeal (9th Circuit)' (2003) 63 ZaöRV 195; JA Frowein, in JA Frowein and W Peukert (eds), *Europäische MenschenRechtsKonvention. EMRK-Kommentar* (2nd edn, 1996) Art 1, para 2 (for the European Convention on Human Rights); WH Meyer and B Stefanova, 'Human Rights, the UN Global Compact, and Global Governance' (2001) 34 Cornell Int'l LJ 501, 514–515.   [144] Dröge (n 88 above) 72; Giegerich (n 89 above) 14.

[145] Giegerich (n 89 above) 306 ff.

[146] *Shelley v Kraemer* 334 US 1 (1948) 19 f. Giegerich (n 89 above) 454.

[147] BVerfGE 7, 198, 205 (1958).

of *Generalklauseln* (general norms) such as § 138 *Bürgerliches Gesetzbuch* (Civil Code),[148] which voids deals among private parties in violation of 'good morals'.[149] A third solution is to interpret human rights norms to contain a duty of the state to protect individuals from violations of their rights by the state and by private parties. This approach is not just commonly applied on the national level,[150] but it is also the approach taken in international human rights law, as shown below. It should be mentioned that discontent with the mere indirect effect of international human rights law on corporations is widespread, but that the efforts undertaken so far have only led to a number of guidelines and initiatives that are not binding on corporations, such as the UN Global Compact,[151] the Draft Norms on the Responsibilities of Transnational Corporations and Other Business Enterprises with regard to Human Rights[152] approved by the Sub-Commission on the Promotion and Protection of Human Rights,[153] and the OECD Guidelines for Multinational Enterprises.[154]

2 Human Rights Obligations of International Organizations

Another question that is quite evidently of eminent importance is whether the WTO itself is bound by international human rights law. If that is the case, it would have to comply with the obligations imposed by that branch of law, eg when providing legal-technical assistance. Any advice on the implementation of the TRIPS Agreement would have to take human rights concerns into account, draft intellectual property laws would have to be in compliance with international human rights law. Another, closely related, issue is the question of whether human rights law can be applied in WTO dispute settlement. This question will be discussed in chapter 5.

---

[148] BGBl I, 42 (2002).

[149] BVerfGE 7, 198, 205 f (1958), B Pieroth and B Schlink, *Grundrechte. Staatsrecht II* (11th edn, 1995) 49 ff.

[150] BVerfG NJW 1987, 2287 (1987) (holding that the state is under a duty to protect life and health against the dangers of AIDS, however the state enjoys wide discretion in the choice of measures and the court will only intervene if the state has not acted at all or if its measures are evidently insufficient); BVerfGE 39, 1, 42 (1975); BVerfGE 88, 203, 251 (1993); Pieroth and Schlink (n 149 above) 26–27.

[151] The Global Compact is an initiative of the Secretary General, K Annan, *Secretary-General Proposes Global Compact on Human Rights, Labour, Environment, in Address to World Economic Forum in Davos*, UN Press Release SG/SM/6881 (1 February 1999).

[152] *Norms on the Responsibilities of Transnational Corporations and Other Business Enterprises with regard to Human Rights*, UN Doc E/CN.4/Sub.2/2003/12/Rev.2 (2003).

[153] *Responsibilities of Transnational Corporations and other Business Enterprises with regard to Human Rights*, Sub-Commission on Human Rights Res 2003/16 (13 August 2003), see also *Responsibilities of Transnational Corporations and Related Business Enterprises with regard to Human Rights*, Human Rights Commission Dec 2004/116 (2004).

[154] Organization for Economic Co-operation and Development (ed), *The OECD Guidelines for Multinational Enterprises. Revision 2000* (2000) 19 (demanding that enterprises should '[r]espect the human rights of those affected by their activities consistent with the host government's international obligations and commitments').

The reader might be somewhat perplexed by the question. After all, if states are bound by human rights law, can they simply extract themselves from their self-imposed bounds by setting up an international organization?[155] The answer to this question is twofold: the first is that international organizations themselves are subjects of international law with their own rights and obligations—at least for the area of law in which they enjoy competencies according to their founding documents.[156] As such they can sign their own treaties and conventions and unless they have done so (and absent special circumstances) they are not bound by a treaty.[157] The WTO has not signed any human rights convention,[158] nor, it should be added, is it incurring any human rights obligations as a specialized agency of the United Nations under the UN Charter, as it is not a specialized agency.

The second part of the answer concerns obligations under general international law. As subjects of international law international organizations are bound by these rules unless the nature of the rule prevents its application to international organizations.[159] This statement comes with a caveat, however. States can both

[155] Schermers and Blocker draw on this perceived paradox and argue with an analogy to state succession to bind international organizations to obligations not signed by them. Furthermore, they state that international organizations, unlike states, possess a weak internal legal order and that they are rarely accepted as parties to conventions and their non-member status does not imply unwillingness to be bound by the rules of a convention. None of these arguments is very convincing, as international organizations possess their own legal personality. HG Schermers and NM Blokker, *International Institutional Law. Unity within Diversity* (3rd edn, 1995) § 1574. The question can also be asked with a national constitutional outlook, focusing on national human rights protection against the acts of international organizations—a question that gained prominence with Security Council Resolutions 1267 (1999) and 1390 (2002) demanding the freezing of bank accounts in the fight against terror. C Walter, 'Grundrechtsschutz gegen Hoheitsakte internationaler Organisationen' (2004) 129 AÖR 39; G Biehler, 'Individuelle Sanktionen der Vereinten Nationen und Grundrechte' (2003) 41 AVR 169; *Lenzing AG v United Kingdom* (App 38817/97) (1998) 94-A DR 136; Court of First Instance of the European Communities, Case T-184/95 *Dorsch Consult Ingenieurgesellschaft mbH v Council of the European Union* [1998] ECR II-667 [74].

[156] *Reparation for Injuries Suffered in the Service of the United Nations*, Advisory Opinion, ICJ Reports 1949, 174, 178 ff (11 April 1949); Epping in Ipsen (n 16 above) 71 ff. States acting within international organizations of course remain bound by their human rights obligations. Hörmann in M Hilf and S Oeter (eds), *WTO-Recht. Rechtsordnung des Welthandels* (2005) 652.

[157] *Contra* HG Schermers, 'The Legal Bases of international Organization Action' in R-J Dupuy (ed), *A Handbook on International Organizations* (2nd edn, 1998) 401, 403. Schermers argues that international organizations are also bound by treaties to which all its member states were parties at the time of the creation of the organization—*nemo plus iuris transferre potest quam ipse habet*. The argument is unconvincing for several reasons: first of all, the organization has its own personality, hence it has its own obligations. Secondly, states are free to modify their treaty obligations and are free to do so by setting up an international organization. Thirdly, rather than simply assuming the organization to be bound by treaties it has not signed it is preferable to conceive the organization as not bound, but the state as being in violation of its own treaty obligations for setting up the organization.

[158] On the reluctance of international organizations to sign human rights instruments, often also spurred by the sentiment that they lack the relevant competence: K Wellens, *Remedies against International Organisations* (2002) 15.

[159] Schermers and Blocker (n 155 above) § 1579; Schermers (n 157 above) 402; M Bedjaoui, 'Du Contrôle de Légalité des Actes du Conseil de Sécurité' in *Nouveaux Itinéraires en Droit. Hommage à François Rigaux* (1993) 69, 82 ff; M Bothe, 'Le Droit de la Guerre et les Nations Unies.

explicitly and implicitly contract out of obligations under general international law. As Koskenniemi states in his study on fragmentation of international law for the ILC:

there is little doubt that most international law (...) is dispositive and that contracting out by establishing a regime is possible and limited only to the extent that such limitation may be received from the *jus cogens* nature or otherwise compelling character of general law.[160]

Pauwelyn, in his work on conflict of norms in public international law, comes to much the same conclusion.[161]

The WTO Agreements are conspicuously silent on human rights law. Even though the preamble to the WTO Agreement recognizes that trade relations 'should be conducted with a view to raising standards of living, ensuring full employment and a large and steadily growing volume of real income' and acknowledges the need to secure the developing countries' share in economic growth, it falls short of mentioning human rights as such. The TRIPS Agreement goes a step further and mentions 'the transfer and dissemination of technology, to the mutual advantage of producers and users of technological knowledge and in a manner conducive to social and economic welfare, and to a balance of rights and obligations' as one of its objectives.[162] It goes on to state that:

Members may, in formulating or amending their laws and regulations, adopt measures necessary to protect public health and nutrition, and to promote the public interest in sectors of vital importance to their socio-economic and technological development, provided that such measures are consistent with the provisions of this Agreement.[163]

The WTO Agreement and its Annexes do not go beyond such erratic references to concerns of relevance to human rights.[164] Nowhere do they mention human rights law explicitly, nowhere do they explicitly contract out of general international law standards of human rights. As such, the WTO is therefore bound by general international law standards of human rights to the extent that WTO law is not contradicting them, implicitly contracting out of them. In case

A Propos des Incidents Armés au Congo' in *Etudes et Travaux de l'Institut Universitaire de Hautes Etudes Internationales, No 5* (1967) 135, 188. In one of the few more thorough studies of the issue Bleckmann disagrees, arguing that international organizations did not participate in the formation of customary international law. However, he potentially wants to apply customary international law to international organizations via an analogy. A Bleckmann, 'Zur Verbindlichkeit des allgemeinen Völkerrechts für internationale Organisationen' (1977) 37 ZaöRV 107 ff; on privileges and immunities of international organizations, see I Scobbie, 'International Organizations and International Relations' in R-J Dupuy (ed), *A Handbook on International Organizations* (2nd edn, 1998) 831 ff; CF Amerasinghe, *Principles of the Institutional Law of International Organizations* (1996) 397 ff.

[160] M Koskenniemi, *Fragmentation of International Law: Difficulties Arising from the Diversification and Expansion of International Law*, ILC(LVI)/SG/FIL/CRD.1/Add.1 (4 May 2004).
[161] Pauwelyn (n 11 above) 200 ff.   [162] Article 7 of the TRIPS Agreement.
[163] Article 8.1 of the TRIPS Agreement.
[164] R Howse and M Mutua, *Protecting Human Rights in a Global Economy. Challenges for the World Trade Organization* (2000).

of a contradiction the WTO remains bound by human rights standards where those have acquired the status of *jus cogens*.

V Conventions

I now turn to the protection of access to medicine under international law. The sources of international law are habitually enumerated along the lines of Article 38 of the Statute of the International Court of Justice. Article 38(1)(a) of the Statute lists as the first source of law 'international conventions, whether general or particular, establishing rules expressly recognized by the contesting states'.

1 ICESCR

With 154 State Parties as of September 2006 the ICESCR is the most widely adopted convention on economic, social, and cultural rights. Of 145 eligible WTO Members that are states[165] only 22 have not ratified the Covenant—among these are the United States of America and South Africa, even though both are signatories to the ICESCR, which obliges them to refrain from acts which would defeat the object and purpose of the treaty according to Article 18(a) of the Vienna Convention. Eighty-five per cent of the WTO Members are thus bound by the ICESCR.

A Access to Medicine as Part of the Right to Health

Access to medicine is protected by the ICESCR as an integral part of the right to health contained in Article 12 of ICESCR, which reads:

(1) The States Parties to the present Covenant recognize the right of everyone to the enjoyment of the highest attainable standard of physical and mental health.
(2) The steps to be taken by the State Parties to the present Covenant to achieve the full realization of this right shall include those necessary for:
    (a) The provision for the reduction of the stillbirth-rate and of infant mortality and for the healthy development of the child;
    (b) The improvement of all aspects of environmental and industrial hygiene;
    (c) The prevention, treatment and control of epidemic, endemic, occupational and other diseases;
    (d) The creation of conditions which would assure to all medical service and medical attention in the event of sickness.

The duties that the rights of the Covenant impose on States Parties are put down in Article 2(1) of the ICESCR:

Each State Party to the present Covenant undertakes to take steps, individually and through international assistance and co-operation, especially economic and technical, to

---

[165] The European Communities, Hong Kong, Macau, and Chinese Taipei are WTO members, but not states.

the maximum of its available resources, with a view to achieving progressively the full realization of the rights recognized in the present Covenant by all appropriate means, including particularly the adoption of legislative measures.

It is appropriate to discuss the scope of the right as it relates to access to medicine first, bearing in mind that it shall be realized progressively, and to then turn to the obligations imposed on State Parties. To what extent patent legislation actually interferes with the right to health and whether such an interference is justified will be examined in the subsequent chapter.

a Content of the Right

In recent years the ICESCR's right to health has gone through a remarkable development. Although it contains a non-exclusive list of steps to be taken by States Parties in Article 12(2) of the ICESCR,[166] its scope seemed too large and vague to enable the right to have a major impact. State practice has since clarified its scope significantly. Drawing on this state practice[167] the Committee on Economic, Social and Cultural Rights drafted General Comment No 14 on the right to health which has had a significant impact on the further development of the right.[168]

The wording of the right as the 'right of everyone to the enjoyment of the highest attainable standard of physical and mental health' is extraordinarily broad, whether health is defined as the absence of disease or, following the definition of the WHO, as 'a state of complete physical, mental and social well-being (...)'.[169] However, it does not go so far as to grant a (purely utopian) right to be healthy:[170] only the highest 'attainable' standard of health, or, as the equally authentic French version puts it more clearly, the *'meilleur état de santé (...) qu'elle soit capable d'atteindre'* is protected—the highest standard of health that a person can reach according to its biological preconditions.[171] To enable a person to reach this standard of health the right has to protect both the socio-economic factors underlying a healthy life, such as food and housing[172] as well as health care, including

---

[166] Toebes (n 38 above) 293; General Comment No 14 (n 117 above) para 7.

[167] '[B]ased on the Committee's experience in examining State parties' reports over many years'. General Comment No 14 (n 117 above).

[168] General Comment No 14 (n 117 above) para 6.

[169] J Montgomery, 'Recognising a Right to Health' in R Beddard and DM Hill (eds), *Economic, Social and Cultural Rights. Progress and Achievement* (1992) 184, 186–187; HD Roscam Abbing, *International Organizations in Europe and the Right to Health Care* (1979) 70 ff.

[170] General Comment No 14 (n 117 above) para 8.

[171] There has been some debate as to whether 'attainable' refers to the available resources of the state. Toebes (n 38 above) 45–46. General Comment No 14 (n 117 above) para 9 opines that 'attainable' includes both limitations. Given the clear wording of the French version, the better view is that the reference to state resources is introduced by Art 2 of the ICESCR. In practice the debate is irrelevant as both limitations are indubitably imposed by the Covenant.

[172] The interpretation is confirmed by the drafting history. General Comment No 14 (n 117 above) para 4. P Hunt, *Economic, Social and Cultural Rights. The Right of Everyone to the Enjoyment of the Highest Attainable Standards of Physical and Mental Health. Report of the Special Rapporteur, Paul Hunt, Submitted in Accordance with Commission Resolution 2002/31*, E/CN.4/2003/58, para 23 (13 February 2003); AR Chapman, 'Monitoring Women's Right to Health under the International Covenant on Economic, Social and Cultural Rights' (1994–1995) 44 Am U L Rev 1157, 1166.

medicine. The right is thus interdependent with other socio-economic rights and, where diseases are life-threatening, closely connected to the right to life.[173]

Article 12(2) of the ICESCR illustrates how medication comes into play. It states that steps to be taken by States Parties to achieve the right to health include those necessary for 'the prevention, treatment and control of epidemic, endemic, occupational and other diseases' and for 'the creation of conditions which would assure to all medical service and medical attention in the event of sickness'. In early medical science drugs played only a marginal role in the treatment of diseases. Nowadays, however, prevention, treatment, and control of most diseases rely on medicine as an integral, vital, indispensable part of the therapy. Treatment of serious infections without antibiotics, of fungal infections without antifungal agents, and increasingly, of viral infections without antiviral agents is unthinkable—it would constitute malpractice.[174] Hence, access to medicine is necessary for the prevention and treatment of most diseases as well as the control of communicable diseases. Medical service and medical attention in the event of sickness equally necessitate the provision of drugs.[175] They are now vital in enabling individuals to reach their 'highest attainable' standard of health and thus an integral part of the right to health, as affirmed in numerous resolutions.[176] The provision of medication, of course, has to be part of the provision of general health services and health facilities.

Adjudicatory bodies in several countries have had the opportunity to clarify that access to medicine is part of the right to health. For the South African Constitution this has been recognized by the Constitutional Court of South Africa in *Minister of Health v Treatment Action Campaign*, in which the court ordered the government to make nevirapine, a drug preventing mother-to-child transmission of HIV, more widely available.[177] The *Tribunal Supremo de Jusicia de Venezuela* held the same under the Venezuelan Constitution in *Cruz Bermúdez v Ministerio de Sanidad y Asistencia Social*, in which it required the government to

---

[173] This relationship is stressed in the jurisprudence of the Corte Constitucional of Colombia that holds economic, social, and cultural rights only enforceable where they are connected to rights such as the right to life or the inviolability of the body: 'Los derechos económicos, sociales o culturales se tornan en fundamentales cuando su desconocimiento pone en peligro derechos de rango fundamental o genera la violación de éstos, conformándose una unidad que reclama protección íntegra, pues las circunstancias fácticas impiden que se separen ámbitos de protección.' Corte Constitucional de Colombia, *Alejandro Moreno Alvarez v Ministerio de Salud* SU.819/99 (1999); Corte Constitucional de Colombia, *Alonso Muñoz Ceballos v Instituto de los Seguros Sociales* T-484–92 (1992).

[174] J Drews, *In Quest of Tomorrow's Medicines. An Eminent Scientist Talks About the Pharmaceutical Industry, Biotechnology, and the Future of Drug Research* (trans D Kramer, 1999) 3 ff.

[175] General Comment No 14 (n 117 above) 17.

[176] Eg *Declaration of Commitment on HIV/AIDS*, GA Res S-26/2 (27 June 2001), UN Doc A/RES/S-26/2 (2001) para 15; *Access to Medication in the Context of Pandemics such as HIV/AIDS, Tuberculosis and Malaria*, Commission on Human Rights Res 2004/26 (16 April 2004) para 1; *Access to Medication in the Context of Pandemics such as HIV/AIDS*, Commission on Human Rights Res 2001/33 (23 April 2001) para 1.

[177] *Minister of Health et al v Treatment Action Campaign et al* 2002 (5) SA 721 (CC); 2002 (10) BCLR 1033 (CC) (5 July 2002).

provide antiretroviral treatment to all HIV-infected patients in Venezuela.[178] The Inter-American Commission on Human Rights has decided to tackle access to medicine in *Jorge Odir Miranda Cortez v El Salvador*, in which the HIV-positive petitioners allege a violation of the right to health, as the government has not provided them with the necessary triple therapy. Even though the Commission found itself not competent *ratione materiae* to examine a violation of the right to health itself, which is contained in Article 10 of the Additional Protocol to the American Convention on Human Rights in the Area of Economic, Social and Cultural Rights (Protocol of San Salvador),[179] it decided that it could consider the Protocol in the interpretation of the provisions of the American Convention on Human Rights and declared the case admissible for alleged violations of, amongst others, social and cultural rights under Article 26 of the American Convention on Human Rights.[180]

Conceptually, access to medicine contains four elements, as stated in General Comment No 14: (a) the availability of the medication in sufficient quantity; (b) the accessibility of the medication to everybody; (c) the acceptability of the treatment with respect to the culture and ethics of the individual; and (d) an appropriate quality of the medication. Accessibility includes physical accessibility, eg the patient cannot be required to travel long distances, accessibility of information about the medication, economic accessibility of the medication, and accessibility of the medication without discrimination.[181] Economic accessibility is of particular importance for this study, as it deals with the issue of drug pricing. General Comment No 14 specifies:

health facilities, goods and services must be affordable for all (...) ensuring that these services, whether privately or publicly provided, are affordable for all, including socially disadvantaged groups. Equity demands that poorer households should not be disproportionately burdened with health expenses as compared to richer households.[182]

These four elements of access to medicine can, at times, come into conflict. Thus, the requirement of an appropriate quality of drugs can hamper the accessibility and availability of the medicine. Most countries require a drug to be approved before it can be brought to the market. The agency responsible for approving the drug, in the United States the Food and Drug Administration

---

[178] Tribunal Supremo de Justicia de Venezuela, *Cruz Bermúdez v Ministerio de Sanidad y Asistencia Social*, Case No 15.789, Decision No 916 (1999). MA Torres, 'The Human Right to Health, National Courts, and Access to HIV/AIDS Treatment: A Case Study from Venezuela' (2002) 3 Chi J Int'l L 105.

[179] Article 19(6) of the Protocol of San Salvador allows individual petitions only for violations of Art 8(a) and Art 13 of the Protocol.

[180] *Jorge Odir Miranda Cortez et al v El Salvador*, Inter-American Commission on Human Rights Report No 29/01. Case 12.249, paras 35 ff, 49 (7 March 2001).

[181] General Comment No 14 (n 117 above) para 12; AE Yamin, 'Not just a Tragedy: Access to Medications as a Right under International Law' (2003) 21 BU Int'l L J 325.

[182] General Comment No 14 (n 117 above) 12.

(FDA), generally requires a demonstration that the drug is both safe and effective.[183] The trials necessary to support such a finding are lengthy and expensive and the availability of the drug during the trials is severely limited. The trials also raise the cost of the drug, as the manufacturer will have to offset the trial costs. The length of the drug trials was highly criticized by AIDS activists during the early AIDS medication trials.[184] Apart from the potential for a real conflict between the components there is also the danger that safety concerns are abused as an argument to curtail accessibility of drugs (eg to favour the innovative pharmaceutical industry).[185]

Health as a human right would lose its contours and its purpose if it protected access to all pharmaceuticals. General Comment No 14 rightly quotes only 'essential drugs' as included within the scope of the right.[186] The WHO maintains a regularly updated list of essential drugs,[187] defined as:

those that satisfy the priority health care needs of the population. They are selected with due regard to public health relevance, evidence on efficacy and safety, and comparative cost effectiveness. (...) The implementation of the concept of essential medicines is intended to be flexible and adaptable to many different situations; exactly which medicines are regarded as essential remains a national responsibility.[188]

Based on its experience with state practice the Committee on Economic, Social and Cultural Rights is of the view that 'a minimum core obligation to ensure the satisfaction of, at the very least, minimum essential levels of each of the rights is

---

[183] For a description of the FDA process see GM Levitt, JN Czaban, and AS Paterson, 'Human Drug Regulation' in DG Adams, RM Cooper, and JS Kahan (eds), *Fundamentals of Law and Regulation. Volume II. An in-depth look at therapeutic products* (1997) 159.

[184] MM Dunbar, 'Shaking up the Status Quo: How AIDS Activists Have Challenged Drug Development and Approval Procedures' (1991) 46 Food Drug Cosm L J 673; MC Lovell, 'Second Thoughts: Do the FDA's Responses to a Fatal Drug Trial and the AIDS Activist Community's Doubts about Early Access to Drugs Hint at a Shift in Basic FDA Policy?' (1996) 51 Food & Drug L J 273.

[185] The point is illustrated by the discussion about President Bush's 'Emergency Plan for AIDS Relief', which restricted spending to FDA approved drugs—ie initially to brand-name drugs. It was repeatedly criticized for the approach and then established an expedited review procedure with the FDA to approve cheap generic fixed-dosed combinations of antiretroviral medicine. In January 2005 the FDA used such a fast-track procedure to approve a triple drug combination produced by Aspen for marketing outside of the United States only. United States Leadership Against HIV/AIDS, Tuberculosis, and Malaria Act of 2003, Pub L 108–25, 117 Stat 711 (27 May 2003); Office of the United States Global AIDS Coordinator (ed), *The President's Emergency Plan for AIDS Relief, U.S. Five-Year Global HIV/AIDS Strategy* (2004); S Lueck, 'White House Gets Pressure on AIDS Plan—Activists, Drug Firms Duel Over Use of Funds For Generic Combination Drugs in Africa' *Wall Street Journal* (25 March 2004); 'Botswana Conference Sparks Debate on Generics' *Bridges Weekly Trade Digest* (31 March 2004); S Lueck, 'White House Aims To Answer Critics Of Its AIDS Fight' *Wall Street Journal* (29 April 2004); DG McNeil, Jr, 'A Path to Cheaper AIDS Drugs for Poor Nations' *NY Times* (26 January 2005). Note that the United States has not ratified the ICESCR and therefore is not bound by it.

[186] General Comment No 14 (n 117 above) para 12(a), 34 (additionally including contraceptives). *Contra* Yamin (n 181 above) 360.

[187] WHO (ed), *Essential Medicines. WHO Model List* (14th edn, 2005).

[188] WHO (ed), *Essential Drugs and Medicines Policy*, at <http://www.who.int/countries/eth/areas/medicines/en/>.

incumbent upon every State party'.[189] The concept is of particular significance when it comes to justifying non-compliance with the right with a lack of financial means as will be shown below. In the domain of access to medicine the Committee considers the provision of essential drugs as defined under the WHO Action Programme on Essential Drugs as well as ensuring access to the drugs on a non-discriminatory basis, especially for vulnerable or marginalized groups as part of these minimum core obligations. The same is true for the adoption and implementation of a national public health strategy and plan of action.[190] The Constitutional Court of South Africa declined to follow the concept of a core content, stating that it simply does not have the data and the experience for determining its scope.[191] The situation is different on the international level, as the Committee profits from its long-standing experience in the examination of state reports.

It should be noted that an effective health policy controls the diseases of the day and attempts to meet the challenges of the future, ie it also includes research.[192] This aspect of the right could provide a basis for arguing that patents are furthering access to medicine, an argument that will be explored in depth in the next chapter.

b Duties imposed on States Parties

It would be illusory to require a state to realize the full extent of the right to health immediately. The Covenant regulates state obligations in its Article 2(1).[193] These obligations are not modified by Article 12(1) of the ICESCR, which provides that States Parties are to 'recognize' the right, rather than stating that 'everyone

---

[189] General Comment No 3 (n 101 above) para 10. On the concept: P Alston, 'Out of the Abyss: The Challenges of Confronting the New UN Committee on Economic, Social and Cultural Rights' (1987) 9 Hum Rts Q 331, 352 ff; E Örücü, 'The Core of Rights and Freedoms: The Limit of Limits' in T Campbell *et al* (eds), *Human Rights: From Rhetoric to Reality* (1986) 37, 45 (referring to the German concept of *Wesensgehalt*).

[190] General Comment No 14 (n 117 above) para 44 (a), (d), (f); Rott (n 117 above) 97.

[191] *Government of the Republic of South Africa and Others v Grootboom and Others* 2001 (1) SA 46 (CC); 2000 (11) BCLR 1169 (CC) para 32 (judgment of 4 October 2000). For criticism DM Chirwa, '*Minister of Health and Others v Treatment Action Campaign and Others*: Its Implications for the Combat against HIV/AIDS and the Protection of Economic, Social and Cultural Rights in Africa' (2003) 9 E Afr J Peace & Hum Rts 174, 187–188.

[192] General Comment No 14 (n 117 above) para 36.

[193] General Comment No 3 (n 101 above) para 9. The duty of progressive realization is at times called an 'obligation of result', requiring states to bring about a result leaving them the choice of means to be distinguished from an obligation of conduct, requiring the performance or omission of a specific determined action. The distinction stems from the International Law Commission's work on State Responsibility: R Ago, 'Sixth Report on State Responsibility' YBILC, II (1977) 3, 8 ff (Art 20). The present author agrees with Dupuy's criticism in P-M Dupuy, 'Reviewing the Difficulties of Codification: On Ago's Classification of Obligations of Means and Obligations of Result in Relation to State Responsibility' (1999) 10 EJIL 371, 375 ff that the distinction is both confusing and unnecessary. As it does not add analytical clarity to the study of human rights, the distinction will not be discussed any further. See also P-M Dupuy, 'The Duty to Protect and to Ensure Human Rights under the International Covenant on Civil and Political Rights—Comment on the Paper by Eckart Klein' in E Klein (ed), *The Duty to Protect and to Ensure Human Rights. Colloquium Potsdam, 1–3 July 1999*, (2000) 391, 321–322.

has' the right. Even though the wording was consciously adopted because it is weaker,[194] for all intents and purposes the difference is naught. 'Recognize' is defined as 'acknowledge the existence, validity, character, or claims of'.[195] A state that acknowledges the right of everyone to health must guarantee the right.

Even though Article 2(1) of the ICESCR provides only for 'achieving progressively the full realization of the rights' in the Covenant, the wording clearly imposes obligations with immediate effect,[196] most significantly the obligation to take steps to the maximum of a State Party's available resources and, in Article 2(2) of the ICESCR the principle of non-discrimination. Read in the light of the purpose of the Covenant, the full realization of the rights, the 'obligation to take steps' means that States Parties have to establish a reasonable action programme towards the full realization of the rights and to start its implementation within a reasonably short time.[197] States have to employ all appropriate means to realize the right, including, but not limited to, legislative measures. The provision leaves the choice of means to the states,[198] but indicates that the rights are relevant for all levels of state action, be it the drafting of health policies, the negotiation of trade agreements, the drafting of a law on social security, or adjudication. Violations can occur through commission (including the repeal or the adoption of legislation) or omission (eg the failure to adopt a national health policy).[199]

To describe states' human rights obligations in more detail it has become habitual to refer to Eide's typology of obligations: the obligations to respect, protect, and to fulfil a right.[200] I will describe these obligations and then turn to the question to what extent a State Party can excuse its poor performance in realizing the right to access to medicine by appealing to the limitation of its obligation by the 'maximum of its available resources'.

aa Obligation to Respect   The duty to respect obligates a state to refrain from interfering with a right and to abstain from discriminatory practices.[201] In the

---

[194] Toebes (n 38 above) 293.

[195] D Thompson (ed), *The Concise Oxford Dictionary of Current English* (9th edn, 1995).

[196] International Commission of Jurists *et al*, *The Limburg Principles on the Implementation of the International Covenant on Economic, Social and Cultural Rights*, UN Doc E/CN.4/1987/17, Annex, para 21 (2–6 June 1986).

[197] General Comment No 3 (n 101 above) paras 1–2; General Comment No 14 (n 117 above) para 30. Simma and von Bennigsen (n 69 above) 1489. Drafting national AIDS programmes was an important part of the programme set up by the WHO's first resolution on AIDS: *Global Strategy for the Prevention and Control of AIDS*, WHA Res 40.26 (5 May 1987); G Behrman, *The Invisible People. How the U.S. Has Slept through the Global AIDS Pandemic, the Greatest Humanitarian Catastrophe of Our Time* (2004) 44–45.   [198] General Comment No 3 (n 101 above) para 4.

[199] General Comment No 14 (n 117 above) para 48.

[200] Eide (n 92 above) paras 66 ff; Koch (n 86 above) 32; General Comment No 14 (n 117 above) para 33. The African Commission additionally assumes an obligation to promote, *Social and Economic Rights Action Centre and the Centre for Economic and Social Rights v Nigeria* (n 114 above). The different existing typologies have been studied in-depth by Sepúlveda, *The Nature of the Obligations under the International Covenant on Economic, Social and Cultural Rights* (2003) 157 ff. The tripartite typology was originally proposed with a different wording by H Shue, *Basic Rights: Subsistence, Affluence & U.S. Foreign Policy* (1980) 52.

[201] Article 2 (2) of the ICESCR; Yamin (n 181 above) 352 ff.

domain of access to medicine that means that a state has to refrain from denying or limiting equal access to essential medicine[202] and from action that interferes with access to medicine. It has been argued that the adoption of patent laws is an act by the state that raises drug prices and thus interferes with the economic accessibility of medicine, a possible violation of the obligation to respect the right.[203] This argument overlooks the fact that the vital action—raising prices—is not taken by the state itself, but by private companies. If the state itself raises drug prices, it indubitably interferes with economic accessibility of medicine and the obligation to respect comes into play. This is the case where, eg, countries impose tariffs on the import of pharmaceuticals, thus raising the prices.[204] If the state only creates the possibility for private parties to interfere with economic accessibility, the question imposes itself to what extent a state is under a duty to prevent private parties from interfering with the right, which is not part of the obligation to respect.

bb Obligation to Protect The obligation to protect requires States Parties to prevent third parties from interfering with the right. General Comment No 14 states that this obligation includes:

inter alia, the duties of States to adopt legislation or to take other measures ensuring equal access to health care and health-related services provided by third parties; to ensure that privatization of the health sector does not constitute a threat to the availability, accessibility, acceptability and quality of health facilities, goods and services; to control the marketing of medical equipment and medicines by third parties (...)[205]

With the increasing privatization of the health care sector the duty to protect plays a key role in the achievement of the right to health. If anything, the importance of the obligation to protect is even greater for access to medicines, as pharmaceuticals are almost entirely manufactured and marketed by the private sector. Given that accessibility and particularly economic accessibility is part of the right to health, the state is under an obligation to make sure that pharmaceutical manufacturers do not limit the accessibility of essential drugs. High prices limit the economic accessibility of the drugs where the patients have to bear the cost. Where a state acquires the drugs for the patients or contributes to a comprehensive health insurance system that provides the drugs to all patients who need them, high prices do not limit economic accessibility—after all the drugs are free for the individual. However, even highly industrialized countries find it increasingly difficult to finance such a system. The policy option is not available at all for poor states. They have no choice but to ensure that prices are adequate, eg by enforcing their

---

[202] General Comment No 14 (n 117 above) para 34.   [203] Yamin (n 181 above) 353 ff.

[204] HE Bale, Jr, 'Consumption and Trade in Off-Patented Medicines' CMH Working Paper Series Paper No WG4: (2001) 3, 10, 20 ff.

[205] General Comment No 14 (n 117 above) para 35; BC Alexander, 'Lack of Access to HIV/AIDS Drugs in Developing Countries: Is There a Violation of the International Human Rights (sic) to Health?' (2001) 8 No 3 Hum Rts Brief 12.

competition rules on the trans-national corporations that produce and then import the drugs into their territory and, if patents have an impact on drug prices, by constructing their patent system in a way that it does not result in excessive pricing.[206]

cc Obligation to Fulfil   The duty to fulfil requires appropriate measures including legislative, administrative, and budgetary ones to work towards the full realization of the right.[207] The right to health has to be given sufficient recognition in the national political and legal system and State Parties have to adopt a national health policy. The provision of a public, private, or mixed health insurance system affordable for all is part of the duty, as is the provision of health information.[208] In the area of medicines states have to provide information on available pharmaceutical treatment for diseases such as HIV/AIDS and they have to adopt a pharmaceutical policy, including a policy on generics.[209] But the duty to fulfil demands further positive measures to be taken, [210] such as the assistance to indigents by providing them with essential medicine. Developed countries are often in a position to even provide essential drugs by buying them from the manufacturer themselves. Even though the focus of this study is on the prices of drugs, it needs to be mentioned that drug prices are only part of the bill a country has to foot: the cost of distributing the drug is often significantly higher than that of the drug itself.[211] Indubitably, the obligation to fulfil entails severe budgetary implications and will therefore quite often be limited by budgetary constraints.

dd Justifying Non-Compliance with Lack of Financial Means   Economic, social, and cultural rights often require budgetary measures by states. But financial resources are limited. The ICESCR takes account of this fact in that States Parties only undertook to take steps towards the full realization of the rights 'to the maximum' of their available resources. Non-compliance with the obligations under the Covenant can thus be excused by a lack of resources. The Committee on Economic, Social and Cultural Rights has specified this standard further with respect to retrogressive measures and core obligations. Where states adopt retrogressive measures, ie measures reducing an already achieved standard of protection of the rights, the state carries the burden of proving that the measures are justified by reference to the totality of the rights provided for in the Covenant in the context of the full use of the State Party's maximum available resources.[212] A State Party that does not comply with the core obligations, including access to essential medicine, is prima facie violating the ICESCR. To justify its non-compliance the State must 'demonstrate that every effort has been made to use all resources that

---

[206] General Comment No 17 (n 55 above) para 35.
[207] Koch (n 86 above) 32; General Comment No 14 (n 117 above) para 33.
[208] General Comment No 14 (n 117 above) para 36.   [209] Yamin (n 181 above) 358–359.
[210] Koch (n 86 above) 32.   [211] Bale (n 204 above) 9.
[212] General Comment No 3 (n 101 above) para 9; General Comment No 14 (n 117 above) para 30.

are at its disposition in an effort to satisfy, as a matter of priority, those minimum obligations'. Even where non-compliance is excused, States Parties have to continue to strive to realize the right, monitor their progress, and protect the vulnerable members of society.[213] General Comment No 14 goes beyond this standard and does not allow a State to justify non-compliance with the core obligations at all.[214] Sadly, however, some developing countries lack the resources to even provide a bare minimum of medical services. Rather than demand the impossible the minimum core concept should be understood as requiring a heightened burden of proof that the state has committed all its available resources.[215]

How states implement the right to access to medicine, eg by financing a general health insurance, by providing the drugs at the government's expense in hospitals, or by trying to reduce the prices of the drugs, is, as far as the right to health is concerned, left to their discretion. Where resources are relevant and the prioritization of resources is at issue, some deference should be given to the decisions of the administration. However, the reasonableness of those decisions should be controlled. Two cases of the Constitutional Court of South Africa properly demonstrate how such a control can be operationalized.

In 1997 the Court had to answer to the request of an indigent diabetic in an irreversible condition and ineligible for a kidney transplant, whose life could be prolonged by regular renal dialysis. He had been refused access to dialysis, because treatment was reserved for patients whose conditions could be remedied or patients eligible for a kidney transplant. The Department of Health had already overspent its budget and the dialysis machines were stretched beyond their capacity by handling the patients eligible for treatment according to the guidelines. Admitting the significant number of people in the situation of the diabetic would have made substantial inroads in the health budget, already burdened by South Africa's HIV/AIDS crisis. The Court upheld the health policies of the state in the name of the larger needs of society and thus denied the request for access to regular renal dialysis.[216]

Five years later the Court had to examine an aspect of South Africa's response to the HIV/AIDS pandemic. The government had restricted the provision of nevirapine, a drug preventing mother-to-child transmission of HIV, to pilot sites, which could offer additional services such as substitution of bottle-feeding for breastfeeding at the option of the mothers. The drug was unavailable for women

---

[213] General Comment No 3 (n 101 above) paras 10 ff.
[214] General Comment No 14 (n 117 above) para 47.
[215] The South African Supreme Court regards the full realization of the core obligations as impossible, *Minister of Health et al v Treatment Action Campaign et al* 2002 (5) SA 721 (CC); 2002 (10) BCLR 1033 (CC) para 35 (judgment of 5 July 2002). Note the interpretation in P Alston and G Quinn, 'The Nature and Scope of States Parties' Obligations under the International Covenant on Economic, Social and Cultural Rights' (1987) 9 Human Rights Quarterly 156, 181 that is somewhat more lenient (entitling a plea to resource scarcity to some deference, but allowing 'some sort of objective scrutiny').
[216] *Soobramoney v Minister of Health, KwaZulu-Natal* 1998 (1) SA 765 (CC); 1997 (12) BCLR 1696 (CC) (27 November 1997).

without access to either private health care or the public pilot sites, albeit their doctors regarded the treatment as indicated. The government argued that it wanted to evaluate the safety and efficiency of the drug as well as the provision of formula-feed along with nevirapine. Costs of the drug itself were not an issue, as the manufacturer had offered it to the government for free for a period of five years. It was demonstrated that administering nevirapine without substituting breast-feeding would save a significant number of infants, but some infants would acquire HIV through breastmilk. The Court ruled that the reasons given by the government did not justify the restrictions of the programme and that the drug should be available where there is the capacity to administer it and its use is medically indicated. The government was ordered to train counsellors and extend testing and counselling facilities to facilitate the use of nevirapine.[217]

The latter case shows the limits of administrative discretion: where the right to health can be realized to a greater extent without committing resources it is unreasonable not to do so. This holding is of particular importance for the question of patent legislation. Where states are financially unable to provide medicine for their population they have to guarantee economic accessibility by other means, eg by strictly enforcing their competition laws or—if patents influence prices—by changing their patent legislation. As these options do not require significant financial resources, states cannot evade their obligation by pleading a lack of resources.

B Enjoyment of the Benefits of Scientific Progress

A further argument in support of access to medicine can be drawn from Article 15(1)(b) of the ICESCR, which reads:

(1) The States Parties to the present Covenant recognize the right of everyone:
    (. . .)
    (b) To enjoy the benefits of scientific progress and its applications;
    (. . .)
(2) The steps to be taken by the States Parties to the present Covenant to achieve the full realization of this right shall include those necessary for the conservation, the development and the diffusion of science and culture. (. . .)

New drugs are part of 'scientific progress' and Article 15 grants everyone the right to enjoy the benefits of this progress and its applications, emphasized by paragraph 2's reference to States Parties' obligation to take the steps necessary for the 'diffusion', ie spreading of science. However, as the right does not add anything beyond the scope of Article 12, it does not need to be discussed in more detail.

2 The WHO

The World Health Organization is an international organization, membership of which is open to all states[218] and territories not responsible for the conduct of their

---

[217] *Minister of Health et al v Treatment Action Campaign et al* 2002 (5) SA 721 (CC); 2002 (10) BCLR 1033 (CC) (5 July 2002).   [218] Article 3 of the WHO Constitution.

international relations. The latter have the status of associate members.[219] The WHO currently boasts 192 member states, including all of the WTO Members that are states but Liechtenstein.

The WHO Constitution was the first international legal document to mention the right to health. The preamble states that:

The enjoyment of the highest attainable standard of health is one of the fundamental rights of every human being without distinction of race, religion, political belief, economic or social condition.

The health of all peoples is fundamental to the attainment of peace and security and is dependent upon the fullest cooperation of individuals and States.

The achievement of any State in the promotion and protection of health is a value to all.

The preamble also adopted a new definition of health that went far beyond the previously held understanding that health is the absence of disease:[220]

Health is a state of complete physical, mental and social well-being and not merely the absence of disease or infirmity.[221]

It has been alleged that the WHO preamble is one of the sources of a binding right to health.[222] The contributions to the discussion that do so usually list the sources of the right to health such as the ICESCR and the WHO preamble and then proceeded to discuss its content. This faulty methodological approach glosses over the differences in the scope of the rights granted under various instruments. Indeed, the WHO preamble should not be listed as a source of the right to health at all, as it is not legally binding: preambles of international agreements set forth the motives of the parties as well as the object and purpose of the treaty. They serve as 'context' for the purposes of treaty interpretation[223] and do not create any legal commitment beyond the treaty's operative part.[224] It is in this context that the WHO Constitution's right to health was referred to in the ICJ's Advisory Opinion on the *Legality of the Use by a State of Nuclear Weapons in Armed Conflict*

---

[219] Article 8 of the WHO Constitution. Y Beigbeder, *The World Health Organization* (1998) 31.

[220] M Vierheilig, *Die rechtliche Einordnung der von der Weltgesundheitsorganisation beschlossenen regulations* (1984) 14.   [221] Preamble WHO Constitution.

[222] Toebes (n 38 above) 33 ('The Constitution of the WHO is therefore binding upon States that are a party to the WHO. States parties will accordingly have to comply with the right to health as set forth in the preamble to the WHO Constitution.'). Shah (n 82 above) 453; A Gupta, *Patent Rights for Pharmaceuticals: TRIPS and the Right to Health at Crossroads*, at <http://users.ox.ac.uk/~edip/gupta.pdf>.

[223] JA Corriente Cordoba, *Valoración jurídica de los preámbulos de los tratados internacionales* (1973) 21; A Maresca, *Il diritto dei trattati. La convenzione codificatrice di Vienna del 23 Maggio 1969* (1971) 355. The ICJ referred to a preamble for treaty interpretation, eg in *Case concerning Rights of Nationals of the United States of America in Morocco (France/United States of America)*, ICJ Report 1952, 176, 196 (27 August 1952).

[224] Treviranus (n 133 above); Daillier and Pellet (n 32 above) 131; C Rousseau, *Droit International Public. Tome I: Introduction et Sources* (1970) 87; I Seidl-Hohenveldern and G Loibl, *Das Recht der Internationalen Organisationen einschließlich der Supranationalen Gemeinschaften* (7th edn, 2000) 247; Aust (n 57 above) 336–337; *Contra* P You, *Le préambule des traités internationaux*, 140 (1941) ('*un engagement plus ou moins général inséré dans le préambule reste un engagement*').

when it interpreted the WHO's functions in the light of the object and purpose of the organization and held that its request for an advisory opinion was not within the scope of its activities in accordance with Article 96(2) of the UN Charter and hence inadmissible.[225] There is nothing in the operative part of the Constitution that would allow us to infer a right to health under the document. This limited legal relevance of the preamble's right to health explains why it received little attention in the drafting process of the Constitution.[226]

Even though it is conceivable that later state practice changes a treaty—indeed, states are free to modify a treaty in violation of its amendment procedures if the decision is taken unanimously[227]—this has not taken place. The World Health Assembly (WHA), one of the three principal bodies of the WHO[228] has adopted numerous resolutions mentioning and reaffirming the right to health,[229] but these resolutions are not legally binding[230] and did not establish a right to health

---

[225] *Legality of the Use by a State of Nuclear Weapons in Armed Conflict*, Advisory Opinion, ICJ Reports 1996, 66, paras 20 ff (8 July 1996).

[226] The right was not mentioned in any of the four proposals submitted to the Technical Preparatory Committee, even though, naturally, they stress the importance of health: *Proposals for the Establishment of an International Health Organization (United Kingdom)* E/H/PC/9 (20 March 1946), 1 Official Records of the World Health Organization 42 (1947); *Proposals for the Establishment of an International Health Organization (USA)* E/H/PC/6 (19 March 1946), 1 Official Records of the World Health Organization 46 (1947); *Proposal for an International Convention Establishing the International Health Organization (France)* E/H/PC/5 (19 March 1946), 1 Official Records of the World Health Organization 49 (1947); *Suggestions Relating to the Constitution of an International Health Organization (Yugoslavia)* E/H/PC/10 (20 March 1946), 1 Official Records of the World Health Organization 54 (1947). It was first included in a draft preamble by a four-member sub-committee of the Technical Preparatory Committee: *Draft of 'Preamble' to the Convention of the World Health Organization*, E/H/PC/W/2 (21 March 1946), 1 Official Records of the World Health Organization 61 (1947) and became part of the Technical Preparatory Committee's proposal after only minor changes. *Proposals for the Constitution of the World Health Organization*, 1 Official Records of the World Health Organization 69 (1947). Neither did the provision elicit debate during the International Health Conference. *Summary Report on Proceedings Minutes and Final Acts of the International Health Conference*, 2 Official Records of the World Health Organization 5 (1948); Abbing (n 169 above) 105–106 (stating that it is realistic to conclude that the objective was to express the need for adequate health measures for a dignified life).

[227] Seidl-Hohenveldern and Loibl (n 224 above) 234. On an international organization's power to adopt legal instruments: J Klabbers, *An Introduction to International Institutional Law* (2002) 197 ff; J Verhoeven, 'Les activités normatives et quasi normatives—élaboration, adoption, coordination' in R-J Dupuy (ed), *Manuel sur les organisations internationales* (2nd edn, 1998) 413 ff; M Diez de Velasco Vallejo, *Las Organizaciones Internacionales* (12th edn, 2002) 140 ff.

[228] Beigbeder (n 219 above) 31.

[229] Eg *Human Rights*, WHA Res 23.41 (21 May 1970) (reaffirming that the right to health is a fundamental human right). Note that the resolution merely requests the Director-General to affirm the WHO's willingness to draft a report on the health aspects of human rights and was consented to as the item 'Co-ordination with the United Nations, the specialized agencies and the International Atomic Energy Agency: Programme matters—Human Rights' (*Fifteenth Plenary Meeting. Thursday, 21 May 1970*, 185 Official Records of the World Health Organization 241 (1970)). See also para I Declaration of Alma-Ata (12 September 1978), in World Health Organization (ed), *From Alma-Ata to the year 2000. Reflections at the midpoint*, 1988 (the Declaration was adopted by the International Conference on Primary Health Care, convened by the WHO and UNICEF and attended by country, UN and NGO delegates, Beigbeder (n 219 above) 24).

[230] The WHA can adopt conventions, agreements (Art 19 f of the WHO Constitution), regulations (Art 21 f of the WHO Constitution) and recommendations (Art 23 of the WHO

under the Constitution. The question whether the constant reaffirmation of the right to health might have contributed to the establishment of the right under customary international law will be examined later on.

3 ICCPR

With an Optional Protocol providing for an individual communication procedure the ICCPR is one of the more potent human right conventions. By September 2006, it has been ratified by 157 nations, 106 of them also parties to the Optional Protocol. As with the ICESCR not all WTO Members that are states have ratified the ICCPR—19 states chose not to do so, among them China, Pakistan, and Singapore, with China having signed the convention.

Article 6(1) of the ICCPR contains the right to life in the following wording:

Every human being has the inherent right to life. This right shall be protected by law. No one shall be arbitrarily deprived of his life.

The obligations imposed on States Parties are laid out in some detail in Article 2 of the Covenant:

(1) Each State Party to the present Covenant undertakes to respect and to ensure to all individuals within its territory and subject to its jurisdiction the rights recognized in the present Covenant, without distinction of any kind, such as race, colour, sex (...).

(2) Where not already provided for by existing legislative or other measures, each State Party to the present Covenant undertakes to take the necessary steps, in accordance with its constitutional processes and with the provisions of the present Covenant, to adopt such legislative or other measures as may be necessary to give effect to the rights recognized in the present Covenant.

(3) Each State Party to the present Covenant undertakes:
   a) To ensure that any person whose rights or freedoms as herein recognized are violated shall have an effective remedy, notwithstanding that the violation has been committed by persons acting in an official capacity;
   b) To ensure that any person claiming such a remedy shall have his right thereto determined by competent judicial, administrative or legislative authorities, or by any other competent authority provided for by the legal system of the State, and to develop the possibilities of judicial remedy;
   c) To ensure that the competent authorities shall enforce such remedies when granted.

A Content of the Right

The right to life, the first substantive right granted by the ICCPR, is the quintessential fundamental human right, a prerequisite for the enjoyment of all other

Constitution). Its resolutions according to Art 23 of the WHO Constitution are not binding. M Vierheilig-Langlotz, 'WHO—World Health Organization' in R Wolfrum and C Philipp (eds), *United Nations: Law, Policies and Practice. New, Revised English Edition. Volume 2* (1995) 1425, 1426–1427; Beigbeder (n 219 above) 71 ff.

human rights.[231] The right is non-derogable, ie even in times of a public emergency threatening the life of the nation it may not be derogated from.[232] The significance of the right is also stressed by its wording: it is an 'inherent' right, a right that the individual 'has' originating in the *jus naturale*, not a right that it 'shall have'.[233] The importance of the right has led many commentators to categorize it as *jus cogens*,[234] a norm accepted and recognized by the international community of states as a whole as a norm from which no derogation is permitted.[235]

Does the 'right to life' include access to medicine? According to the traditional view such a broad reading of the right to life is unjustified, the right is limited to prohibiting the state from killing persons and imposing a duty to protect persons from murder. It does not guarantee an appropriate standard of living, food, housing, or medical care.[236] Textually, this view argues either with the last sentence of Article 6(1) of the ICCPR or with the fact that Article 6 protects the 'right to life' and not 'life'.[237] But a distinction between 'right to life' and 'life' is not only artificial, it also seems unclear why such a distinction should support a limitation of the right. Also, there is no plausible reason why the first sentence of Article 6(1) should not have a broader content than the provision's last sentence. There is no reason why a lack of food or medical services should be less significant for the right to life than insufficient penal laws on murder. To be effective, the right to life has to extend to the basic conditions of life, the components necessary for survival, even if that part of the right is to some extent coextensive with economic, social, and cultural rights.[238] This includes access to life-saving medicine, a scope that is somewhat narrower than access to medicine under the right to health. Such a broader reading has also been adopted by the Human Rights Committee,

---

[231] Human Rights Committee, General Comment No 6/16 (27 July 1982), para 1, MJ Bossuyt, *Guide to the 'Travaux Préparatoires' of the International Covenant on Civil and Political Rights*, 115 (1987); Dinstein (n 143 above) 114; Nowak (n 135 above) Art 6 para 1; Inter-American Court of Human Rights, *Villagrán Morales v Guatemala (Caso de los 'niños de la Calle')*, 1999 Inter-Am Ct HR (SerC) No 63, para 144 (19 December 1999); *Human Rights and Scientific and Technological Developments*, GA Res 37/189A (18 December 1982), UN GAOR, 37th Sess, Supp No 51, at 206, UN Doc A/37/51 (1982), paras 1, 6; E Klein, 'Bedeutung des Gewohnheitsrechts für den Menschenrechtsschutz' in E Klein (ed), *Menschenrechtsschutz durch Gewohnheitsrecht. Kolloquium 26.-28. September 2002 Potsdam* (2003) 11, 17.   [232] Article 4 of the ICCPR.

[233] Nowak (n 135 above) Art 6 para 2.

[234] BG Ramcharan, 'The Right to Life' (1983) 30 NILR 297, 307, 308, 311ff; R Higgins, 'Derogations under Human Rights Treaties' (1976–1977) 48 BYIL 281, 282; *Report of the Economic and Social Council. Protection of Human Rights in Chile*, UN Doc A/37/564, para 22 (1982).

[235] Article 53 of the Vienna Convention on the Law of Treaties.

[236] Dinstein (n 143 above) 115; F Przetacznik, 'The Right to Life as a Basic Human Right' (1976) 9 Hum Rts J 585, 586–587, 603; N Robinson, *The Universal Declaration of Human Rights* (1958) 106 (concerning the UDHR).

[237] For the European Convention on Human Rights: JES Fawcett, *The Application of the European Convention on Human Rights* (2nd edn, 1987) 37.

[238] Ramcharan (n 234 above) 305 ff; Yamin (n 181 above) 330 ff; B Gammie, 'Human Rights Implications of the Export of Banned Pesticides' (1994) 25 Seton Hall L Rev 558, 585.

which rejected the restrictive interpretation building on its experience in the examination of state reports:

it would be desirable for States parties to take all possible measures to reduce infant mortality and to increase life expectancy, especially in adopting measures to eliminate malnutrition and epidemics.[239]

The position that access to life-saving medicine is part of the right to life is further supported by a survey of the right to life in other documents. Thus, according to a concurring opinion of two judges of the Inter-American Court of Human Rights, the right to life under the American Convention on Human Rights includes the right to live with dignity.[240] The African Commission on Human and Peoples' Rights has adopted a broad interpretation of the right to life in *Social and Economic Rights Action Centre and the Centre for Economic and Social Rights v Nigeria*, citing, amongst others, destruction of farms on which the survival of the Ogonis depends as well as pollution and environmental degradation to such an extent that it made living in the territory 'a nightmare' as violations of the right to life.[241] The right to life under the ECHR is worded somewhat more narrowly and has generally been interpreted accordingly.[242] However, the European Commission of Human Rights explicitly did not rule on whether the right to life includes a positive duty to provide free medical services to indigents,[243] and did hold in the context of a vaccination scheme that states have to take appropriate steps to safeguard life.[244]

National courts, too, are embracing a broader approach, often explicitly ruling on the question of access to medicine. The right to life under the Indian Constitution has been held to include a right to livelihood and a right to live with human dignity. The protection of health has been adjudged to be among the minimum requirements of the thus understood right to life.[245] Access to life-saving

---

[239] General Comment No 6/16 (n 231 above) para 5.

[240] Inter-American Court of Human Rights, *Villagrán Morales v Guatemala (Caso de los 'niños de la Calle')*, 1999 Inter-Am Ct HR (SerC) No 63, Voto Concurrente Conjunto de los jueces A A Cançado Trindade y A Abreu Burelli, para 4 (19 November 1999). *Contra* Yamin (n 181 above) 334 the case *Jorge Odir Miranda v El Salvador* (n 180 above) cannot be cited in support of the proposition here advanced, as it explicitly left the question of the admissibility with respect to the right to life open.

[241] *Social and Economic Rights Action Centre and the Centre for Economic and Social Rights v Nigeria* (n 114 above) para 67.

[242] C Grabenwarter, *Europäische Menschenrechtskonvention* (2003) 147 ff; P van Dijk and GJH van Hoof, *Theory and Practice of the European Convention on Human Rights* (3rd edn, 1998) 296 ff; T Opsahl, 'The Right to Life' in RSJ Macdonald, F Matscher, and H Petzold (eds), *The European System for the Protection of Human Rights* (1993) 207.

[243] European Commission of Human Rights, *X v Ireland* (App 6839/74) (1976) 7 DR 78, 79; M O'Boyle, 'The Development of the Right to Life' in DP Björgvinsson *et al* (eds), *Afmælisrit Þór Vilhjálmsson. Sjötugur. 9. Júní 2000* (2000) 65.

[244] European Commission of Human Rights, *X v United Kingdom* (App 7154/75) (1978) 14 DR 31, 32.

[245] D De, *The Constitution of India. Volume I Articles 1–104* (2002) 805, 842–843, 866–867. Shah (n 82 above) 475 ff.

medicine is part of this right. The *Sala Constitucional* of Costa Rica reasoning that the right to life is a right to a dignified life ruled that health is part of the right to life and that the state therefore has to provide AIDS medicine.[246] Other courts have similarly included access to AIDS medicine in the right to life.[247] Even though the right to life under the German *Grundgesetz* includes a guarantee of the means for basic subsistence, commentators have doubted whether it grants an individual claim to medical care.[248] However, the *Bundesverfassungsgericht* has ruled in the context of the AIDS pandemic that the objective content of the right to life imposes a duty on the state to protect society from the disease, albeit the Court can only rule against the state where it does not act at all or acts in a manifestly insufficient manner.[249] In another case, the court emphasized that the judiciary has to pay due attention to the right to life when considering whether the state has to pay for the medical treatment of an individual.[250]

B Duties Imposed on States Parties

Article 6(1) of the ICCPR does not just establish the right to life, it also explicitly demands that the right be protected by law. This takes up and does not limit[251] the obligations in Article 2(1) of the ICCPR to respect and ensure the rights in the Covenant. These duties, both of which have immediate effect for all States Parties,[252] include the negative obligation to refrain from violations of the right as well as the positive duty to take measures to fulfil the legal obligation and to protect individuals against violations of the right by the state and by private parties.[253] Again we encounter the obligations to respect, protect,[254] and fulfil.[255] The duty to protect resonates through the cases of the Human Rights Committee.[256] The

---

[246] C Chinchilla Sandí, 'Artículo 21' in N Cheves Aguilar and C Araya Pochet (eds), *Constitución Política Comentada de Costa Rica* (2001) 54.

[247] Eg Corte Constitucional de Colombia, *Juan Guillermo Gómez Morales v Ministerio de Salud*, T-328/98 (1998).

[248] HD Jarass in HD Jarass and B Pieroth, *Grundgesetz für die Bundesrepublik Deutschland*, (7th edn, 2004) Art 2 para 69; P Kunig in I von Münch and P Kunig (eds), *Grundgesetz-Kommentar. Band 1 (Präambel bis Art. 20)* (4th edn, 1992) Art 2 para 60; C Starck, in H v Mangoldt, F Klein, and C Starck (eds), *Das Bonner Grundgesetz. Kommentar. Band 1: Präambel, Artikel 1 bis 19* (4th edn, 1999) Art 2 paras 192 ff.   [249] BVerfG NJW 1987, 2287 (1987).

[250] BVerfG NJW 2003, 1236 (2002).

[251] At a first glance the wording 'protected by law' is more limited that that of Art 2(2) of the ICCPR demanding legislative or other measures. However, to read Art 6(1) of the ICCPR as a restriction of the general obligations would run counter to the effective protection of human rights. Statement by Tomuschat in the *443rd Meeting of the Human Rights Committee*, Yearbook of the Human Rights Committee 1983–1984. Volume 1, 204, para 55 ('it was not only for the legislator, but for all State authorities—the executive, the police, the military—actively to protect life'); *Guillermo Ignacio Dermit Barbato and Hugo Haroldo Dermit Barbato v Uruguay*, Communication No 84/1981, UN Doc A/38/40 (1983), printed in Yearbook of the Human Rights Committee 1983–1984. Volume I, 419, 488.   [252] General Comment No 31 [80] (n 87 above) para 5.

[253] Article 2(2) of the ICCPR; General Comment No 31 [80] (n 87 above) paras 5 ff.

[254] Klein (n 135 above) 301–302.   [255] Eide (n 92 above).

[256] Eg *W Delgado Páez v Colombia*, Communication No 195/1985, in Yearbook of the Human Rights Committee 1989–1990. Volume II, 396, para 5.6; *Herrera Rubio v Colombia*, Communication

immediate effect of the obligations was confirmed by the Human Rights Committee when it did not allow tense economic circumstances as a justification for poor prison conditions in violation of the Covenant.[257]

States Parties are obligated to create a legal order in which access to life-saving medicine is guaranteed. This includes measures to prevent private parties from hampering access to life-saving medicine.[258] Although the scope of the right is smaller with respect to the medicines covered, I can refer to the obligations imposed by the right to health for the types of obligations imposed by the right.

4 Universal Declaration of Human Rights

One of the most significant sources of international human rights law, the UDHR, has not been mentioned so far. In fact, it is technically incorrect to mention it under the heading of 'Conventions' at all. It is a Resolution of the General Assembly of the United Nations, not a treaty. The relevant rights contained in the UDHR are verbatim:

Art 3

Everyone has the right to life, liberty and security of person. (...)

Art 22

Everyone, as a member of society, has the right to social security and is entitled to realization, through national effort and international co-operation and in accordance with the organization and resources of each State, of the economic, social and cultural rights indispensable for his dignity and the free development of his personality. (...)

Art 25

(1) Everyone has the right to a standard of living adequate for the health and well-being of himself and of his family, including food, clothing, housing and medical care and necessary social services, and the right to security in the event of unemployment, sickness, disability, widowhood, old age or other lack of livelihood in circumstances beyond his control. (...)

Art 27

(1) Everyone has the right freely to participate in the cultural life of the community, to enjoy the arts and to share in scientific advancement and its benefits.

No 161/1983, in Yearbook of the Human Rights Committee 1987–1988. Volume II, 430 para 10.3; *Guillermo Ignacio Dermit Barbato and Hugo Haroldo Dermit Barbato v Uruguay*, Communication No 84/1981, UN Doc A/38/40 (1983), in Yearbook of the Human Rights Committee 1983–1984. Volume I, 419, 488; *Nydia Bautista de Arellana v Colombia*, Communication No 563/1993, printed in UN GAOR, 51st Sess, Supp No 40, at 132, UN Doc A/51/40, para 8.3 (1997).

[257] Klein (n 135 above) 299.
[258] F Menghistu, 'The Satisfaction of Survival Requirements' in BG Ramcharan (ed), *The Right to Life in International Law* (1985) 63 ff (arguing that there is no meaningful difference between depriving a person of basic needs and thus killing him or executing him wrongfully); LO Gostin and Z Lazzarini, *Human Rights and Public Health in the AIDS Pandemic* (1997) 12–13 (emphasizing that vaccines and treatment have to be made available to everybody). Far more expansive propositions are submitted by Ramcharan (n 234 above) 302 ff. However, his submissions include the ones made here, ibid 304.

As a resolution of the General Assembly of the United Nations the UDHR is, if the UN Charter is taken seriously, merely a 'recommendation'[259] and as such not binding.[260] Nevertheless, most scholars agree that the UDHR has obtained at least some legal effect. Some authors argue that the UDHR, possibly along with the Covenants and other human rights instruments, has become part of customary international law[261]—an argument that will be pursued below. Sohn favours another highly noteworthy approach: he regards the UDHR and the Covenants as interpretations of the human rights provisions of the UN Charter, ie Articles 55–56 of the UN Charter. This would put the UDHR squarely under the heading of treaty law. He refers to state practice to back up his argument: not only have states invoked the UDHR as soon as it was passed, the International Conference on Human Rights at Teheran proclaimed the Declaration to constitute 'an obligation for the members of the international community'. Many later resolutions are based both on the Charter and the UDHR.[262] The ICJ, too, applied the Charter and the UDHR simultaneously in the *United States Diplomatic and Consular Staff in Tehran* case.[263] If this argument were to be followed, the UDHR and the Covenants would be binding on all UN member states. However, it is already doubtful whether the mere mention of human rights in the Charter is a sufficiently solid ground to accommodate the whole area of human rights and make them binding for all UN members.[264] What is more, the General Assembly does not have the power to make authentic and binding interpretations of the Charter. Such a power is simply not contained in the Charter—in fact, a Belgian proposal to incorporate it was explicitly rejected.[265]

---

[259] Article 10–14 of the UN Charter.

[260] Hailbronner and Klein, in B Simma (ed), *The Charter of the United Nations. A Commentary. Volume I* (2nd edn, 2002) Art 10 paras 44 ff.

[261] MS McDougal, HD Lasswell and L-C Chen, *Human Rights and World Public Order. The Basic Policies of an International Law of Human Dignity* (1980) 273, 274, 325 (concerning the UDHR); K Oellers-Frahm, 'Comment: The erga omnes Applicability of Human Rights' (1992) 30 AVR 28 (claiming that most treaty-based human rights have to be qualified as customary international law). For a general overview see T Meron, *Human Rights and Humanitarian Norms as Customary Law* (1991) 79 ff; A Bleckmann, 'Zur originären Entstehung gewohnheitsrechtlicher Menschenrechtsnormen' in E Klein (ed), *Menschenrechtsschutz durch Gewohnheitsrecht. Kolloquium. 26.-28. September 2002. Potsdam* (2003) 29; K Doehring, 'Gewohnheitsrechtsbildung aus Menschenrechtsverträgen' in E Klein (ed), *Menschenrechtsschutz durch Gewohnheitsrecht. Kolloquium. 26.-28. September 2002. Potsdam* (2003) 84.

[262] LB Sohn, 'The Human Rights Law of the Charter' (1977) 12 Tex Int'l L J 129, 132 ff; LB Sohn, 'The New International Law: Protection of the Rights of Individuals Rather than States' (1982–1983) 32 Am U L Rev 1, 16; T Buergenthal, 'International Human Rights Law and Institutions: Accomplishments and Prospects' (1988) 63 Wash L Rev 1, 9. Proclamation of Teheran, (n 34 above) para 2; E de Wet, *The Chapter VII Powers of the United Nations Security Council* (2004) 199.

[263] *United States Diplomatic and Consular Staff in Tehran (United States of America/Iran)*, Judgment, ICJ Reports 1980, 3, para 91 (24 May 1980).

[264] B Simma, 'Die Erzeugung ungeschriebenen Völkerrechts: *Allgemeine Verunsicherung—klärende Beiträge Karl Zemaneks*' in K Ginther et al (eds), *Völkerrecht zwischen normativem Anspruch und politischer Realität. Festschrift für Karl Zemanek zum 65. Geburtstag* (1994) 95, 108–109.

[265] Hailbronner and Klein in B Simma (ed), *The Charter of the United Nations. A Commentary. Volume I* (2nd edn, 2002) Art 10, para 46.

5 Other Agreements

The ICESCR and the ICCPR are not the only conventions that protect the right to access to medicine.[266] Article 24 of the United Nations Convention on the Rights of the Child contains a right to health for children. Article 25 of the International Labour Organization Convention No 169 concerning Indigenous and Tribal Peoples in Independent Countries guarantees the right to health for indigenous and tribal peoples. Gender-specific health provisions can be found in the Convention on the Elimination of All Forms of Discrimination against Women. Race-discrimination in health care is tackled by Article 5(e)(iv) of the International Convention on the Elimination of All Forms of Racial Discrimination. Furthermore, many regional documents protect health and/or life, such as the African Charter on Human and Peoples' Rights (Banjul Charter),[267] the ECHR,[268] the European Social Charter,[269] the Charter of Fundamental Rights of the European Union,[270] the American Declaration of the Rights and Duties of Man,[271] the American Convention on Human Rights,[272] the Protocol of San Salvador.[273] As the scope of protection of all of these instruments is limited either *ratione materiae* or *ratione loci*, they will not be discussed in any detail.

VI General International Law

The next question that merits discussion is whether access to medicine is part of general international law, ie in the words of Article 38(1) of the Statute of the International Court of Justice 'international custom, as evidence of a general practice accepted as law' and 'the general principles of law recognized by civilized nations'. The body of general international law, ie customary international law and general principles of law, binds all states, albeit a customary rule is not binding on a state that persistently objected to it.[274]

---

[266] A number of documents are contained in G Alfredsson and K Tomaševski (eds), *A Thematic Guide to Documents on Health and Human Rights. Global and Regional Standards Adopted by Intergovernmental Organizations, International Non-Governmental Organizations and Professional Associations* (1998); DP Fidler, *International Law and Public Health: Materials on and Analysis of Global Health Jurisprudence* (2000).

[267] Article 4 of the Banjul Charter (life); Article 16 of the Banjul Charter (health).

[268] Article 2 of the ECHR (life).   [269] Article 11 of the European Social Charter (health).

[270] Article 2 of the Charter of Fundamental Rights (life), Article 35 of the Charter of Fundamental Rights (health care). The Charter has not come into force.

[271] Article I of the Declaration (life).   [272] Article 4 of the American Convention (life).

[273] Article 10 of the Protocol of San Salvador (health).

[274] There is an increasing tendency to regard customary international norms as binding on all states regardless of individual consent. Weil (n 94 above) 433 ff (criticizing this tendency). Nevertheless, the law remains that states consistently and timely objecting to a rule of customary international law are not bound by it, *Colombian-Peruvian Asylum Case (Colombia/Peru)*, Judgment, ICJ Reports 1950, 266, 277–278 (20 November 1950); *Fisheries case (United Kingdom/Norway)*, Judgment, ICJ Reports 1951, 116, 131 (18 December 1951).

1 Customary International Law

As the language of the Statute of the International Court of Justice suggests, customary international law arises where two components are present: an objective component—state practice—and a subjective one. The subjective element, known as *opinio juris sive necessitatis*, requires, in the words of the ICJ, that the 'States concerned must (...) feel that they are conforming to what amounts to a legal obligation'[275] and not just following a tradition or usage.[276]

A Treaties and Customary International Law

To some the discussion of customary law might seem peculiar given that there are treaties on human rights law. Could it not be argued that these 'overrule' customary law or function as *lex specialis*?[277] In the *Nicaragua* case the ICJ explicitly ruled on this question and held that norms of customary international law and of treaty law have a separate existence, even if they have the same content and even if they both bind the same state.[278] To treat the two sources separately is more than a mere academic exercise: even though the universal human rights treaties have been widely embraced, not all states have ratified them. Customary international law, on the other hand, binds every state with the exception of 'persistent objectors'. Moreover, numerous countries treat customary international law as the law of the land whereas they require treaty law to be transposed into national law.[279]

Notwithstanding their 'separate existence' the two sources interact with each other: customary international law can modify treaty rules[280] and, more significant

---

[275] *North Sea Continental Shelf (Federal Republic of Germany/Denmark; Federal Republic of Germany/Netherlands)*, Judgment, ICJ Reports 1969, 3, para 77 (20 February 1969); *The Case of the SS 'Lotus' (French Republic/Turkish Republic)*, PCIJ Reports 1927, Ser A, No 10, 28 (7 September 1927).

[276] There is much uncertainty about the concept of customary international law. This uncertainty combined with the large number of precedents in the history of international relations creates a treasure trove for arguing customary law claims, so caution is warranted in the analysis. M Koskenniemi, *From Apology to Utopia. The Structure of International Legal Argument* (1989) 363. On customary international law generally: Brownlie (n 17 above) 6 ff; Verdross and Simma (n 17 above) 345 ff; P-M Dupuy, *Droit International Public* (5th edn, 2000) 301 ff; M Byers, *Custom, Power and the Power of Rules. International Relations and Customary International Law* (1999) 44; C de Visscher, *Théories et Réalités en Droit International Public* (3rd edn, 1960) 188 ff.

[277] This is implied by H Dreier, 'Kontexte des Grundgesetzes' (1999) DVBl 667, 675.

[278] *Military and Paramilitary Activities in and against Nicaragua (Nicaragua/United States of America)*, Merits, Judgment, ICJ Reports 1986, 14, para 178 (27 June 1986); Watts (n 57 above) 261; *United States Diplomatic and Consular Staff in Tehran (United States of America/Iran)*, Judgment, ICJ Reports 1980, 3, para 62 (24 May 1980); Art 43 of the Vienna Convention on the Law of Treaties.

[279] Meron (n 261 above) 3–4, 79–80.

[280] *Case concerning the Temple of Preah Vihear (Cambodia/Thailand)*, Merits, ICJ Reports 1962, 6, 33–34 (15 June 1962) (admitting a later document as an interpretation of an earlier treaty); *Legal Consequences for States of the Continued Presence of South Africa in Namibia (South West Africa) notwithstanding Security Council Resolution 276 (1970)*, Advisory Opinion, ICJ Reports 1971, 16, para 22 (21 June 1971) (on the practice of abstention of permanent members in Security Council voting); Byers (n 276 above) 172 ff; GM Danilenko, *Law-Making in the International Community* (1993) 162 ff (listing the arguments *contra*).

for this study, a treaty norm can give rise to a norm of customary international law, which, unlike the treaty norm (*pacta tertiis*), binds states that are not parties to the treaty.[281] Many of the details of this process are still unclear.

B State Practice

The concept of customary law evokes a practice hardening into law. While this sociological premise largely holds true for public international law it poses two problems. The first one concerns the question of what acts of the state are to count as state practice. Possible answers range from D'Amato's claim that only acts and not statements of states can be admitted as practice[282] to Akehurst's assertion that any act or statement by a state from which its view can be inferred counts as state practice,[283] including press releases, state legislation, international and national judicial decisions, the practice of international organs, and resolutions of the United Nations General Assembly.[284]

The second problem is the required duration of the practice. Some authors require the practice to be of a certain duration, consistency, and generality.[285] This is well in line with common perceptions of custom as a practice going back to times immemorial. But the exigencies of our quickly changing times and the frequency of international conferences at which numerous states can voice their opinions on what the law is might well indicate otherwise, particularly with respect to resolutions and conventions becoming part of customary international law. In the *North Sea Continental Shelf Cases* the ICJ stated that:

it might be that, even without the passage of any considerable period of time, a very widespread and representative participation in the convention might suffice of itself, provided it included that of States whose interests were specially affected, [to make a norm-creating conventional rule enter customary international law].[286]

Cheng, famously, is ready to discard the durational requirement completely and accept the creation of 'instant customary law'.[287] The acceptability of such a

[281] Article 38 of the Vienna Convention on the Law of Treaties. Weil (n 94 above) 434 ff; Meron (n 261 above) 81.

[282] A D'Amato, *The Concept of Custom in International Law* (1971) 88; A D'Amato, 'Trashing Customary International Law' (1987) 81 AJIL 101, 102 (cited as D'Amato CIL); K Wolfke, *Custom in Present International Law* (2nd edn, 1993) 41–42, 84.

[283] M Akehurst, 'Custom as a Source of International Law' (1974–1975) 47 BYIL 1 ff; *Case concerning Rights of Nationals of the United States of America in Morocco* (n 223 above) 200 (examining diplomatic correspondence as state practice).   [284] Brownlie (n 17 above) 6.

[285] Brownlie (n 17 above) 7–8.

[286] *North Sea Continental Shelf* (n 275 above) para 73; *South West Africa, Second Phase (Ethiopia/South Africa; Liberia/South Africa)*, Judgment, ICJ Reports 1966, 6, 250, 291 (18 July 1966) (Dissenting Opinion Judge Tanaka); ME Villiger, *Customary International Law and Treaties* (1985) 24.

[287] B Cheng, 'Some Remarks on the Constituent Element(s) of General (or So-called Customary) International Law', in A Anghie and G Sturgess (eds), *Legal Visions of the 21st Century: Essays in Honour of Judge Christopher Weeramantry* (1998) 377, 385; B Cheng, 'United Nations Resolutions on Outer Space: "Instant" International Customary Law?' (1965) 5 Indian J Int'l L 23, 35 ff.

proposition depends very much on the view of *opinio juris* one prefers to adopt: adherents of a consensual notion of international law who regard custom as nothing but a tacit sort of treaty will have no problem accepting the instant meeting of the minds of states, so to speak.

Given the wide range of positions, dressing up a concise argument on state practice with respect to access to medicine seems preposterous. All the more so because human rights law is quite particular in many respects: no other area is so inextricably linked to morality, no other area can point to so many various documents affirming, reaffirming and re-reaffirming concepts that have already been reaffirmed a hundred times over. What is more significant for the legal task ahead is that state practice in international law is usually found in the international relations of states, but practice in the area of human rights concerns the treatment by a state of its own nationals.[288] The degree to which morality permeates human rights law makes Koskenniemi doubt the value of technical legal arguments altogether:

Some norms seem so basic, so important, that it is more than slightly artificial to argue that states are legally bound to comply with them simply because there exists an agreement between them to that effect, rather than because (...) noncompliance would shock ... the conscience of mankind and be contrary to elementary considerations of humanity.[289]

But this consideration does not help in clarifying the scope of customary human rights law, as it fails to answer precisely what would shock the conscience of mankind. Arguably, practice has a large influence on determining the scope of these considerations of humanity: slavery, an inhuman abuse that certainly shocks the conscience of mankind, was widely practiced in the past. This is not to deny the enormous importance of moral considerations in the area of human rights as customary law. Indeed, the impact of morality can hardly be overestimated: whereas in other areas states will be quite willing to reject rules, in human rights law they tread more carefully, afraid of a backlash in public opinion, afraid to end up on the morally and ethically wrong side. Publicly, they will almost always deny that they breached their human rights obligations rather than refuse to accept the rule as such. But the effect of this is simply that some human rights norms have obtained the necessary *opinio juris* (or possibly *opinio necessitatis*) to enter customary international law—an issue that will be treated more fully in the discussion on the requirement of *opinio juris*.

The wide variety of doctrinal positions on customary law seems to permit the assertion that the whole International Bill of Human Rights (along with the right to life and the right to health) has become customary international law.[290] With

288 O Schachter, 'International Law in Theory and Practice. General Course in Public International Law' (1982–V) 178 RdC 9, 334.

289 M Koskenniemi, 'The Pull of the Mainstream' (1989–1990) 88 Michigan L Rev 1946–1947 (internal quotation marks omitted).

290 WP Gormley, 'The Right to Life and the Rule of Non-Derogability: Peremptory Norms of *jus cogens*' in BG Ramcharan (ed), *The Right to Life in International Law* (1985) 120.

respect to state practice two arguments could do that trick: one relies on the *North Sea Continental Shelf Cases'* passage just quoted. The very widespread and representative participation in the human rights conventions, the immediate approval of both the negotiating states and the world community at large arguably let the whole International Bill enter customary international law.[291] But the conclusion is rash. States are free to choose whether they want to enter into treaty obligations. If they choose not to, the principle of *pacta tertiis nec nocent nec prosunt* protects them from any harmful effects of the treaty.[292] To extend treaty obligations to them under the guise of customary law not only violates this central element of treaty law,[293] it is also logically erroneous: it alleges a form of tacit consent to surmount a quite definite absence of willingness to ratify a treaty. A similar argument applies to the position that the UDHR has become customary international law: even if all states agreed to a non-binding resolution this by itself means hardly more than that all states agreed to a non-binding resolution. To argue that wide agreement by itself makes the non-binding resolution binding overlooks that states might have agreed because the resolution is non-binding.

A second (and enhanced) argument consists of dressing up a list of all the conventions, resolutions, statements, and documents emanating from states, UN human rights bodies and other bodies repeating, citing, and reaffirming the UDHR, the ICCPR and the ICESCR. Surely this must be sufficient state practice to back up the customary international law status of those documents.[294] But one should not allow the sheer number of repetitions to dazzle and overwhelm one's senses. The first intricate argument against admitting this plethora of state practice dismisses documents, statements, and other behaviour emanating from states that are legally bound by the human rights documents. Arguably, their practice only shows that they try to comply with their obligations. What has to be scrutinized according to this argument is the state practice *dehors* the treaty, ie state practice of non-party states.[295] In my opinion, this first counter-argument misperceives customary international law. Customary law as a source of law is based on the evolution of a behaviour to a habit that solidifies and raises expectations of that behaviour in others until, ultimately, *opinio juris* arises. Even where treaties

---

[291] LB Sohn, '"Generally Accepted" International Rules' (1986) 61 Wash L Rev 1073, 1077–1078; G Abi-Saab, 'La Coutume dans Tous ses États ou le Dilemme du Développement du Droit International Général dans un Monde Éclaté' in HC Batiffol *et al* (eds), *Le Droit International à l'Heure de sa Codification. Études en l'Honneur de Roberto Ago. I* (1987) 53, 64; A Cassese, *International Law in a Divided World* (1986) 183–184 (but regarding the UDHR as formally non-binding).

[292] Article 35 of the Vienna Convention on the Law of Treaties.

[293] RR Baxter, 'Multilateral Treaties as Evidence of Customary International Law' (1968) 41 BYIL 275, 286.

[294] A D'Amato, 'Human Rights as Norms of Customary international Law', in A D'Amato (ed), *International Law: Prospect and Process* (1987) 123 ff; L-C Chen, 'Protection of Persons (Natural and Juridical)' (1989) 14 Yale J Int'l L 542, 546–547; Schachter (n 288 above) 334–335; Meron (n 261 above) 89.

[295] H Waldock, 'General Course on Public International Law' (1962–II) 106 RdC 5, 84; RR Baxter, 'Treaties and Custom' (1970–I) 129 RdC 27, 64–65; H Lauterpacht, *International Law. A Treatise. By L. Oppenheim. Vol. I.—Peace* (8th edn, 1955) 28.

exist, such expectations, the understanding of the norm as being deeper and stronger than just based on the treaty, can arise. But apart from these abstract considerations, D'Amato has shown that the argument leads to an absurd result: the more support a convention has garnered, the more difficult it is to find state practice outside of the convention and hence the more unlikely it would be to pass into customary international law.[296]

However, a second line of reasoning against this showing of state practice for the International Bill of Human Rights ultimately prevails. This line of reasoning firstly concerns the acts included in the analysis of state practice: many of the documents referred to are non-binding. It must be assumed that states agreed to them fully aware that they did not commit themselves legally.[297] It is dubitable that custom can arise from them. As Weil put it so eloquently: thrice nothing is still nothing.[298] What is worse is that, secondly, the showing of state practice referred to 'paper practice' only and excluded the deeds of states from the analysis. An analysis including such deeds shows a different level of compliance for different rights. A glance at the numerous reports of human rights organizations indicates that some human rights provisions are commonly violated by states. What to do in this conundrum: admit the sad reality of non-adherence or take heed of the lip service that states pay to human rights and hold them to their words?[299] Simma cautions against the all too hasty reliance on paper practice only. Sole reliance on paper practice supports claims for norms that have not withstood the test of time, '*coutume sauvage*', and depart from the '*coutume sage*' of the olden days deduced from the actual deeds of states.[300] According to Simma, if there is any customary international human rights law, it is not the substantive standards, but the *droit de regard*, entitling the United Nations to respond to gross violations of human rights, eg through decisions of the human rights bodies.[301] Whereas Simma, nevertheless, considers paper practice as state practice[302] others do not even want to go that far, as has already been stated. Wolfke represents this position and he summarized it in a brilliant, if somewhat cynical, manner:

repeated verbal acts are also acts of conduct in their broad meaning and can give rise to international customs, but only to customs of making such declarations (...).[303]

But despite the pointed language Wolfke's argument is mistaken. Customary international law requires the analysis of all available practice. A state's verbal

[296] D'Amato (n 294 above) 129.

[297] Weil (n 94 above); G Arangio-Ruiz, 'The Normative Role of the General Assembly of the United Nations and the Declaration of Principles of Friendly Relations' (1972–III) 137 RdC 419, 444 ff.   [298] Weil (n 94 above).

[299] Bleckmann (n 261 above) 31.

[300] Simma (n 264 above) 105 ff; R-J Dupuy, 'Coutume Sage et Coutume Sauvage' in R Ago *et al* (eds), *La Communauté Internationale. Mélanges Offerts à Charles Rousseau* (1974) 75; GJH van Hoof, *Rethinking the Sources of International Law* (1983) 107–108; AM Weisburd, 'Customary International Law: The Problem of Treaties' (1988) 21 Vand J Transnat'l L 1, 10–11.

[301] B Simma and P Alston, 'The Sources of Human Rights Law: Custom, Jus Cogens, and General Principles' (1992) 12 Australian Y B Int'l L 82, 88 ff.   [302] Simma (n 264 above) 98 ff.

[303] Wolfke (n 282 above) 42.

affirmation of the existence of a right bears on the right itself and cannot automatically be taken as empty words. In practice, too, state practice often consists of statements on the existence *vel non* of a norm of customary international law.[304] However, a state's deeds are equally relevant. This does not imply that any given contrary act vitiates a whole body of state practice supporting a norm. The state practice only needs to be consistent and dense.[305] A dense and consistent paper practice is highly significant for a showing of state practice, as a state can be held to its word, but it is not sufficient where there is no non-paper practice. However, mere instances of non-compliance that are condemned by the international community do not prevent the development of a customary norm.[306]

Here I would like to submit a note of caution against the common belief that non-paper state practice disproves most norms of customary international human rights law. Orthodox scholarship examines this practice with an inherent bias against such norms, due to the selection of the non-paper practice. Even though a wide definition of non-paper practice might include national court decisions and possibly even national legislation, the decisive factor remains the establishment of 'the facts on the ground', the de facto compliance with the right. I will not bore the reader with the obvious workload difficulties of such a Herculean task, of rather more interest are the conceptual difficulties. Human rights elicit attention solely where they are violated. Such reports are the point of departure for orthodox claims that actual non-paper practice does not bear out customary human rights norms. A fair evaluation has to establish instances of compliance with the right as well as instances of its violation.[307]

It is rather self-evident that the scrutiny of state practice, including non-paper practice, will yield different results for different rights and will not support a claim that the whole International Bill of Rights has entered customary international law.[308]

The examination of state practice on access to medicine starts with a look at the 'right to health' and the 'right to life'. The right to health is contained in some 60 national constitutions,[309] but there is insufficient non-paper practice to support it as a whole.[310] In contrast, the right to life is commonly mentioned as a part of

---

[304] Bleckmann (n 261 above) 32; Simma (n 264 above) 101.

[305] *Military and Paramilitary Activities in and against Nicaragua* (n 278 above) para 186; A Kiss, 'The Role of the Universal Declaration of Human Rights in the Development of International Law (1988) Bull of Hum Rts Special Issue. Fortieth Anniversary of the Universal Declaration of Human Rights 47, 48.   [306] Kiss (n 305 above).

[307] This, of course, is a rather impossible task. There are millions of instances a day where a state does not kill its citizens and where the citizens do have access to medicine. Not all of these are relevant to the analysis. Instead, the cases where the right in question did or should have made a difference would have to be isolated. On the futility of such an enterprise A van Aaken, '*Rational Choice' in der Rechtswissenschaft. Zum Stellenwert der ökonomischen Theorie im Recht* (2003) 118–119.

[308] Schachter (n 288 above) 334 ff.   [309] Hunt (n 172 above) para 20.

[310] *Flores et al v Southern Peru Copper Corporation* 343 F3d 140, 160 (2nd Cir, 2003) (reaching the same conclusion, but arguing that the right is too vague, nebulous, and infinitely malleable); SD Jamar, 'The International Human Right to Health' (1994) 22 SUL Rev 1, 49–50. *Contra* (but failing to address non-paper practice) ED Kinney, 'The International Human Right to Health: What

customary international law. State practice consists not just of numerous international conventions mentioning the right to life,[311] resolutions,[312] and national constitutions,[313] but also a rich body of both national and international case law.[314] Numerous violations of the right are documented by NGOs such as Amnesty International,[315] but they are often condemned by other states. It would be wrong, however, to simply assume that the scope of the customary right to life is coextensive with the one under the ICCPR.[316] It is far from clear whether the right's positive component, of which access to life-saving medicine is a part, has also entered customary international law. Bleckmann rightly stated that the application of a customary norm in state practice defines the precise bounds of

Does this Mean for Our Nation and World?' (2001) 34 Ind L Rev 1457, 1464–1465. Note that the ICESCR has not been ratified by the US which is sceptical towards economic, social, and cultural rights. P Alston, 'U.S. Ratification of the Covenant on Economic, Social and Cultural Rights: The Need for an Entirely New Strategy' (1990) 84 AJIL 365, 366 ff; R Copelon, 'The Indivisible Framework of International Human Rights: A Source of Social Justice in the U.S.' (1998) 3 NY City L Rev 59, 63 ff; *Interpretative Statements for the Record by the Government of the United States of America*, I) First Paragraph, in *Report of the World Food Summit. 13–17 November 1996*. UN Doc WFS 96/REP Part One (1996).

[311] For example: Art I of the American Declaration of the Rights and Duties of Man; Art 2(1) of the ECHR; Art 6(1) of the ICCPR; Art 4(1) of the ACHR; Art 4 of the African Charter on Human and Peoples' Rights; Art 6(1) of the Convention on the Rights of the Child; Art 2(1) of the Charter of Fundamental Rights of the European Union.

[312] For example Art 3 of the UDHR, *Declaration on the Protection of All Persons from Enforced Disappearance*, GA Res 47/133 (18 December 1992), UN GAOR, 47th Sess, Supp No 49, at 207, UN Doc A/RES/47/133 (1993), Art 1(2) (adopted without a vote); *Declaration on the Elimination of Violence against Women*, GA Res 48/104, UN GAOR, 48th Sess, Supp No 49, at 217, UN Doc A/RES/48/104 (1994), Art 3(a) (adopted without a vote); UN World Food Conference, *Universal Declaration on the Eradication of Hunger and Malnutrition*, Report of the World Food Conference, Rome 5–16 November 1974, UN Doc E/CONF.65/20 (1975) (16 November 1974) (adopted without a vote).

[313] Documents are collected in A Weber, *Menschenrechte. Texte und Fallpraxis* (2004). Examples include (in various wordings) Algeria (Art 34(1)); Brazil (Art 5); Bulgaria (Art 28); Canada (Art 7); Chile (Art 19, No 1); Czech Republic (Art 6); Estonia (§ 16); Finland (§ 7); Germany (Art 2(2)); India (Art 21); Ireland (Art 40(3.2)); Japan (Art 13); Namibia (Art 6); Poland (Art 38); Portugal (Art 24(1)); Russia (Art 20(1)); South Africa (§ 11); Spain (Art. 15); Switzerland (Art 10); Thailand (§ 31); Tunisia (Art 5); United States of America (XIVth Amendment § 1).

[314] Commission on Human Rights, *Question of Human Rights in Chile*, UN Doc E/CN.4/1983/9, para 19 (1983) ('The international community therefore considers the right to life in the context of jus cogens in international human rights law', emphasis deleted); Nowak (n 135 above) Art 6; Dinstein (n 143 above) 115; Gormley (n 290 above) 121; BG Ramcharan, 'The Concept and Dimensions of the Right to Life' in BG Ramcharan (ed), *The Right to Life in International Law* (1985) 1, 3; HA Kabaalioğlu, 'The Obligations to "Respect" and to "Ensure" the Right to Life' in BG Ramcharan (ed), *The Right to Life in International Law* (1985) 160, 161; A Redelbach, 'Protection of the Right to Life by Law and by other Means' in BG Ramcharan (ed), *The Right to Life in International Law* (1985) 182, 185.

[315] Amnesty International (ed), *Amnesty International Report 2003* (2003).

[316] M Bothe, *Das völkerrechtliche Verbot des Einsatzes chemischer und bakteriologischer Waffen. Kritische Würdigung und Dokumentation der Rechtsgrundlagen* (1973) 38–39; such an approach was adopted by AP Kearns, 'The Right to Food Exists via Customary International Law' (1998) 22 Suffolk Transnat'l L Rev 223.

the norm.[317] The common core of the paper practice is only a first step in this analysis.[318]

While state practice concerning individual access to medicine under the right to life (outside the question of asylum for lack of medical services in the home country[319]) can hardly be deemed dense, the same cannot be said with respect to access to life-saving medicine in national health emergencies, namely pandemics such as HIV/AIDS, tuberculosis, and malaria.[320] This dovetails with the position of the Restatement (Third) of the Foreign Relations Law of the US, that considers 'a consistent pattern of gross violations of internationally recognized human rights' (as compared to single instances of violations) as a violation of customary international law[321] and regards all rights protected by the principal International Covenants as relevant for such gross violations.[322]

In the context of the AIDS pandemic the General Assembly of the United Nations[323] stressed in several resolutions 'the importance of making these technologies and pharmaceuticals available as soon as possible and at an affordable cost' and requested efforts of the UN System to collaborate to promote access of all to therapeutic technologies and pharmaceuticals.[324] Its special session on HIV/AIDS in 2001 resulted in a resolution that was adopted without a vote[325] and in which government representatives declared their commitment to 'address factors affecting the provision of HIV-related drugs, including anti-retroviral drugs, inter alia, affordability and pricing, including differential pricing, and

---

[317] A Bleckmann, 'Zur Feststellung und Auslegung von Völkergewohnheitsrecht' (1977) 37 ZaöRV 504. Note that US courts require a rule of customary international law to be clear and unambiguous rather than a mere abstract right or liberty devoid of articulable or discernable standards: *Hilao et al v Estate of Marcos (In re Estate of Ferdinand Marcos, Human Rights Litigation)* 25 F3d 1467, 1475 (9th Cir, 1994); *Filartiga v Pena-Irala* 630 F 2d 876, 884 (2nd Cir, 1980).

[318] Bleckmann (n 317 above) 524 ff.

[319] European Court of Human Rights, *D v United Kingdom* Application 30240/96, (1997) 24 EHRR 423 (2 May 1997); United Kingdom Court of Appeal (Civil Division), *N v Secretary of State for the Home Department*, 43 ILM 115 (2004) (16 October 2003).

[320] Pandemics hit closer to home as infectious diseases know no frontier. Here it is most evident that health is a public good. MW Zacher, 'Global Epidemiological Surveillance. International Cooperation to Monitor Infectious Diseases' in I Kaul and I Grunberg and MA Stern (eds), *Global Public Goods. International Cooperation in the 21st Century* (1999) 266, 268–269.

[321] American Law Institute, *Restatement of the Law Third. The Foreign Relations Law of the United States. Volume 2*, § 702 (1987). [322] Ibid § 702 comment 'm'.

[323] *Prevention and control of acquired immune deficiency syndrome (AIDS)*, GA Res 42/8 (26 October 1987), UN GAOR, 42nd Sess, Supp No 49, at 19, UN Doc A/RES/42/8 (1987) (adopted without a vote).

[324] *Prevention and control of acquired immunodeficiency syndrome (AIDS)*, GA Res 44/233 (22 December 1989), UN GAOR, 44th Sess, Supp No 49, I, at 158, UN Doc A/RES/44/233 (1989) (adopted by consensus); *Prevention and control of acquired immunodeficiency syndrome (AIDS)*, GA Res 45/187 (21 December 1990), UN GAOR, 45th Sess, Supp No 49, I, at 114, UN Doc A/RES/45/187 (1990) (adopted without a vote); *Prevention and control of acquired immunodeficiency syndrome (AIDS)*, GA Res 46/203 (20 December 1991), UN GAOR, 46th Sess, Supp No 49, I, at 139, UN Doc A/Res/46/203 (1991) (adopted without a vote).

[325] *Declaration of Commitment on HIV/AIDS* (n 176 above) (adopted without a vote, General Assembly, Twenty-sixth special session, UN Doc A/S-26/PV.8 (2001)).

technical and health-care system capacity' as well as to make every effort to progressively provide treatment including anti-retroviral therapy.[326] Access to treatment was explicitly framed as a human rights issue.[327] An even clearer expression of states' obligations to safeguard access to (life-saving) medicine in the context of pandemics came in December 2003, when the General Assembly adopted Resolution 58/179 that calls upon states to pursue policies promoting availability, accessibility, and affordability of safe pharmaceutical products to treat pandemics such as HIV/AIDS, tuberculosis, and malaria and to develop and implement national strategies to progressively realize access for all to comprehensive treatment for all individuals infected. The resolution, in so many words, mentions all three obligations of human rights law, stating that states should adopt legislation in accordance with applicable international law to safeguard access to the relevant pharmaceutical products from any limitation by third parties and take all appropriate measures, to the maximum of the resources allocated for this purpose, to promote effective access to preventive, curative, or palliative pharmaceutical products. States are furthermore called upon to take all appropriate measures to promote research and development of new and more effective drugs. The resolution was adopted by 181 votes to one, the United States being the sole dissenter.[328] Finally in 2006, the General Assembly adopted Resolution 60/262 reaffirming that 'access to medication in the context of pandemics, such as HIV/AIDS' is a fundamental element of the right to health,[329] and committing states to scale up access programmes towards universal access to treatment.[330] Similar statements concerning access to medicine have been made by the WHO,[331] by United Nations human rights bodies,[332] and by innumerable

---

[326] Ibid Annex para 55.   [327] Ibid Annex para 58.

[328] *Access to medication in the context of pandemics such as HIV/AIDS, tuberculosis and malaria* (n 5 above) adopted with the sole dissent of the United States, General Assembly, Fifty-eighth session, UN Doc A/58/PV.77 (2003).

[329] *Political Declaration on HIV/AIDS*, GA Res, UN Doc A/RES/60/262 (15 June 2006), para 12.

[330] Ibid para 49.

[331] *Global Health-sector Strategy for HIV/AIDS*, WHA resolution 56.30 (28 May 2003) (exhorting member states 'as a matter of urgency' to fulfil their obligations under the Declaration of Commitment on HIV/AIDS of the General Assembly, including those related to access to care and treatment), *Ensuring Accessibility of Essential medicines*, WHA resolution 55.14 (18 May 2002) (urging member states to reaffirm their commitment to increase access to medicines); *Scaling up Treatment and Care within a Coordinated and Comprehensive Response to HIV/AIDS*, WHA resolution 57.14 (22 May 2004) (urging member states to pursue policies promoting affordability and availability of relevant medicines as a matter of priority). Today, the Joint United Nations Programme on HIV/AIDS (UNAIDS), a joint programme of specialized agencies set up by ECOSOC Resolution 1994/24, in ESCOR 1994 Supp 1, at 42 is coordinating the response to the HIV/AIDS pandemic.

[332] Eg *Access to medication in the context of pandemics such as HIV/AIDS*, Commission on Human Rights Res 2001/33 (23 April 2001) (recognizing that access to medication in the context of pandemics is a fundamental element for achieving the full realization of the right to health and calling on states to promote availability and accessibility of pharmaceuticals) (adopted 52 votes to none, with the United States abstaining, Commission on Human Rights, Report on the Fifty-Seventh Session, ESCOR 2001, Supplement No 3, UN Doc E/CN.4/2001/167, 410 (2001)); *Access to Medication in the Context of Pandemics such as HIV/AIDS, Tuberculosis and Malaria*, Commission on Human Rights Res 2004/26, para 6 b (16 April 2004) (recognizing that access to medicine in the context of

conferences on the issue.[333] The fact that several national constitutional courts, eg those of South Africa and Colombia, have safeguarded access to medicine in the context of the AIDS pandemic as a human right has already been mentioned.

Despite the favourable paper practice the access situation remains bleak: in 2004 a journalist wrote that only one per cent of the people who need AIDS medication in southern Africa actually have access to it.[334] Bearing in mind, however, that a customary right to access to medicine would include resource limitations just as the right to health under the ICESCR, this fact alone does not prevent the development of a customary norm guaranteeing access. What is more important is states' efforts to guarantee access and international reaction to states' ignoring access to medicine in national health emergencies. Practice here supports a right to access to life-saving medicine in national health emergencies. Most countries are working hard towards universal access to treatment for AIDS, as is evidenced by state reactions to the WHO access initiative '3 by 5'.[335] Even the US, the only major democracy that generally fails to recognize a universal entitlement to health care, has established a programme to achieve universal AIDS treatment;[336] China reportedly established a similar programme.[337] States that fail to provide access to medicine do not argue that they do not have to guarantee access—they engage in denial. Thus, when South Africa's President Mbeki refused to make AIDS medication available he argued that HIV does not cause AIDS.[338] Some countries have denied that the epidemic has reached them.[339] Public pressure on such countries has grown enormously in recent years.[340] This state practice suffices to support a customary international law norm guaranteeing access to life-saving medication in the face of national health emergencies, particularly pandemics.

pandemics such as HIV/AIDS is a fundamental element for achieving progressively the right to health) (adopted without a vote); *Access to medication in the context of pandemics such as HIV/AIDS*, Commission on Human Rights Res 2002/32 (22 April 2002); *The right of Everyone to the Enjoyment of the Highest Attainable Standard of Physical and Mental Health*, Commission on Human Rights Res 2003/28 (22 April 2003) (urging states to fulfil the right to health); *Access to medication in the context of pandemics such as HIV/AIDS, tuberculosis and malaria*, Commission on Human Rights Res 2003/29 (22 April 2003) (calling upon states to pursue policies promoting availability and accessibility of safe medication in the context of pandemics); Committee on Economic, Social and Cultural Rights, General Comment No 14 (n 117 above), General Comment No 17 (n 55 above).

333 An overview can be found in *Declaration of Commitment on HIV/AIDS* (n 176 above) para 6.

334 A-C D'Adesky, *Moving Mountains. The Race to Treat Global AIDS* (2004) 11.

335 WHO (ed), *3 by 5 Progress Report. December 2003 through June 2004* (2004) 23.

336 Ryan White CARE program, Ryan White Comprehensive AIDS Resources Emergency Act of 1990, Pub L 101–381 as amended by the Ryan White CARE Act Amendments of 1996, Pub L 104–146 and the Ryan White CARE Act Amendments of 2000, Pub L 106–345; AR Chapman, 'Conceptualizing the Right to Health: A Violations Approach' (1998) 65 Tenn L Rev 389.

337 'China verabschiedet erstes Aids-Gesetz' *FAZ* (30 August 2004).

338 A Meldrum, 'Call for "dishonest" Mbeki to apologise for Aids gaffe' *The Observer* (28 September 2003); MW Makgoba, 'HIV/AIDS: The Peril of Pseudoscience' (2000) 288 Science 1171; GJ Annas, 'The Right to Health and the Nevirapine Case in South Africa' (2003) 348 New Eng J Med 750.

339 X Lei, 'China: Sars and the Politics of Silence. SARS is Making a Change' (2003) 50 World Press Review, July 2003.

340 D'Adesky (n 334 above); A Park, 'China's Secret Plague' *Time Magazine* (15 December 2003).

The US position deserves some further comment. It could be argued that because of its rejection of universal health care as a national policy and its alleged track record of objection to binding, resource-constraining economic, social, and cultural rights in the context of access to medicine, eg to General Assembly Resolution 58/179,[341] it cannot be bound by the right to access to medicine. But US practice on the point is more subtle than its critics allege: while the United States objected to sweeping claims concerning the right to health it did not vote against resolutions aiming to tackle specific pandemics, such as HIV/AIDS.[342] Indeed, on several occasions it explicitly took the stance that access to medicine in pandemics should not be restricted, as illustrated by the following two examples. In December 1999 President Clinton announced that the United States would 'implement its health care and trade policies in a manner that ensures that people in the poorest countries won't have to go without medicine they so desperately need'.[343] The statement was backed up by an executive order issued by President Clinton in May 2000 that forbids the United States to seek the revision of intellectual property laws of Sub-Saharan African countries that promote access to HIV/AIDS pharmaceuticals and are TRIPS compliant.[344] Later, when the United States attacked Brazil's patent laws in the WTO, it made a point of mentioning in the Mutually Agreed Solution reached in 2001 that the US concerns 'were never directed' at Brazil's HIV/AIDS programme, a 'bold and effective' effort.[345]

---

[341] Note also *Interpretative Statements for the Record by the Government of the United States of America* (n 310 above); *Flores et al v Southern Peru Copper Corporation* (n 310 above). However, there are indications that this attitude might change. Numerous recent bills in Congress try to expand health care, some even invoke a right to health: *Healthcare Equality and Accountability Act*, s 1833, 108th Congress, 6 November 2003; *Afghan Women Security and Freedom Act of 2004*, s 2032, 108th Congress, 27 January 2004 (finding that the Taliban regime denied women the most basic human rights, including the right to health care); *Expressing the sense of the Congress that access to basic health care services is a fundamental human right*, H Con Res 56, 103rd Congress, 2 March 1993; Chapman (n 336 above) 393–394.   [342] N 323 ff, 328 ff above.

[343] WJ Clinton, 'Remarks at a World Trade Organization Luncheon in Seattle, December 1, 1999' in Office of the Federal Register National Archives and Records Administration (ed), *Public Papers of the Presidents of the United States. William J. Clinton. 1999 (in Two Books). Book II—July 1 to December 31, 1999* (2001) 2189, 2192.

[344] Section 1(a) Executive Order No 13155, *Access to HIV/AIDS Pharmaceuticals and Medical Technologies* (10 May 2000).

[345] *Brazil-Measures Affecting Patent Protection. Notification of Mutually Agreed Solution*, WT/DS199/4 (19 July 2001). Further state practice stems from actions within the WTO relating to the TRIPS Agreement and access to medicine and clearly implies different US behaviour in different disease areas: RB Zoellick, 'Letter to Trade Ministers dated December 27, 2002' in *InsideHealthPolicy.com* (17 January 2003) (complaining about a possible expansion of the scope of diseases covered under the Doha Declaration); Council for TRIPS, *Moratorium to Address Needs of Developing and Least-Developed Members with no or Insufficient Manufacturing Capacities in the Pharmaceutical Sector. Communication from the United States*, IP/C/W/396 (14 January 2003) (declaring a moratorium on dispute settlement for Art 31(f) of the TRIPS Agreement for economies facing a grave public health crisis associated with HIV/AIDS, malaria, tuberculosis, or other infectious epidemics of comparable scale and gravity); DR Andresen (US Embassy Singapore), 'US Active in Helping Poorer Nations Tackle Health Crises' IP-Health (27 January 2003); RB Zoellick, 'Statement of Robert B. Zoellick, U.S. Trade Representative before the Committee on Ways and Means of the House of Representatives' IP-Health (26 February 2003) (emphasizing US commitment to help poor countries obtain medication);

C Opinio juris

State practice by itself evidences solely a usage of states. There must be something that raises this usage from the level of an empirical statement about what states do to a normative rule about what states have to do. The content of this second component of customary law, *opinio juris sive necessitatis*, is the subject of much debate. For consensualists like Anzilotti[346] the answer must appear simple. For them all international law is based on the consent of states,[347] *opinio juris* is the tacit consent of states. In practice they infer this consent, ie they accept acquiescence as consent, and only exempt states from the rule that persistently object to its formation.[348] Other authors reject the consensual premise to be able to include the majority of 'passive states'.[349] Even natural law notions rear their head in the debate.[350] The majority view on *opinio juris* has been expressed by the ICJ in the *North Sea Continental Shelf Cases* in the following terms:

the acts (. . .) must also be such, or be carried out in such a way, as to be evidence of a belief that this practice is rendered obligatory by the existence of a rule of law requiring it. (. . .) The states concerned must therefore feel that they are conforming to what amounts to a legal obligation.[351]

Scholars have had an extraordinarily hard time coming to terms with this notion. The problems begin with proving *opinio juris*. Obviously, any such proof will have to recur to verbal acts of state officials. Peculiarly, the same acts could also evidence state practice. Mendelson strongly cautions against using the same act for both purposes. Such an approach, he asserts, is incompatible with the two-prong test of customary international law.[352] Even if this difficulty is overcome, the next challenge already lies ahead. The *opinio juris* formula premises the development of a new customary norm on the belief of a state that it is legally bound by the norm. But how can this be if the norm is not yet in existence? Are we really to demand that states mistakenly assume the existence of a binding norm?[353] In the

---

Understanding between Canada and the United States regarding the implementation of the Decision of the WTO General Council of August 30, 2003 and NAFTA (16 July 2004); USTR Press Release, 'United States Welcomes Negotiations Leading to Positive Outcome on Enhancing Access to Medicines' (6 December 2005).

[346] Anzilotti (n 15 above) 41 ff.

[347] *The Case of the S.S. 'Lotus'* (n 275 above) 18 ('The rules of law binding upon States therefore emanate from their own free will as expressed in conventions or by usages generally accepted as expressing principles of law').   [348] Byers (n 276 above) 142–143.

[349] G Scelle, *Manuel de Droit International Public* (1948) 575.

[350] JC Bluntschli, *Das moderne Völkerrecht der civilisirten Staten als Rechtsbuch dargestellt* (2nd edn, 1872) 58–59.   [351] *North Sea Continental Shelf* (n 275 above) para 77.

[352] MH Mendelson, 'The Formation of Customary International Law' (1998) 272 RdC 155, 206–207; J Kammerhofer, 'Uncertainty in the Formal Sources of International Law: Customary International Law and Some of its Problems' (2004) 15 EJIL 523, 526.

[353] The question of such an error in the formation of customary law has been discussed by F Geny, *Méthode d'Interprétation et Sources on Droit Privé Positif. Essai Critique. Tome Premier* (2nd edn, 1919) 367 ff (albeit for private law).

face of these challenges Kelsen initially wanted to abandon the notion of *opinio juris* altogether.[354] The alleged difficulties disappear, however, if the development of customary law is conceived as a process and such notions as legitimate expectations and soft law are borne in mind. Through repetition acts give rise to a usage, usage begins to raise expectations of a certain behavioural pattern, and ultimately what was a mere fact hardens to soft and then to hard law. Criticism of using verbal practice for both the *opinio juris* and the state practice element suggest a static approach. In fact, where such verbal acts evince both elements they can be used as evidence for both elements. Often *opinio juris* can be inferred from paper practice.[355] Moral considerations, too, are not misplaced here, for which nation would publicly take a stance against the right to life or access to medicine? Given the numerous documents in which states explicitly guarantee access to medicine in pandemics I have no doubt that *opinio juris* exists and that access to life-saving medicine in national health emergencies, particularly in pandemics, is part of customary international law.

2 General Principles

'[G]eneral principles of law recognized by civilized nations'[356] are, as a source of international law, to be examined after treaties and customary law.[357] Doctrine admits several types of general principles. First and foremost they can be derived from principles recognized *in foro domestico*, ie common rules in a large majority of states representing all legal systems. The restriction of the comparative exercise to 'civilized nations' is a remnant of eurocentristic views that are no longer relevant. The second category of general principles is general principles of the international legal order arising directly and only in international relations.

Distinguishing general principles and customary law is not a simple task. If anything can be deduced from the vague definitions of general principles, it is that these can be more general than customary rules.[358] It is far from settled whether human rights can be admitted as general principles. Most established general principles stem from the branch of private law, such as the principle of good faith or the law of unjust enrichment.[359] The predominance of private

---

[354] H Kelsen, 'Théorie du Droit International Coutumier' (1939) 1 Revue Internationale de la Théorie du Droit Nouvelle Série, 253, 263 ff; P Guggenheim, *Les deux Éléments de la Coutume en Droit International*, in *La Technique et les Principes du Droit Public. Études en l'Honneur de Georges Scelle. Tome Premier* (1950) 275, 283.   [355] Wolfke (n 282 above) 70.

[356] Article 38 (c) of the ICJ Statute.

[357] This does not imply an inferiority of general principles in the sense of a hierarchy. RA Billib, *Die allgemeinen Rechtsgrundsätze gemäß Art. 38 I c des Statuts des Internationalen Gerichtshofes—Versuch einer Deutung* (1972) 168–169.

[358] On general principles H Mosler, 'General Principles of Law' in R Bernhardt (ed), *Encyclopedia of Public International Law, II* (1995) 511; H von Heinegg, in Ipsen (n 16 above) 198 ff; Billib (n 357 above); B Cheng, *General Principles of Law as Applied by International Courts and Tribunals* (1953).

[359] Bleckmann (n 261 above) 38–39; E Fanara, *Gestione di affari e arricchimento senza causa nel diritto internazionale* (1966); R Yakemtchouk, *La Bonne Foi dans la Conduite Internationale des États* (2002) 72 ff.

law principles is an acknowledgement of the contract—treaty analogy. But there is nothing inherent in the notion of general principles itself that would limit it to private law principles.[360] In their seminal study on the issue Simma and Alston convincingly argue that human rights can be general principles. Both categories of principles are open to human rights: recognition *in foro domestico*, or as basic considerations that have obtained general acceptance or recognition by states on the international plane.[361] The old objection that human rights are within the exclusive domestic jurisdiction of states has long been overcome.[362]

The inclusion of human rights in the ambit of general principles gains some support from the *Corfu Channel* case of the ICJ, in which it recognized 'elementary considerations of humanity' as a general principle, but with little regard to the method used to discern the principle:

The obligations incumbent upon the Albanian authorities consisted in notifying, for the benefit of shipping in general, the existence of a minefield in Albanian territorial waters and in warning the approaching British warships of the imminent danger to which the minefield exposed them. Such obligations are based (...) on certain general and well-recognized principles, namely: elementary considerations of humanity, even more exacting in peace than in war (...).[363]

Similarly, in the *Genocide Convention* case the ICJ held that 'the principles underlying the Convention are principles which are recognized by civilized nations as binding on States, even without any conventional obligation'.[364] The German *Bundesverfassungsgericht* considers a minimum human rights standard as part of general international law.[365]

The wide acceptance of human rights makes it plausible to follow the new trend to accept basic human rights as general principles.[366] The national practice scrutinized in the analysis of the customary law status of access to medicine allows the conclusion that access to life-saving medicine in national health emergencies is also a general principle of law.

---

[360] Mosler (n 358 above) 512, 521.

[361] Simma and Alston (n 301 above) 102 ff; Generally: B Vitanyi, 'Les positions doctrinales concernant le sens de la notion de "principes généraux de droit reconnus par les nations civilisées"' (1982) 86 Revue Générale de Droit International Public 48, 85 ff (discussing the genesis of general principles).

[362] *Interpretation of Peace Treaties*, Advisory Opinion, ICJ Reports 1950, 65, 70–71 (30 March 1950); Meron (n 261 above) 106.

[363] *Corfu Channel Case (United Kingdom/Albania)*, Merits, Judgment, ICJ Rep 1949, 4, 22 (9 April 1949).

[364] *Reservations to the Convention on Genocide*, Advisory Opinion, ICJ Reports 1951, 15, 23 (28 May 1951).

[365] BVerfGE 46, 342, 362 (1977); BVerfGE 60, 253, 304 (1982).

[366] Mosler (n 358 above) 525; Simma and Alston (n 301 above) 102 ff; Meron (n 261 above) 88 f; Waldock (n 295 above) 198; JP Humphrey, 'The Universal Declaration of Human Rights: Its History, Impact and Juridical Character' in BG Ramcharan (ed), *Human Rights: Thirty Years After the Universal Declaration* (1979) 21, 29.

VII Conclusion on Human Rights

It has been demonstrated that access to medicine is now guaranteed by several sources of international law. However, the scope of the right varies for the different sources: the ICESCR protects access to essential medicine, the ICCPR access to life-saving medicine, and general international law access to life-saving medicine in national health emergencies, particularly in pandemics.

A vital part of the accessibility of medicine is their economic accessibility, ie the affordability of medicine. States are under an obligation to respect, protect, and fulfil such accessibility. States can meet these obligations in one of two ways: they can either assist individuals in buying such medicine by buying the medicine for them, granting financial aid to buy medicine, or financing a comprehensive health care system, or they can guarantee an adequate level of the price of medicine. Developing countries will have to adopt the latter route. This entails protecting access to medicine also from excessive pricing by pharmaceutical companies.

4

Conflict between Patents and Access to Medicine

Having determined the scope of the protection of access to medicine, this chapter will, at first, turn to whether the obligation to adopt patent laws interferes with this right (I). The allegation by developing countries, scholars, NGOs, and several international bodies—self-evident to the extent of being banal to some, hotly contested by others—is that introducing patents on pharmaceuticals in developing countries will result in higher prices, interfering with economic accessibility in developing countries that cannot afford to provide expensive drugs for their populations. The first part of this chapter will examine the merits of the claim in light of microeconomic theory (1) and by surveying empirical studies that have been conducted on the issue (2). Finally, it addresses the challenge that the price effect is de minimis and that public attention should be focused on other issues (3), concluding that patents interfere with the right to acess to medicine.

In part II, an additional aspect of the debate needs to be explored, namely whether the interference with access can be justified. A possible justification that has attracted little attention is the right of authors to benefit from the protection of the moral and material interest resulting from their scientific productions (1). The more common justification relies on the necessity of patents as an incentive for research on future medication (2). This part will conclude, however, that pharmaceutical patents in developing countries unjustifiably interfere with access to medicine.

While, directly, this finding concerns the rights and obligations of developing countries only, part III will show that other countries are concerned, too, as international law imposes a duty on other states to cooperate in the achievement of the full realization of human rights.

This result both concludes the view of patents through the glasses of a human rights scholar and sets the stage for a change in the point of view. Departing from the concrete question examined so far, part IV will inquire what the finding implicates for the larger question of the relationship between the TRIPS Agreement and human rights law under the heading of regime conflict.

I Interference of Patents with Access to Medicine due to Price Effects

A state interferes with a human right if it limits the exercise of that right, ie if it encroaches upon the right or fails to fulfil a positive duty associated with the right.[1] As chapter 3 has shown, states must guarantee the economic accessibility of medicine and developing countries can only do so by guaranteeing a reasonable price level. Providing corporations with the possibility to patent pharmaceuticals is allegedly counterproductive in this respect, since it results in a higher price level of those products. If such a price effect can be shown, patents would indeed interfere with the right to access to medicine at least in developing countries, as higher prices reduce the accessibility of the medicine for the poor and this effect cannot be compensated by developing countries, which lack the resources to pay for the higher prices themselves. This part takes on the task of verifying the allegation both on a theoretical economic level and on an empirical level. The claim that the higher prices are justified as an incentive to encourage further research and that without such incentives many of the drugs would not be available will be examined later on.

1 Microeconomic Theory

To gauge the effect that patents have on prices, this study will first examine how prices are set in a perfectly competitive, unregulated market, ie a market without patents (A). That situation will then be compared with monopoly pricing (B), assuming *arguendo* that patents result in monopoly pricing. To what extent this assumption is true will be discussed in (C). Finally, (D) will inquire into whether the results of the investigation are also true with respect to developing countries.

A Competitive Market

The 'perfectly competitive, unregulated market' is an ideal fulfilling several conditions: a large number of small companies compete against each other for market share in one product. The products of the companies are identical so that buyers are indifferent as to which supplier they purchase from. Because the number of

---

[1] Article 4 of the ICESCR adopts the approach of examining a limitation of the right and then a possible justification. For positive obligations the concept of interference and justification of the interference is not always used. Thus, the European Court of Human Rights inquires instead whether a fair balance has been struck between the general interest of the community and the interest of the individual. ME Villiger, *Handbuch der Europäischen Menschenrechtskonvention* (EMRK) (2nd edn, 1999) 344–345; for German law HD Jarass and B Pieroth, *Grundgesetz für die Bundesrepublik Deutschland. Kommentar* (7th edn, 2004) Vorb vor Art 1 paras 24 ff.

competitors is large, a change in output by one of them has no effect on the overall market supply and on the market price of the product. Also, there are no barriers to enter or exit the market. Finally, information about alternative suppliers is readily available and both buyers and sellers are mobile. In such a market, goods will be priced at marginal cost.

Single companies in this market are 'price takers', ie they do not have an influence on the price. The market price is a constant in their decision-making process.[2] At a higher price the company would be unable to sell any products. It therefore has no incentive to raise the price. At the current market price it can sell as many products as it wants to due to the insignificance of the size of its own production compared to overall market supply. Hence, it also has no incentive to lower the price.[3]

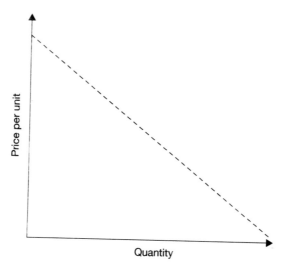

Fig 4.1. The Demand Curve

The prices are set by the 'invisible hand' of the market, the workings of the laws of supply and demand, ensuring that resources are used efficiently.[4] The law of demand follows a simple pattern: the quantity in which a good is consumed falls as the price rises. The demand curve varies depending on a number of factors

---

[2] NT Skaggs and JL Carlson, *Microeconomics. Individual Choice and Its Consequences* (2nd edn, 1996) 286; E von Böventer *et al*, *Einführung in die Mikroökonomie* (7th edn, 1991) 224.
[3] JM Perloff, *Microeconomics* (1999) 242–243.
[4] W Nicholson, *Microeconomic Theory. Basic Principles and Extensions* (7th edn, 1998) 501. For the definition of efficient (Pareto Efficiency) ibid 502 (if it is not possible to make one person better off without making someone else worse off).

including consumer income and price of other goods, especially of similar goods satisfying the same desire of the consumer, so-called 'substitutes'. The demand for a good decreases when the price of substitutes falls.[5]

An important characteristic of the demand curve is its so-called 'elasticity'. Elasticity is defined as the number of percentage points that the quantity demanded decreases at a one per cent price increase.[6] Demand is dubbed 'perfectly inelastic' if the quantity demanded is absolutely insensitive to a price change. It is 'perfectly elastic' if the available quantity will be bought at one price, none at a higher price, and infinite amounts at any lower price.[7] The demand curve for many drugs is inelastic—especially in the case of unique, life-saving drugs: patients are willing to pay almost any price. In these circumstances, demand drops only when the available financial means of the patients are exhausted. On the other hand lower prices will not raise the demand for essential drugs significantly as patients rarely buy many more drugs than they have to take merely because they are cheap.

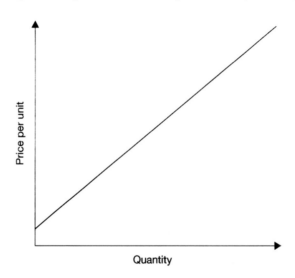

Fig 4.2. The Supply Curve

The supply curve—the other component of the famous 'law of supply and demand'—reflects the quantity of the good that producers are willing to sell at a given price. When the market price of a good is higher, companies are willing to produce more than if the price were lower because they can make more money.[8] The exact supply curve depends on a number of factors, such as the cost of raw materials,

    [5] Skaggs and Carlson (n 2 above) 65.
    [6] RS Pindyck and DL Rubinfeld, *Microeconomics* (5th edn, 2001) 30. Mathematically: $E_p = (\Delta Q/Q)/(\Delta P/P)$ where Q means quantity and P means price.
    [7] Skaggs and Carlson (n 2 above) 151.   [8] Skaggs and Carlson (n 2 above) 66.

production costs, etc. Firms are willing to supply one more unit of the good if they expect to receive a price that covers or exceeds their 'marginal cost', ie the additional cost it takes to produce that unit.[9] The supply curve therefore is the marginal cost curve.[10]

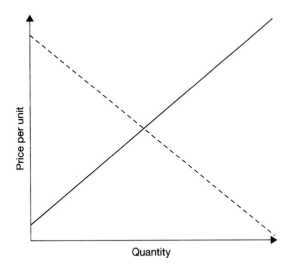

Fig 4.3. Price Setting in a Perfectly Competitive Market

In a perfectly competitive market, the 'invisible hand' drives the price to where the supply and the demand curves intersect, meaning that the good is priced at marginal cost. The graph illustrates that prices below the equilibrium price lead to excess demand. Producers and retailers will mark up prices as their stocks are depleted, which then drives the market back to the equilibrium price. Prices above the equilibrium price lead to excess supply; retailers reduce their orders; producers, competing against each other, lower prices to sell their products—the price is pushed towards the equilibrium price. Thus, in a perfectly competitive environment the good will be priced at the marginal cost.

Even though the prices of a good in a perfectly competitive market are generally advantageous for consumers, they are not optimal in all situations. At times they might not reflect all costs or benefits involved. Where such 'externalities'[11] are not internalized, the unregulated market is inefficient. That is what economists term a 'market failure'.

Inventions are a textbook example of a market failure. An inventor puts time and money into the research and development of a product. Without patent

⁹ Pindyck and Rubinfeld (n 6 above) 80.   ¹⁰ Skaggs and Carlson (n 2 above) 67.
¹¹ Pindyck and Rubinfeld (n 6 above) 294.

protection, competitors could free-ride on the efforts of the inventor, copying the invention through reverse engineering and saving the research and development costs while reaping the benefits of the inventor's efforts. They can then undercut the inventor because their costs of producing the product were lower than the inventor's. Consequently, inventors will not have an incentive to invent because they will not receive a return on their investment of time and money.

Patents help resolve this market failure. The necessity for a mechanism to internalize research and development costs in the pharmaceutical industry is uncontested, given the staggering amount of these costs. A commonly cited study by DiMasi based on confidential data puts the price tag for the development of a drug (including failed research and cost of capital) at $802m in 2000, up from $231m in 1987.[12] The figure has been criticized as inflated,[13] with other studies putting the figure at $194m in 1990 dollars (US Congress' Office of Technology Assessment)[14] or significantly lower.[15] A non-partisan estimate based on data culled from sources in addition to that provided by the pharmaceutical industry is the Global Alliance for TB Drug Development's calculation of the cost of discovering and developing a new anti-tuberculosis drug (including the cost of failure): $115m–$240m.[16] Whichever figure turns out to be closer to the truth, it cannot be disputed that the costs involved are substantial.

B Monopoly Pricing

A patent holder can prevent third parties from 'making, using, offering for sale, selling or importing for these purposes' the product.[17] These rights make the patent holder the only one who can supply the product, ie a monopoly supplier.[18]

---

[12] JA DiMasi, RW Hansen and HG Grabowski, 'The Price of Innovation: New Estimates of Drug Development Costs' (2003) 22 J Health Econ 151, 180; JA DiMasi *et al*, 'Cost of Innovation in the Pharmaceutical Industry' (1991) 10 J Health Econ 107.

[13] DW Light and J Lexchin, 'Will Lower Drug Prices Jeopardize Drug Research? A Policy Fact Sheet' (2004) Am J of Bioethics 4(1), W3, W4; M Goozner, *The $800 Million Pill: The Truth Behind the Cost of New Drugs* (2004).

[14] US Congress, Office of Technology Assessment, *Pharmaceutical R&D: Costs, Risks and Rewards* (1993) 1 (for drugs reaching the market in the 1980s). Perloff (n 3 above) 402.

[15] $108m 93% of the time, $400m 7% of the time; in between $57m and $71m. Light and Lexchin (n 13 above) W4; Public Citizen (ed), *Rx R&D Myths: The Case Against the Drug Industry's R&D 'Score Card'* (2001) i. Note that this report met with substantial criticism in an evaluation commissioned by the Pharmaceutical Research and Manufacturers of America (PhRMA): Ernst & Young, *Pharmaceutical Industry R&D Costs: Key Findings about the Public Citizen Report* (2001). The Consumer Project on Technology analyzed filings for tax credits with the US Internal Revenue Service (IRS), concluding that pre-tax expenditures on clinical testing including the costs of failures was only $7.9m per approved orphan drug—much lower than the figures that the DiMasi study used for this item: J Love and M Palmedo, *Cost of Human Use Clinical Trials: Surprising Evidence from the US Orphan Drug Act* (2001).

[16] The Global Alliance for TB Drug Development, *Executive Summary for the Economics of TB Drug Development*, 16 (2001), at <http://www.tballiance.org/downloads/publications/TBA_Economics_Report_Exec.pdf>.   [17] Article 28.1(a) of the TRIPS Agreement.

[18] The question whether patents are monopolies will be dealt with below. As here: Perloff (n 3 above) 398.

A monopoly is commonly understood as a situation in which there is only one supplier of a good that is lacking close substitutes. A monopoly supplier is a price maker—as the sole supplier of the good, it can set its price. The output of the supplier is the total market supply, the demand it meets is the market demand curve. A monopolist is free to choose between producing a larger quantity of the good to be sold at a lower price or producing a smaller quantity to be sold at a higher price. In a free market system it will select the market price promising the highest profit.

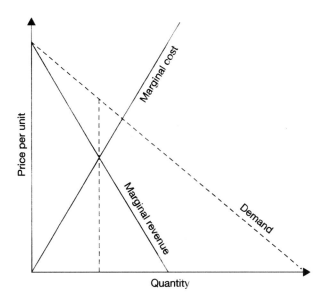

Fig 4.4. Price Setting for a Monopoly

To determine this price a 'marginal revenue' curve has to be plotted. The total revenue of the monopolist at a quantity q is price p $\times$ quantity q, with p being the price value of q on the demand curve. Its marginal revenue is the additional revenue the monopolist obtains from selling one more unit of the good: marginal revenue = ΔR (increase in revenue)/Δq (increase in quantity). When a corporation increases its production quantity by one unit in a fully competitive situation, it can charge the same price as for all the other goods it sells and its revenue thus increases by 1 $\times$ p (price). But when a monopoly supplier increases its production quantity it has to decrease the price to be able to sell the additional unit of goods, because the monopoly supplier's demand curve is the downward sloping market demand curve. It will thus run a marginal revenue that is less than the price charged at the old quantity. Assuming a linear demand curve, the appearance of the marginal revenue curve can be figured out quickly: mathematically a linear demand curve can be written as $p = a - bq$. The revenue of the monopolist is $r = pq$. Inserting the price equation yields $r = (a - bq)q = aq - bq^2$. To obtain the marginal revenue I differentiate the equation with respect to q: marginal revenue $= a - 2bq$. The demand curve and the marginal revenue curve thus both intersect the price axis at a, both slope downward, but the price curve with a slope of b, the marginal revenue curve with a slope of $2b$. The monopolist will now select the quantity of the dot where the marginal revenue curve and the marginal cost curve (I chose a linear curve) intersect and select the price on the demand curve for that quantity as it cannot change the demand curve, which is the market's demand curve. At smaller quantities the marginal revenue is greater than the marginal cost and the monopolist could make a greater profit by producing more. At greater quantities the marginal revenue is below the marginal cost, so the profit would be increased by lowering the output.[19] The market price in a competitive environment is, as already demonstrated, the price where the marginal cost curve and the demand curve intersect. The graph demonstrates that a monopolist sells a lower quantity of goods than would be sold in a competitive environment at a higher price to maximize its profit. A monopoly environment thus leads to higher prices and lower sold quantities of the good. Economists have shown that the difference in pricing and output levels do not only lead to greater profits of the producer, but that a loss of welfare is involved ('deadweight loss').[20] But competitive pricing does not just lower the prices to marginal costs, it also lowers the marginal costs: as competitors appear on the scene corporations have a motivation to produce more efficiently,[21] such as by investing resources into more efficient production processes. In a monopoly situation inefficient processes often remain unchanged.

The application of the comparison between monopoly and competitive pricing to patent law can be attacked from two sides: first of all it assumes the existence of a good that can be subject to competitive or monopoly pricing—the rationale of patent law alleges that without granting a monopoly right the good would not have been invented so that the competitive situation is merely fictitious.[22] This challenge will be answered in the section on justification. The second attack, which I will turn to momentarily, is directed at classifying patents as monopolies.

C Patents as Monopolies—other Pricing Factors

The patent expert and professor of law Kitch concludes that 'the common perception that patents confer monopolies is false'.[23] Monopolies, according to Kitch,

---

[19] Perloff (n 3 above) 370 ff.

[20] Perloff (n 3 above) 386 ff.

[21] H Leibenstein, 'Allocative Efficiency vs. "X-Efficiency"' (1966) 56 Am Econ Rev 392, 398 ff.

[22] KE Maskus, *Intellectual Property Rights in the Global Economy* (2000) 28 ff.

[23] EW Kitch, 'Patents: Monopolies or Property Rights?' (1986) 8 Res in L & Econ 31.

are characterized by a downward sloping demand curve of the seller. This is not necessarily the case for patents for three reasons: (1) Patented products only rarely monopolize a market, as they face competition by substitutes. Thus, a pharmaceutical company might hold a patent on a drug, but competitors usually supply other chemical entities with the same or a similar effect;[24] (2) even radically new products without substitutes do not reap monopoly rents immediately, as they often replace other products and have to overcome a reluctance of the system to switch technologies and abandon the investment made into the old technology; (3) as the patent holder is aware of the fact that the patent will run out, it will prepare for the competition by trying to capture a large market share during the patent term—and thus not impose high prices.

Pharmaceutical patents are somewhat particular in this respect. Patients show no reluctance to buy new drugs against their sufferings and they are willing to pay dearly for important new drugs, so that a new drug will quickly capture the relevant market despite relatively high prices.[25] Hence only Kitch's first argument is relevant for the pharmaceutical market. The availability of substitutes (and thus of competition) moves the price setting from monopoly pricing towards competitive pricing.[26] However, because patents limit the number of competitors in the market, the competitive level will not be reached and the price will still be higher than in a competitive setting.

It should be noted that patents are far from the only factor influencing drug pricing. Hardly any area is as regulated as health care and most of these regulations influence drug pricing one way or another. Government price controls can lower prices significantly. Wide availability of health insurance takes the pressure off the individual to pay attention to prices, however, where insurance systems impose a limit on the price they will reimburse this limit can have a similar effect as a governmental price control. Often insurance systems or government health care systems buy drugs or negotiate drug prices. Such a situation, in which there is only one (or at least only one significant) buyer of a company's product is called a 'monopsony' situation—and it enables the buyer to negotiate significantly lower prices.[27] It is extremely difficult to predict the resulting price. Any economic study

---

[24] The effect of competition between different patented products in therapeutic competition for the treatment of one disease is examined by FR Lichtenberg and TJ Philipson, 'The Dual Effects of Intellectual Property Regulations: Within- and Between- Patent Competition in the US Pharmaceuticals Industry' NBER Working Paper 9303 (2002).

[25] After the patent expires and generics become available many patients continue to prefer the brand-name drug, fearing the generic to be of lesser quality. This explains why many of the original manufacturers continue to provide the brand-name drug and at the same time produce a generic. Perloff (n 3 above) 489–490.

[26] SF Ellison *et al*, 'Characteristics of Demand for Pharmaceutical Products: An Examination of four Cephalosporins' (1997) 28 RAND J of Econ 426, 445; on monopsony power and the potential of bulk purchasing, also by international organizations: C Grace, *Equitable Pricing of Newer Essential Medicines for Developing Countries: Evidence for the Potential of Different Mechanisms* (2003) 16 ff.

[27] JH Barton, 'Differentiated Pricing of Patented Products' CMH Working Paper Series, Paper No WG4: (2001) 2, 4.

that analyzes the effect of just one price-building factor simplifies reality significantly. Nevertheless, this study is solely concerned with patents and their influence on pricing and thus has to isolate the effect of patents on pricing.

D Pricing in Developing Countries

The model so far assumes one single market and can adequately describe pricing for a product in one market. For developing countries such a model would capture the pricing of medicine for diseases prevalent only in developing countries. Two different models are necessary to understand drug pricing in developing countries for patented medicine against global diseases. The first model assumes that markets are strictly separated, whether by granting patents that allow the patent holder to ban parallel imports or by other means such as drug approval.[28] In such a market the seller of a drug optimizes its price against the national demand curve. This can imply lower prices in lower-income countries, a system that is referred to as 'tiered pricing', 'equitable pricing', or—more popular with economists—'discriminatory pricing' or 'Ramsey pricing'. The system is elegant in that richer countries contribute more towards the cost of research and development than poorer ones and it has been widely praised by economists.[29] The suggestion of some scholars, however, that it would result in marginal pricing in developing countries[30] is untenable. It would merely result in monopoly pricing for each national market separately by patent holders[31]—and the assumption that the monopoly price in least-developed countries is necessarily very close to the marginal price is false. Barton has rightly pointed out that the tiered price in developing countries is not necessarily lower than the price in a developed country: many developing and least-developed countries have a skewed income distribution and at times a higher price, catering only to the wealthier part of the population, can be more profitable for the supplier than a lower one.[32]

---

[28] Ibid.

[29] Much has been said about differential pricing, eg PM Danzon, 'Differential Pricing for Pharmaceuticals: Reconciling Access, R & D and Patents' CMH Working Paper Series, Paper No WG2: (2001) 10; FM Scherer and J Watal, 'Post-Trips Options for Access to Patented Medicines in Developing Countries' CMH Working Paper Series, Paper No WG41, 48–49 (2001); PM Danzon and A Towse, *Differential Pricing for Pharmaceuticals: Reconciling Access, R & D and Patents* (2003); WHO and WTO (eds), *Report of the Workshop on Differential Pricing and Financing of Essential Drugs, 8–11 April 2001, Høsbjør, Norway* (2001). The workshop presentations are accessible as WHO (ed), *WHO-WTO Workshop on Differential Pricing and Financing of Essential Drugs, Høsbjør, 2001* (2001). The EU has adopted a regulation to enable pharmaceutical companies to engage in differential pricing also for certain generic medication. The regulation prohibits the re-importation of drugs on a 'tiered' price list that carry a special logo. Council Regulation (EC) 953/2003 of 26 May 2003 to Avoid Trade Diversion into the European Union of Certain Key Medicines [2003] OJ L135/5 (3 June 2003); in-depth: K Gamharter, *Access to Affordable Medicines. Developing Responses under the TRIPS Agreement and EC Law* (2004) 252 ff.   [30] Danzon (n 29 above) 2.

[31] Maskus (n 22 above) 33.

[32] Barton (n 27 above) 4; KE Maskus and M Ganslandt, 'Parallel Trade in Pharmaceutical Products: Implications for Procuring Medicines for Poor Countries' in B Granville (ed), *The*

The situation is potentially worse in the second model in which national markets are interconnected. In this model the price of one national market 'leaks' into another one. Such leakage may occur because of 'parallel imports', ie a drug placed on a low-price market by the manufacturer is imported by a third party into higher priced markets spoiling the prospect for price discrimination, or because of reference pricing in which governments adopt price regulations that assure that their national prices are not much higher than other national prices. Here a monopolist might threaten to limit the supply for the market with the lower price to prevent the medicine from leaving the country[33] or it might simply set a unitary high price to prevent a loss of sales in the high-price country.[34] All of the models indicate that drug prices in developing countries for patented medicines are higher than if patents were not available. The reader might exclaim at this point that without patents many of these drugs would never have been invented. The claim is certainly not without merit and it will be examined later as a justification for the interference with access to medicine. However, the interference itself exists—it is due to the higher price of the already invented medicine under patent protection as compared to the price that this medicine would have without patent protection. Of particular political importance is the fact that the monopoly rents collected due to TRIPS-induced strengthening of patent legislation are commonly transferred from developing to developed countries. Maskus estimated a significant rent transfer from countries such as Brazil and India to the United States as the largest beneficiary, but also to countries such as Germany.[35]

Economics of Essential Medicines (2002) 57, 78; FM Scherer and J Watal, 'The Economics of TRIPS Options for Access to Medicines' in B Granville (ed), *The Economics of Essential Medicines* (2002) 32, 38 ff. Many commentators have failed to recognize this somewhat perplexing fact. Eg A Subramanian, 'The AIDS Crisis, Differential Pricing of Drugs, and the TRIPS Agreement. Two Proposals' (2001) 4 J World Intell Prop 323, 324; N Gallus, 'The Mystery of Pharmaceutical Parallel Trade and Developing Countries' (2004) 7 J World Intell Prop 169, 173 ff. Note that some authors suggest solving the problem by applying price discrimination also within the country, a proposal which is difficult to implement. For a critical assessment of differential pricing see E t'Hoen and S Moon, 'Pills and Pocketbooks: Equity Pricing of Essential Medicines in Developing Countries' WHO-WTO Workshop on Differential Pricing and Financing of Essential Drugs (2001).

[33] Even though it is hard to see how the realization of the threat would actually prevent the exportation of drugs such threats have been floating in the air in the debate about the exportation of cheap Canadian drugs to elderly US citizens. Similar action was taken by Bayer in the 1990s when wholesalers in Spain and France, where the Bayer drug Adalat was under governmental price control, began placing increasingly large orders to export the drug to the United Kingdom at a significant profit. Bayer reacted by fulfilling orders only to a level determined by the orders of previous years. Judgment of the Court of First Instance, Case T-41/96 *Bayer AG v Commission* [2001].

[34] Danzon (n 29 above); Scherer and Watal (n 29 above). Whether such a course could actually be taken depends on the power and negotiation strength of the country and the company involved as well as the reaction of the general public.

[35] Canada, the United Kingdom, and Japan are also on the losing end of the scale. Maskus (n 22 above) 184.

2 Empirical Studies and Extrapolations

Empirical studies on the price effect of patents abound, though some economists lament their lack of methodological rigour.[36] It has been shown repeatedly that generics are priced significantly lower than branded drugs. Studies in the United States estimate that the price of the first generic entrant is at roughly 60 per cent of the branded drug, and drops to 17 per cent when 20 generics have entered the market.[37] The substantial experience with compulsory licensing of pharmaceuticals—long practiced in countries such as the United Kingdom and Canada—affirms this finding.[38] The availability of substitutes also results in lower prices, though the effect is more limited.[39]

Anecdotal evidence strongly supports that patents lead to higher prices in developing countries. This is not just evinced by instances in which governments threatened to impose compulsory licences and managed to achieve significant price reductions, but even more significantly by Brazil's HIV/AIDS programme. By manufacturing HIV/AIDS drugs in its own government labs rather than procuring branded (and patented) drugs, Brazil achieved a 70 per cent reduction in drug prices by 2001.[40] The complainants in a case before the South African Competition Commission charging GlaxoSmithKline and Boehringer Ingelheim with excessive pricing of antiretrovirals to the detriment of consumers in violation of the South African Competition Act compared the international best price offer of the branded product with the price of a WHO prequalified generic and found the branded drug generally priced at approximately 230 per cent of the generic.[41]

---

[36] Scherer and Watal (n 29 above) 5, 8.

[37] RE Caves, MD Whinston and MA Hurwitz, 'Patent Expiration, Entry, and Competition in the U.S. Pharmaceutical Industry' Brookings Papers on Economic Activity, Microeconomics (1991), 1, 35–36; see also J Stanton, 'Comment: Lesson for the United States from Foreign Price Controls on Pharmaceuticals' (2000) 16 Conn J Int'l L 149, 158; R Goldberg, 'Pharmaceutical Price Controls: Saving Money Today or Lives Tomorrow' (1993) IPI Policy Report No 123, 10 (estimating generic prices at 10%–20% of the branded price).

[38] Consumer and Corporate Affairs Canada, *Compulsory Licensing of Pharmaceuticals. A Review of Section 41 of the Patent Act* (1983) 39 ff; DJ Fowler and MJ Gordon, *The Effect of Public Policy Initiatives on Drug Prices in Canada, 10 Canadian Public Policy—Analyse de Politiques* (1984) 64, 71; Canadian Drug Manufacturers Association, 'Bill C-91: An Act to Amend the Patent Act. Position Paper' in Canadian Drug Manufacturers Association (ed), *Preliminary Submissions of the Canadian Drug Manufacturers Association Regarding Intellectual Property Rights in the Dunkel Draft Tabled on December 21, 1991 in the General Agreement on Tariffs and Trade ('Gatt') Negotiations* (1993) 3; Scherer and Watal (n 29 above) 15 ff; but see RP Rozek, 'The Effects of Compulsory Licensing on Innovation and Access to Health Care' (2000) 3 J World Intell Prop 889, 909 (concluding that compulsory licensing did not reduce prices, but damaged research). On the economic background: FM Scherer, 'The Economic Effects of Compulsory Patent Licensing' in R Towse and R Holzhauer (eds), *The Economics of Intellectual Property Volume II. Patents* (2002) 315, 350 ff.

[39] Scherer and Watal (n 29 above) 7; Ellison (n 26 above); JA DiMasi, 'Price Trends for Prescription Pharmaceuticals: 1995–1999' Tufts Center for the Study of Drug Development (2000).

[40] A-C D'Adesky, *Moving Mountains. The Race to Treat Global AIDS* (2004) 28 ff.

[41] Competition Commission of South Africa, *Hazel Tau et al v GlaxoSmithKline, Boehringer Ingelheim et al*, Competition Commission, Statement of Complaint in Terms of Section 49B(2)(b) of the Competition Act 89 of 1998. Law and Treatment Access United of the AIDS Law Project and

Many studies compare the price of branded drugs in countries with patent protection (usually the United States) with the price of generic equivalents in countries without such protection (usually India) and find enormous mark-ups. However, these studies fail to isolate the effect of patents on the price.[42] Nevertheless, most rigorous economic studies concur that patents would lead to significant price increases, generally over 100 per cent.[43]

Rozek and Berkowitz disagree, however. They compared the price development of pharmaceutical products between 1989 and 1996 in nine developing countries, five of which had strengthened intellectual property protection, and concluded that the introduction of intellectual property protection in the countries studied had no measurable impact on real or nominal prices of drugs that came on the market before the introduction of intellectual property protection.[44] However, the study is not convincing, because it focuses on existing products[45] and because all of the countries studied applied more or less stringent price controls—and thus the study cannot claim to isolate the effect of patents. The wide variety of studies predicting a significant increase in drug prices is more convincing.

Since patents lead to higher prices for pharmaceuticals, they reduce the accessibility of the medicine for the poor. Developed countries have the financial means to assist their populace in the provision of expensive patented medicine, and are under an obligation to do so. Whether they fail to comply with this obligation is beyond the scope of this inquiry. However, developing countries lack the resources to cover the additional price tag (indeed, they often cannot even cover the costs of generics) and hence can only safeguard access to medicine by guaranteeing an adequate price level. As patent rights raise this price level, patents interfere with access to medicine in developing countries.

Treatment Action Campaign, *The Price of Life. Hazel Tau and Others vs GlaxoSmithKline and Boehringer Ingelheim: A Report on the Excessive Pricing Complaint to South Africa's Competition Commission* (2003). Litigation alleging excessive drug pricing is proliferating, see, eg, M Santora, 'City Sues Drug Companies, Claiming Medicaid Fraud' *NY Times* (6 August 2004).

[42] WHO and WTO, *WTO Agreements & Public Health. A Joint Study by the WHO and the WTO Secretariat* (2002) 94.

[43] Eg S Chaudhuri and PK Goldberg and P Jia, 'The Effects of Extending Intellectual Property Rights Protection to Developing Countries: A Case Study of the Indian Pharmaceutical Market' NBER Working Paper 10159 (2003) 31 (estimating price increases for India of in-between 200% and 750%); C Fink, 'How Stronger Patent Protection in India Might Affect the Behavior of Transnational Pharmaceutical Industries' World Bank Working Paper No 2352 (2000) 42 (suggesting price increases for India of well over 200%); R Döbert, W van den Daele and A Seiler, 'Access to Essential Medicines—Rationality and Consensus in the Conflict Over Intellectual Property Rights' WZB discussion papers No SP IV 2003-108 (2003) 74 (juxtaposing different assertions); P Challú, 'The Consequences of Pharmaceutical Product Patenting' (1991) 15–2 World Competition 65, 88 ff; CM Correa, *Intellectual Property Rights, the WTO, and Developing Countries. The TRIPS Agreement and Policy Options* (2000) 35.

[44] RP Rozek and R Berkowitz, 'The Effects of Patent Protection on the Prices of Pharmaceutical Products—Is Intellectual Property Protection Raising the Drug Bill in Developing Countries?' (1998) 2 J World Intell Prop 179.

[45] Scherer and Watal (n 29 above) 5; J Dumoulin, 'Les Brevets et le Prix des Médicaments' (2000) RIDE 45, 60–61.

3 Severity of the Access Impact

Several authors have argued that the focus of the access debate on patents is badly misplaced and that, compared to other factors, the impact of patents is de minimis: 95 per cent of the WHO's essential drugs have never been or are no longer patented and most AIDS, malaria, or tuberculosis medication is not patented in the countries that are hardest hit.[46] Attaran and Gillespie-White surveyed the patent situation[47] of 15 antiretrovirals in Africa in 2001 and found that most of the drugs were patented in few African countries. They also found that in the countries that had granted patents, only a few drugs were in fact patented. Three companies, however, patented their products in up to 37 of the 53 surveyed countries. South Africa, for its part, protected 13 of the 15 surveyed drugs.[48]

But the reluctance to patent drugs in all markets where patents are available does not imply that patents pose no obstacle to access: a company need only obtain patents in all markets with the capacity to produce the drug, because it can then use the patent to prevent others from manufacturing the drug without its consent. Many developing countries do not have the capacity to manufacture drugs.

Where such capacities exist, moverover, they are almost always limited to producing finished products. A 1992 study listed only 12 developing countries as having the capacity to also produce the therapeutic ingredients.[49] It is solely these countries that are of interest in the debate over patents and access to medicine—a fact that is sometimes obscured. Voluntary programmes by drug companies to make drugs more available by reducing prices, giving them away, or granting licences to produce the drug are laudable and increasingly common,[50] but do not resolve the issue. In a market economy, pharmaceutical companies (much like

---

[46] J Straus, 'Patentschutz durch das TRIPS-Abkommen—Ausnahmeregelungen und—praktiken und ihre Bedeutung, insbesondere hinsichtlich pharmazeutischer Produkte' in Stiftung Gesellschaft für Rechtspolitik and Institut für Rechtspolitik (eds), *Bitburger Gespräche. Jahrbuch 2003* (2003) 117, 132.

[47] The study counted a drug as protected if it was protected by a product patent, a process patent, a use patent, or exclusive marketing rights.

[48] A Attaran and L Gillespie-White, 'Do Patents for Antiretroviral Drugs Constrain Access to AIDS Treatment in Africa?' (2001) 286 JAMA 1886. Similar results were obtained by International Intellectual Property Institute, *Patent Protection and Access to HIV/AIDS Pharmaceuticals in Sub-Saharan Africa* (2000) 36 ff; see P Boulet, J Perriens and F Renaud-Théry, 'Patent Situation of HIV/AIDS-related Drugs in 80 Countries' UNAIDS/WHO (2000).

[49] WA Kaplan *et al, Is Local Production of Pharmaceuticals a Way to Improve Pharmaceutical Access in Developing and Transitional Countries? Setting a Research Agenda (Draft)*, Boston University School of Public Health (2003) 8; European Federation of Pharmaceutical Industries and Associations, *Local Production: Protectionism, Technology Transfer or Improved Access?*, at <http://www.efpia.org/4_pos/access/localprod.pdf>.

[50] Attaran and Gillespie-White (n 48 above) 1891; European Federation of Pharmaceutical Industries and Associations, *Partnerships for the Developing World (Summary of Industry Contributions)* (2002). On the experiences with one such programme: JL Struchio and BD Colatrella, 'Successful Public-Private Partnerships in Global Health: Lessons from the MECTIZAN Donation Program' in B Granville (ed), *The Economics of Essential Medicines* (2002) 255.

generic manufacturers) are in the business for profit, and there is little incentive for them to reject monopoly rents.

Yet, there is an important facet of the issue of access to medicine that scholars regarding the impact of patents as minimal have drawn attention to and that has to be borne in mind: the abolition of patent rights is not likely to solve all access problems. Access to medicine is multifaceted. It requires a health system with qualified personnel, capacity to distribute the drugs, testing facilities, and other, related capacity to effectively administer the drugs. In many countries, even basic infrastructure—such as access to water—is lacking. These are formidable obstacles, and the political leadership of some countries may lack the means and/or the will to overcome them. To wit, the funding necessary to solve these problems is often well above what would be necessary to acquire patented drugs.[51]

But the question whether patents impede access is not negated by the fact that other factors impede access even more.[52] The complaints often voiced by the pharmaceutical industry that in some nations with acute health emergencies the military budget is bloated at the expense of the health budget and that the government's own tariffs on the drug inflate the price are correct and must be seconded.[53] Yet, the problems involved with drug patents should not be underestimated: a government that can afford to provide drugs only to a fraction of the population saves a significant amount of money if the drug prices are cut in half (as a conservative evaluation of the studies above suggests they would be). This money can be invested in supplying a larger portion of the population with medicine or in upgrading the necessary infrastructure. The amounts involved can be significant, as drugs can constitute an important portion of the health budget.[54] Cheaper drug prices will also help overcome government reluctance to act, as it is likely that exorbitant drug prices discourage governments from tackling treatment and make

---

[51] Attaran and Gillespie-White (n 48 above) 1890; HE Bale, Jr, 'Consumption and Trade in Off-Patented Medicines' CMH Working Paper Series Paper No WG4: (2001) 3; HE Bale, Jr, 'Patents, Patients and Developing Countries: Access, Innovation and The Political Dimensions of Trade Policy' in B Granville (ed), *The Economics of Essential Medicines* (2002) 100; KE Maskus, 'Ensuring Access to Essential Medicines: Some Economic Considerations' (2001–2002) 20 Wis Int L Rev 563, 567; RP Rozek and N Tully, 'The TRIPS Agreement and Access to Health Care' (1999) 2 J World Intell Prop 813.   [52] Attaran and Gillespie-White (n 48 above) 1890.

[53] HE Bale, Jr, 'Consumption and Trade in Off-Patented Medicines' CMH Working Paper Series Paper No WG4: (2001) 3.

[54] Expenditure for medicine is the largest single expenditure category for the South African medical scheme—at 29% of the total expenditure in 1998/99. In the United States, prescription drugs accounted for 10% of the nation's $1.88 trillion health expenditures in 2004. Depending on the incentives set within their health system some countries reach exorbitant percentages (China: 52%). One study cites this percentage as 7%–30% for developed and transition countries and 24%–66% for developing countries. J Doherty *et al*, 'Health Care Financing and Expenditure' in P Ijumba (ed), *South African Health Review 2002* (2003) 13, 31–32; Alliance for Health Reform, *Covering Health Issues: A Sourcebook for Journalists* (2006) 113; Ernst & Young, *Health Care Systems and Health Market Reform in the G20 Countries* (2003); K Floyd and C Gilks, *Cost and Financing Aspects of Providing Anti-retroviral Therapy: A Background Paper*, Worldbank (1998); G Velásquez, 'Médicaments Essentiels et Mondialisation' (2000) RIDE 37, 40.

them set different priorities.[55] The interference of patents in developing countries with access can thus hardly be held to be de minimis.

II Justification of the Interference

Very few rights are absolute in the sense that any interference with them violates the right. Most human rights provisions can be limited if certain conditions are fulfilled. This means that the interference of patents in developing countries with the right to access to medicine could be justified under human rights law. The International Covenant on Civil and Political Rights (ICCPR) allows derogations in times of an emergency threatening the life of a nation for many of its provisions under its Article 4. Some rights also contain limitation clauses and where states limit the right in compliance with the limitation clause and the principle of proportionality their interference with the right is regarded as justified and there is no violation of the right.[56] The International Covenant on Economic, Social, and Cultural Rights (ICESCR) contains a general limitation clause in its Article 4 that provides:

in the enjoyment of those rights provided by the State in conformity with the present Covenant, the State may subject such rights only to such limitations as are determined by law only in so far as this may be compatible with the nature of these rights and solely for the purpose of promoting the general welfare in a democratic society.

The Limburg principles, written by a group of experts convened by the International Commission of Jurists, stress that the article was not meant to introduce limitations on rights affecting the subsistence or survival of the individual.[57] The ICCPR does not contain such a general limitation clause. Nor does the right to life contain a limitation clause that is related to patent law.

However, this does not imply that no justification is available. At times, the freedoms identified in the Covenant can conflict, requiring balancing them against one another. An example that has excited much attention in German literature is the situation in which a hostage taker threatens to kill the hostage, and a police officer has the possibility to kill the hostage taker. Can the state agent kill and infringe the right to life of the hostage taker? Must the officer kill to protect the life of the hostage?[58] In such cases a balance needs to be struck between the colliding rights. Such a limitation of the rights of one person by the rights of others is inherent in the concept of rights—some authors would argue that it is

---

[55] Döbert, van den Daele and Seiler (n 43 above) 73.
[56] M Nowak, *Introduction to the International Human Rights Regime*, 56 ff (2003).
[57] International Commission of Jurists *et al*, *The Limburg Principles on the Implementation of the International Covenant on Economic, Social and Cultural Rights*, UN Doc E/CN.4/1987/17, Annex, para 47 (2–6 June 1986). On the provision see also MCR Craven, *The International Covenant on Economic, Social and Cultural Rights. A Perspective on its Development* (1995) 312, 254–255, 282–283.
[58] H Witzstrock, *Der polizeiliche Todesschuß* (2001).

not a question of the limitation of the right but rather part of the definition of the scope of the right.[59] Whether examining a justification under Article 4 of the ICESCR or under colliding rights, a possible colliding value needs to be identified to justify the interference. Article 4 of the ICESCR frames this requirement as 'promoting the general welfare in a democratic society', the ICCPR and customary law require a colliding human right.

1 Protection of the Inventor's Material Interests

The first colliding right that could justify patent laws in developing countries is the right of authors to benefit from the protection of the moral and material interest resulting from scientific productions contained in Article 15 of the ICESCR, which reads:

(1) The States Parties to the present Covenant recognize the right of everyone:
> (...)
>> (c) To benefit from the protection of the moral and material interests resulting from any scientific, literary or artistic production of which he is the author.

(2) The steps to be taken by the States Parties to the present Covenant to achieve the full realization of this right shall include those necessary for the conservation, the development and the diffusion of science and culture. (...)

The Universal Declaration of Human Rights (UDHR) contains a similar provision in Article 27(2). A whole number of questions have to be answered in respect of a possible justification of the interference of patents in developing countries with access to medicine with this right, eg can a right that is contained in the ICESCR justify an interference with the right to life under the ICCPR? However, it suffices to determine the scope of protection of Article 15(1)(c) of the ICESCR to see that this approach of justification clearly fails.

Article 15(1)(c) of the ICESCR has long been dormant. It has already been stated above that natural law arguments in intellectual property law held large sway during the French Revolution and influenced the subsequent development of intellectual property law, but have since taken the backseat to utilitarian considerations with the exception of moral rights in copyright law. Only recently have human rights aspects regained more attention with commentators. Some of these authors have argued that Article 15(1)(c) is broad enough to cover at least patents, copyright, and utility models.[60] A proper understanding of Article 15(1)(c)

---

[59] For the ECHR: P van Dijk and GJH van Hoof, *Theory and Practice of the European Convention on Human Rights* (3rd edn, 1998) 764; For German constitutional law: A Bleckmann, *Staatsrecht II— Die Grundrechte* (4th edn, 1997) 473 ff; M Winkler, *Kollission verfassungsrechtlicher Schutznormen. Zur Dogmatik der 'verfassungsimmanenten Grundrechtsschranken'*, (2000) 20 ff; M Sachs, *Verfassungsrecht II. Grundrechte* (2000) 133 ff; R Alexy, *Theorie der Grundrechte* (1994) 249 ff.

[60] W Fikentscher, *Wirtschaftsrecht. Band I Weltwirtschaftsrecht Europäisches Wirtschaftsrecht* (1983) 263; W Meng, 'GATT and Intellectual Property Rights—The International Law Framework' in G Sacerdoti (ed), *Liberalization of Services and Intellectual Property in the Uruguay Round of GATT. Proceedings of the Conference on 'The Uruguay Round of GATT and the Improvement of the Legal Framework of Trade in Services'*, Bergamo, 21.–23. September 1989 (1990) 57, 68.

however, has to differentiate between the scope of this provision and modern-day intellectual property law. Article 15 protects the moral and material interest of authors—which is not coextensive with modern-day 'patents' or 'copyrights'.[61] The ICESCR does not elevate modern day intellectual property law lock, stock, and barrel to a human right.

Intellectual property law goes beyond the moral and material interests of authors and has rightly been conceptualized by Drahos as 'instrumental' rather than 'fundamental'. Modern day intellectual property rights are only the means to achieve a larger societal goal, namely the advancement of society for the benefit of its constituents. It is merely this goal that harks back to fundamental human rights values.[62] Intellectual property rights, however, are, with the exception of trademarks, temporary in nature, limited by a term the length of which has been fixed arbitrarily. They can be assigned and revoked—and are thus quite different from 'fundamental' human rights.

Article 15(1)(c) of the ICESCR is such a fundamental human right, but it does not protect 'patents' or 'copyrights' as such. Instead, it protects the right of the author to benefit from the protection of the moral and material interests resulting from his scientific, literary, or artistic productions—a point which needs further clarification.

A *Author—Scope* ratione personae

Article 15(1)(c) of the ICESCR protects an author's moral and material interest in his or her qualifying products. The wording clearly addresses natural persons only: the provision speaks of 'everyone', 'the author', and 'he'.[63]

The first point of inquiry is whether pharmaceutical companies can rely on this provision at all. Many national human rights provisions allow legal entities to rely on them at least if the provisions are closely related to property notions—after all, property as a human right protects the owner of the property and ownership rights are of identical content whether the owner is a natural person or a legal entity.[64] The situation with respect to Article 15(1)(c) of the ICESCR is

---

[61] Committee on Economic, Social and Cultural Rights, General Comment No 17, para 2.

[62] P Drahos, 'The Universality of Intellectual Property Rights: Origins and Development' in WIPO (ed), *Intellectual Property and Human Rights. A Panel Discussion to commemorate the 50th Anniversary of the Universal Declaration of Human Rights. Geneva, November 9, 1998* (1999) 13; Committee on Economic, Social and Cultural Rights, *Substantive Issues Arising in the Implementation of the International Covenant on Economic, Social and Cultural Rights. Follow-up to the day of general discussion on article 15.1 (c). Monday, 26 November 2001*, E/C.12/2001/15 (14 December 2001) para 6.

[63] US and German patent laws recognize that the inventor can only be a natural (or several natural) person(s): cf 35 USC § 102(f); M Barrett, *Intellectual Property. Patents, Trademarks & Copyrights* (2000) 36; AR Miller and MH Davis, *Intellectual Property in a Nutshell. Patents, Trademarks, and Copyright* (3rd edn, 2000) 103–104. § 6 PatG; DPA (1951) GRUR 577; BGH (1966) GRUR 558, 560, H Hubmann and H-P Götting, *Gewerblicher Rechtsschutz* (7th edn, 2002) 140. Note that the situation was different before a change in the German Patent Act in 1936, with the *Reichsgericht* allowing so-called 'corporate inventions'.

[64] Eg the basic rights of the German *Grundgesetz* apply to domestic legal entities 'to the extent that the nature of such rights permits' (Art 19(3) of GG); trans DP Kommers, *The Constitutional*

different: it is not just the language of the provision that fails to mention corporations as possible beneficiaries; the history of international human rights law indicates that the provision was meant for the benefit of individuals. Drawing on its knowledge of state practice, the Committee on Economic, Social and Cultural Rights commented that under 'the existing international treaty protection regimes, legal entities are included among the holders of intellectual property rights. However, (. . .) their entitlements, because of their different nature, are not protected at the level of human rights'.[65] The proposition that legal entities do not benefit from the protection of universal international human rights instruments with the exception of certain rights such as trade union rights is now generally accepted, as indicated by its inclusion in the US Restatements on Foreign Relations Law.[66]

B Interests of Inventors—Scope ratione materiae

It is also doubtful whether inventors can rely on the ICESCR. The term 'author' of a 'scientific, literary or artistic production' seems to imply that the provision is concerned with the protection of writers of scientific tractates only. This is also the understanding of the German government.[67] The argument is buttressed by the fact that the language in the ICESCR is reminiscent of that in several treaties in the domain of copyright law: the Universal Copyright Convention[68] protects the 'rights of authors and other copyright proprietors in literary, scientific and artistic works (. . .)'. Similarly, the scope of the Berne Convention for the Protection of Literary and Artistic Works[69] includes 'every production in the literary, scientific and artistic domain'. An even clearer indication of the fact that inventions are not protected by the language of Article 15(1)(c) is the terminology of Article XIII of the American Declaration of the Rights and Duties of Man:[70] that provision explicitly extents protection to inventions *and* literary, scientific, or artistic works.[71]

Textually, an exclusion of inventors from the right would rely on a definition of 'author' of 'scientific production' that excludes inventions. Given that 'author' is

---

Jurisprudence of the Federal Republic of Germany (2nd edn, 1997) 507 ff; for the application on the protection of property: H-J Papier, in T Maunz *et al* (eds), *Grundgesetz. Kommentar. Band II Art. 12–20* (loose-leaf, last updated February 2003) Art 14, paras 206 ff, 217.

65 General Comment No 17 (n 61 above) para 7.

66 American Law Institute, *Restatement of the Law Third. The Foreign Relations Law of the United States. Volume 2*, (1987) § 701 Reporters' note 6 (at 158); concerning the ICCPR: T Buergenthal, 'To Respect and to Ensure: State Obligations and Permissible Derogations' in L Henkin (ed), *The International Bill of Rights. The Covenant on Civil and Political Rights* (1981) 72, 73. Note that the situation can be different with respect to regional instruments.

67 Bundesregierung, *Denkschrift zum Internationalen Pakt über wirtschaftliche, soziale und kulturelle Rechte vom 19. Dezember 1966*, BT-Drucks 7/658, 18, 27 (1973).

68 Article I of the Convention. 69 Articles 1, 2 (1) of the Convention.

70 American Declaration of the Rights and Duties of Man (1948), OAS, *Basic Documents Pertaining to Human Rights in the Inter-American System*, OEA/Ser L/V/I.4 Rev 9, at 17 (2003).

71 P Buck, *Geistiges Eigentum und Völkerrecht*, 220–221 (1994).

defined as both 'writer of a literary work' and 'one that originates or creates',[72] it would have to exclude inventions from 'scientific production'. It could only do so by defining a 'scientific production' as a work of basic or theoretical science, as opposed to applied science.[73] Such a separation is untenable. The large amount of patents held by university institutes[74] shows that basic science and applied 'inventions' are inextricably linked—it would be an oddity to claim that an author is protected under the ICESCR if he publishes an article on a genetic problem in a journal, whereas he is not protected if he uses the same article as a disclosure in a patent application.

The context of Article 15(1)(c) supports this position: Article 15(1)(b) contains a right to enjoy the benefits of scientific progress and its applications, clearly including inventions as the 'applications' of scientific progress. Article 15(2) stresses the link between the two provisions: it speaks of 'the full realization of this right', apparently regarding the provisions of Article 15(1) (a), (b), and (c) as inextricably linked, if not as a unitary right. Even though the sub-paragraphs of Article 15(1) contain separate rights, they are closely interlinked and limit each other. Thus, the fact that Article 15(1)(b) includes inventions is some indication to the fact that Article 15(1)(c) does the same.

What little practice there is on the provision also points towards a protection of inventors. Thus, the Committee on Economic, Social and Cultural Rights regards inventions as within the scope of the provision in its statement about Article 15(1)(c) in preparation of a General Comment and mentions innovations as within the scope of the norm in its General Comment No 17.[75] The *travaux préparatoires* are surprisingly silent on the provision that was modelled on the UDHR: even though its inclusion was hotly contested, it incited little debate on its substance. However, during the discussions some delegations made references to rights of the inventor or patents, evidently assuming that inventors' interests were included in the scope of the provision.[76]

---

[72] FC Mish *et al* (eds), *Merriam-Webster's Collegiate Dictionary* (10th edn, 1998).

[73] Buck (n 71 above) 221.

[74] The interplay of basic and applied research is illustrated by the history of AIDS research described in chapter 1. The importance of patents for universities can be gauged by looking at University of California, *Technology Transfer Program. 2002 Annual Report* (2002) (noting that the University of California holds more than 3,000 US patents, receiving licensing fees of $100m in 2002).

[75] Follow-up to the day of general discussion on Article 15.1(c) (n 62 above); General Comment No 17 (n 61 above) para 9. See also United Nations High Commissioner for Human Rights, *Economic, Social and Cultural Rights. The Impact of the Agreement on Trade-Related Aspects of Intellectual Property Rights on Human rights. Report of the High Commissioner*, UN Doc E/CN.4/Sub.2/2001/13 (27 June 2001) para 10 ff; D Weissbrodt and K Schoff, 'Human Rights Approach to Intellectual Property Protection: The Genesis and Application of Sub-Commission Resolution 2000/7' (2003) 5 MIPR 1, 3; Max Planck Institute for Foreign and International Patent, Copyright and Competition Law, *Comment of the Max Planck Institute*, in *Economic, Social and Cultural Rights. Intellectual Property Rights and Human Rights. Report of the Secretary General*, UN Doc E/CN.4/Sub.2/2001/12 (14 June 2001).

[76] Buck (n 71 above) 225–226; AR Chapman, 'Approaching Intellectual Property as a Human Right: Obligations Related to Article 15 (1) (c)' in UNESCO (ed), 35 *Copyright Bulletin Approaching*

C Moral and Material Interests

Article 15(1)(c) of the ICESCR protects the 'moral' and 'material' interests of inventors. Moral interests, a subject of enormous debate for authors of literary works,[77] are non-material interests stemming from the intimate connection of the inventor with his work. They include, for example, the right of the inventor to be named as such. It is the protection of the material interests of the inventor, however, that is of relevance for the conflict with the right to health.

The provision protects the inventor's material interest. As such, the provision is meant to insure that the inventor can reap the fruits of his labour as adequate remuneration. It is a true human right and has little in common with the interests protected by modern day patent law. Modern patents ensure that the inventor, or more commonly the corporation he works for, obtains a sufficient amount of money to have an incentive to invent. Pharmaceutical patents are rarely ever owned by the inventor. Nor are the enormous costs necessary to sustain inventive activity shouldered by the inventor. The Committee on Economic, Social and Cultural Rights notes that 'intellectual property regimes, although they traditionally provide protection to individual authors and creators, are increasingly focused on protecting business and corporate interests and investments', and regards these interests as outside the scope of human rights protection.[78] Patents are, as has been shown at length in chapter 2, utilitarian tools to advance a policy, not human rights instruments. The interests of the inventor as a person are the ones at the heart of the human rights provision. Patents in the hands of inventors are partly a means to achieve the goals of the human rights provision,[79] but the human rights provision does not protect modern day patents to the full extent.

It could be argued that all modern day patents—even those in the hands of legal entities—are necessary to protect the inventors' material interests, as without such patents companies would not invest in inventive activity and employ inventors, thus leaving them without a livelihood. But this would turn Article 15(1)(c) into a protection of our current-day organization of inventive activity, something that is beyond the scope of human rights law. The provision merely protects the livelihood of inventors, which is sufficiently protected if protection is granted to the inventor only.

D The Right in the Conflict with Access to Medicine

It has already become clear that Article 15(1)(c) of the ICESCR offers very little ground to stand on as a justification for an interference with the right to access to

---

Intellectual Property as a Human Right (2001) 4, 10 ff; M Green, *Drafting History of the Article 15 (1) (c) of the International Covenant on Economic, Social and Cultural Rights*, UN Doc E/C.12/2000/15 (2000).

77 F Abbott, T Cottier and F Gurry, *The International Intellectual Property System. Commentary and Materials. Pt One* (1999) 1085 ff.

78 Follow-up to the day of general discussion on Article 15.1 (c) (n 62 above) 6.

79 General Comment No 17 (n 61 above) para 16.

medicine. It does not protect patents as such, nor does it protect pharmaceutical companies. What little there remains of a possible justification is defeated by the fact that Article 15 tries to achieve a balance between the protection of the interest of the inventor and public access to the invention—this is indicated both by Article 15(1)(a), (b) and by paragraph 2 of the provision.[80] The Convention thus warrants a flexible approach—the precise balance between public access to the invention and protection of the inventor's interests has to take the context of Article 15 into account. Other human rights provisions are part of this context. If no other rights are at risk from the protection of the inventor's interests, the pendulum swings towards the protection of these interests. If other rights are at risk from a lack of diffusion—such as the right to health or the right to food—the pendulum swings towards supporting diffusion and access to the benefits of the new technology. Article 15(1)(c) therefore does not justify the interference of patent laws with the right to access to medicine.

Patent holders could also try to base their human rights claims on regional instruments, some of which explicitly mention the interests involved, eg the American Declaration of the Rights and Duties of Man[81] and the Charter of Fundamental Rights of the European Union,[82] some of which protect intellectual property interests as property.[83] As with the right to access to medicine, this study is limited to the universal human rights instruments.

2 Justification as an Incentive for Future Research

The second and far more complicated question is whether patents in developing countries can be justified by the fact that they provide an incentive for further research and have provided an incentive for past research: without patents, the medicine that we now want to make available would never have been developed, or so the claim goes. Legally, the rights in question in this justification are the very same that patents are interfering with: patents would be protected to safeguard access to future (new) medicine. At stake is the balance between the medicine for the diseases of today and those of tomorrow. With lives and livelihoods at stake on both sides, it can come as no surprise that proponents of each position exchange invectives.

---

[80] General Comment No 17 (n 61 above) paras 4, 35; Drahos (n 62 above) 24; Weissbrodth and Schoff (n 75 above). The fact that Art 15(1)(c) of the ICESCR received less support than the other provisions of the Article during the drafting process does not support a hierarchy within the norm, *contra* Chapman (n 76 above) 12–13.

[81] Article XIII (protecting the moral and material interests as regards an author's inventions or literary, scientific, or artistic works).   [82] Article 17 (2) (protecting intellectual property), not in force.

[83] The European Commission of Human Rights held patents to be protected as property under Art 1 of the Protocol No 1 to the Convention for the Protection of Human Rights and Fundamental Freedoms in *Smith Kline and French Laboratories Ltd v Netherlands* (App 12633/87) (1990) 66 DR 70, 79; W Peukert in JA Frowein and W Peukert (eds), *Europäische MenschenRechtsKonvention. EMRK-Kommentar* (2nd edn, 1996) Art 1 des 1. ZP para 6.

Any justification of patents through this argument relies on the fact that patents actually *do* spur research and innovation in the pharmaceutical industry. With research and development costs of new drugs, as already mentioned, falling between $115m and $802m, it is rather self-evident that without the opportunity to recoup this cost there would be no incentive to innovate in the future.[84] The incentive argument disfavours any exception to patent law. If exceptions for medicine for particularly serious diseases are made, the incentive to innovate is lost in the area where it is needed most.

Nevertheless, there have been voices criticizing the patent system as a whole. First of all they point out that even a well-functioning patent office like that of the United States grants many patents that should not be granted.[85] But even if the quality of patent examination were better, there is much debate whether the innovations made because of patents compensate for the welfare losses incurred—with a study denying positive welfare effects from patents for every study that shows such welfare effects.[86] Finally, the often-adduced argument that 'patents are good for innovation' does not say anything about the limits on patents: it favours prolonging patents beyond all bounds and is silent on how much of a profit is a sufficient incentive, a pertinent question as the pharmaceutical industry ranks among the most profitable businesses.[87] It fits well into this picture that the TRIPS Agreement's 20-year patent term does not rely on economic studies, but rather historic coincidence and goes back to the Belgium patent legislation passed in 1854.[88]

[84] FM Scherer, 'Le Système des Brevets et l'Innovation dans le Domaine Pharmaceutique' (2000) RIDE 109; FE Muennich, 'Les Brevets Pharmaceutiques et L'Accès Aux Médicaments' (2000) RIDE 71; HE Bale, Jr, 'Patents, Patients and Developing Countries: Access, Innovation and The Political Dimensions of Trade Policy' in B Granville (ed), *The Economics of Essential Medicines* (2002) 100, 102 ff.

[85] One study shows that a mere 54% of the patents litigated to judgment are found to be valid. It can be supposed that in countries with a less well-established patent office a majority of the patents granted are of doubtful validity. J Love, *Compulsory Licensing: Models for State Practice in Developing Countries, Access to Medicine and Compliance with the WTO TRIPS Accord*, prepared for the United Nations Development Programme, para 8, at <http://www.cptech.org/ip/health/cl/recommended-statepractice.html> (2001).

[86] Thus, one study shows that the introduction of pharmaceutical product patents in Italy in 1978 led to approximately 200% higher prices for medicine, but neither to a growth of the expenditure on research and development nor to an accelerated introduction of new products. On the other hand, survey evidence from India suggests higher expenditure on research and development in anticipation of the introduction of product patents. Scherer and Watal (n 29 above) 11; FM Scherer and S Weisburst, *Economic Effects of Strengthening Pharmaceutical Patent Protection in Italy*, IIC 1995, 1009; K Timmermans and T Hutadjulu, *The TRIPS Agreement and Pharmaceuticals, Report of an ASEAN Workshop on the TRIPs Agreement and its Impact on Pharmaceuticals. Jakarta, 2–4 May 2000* (2000) 24.

[87] In Fortune's 2006 ranking the pharmaceutical industry was ranked as the fifth most profitable industry out of 50 industries with a profitability of 15.7% of revenues. *Top Industries*, Fortune, 17 April 2006. This criticism has been voiced since the 1960s as is recounted in C Crampes, 'La Recherche et la Protection des Innovations dans le Secteur Pharmaceutique' (2000) RIDE 125, 135.

[88] S Lapointe, 'L'histoire des brevets' (2000) 12 Les Cahiers de propriété intellectuelle 633, 649. Economic literature on the optimal patent term is inconclusive and fraught with restrictive assumptions, because as Nordhaus states, '[the] determination of the optimal [patent] life is extremely difficult'. WD Nordhaus, *Invention, Growth, and Welfare. A Theoretical Treatment of Technological Change*

But if nothing else has changed from the days when Machlup attested to the US Congress that on the economic facts it would be irresponsible to introduce a patent system if none were in place,[89] the investment costs necessary for research and development have exploded. For this reason even most activists today rightly agree that some form of patent system is necessary.

The less radical reformists argue convincingly that the incentives set by the patent system need to be recalibrated. As in any industry, the pharmaceutical industry does research where money can be made with a sufficient probability. Drews, the former president of global research at Hoffmann-La Roche, thinks that such an approach is not compatible with the philosophy of research. He argues that marketing should be inspired by new research, not research submitted to the instructions of marketing. 'What, then, will it mean to subordinate research to the requirements of the market? It means that long-range problems have been subordinated to short-term needs, that the innovative must take a back seat to the tried and true (...).'[90] Areas offering particularly attractive and probable returns on research investments seem to be (1) 'life-style drugs', ie drugs that can be marketed to a large share of the population, but that are not targeting serious diseases;[91] (2) minor (but patentable) improvements on existing drugs the patents on which are running out, in an attempt to channel patients to the new patented drug and save the already established market for a patented product;[92] (3) the modification of chemical entities marketed by competitors to obtain a competing drug in an already existing market.[93] Several numbers support the finding: the UNDP estimates that 70 per cent of drugs with therapeutic gain were produced

(1969) 86, M Rafiquzzaman, 'The Optimal Patent Term under Uncertainty' (1987) 5 Int'l J of Indus Org 233; R Gilbert and C Shapiro, 'Optimal Patent Length and Breadth' (1990) 21 RAND J of Econ 502, 507 (suggesting long but weak patents); P Klemperer, 'How Broad Should the Scope of Patent Protection Be?' (1990) 21 RAND J of Econ 113 (favouring short and strong patents).

[89] F Machlup, *An Economic Review of the Patent System, Study of the Subcommittee on Patents, Trademarks, and Copyrights of the Committee on the Judiciary, United States Senate, Eighty-Fifth Congress, Second Session* (1958) 80.

[90] J Drews, *In Quest of Tomorrow's Medicines* (trans D Kramer, 2003) 234.

[91] Investment in direct-to-consumer and professional advertising by pharmaceutical companies in the United States ($15.7b in 2000) rose faster between 1996 and 2000 than investment in research and development ($25.7b in 2000). Advertising is mostly done for non-essential medication. However, several other factors contribute to a complex set of market failures, including the human psyche: studies have shown that patients are more content when receiving a positive diagnosis. S Woloshin *et al*, 'Direct-to-Consumer Advertisements for Prescription Drugs: What Are Americans Being Sold?' (2001) 358 Lancet 1141; Goozner (n 13 above) 230, 233; S Vaisrub, 'The Magic of a Name' (1980) 243 JAMA 1931.

[92] European Generic Medicines Association, *Tangled Patent Linkages Reduce Pharmaceutical Innovation. 6,730 patents for 27 pharmaceutical inventions*, EGA Press Release, at <http://www .EGAgenerics.com/pr-2004-07-01.htm> (1 July 2004); Goozner (n 13 above) 219 ff.

[93] In a Senate hearing in the early 1960s the retired former head of research at EJ Squibb estimated that more than half of the corporate drug research fell into that category. Goozner (n 13 above) 209 ff, 214. The pharmaceutical industry contests these figures, stating that 20% of its research budget goes towards improving and/or modifying existing products, whereas 80% is directed at the advancement of scientific knowledge and the development of new products. AF Holmer, 'Innovation Is Key Mission' *USA Today* (31 May 2002).

with government involvement.[94] And while the US PTO granted 6,730 pharmaceutical patents in 2000, the FDA only registered 27 new chemical entities during that period.[95] Even the value of these to society is not always high: of the 144 new molecular entities[96] introduced in the United States from 1978–1987 only 14 had no close substitute in their therapeutic class.[97] A 2002 study by the National Institute for Health Care Management found that only 24 per cent of the 1,035 drug applications approved by the FDA in between 1989 and 2000 were priority reviews, signifying a medical advance, and the percentage is falling.[98] But these numbers, however convincing they look at first sight, are not always so clear upon closer examination. Thus, the pharmaceutical industry took offence at the use of FDA data by the 2002 study, stating that if every drug would be submitted to priority review, the purpose of establishing such a review would be defeated. Hence the FDA status is not dispositive in considering the real value of a drug.[99]

Fortunately, it is not necessary to sift through the myriad studies on the merits of the patent system as a whole for the purposes of this study and to solve the hydra-headed problems involved in constructing (or abolishing) a patent system—a task that has eluded economists and lawyers ever since the patent system was invented. Only the merits of pharmaceutical patents in developing countries are within the purview of the study. For this reason two questions need to be distinguished: whether pharmaceutical patents in developing countries are necessary as an incentive for the development of medication that will be used for global diseases and whether pharmaceutical patents are necessary as an incentive for the development of cures of diseases prevalent solely in developing countries.

The paramount determinant in this evaluation is the insignificant role that developing countries' markets play in the world economy. Most major drug companies achieve over 80 per cent of their sales in the United States, Canada, the European Union, and Japan alone.[100] The share of the profits is even higher, as those markets are often the highest-priced. Africa is particularly negligible as a market—it represents just 1.1 per cent of the global market.[101] With these figures

[94] UNDP, *Human Development Report 1999* (1999) 69; CM Correa, 'Some Assumptions on Patent Law and Pharmaceutical R&D' (2001) Quaker United Nations Office—Geneva—Occasional Paper 6, 2.   [95] European Generic Medicines Association (n 92 above).

[96] The study found 195 new molecular entities launched, but had to exclude several of them for various reasons.

[97] ZJ Lu and WS Comanor, 'Strategic Pricing of New Pharmaceuticals' (1998) 80 Review of Econ & Statistics 108, 112–113; Scherer and Watal (n 29 above) 7.

[98] National Institute for Health Care Management Research and Education Foundation, *Changing Patterns of Pharmaceutical Innovation* (2002) 3.

[99] Pharmaceutical Research and Manufacturers Association, *NIHCM's Report on Pharmaceutical Innovation: Fact vs. Fiction, a preliminary report* (2002) 3.

[100] The 2002 figures are: Aventis: 82% (United States, Canada, Western Europe, and Japan) (Aventis, *2002 Annual Report* (2002) 56); GlaxoSmithKline: 86.9% (United States, Canada, Europe, and Japan) (GlaxoSmithKline, *The Impact of Medicines. Annual Report 2002* (2002) 13); Roche: 77.8% (Switzerland, the European Union, North America, and Japan) (Roche, *Annual Report 2002* (2002) 88); Eli Lilly: 78.5% (United States and Western Europe) (Eli Lilly & Co, *Developing Innovation. Annual Report 2002* (2002) 30); Merck: 80.5% (United States and Western Europe) (Merck & Co, Inc, *Annual Report 2002* (2002) 23).

[101] Attaran and Gillespie-White (n 48 above) 1890.

it is highly unlikely that the profits in least-developed countries or in developing countries are necessary to maintain research and development expenditure—their marginal contribution to the research and development costs is negligible. The research that is done on diseases that are spread globally would also be done (and has been done for a long time) without patents being available in developing country markets.

Developing countries' marginal contribution to pharmaceutical companies' profits is confirmed by the fact that the pharmaceutical industry does relatively little research on priority health concerns in the developing world, which are different from those in developed countries.[102] The research would simply not pay. The diseases in those countries are thus neglected—much like rare diseases in the developed world, which are targeted by so-called 'orphan drugs'. The current situation can be illustrated by numbers that speak in the clearest of terms: the UNDP has stated that only 0.2 per cent of the global health-related research and development goes to pneumonia, diarrhoeal diseases, and tuberculosis, which account for 18 per cent of the global disease burden and concluded: 'Tighter control of innovation in the hands of multinational corporations ignores the needs of millions. From new drugs to better seeds for food crops, the best of the new technologies are designed and priced for those who can pay. For poor people, the technological progress remains far out of reach.'[103] Only one per cent of the new chemical entities developed between 1975 and 1997 were for the treatment of tropical diseases.[104] Some hope that the introduction of patents in developing markets can change the situation,[105] enlarge the incentive for the pharmaceutical industry, spur foreign direct investment,[106] and enable the local industry to do research on these neglected diseases.[107]

---

[102] Correa (n 94 above) 5; JO Lanjouw and IM Cockburn, 'New Pills for Poor People? Empirical Evidence after GATT' (2001) 29 World Development 265, 266; EFM 't Hoen, 'The Responsibility of Research Universities to Promote Access to Essential Medicines' (2003) 3 Yale J Health Pol'y L & Ethics 293, 295. Taking account of this distinction Lanjouw has proposed to make pharmaceutical companies choose whether to patent a product in the developed or in the developing world. JO Lanjouw, 'A Patent Policy Proposal for Global Diseases, CMH Working Paper Series' Paper No WG2: (2001) 11.   [103] UNDP (n 94 above) 68–69.

[104] M Byström and P Einarsson, *TRIPS—vad betyder WTOs patentavtal för de fattiga ländernas människor och miljö?* (2002) Diakonia Forum Syd Svenska Naturskyddsföreningen, 37.

[105] AO Sykes, 'TRIPs, Pharmaceuticals, Developing Countries, and the Doha "Solution"' (2002) John M Olin Law & Economics Working Paper No 140 (2nd series), 3; G Saint-Paul, 'To What Extent Should Less-Developed Countries Enforce Intellectual Property?' CEPR Discussion Paper No 4713 (2004). More cautious: CA Primo Braga, C Fink and C Paz Sepulveda, 'Intellectual Property Rights and Economic Development' World Bank Discussion Paper No 412 (2000) 28 (pointing out that there is limited evidence regarding the usefulness of the patent system in promoting the creation of new knowledge in developing countries).

[106] CA Primo Braga and C Fink, 'Reforming Intellectual Property Rights Regimes: Challenges for Developing Countries' (1998) 1 JIEL 537, 542; C Mariot Kalanje, 'Intellectual Property, Foreign Direct Investment and the Least-Developed Countries. A Perspective' (2002) 5 J World Intell Prop 119, 126–127; in-depth: C Fink and CA Primo Braga, 'How Stronger Protection of Intellectual Property Rights Affects International Trade Flows' World Bank Working Paper No 2051 (1999) 13 (with an ambiguous outcome).

[107] O Lippert, 'A Market Perspective on Recent Developments in the TRIPS and Essential Medicines Debate' in B Granville (ed), *The Economics of Essential Medicines* (2002) 3, 24–25.

But the available evidence indicates that the hopes do not bear out. Newly available patent laws have done and by themselves will probably do little to change the situation.[108] The incremental incentive provided by additional patent protection is unlikely to produce much more investment in research and development for tropical diseases by global corporations as long as the profits are to be made elsewhere.[109] The hopes for local industries to be set up in the developing world and do that research are similarly inflated.[110] Most national pharmaceutical industries lack the capacity to do research at all.[111] Where such capacities exist the research will not target developing markets, either: a recent study shows that as of 1999 only 16 per cent of the growing pharmaceutical research and development investments in India went towards tropical diseases and half of these 16 per cent studied the improvement of products for diseases of global incidence.[112] Economists therefore increasingly concur that the welfare effects of the introduction of new patent laws are negative in the developing world. Scherer illustrates this by stating that stronger patent protection in the developing world would lead to 18 drugs instead of 15 for this market, but the welfare transfer due to patent protection could only be offset by a three-fold increase.[113]

The research priorities of the drug companies follow economic rationales: the developing countries' industry is faced with the same choice as the industry in developed countries—to research for the developed or for the developing countries' markets. As developing countries' markets lack the financial capital to acquire expensive drugs, the fact that monopoly rents can be collected is of little relevance—developed country markets remain more attractive. For this reason a number of well-known economists have proposed setting up funds to put money in the market and acquire drugs or finance research for neglected diseases directly.[114] Three highly visible expert commissions showed similar doubts concerning the

---

[108] Correa (n 94 above) 5; Lanjouw and Cockburn (n 102 above) 287; HE Kettler, 'Using Intellectual Property Regimes to Meet Global Health R&D Needs' (2002) 5 J World Intell Prop 655, 667 ff Maskus (n 51 above) 568.

[109] AV Deardorff, 'Welfare Effects of Global Patent Protection' (1992) 59 Economica 35, 49; World Health Organization, 'Investing in Health Investing in Development. Paper Prepared by WHO for the UN Conference on Financing for Development Mexico, March 2002' (2002) 12. The Congress' Office of Technology Assessment on Patent-Term Extension concluded that patent-term extension in the United States would not increase the economic attractiveness of research on drugs with small markets. Office of Technology Assessment, *Patent-Term Extension and the Pharmaceutical Industry* (1981) 45.

[110] LG Branstetter, 'Do Stronger Patents Induce More Local Innovation?' (2004) 7 JIEL 359.

[111] Kaplan (n 49 above).

[112] Lanjouw and Cockburn (n 102 above) 281; Scherer and Watal (n 29 above) 11; HE Kettler and R Modi, 'Building Local Research and Development Capacity for the Prevention and Cure of Neglected Diseases: The Case of India' (2001) 79 Bulletin of the WHO 742, 745.

[113] FM Scherer, *The Patent System and Innovation in Pharmaceuticals* (1998); Scherer (n 84 above) 117 ff; W Jack and JO Lanjouw, *Financing Pharmaceutical Innovation: When Should Poor Countries Contribute?* (2003). Many economists conclude that patents are necessary, yet not sufficient as an incentive, eg HE Kettler and C Collins, 'Using Innovative Action to Meet Global Health Needs through Existing Intellectual Property Regimes' UK Commission on Intellectual Property Rights Study Paper 2b.

[114] M Kremer, 'Creating Markets for New Vaccines. Pt I: Rationale' (2001) 1 Innovation Policy and the Economy 35; M Kremer, 'Creating Markets for New Vaccines: Pt II: Design Issues' (2001) 1

viability of intellectual property rights as a sole incentive for research and development on neglected diseases. The Commission on Macroeconomics and Health, set
up by the WHO and chaired by Columbia economist Sachs concluded that:

[p]oor-country governments lack the means to subsidize R&D, and patent protection
means little when there is no significant market at the end of the process. The result is that
the R&D for diseases specific to poor countries (. . .) tends to be grossly underfinanced.
The poor countries benefit from R&D mainly when the rich also suffer from the same
diseases![115]

It goes on to state that '[a]ssuming that a patent holder chooses neither to offer an
essential medicine on a no-profit basis nor to license the medicine to a generics
producer, the low-income country will still need a way to ensure access at low
cost'.[116] The UK Commission on Intellectual Property Rights under the aegis of
Stanford law professor Barton came to a similar conclusion:

Regardless of the intellectual property regime prevailing in developing countries, in reality
there is little commercial incentive for the private sector to undertake research of specific
relevance to the majority of poor people living in low income countries. Accordingly, little
such work is done by the private sector.[117]

Finally, the Commission on Intellectual Property Rights, Innovation and
Public Health set up by the WHO opined that:

where the market has very limited purchasing power, as is the case for diseases affecting
millions of poor people in developing countries, patents are not a relevant factor or effective in stimulating R&D and bringing new products to market.[118]

It would be preposterous to claim that this study states the answer to the economic problem of patenting in the developing world. As Sykes wrote in 2002:
'The ultimate wisdom of measures that relax intellectual property protection for
pharmaceuticals in developing countries turns on complex matters, including
empirical issues about which one can only hazard an educated guess.'[119] The
conclusion can only be that it is unlikely that patents in developing countries will

Innovation Policy and the Economy 73; JD Sachs, 'A New Global Effort to Control Malaria' (2002)
298 Science 122, 123; JD Sachs, 'A Global Fund for the Fight Against AIDS' *Washington Post* (7 April
2001); JD Sachs, 'Financing Global Public Goods: Approaches to Health' in I Kaul, K Le Goulven
and M Schnupf (eds), *Global Public Goods Financing: New Tools for New Challenges. A Policy Dialogue*
(2002). The approach has been adopted with the Global Fund to Fight AIDS, Tuberculosis, and
Malaria (The Framework Document of the Global Fund to Fight AIDS, Tuberculosis and Malaria).
NEPAD committed to increase public R&D spending in Africa to at least 1% of the GDP. *Africa
vows to step up investment in R&D* (2004) 2 A World of Science 8.

[115] Commission on Macroeconomics and Health, *Macroeconomics and Health: Investing in Health
for Economic Development* (2001) 77.   [116] Ibid 90.
[117] Commission on Intellectual Property Rights, *Integrating Intellectual Property Rights and
Development Policy* (2002) 32. For criticism of the report: RS Crespi, 'IPRs Under Siege: First
Impressions of the Report of the Commission on Intellectual Property Rights' (2003) 25 EIPR 242,
245–246.
[118] Commission on Intellectual Property Rights, Innovation and Public Health, *Public Health.
Innovation and Intellectual Property Rights* (2006) 22.   [119] Sykes (n 105 above) 2–3.

lead to significantly more research and hence to more drugs for neglected diseases, but that some uncertainty prevails.[120] However, this suffices to give a preliminary response to the issue of justification: a certain interference with access to medicine can hardly be justified with an improbable additional benefit some time in the future.

However, the analysis raises the question as to why the pharmaceutical industry has lobbied so strongly to make patents available in developing countries if their markets are so insignificant. Of course, it might have pondered the future prospects of such markets, but it is more likely that the industry wanted to prevent 'price leakage' to the developed world, ie it wanted to prevent the prices it set for the developing world from leaking to the developed world. As stated above such leakage can occur where products sold at a low price in the developing world are imported into a developed country (parallel imports). Also, a developed country may engage in reference pricing for medication and include prices in developing countries as a reference. These fears of the industry should not be taken lightly. Developed countries' markets are essential for the industry and profits there finance its research and development. However, neither of these two fears can justify patent laws in developing countries from the human rights standpoint: it is up to the importing developed country, and not to the developing country, to prevent parallel imports from developing countries and, equally, it is the developed countries that have to abstain from using developing countries' prices in reference pricing. More often than not developed countries abstain from allowing such measures. They prove less resilient to what could be termed 'psychological price leakage'. Most developed countries are in a constant process of restructuring their health systems in the face of an ageing population and exploding health care costs. Political pressure to control costs is immense. The knowledge that a generic manufacturer offers a drug at a fraction of the cost of the brand-name manufacturer will inevitably lead to politicians pressuring drug companies to reduce prices, even if the political elite is well aware of the fact that adequate profits are necessary for the pharmaceutical industry to sustain its research and development efforts. Without generics, there is no way of disproving an industry claim that high prices are justified by intricate and expensive production processes[121] and that lower prices charged in the developing world are below the costs. The pressure on the pharmaceutical industry to lower prices would ease, preserving not only the profits of the industry, but also the industry's incentive to do research. However desirable, such rational ignorance is hardly a justification to deny access to medicine. It is up to the democratic process in industrialized countries to preserve the industry's incentive for research even where the decision-makers and the population are

---

[120] AO Sykes, 'International Trade and Human Rights: An Economic Perspective' (2003) John M Olin Law & Economics Working Paper No 188 (2nd series), 20 ff; FM Abbott, 'The Enduring Enigma of TRIPS: A Challenge for the World Economic System' (1998) 1 JIEL 497, 520–521.

[121] Pricing of AZT can serve as an example (chapter 1 above). The price of the drug fell significantly when generic competitors showed that the medicine could be produced for a fraction of the price initially charged.

fully aware of the true amount of the monopoly rents collected by the pharmaceutical industry. I conclude that patents in developing countries interfere with access to medicines without a justification.

III Effects on Third Parties: Duty to Cooperate

This conclusion concerns first and foremost the relationship between a country's human rights obligations and its obligation to adopt patent laws. But, as stated above, many developing countries cannot achieve much by tampering with or abolishing their own patent laws, as they often do not have the facilities to produce medicine at all—they have to rely on the industry of third countries to obtain generics. Does international human rights law oblige these third countries to allow their industry to provide the needed generics? A related question concerns the negotiation tactics of third countries. Developed countries use their strong negotiating positions in many fora to strengthen patent protection—also for pharmaceuticals. Does human rights law prohibit their doing so? Both of these questions raise the issue of whether states are under an obligation to cooperate in the achievement of the full realization of human rights.

The appeal of such an obligation is immense—it harks back to the highest aspirations of mankind, the idea that man should stand in for his fellow man. It rings through history and philosophy from Grotius' *appetitus societatis*[122] and Rousseau's social contract[123] to the motto of the French Republic that includes *fraternité* alongside *liberté* and *égalité*. Vattel famously declared:

les Nations n'étant pas moins soumises aux lois naturelles que les particuliers (...), ce qu'un homme doit aux autres hommes, une Nation le doit, à sa manière, aux autres Nations (...). Tel est le fondement de ces devoirs communs, de ces offices d'humanité, auxquels les Nations sont réciproquement obligées les unes envers les autres. Ils consistent en général à faire pour la conservation et le bonheur des autres tout ce qui est en notre pouvoir, autant que cela peut se concilier avec nos devoirs envers nous-mêmes.[124]

Rawls' took up the idea and declared: 'Well-ordered peoples have a *duty* to assist burdened societies.'[125]

---

[122] H Grotius, *De iure belli ac pacis*, prologomena (1646). Pufendorf deduced duties of men towards other men from common obligations with which God wanted to join men together, S von Pufendorf, *Über die Pflicht des Menschen und des Bürgers nach dem Gesetz der Natur* (trans K Luig 1994) Kapitel 6 § 1.

[123] J-J Rousseau, 'Politique du Contrat Social ou Principes du Droit Politique' in H Guillemin (ed), *Du Contrat Social* (1973) 59 Liv I Chap IX.

[124] E de Vattel, *Le Droit des Gens, ou Principes de la Loi Naturelle, Appliquée à la Conduite et aux Affaires des Nations et des Souverains* (1839) liv II, § 2. (As nations are just as much subject to natural law as individuals (...), a nation owes, in its own way, to other nations what man owes to other men (...). That is the foundation of these common duties, of these offices of mankind, which nations are bound by in reciprocity one towards the others. In general, they consist of doing everything within our power for the conservation and the happiness of others, to the extent that this can be conciliated with our duties towards ourselves (translation by author).)

[125] (Emphasis in original); J Rawls, *The Law of Peoples. With 'The Idea of Public Reason Revisited'*, (1999) 106.

Legally, the duty to cooperate in the realization of human rights is contained in Articles 1(3), 55(b), (c), and 56 of the UN Charter, and was reiterated by the UN General Assembly Declaration on Principles of International Law Concerning Friendly Relations and Co-operation among States in Accordance with the Charter of the United Nations[126] and in other (non-binding) resolutions.[127] All WTO Members that are states are also members of the UN and therefore bound by the UN Charter. The duty to cooperate in the realm of the ICESCR finds an additional source in Article 2(1) of that Covenant that imposes an obligation of international assistance and cooperation on States Parties and covers the right to access to medicine under the ICESCR as described in chapter 3.

However, the content of the duty to cooperate is in dispute. The language of the UN Charter remains vague: the members pledge to take joint and separate action for the achievement of the promotion of universal respect for and observance of human rights and fundamental freedoms.[128] The language of the ICESCR is not much clearer. Therefore, the legal duty to cooperate has understandably met with considerable scepticism—despite its long and noble heritage. Its vagueness, the myriad ways to feign compliance and the difficulty to enforce the obligation seem to put cooperation into the realm of wishful thinking rather than that of positive law.[129]

Such doubts are particularly pronounced in discussions about the existence of a 'general obligation to co-operate',[130] however they are less warranted for a duty to cooperate in reaching a specific goal, particularly in realizing human rights obligations. In such a context the obligations imposed take a clearer form.[131]

Cooperation of states in the achievement of the right to access to medicine, ie states working together towards the realization of the right whether in an

---

[126] UNGA res 2625 (XXV), 24 October 1970. R Rosenstock, 'The Declaration of Principles of International Law concerning Friendly Relations: A Survey' (1971) 65 AJIL 713, 729–730; M Šahović, 'Codification des Principes du Droit International des Relations Amicales et de la Coopération entre les États' (1972—III) 137 RdC 243; E McWhinney, 'The Concept of Co-operation' in M Bedjaoui (ed), *International Law: Achievement and Prospects* (1991) 425.

[127] *Declaration on the Right to Development*, GA Res 41/128 (4 December 1986), UN GAOR, 41th Sess, Supp No 53, at 168, UN Doc A/41/53, Art 3 (3), Art 4, Art 6 (1); Art 8 ff *Charter of Economic Rights and Duties of States*, UNGA res 3281 (XXIX) (12 December 1974); C Tomuschat, 'Die Charta der wirtschaftlichen Rechte und Pflichten der Staaten. Zur Gestaltungskraft von Deklarationen der UN-Generalsammlung' (1976) 36 ZaöRV 445, 457 ff.

[128] T Buergenthal, *International Human Rights in a Nutshell* (2nd edn, 1995) 24–25.

[129] B Graf zu Dohna, *Die Grundprinzipien des Völkerrechts über die freundschaftlichen Beziehungen und die Zusammenarbeit zwischen den Staaten* (1973) 188–189; G Arangio-Ruiz, 'The Normative Role of the General Assembly of the United Nations and the Declaration of Principles of Friendly Relations' (1972—III) 137 RdC 419, 573–574; H Neuhold, 'Die Pflicht zur Zusammenarbeit zwischen den Staaten: Moralisches Postulat oder völkerrechtliche Norm?' in H Miehsler *et al* (eds), *Ius Humanitatis. Festschrift zum 90. Geburtstag von Alfred Verdross* (1980) 575.

[130] A forceful statement in favour of such a general obligation is P-M Dupuy, 'The Place and Role of Unilateralism in Contemporary International Law' (2000) 11 EJIL 19, 22–23; much more doubtful: R Wolfrum, 'International Law of Cooperation' in R Bernhardt (ed), *Encyclopedia of Public International Law, II, 2* (1995) 1242, 1243 ff.

[131] J Delbrück and R Wolfrum, *Völkerrecht. Begründet von Georg Dahm. Band I/3 Die Formen des völkerrechtlichen Handelns; Die inhaltliche Ordnung der internationalen Gemeinschaft* (2nd edn, 2002) 851 ff.

institutional or in a bilateral setting,[132] addresses the global imbalances in access to medicine that are currently all too obvious. In the context of the ICESCR the Committee on Economic, Social and Cultural Rights implicitly falls back on the tripartite typology of human rights obligations to determine the content of the duty to cooperate, a helpful approach for the duty in the area of human rights in general. This means that states may not interfere with access to medicine in other states to the extent that they are bound by such a right, eg they may not pressure other States Parties to adopt regulations that would hamper access to medicine. As patents in developing countries have such an effect, other countries have to abstain from pressuring developing countries that want to make use of TRIPS Agreement flexibilities. It additionally means that, where possible, states have to prevent third parties from violating the right in other states, again to the extent the states are bound by the right. It finally means that states have to help other states to fulfil the right depending on the availability of resources and to the extent that they are bound by the right.[133]

The last of these obligations is the vaguest. Developing countries have attempted repeatedly to construct an obligation to grant development aid. But while there is an obligation of solidarity going beyond mere token cooperation, it is difficult to give a precise definition to its scope:[134] is technical aid sufficient? Or is there a duty to pay development aid? If so, what amount is necessary? Developed countries insist that development aid is granted on a purely voluntary basis and it is simply unrealistic to assume the contrary.[135] But the question asked at the beginning of

---

[132] L Fisler Damrosch, 'Obligations of Cooperation in the International Protection of Human Rights' in J Delbrück (ed), *International Law of Cooperation and State Sovereignty. Proceedings of an International Symposium of the Kiel Walther-Schücking-Institute of International Law May 23–26, 2001* (2002) 15, 24.

[133] Committee on Economic, Social and Cultural Rights, General Comment No 14 (2000), paras 38 ff.

[134] P Rott, *Patentrecht und Sozialpolitik unter dem TRIPS-Abkommen* (2002) 102–103; *Declaration on the Right to Development*, GA Res 41/128 (4 December 1986), UN GAOR, 41st Sess, Supp No 53, at 186, UN Doc A/41/53; Para IX Declaration of Alma-Ata (12 September 1978), in WHO (ed), *From Alma-Ata to the year 2000. Reflections at the midpoint* (1988). The idea that the rich have to pay more than the poor in many respects is now rather common, though falling short of being a norm of customary international law: CD Stone, 'Common but Differentiated Responsibilities in International Law' (2004) 98 AJIL 276. The European Communities have included human rights as an objective in their developmental policies. Council Regulation (EC) 975/1999 of 29 April 1999 Laying down the Requirements for the Implementation of Development Cooperation Operations which Contribute to the General Objective of Developing and Consolidating Democracy and the Rule of Law and to that of Respecting Human Rights and Fundamental Freedoms [1999] OJ L120/1 (8 May 1999).

[135] F Menghistu, 'The Satisfaction of Survival Requirements' in BG Ramcharan (ed), *The Right to Life in International Law* (1985) 63, 76; EU Petersmann, '"Entwicklungsvölkerrecht", "Droit International Du Développement", "International Economic Development Law": Mythos oder Wirklichkeit' (1974) 17 GYIL 145, 165 ff; DE Buckingham, 'A Recipe for Change: Towards an Integrated Approach to Food under International Law' (1994) 6 Pace Int'l L Rev 285, 301 (concerning food assistance); R Schütz, *Solidarität im Wirtschaftsvölkerrecht* (1994) 102 ff; but see Art 22 of the Charter of Economic Rights and Duties of States (n 127 above).

this part shows that there are other, and for this topic more pertinent, ways to assist a state in realizing access to medicine. Many countries do not have the technology base to produce generics. Competitors of the patent holder in third states could do so, but are legally prevented from manufacturing generics by patents granted in the third state. The third state, however, can adapt its patent laws to enable its industry to manufacture the necessary generics for the market of the developing country.[136] I will examine the legal intricacies involved in such an approach on the patent law side in chapter 5, but it should already be mentioned that this solution is envisaged by the December 2005 WTO amendment. Several countries have amended their patent legislation to implement the approach.[137] The adoption of such legislation is not just laudable, but a way to comply with the obligation to cooperate. The importance of the obligation in the context of the ICESCR has been stressed by the Committee on Economic, Social and Cultural Rights that regards it as a core obligation of states that are in a position to assist other states.[138]

IV A Conflict between the Patent and the Human Rights Regime?

The conclusion on the human rights side does not conclude the study, though. It merely imposes a change of perspectives. So far, two separate bodies of law have been analyzed: at first, the study described the basics of international patent law, its philosophy, and its history and showed that it imposes the obligation to adopt minimum patent standards on all WTO Members. The study then turned to international human rights law and found that it guarantees access to medicine under several of its sources. This chapter has demonstrated that pharmaceutical patents in developing countries unjustifiably interfere with access to medicine. The linkage between these two bodies of law in the study is clear: the TRIPS Agreement obliges developing countries to grant patents, but doing so would violate their human rights obligations.

The two bodies of law are in conflict. Some authors disagree with this statement, pointing to the 'flexibilities' of the TRIPS Agreement, eg parallel imports and compulsory licenses, and to Articles 7, 8.1 of the TRIPS Agreement that explicitly refer to health care measures and recognize dissemination, welfare, and development concerns. How can I claim that there is a conflict between access to medicine and the TRIPS Agreement before interpreting these flexibilities that are regarded by many to provide the necessary balance between access to medicine

---

[136] AE Yamin, 'Not just a Tragedy: Access to Medications as a Right under International Law' (2003) 21 BU Int'l L J 325, 368.   [137] Chapter 5.
[138] General Comment No 14 (n 133 above) para 45. Committee on Economic, Social and Cultural Rights, General Comment No 3 (1990), paras 13–14.

and patent protection and have led thoughtful commentators such as Rott in his study on social concerns in the TRIPS Agreement to conclude:

Auch die Menschenrechte, insbesondere das Recht auf Leben, das Recht auf Gesundheit und das Recht auf Nahrung, sind unausgesprochen im TRIPS-Abkommen reflektiert. (...) Das TRIPS-Abkommen sollte als Beitrag zur Rationalisierung der Handelsbeziehungen, vor allem aber als Schritt zu einer neuen Harmonisierung des internationalen Patentrechts (als Teil des internationalen Wirtschaftsrechts) unter Einschluss der Menschenrechte, sozialpolitischer Ziele und des Entwicklungsvölkerrechts angesehen werden.[139]

To understand why I can submit that there is a conflict between the international human rights regime and the international patent regime even before analyzing the flexibilities of the latter it is necessary to have a closer look at the notion of conflict between international legal regimes. The terms 'conflict' and 'international legal regime' will be defined in the next section. It is the notion of conflict used in the study that explains why it is possible to claim that there is a regime conflict even before the flexibilities of the TRIPS Agreement are examined (1). The problem of regime conflict is rooted in the structure of the international order. Structural changes in that order have changed both the *quantity*, but also the *quality* of such conflicts. One of the most important developments in this regard is the development of a normative hierarchy. This development, however, is put at risk by the institutional fragmentation of international law that establishes a factual hierarchy besides and independent from the normative hierarchy. This factual hierarchy suggests that the WTO regime is decisive for the outcome of the conflict between patents and human rights (2).

1 Conflict of International Legal Regimes: Terminology

Before I can stride into the difficult terrain of conflicts of international legal regimes, the terms 'regime' and 'conflict' need to be defined. But before doing so it will be necessary to say a few words about the structure of international law, a topic that will be discussed in more detail in part 2.

A Fragmentation of International Law

Law-making in the international community proceeds in a decentralized manner. International law has never known a central law-making body.[140] Where new legal norms are needed, states—the traditional subjects of international law—enter

---

[139] 'Human rights, too, particularly the right to life, the right to health and the right to food, are implicitly reflected in the TRIPS Agreement. (...) The TRIPS Agreement should be regarded as a contribution to the rationalization of trade relations, but especially as a step on the way to a new harmonization of international patent law (as a part of international economic law) including human rights, sociopolitical objectives and international developmental law.' Rott (n 134 above) 335 ff (translation by author); see W Wendland, *La Propriété Intellectuelle et les Droits de l'Homme*, UN Doc E/CN.12/2000/19, paras 38 ff (2000).

[140] The Security-Council, though, seems to have taken that role concerning international terrorism.

into bilateral or multilateral treaties. Separate issues are thus regulated by separate legal instruments and rarely are all of these instruments embraced by the same states. Only customary law and general principles bind all states (with few exceptions).[141]

The multiplication of legal instruments regulating separate issue areas has accelerated to a speed that is nothing short of astonishing. Tomuschat speaks of the international society's 'insatiable hunger for legal norms'.[142] A growing number of these instruments are administered by international organizations created for that purpose. Some of these organizations even boast an adjudicatory system, so that a multiplication of courts joins that of legal norms.[143] But the family of legal norms is not just growing, it is also diversifying: 'soft law' in all shades and colours joined 'hard law',[144] regionalism adds local colour,[145] and even the once rock-solid dogma that states and states alone are the legislators in the international system has suffered noticeable cracks:[146] international organizations have taken up the law-making business and the growing literature on the *lex mercatoria*[147] as

---

[141] Because of this lack of generality Jennings and Watts consider the term 'law' as inappropriate. R Jennings and A Watts, *Oppenheim's International Law. Volume I Peace. Introduction and Pt 1* (9th edn, 1992) 31; J Combacau and S Sur, *Droit International Public* (5th edn, 2001) 25. For parties to a convention, however, the effect of the convention is like that of law, as is illustrated by Art 1134 of the French Code Civil that reads: 'Les conventions légalement formées tiennent lieu de loi à ceux qui les ont faites.' (The legally formed contracts hold the place of law for those that have made them (translation by author).)

[142] C Tomuschat, 'International Law: Ensuring the Survival of Mankind on the Eve of a New Century. General Course on Public International Law' (1999) 281 RdC 9, 306.

[143] R Wolfrum, 'Konkurrierende Zuständigkeiten internationaler Streitentscheidungsinstanzen: Notwendigkeit für Lösungsmöglichkeiten und deren Grenzen' in N Ando *et al* (eds), *Liber Amicorum Judge Shigeru Oda. Volume 1* (2002) 651; M Pinto, 'Fragmentation or Unification among International Institutions: Human Rights Tribunals' (1998–1999) 31 NYU J Int'l L & Pol 833; JH Jackson, 'Fragmentation or Unification among International Institutions: The World Trade Organization' (1998–1999) 31 NYU J Int'l L & Pol 823; P-M Dupuy, 'The Danger of Fragmentation or Unification of the International Legal System and the International Court of Justice' (1998–1999) 31 NYU J Int'l L & Pol 791; G Guillaume, 'La Cour Internationale de Justice. Quelques Propositions Concrètes à l'Occasion du Cinquantenaire' (1996) 100 RGDIP 323, 329 ff; G Guillaume, 'The Future of International Judicial Institutions' (1995) 44 ICLQ 848.

[144] G Abi-Saab, 'Éloge du "Droit Assourdi". Quelques Réflexions sur le Rôle de la *Soft Law* en Droit International Contemporain' in *Nouveaux Itinéraires en Droit. Hommage à François Rigaux* (1993) 59; H Hillgenberg, 'A Fresh Look at Soft Law' (1999) 10 EJIL 499; U Fastenrath, 'Relative Normativity in International Law' (1993) 4 EJIL 305.

[145] Regional norms exist in many areas of international law, eg human rights (C Zanghì, *La Protezione Internazionale dei Diritti dell'Uomo* (2002) 97 ff) and trade law (P Demaret, J-F Bellis, and G García Jiménez (eds), *Regionalism and Multilateralism after the Uruguay Round. Convergence, Divergence and Interaction* (1997); P van Dijk and S Sideri (eds), *Multilateralism versus Regionalism: Trade Issues after the Uruguay Round* (1996)). Delmas-Marty speaks of 'un monde qui a été "cassé"' (a world that has been broken (translation by author)). M Delmas-Marty, *Trois Défis pour un Droit Mondial* (1998) 27.

[146] P Zumbansen, 'Die vergangene Zukunft des Völkerrechts' (2001) 34 Kritische Justiz 46; A-M Slaughter, *A New World Order* (2004).

[147] G Teubner, '"Global Bukowina": Legal Pluralism in the World Society' in G Teubner (ed), *Global Law without a State* (1996) 3; KP Berger, *The Creeping Codification of the Lex Mercatoria* (1999).

well as on that amorphous California corporation ICANN[148] that governs the internet seems to suggest that corporations, too, are not just poised to get their bite of the apple, but have long since started eating it. I do not mean to suggest that all of these peculiar characters deserve to be admitted to the family of international legal norms, much of this area remains subject to debate.[149] My intention is to convey to the reader the sense that international law is diversifying and building different, possibly contradictory regulatory areas, some of them endowed with adjudicatory mechanisms.[150] The phenomenon is sufficiently wide-spread to have attracted the attention of the ILC that established a study group on the 'fragmentation' of international law under the chairmanship of Simma and, upon his departure for the ICJ, Koskenniemi.[151]

B International Legal Regimes

The compartmentalization of international law into separate and specialized functional fields has attracted interest outside the legal field. In the footsteps of famed sociologist Luhmann scholars apply general systems theory to the field to study the differentiation of sub-systems of international law and their interaction.[152] International relations scholars have used a 'regime theory' approach to analyze the conditions for the formation and maintenance of international regimes.[153] It is this latter approach that has formed the terminology. The standard definition of 'international legal regime' or 'regime' has been elaborated by Krasner:

Regimes can be defined as sets of implicit or explicit principles, norms, rules, and decision-making procedures around which actors' expectations converge in a given area of international relations. Principles are beliefs of fact, causation and rectitude. Norms are standards of behavior defined in terms of rights and obligations. Rules are specific prescriptions or

---

[148] AM Froomkin, 'ICANN 2.0: Meet the New Boss' (2003) 36 Loy LA L Rev 1087; JP Kesan, 'Private Internet Governance' (2003) 35 Loy U Chi L J 87.

[149] P Weil, 'Towards Relative Normativity in International Law' (1983) 77 AJIL 413; J Klabbers, 'The Undesirability of Soft Law' (1998) 67 Nordic J Int'l L 381.

[150] G Abi-Saab, 'Fragmentation or Unification: Some Concluding Remarks' (1998–1999) 31 NYU J Int'l L & Pol 919; M Koskenniemi and P Leino, 'Fragmentation of International Law? Postmodern Anxieties' (2002) 15 LJIL 553.

[151] M Koskenniemi, *Fragmentation of International Law: Difficulties Arising from Diversification and Expansion of International Law. Study on the 'Function and scope of the lex specialis rule and the question of "self contained regimes"': Preliminary report*, UN Doc ILC(LVI)/SG/FIL/CRD.1/Add.1, para 109 (4 May 2004); M Koskenniemi, *Fragmentation of International Law: Difficulties Arising from the Diversification and Expansion of International Law. Report of the Study Group of the International Law Commission*, UN Doc A/CN.4/L.682 (13 April 2006) (hereinafter: Koskenniemi 2); Study Group of the ILC, *Fragmentation of International Law: Difficulties Arising from the Diversification and Expansion of International Law. Report of the Study Group of the International Law Commission*, UN Doc A/CN.4/L.702 (18 July 2006).

[152] S Oeter, 'International Law and General Systems Theory' (2001) 44 GYIL 72; A Fischer-Lescano and G Teubner, 'Regime-Collisions: The Vain Search for Legal Unity in the Fragmentation of Global Law' (2004) 25 Michigan J Int'l L 999; An introduction to the field is N Luhmann, *Einführung in die Systemtheorie* (2nd edn, 2004).

[153] RO Keohane, 'The Demand for International Regimes' (1982) 36 International Organization 325; RO Keohane and JS Nye, *Power and Interdependence* (2nd edn, 1989); B Kohler-Koch,

proscriptions for action. Decision-making procedures are prevailing practices for making and implementing collective choice.[154]

Note that, as understood here, international legal regimes might include, but do not necessarily include, an institutional structure. Taken together, the regimes form the international legal system that itself possesses a certain degree of unity and cohesion.[155] The terminology exhibits some flexibility: human rights can certainly be understood as a regime, the TRIPS Agreement, however, could be part of the intellectual property regime or the world trade regime. Both of these classifications are justified and have been alluded to so far. Legally, however, it must be remembered that the TRIPS Agreement is part of the WTO Agreements and subject to its rules—thus the conflict is, strictly speaking, between the world trade and the human rights regimes.

C Conflict

Law cannot be detached from the realities of life. It is the tool to solve problems that occur in life. As Jhering phrased it: 'purpose is the creator of all law, (...) there is no norm that does not owe its existence to a purpose, ie a practical objective.'[156] The questions that life puts to the legal system can rarely be very neatly compartmentalized. Hence, it should not come as a surprise that the legal regimes are not disconnected entities when it comes to solving real-life issues, but they interfere with each other, influence each other, and sometimes come into conflict. The situation is reminiscent of the area of conflict of laws, the area of law containing the rules on how to deal with a situation in which the separate legal systems of municipal law touch each other. Yet, the separation of regimes in international law often follows a functional, not a locational rationale. The interplay between regimes is not uncommon in international law: a state imposing economic sanctions for a violation of environmental law might infringe trade obligations.[157] A government's

---

'Zur Empirie und Theorie internationaler Regime' in B Kohler-Koch (ed), *Regime in den internationalen Beziehungen* (1989) 17; A-M Slaughter, 'International Law and International Relations' (2000—I) 285 RdC 9; A-M Slaughter, 'An International Relations Approach' (2001) 95 AJIL 25.

[154] SD Krasner, 'Structural Causes and Regime Consequences: Regimes as Intervening Variables' (1982) 36 International Organization 185, 186; see N Matz, *Wege zur Koordinierung völkerrechtlicher Verträge. Völkervertragsrechtliche und institutionelle Ansätze* (2005) 359 ff; RA Coate, *Global Issue Regimes* (1982) 45 ff; E Klein, 'International Régimes' in R Bernhardt (ed), *Encyclopedia of Public International Law, II* (1995) 2, 1354 (limiting the term to treaty-based settlements defining the status of a certain area and intended to form part of the international order); EB Haas, 'Why Collaborate? Issue-Linkage and International Regimes' (1980) 32 World Politics 357, 358; J Neumann, *Die Koordination des WTO-Rechts mit anderen völkerrechtlichen Ordnungen. Konflikte des materiellen Rechts und Konkurrenzen der Streitbeilegung* (2002) 50 ff (limiting the term to treaty-based systems founding international organizations not having a legal personality under international law).

[155] G Abi-Saab, 'Cours Général de Droit International Public' (1987—VII) 207 RdC 9, 105 ff; Y Shany, *The Competing Jurisdictions of International Courts and Tribunals* (2003) 87.

[156] R von Jhering, *Der Zweck im Recht. Erster Band* (4th edn, 1904) V.

[157] The relationship between trade and environment is much discussed. R Wolfrum (ed), *Enforcing Environmental Standards: Economic Mechanisms as a Viable Means?* (1996); PK Rao, *The*

taking of intellectual property might fall foul of human rights obligations,[158] international investment law,[159] and/or international patent law. Security Council action under Chapter VII of the UN Charter can raise questions under human rights or humanitarian law.[160] Even such seemingly non-related regimes as the environmental and the security regimes have their points of connection. A 2003 study solicited by the Pentagon examined the impact of climate change on security and concludes that climate change should be considered a security concern.[161] Whereas these examples concern the normative aspect of regime conflict, there is also an institutional aspect of the topic focusing on the coordination of institutions including different international courts and tribunals.[162] However, this study focuses on normative aspects.

a Definition of Conflict

The notion of 'conflict' has gained more attention in recent years. A precondition for conflict to arise between norms is that a state or other subject of public international law is bound by two norms, stemming from any source of public international law, which are applicable *ratione materiae, ratione personae*,[163] and *ratione temporis* ('*Normkonkurrenz/Interferenza*').[164] In other words, there must be at least some overlap[165] in the subject matter regulated by the norm, meaning that both norms apply to the factual situation rather than that both norms are from the same area of law. Furthermore, at least one subject of international law must be bound by both norms and the norms must, according to the principles

---

World Trade Organization and the Environment (2000); A Kiss, D Shelton and K Ishibashi, *Economic Globalization and Compliance with International Environmental Agreements* (2003).

[158] N 83 above.   [159] Chapter 5 below.

[160] D Starck, *Die Rechtmäßigkeit von UNO-Wirtschaftssanktionen in Anbetracht ihrer Auswirkungen auf die Zivilbevölkerung. Grenzen der Kompetenzen des Sicherheitsrats am Beispiel der Maßnahmen gegen den Irak und die Bundesrepublik Jugoslawien* (2000); E de Wet, *The Chapter VII Powers of the United Nations Security Council* (2004).

[161] P Schwartz and D Randall, *An Abrupt Climate Change Scenario and Its Implications for United States National Security* (2003).

[162] ILC, *Report of the Study Group on Fragmentation of International Law: Difficulties arising from the Diversification and Expansion of International Law*, UN Doc A/CN.4/L.644, para 6 (18 July 2003); Matz (n 154 above). Problems of institutional coordination can even arise within one legal order like the UN: G Arangio-Ruiz, 'The ICJ Statute, the Charter and Forms of Legality Review of Security Council Decisions' in L Chand Vohrah *et al* (eds), *Man's Inhumanity to Man. Essays on International Law in Honour of Antonio Cassese* (2003) 41; MI Papa, *I Rapporti Tra la Corte Internazionale di Giustizia e il Consiglio di Sicurezza* (2006).

[163] Where two treaties set out inconsistent systems, but the obligations flowing from these systems are owed to different parties there is no conflict. GG Fitzmaurice, 'Third Report on the Law of Treaties' in YBILC, II (1958) 20, 44.

[164] J Delbrück and R Wolfrum, *Völkerrecht. Begründet von Georg Dahm. Band I/3 Die Formen des völkerrechtlichen Handelns; Die inhaltliche Ordnung der internationalen Gemeinschaft* (2nd edn, 2002) 680 ff; F Klein, 'Vertragskonkurrenz' in H-J Schlochauer (ed), *Wörterbuch des Völkerrechts. Begründet von Professor Dr. Karl Strupp*, 555 (2nd edn, 1962); McNair, *The Law of Treaties* (1961) 214 ff.

[165] Volken demands an identical scope of application, but there is no reason why an overlap should not suffice for *Normkonkurrenz* to arise. P Volken, *Konventionskonflikte im internationalen Privatrecht* (1977) 236.

of intertemporal law, both be valid.[166] Also, where norms are applicable under different circumstances (eg in times of peace or of war) no *Normkonkurrenz* arises between the two norms.[167] The study has already shown that the TRIPS Agreement and access to medicine possess the required overlap, as many states are bound by both rules and both rules demand to be applied in the same factual situation—the question whether to grant pharmaceutical patents.

Normkonkurrenz is a necessary, yet not sufficient condition for a conflict to arise. The norms also have to be contradictory—a notion that seems simple to define only at first sight. The definition that Jenks formulated in his ground-breaking study on the topic of conflict between law-making treaties in 1953 has become a staple: 'A conflict in the strict sense of direct incompatibility arises only where a party to the two treaties cannot simultaneously comply with its obligations under both treaties.' Norm 'A' obliges the state to do what norm 'B' prohibits.[168] Kelsen held a similar view.[169]

But this strict definition of conflict is rightly being perceived as unduly narrow. In his study on conflicts of norms, Pauwelyn has established an elaborate typology of normative conflict that would deserve to be repeated in full. However, suffice it to say for our purposes that he, amongst others, argues that a norm containing a permission, ie an option to take a certain course of action or not, is in conflict with a norm that commands or prohibits said course of action. Assume that norm 'A' states that 'countries are prohibited from imposing tariffs on food products'. Norm 'B' provides that 'states *may* impose tariffs on meat'. Under the narrow definition there is no conflict, as a state can comply with both norms by following the command or prohibition: a state that does not impose tariffs on food products complies with a norm permitting it to impose tariffs on meat. But to impose this as the standard solution, as would be done by stating there is no conflict, deprives the permission of its meaning. The permission to impose tariffs on meat could never be used. Thus, the solution runs counter to the well-established principle of effective interpretation, stating that every provision of a treaty is supposed to have a meaning (*ut res magis valeat quam pereat*).[170]

---

[166] F Capotorti, 'Interferenze fra la Convenzione Europea dei Diritti dell'Uomo ed Altri Accordi, e Loro Reflessi negli Ordinamenti Interni' in Instituto di Diritto Internazionale e Straniero della Università di Milano (ed), *Comunicazioni e Studi. Volume Dodicesimo* (1966) 115, 117; J Pauwelyn, *Conflict of Norms in Public International Law. How WTO Law Relates to other Rules of International Law* (2003) 164 ff.

[167] W Karl, 'Treaties, Conflict Between' in R Bernhardt (ed), *Encyclopedia of Public International Law, IV, 2* (2000) 935, 936.

[168] W Jenks, 'The Conflict of Law-Making Treaties' (1953) 30 BYIL 401, 426, 427; Delbrück and Wolfrum (n 164 above) 682; SA Sadat-Akhavi, *Methods of Resolving Conflicts between Treaties* (2003); WH Wilting, *Vertragskonkurrenz im Völkerrecht* (1996) 4; Waldock in ILC, '742nd Meeting. Law of Treaties' YBILC, I (1964) 119, 125.

[169] H Kelsen, *General Theory of Norms* (trans M Hartney, 1991) 123.

[170] The principle is commonly applied both by the ICJ and the WTO Appellate Body: *Territorial Dispute (Libyan Arab Jamahiriya/Chad)*, Judgment, ICJ Reports 1994, 6, para 51 (3 February 1994); *Aegean Sea Continental Shelf*, Judgment, ICJ Reports 1978, 3, para 52 (19 December 1978); *Legal Consequences for States of the Continued Presence of South Africa in Namibia (South West Africa)*

To avoid this outcome, Pauwelyn regards the constellation as one of conflict.[171] This does not imply that in the end the result could never be to impose the obligation, it only implies that upon identification of the conflict all of the tools that are available for resolving a conflict have to be applied and the outcome might, but need not, be different. Koskenniemi, in his report as chairman for the ILC Study Group on Fragmentation of International Law, also favours a broad definition of conflict.[172] It is under such a broad definition that I can assert a conflict between the TRIPS Agreement and access to medicine before the flexibilities the TRIPS Agreement offers are described. The TRIPS Agreement obliges WTO Members to introduce patents and permits them to make use of certain exceptions. The permission to make use of certain exceptions conceptually is both a right to use the exceptions and a right not to use the exceptions. In short, the Agreement grants an option. As patents in developing countries unjustifiably interfere with access to medicine developing countries could only escape the verdict of violating their human rights obligations by making use of the exceptions (and even this only if the exceptions are sufficiently broad). But the obligation to use the exception nullifies the aspect of the norm granting Members a right not to use the exception. What used to be a *may* would turn into a *must*—a conflict under the broad definition of conflict herein favoured.

The notion of 'conflict' has also been at issue in several WTO cases. Panels had the opportunity to interpret the term in the context of provisions of WTO law that state which rule prevails in case of a conflict between norms contained in different WTO agreements.[173] Absent a conflict both norms apply. So far, both

---

notwithstanding Security Council Resolution 276 (1970), Advisory Opinion, ICJ Reports 1971, 16, para 66 (21 June 1971); *Lighthouse Case Between France and Greece (France/Greece)*, PCIJ Reports 1934, Ser A/B, No 62, 27 (17 March 1934); *Japan—Taxes on Alcoholic Beverages*, WT/DS8, 10, 11/AB/R (1996); *United States—Standards for Reformulated and Conventional Gasoline*, WT/DS2/AB/R (1996) (*United States—Gasoline*); *Canada—Measures Affecting the Importation of Milk and the Exportation of Dairy Products*, WT/DS103, 113/AB/R, para 133 (1999); *Argentina—Safeguard Measures on Imports of Footwear*, WT/DS121/AB/R, para 88 (1999); *Korea—Definitive Safeguard Measure on Imports of Certain Dairy Products*, WT/DS98/AB/R, para 80 (1999); *European Communities—Measures Affecting Asbestos and Asbestos-containing Products*, WT/DS135/AB/R, para 115 (2001) (*EC—Asbestos*).

171 J Pauwelyn, 'The Role of Public International Law in the WTO: How Far Can We Go?' (2001) 95 AJIL 535, 550–551; Pauwelyn (n 166 above) 175 ff (defining conflict as a relationship between two norms where one norm constitutes, has led to or may lead to a breach of the other); J Pauwelyn, 'Cross-agreement Complaints before the Appellate Body: A Case Study of the EC-Asbestos Dispute' (2002) 1 World Trade Review 63, 78 ff; Neumann (n 154 above) 60 ff.

172 Koskenniemi 2 (n 151 above) paras 21 ff.

173 Interpretative Note to Annex 1A of the Marrakesh Agreement Establishing the World Trade Organization provides: 'In the event of conflict between a provision of the General Agreement on Tariffs and Trade 1994 and a provision of another agreement in Annex 1A to the Agreement Establishing the World Trade Organization (...), the provision of the other agreement shall prevail to the extent of the conflict.'; Art 1.2 of DSU reads: '(...) In disputes involving rules and procedures under more than one covered agreement, if there is a conflict between special or additional rules and procedures of such agreements under review (...) the Chairman of the Dispute Settlement Body (...), in consultation with the parties to the dispute, shall determine the rules and procedures to be followed (...).'

approaches to interpreting 'conflict' have been used. In *EC—Bananas*[174] the WTO Panel adopted the broad interpretation of conflict, explicitly including 'the situation where a rule in one agreement prohibits what a rule in another agreement explicitly permits' in its definition.[175] The Panels in *Indonesia—Automobiles* and *Turkey—Textiles* arguably preferred the narrow definition, regarding only mutually exclusive obligations as being in conflict.[176]

The Appellate Body has not studied the issue in depth. The most thorough analysis so far is *Guatemala—Cement (I)*,[177] in which the Appellate Body had to tackle an interference between special rules for dispute settlement contained in Article 17 of the Anti-Dumping Agreement and the general rules of dispute settlement contained in the Dispute Settlement Understanding (DSU), a situation which is governed by Article 1.2 of the DSU. The Appellate Body held that:

it is only where the provisions of the DSU and the special or additional rules and procedures of a covered agreement *cannot* be read as *complementing* each other that the special or additional provisions are to *prevail*. A special or additional provision should only be found to *prevail* over a provision of the DSU in a situation where adherence to the one provision will lead to a violation of the other provisions, that is, in the case of a *conflict* between them.[178]

Different commentators found the statement to be in support of different definitions of conflict. Some authors regard the latter part of the ruling as a straightforward application of the narrow definition.[179] Others point out that the holding can be read to conform to the broader definition: a state making use (or not making use) of a right arguably adheres to the right. If its choice leads to a violation of the command contained in the second norm, the definition concludes that there is a conflict.[180] Given that the Appellate Body in *US—Cotton* found an 'explicit carve-out or exemption' under the Agreement on Agriculture to prevail over the discipline of the SCM Agreement[181] I would conclude that the Appellate Body

---

[174] *European Communities—Regime for the Importation, Sale and Distribution of Bananas. Complaint by the United States*, WT/DS27/R/USA (1997) (*EC—Bananas*).

[175] Ibid para 7.159.

[176] *Indonesia—Certain Measures Affecting the Automobile Industry*, WT/DS54/R, WT/DS55/R, WT/DS59/R, WT/DS64/R, para 14.28 footnote 649 (1998) (*Indonesia—Automobiles*); *Turkey—Restrictions on Imports of Textile and Clothing Products*, WT/DS34/R, para 9.92 ff (1999) (*Turkey—Textiles*). The Panel's reference to the principle of effective interpretation mitigates in favour of the broad definition of conflict, so that some authors argue that the Panel did, in effect, apply a broad definition. Neumann (n 154 above) 61–62; D Falke, 'Vertragskonkurrenz und Vertragskonflikt im Recht der WTO: Erste Erfahrungen der Rechtsprechung 1995–1999' (2000) 3 ZeuS 307, 329–330, but see Pauwelyn (n 166 above) 193–194.

[177] *Guatemala—Anti-Dumping Investigation Regarding Portland Cement from Mexico*, WT/DS60/AB/R (1998) (*Guatemala—Cement (I)*).

[178] (Emphasis in original) ibid para 65.

[179] G Marceau, 'Conflicts of Norms and Conflicts of Jurisdictions' (2001) 35 JWT 1081, 1085; E Montaguti and M Lugard, 'The GATT 1994 and other Annex 1A Agreements: Four Different Relationships?' (2000) 3 JIEL 473, 476.

[180] Pauwelyn (n 166 above) 195; Neumann (n 154 above) 62; B Eggers and R Mackenzie, 'The Cartagena Protocol on Biosafety' (2000) 3 JIEL 525, 540.

[181] *United States—Subsidies on Upland Cotton*, WT/DS267/AB/R (3 March 2005), para 532 (*US—Cotton*).

tends towards the broader definition. It is likely that the Appellate Body has not had the last word on the matter.

Before concluding that there is a conflict, however, the Appellate Body tries to interpret two interfering norms of international law in a way that would avoid a conflict—a principle of interpretation known as the 'presumption against conflicts' that is well-established in international law.[182] Its approach to Article 17.5 of the Anti-Dumping Agreement is exemplary. The provision contains certain requirements for a panel request—as does Article 6.2 of the DSU. Rather than reading Article 17.5 of the Anti-Dumping Agreement as supervening Article 6.2 of the DSU the Appellate Body simply held that that a panel request under the Anti-Dumping Agreement has to comply with the requirements of both of the provisions.[183] WTO law aficionados will recall the Appellate Body applied the same principle in *Argentina—Footwear*.[184] The peculiar problem in the case was that Article XIX:1(a) of the GATT allows safeguard measures only when an increase in imports is a result of unforeseen developments, but the Agreement on Safeguards fails to mention this requirement. The Appellate Body held that there was no conflict between the two Agreements, rather, both provisions had to be applied cumulatively.[185]

The presumption against conflicts holds an interesting place in the definition of conflict and exposes a problem involved in the orthodox definition of conflict. Commentators, much like the Appellate Body, regard it as a technique to avoid conflicts.[186] Thus, a conflict can exist only if the presumption fails. But the application of the presumption shows that this approach is somewhat circular: the presumption dictates that among several possible interpretations of a norm the meaning that does not conflict with the other norm has to be chosen.[187] Hence, the presumption only comes into play if a conflict exists—a catch-22: before it can be determined that there is a conflict the presumption against conflicts has to be applied, but the presumption only comes into play if there is a conflict. The

---

[182] *Canada—Term of Patent Protection*, WT/DS170/R, para 6.45 (2000); *United States—Section 110 (5) of the US Copyright Act*, WT/DS160/R, para 6.66 (2000); *Canada—Certain Measures Concerning Periodicals*, WT/DS31/AB/R (1997); *EC—Bananas* (n 174 above) paras 219 ff; *Case Concerning Right of Passage over Indian Territory (Preliminary Objections)*, ICJ Rep 1957, 125, 142 (26 November 1957). The notion is distinct from but very similar to the presumption against conflict concerning national and international law. *United States—Anti-Dumping Act of 1916. Complaint by Japan*, WT/DS162/R, para 3.46 (2000).

[183] *Guatemala—Cement (I)* (n 177 above) paras 74 f.

[184] *Argentina—Safeguard Measures on Imports of Footwear*, WT/DS121/AB/R, para 89 (1999) (*Argentina—Footwear*).

[185] Ibid para 89; *Korea—Definitive Safeguard Measure on Imports of Certain Dairy Products*, WT/DS98/AB/R, paras 76 ff (1999); *United States—Definitive Safeguard Measures on Imports of Certain Steel Products*, WT/DS248, DS249, DS251, DS252, DS253, DS254, DS258, DS259/AB/R, para 275 (2003). The holding has been criticized by RH Steinberg, 'Judicial Lawmaking at the WTO: Discursive, Constitutional, and Political Constraints' (2004) 98 AJIL 247, 253–254; AO Sykes, 'The Persistent Puzzles of Safeguards: Lessons from the Steel Dispute' (2004) 7 JIEL 523, 539–540.   [186] Pauwelyn (n 166 above) 240 ff.

[187] On the limits of such an interpretation Pauwelyn (n 166 above) 244 ff.

application of the presumption also raises problems that are very similar to those that occur in solving conflicts, such as whether the application of the presumption on two treaties that have not been signed by the same states would violate the principle of *pacta tertiis*—that a treaty is not supposed to burden a third party.

It seems to me that the definition of the notion of conflict depends largely on the purpose for which the definition is needed. Are we trying to identify cases in which only one of two norms can survive or are we trying to identify cases in which the interference of two norms might limit the scope of one or both of them to some extent, remaining within the bounds of an appropriate interpretation. In the latter case the presumption against conflicts would have to be regarded as a conflict-solution rather than a conflict-avoidance technique. In any event, however, a broad definition of conflict seems more appropriate to realize the objective of conventions and therefore I can conclude that the TRIPS Agreement conflicts with access to medicine.

b Typologies of Conflicts

The interest in the topic of normative conflict in public international law is immense. To gain a better grasp on such conflicts, scholars have developed numerous typologies. It is helpful to locate the conflict that is the subject of this study within two of these typologies. One distinguishes conflicts as to the sources involved, the other as to the severity of the conflict within regimes.

The conflicting norms can stem from all possible sources of public international law: a norm of general international law can conflict with a treaty norm. The conflict can be between bilateral treaties involving the same parties (contract 1 between A and B, contract 2 between A and B) or different parties (AB; BC). The most complex problems are posed by conflicts between multilateral treaties, such as the WTO Agreements and human rights instruments, or conflicts between bilateral and multilateral treaties. Again, the conflict can involve treaties with identical parties (ABC; ABC), but it can also involve treaties with differing parties, either because only some parties of the first multilateral agreement have also ratified the second one (ABC; AB) or because the parties are only partially identical (ABC; ABD).[188] At times, it is possible to resolve a multilateral agreement into bundles of bilateral treaty relations, resulting in a number of bilateral commitments and a situation of conflicting 'virtual' bilateral agreements, which allows the application of a conflicting treaty *inter se*. At other times it is not possible to do so as the obligations are more than just bilateral commitments, they are owed to all other parties (*erga omnes partes*) of the agreement, the agreement is an integral one and therefore an *inter se* application of the conflicting treaty is not permissible.[189] It is

---

[188] Numerous examples for conflicts among treaties are mentioned in the early works on such conflicts, eg C Rousseau, 'De la Compatibilité des Normes Juridiques Contradictoires dans l'Ordre International' (1932) 39 RGDIP 133, 137 ff, Jenks (n 168 above) 407 ff.

[189] Article 30(4) of the Vienna Convention on the Law of Treaties. The provision is premised on the possibility of resolving the multilateral treaty into bundles of bilateral commitments. Wilting (n 168 above) 99; M Zuleeg, 'Vertragskonkurrenz im Völkerrecht. Teil I: Verträge zwischen souveränen

particularly these latter agreements that cause great conceptual problems—they will be discussed in more detail below. The conflict discussed here plays between human rights obligations, which either stem from general international law or multilateral agreements, and another multilateral agreement: the TRIPS Agreement. Where the human rights obligations stem from treaty law the parties to the human rights agreements and the TRIPS Agreement are only partly identical, albeit over 80 per cent of the Members of the WTO are bound by the human rights treaties analyzed.

The second typology of conflict distinguishes between conflicts of norms and conflict of regimes in their totality (systemic conflict). In a given case they might be hard to tell apart, as in concrete situations a systemic conflict materializes as a conflict of norms. However, systemic conflicts reflect a clash between fundamental principles or goals of two regimes, rather than merely single norms. They are deeply rooted in the regimes that clash and coordinating mechanisms will have to be found to try to realize the goals of both regimes to the fullest—if that is possible at all.[190] Locating the conflict between the TRIPS Agreement and access to medicine in this typology—a mere conflict of norms or a systemic conflict between the WTO and the human rights regime—opens Pandora's box. Anyone sufficiently interested in the world trading system to pick up a study like the one at hand will be familiar with the debate that the topic 'WTO and human rights' has sparked. It pits activists that wholeheartedly agree with the 'nightmare report' prepared for the Sub-Commission on the Promotion and Protection of Human Rights and concluding that 'for certain sectors of humanity—particularly the developing countries of the South—the WTO is a veritable nightmare'[191] against neoliberals that assert that 'a more open trading system generally tends to promote most of the concerns that come under the rubric of human rights'.[192] I submit that WTO

Staaten' (1977) 20 GYIL 246, 261; Pauwelyn (n 166 above) 52 ff; J Pauwelyn, 'The Nature of WTO Obligations' Jean Monnet Working Paper No 1/02 (2002) (showing that WTO obligations are of the bilateral type, but explicitly not deciding whether the same is true for TRIPS Agreement obligations).

[190] Matz (n 154 above) 10 ff; Neumann (n 154 above) 63 ff; S Kadelbach, *Allgemeines Verwaltungsrecht unter europäischem Einfluß* (1999) 32 ff ('*Systemkonflikte*'); CM Pontecorvo, 'Interdependence between Global Environmental Regimes: The Kyoto Protocol on Climate Change and Forest Protection' (1999) 59 ZaöRV 709, 739 ('conflicts' between the goals of multilateral treaties); R Wolfrum, 'Coordination among Multilateral Agreement through Treaty Provisions' in P-T Stoll and B Berger (eds), *International Governance for Environment and Sustainable Development. Goettingen Workshop 10–11 December 2001 in Goettingen, Germany* (2001) 19.

[191] J Oloka-Onyango and D Udagama, *The Realization of Economic, Social and Cultural Rights. Globalization and its Impact on the Full Enjoyment of Human Rights*, UN Doc E/CN.4/Sub.2/2000/13, para 15 (2000); later reports focus on particular instances of normative conflict rather than alleging a systemic conflict: J Oloko-Onyango and D Udagama, *Economic, Social and Cultural Rights. Globalization and its Impact on the Full Enjoyment of Human Rights*, UN Doc E/CN.4/Sub.2/2001/10, para 14 ff (2001); High Commissioner for Human Rights, *Economic, Social and Cultural Rights. Globalization and its impact on the full enjoyment of human rights*, UN Doc E/CN.4/2002/54 (2002); Sub-Commission on the Promotion and the Protection of Human Rights, *Liberalization of Trade in Services, and Human Rights*, Sub-Commission on Human Rights Res 2001/4 (15 August 2001).

[192] AO Sykes (n 120 above) 2. Sykes continues 'And to the extent that exceptions arise, conventional economic arguments regarding optimal policy instruments strongly counsel against curtailment

law is not in a systemic conflict with the human rights regime. Nor, however, does WTO law automatically advance human rights interests. Areas of possible conflict between the regimes are numerous.

Even between patents under the TRIPS Agreement and human rights law alone a number of possible conflicts have been identified. Granting gene patents[193] can interfere with the freedom of research,[194] particularly as gene fragments can serve as research tools.[195] Similarly such patents can conflict with the right to food[196] by preventing farmers (through licensing agreements or through a 'terminator' gene) from saving seeds from one harvest for planting them the next year.[197] The most widely discussed problem arises in the area of traditional knowledge of indigenous communities. Such knowledge is rarely patentable as it is commonly neither new, nor is the inventor known. Not only does the knowledge of indigenous communities thus go unprotected, it is also often exploited by corporations from developed countries that acquire the knowledge from the indigenous community and obtain patents on downstream inventions improving on the indigenous knowledge without letting the indigenous communities share in the profits. The situation is commonly held to be unsatisfactory with respect to the protection of indigenous people.[198]

of open trade as a solution, and instead argue for tailored measures that directly address the issue in question.'

[193] The US PTO as well as the European Patent Office and the Japanese Patent Office grant gene patents as product patents, regarding the gene, a nucleic acid molecule, as a compound. Whether the patent will be granted also depends on the other requirements of patentability, particularly the utility requirement. EPO and JPO and US PTO, *Trilateral Project B3b. Comparative Study on Biotechnology Patent Practices* (2000). Whether this approach to patentability is prescribed by TRIPS is far from certain.

[194] The Committee on Economic, Social and Cultural Rights considers this freedom to be part and parcel of the right to education under Art 13 of the ICESCR. Committee on Economic, Social and Cultural Rights, General Comment No 13 (1999), paras 38 f.

[195] R Wolfrum and P-T Stoll and S Franck, *Die Gewährleistung freier Forschung an und mit Genen und das Interesse an der wirtschaftlichen Nutzung ihrere Ergebnisse* (2002); MA Heller and RS Eisenberg, 'Can Patents Deter Innovation? The Anticommons in Biomedical Research' (1998) 280 Science 698; more ambiguous: A Gambardella, L Orsenigo and F Pammolli, 'Global Competitiveness in Pharmaceuticals. A European Perspective' European Commission Enterprise Papers No 1—2001, 77 f (2001).   [196] Article 11 of the ICESCR.

[197] K Aoki, 'Weeds, Seeds & Deeds: Recent Skirmishes in the Seed Wars' (2003) 11 Cardozo J. Int'l & Comp L 247; Rott (n 134 above) 62 ff; PC Carstensen, 'Concentration and the Destruction of Competition in Agricultural Markets: The Case for Change in Public Policy' (2000) Wis L Rev 531, 540.

[198] The protection of indigenous people is also regarded as unsatisfactory, given that the main instrument, the Convention Concerning Indigenous and Tribal Peoples in Independent Countries, has only been ratified by 17 countries and that the application of the right of self-determination contained in the common Art 1 of the ICCPR and ICESCR to indigenous peoples is contested. Article 8(j) of the International Convention on Biological Diversity commits member states to 'encourage' benefit-sharing arising from the utilization of traditional knowledge, too weak a provision to solve the conundrum. R Wolfrum, 'The Protection of Indigenous Peoples in International Law' (1999) 59 ZaöRV 369; A von Hahn, *Traditionelles Wissen indigener und lokaler Gemeinschaften zwischen geistigen Eigentumsrechten und der* public domain (2004) particularly 83 ff.

2 Conflict of International Legal Regimes: Towards Hierarchy?

A conflict between human rights law and WTO law can be approached in three different ways: (1) it can be studied under general international law; (2) the role of WTO law within the human rights regime can be explored; and, (3) the role of human rights law within the WTO regime can be examined. I submit that the last of these approaches is the most important one and will focus on it in the subsequent chapter. To explain this restriction some more background on regime conflicts in international law is required.

Above, the phenomenon of decentralized law-making in international law and the fragmentation of international law was introduced. It is now time to have a closer look at this phenomenon. The starting point is the 'traditional' setting of international law, commonly known as a 'law of co-existence' in which legal relations were largely reciprocal and the resolution of normative conflicts followed a bilateral model (A). The introduction of community values into this system has caused an upheaval that has not yet settled—in particular it has introduced a hierarchy into the normative system commonly associated with the terms *erga omnes* obligations and *jus cogens* (B). Much is to be learned in this respect from three different projects of the International Law Commission: its work on the law of treaties, on state responsibility, and on fragmentation of international law. But the notion of community values had another effect, too: it began a process of institutionalization of international legal regimes, resulting in a de facto hierarchy of regimes that is entirely independent from the normative hierarchy (C). The interplay between the WTO and the human rights regimes illustrates that the institutional fragmentation is perceived as particularly awkward where the de facto hierarchy puts the regime at a lower level that is generally preferred by the normative hierarchy (D).

A Law of Coexistence and Reciprocity—A Law without Hierarchy

In the classical system of international law states are the subjects and the central units of decision-making. Sovereign[199] and equal they are both the law-makers and the law-takers. They decide on what the law will be by consensus.[200] Where a

---

[199] The term 'sovereign' stems from Bodin according to whom the monarch was sovereign. He conceived sovereignty as the absolute power of the states—its internal workings were not to be meddled with by other states and its independence from foreign power had to be guaranteed. J Bodin, *Sechs Bücher über den Staat. Buch I-III* (trans B Wimmer, 1981) 205; WG Grewe, *The Epochs of International Law* (trans M Byers, 2000) 163 ff.

[200] D Anzilotti, *Corso di Diritto Internazionale (Ad uso degli studenti dell'Università di Roma). Volume Primo: Introduzione—Teorie Generali* (3rd edn, 1928) 42–43; B Conforti, *Diritto Internazionale* (5th edn, 1997) 6–7; C Rousseau, *Droit International Public. Tome I Introduction et Sources* (1970) 57–58; L Oppenheim, *International Law. A Treatise. Vol. I. Peace* (2nd edn, 1912) 16–17. For criticism see J Delbrück and R Wolfrum, *Völkerrecht. Begründet von Georg Dahm. Band I/1. Die Grundlagen. Die Völkerrechtssubjekte* (2nd edn, 1989) 34 ff; K Doehring, *Völkerrecht* (2nd edn, 2004) 5 ff.

state has not agreed to a treaty norm, the principle of *pacta tertiis nec nocent nec prosunt* prevents it from suffering any adverse effects from the treaty. Simma, who refers to this system as one of 'bilateralism', has described the old state of the law admirably in his Hague lecture:

basically, international legal obligations existed, and still exist, at the level of relations between States individually. In other words, international law does not generally oblige States to adopt a certain conduct in the absolute, *urbi et orbi*, as it were, but only in relation to the particular State or States (or other international legal persons) to which a specific obligation under treaty or customary law is owed. (. . .) What I have said about the way in which international legal obligations 'run' between States is also valid for the traditional patterns of responsibility and enforcement attached to the primary rules: the principle is that it is up to each State to protect its own rights.[201]

The enforcement system, too, was bilateral in nature: the injured state and only the injured state could renounce the claim, demand damages, suspend, or renounce the treaty that its co-contractant violated.[202] Even though bilateral treaties come to mind first as an embodiment of this system, customary law followed the same reciprocal tenet.[203] Even multilateral treaties, which appeared with the Congress of Vienna in 1815,[204] structurally were nothing but a bundle of bilateral obligations which generally followed the rules of reciprocity.[205] Notions of non-intervention into internal affairs, perceived as a corollary of sovereignty, determined the purpose of international law: delimiting the responsibilities of the states, regulating coexistence. The subject matters international law governed were limited—diplomatic conduct, the high seas, immunities of states, recognition of states and governments, territorial questions, questions of war and neutrality as well as the protection of citizens in other states.[206]

This 'law of coexistence' is at the core of the present system of international law, arising together with the modern state in the early 16th century in northern Italy. But its roots are much older than that, going back to the first international treaties we know of—between Ebla and Ashur in the middle of the third millennium BC[207] and—better known—between Ramses II and Hattusili III in 1270 BC.[208]

---

[201] (Emphasis in original, footnotes omitted) B Simma, 'From Bilateralism to Community Interest in International Law' (1994—VI) 250 RdC 217, 230–231.

[202] Ibid; P-M Dupuy, 'L'Unité de l'Ordre Juridique International. Cours Général de Droit International Public (2000)' (2002) 297 RdC 9, 83–84.

[203] B Simma, *Das Reziprozitätselement in der Entstehung des Völkergewohnheitsrecht* (1970), Simma (n 201 above) 232.   [204] Dupuy (n 202 above) 81.

[205] B Simma, *Das Reziprozitätselement im Zustandekommen völkerrechtlicher Verträge* (1972) 154, 155.

[206] R Wolfrum, 'Entwicklung des Völkerrechts von einem Koordinations- zu einem Kooperationsrecht' in P-C Müller-Graff and H Roth (eds), *Recht und Rechtswissenschaft. Signaturen und Herausforderungen zum Jahrtausendbeginn. Ringvorlesung der Juristischen Fakultät der Ruprecht-Karls-Universität Heidelberg* (2000) 421; W Friedmann, *The Changing Structure of International Law* (1964) 4–5.

[207] The treaty was mostly commercial in nature. K-H Ziegler, *Völkerrechtsgeschichte* (1994) 15.

[208] A peace treaty concluded after the battle of Qadesh. E Edel, *Der Vertrag zwischen Ramses II. von Ägypten und Hattušili III. von Hatti* (1997).

Its basis of sovereign equality endures to this day as a fundamental principle contained in the UN Charter.[209]

Even though the topic of regime conflict is treated in the works of the great classic internationalists from Grotius[210] to Vattel,[211] it did not receive much attention during this period: in 1953 Jenks remarked that the formulation of coherent principles had hardly begun.[212] The reason for this is quite clear: quantitatively, conflicts were less common than today, as public international law only contained a relatively small number of regimes.

The rules for solving regime conflicts in such a system cannot but depart from the assumption that all provisions are of equal status, whatever source of international law they arise from, ie customary norms are not inferior to treaty norms, as all norms are founded on the consent of the states.[213] Nor can a hierarchy stem from the special status of the law-maker, as all states are equal. Thus, a hierarchy can only arise from the content of the norm, from its regulating some special, particular subject matter. However, the subjects that today are commonly perceived as being of some superior quality—particularly human rights—were regarded as outside the scope of international law as they would interfere with the sovereignty of states and thus meddle with internal affairs. As all conflicts in this system are of the bilateral type, it is not surprising that the solutions to normative conflict were inspired not just by an analogy to a conflict between municipal laws, but also between contracts.[214]

The former analogy prevailed for conflicts of treaties (or other norms) binding the same parties, which were solved by interpretation to avoid conflict, the *lex posterior* rule according to which later laws prevail over earlier ones, the *lex specialis* rule according to which the special law prevails over the general one, and the attempt to determine the legislative opinion.[215] For a conflict between two treaties that one state concluded with two different partners (AB-BC) Lauterpacht followed the contract analogy in his first two reports on the law of treaties for the ILC and suggested that the first treaty prevails over the second one on the claim that the state no longer has the capacity to contract on the issue (*nemo plus juris*

---

[209] Article 2 No 1 of the UN Charter, see Art 2 No 7 of the UN Charter.

[210] Grotius (n 122 above) lib II, cap XVI, § XXVIII ff.

[211] De Vattel (n 124 above) liv II, chap XVII, § 311 ff.

[212] Jenks (n 168 above) 405–406.

[213] Pauwelyn (n 166 above) 94; N Kontou, *The Termination and Revision of Treaties in the Light of New Customary International Law* (1994) 21; M Akehurst, 'The Hierarchy of the Sources of International Law' (1974–1975) 47 BYIL 273, 274–275; E Roucounas, 'Engagements Parallèles et Contradictoires' (1987—VI) 206 RdC 9, 57; W Czapliński and G Danilenko, 'Conflict of Norms in International Law' (1990) 21 NYIL 3, 7.

[214] The difference between these two analogies runs as a fine thread through many of the problems currently experienced. It is also at the core of the well-known distinction between law-making and common treaties going back to Bergbohm and Triepel that is somewhat out of *vogue* nowadays. H Triepel, *Völkerrecht und Landesrecht* (1899) 45 ff.

[215] Jenks (n 168 above) 436 ff; K Larenz and C-W Canaris, *Methodenlehre der Rechtswissenschaft* (3rd edn, 1995) 87 ff; E Sciso, *Gli Accordi Internazionali Confliggenti* (1986) 17 ff.

transfere potest quam habet).²¹⁶ This approach was abandoned by Fitzmaurice's third report on the law of treaties that considered both treaties as valid and accordingly envisioned damages to the party whose treaty is broken.

His approach prevailed and found its way into the Vienna Convention on the Law of Treaties (Vienna Convention),²¹⁷ to a great extent also for multilateral obligations: Article 30 of the Vienna Convention on conflicts between successive treaties relating to the same subject matter stipulates that absent a provision to the contrary²¹⁸ the later treaty governs the relations between parties to both treaties,²¹⁹ the treaty to which both states are parties governs where one state is only party to one of the treaties, but the other is party to both of them.²²⁰

B Law of Cooperation and Community Interests—Hierarchy in International Law

As Rosenne stated in his 2001 Hague lecture, the system of international law that existed 100 years ago and is associated with the Peace of Westphalia has been swept away.²²¹ It might be more correct to state that the system never existed but as a paradigm. Its very foundations are doubtful. Does the notion of sovereignty make sense in a world in which nations are interdependent and interact?²²² Is equality of states realistic or even desirable with countries as disparate as Tuvalu with all of 11,468 inhabitants and China with more than 100,000 times that population?²²³ But it is the new realities of a growing interdependence of nations resulting from drastically reduced transportation costs, technological changes and their consequences, and new means of mass communications that have driven the point home.

In the brave new world states awake to find that they cannot solve the problems of the day on their own. War and modern weaponry threaten everybody, as the two World Wars have shown, and require states to work together. The same holds

---

²¹⁶ H Lauterpacht, 'Report on the Law of Treaties' in YBILC, II (1953) 90, 156 (modifying the principle where the subsequent treaty partakes of the nature of a general rule of international law of a legislative character); H Lauterpacht, 'Règles Générales du Droit de la Paix' (1937—IV) 82 RdC 99, 308 ff.   ²¹⁷ Fitzmaurice (n 163 above) 27.

²¹⁸ Article 30(2) of the Vienna Convention.

²¹⁹ Article 30(3), (4)(a), 59 of the Vienna Convention.

²²⁰ Article 30(4)(b), but see Art 41 of the Vienna Convention.

²²¹ S Rosenne, 'The Perplexities of Modern International Law. General Course on Public International Law' (2001) 291 RdC 9, 23.

²²² JH Jackson, 'Sovereignty-Modern: A New Approach to an Outdated Concept' (2003) 97 AJIL 782; SD Krasner, *Sovereignty. Organized Hypocrisy* (1999) 220; D Palmeter, 'National Sovereignty and the World Trade Organization' (1999) 2 J World Intell Prop 88. To some, the defence of sovereignty has become a rallying cry: B Barr, 'Protecting National Sovereignty in an Era of International Meddling: An Increasingly Difficult Task' (2002) 29 Harv J on Legis 299; American Sovereignty Restauration Act of 2003, HR 1146, 108th Congress (16 sponsors) (not in force).

²²³ N Krisch, 'More Equal than the Rest? Hierarchy, Equality and US Predominance in International Law' in M Byers and G Nolte (eds), *United States Hegemony and the Foundations of International Law* (2003) 135; R Wolfrum, 'Comment on Chapters 10 and 11' in M Byers and

true for environmental problems such as the depletion of the ozone layer or climate change,[224] international transportation,[225] international communication,[226] terrorism,[227] and scores of other topics.[228] The recourse to protectionism in the inter-war period led states to internationalize economic policies in the belief that only internationalization could prevent the misplaced policies[229] and after World War II states opened up human rights to internationalization, regarding them as a concern for all of humanity—the 'international community'. Even though the latter notion is hard to grasp, at times connoting some mythical entity of its own, at times nothing but the collectivity of states,[230] it has entered international law for good and left a deep and lasting impact. In pursuit of community interests states will have to cooperate, law has to take account of this and, as Friedmann observed, become a law of cooperation.[231] The changes in the legal regime are plentiful and go well beyond what is necessary to consider for this study. I will focus on the notion of hierarchy that is most relevant in the area of regime conflict.

With the growing interdependence, more areas opened up to regulation and the number of international regimes multiplied, creating, in its wake, the potential for numerous regime conflicts. Many of the new multilateral treaties and also customary norms cannot be aptly described by the bilateral paradigm. Admittedly, multilateral treaties already occupied a somewhat awkward place in the traditional bilateral system: the rule of *lex posterior*, for example, is hard to apply where different parties accede to a multilateral treaty at different times making it possible that

---

G Nolte (eds), *United States Hegemony and the Foundations of International Law* (2003) 356; The data is taken from CIA, *The World Factbook 2004* (2004).

[224] Montreal Protocol on Substances that Deplete the Ozone Layer; Kyoto Protocol to the United Nations Framework Convention on Climate Change; R Wolfrum, 'Purposes and Principles of International Environmental Law' (1990) 33 GYIL 308.

[225] International Air Services Transit Agreement.

[226] A Noll, 'International Telecommunication Union' in R Bernhardt (ed), *Encyclopedia of Public International Law II, 2* (1995) 1379; Friedmann (n 206 above) 16 ff.

[227] International Convention for the Suppression of the Financing of Terrorism and actions by the Security Council.

[228] P Malanczuk, 'Globalization and the Future Role of Sovereign States' in F Weiss and E Denters and P de Waart, *International Economic Law with a Human Face* (1998) 45.

[229] P Sutherland *et al*, *The Future of the WTO. Addressing Institutional Challenges in the New Millennium* (2004) paras 108 ff; RE Hudec, *The GATT Legal System and World Trade Diplomacy* (1990) 5 ff. Petersmann has shown how international trade law prevents special interest from cajoling national legislatures into passing wealth-reducing protective measures, a 'constitutional function' of world trade law. E-U Petersmann, *Constitutional Functions and Constitutional Problems of International Economic Law* (1991) 96 ff.

[230] C Tomuschat, 'Die internationale Gemeinschaft' (1995) 33 AVR 1; R-J Dupuy, 'Communauté Internationale et Disparités de Développement' (1979—IV) 165 RdC 21, 195 ff; B Simma and AL Paulus, '*The "International Community": Facing the Challenge of Globalization*' (1998) 9 EJIL 266; AL Paulus, *Die internationale Gemeinschaft im Völkerrecht. Eine Untersuchung zur Entwicklung des Völkerrechts im Zeitalter der Globalisierung* (2001).   [231] Friedmann (n 206 above) 3.

a treaty that is the *lex posterior* for one party is actually the earlier treaty for the other.[232] The notion of community interest challenges the whole concept of the bilateral paradigm by granting obligations *erga omnes* status, a status that acknowledges that not just the state whose rights were breached has an interest in the protection of those rights, but also third states (a). It also introduces a normative hierarchy into the international order—the concept of *jus cogens* (b). The impact of community interest has been particularly close to the heart of a number of German scholars, as illustrated by Frowein's,[233] Simma's,[234] and Tomuschat's[235] Hague lectures and Paulus' doctoral thesis.[236]

a *Erga Omnes* Obligations—Integral Treaties

The legal recognition that some norms do not fit within a bilateral paradigm and that third states beyond the state suffering from the breach have an interest in the compliance with the norm is the notion of *erga omnes* obligations. It goes back to an *obiter dictum*[237] of the ICJ in the *Barcelona Traction* case reading:

> an essential distinction should be drawn between the obligations of a State towards the international community as a whole, and those arising vis-à-vis another State in the field of diplomatic protection. By their very nature the former are the concern of all States. In view of the importance of the rights involved, all States can be held to have a legal interest in their protection; they are obligations *erga omnes*.
>
> 34. Such obligations derive, for example, in contemporary international law, from the outlawing of acts of aggression, and of genocide, as also from the principles and rules concerning the basic rights of the human person, including protection from slavery and racial discrimination. Some of the corresponding rights of protection have entered into the body of general international law (. . .); others are conferred by international instruments of a universal or quasi-universal character.[238]

The popularity of this *obiter* far eclipsed that of the judgment itself: the concept of *erga omnes* norms was taken up in other decisions of the Court[239] and soon became a staple among internationalists, even though it has caused some difficulty, stemming on the one hand from the fact that the obligations are owed 'towards the international community as a whole', seeming to imply some community mechanism for

---

[232] EW Vierdag, 'The Time of the "Conclusion" of a Multilateral Treaty: Article 30 of the Vienna Convention on the Law of Treaties and Related Provisions' (1988) 59 BYIL 75.

[233] JA Frowein, 'Reactions by not Directly Affected States to Breaches of Public International Law' (1994—IV) 248 RdC 345.   [234] Simma (n 201 above).

[235] C Tomuschat, 'Obligations Arising for States without or against Their Will' (1993—IV) 241 RdC 209.   [236] Paulus (n 230 above).

[237] M Ragazzi, *The Concept of International Obligations* Erga Omnes (1997) 5 ff.

[238] (Emphasis in original) *Barcelona Traction, Light and Power Company, Limited (Belgium/Spain)*, Second Phase, Judgment, ICJ Reports 1970, 32, paras 33 f (5 February 1970).

[239] S Forlati, 'Azioni Dinanzi alla Corte Internazionale di Giustizia Rispetto a Violazioni di Obblighi Erga Omnes' (2001) 84 Rivista di Diritto Internazionale 69; C Annacker, *Die Durchsetzung von erga omnes Verpflichtungen vor dem Internationalen Gerichtshof* (1994).

their enforcement,[240] on the other from the unclear connection with numerous other notions commonly mentioned in the same breath such as *jus cogens*, international crimes,[241] and integral obligations. The numerous studies on the subject[242] and the work of the International Law Commission on state responsibility[243] have clarified some points, however. *Erga omnes* status is a rule of *jus standi*. Every state can invoke a violation of *erga omnes* norms, as illustrated by Portugal's invocation of the self-determination of the people of East Timor in the ICJ's *East Timor* case.[244] A similar phenomenon can be observed within treaty regimes for all States Parties, as recognized by Article 48(1)(a) of the ILC Draft Articles on State Responsibility,[245] with the consequence that every State Party can invoke the violation of these obligations *erga omnes partes*. For human rights norms, the *erga omnes (partes)* character is of particular importance—it is a characteristic of human rights norms as opposed to the law of aliens that they protect the citizens of the violating nation. Who could invoke a violation of the human rights norms if not other states under the doctrine of *erga omnes* norms?[246]

---

[240] P Picone, 'Interventi delle Nazioni Unite e Obblighi Erga Omnes' in P Picone (ed), *Interventi delle Nazioni Unite e Diritto Internazionale* (1995) 517, 528 ff; P Picone, 'Nazioni Unite e Obblighi "erga omnes"' (1993) 48 La Communitá internazionale 709, 715 ff.

[241] The concept was contained in Art 19(2) of the ILC's Draft Articles on State Responsibility and later dropped. It recognized the fact that a breach of an obligation essential for the protection of fundamental interests of the international community should carry different consequences from normal violations of international law. Riphagen suggested that for international crimes all other states are injured states. ILC, 'Report of the International Law Commission on the work of its twenty-eighth session 3 May–23 July 1976' in YBILC, II (1976) Pt 2, 1, 95; W Riphagen, 'Fifth Report on the Content, Forms and Degrees of International Responsibility (Pt 2 of the Draft Articles)' in YBILC, II (1984) Pt 1, 1, 3 Art 5(e); J Crawford, *The International Law Commission's Articles on State Responsibility. Introduction, Text and Commentaries*, 37 (2002).

[242] Frowein (n 233 above) 405 ff; JA Frowein, 'Obligations Erga Omnes' in R Bernhardt (ed), *Encyclopedia of Public International Law, III, 2* (1997) 757; Simma (n 201 above) 293 ff; P Picone, 'Obblighi Reciproci ed Obblighi *erga omnes* degli Stati nel Campo della Protezione Internazionale dell'Ambiente Marino dall'Inquinamento' in V Starace (ed), *Diritto Internazionale e Protezione dell'Ambiente Marino* (1983) 15; G Gaja, 'Obligations *Erga Omens*, International Crimes and *Jus Cogens*: A Tentative Analysis of Three Related Concepts' in JHH Weiler and A Cassese and M Spinedi (eds), *International Crimes of States. A Critical Analysis of the ILC's Draft Article 19 on State Responsibility* (1989) 151; A de Hoogh, *Obligations* Erga Omnes *and International Crimes. A Theoretical Inquiry into the Implementation and Enforcement of the International Responsibility of States* (1996); A Gattini, 'A Return Ticket to "Communitarisme", Please' (2002) 13 EJIL 1181.

[243] The notion is particularly clear in Art 48(1) of the 2001 Articles on State Responsibility, which reads: 'Any State other than an injured State is entitled to invoke the responsibility of another State in accordance with paragraph 2 if: (a) the obligation breached is owed to a group of States including that State, and is established for the protection of a collective interest of the group; or (b) the obligation breached is owed to the international community as a whole.'

[244] *Case concerning East Timor (Portugal/Australia)*, ICJ Reports 1995, 90, para 29 (30 June 1995). However, the invocation failed, as the Court opined it could not overcome the lack of consent to jurisdiction by Indonesia.   [245] N 243 above.

[246] The *erga omnes* character of all human rights norms is not undisputed, particularly in the light of the ICJ's statement that 'the instruments which embody human rights do not confer on States the capacity to protect the victims of infringements of such rights irrespective of their nationality' in Barcelona Traction (n 238 above) para 94. H-M Empell, *Die Staatengemeinschaftsnormen und ihre Durchsetzung. Die Pflichten erga omnes im geltenden Völkerrecht* (2003) 195 ff.

Where a treaty's obligation runs *erga omnes partes* it is no longer possible to dissolve the treaty into a number of virtual bilateral relationships—the treaty is called an 'integral' treaty. The classical bilateral enforcement structure breaks down for such treaties, as Fitzmaurice noted in his reports on the Law of Treaties. Whereas in the bilateral paradigm a party could respond to another party's violation of a treaty by suspending its own obligations this would lead to absurd results in the case of integral treaties: a violation of the Genocide Convention by one party does not relieve other parties of the obligation not to commit genocide.[247] *Inter se* modifications, letting a conflicting later bilateral treaty prevail for the two parties to it, or applying a different treaty in the dealings of a party to the *erga omnes partes* agreement with a third party runs into stormy waters, as the obligations are not just owed within a bilateral relationship. As Judge Anzilotti stated in his individual opinion in the *Customs Régime Between Germany and Austria* case concerning Article 88 of the Treaty of Saint-Germain:

It is an arguable question whether the States who in 1922 signed the Geneva Protocol were in a position to modify *inter se* the provisions of Article 88, which provisions (. . .) form an essential part of the peace settlement and were adopted not in the interests of any given State, but in the higher interest of the European political system and with a view to the maintenance of peace.[248]

A similar argument can be made in the area of human rights, as indicated by the ICJ concerning the Genocide Convention:

The Convention was manifestly adopted for a purely humanitarian and civilizing purpose. (. . .) In such a convention the contracting States do not have any interests of their own; they merely have, one and all, a common interest, namely, the accomplishment of those high purposes which are the *raison d'être* of the convention. Consequently, in a convention of this type one cannot speak of individual advantages or disadvantages to States, or of the maintenance of a perfect contractual balance between rights and duties.[249]

The Vienna Convention regards *inter se* modifications explicitly as impermissible where treaties protect community interests.[250] But what to make of the modifying treaty? Fitzmaurice's instinct to simply nullify any conflicting treaty a party to an integral treaty signs was successfully countered during the ILC project on the law

---

[247] Fitzmaurice distinguished between integral obligations in which the obligation of each party is independent of the performance by any of the others (eg the Genocide Convention), interdependent obligations in which the obligation of each party is dependent on a corresponding performance by all the parties (eg disarmament conventions) and traditional reciprocal obligations. Fitzmaurice (n 163 above) 27, 44 (Art 19 of the Articles).

[248] (Emphasis in original) Individual Opinion Judge Anzilotti, *Customs Régime Between Germany and Austria*, Advisory Opinion, PCIJ Reports 1931, Ser A/B, No 41, 64 (5 September 1931); see also Separate Opinion Judge Schücking, *The Oscar Chinn Case (United Kingdom/Belgium)*, PCIJ Reports 1934, Ser A/B, No 63, 148 (12 December 1934).

[249] *Reservations to the Convention on Genocide*, Advisory Opinion, ICJ Reports 1951, 15, 23 (28 May 1951).   [250] Article 41(1)(b) of the Vienna Convention.

of treaties by Waldock who accepted nullity only for violations of *jus cogens*.[251] Today, there is general agreement that an agreement conflicting with an integral agreement is not void, unless the integral agreement is *juris cogentis*.[252]

b *Jus cogens*

This leads to another instance, the clearest instance, of normative hierarchy: *jus cogens* or peremptory norms.[253] They build the value base of international law, the non-derogable core rules. Unlike *erga omnes* obligations, which merely give all states standing in case of their violation, the violation of a norm *juris cogentis* voids the agreement that violates it. Even though the two concepts are separate, there is one connection: all norms *juris cogentis* are also *erga omnes*, however not all *erga omnes* obligations are *juris cogentis*.[254]

Apart from Article 103 of the UN Charter establishing the priority of the Charter[255] *jus cogens* is the only clear instance of normative hierarchy in international law. The concept of superior norms in the international order is as old as international law and builds on natural law ideas as well as the private law distinction between *jus strictum* and *jus dispositivum*. Even though the principle of *jus cogens* is well-recognized in international law, as the ILC stated in its Articles on State Responsibility,[256] it is far from clear which norms are part of *jus cogens*. Article 53 of the Vienna Convention gives a first hint by defining *jus cogens*:

A treaty is void if, at the time of its conclusion, it conflicts with a peremptory norm of general international law. For the purposes of the present Convention, a peremptory norm of general international law is a norm accepted and recognized by the international community of States as a whole as a norm from which no derogation is permitted and which can be modified only by a subsequent norm of general international law having the same character.

Thus, only norms of general international law can be *juris cogentis*. The test to find out which customary norm has achieved such a status is a substantive one, ie one concerning the content of the norm. The reference to the international community in the Vienna Convention is reminiscent of the test for *erga omnes* norms and

---

[251] Wilting (n 168 above) 96 ff.

[252] Sciso (n 215 above) 189; Wilting (n 168 above) 110 f; C Feist, *Kündigung, Rücktritt und Suspendierung von mulitlateralen Verträgen* (2001) 195 ff; Zuleeg (n 189 above) 250 .

[253] Several other notions appear from time to time, eg *ordre public*, but none of these are clearly defined nor are they clearly distinguishable from *jus cogens*. The debate is not helped by adding more and more layers of hierarchy into the debate without ever proving them in practice. On *jus cogens* JA Frowein, '*jus cogens*' in R Bernhardt (ed), *Encyclopedia of Public International Law, III, 1* (1997) 65; G Gaja, '*Jus Cogens* beyond the Vienna Convention' (1981) 172 RdC 271; L Hannikainen, *Peremptory Norms* (jus cogens) *in International Law* (1988).

[254] M Byers, 'Conceptualising the Relationship between Jus Cogens and Erga Omens Rules' (1997) 66 Nordic J Int'l L 211, 212. Human rights norms arguably all have *erga omnes* character or *erga omnes partes* where derived from treaties, but are not all *jus cogens*.

[255] R Bernhardt, in B Simma *et al* (eds), *The Charter of the United Nations. A Commentary. Volume II*, (2nd edn, 2002) Art 103.

[256] Commentary to Art 26, para 5, Art 40, para 2 in Crawford (n 241 above).

it can be hardly surprising that the leading treatises on the topics discuss the same cases for both topics.[257]

Doctrine has busily cited numerous candidates for *jus cogens* status. Suffice it to refer to the commentary of the ILC's Articles on State Responsibility that lists, by way of example, the prohibition of aggression, the prohibitions against slavery and the slave trade, genocide, racial discrimination, *apartheid*, torture, the basic rules of international humanitarian law as well as the obligation to respect the right of self-determination.[258] Practice is far more cautious. While many courts have made *jus cogens* based arguments,[259] Kadelbach showed in 1991 that no existing treaty has been declared null and void for a violation of *jus cogens* by international tribunals. The closest a tribunal ever got was in one of the Nuremberg trials. A defendant had relied on an alleged agreement between the *Reich* and Vichy France allowing forced labour of French prisoners of war in the defence industry. The tribunal dismissed this defence as any such treaty would be 'manifestly *contra bonus mores (sic)* and hence void'.[260] But the discussion took place in the hypothetical as the defence was unable to produce the treaty. Even though falling short of actually applying the doctrine, the ICJ has mentioned *jus cogens* (though often not using the term) a number of times, eg in the *North Sea Continental Shelf* case, the *Nicaragua* case, and the Advisory Opinion on the *Legality of the Threat or Use of Nuclear Weapons*.[261]

The consequence of a violation of *jus cogens* is, as stated in Article 53 of the Vienna Convention, the nullity of the whole contravening treaty—a doubtful and much criticized[262] solution, particularly in the light of modern complex treaties that contain numerous provisions pertaining to various subject matters and that could inadvertently violate *jus cogens* in a peripheral detail. The better view is that clauses that do not violate *jus cogens* remain valid.[263] The Vienna Convention also prescribes a procedure for declaring a treaty void.[264] It has been much discussed

---

[257] S Kadelbach, *Zwingendes Völkerrecht* (1992) 109 ff.   [258] (N 241 above) Art 40 para 4 f.

[259] Koskenniemi 2 (n 151 above) paras 361 ff.

[260] US Military Tribunal, Nuremberg, 'Trial of Alfried Felix Alwyn Krupp von Bohlen und Halbach and Eleven Others, Casse No. 58' in United Nations War Crimes Commission (ed), *Law Reports of Trials of War Criminals* (17 November 1947–30 June 1948) vol X, 69, 141.

[261] *North Sea Continental Shelf (Federal Republic of Germany/Denmark; Federal Republic of Germany/Netherlands)*, Judgment, ICJ Reports 1969, 3, para 72 (20 February 1969); *Military and Paramilitary Activities in and against Nicaragua (Nicaragua/United States of America)*, Merits, Judgment, ICJ Reports 1986, 14, para 190 (27 June 1986); *Legality of the Threat or Use of Nuclear Weapons*, Advisory Opinion, ICJ Reports 1996, 226, para 83 (8 July 1996). Individual judges have frequently referred to *jus cogens*. Koskenniemi 2 (n 151 above) paras 377 ff.

[262] U Scheuner, 'Conflict of Treaty Provisions with a Peremptory Norm of General International Law' (1969) 29 ZaöRV 28, 35 ff; E Schwelb, 'Some Aspects of International *jus cogens* as Formulated by the International Law Commission' (1967) 61 AJIL 946, 971–972; P Cahier, 'Les Caractéristiques de la Nullité en Droit International et Tout Particulièrement dans la Convention de Vienne de 1969 sur le Droit des Traités' (1972) 76 RGDIP 645, 688–689; EP Nicoloudis, *La Nullité de jus cogens et le Developpement Contemporain du Droit International Public* (1974) 114–115; A Gómez Robledo, 'Le *jus cogens* International: Sa Genèse, sa Nature, ses Fonctions' (1981—III) 172 RdC 9, 121–122.

[263] Koskenniemi 2 (n 151 above) para 364 n 506.

[264] Articles 65 ff of the Vienna Convention.

whether in the case of violations of *jus cogens* this procedure is merely declaratory. It is reasonable to assume so,[265] as the opposite view would force a party to comply with a treaty violating *jus cogens* until the violation has been determined. Given the effect of *jus cogens*, it can rightly be stated that *jus cogens* has a constitutional function in the sense of setting down norms of higher status—states are free to conclude treaties and contract out of both customary international law and treaty law, but only to the extent that they do not violate *jus cogens*.

c Non-consenting States and Community Interests

Even though not all the dots have been connected, yet, a picture of an international order based on community values seems to be emerging. But there is an unseemly spot in the picture: who determines what 'community values' are and what happens if some states disagree? We all favour human rights protection and speak of universal values, but what can be done if Myanmar is reluctant to sign human rights agreements? Everybody can quickly agree that climate change is a community concern, but of what use is such a determination in light of the US refusal to sign the Kyoto protocol? In the end there are very few treaty regimes, including treaties commonly regarded as protecting community interests, that attract a universal following. Divergent participation heightens the problem of regime conflict, as such a conflict is easier to solve where all parties have signed on to both of the conflicting obligations. Even such 'universal' regimes as the human rights covenants and the WTO do not have an identical membership: as mentioned in chapter 3 only roughly 85 per cent of the WTO Member States have also ratified the human rights covenants. The reasons why some states fail to join an almost universal consensus are manifold and range from free-rider benefits that a lone holdout state can gain if others take care of reaching the community goals to the simple but sobering fact that at times some states do *not* agree with an approach enjoying near-unanimous support or even with a purportedly universal goal.

So what can be done to achieve *real* universality in the adherence to treaty regimes? At times a treaty can be constructed in a way that non-adherence comes at a prohibitive cost. This is true for the WTO Agreements that promise access to the most important economic markets in the world, but also, for example, for the Basel Convention on the Control of Transboundary Movements of Hazardous Wastes and their Disposal that generally prohibits the export of waste to and the import of waste from non-parties.[266] At other times public or political pressure can induce other states to adhere to a treaty.

---

[265] Kadelbach (n 257 above) 324 f; R Jennings, 'Nullity and Effectiveness in International Law' in R Jennings (ed), *Cambridge Essays in International Law. Essays in Honour of Lord McNair* (1965) 64, 66 ff; Gaja (n 253 above) 285–286; *contra* G Morelli, 'Aspetti Processuali della Invalidità dei Trattati' (1974) 57 Rivista di Diritto Internazionale 5, 9.

[266] Article 4(5) of the Basel Convention. J Jekewitz, 'The Implementation of the Basel Convention in German National Environmental Law as an Example for the Use of the Economic Mechanisms' in R Wolfrum (ed), *Enforcing Environmental Standards: Economic Mechanisms as Viable Means?* (1996) 395, 408.

However, under traditional international law the technical legal avenues to achieve this goal are blocked: attempts to impose treaty obligations on third states[267] have to fail as states have to consent to be bound by them and the *pacta tertiis* principle prevents any negative effect on states that did not express their consent. Nevertheless, so-called 'objective regimes'—treaties governing the administration or status of certain areas, such as Antarctica—at times are considered to impose obligations on third states.[268] Another approach is the liberal use of customary international law. But the reasoning to endow the relevant norms with customary status has to proceed carefully to avoid circularity. There is a risk that a value is embraced as a community value despite the fact that some states have *not* signed a certain convention and then that value is argued to have entered general international law, because it is generally accepted, imposing the value on the state that has not signed. The discussion of access to medicine in chapter 3 certainly comes to mind, where the pitfall of circularity was avoided by examining the position of countries like the United States that have not ratified the ICESCR with the utmost care and finding that it only accepts a part of the right to access to medicine as guaranteed by the ICESCR.

Finding a lasting solution to the problem of lacking generality is a tightrope act from a bilateral past to a 'constitutionalized' world with fundamental values, the risk of falling into the pitfalls of politics always present. Anyone daring to climb onto the tightrope must be aware, however, that a constant intercultural debate is necessary to determine whether a goal is really a community goal and that a similar debate is needed to analyze whether consent can be reached as to the means necessary to reach the goal.

C Institutionalization, Factual Hierarchy

The presentation so far has conveyed the impression of an international system that is proceeding, albeit in a disorderly and haphazard manner, towards a structure that could be dubbed constitutional in the sense that it consists of normal rules and *jus cogens* rules with a hierarchically superior status. The 'constitutional' paradigm has gained wide popularity and produced valuable insights into the changing structures of the international system.[269] It seems only natural to envision a world constitutive process, focusing on the UN and its Charter.[270]

---

[267] R Jennings, 'Treaties as "Legislation"', in G Abi-Saab (ed), *Collected Writings of Sir Robert Jennings. Volume 2* (1998) 719.

[268] R Wolfrum, 'Le Régime de l'Antarctique et les États Tiers' in *La Mer et Son Droit. Mélanges Offerts à Laurent Lucchini et Jean-Pierre Quéneudec* (2003) 695; R Wolfrum, *Die Internationalisierung staatsfreier Räume. Die Entwicklung einer internationalen Verwaltung für Antarktis, Weltraum, Hohe See und Meeresboden* (1984); I Brownlie, *Principles of Public International Law* (6th edn, 2003) 254 ff, 599.

[269] JA Frowein, 'Konstitutionalisierung des Völkerrechts' in Deutsche Gesellschaft für Völkerrecht (ed), *Völkerrecht und Internationales Privatrecht in einem sich globalisierenden internationalen System—Auswirkungen der Entstaatlichung transnationaler Rechtsbeziehungen* (2000) 427.

[270] B Fassbender, 'The United Nations Charter as Constitution of the International Community' (1998) 36 Colum J Transnat'l L 529; P-M Dupuy, 'The Constitutional Dimension of the Charter of the United Nations Revisited' (1997) 1 Max Planck UNYB 1, 30 ff; more critical: MJ Herdegen, 'The "Constitutionalization" of the UN Security System' (1994) 27 Vand J Transnat'l L 135.

But, as Walter observed, the disaggregation of international law into sectorally organized regimes stands in the way of such a world constitutive process.[271] To increase the effectiveness of these sectorally organized regimes states can choose to endow them with an organizational structure and an adjudication and enforcement system, thus stabilizing the regimes—to apply the constitutional paradigm, it is appropriate to speak of several constitutions rather than one constitution.[272] The constitutional documents of the adjudicatory bodies commonly limit their jurisdiction to claims arising under the norms of the regime, but they can also define which law the tribunal is empowered to apply and limit the applicable law to the legal rules of the regime[273]—a natural consequence of the validity of treaties contracting out of customary law and out of treaty law even if the treaty that is contracted out of is of an integral nature. The only limit to the process is *jus cogens*, which consequently has to be applied by all tribunals.

Risks of conflict between the different tribunals arise whether their applicable law is identical or not: where different tribunals apply the same law, there is a risk that they interpret the same rule differently, as illustrated by the *Loizidou*[274] case in which the European Court of Human Rights' holding on the effect of territorial reservations differed from the standards set by the ICJ, or by the *Tadić*[275] case in which the International Criminal Tribunal for the former Yugoslavia rejected the ICJ's effective control test for the question of state responsibility for acts of military groups laid down in the *Nicaragua* case.[276]

Where the applicable law of the different tribunals is limited to the legal rules of their regimes—or where the constitutive document of the tribunal imposes a hierarchy of the norms to be applied by the tribunal[277]—the issue is a different one.

---

[271] C Walter, 'Constitutionalizing (Inter)national Governance—Possibilities for and Limits to the Development of an International Constitutional Law' (2001) 44 GYIL 170, 189.

[272] The concept of constitutionalization has been discussed for several regimes. DZ Cass, 'The "Constitutionalization" of International Trade Law: Judicial Norm-Generation as the Engine of Constitutional Development in International Trade' (2001) 12 EJIL 39; HL Schloemann and S Ohlhoff, '"Constitutionalization" and Dispute Settlement in the WTO: National Security as an Issue of Competence' (1999) 93 AJIL 424; E-U Petersmann, 'Human Rights and International Economic Law in the 21st Century. The Need to Clarify their Interrelationships' (2001) 4 JIEL 3; C Walter, 'Die Europäische Menschenrechtskonvention als Konstitutionalisierungsprozeß' (1999) 59 ZaöRV 961. The concept should be employed carefully as highlighted by R Howse and K Nicolaidis, 'Legitimacy through "Higher Law"? Why Constitutionalizing the WTO Is a Step too Far' in T Cottier and PC Mavroidis (eds), *The Role of the Judge in International Trade Regulation. Experience and Lessons for the WTO* (2003) 307.

[273] On the proliferation of tribunals: M Shahabuddeen, 'Consistency in Holdings by International Tribunals' in N Ando *et al* (eds), *Liber Amicorum Judge Shigeru Oda. Volume 1* (2002) 633; B Kingsbury, 'Is the Proliferation of International Courts and Tribunals a Systematic Problem?' (1999) 31 NYU J Int'l L & Politics 679; JI Charney, 'Is International Law Threatened by Multiple International Tribunals?' (1998) 271 RdC 101.

[274] *Loizidou v Turkey*, Preliminary Objections, 310 ECHR (1995) Series A (23 March 1995).

[275] *Prosecutor v Duško Tadić*, Appeals Chamber, Judgment, Case No IT-94-1-A, paras 99 ff, 115 ff (15 July 1999).

[276] *Military and Paramilitary Activities in and against Nicaragua (Nicaragua/United States of America)*, Merits, Judgment, ICJ Reports 1986, 14, para 115 (27 June 1986).

[277] Eg Art 293(1) of the UNCLOS: 'A court or tribunal having jurisdiction under this section shall apply this Convention and other rules of international law not incompatible with this Convention.'

Even if the facts of the case raise questions under several regimes, the tribunal will only apply the rules (or give preference to the rules) of its own regime. Consequently it will *not* apply the general international law rules for normative conflict. As Böckenförde has rightly pointed out, clearing up some misperceptions in doctrine, this does not affect the standing of the rules under international law; it does not impose a normative hierarchy between the norms.[278] The approach is illustrated by Judge Wolfrum's Separate Opinion in the *MOX Plant* case. The dispute before the International Tribunal for the Law of the Sea (ITLOS) involved the United Nations Convention on the Law of the Sea (UNCLOS), the OSPAR Convention and European Law.[279] Accordingly parts of the case or the whole case had been brought before an arbitral tribunal under Annex VII of the UNCLOS,[280] an arbitral tribunal under the OSPAR Convention[281] and the European Court of Justice.[282] Judge Wolfrum stated pointedly that with the exception of the Annex VII tribunal the procedures do not settle disputes under the UNCLOS: 'The dispute settlement system under the OSPAR Convention is designed to settle disputes concerning the interpretation and application of that Convention and not concerning the Convention on the Law of the Sea.'[283] The same can be said for the Court of Justice of the European Communities. The *MOX Plant* case was not the only one involving adjudicatory bodies of different regimes: ITLOS' *Swordfish* Case pinned the world trade order against UNCLOS and also occupied the WTO dispute settlement mechanism.[284] In *Argentina—Poultry* a WTO Panel had to discuss a measure the legality of which had already been challenged before a MERCOSUR Ad Hoc Arbitral Tribunal.[285] The result of this proliferation of

[278] M Böckenförde, 'Zwischen Sein und Wollen—Über den Einfluss umweltvölkerrechtlicher Verträge im Rahmen eines WTO-Streitbeilegungsverfahrens' (2003) 63 ZaöRV 971, 974–975.

[279] ITLOS, *The MOX Plant Case (Ireland v United Kingdom)*, Case No 10, Request for Provisional Measures, Order of 3 December 2001.

[280] Permanent Court of Arbitration, *The MOX Plant Case (Ireland v United Kingdom)*, Order No 3 (24 June 2003).

[281] Permanent Court of Arbitration, *Dispute Concerning Access to Information under Article 9 of the OSPAR Convention (Ireland v United Kingdom)*, Final Award (2 July 2003); M Fitzmaurice, 'Current Legal Development. OSPAR Tribunal' (2003) 18 The International Journal of Marine and Coastal Law 541.

[282] Case C-459/03 *Commission v Ireland* [2004] OJ C7/24 (10 January 2004); R Churchill and J Scott, 'The MOX Plant Litigation: The First Half-Life' (2004) 53 ICLQ 643.

[283] ITLOS, *The MOX Plant Case (Ireland v United Kingdom)*, Case No 10, Request for Provisional Measures, Order of 3 December 2001, Separate Opinion Judge Wolfrum.

[284] ITLOS, *Case concerning the Conservation and Sustainable Exploitation of Swordfish Stocks in the South-Eastern Pacific Ocean (Chile v European Community)*, Case No 7; *Chile—Measures Affecting the Transit and Importation of Swordfish, Request for Consultations by the European Communities*, WT/DS193/1 (26 April 2000). P-T Stoll and S Vöneky, 'The Swordfish Case: Law of the Sea v. Trade' (2002) 62 ZaöRV 21; M Rau, 'Comment: The Swordfish Case: Law of the Sea v. Trade' (2002) 62 ZaöRV 37.

[285] *Argentina—Definitive Anti-Dumping Duties on Poultry from Brazil*, WT/DS241/R (2003) (*Argentina—Poultry*); *Laudo del Tribunal Arbitral sobre la controversia entre la República Federativa de Brasil (Parte Reclamante) y República Argentina (Parte Reclamada) identificada como controversia sobre 'Aplicación de Medidas Antidumping contra la exporación de pollos enteros, provenientes de Brasil, Resolución No 574/2000 del Ministerio de Economía de la República Argenina'* (21 May 2001) (*Laudo IV—Pollos—de Brasil a Argentina*).

tribunals is that a state can be faced with two rulings that turn out to be contradictory, each clarifying the rules under one regime only.

The consequences of this institutional structure have been neglected so far. Logically, it results in a 'factual hierarchy' of regimes, a hierarchy that, even though completely independent from the normative hierarchy, is still real: some regimes boast strong enforcement mechanisms with the possibility of sanctions, others are enforced by shaming states into compliance, yet other regimes do not have an enforcement or adjudication mechanism at all. It is reasonable to conclude that in cases of regime conflicts states will tend to abide by the rules of the regime with the strongest enforcement mechanism. Even though technically it is correct to state that this does not change the relationship of the regimes under general international law and that under general international law the outcome might be different, it is unrealistic to leave it at that. If a state will abide by the solutions imposed by the regime with the strong enforcement mechanism and it is this mechanism that determines what will happen in fact, *peu importe* what doctrine holds dear. As Justice Holmes once put it: a bad man 'does not care two straws for the axioms or deductions, but that he does want to know what the (. . .) courts are likely to do in fact.'[286]

While this state of affairs at first sight is entirely displeasing and random one should not rush to conclusions. First of all, regime conflicts are a necessary corollary of the way the international order is constructed:[287] if some regimes are endowed with weak enforcement systems, this is simply because states could not agree to set up a stronger one.[288] Secondly, there is some benefit to be gained by keeping regimes separate, namely the benefit of specialization. A specialized dialogue can develop to tackle regime-specific issues and attention is focused on one issue only, even at the disadvantage of a weak enforcement mechanism. This point is illustrated by the WTO and the human rights regime: human rights would benefit from a much stronger enforcement system if turned over to the WTO, but the human rights regime could, nevertheless, be on the losing side as the WTO culture is more sceptical towards human rights and might interpret them too restrictively.[289]

Nevertheless, the risk of incoherent and contradictory results cannot be denied. To some extent it can be mitigated by coordinating the different adjudicatory mechanisms—be it by clearly delineating the jurisdiction of the tribunals and giving the case to the tribunal best suited for it or by taking account of other tribunals' rulings even though they involved different regimes.[290] But the basic problem remains. Two solutions offer themselves: we can either live with the possibility of contradictory outcomes of adjudicatory proceedings as a consequence of the structure of the international system, relying on the fact that real regime conflicts

---

[286] OW Holmes, 'The Path of the Law' (1996–1997) 110 Harv L Rev 991, 994.

[287] Koskenniemi and Leino (n 150 above) 560 ff.

[288] P Alston, 'Resisting the Merger and Acquisition of Human Rights by Trade Law: A Reply to Petersmann' (2002) 13 EJIL 815, 833 ff.

[289] R Howse, 'Human Rights in the WTO: Whose Rights, What Humanity? Comment on Petersmann' (2002) 13 EJIL 651, 656.   [290] Neumann (n 154 above) 513 ff.

are not a common occurrence.[291] Or we can refuse to accept the incoherence and try to make tribunals apply the full panoply of international law—at the risk of forcing the wording of the rules on the law the tribunals may apply.[292]

D 'Soft-enforced' Human Rights Meet 'Hard-enforced' WTO

The characterization with respect to the paradigms described above of the two regimes involved in the conflict that is the subject of this study explains why the rest of the study will focus on an analysis to what extent human rights law can be taken into account within the WTO system.

a The WTO Regime

The WTO regime will first be analyzed with respect to normative hierarchy, then with respect to factual hierarchy. In addition, as the WTO regime offers a particularly high potential for conflicts with other regimes, a survey of the normative solutions that the regime offers for such conflicts will be undertaken.

aa Normative Hierarchy: An Instrumental Order of the Bilateral or Integral Type? The WTO Regime consists of two different types of rules, as Petersmann observed. The old GATT agreement, still at the core of the WTO and the focus of interest for most trade lawyers, follows the tenets of negative integration:[293] it prohibits governments from taking certain measures such as quantitative restrictions.[294] Pauwelyn analyzed the rules of this regime to determine whether WTO obligations are bilateral in nature or integral. His test was whether the breach of an obligation to one state necessarily affects the rights and obligations of all other states. He found that most WTO obligations remain bilateral in nature, concurring with an earlier study by Hahn, because (a) of the bilateral nature of trade and consequently of market access, which is necessarily access for a product from country A to market B, (b) trade is an instrument to increase welfare, rather than a value in itself,[295] (c) the concessions made in the WTO are negotiated bilaterally and only then multilateralized, and, most importantly, (d) WTO obligations are enforced exclusively bilaterally in WTO dispute settlement, in which one state claims nullification or impairment of benefits accruing to it by another state and which ultimately results in a classical reciprocal enforcement measure, namely the possibility of suspension of concessions or other obligations under the Marrakesh Agreement Establishing the World Trade Organization.[296] Petersmann, who has emphasized

---

[291] Böckenförde (n 278 above).
[292] Pauwelyn (n 166 above). This would not exclude the risk of different interpretations of the same rule by different tribunals.
[293] The terminology has been introduced by J Tinbergen, *International Economic Integration* (2nd edn, 1956) 122.   [294] Article XI of the GATT.
[295] FJ Garcia, 'The Global Market and Human Rights: Trading Away the Human Rights Principle' (1999) 25 Brook J Int'l L 51, 64 ff.
[296] Article XXIII:1 of the GATT; Art 22 of the DSU; J Pauwelyn, The Nature of WTO Obligations (n 189 above) 15 ff; M Hahn, *Die einstige Aussetzung von GATT-Verpflichtungen als Repressalie* (1996) 152.

throughout his work that the WTO system serves to protect economic freedoms of individuals,[297] might disagree. It is important to note, however, that any protection of economic freedoms of individuals by the WTO is merely a reflex, albeit an intended one, of the world trade order. WTO law does not confer trade rights on individuals in the sense that human rights law does, and remains an instrumental order based on utilitarian ideas.

The other type of rules of WTO law require active state measures, they harmonize internal legislation and provide for *positive integration*.[298] The TRIPS Agreement is the most significant example of this type of rules. With respect to these rules Pauwelyn considers a classification as integral obligations possible. However, from a technical legal standpoint there is no reason to consider these obligations as different from GATT obligations: contrary to public perception, the TRIPS Agreement does not require full harmonization, it requires the application of its standards only for nationals of other Members,[299] and thus stays within a bilateral structure in which the state whose nationals do not receive such treatment can complain. Also, the TRIPS Agreement does not protect human rights, even though a core of the intellectual property rights contained in the agreement is protected by human rights law. As already demonstrated, modern intellectual property law is an instrumental order that serves utilitarian goals, much like GATT law.

Nevertheless, a classification of the TRIPS Agreement as purely reciprocal is clearly overly technical and neglects an important practical aspect. The classification of the agreement as bilateral would allow *inter se* modifications of the Agreement resulting in a state having to adopt different standards of intellectual property protection for foreigners coming from different countries. However, no modern state that I am aware of actually ever contemplated establishing such an order—and the construction of such a system would be so cumbersome, given that states would have to comply with the most-favoured nation clause, that states are unlikely to ever do so. It is much likelier that states had the intention to establish, at least in this respect, a harmonized system. Hence, the TRIPS Agreement should be regarded as an integral agreement, even though it only provides for minimum standards.

None of the two types of rules, however, are *juris cogentis*, as both of them pursue instrumental purposes, rather than protecting values in themselves. The whole culture of trade law illustrates that the rules involved can hardly be *juris cogentis*, as the process of trade negotiations by necessity involves trade-off, something that is impermissible with respect to *jus cogens*. The mere fact that economic theory teaches that all states stand to gain from free trade only means that states set up the

---

[297] E-U Petersmann, 'From the Hobbesian International Law of Coexistence to Modern Integration Law: The WTO Dispute Settlement System' (1998) 1 JIEL 175, 176 ff; E-U Petersmann, 'Time for a United Nations "Global Compact" for Integrating Human Rights into the Law of Worldwide Organizations: Lessons from European Integration' (2002) 13 EJIL 621, 639 ff, 643–644; E-U Petersmann, 'The WTO Constitution and Human Rights' (2000) 3 JIEL 19.
[298] E-U Petersmann, 'From "Negative" to "Positive" Integration in the WTO: Time for "Mainstreaming Human Rights" into WTO Law?' (2000) 37 Common Market Law Review 1363, 1364–1365.   [299] Article 1.3 of the TRIPS Agreement.

system in their own interest, it does not imply the existence of some community interest beyond this.

bb The WTO in the Factual Hierarchy of Regimes: A Powerhouse   In the factual hierarchy of international regimes the WTO regime is much stronger than in the normative one, in fact—it is second to none. Experts fall into superlatives to describe the effectiveness of its dispute settlement mechanism and enforcement system. 'The dispute settlement system negotiated during the Uruguay Round seems to me still today an extraordinary achievement that comes close to a miracle.' (Ehlermann)[300] 'After [the first] five years of WTO existence, one can now say that the WTO dispute procedures are clearly considered a success. (...) There has (...) been a high level of compliance up to this point.' (Jackson)[301] 'The dispute settlement procedures in the 1994 WTO Agreement are the most ambitious worldwide system for the settlement of disputes among more than 130 states ever adopted in the history of international law.' (Petersmann)[302] It is 'the most complete system of international dispute resolution in history' (Lowenfeld).[303] 'For the most part, it is now *simply assumed* that trade disputes between and among the Members of the WTO will be resolved through the arrangements of WTO dispute settlement.' (Bacchus)[304] All Members are subject to compulsory jurisdiction, a quasi-judicial proceeding with independent appellate review, quasi-automatic rulings in a short time span, which can ultimately result in the authorization of compensation and the suspension of concessions.[305] Numerous disputes have been brought to and settled by the mechanism. To describe their outcome I will defer to the colourful prose of Bacchus:

Many—perhaps even most—of the international trade disputes that are brought to the attention of the WTO are resolved in a 'positive solution' without formal consultations. Most of the disputes that result in formal consultations are resolved without the formal establishment of a panel (...). Furthermore, almost all of the trade disputes that are addressed by a panel and, if appealed, by the Appellate Body, result in what all the WTO Members that are

---

[300] C-D Ehlermann, 'Six Years on the Bench of the "World Trade Court". Some Personal Experiences as Member of the Appellate Body of the World Trade Organization' in F Ortino and E-U Petersmann, *The WTO Dispute Settlement System 1995–2003* (2004) 499, 529.

[301] JH Jackson, 'International Economic Law: Jurisprudence and Contours' (1999) 93 ASIL Proceedings 98, 102.

[302] Petersmann, Hobbesian International Law of Coexistence (n 297 above) 183.

[303] AF Lowenfeld, *International Economic Law* (2002) 150.

[304] J Bacchus, '"Woulda, Coulda, Shoulda": The Consolations of WTO Dispute Settlement' in J Bacchus, *Trade and Freedom* (2004) 361, 367.

[305] Article 22 of the DSU; Petersmann, Hobbesian International Law of Coexistence (n 297 above) 183. For an overview over WTO dispute settlement see R Wolfrum, 'Das Internationale Recht für den Austausch von Waren und Dienstleistungen' in R Schmidt (ed), *Öffentliches Wirtschaftsrecht* (1996) 535, 623 ff; MJ Trebilcock and R Howse, *The Regulation of International Trade* (2nd edn, 1999) 58 ff; P Picone and A Ligustro, *Diritto dell' Organizzazione Mondiale del Commercio* (2002) 575 ff; R Howse, 'The Most Dangerous Branch? WTO Appellate Body Jurisprudence on the Nature and Limits of the Judicial Power' in T Cottier and PC Mavroidis (eds), *The Role of the Judge in International Trade Regulation. Experience and Lessons for the WTO* (2003) 11.

parties to those disputes agree is a 'positive solution' within a reasonable period of time after the adoption of the dispute settlement reports by the Dispute Settlement Body. (...) So we know that the difficulties, thus far, have been, in fact, in only a mere handful of disputes. We could count them on the fingers of the hand we might use to strum a bass fiddle.[306]

The effective dispute-settlement and enforcement mechanism does not just lead to a level of compliance that is generally considered as outstanding, it also means that where another regime clashes with WTO law the outcome of the WTO proceeding will most likely be determinative of a state's real-life behaviour, whatever the other regime orders.

cc The WTO and Regime Conflict   It is not only its strong position in the factual hierarchy of regimes, it is also its exceptional breadth that makes the WTO regime occupy a prominent position in the topic of regime conflicts. One has the impression that there is hardly any regime with which the WTO might not potentially come into conflict: Neumann's comprehensive survey lists potential conflicts with numerous multilateral environmental agreements ranging from the Convention on International Trade in Endangered Species of Wild Fauna and Flora (CITES) to the Cartagena Protocol on Biosafety to the Convention on Biological Diversity, as well as conflicts with labour standards, human rights, WIPO Treaties, the Universal Postal Convention, the telecommunications, finance, and development regimes.[307]

The extraordinary vulnerability of the WTO regime to regime conflict is due to the fact that almost any regulation has the potential to affect trade, just as trade rules have the potential to affect almost any other area of regulation, not to speak of trade sanctions as an enforcement mechanism, which naturally affect trade. Pauwelyn has rightly stated that trade rules 'cut across almost all other rules of international law'.[308] Anyone who doubts that so many areas of regulation can have potential trade effects is advised to survey the literature on WTO enlargement that suggests including many a regime in the WTO on the grounds of its trade effects.[309] Many seem to perceive the development of the WTO according to the 'bicycle theory': the world trading system must move forward, or it will fall.[310] At times, though, it appears more like an avalanche: what once began as a small snowball has, over time, started to swallow other areas of regulation. Arguments

---

[306] (Emphasis deleted) Bacchus (n 304 above) 368.   [307] Neumann (n 164 above).

[308] Pauwelyn (n 166 above) 20. Note also S Charnovitz, 'Trade Measures and the Design of International Regimes' in S Charnovitz (ed), *Trade Law and Global Governance* (2002) 27; DW Leebron, 'Linkages' (2002) 96 AJIL 5.

[309] S Charnovitz, 'Triangulating the World Trade Organization' (2002) 96 AJIL 28; JP Trachtman, 'Institutional Linkage: Transcending "Trade and ..."' (2002) 96 AJIL 77; K Bagwell, PC Mavroidis and RW Staiger, 'It's a Question of Market Access' (2002) 96 AJIL 56; R Howse, 'From Politics to Technocracy—and Back Again: The Fate of the Multilateral Trading Regime' (2002) 96 AJIL 94; FJ Garcia, 'Trade Linkage Phenomenon: Pointing the Way to the Trade Law and Global Social Policy of the 21st Century, The Symposium on Linkage as Phenomenon: An Interdisciplinary Approach: Introduction' (1998) 19 U Pa J Int'l Econ L 201.

[310] J Bacchus, 'The Bicycle Club: Affirming the American Interest in the Future of the WTO' in J Bacchus, *Trade and Freedom* (2004) 329.

about WTO enlargement are legion. As I have argued more extensively elsewhere, after the inclusion of the TRIPS Agreement the attempt to exclude an area from the trade ambit on substantive grounds will be doomed to fail in many cases.[311]

WTO negotiators were not unaware of the potential of trade law to come into conflict with other regulatory areas. They provided for a resolution for regime conflict within the GATT context, but failed to do so within the TRIPS Agreement.

Thus, the GATT explicitly accounts for the possibility of non-trade values supervening GATT rules. Besides the security exceptions contained in Article XXI of the GATT,[312] it is especially Article XX of the GATT that exempts certain measures from GATT compliance. A violation of a GATT obligation can be justified under that provision if (1) the measure falls under one of the enumerated policies such as those 'necessary to protect human, animal or plant life or health' and 'relating to the conservation of exhaustible natural resources if such measures are made effective in conjunction with restrictions on domestic production or consumption' and (2) the measure complies with the requirements of the *chapeau* of Article XX. The *chapeau* prevents abuse of the exception. It requires that the measures 'are not applied in a manner which would constitute a means of arbitrary or unjustified discrimination between countries where the same conditions prevail, or a disguised restriction on international trade'. Under the old GATT 1947 appeals to Article XX commonly failed, as panels had adopted a narrow interpretation of that provision.[313] Appellate Body Reports under GATT 1994 (which contains amongst others the provisions of GATT 1947) indicate that chances of a policy to be upheld under Article XX GATT have improved.

In addition, the SPS and the TBT Agreements elaborate specific rules for the application of Article XX(b) of the GATT in the area of sanitary or phytosanitary measures and technical barriers to trade.

Several aspects of Article XX as it stands today are relevant to the issue of regime conflict. The first important observation is that compliance with Article XX justifies the violation of any and all other GATT obligations.[314] The second is that governments enjoy considerable leeway in making use of the exceptions, as long as the policy falls within one of the enumerated policy areas. This had been put in doubt, not just by the fact that all measures will have to comply with the requirements of the *chapeau*,[315] but particularly because some policy areas require measures

---

[311] HP Hestermeyer, 'The Language of Trade Linkage. Lessons for the Singapore Issues Learned from TRIPS' in A Steinmann and F Höhne and P-T Stoll (eds), *Die WTO vor neuen Herausforderungen* (2005) 139.

[312] JH Jackson, *The World Trading System. Law and Policy of International Economic Relations*, (2nd edn, 1997) 229 ff.

[313] *Thailand—Restrictions on Importation of and Internal Taxes on Cigarettes*, DS10/R—37S/200 (1990) (*Thailand—Cigarettes*), paras 72 ff; *United States—Restrictions on Imports of Tuna*, DS21/R—39S/155 (1991), paras 5.22 ff (*US—Tuna I*, not adopted); *United States—Restrictions on Imports of Tuna*, DS29/R (1994), paras 5.11 ff (*US—Tuna II*, not adopted).

[314] *United States—Gasoline*, WT/DS2/AB/R (1996) 24.

[315] P-T Stoll and F Schorkopf, *WTO—Welthandelsordnung und Welthandelsrecht* (2002) 64 ff.

to be 'necessary' for a policy goal, ie there may not be an 'alternative measure consistent with the General Agreement, or less inconsistent with it, which [the Member] could reasonably be expected to employ to achieve its (. . .) policy objectives'.[316] Scholars interpreted this requirement to include trade-offs among the non-trade value and trade, ie the trade burden is measured against the non-trade benefits.[317] But in two cases concerning health protection, under Article XX and under the SPS Agreement, the Appellate Body made it clear that Members remain free to determine the level of health protection they want to attain.[318] This clearly implies that the Appellate Body will not venture into balancing the trade detriments and the non-trade benefits.[319]

Article XX of the GATT thus offers an attractive solution for conflicts with other regimes: where another regime comes into conflict with the trade regime, but it falls under the policies enumerated by Article XX and complies with the *chapeau*, Article XX solves any conflict in favour of the non-trade regime.[320]

The Appellate Body Report in *US—Shrimp* demonstrates how the solution can be operationalized. The Appellate Body referred to UNCLOS, the Convention on Biological Diversity, CITES, and two environmental law resolutions in interpreting the term 'exhaustible natural resources' in 'relating to the conservation of exhaustible natural resources if such measures are made effective in conjunction with restrictions on domestic production or consumption', one of the Article XX policies. It held the term to include living and non-living exhaustible natural resources, such as sea-turtles.[321]

Taking a measure to comply with another treaty regime also helps to show that the measure is not applied in a manner which would constitute a means of arbitrary or unjustified discrimination between countries where the same conditions prevail, ie it helps to show compliance with Article XX's *chapeau*.[322] Human rights as such are not mentioned among Article XX's non-trade policies, hardly surprising given that, when the GATT was negotiated, human rights had barely started

---

[316] *Thailand—Cigarettes*, para 75, *United States—Section 337 of the Tariff Act of 1930*, L/6439—36S/345 (1989), para 5.26, both cited with approval in *EC—Asbestos*, paras 170 f.

[317] JP Trachtman, 'Trade and . . . Problems, Cost-Benefit Analysis and Subsidiarity' (1998) 9 EJIL 32. Critical: Garcia (n 295 above) 83 ff.

[318] For Art XX: *EC—Asbestos*, para 168. For the SPS: *Australia—Measures Affecting Importation of Salmon*, WT/DS18/AB/R (1998), para 199; J Pauwelyn, 'Does the WTO Stand for "Deference to" or "Interference with" National Health Authorities When Applying the Agreement on Sanitary and Phytosanitary Measures (SPS Agreement)?' in T Cottier and PC Mavroidis (eds), *The Role of the Judge in International Trade Regulation. Experience and Lessons for the WTO* (2003) 175; FJ Garcia, 'The *Salmon Case*: Evolution of Balancing Mechanism for Non-Trade Values in WTO' Boston College Law School Public Law and Legal Theory Research Paper No 19 (2003).

[319] PJIM de Waart, 'Quality of Life at the Mercy of WTO Panels: GATT's Article XX and Empty Shell?' in F Weiss and E Denters and P de Waart (eds), *International Economic Law with a Human Face* (1998) 109, 123 ff.

[320] However, a state trying to justify its regulations by public health interest still is in the defensive. CM Correa, 'Implementing National Public Health Policies in the Framework of WTO Agreements' (2000) 34 JWT 89, 108.

[321] *United States—Import Prohibition of Certain Shrimp and Shrimp Products*, WT/DS58/AB/R (1998), paras 130 f (*US—Shrimp*).   [322] Ibid paras 166–167.

to make an appearance in international law. However, several human rights concerns can be accommodated under the existing policy headings,[323] particularly measures 'necessary to protect public morals', 'necessary to protect human, animal or plant life or health', or 'relating to the products of prison labour'.

The TRIPS Agreement offers no such comprehensive exemption from patentability outside of the area of national security (Article 73 of the TRIPS Agreement). Article 27.3 of the TRIPS Agreement removes only certain areas, such as diagnostic methods, plants, and animals from the field of patentability. Article 27.2 of the TRIPS Agreement seems to provide an exception resembling Article XX of the GATT by allowing the exclusion from patentability of inventions, the prevention of the commercial exploitation of which within the Member is necessary to protect *ordre public* or morality, including to protect human, animal, or plant life or health, or to avoid serious prejudice to the environment, provided that such exclusion is not made merely because the exploitation is prohibited by domestic law. But it only applies where the risk for the policy results from the *commercial exploitation* of the invention, not where the patentability itself poses a risk to one of the enumerated policy goals.[324] The TRIPS Agreement's flexibilities generally do not provide for the exclusion from patentability, but rather for a limitation of patent rights. They will be treated below. There is thus no comparable mechanism to Article XX of the GATT giving preference to certain non-trade values. Regime conflicts with the TRIPS Agreement are consequently less likely to be solved by a close and careful interpretation of the TRIPS Agreement.

b The Human Rights Regime
The second regime partaking in the conflict at issue could not be more different: where the WTO regime is instrumental and utilitarian, the human rights regime is moral, it is an end in itself. Where the WTO regime is endowed with the arguably strongest enforcement system in international law, that of the human rights system relies largely on public pressure, 'shaming' a country into compliance. The differences merit a more detailed study.

aa Normative Hierarchy: Law of Values   Human rights law is fundamentally different from world trade law. Whereas the latter order is utilitarian, a means to further the well-being of mankind, the former represents the end in itself, it tries to formulate the essential freedoms and needs of man. It is an order deeply entrenched in morality. Not only does human rights law transgress the old dogma that, with few exceptions, the state is the only subject of international law. As de Frouville emphasizes in his study on the intangibility of human rights, human rights law raises the question of the role of humanity in international law at large.[325] Authors

---

[323] R Howse and M Mutua, *Protecting Human Rights in a Global Economy. Challenges for the World Trade Organization* (2000); Garcia (n 295 above) 79 ff.

[324] D Gervais, *The TRIPS Agreement: Drafting History and Analysis* (2nd edn, 2003) 2.261.

[325] O de Frouville, *L'Intagibilité des Droits de L'Homme en Droit International. Regime Conventionnel des Droits de l'Homme et Droits des Traités* (2004).

have claimed to identify numerous specificities of human rights norms, such as the impermissibility of reservations in human rights treaties. The notion that human rights occupy a superior place in the hierarchy of norms of international law has an almost irresistible allure, all the more so as we are accustomed to such a notion by domestic constitutional law. Do not human rights norms 'recognize' rather than 'create' human rights, pointing to a right pre-existing in nature, or maybe a transcendental notion of the aspirations that we all carry inside? Would not a legislator lose its legitimacy if it decided to disregard these norms?[326] Is it not all but natural to grant norms that guarantee the freedoms and needs of individuals precedence over norms that are merely instrumental and serve these goals only indirectly?[327] As an aspiration and goal at this abstract level this thought is almost impossible not to agree with. Accordingly, the idea that the economic order may not infringe human rights standards reverberates through the literature.[328]

But by giving in to such impulses one would fall into a trap that Pellet has referred to as *Droits-de-l'Hommisme*. He describes this phenomenon as the admirable mindset of human rights lawyers or even more so of human rights activists, struggling to bring relief to the downtrodden and using human rights law as a tool in their fight. Two risks flow from the agenda: the (erroneous) belief that human rights require special legal techniques, quite distinct from those applied in other legal areas, and the tendency to hang on to new lines of thinking and to regard them as binding law.[329] I cannot but agree that some of the claims raised under human rights law seem to rely on wishful thinking[330] rather than legal reasoning. Overly broad claims can do more bad than good, particularly in regime conflict, as the repetition of overly broad claims might have contributed to the critical view of human rights that has long been prevalent within the WTO.

The structure of current international law makes it difficult to accommodate all hierarchical claims of human rights law. Two routes seem available. The first is to regard the International Bill of Human Rights as an interpretation of the UN Charter's human rights provisions. It would thus arguably obtain a superior status in the hierarchy of norms by partaking in the effect of Article 103 of the UN Charter that provides that '[i]n the event of a conflict between the obligations of the Members of the United Nations under the present Charter and their obligations under any other international agreement, their obligations under the present

---

[326] Ibid 16 ff.   [327] Garcia (n 295 above) 69 ff.

[328] The discussion on the relationship between human rights and trade also covers the positive welfare effects of the WTO itself—making for a complex relationship. AH Qureshi, 'International Trade and Human Rights from the Perspective of the WTO' in F Weiss, E Denters and P de Waart (eds), *International Economic Law with a Human Face* (1998) 159; H Lim, 'Trade and Human Rights. What's at Issue?' (2001) 35 JWT 275; Howse and Mutua, *supra* n 323; E-U Petersmann, 'Challenges to the Legitimacy and Efficiency of the World Trading System: Democratic Governance and Competition Culture in the WTO' (2004) 7 JIEL 585, 588 ff; E-U Petersmann, 'Human Rights and the Law of the World Trade Organization' (2003) 37 JWT 241.

[329] A Pellet, *Droits de l'Hommisme et Droit international*, Droits fondamentaux (2001) 1.

[330] K Doehring, 'Die undifferenzierte Berufung auf Menschenrechte' in U Beyerlin (ed), *Festschrift für Rudolf Bernhardt* (1995) 355.

Charter shall prevail'. The premise of this approach has been discussed in the preceding chapter where I concluded that it is a considerable overinterpretation of the Charter's sparse human rights provisions.

The second route that would allow us to regard human rights law as superior to other international law would be to categorize it as *jus cogens*. But while all human rights obligations arguably are of the *erga omnes* type, the situation is quite different with regard to *jus cogens*. Although human rights norms have always been among the favourite discussion items for inclusion in this category, only very few norms actually fall into this category. Given the lack of precedents it would seem preposterous to dress up a comprehensive list of the norms that qualify. I sadly have to conclude that most human rights norms remain on the same legal level as other international norms.

bb Factual Hierarchy: Soft Enforcement   Even though most states seem eager to dispel any doubt that they might not be in compliance with human rights law and despite the disproportionate stigma involved with human rights violations as compared with violations of trade law, the enforcement mechanism of international human rights law is far less effective than that of WTO law. As stated above, the human rights monitoring and enforcement mechanisms commonly rely on shaming violators into compliance rather than threatening sanctions, as is the case under WTO law.[331] Enforcement of human rights law is further hampered by the fact that, unlike with economic law, the most common case of a state's violation of human rights law—namely a violation of the rights of its own citizens—does not harm other states directly,[332] which therefore lack an incentive to complain about the violation.

In light of this it is no surprise that some authors have doubted the efficiency of human rights instruments, wondering whether some of the states that decide in favour of ratifying human rights treaties do so merely in response to international pressure and to improve their image, rather than to engage in a sincere process of movement towards full compliance with human rights.[333]

cc Human Rights and Regime Conflict   Whereas the WTO regime is broad as to its subject matter, human rights law defies the separation of regimes altogether. By their very purpose human rights have the potential to reach all human behaviour, and as all regulation is ultimately aimed at human behaviour, human rights law has the potential to influence all regimes. Human rights are the fine thread that runs

---

[331] Alston (n 288 above) 833 ff.

[332] OA Hathaway, 'Do Human Rights Treaties Make a Difference?' (2002) 111 Yale LJ 1935, 1938.

[333] D Kennedy, 'The International Human Rights Movement: Part of the Problem?' (2002) 15 Harv Hum Rts J 101; Hathaway (n 332 above) 1989 ff. Hathaway attempts to quantify compliance, but does so on the basis of doubtful data. For criticism: R Goodman and D Jinks, 'Measuring the Effects of Human Rights Treaties' (2003) 14 EJIL 171, her reply is OA Hathaway, 'Testing Conventional Wisdom' (2003) 14 EJIL 185.

through all areas of law. Human beings can engage in all sorts of different behaviour, subject to many different regimes, but human rights are never far behind—they are seated in the human being as a person. The allegation of some scholars that international law has irreparably split into separate regimes[334] is therefore wrong as to human rights law.[335] With human rights law potentially reaching any and all human behaviour, the potential for conflict with other regimes is particularly great. It is precisely in these conflicts that human rights law can fulfil one of its functions: protecting individuals from regulation that would infringe their rights. Even though normally this function only comes into play on a national level, with an increasing amount of substantive legislation-type law on the international level there is a need for this function to be transported to the international level.

c Perplexity

With human rights law, the utilitarian and instrumental WTO order meets a legal regime fundamentally based on morality and aspiring superior status. In an international system with more and more norms resembling national laws it seems only natural to allow human rights a similar effect on such norms as they have in national law: influencing their interpretation and, where there is a conflict, invalidating those norms. However, current international law cannot accommodate such a claim, as normative hierarchy in international law is underdeveloped.

The normative hierarchy of WTO and human rights law stands in stark contrast to the factual hierarchy of regimes, as the factual hierarchy clearly favours the WTO regime with its strong adjudication and enforcement mechanism. It is a recipe for perplexity: while the claim of normative superiority of human rights law has strong emotional (but far less legal) appeal, state behaviour will be largely dominated by the tenets of WTO law. The question to be tackled in the next chapter is whether there is a way to make human rights law count within the WTO system, as it is that system that will determine the behaviour of states.

---

[334] Fischer-Lescano and Teubner (n 152 above).　　　[335] De Frouville (n 325 above) 11.

5

Access to Medicine as a Human Right in the WTO Order

Having shown that states are likely to comply with the WTO system due to its strong enforcement mechanism I now turn to the question of to what extent access to medicine as a human right is accommodated within the WTO system. The study will proceed in several steps. First, it will analyze to what extent the right to access to medicine can be applied within the WTO dispute settlement mechanism (I). That part will show that the right cannot be relied on as a defence to a claim of an infringement of the TRIPS Agreement; it can only be used in the interpretation of the TRIPS Agreement. This interpretative approach is more concrete than the interpretation of the TRIPS Agreement in the light of the object and purpose of the Agreement, which includes health concerns. Using the interpretative approach introduced in part I, part II will describe the flexibilities of the TRIPS Agreement before its amendment, which at the time of writing is not yet in force. It will show where a human rights-based interpretation can serve as an argument for granting more discretionary space to Members for taking measures to safeguard access to medicine. However, it will also indicate the weakness of the approach, namely that it is just one argument amongst several and that states taking such measures still risk the threat of WTO litigation. This has been recognized by the WTO, which has taken three important decisions on the topic of TRIPS and access to medicine including the decision to amend the TRIPS Agreement (III), implicitly recognizing its own responsibility for the right to health. The content of these decisions will be analyzed, as will their legal quality, demonstrating that the WTO has made some progress towards accommodating access to medicine. What is just as important as the content of the decisions, though, is that the WTO has shown an astonishing willingness to disregard its own decision-making rules when deciding on the issue. Part IV will argue that the current situation is still not satisfactory and that ultimately either the Appellate Body or the political decision-making bodies will have to take a clearer and more courageous stance on human rights within the WTO system. It will also point out, however, that this will not be the end of the debate—new threats already undermine flexible solutions found within the WTO system: so-called 'TRIPS-plus' obligations incurred in other fora.

I Access to Medicine as a Human Right within
WTO Dispute Settlement

The question of the application of the right to access to medicine within the WTO dispute settlement mechanism can arise in two different procedural constellations: (1) a Member could invoke its human rights obligations in its defence against a claim that it does not provide for (sufficient) protection of pharmaceutical patents in violation of the TRIPS Agreement; or (2) a Member could commence a WTO dispute settlement proceeding against another Member that does grant pharmaceutical patents, alleging a violation of that Member's human rights obligations.

At first glance both of these constellations seem to require the resolution of the conflict between access to medicine and the TRIPS Agreement that was described in the last chapter. As discussed there, public international law offers a set of rules to resolve conflicts between obligations, even though that set of rules is poorly developed. It seems all but natural to apply these rules to the conflict at hand. However, the last chapter also stated that a number of international tribunals may only apply a subset of international law. Where a tribunal is only empowered to apply one of the conflicting norms it does not have to deal with the rules for regime conflict under general international law—it will merely apply the rule it is empowered to apply. The decision of the tribunal can thus differ from the resolution of the regime conflict that general international law would have imposed. If the tribunal's decision benefits from a strong enforcement system, the outcome of the conflict under general international law can be irrelevant as states will likely comply with the tribunal's decision. As this is the case with the WTO system, the decisive question to examine is to what extent the WTO dispute settlement body can apply the human rights norm of access to medicine.

Put in more general terms, the question that needs to be addressed is the question of the use of non-WTO law within the WTO system. Scholars have asked this question with respect to several legal regimes, eg the applicability of environmental law within the WTO system or the applicability of human rights law within the WTO system. Due to the limited hierarchization of international law the answer will be identical for all non-WTO law, as long as a particular norm has not attained *jus cogens* status. I will tackle the issue by first distinguishing five different intensities of the applicability of non-WTO law within the WTO dispute settlement mechanism (1). One of these, the concept that WTO law is entirely separate from the body of public international law, is now universally rejected (2). A decision among the other four models of application can only be made after a thorough examination of two separate issues: the jurisdiction of WTO adjudicating bodies (3), the discussion of which will eliminate one more model, and the question of 'applicable law' (4). The section will conclude that the right to access to medicine can only be taken into account for the purpose of interpretation. Section 5 will show that the solution proposed is in accord with WTO jurisprudence. Section 6, finally, will discuss the possibilities of the concept of access to medicine as *jus cogens* within WTO dispute settlement.

1 Five Models for the Use of Non-WTO Law in WTO Dispute Settlement

The question of the use of non-WTO law in the WTO dispute settlement mechanism has started to receive considerable attention.[1] In numerous insightful studies scholars have proposed what I consider to be five different approaches:

(1) A commonly discussed conception of the WTO is that of the WTO regime as a regime apart, entirely outside the system of international law and untouched by it. According to this conception the WTO adjudicating bodies could not apply any non-WTO law. The buzz-word for this conception is that of a 'self-contained regime'.[2]

(2) Most scholars consider the role of non-WTO law within the WTO dispute settlement regime as rather limited. They argue that, apart from explicit references to non-WTO law, the Dispute Settlement Understanding (DSU) allows for the use of non-WTO law only to clarify the meaning of a provision of WTO law, or to be more precise of the 'covered agreements'.[3]

(3) Going a step further, Bartels regards non-WTO law as applicable by WTO adjudicating bodies, but considers Articles 3.2, 19.2 of the DSU as conflict rules, giving norms of the WTO covered agreements precedence over non-WTO norms in case of conflict. WTO adjudicating bodies would thus be free

---

[1] J Pauwelyn, 'The Role of Public International Law in the WTO: How Far Can We Go?' (2001) 95 AJIL 535; DM McRae, 'The WTO in International Law: Tradition Continued or New Frontier?' (2000) 3 JIEL 27; L Bartels, 'Applicable Law in WTO Dispute Settlement Proceedings' (2001) 35 JWT 499; JP Trachtman, 'The Domain of WTO Dispute Resolution' (1999) 40 Harv Int'l L J 333; D Palmeter and PC Mavroidis, 'The WTO Legal System: Sources of Law' (1998) 92 AJIL 398; G Marceau, 'Conflict of Norms and Conflicts of Jurisdiction. The Relationship between the WTO Agreements and MEAs and other Treaties' (2001) 35 JWT 1081; M Böckenförde, 'Zwischen Sein und Wollen—Über den Einfluss umweltvölkerrechtlicher Verträge im Rahmen eines WTO-Streitbeilegungsverfahrens' (2003) 63 ZaöRV 971.

[2] DM McRae, 'The Contribution of International Trade Law to the Development of International Law' (1996) 260 RdC 99; P Weil, 'Le Droit International Économique Mythe ou Réalité?' in Société Française pour le Droit International (ed), *Aspects du Droit International Économique. Élaboration—Controle—Sanction. Colloque d'Orléans 25–27 Mai 1971* (1972) 1, 29 ff; McRae (n 1 above) 27.

[3] Böckenförde (n 1 above) 993 ff; G Marceau, 'WTO Dispute Settlement and Human Rights' (2002) 13 EJIL 753, 773 ff; G Marceau, 'A Call for Coherence in International Law. Praises for the Prohibition Against "Clinical Isolation" in WTO Dispute Settlement' (1999) 33 JWT 87, 107; Trachtman (n 1 above) 342–343; RE Hudec, 'The Relationship of International Environmental Law to International Economic Law' in FL Morrison and R Wolfrum (eds), *International, Regional and National Environmental Law* (2000) 133, 151–152; J Neumann, *Die Koordination des WTO-Rechts mit anderen völkerrechtlichen Ordnungen. Konflikte des materiellen Rechts und Konkurrenzen der Streitbeilegung* (2001) 364; E-U Petersmann, 'Human Rights and the Law of the World Trade Organization' (2003) 37 JWT 241, 248; Hörmann in M Hilf and S Oeter (eds), *WTO-Recht. Rechtsordnung des Welthandels* (2005) 653.

to apply non-WTO law, however such law could not 'add to or diminish the rights and obligations provided' in the WTO agreements.[4]

(4) In an article that has stirred much interest Pauwelyn proposed the application of the entire *corpus* of international law within the WTO dispute settlement mechanism. Should a conflict between non-WTO law and WTO law arise, the adjudicating body has to apply general international law governing the conflict of norms and can determine the conflict in favour of non-WTO law, thus setting aside the relevant WTO norm in the case at hand.[5] According to this approach, in cases of conflict between WTO law and non-WTO law a panel cannot rule against a Member that does not abide by the WTO rule if the non-WTO rule prevails under general international law.

(5) Finally, some authors have proposed *de lege ferenda* to enforce other norms in WTO dispute settlement, ie to allow WTO adjudicating bodies to entertain claims of violations of non-WTO law. The aim of such a proposal is to use the strong enforcement mechanism of the WTO for other regimes that lack such a mechanism.[6]

2 The WTO: A Self-contained Regime?

The first of the proposed five levels of integration of non-WTO law within the WTO order stands out, not just because of its radical rejection of such integration, but also because it does not seem to be supported by anybody.[7] But even though the view is universally rejected, it has become such a common *topos* that it deserves some discussion.

At the root of the idea of a 'self-contained' world trade regime is the fact that the fathers of international economic law rarely thought about their creation in terms

---

[4] Bartels (n 1 above) 499 ff.   [5] Pauwelyn (n 1 above) 577.

[6] With respect to human rights see E-U Petersmann, 'The WTO Constitution and Human Rights' (2000) 3 JIEL 19, 20; P Alston, 'Resisting the Merger and Acquisition of Human Rights by Trade Law: A Reply to Petersmann' (2002) 13 EJIL 815, 833 ff; with respect to core labour standards see H-M Wolffgang and W Feuerhake, 'Core Labour Standards in World Trade Law. The Necessity for Incorporation of Core Labour Standards in the World Trade Organization' (2002) 36 JWT 883, 900; C McCrudden and A Davies, 'A Perspective on Trade and Labor Rights' (2000) 3 JIEL 43, 59 ff; K Addo, 'The Correlation Between Labour Standards and International Trade. Which Way Forward?' (2002) 36 JWT 285, 293 ff. Generally on enlarging the WTO: JP Trachtman, 'Institutional Linkage: Transcending "Trade and ..."' (2002) 96 AJIL 77; S Charnovitz, 'Triangulating the World Trade Organization' (2002) 96 AJIL 28; HP Hestermeyer, 'The Language of Trade Linkage. Lessons for the Singapore Issues Learned from TRIPS' in A Steinmann, F Höhne, and P-T Stoll (eds), *Die WTO vor neuen Herausforderungen* (2005) 139.

[7] G Schwarzenberger, 'The Principles and Standards of International Economic Law' (1966–I) 117 RdC 1, 5; Pauwelyn (n 1 above) 535; Palmeter and Mavroidis (n 1 above) 413; I Seidl-Hohenveldern, *International Economic Law* (3rd edn, 1999) 29. Pauwelyn considers Bello to be a possible exception, because of her statement that 'WTO rules are simply not "binding" in the traditional sense', but this statement only pays tribute to the debate about the enforcement deficit of public international law. J Bello, 'The WTO Dispute Settlement Understanding: Less Is More' (1996) 90 AJIL 416 f; Pauwelyn (n 1 above) 538; Böckenförde (n 1 above) 975.

of international law. Diplomacy and economics took precedence. The director of the legal affairs division of the GATT and WTO until 1995, Roessler, recounts that in 1973 his question about the creation of a legal service was answered by the statement that GATT believes in pragmatism, not in law.[8] In line with this philosophy the GATT dispute settlement mechanism was more of a tool to exert diplomatic pressure on states with inappropriate trade policies than a legal adjudication procedure.[9]

The fallacy of the conception of the WTO being outside the regime of international law is already indicated by the misnomer 'self-contained regime'. The notion has never been meant to imply that a regime is outside the international legal system. It was used by the Permanent Court of International Justice (PCIJ) in the *Wimbledon* case with respect to the provisions relating to the Kiel Canal in the Treaty of Versailles. The Court stated that these provisions could not be supplemented and interpreted by the aid of the provisions of the Treaty of Versailles referring to the inland navigable waterways of Germany.[10] At its origin the notion of 'self-contained' thus meant little more than that there were specific rules for a specific situation, having priority over other, more general ones.[11] The notion reappeared and was narrowed down[12] in the ICJ's *Tehran Hostages* case, when Iran, which did not appear before the Court, in letters to the Court defended the hostage-taking of US diplomatic and consular staff and other US nationals with alleged US interference in the internal affairs of Iran, including CIA involvement in the *coup d'état* of 1953. The Court ruled that 'diplomatic law itself provides the necessary means of defense against, and sanction for, illicit activities by members of diplomatic or consular missions':[13]

The rules of diplomatic law, in short, constitute a self-contained régime which, on the one hand, lays down the receiving State's obligations regarding the facilities, privileges and immunities to be accorded to diplomatic missions and, on the other, foresees their possible abuse by members of the mission and specifies the means at the disposal of the receiving State to counter any such abuse.[14]

---

[8] F Roessler, 'Foreword' in RE Hudec (ed), *Essays on the Nature of International Trade Law* (1999) 10.
[9] RE Hudec, 'The GATT Legal System: A Diplomat's Jurisprudence' in RE Hudec (ed), *Essays on the Nature of International Trade Law* (1999) 17; JH Jackson, *Restructuring the GATT System* (1990) 59 ff; RE Hudec, 'GATT or GABB? The Future Design of the General Agreement on Tariffs and Trade' in RE Hudec (ed), *Essays on the Nature of International Trade Law* (1999) 77.
[10] *The S.S. Wimbledon*, PCIJ Reports 1923, Ser A, No 1, 23–24 (17 August 1923).
[11] M Koskenniemi, *Fragmentation of International Law: Difficulties Arising from Diversification and Expansion of International Law. Study on the 'Function and scope of the lex specialis rule and the question of "self contained regimes"': Preliminary report*, ILC(LVI)/SG/FIL/CRD.1/Add.1, para 109 (4 May 2004).
[12] M Koskenniemi, *Fragmentation of International Law: Difficulties Arising from the Diversification and Expansion of International Law. Report of the Study Group of the International Law Commission*, UN Doc A/CN.4/L.682, paras 128 ff (13 April 2006) (identifying three not clearly distinguishable meanings of the term).
[13] *United States Diplomatic and Consular Staff in Tehran (United States of America/Iran)*, Judgment, ICJ Reports 1980, 3, 38 (24 May 1980).   [14] Ibid 40.

The notion was taken up by Special Rapporteur Riphagen in his work on state responsibility. He envisaged a system in which the general rules on state responsibility would be applicable as default rules where and to the extent states had not regulated the consequences of a breach of an obligation in a 'subsystem' or 'special regime' together with the obligation. He saw a subsystem as a system that contains primary rules, the rules on the consequences of a breach of the primary rules and enforcement norms. Simma has much elucidated Riphagen's prose by defining a self-contained regime as a subsystem with a 'full (exhaustive and definitive) set of secondary rules',[15] ie a subsystem excluding 'more or less totally the application of the general legal consequences of wrongful acts'.[16] The International Law Commission's (ILC) Articles on State Responsibility now allow such regimes in Article 55: 'These articles do not apply where and to the extent that the conditions for the existence of an internationally wrongful act or the content or implementation of the international responsibility of a State are governed by special rules of international law.' The Commentary to the Article explicitly mentions the WTO's DSU.[17]

As the term self-contained regime implies, states can contract out of rules of international law (with the exception of *jus cogens*) and establish a functionally specialized regime in which some other norms of international law are not applicable. However, it is hard to conceive how an international treaty could contract out of all of international law—such an event could only be described in revolutionary terms, something that might be argued in the case of EU law. The WTO Agreements clearly show that WTO Members did not contract out of international law as a whole.[18] Article 3.2 of the DSU states that the dispute settlement system serves to clarify the existing provisions of the covered agreements 'in accordance with customary rules of interpretation of public international law'. Furthermore, the TRIPS Agreement contains numerous references to other international agreements such as the Paris Convention, the Berne Convention, and the Rome Convention.[19] The Appellate Body duly acknowledged that 'the General Agreement is not to be read in clinical isolation from public international law'.[20]

3 Jurisdiction

As with national courts, one of the first questions that a WTO panel has to decide is whether it has jurisdiction, ie the power to decide the case.[21] Where jurisdiction

---

[15] B Simma, 'Self-contained Regimes' (1985) 16 NYIL 111, 117.   [16] Ibid.

[17] J Crawford, *The International Law Commission's Articles on State Responsibility. Introduction, Text and Commentaries* (2002) at Art 55 para 3. In-depth: Simma (n 15 above); A Marschik, *Subsysteme im Völkerrecht. Ist die Europäische Union ein 'Self-Contained Regime'?* (1997); PJ Kuyper, 'The Law of GATT as a Special Field of International Law. Ignorance, further Refinement or Self-contained System of International Law?' (1994) 25 NYIL 227, 251 ff; J Pauwelyn, *Conflict of Norms in Public International Law. How WTO Law Relates to other Rules of International Law* (2003) 35 ff.

[18] Hilf and Oeter in Hilf and Oeter (eds) (n 3 above) 705.

[19] Article 1.3 of the TRIPS Agreement.

[20] *United States—Standards for Reformulated and Conventional Gasoline*, WT/DS2/AB/R, p 17 (1996) (*US—Gasoline*).   [21] BA Garner, *Black's Law Dictionary* (7th edn, 2000).

exists, WTO dispute settlement takes precedence over other dispute resolution fora according to Article 23.1 of the DSU.[22] Even though many authors at times use the terms 'apply' or 'enforce' a law and 'have jurisdiction' over it interchangeably, the question of jurisdiction is distinct from that of the applicable law and poses itself at an earlier stage: The question of jurisdiction determines whether the panel can accept the case; only after it has done so does the panel have to determine which law it will apply to decide about the claims of the complainant.

A Violation Complaints

WTO panels have limited subject matter jurisdiction. This follows from Article 1.1 of the DSU, according to which the DSU only applies to disputes brought pursuant to the consultation and dispute settlement provisions of the 'covered agreements', which are the agreements listed in Appendix 1 of the DSU, mainly the GATT, GATS, and the TRIPS Agreement. The dispute settlement provisions of these agreements allow for complaints about violations of the covered agreements and generally also for two other types of complaints: non-violation and situation complaints.[23] Leaving aside the last two types of complaints for the moment, the WTO dispute settlement mechanism therefore only has jurisdiction over claims of violations of the covered agreements. Non-WTO provisions that are explicitly incorporated by the covered agreements (such as certain provisions of the Berne and Paris Convention under the TRIPS Agreement) have to be regarded as part of those agreements. Since the human rights agreements are not covered agreements, WTO panels have no jurisdiction over claims of violations of human rights law.

One commentator has argued that parties could enlarge the scope of jurisdiction and submit non-WTO claims if both parties to the dispute explicitly agree on non-standard terms of reference pursuant to Article 7.3 of the DSU.[24] However, Article 1 of the DSU does not provide for such an exception in the case of non-standard terms of reference, so that such a possibility cannot be admitted.[25] Also, it would seem improper to use a specialized dispute settlement procedure such as the WTO dispute settlement system for issues entirely outside of its area of specialization.

B Non-Violation Complaints

A Member could, however, attempt to bring a claim concerning human rights violations under the non-violation complaint procedure. Such a complaint requires that a measure attributable to the respondent party nullifies or impairs a benefit

---

[22] *United States—Sections 301–310 of the Trade Act of 1974*, WT/DS152/R, para 7.43 (1999).
[23] Articles XXII, XXIII of the GATT; Art 64 of the TRIPS Agreement. On non-violations and situation complaints within the TRIPS Agreement context see P-T Stoll and F Schorkopf, *WTO. World Economic Order, World Trade Law* (2006) 223.   [24] Pauwelyn (n 1 above) 554.
[25] Böckenförde (n 1 above) 981, footnote 39. Pauwelyn himself is more ambiguous on the issue now: Pauwelyn (n 17 above) 444. In *Canada—European Communities—Article XXVIII Rights*, DS12/R (1990) the arbitrator considered claims under the bilateral agreement between the parties on wheat due to its close connection with the GATT, its consistency with GATT objectives and the consensual request of recourse to the GATT Arbitration procedures. However, the case was decided before the Uruguay Round, ie not under the DSU.

accruing to the complaining party under the relevant agreement contrary to the reasonable expectations of the complaining party at the time the agreement was made.[26] The argument would proceed along the lines that the violation of human rights standards adversely affects the competitive relationship between the products of the parties and that this violation could not have been foreseen at the time the commitment was negotiated.[27] Such an argument is not without precedents. When the United States imposed trade sanctions on Brazil in 1988, the 'non-violation nullification' argument was made with respect to intellectual property protection, arguing that a lack of intellectual property protection by Brazil nullified or impaired the trade concessions the United States had obtained.[28] However, the non-violation complaint is an 'exceptional'[29] one. It would circumvent the limited subject-matter jurisdiction of WTO panels if any violation of international law could simply be invoked via the non-violation complaint mechanism, arguing that the competitive relationship between products of the party in breach and the complaining parties is upset.[30] The same argument prevents the justification of unilateral trade sanctions for human rights violations as 'social dumping' or 'subsidies in the form of weak social standards'.[31] Thus, even under this procedure WTO panels have no jurisdiction to hear claims concerning the violation of human rights. *De lege lata* the approach listed as number 5 therefore has no basis in the WTO Agreements.

C De Lege Ferenda

At times it is argued that WTO panels *should* have jurisdiction to rule on human rights violations. Such an extension of WTO panel jurisdiction would allow the use of the strong WTO enforcement mechanism along with the possibility of trade sanctions for the benefit of human rights law, thus enhancing the weak human rights enforcement mechanism. A number of arguments militate against such an extension. First of all, the world trade philosophy, in which trade-offs feature prominently, is hardly compatible with the philosophy of human rights law that imposes non-negotiable standards. Furthermore, the enforcement of human rights standards by WTO dispute settlement would require major changes in the dispute resolution process. Would only inter-state complaints be permissible? Or would individuals have standing? How would the trade sanctions be calculated? Certainly retaliating for violations of WTO law by suspending human rights obligations would not be permissible, but what WTO benefits should be suspendable for

---

[26] *Korea—Measures Affecting Government Procurement*, WT/DS163/R, para 7.85 (2000) (*Korea—Government Procurement*); in-depth: Council for TRIPS, *Non-Violation Complaints and the TRIPS Agreement*, IP/C/W/124, paras 30 ff (28 January 1999).   [27] Pauwelyn (n 1 above) 559.

[28] Chapter 2.

[29] *European Communities—Measures Affecting Asbestos and Asbestos-containing Products*, WT/DS135/AB/R, para 186 (2001) (*EC—Asbestos*).

[30] With a different argument Marceau, *Human Rights* (n 3 above) 768.

[31] Such measures are advocated by R Wai, 'Countering, Branding, Dealing: Using Economic and Social Rights in and around the International Trade Regime' (2003) 14 EJIL 35, 60.

human rights violations? Arguably, all of these practical problems could ultimately be overcome, but it is unlikely to happen. Alston has rightly pointed out that governments have persistently refused to enhance the human rights enforcement mechanism. There is no reason to assume that they would change their mind merely because human rights enforcement would take place within the WTO setting.[32] One reason that makes such a development all the more unlikely to occur is the fear of developing countries that developed countries would use human rights arguments as a guise for protectionism, denying market access to developing nations.[33]

4 Applicable Law

Once a WTO panel has accepted a case, it has to decide which law it is empowered to apply. Often, the treaty setting up a tribunal also determines the rules the tribunal has to apply.[34] It is worthwhile looking at some examples of how treaties determine the applicable law.

A Examples of Provisions

The ICJ statute determines the law applicable by the ICJ in its Article 38(1). The provision has become the *locus classicus* for an enumeration of the sources of international law. But the ICJ is not the only court that can apply the whole *corpus* of international law. The adjudicating bodies of the MERCOSUR, one of the two Latin American Regional Trade Agreements, can apply a number of enumerated MERCOSUR documents and principles and provisions of international law applicable to the matter.[35] The United Nations Convention on the Law of the Sea (UNCLOS), too, empowers a court or tribunal under the Convention to apply international law. However, it also establishes a hierarchy for the purposes of adjudication under the Convention: 'A court or tribunal having jurisdiction under this section shall apply this Convention and other rules of international law not incompatible with this Convention.'[36]

The examples of the MERCOSUR dispute settlement protocol and UNCLOS show that the questions of applicable law and jurisdiction are two separate issues. The fact that the jurisdiction of WTO panels is limited to claims under WTO covered agreements does not necessarily imply that those panels may only apply WTO law.[37] Unlike many other agreements setting up tribunals, the DSU does

---

[32] Alston (n 6 above) 833–834.

[33] Wai (n 31 above) 51 ff; Petersmann (n 3 above) 280; Hilf and Oeter in Hilf and Oeter (eds) (n 3 above) 708. [34] I Brownlie, *Principles of Public International Law* (6th edn, 2003) 672 ff.

[35] Article 34 (1) of the Protocolo de Olivos para la Solución de Controversias en el MERCOSUR (translation by author). The Tribunal Permanente de Revisión of MERCOSUR has later ruled that the application of international law can only be of subsidiary nature or at most complementary. Tribunal Permanente de Revisión, *Laudo No 1/2005*, para 9. [36] Article 293(1) of the UNCLOS.

[37] Pauwelyn (n 1 above) 560. Marceau seems to confuse these two issues when she writes that the WTO adjudicating bodies 'are not courts of general jurisdiction and they cannot interpret and apply all treaties involving WTO Members'. Marceau, *Human Rights* (n 3 above) 777.

not contain a provision that is entitled 'applicable law'. However, the lack of this precise wording hardly amounts to evidence that the DSU fails to determine the applicable law. A closer look at the provisions of the DSU is warranted.

B Article 7 of the DSU

A panel is established on the request of the complaining party, made in writing and providing a brief summary of the legal basis of the complaint.[38] Unless the parties to the dispute agree otherwise, Article 7.1 of the DSU endows a panel with the following standard terms of reference:

> To examine, in the light of the relevant provisions in (name of the covered agreement(s) cited by the parties to the dispute), the matter referred to the DSB by (name of party) in document … and to make such findings as will assist the DSB in making the recommendations or in giving the rulings provided for in that/those agreement(s).

The panel thus addresses the relevant provisions in 'any covered agreement or agreements cited by the parties to the dispute'.[39] However, according to Articles 7.3, 7.1 of the DSU, the parties can agree to non-standard terms of reference.

Many scholars read the terms 'to examine, in the light of the relevant provisions in (name of the covered agreement(s) cited by the parties to the dispute)' as limiting the applicable law to the covered agreements.[40] Both Bartels and Pauwelyn dispute this function of Article 7.1 of the DSU. They argue that the wording of Articles 7.1 and 7.2 might specifically point panels towards the covered agreements, but it does not exclude the application of other law. Short of a 'contracting out' of wider international law, the other rules of international law remain applicable by the panel.[41] They cite for support a statement by the Panel in *Korea— Government Procurement*:

> [t]he purpose of the terms of reference is to properly identify the claims of the party and therefore the scope of a panel's review. We do not see any basis for arguing that the terms of reference are meant to *exclude* reference to the broader rules of customary international law in interpreting a claim properly before the Panel.[42]

Even though I agree that wider international law needs to be contracted out of to lose its applicability, I fail to see how this has not been done in Article 7 of the DSU.[43] If Article 7.1 goes to the applicable law, and Pauwelyn half-heartedly seems

---

[38] Article 6 of the DSU.   [39] Article 7.2 of the DSU.

[40] Böckenförde (n 1 above) 979; Trachtman (n 1 above) 342; Marceau, *Call for Coherence* (n 3 above) 110; J Cameron and KR Gray, 'Principles of International Law in the WTO Dispute Settlement Body' (2001) 50 ICLQ 248, 263. Palmeter and Mavroidis regard Art 7 of the DSU as covering the applicable law, but consider other international instruments, customs, general principles, and the teachings of publicists also to be relevant sources of WTO law. Palmeter and Mavroidis (n 1 above) 399.   [41] Pauwelyn (n 1 above) 561–562; Bartels (n 1 above) 505.

[42] *Korea—Government Procurement* (n 26 above) para 7.101 footnote 755; Pauwelyn (n 1 above) 562; Bartels (n 1 above) 504.

[43] Koskenniemi concludes that there is little reason to 'depart from the view that general international law supplements WTO law unless it has been specifically excluded and that so do other treaties which

to agree that it does,[44] it merely mentions the 'name of the covered agreement(s) cited by the parties'. This excludes non-WTO law. Provisions on the applicable law generally enumerate the law that is applicable and *not* the law that is not applicable. The opposite point of view would render the mention of the covered agreements in Article 7.1 superfluous—a result that is to be avoided in treaty interpretation according to the principle of effective interpretation. The Panel statement does not challenge this argument, because the sentence does not support the application of non-WTO law, it supports its use for interpretative purposes.[45]

Bartels notes furthermore that the possibility of non-standard terms of reference, ie terms of reference agreed upon by the parties according to Articles 7.3 and 7.1, strongly supports that Article 7 does not limit the applicable sources of law.[46] It is not entirely clear why this should be so. Non-standard terms of reference allow parties to include non-WTO law as applicable law by consent. The fact that the DSU allows parties to do so by consent implies that absent this consent (ie under the standard terms of reference) non-WTO rules are not applicable.[47]

One could take exception to this and adduce that Article 7 only declares the 'relevant' provisions of the covered agreements to be applicable. A provision that is not applicable according to the conflict rules under general international law could not be called relevant, so that international law *in toto* has to be applied to determine the relevant provisions of the covered agreements. But this argument misperceives the concept of 'applicable law': parties are free to determine the applicable rules according to which they want to resolve a conflict between them, as long as those do not violate *jus cogens*. This determination would be undermined if in a next step the panel would have to apply the general rules of international law to find out whether another rule prevails over the 'applicable law' on the level of international law.

It deserves notice that Pauwelyn rejects the possibility of restricting *ex ante* the applicable law for any international tribunal. Any such restriction, he argues, would inevitably create small isolated pockets of international law, delinked from international law, and threaten both the unity of international law and the principle of *pacta sunt servanda*.[48] But this argument overestimates the role of international law: international law traditionally relies on the agreement between parties. Where they want to create a 'pocket' in terms of specialized substantive rules, they are free to do so. It also cannot be argued that the limitation of the applicable law within WTO Dispute Settlement would 'freeze' WTO law in time, namely in 1994:[49] first of all

---

should, preferably, be read in harmony with the WTO covered treaties'. However, he does not analyze the significance of Art 7 of the DSU. M Koskenniemi, *Fragmentation of International Law: Difficulties Arising from the Diversification and Expansion of International Law. Report of the Study Group of the International Law Commission*, UN Doc A/CN.4/L.682, para 169 (13 April 2006).

[44] Pauwelyn (n 1 above) 561 ('DSU Article 7 is more directed to applicable law').

[45] Böckenförde (n 1 above) 980.

[46] Bartels (n 1 above) 505. The passage is not entirely clear, as in the passage Bartels seems to confuse applicable law and jurisdiction.   [47] Böckenförde (n 1 above) 980.

[48] Pauwelyn (n 1 above) 564; Pauwelyn (n 17 above) 461.   [49] Pauwelyn (n 17 above) 461.

the Marrakesh Agreement Establishing the World Trade Organization (hereinafter: the WTO Agreement) explicitly provides for the possibility of amendments (Art X), authoritative interpretations (Art IX:2), and waivers (Art IX:3), but maybe more importantly the process of treaty interpretation is not static and allows for changes in the meaning of the terms.

C Article 11 of the DSU

More ammunition for the debate is provided by Article 11 of the DSU determining the functions of a panel in the relevant part as follows:

a panel should make an objective assessment of the matter before it, including an objective assessment of the facts of the case and the applicability of and conformity with the relevant covered agreements, and make such other findings as will assist the DSB in making the recommendations or in giving the rulings provided for in the covered agreements.

It has been argued that this provision forces a panel to rule whether a provision is applicable according to the conflict rules contained in general international law. To enable the panel to reveal the applicable rules of the covered agreements (and to do so objectively) it would have to apply the whole *corpus* of international law.[50]

However, conceptually Article 11 cannot play the role that would thus be assigned to it. Article 7 of the DSU puts down the mandate of a panel and the panel performs its function according to Article 11 within its mandate. The mention of 'applicability' of the relevant agreements has to be read together with the first part of the sentence: the panel has to decide the applicability of the agreements to the matter before it as a part of the normal judicial reasoning that tests the applicability of the law to the facts.[51]

D Article 3.2 of the DSU

One of the key provisions to the debate about non-WTO law within the WTO dispute settlement system is Article 3.2 of the DSU. It states in part that the dispute settlement of the WTO:

serves to preserve the rights and obligations of Members under the covered agreements, and to clarify the existing provisions of those agreements in accordance with customary rules of interpretation of public international law. Recommendations and rulings of the DSB cannot add to or diminish the rights and obligations provided in the covered agreements.

Article 19.2 of the DSU reiterates that 'the panel and Appellate Body cannot add to or diminish the rights and obligations provided in the covered agreements'. Again, scholars disagree on the functions of these provisions.

a The Function of Article 3.2 of the DSU

Bartels considers Articles 3.2 and 19.2 of the DSU to be conflict rules, giving precedence to WTO law in cases of conflict with non-WTO law, both of which

---

[50] Pauwelyn (n 1 above) 562; Bartels (n 1 above) 505–506.
[51] Böckenförde (n 1 above) 981.

are, according to him, part of the applicable law.[52] Pauwelyn, too, does not see any restriction of the applicable law in the provision and regards the function of the preservation of the rights and obligations under the covered agreements as a mere reference to the limited jurisdiction of the panels.[53] But he does not regard the terms 'cannot add to or diminish the rights and obligations provided in the covered agreements' as implying that the norms serve as conflict rules: rather, he sees those terms as stressing the principle that panels may not change WTO law.[54] Given the view taken here on the function of Article 7 of the DSU it seems natural to interpret Article 3.2 of the DSU as clarifying the scope of the applicable law: international law as a whole is not part of the applicable law, but the applicable law (namely WTO law) has to be interpreted in accordance with customary rules of interpretation of public international law.[55] The prohibition of adding to or diminishing the rights under the covered agreements reiterates the idea that non-WTO law may not be applied,[56] as that would change (either add to or diminish) the obligations under WTO law.[57]

b The Approach Prescribed by the DSU: Use of International Law for Interpretation

The above interpretation of the DSU shows that international law *in toto* is not part of the applicable law in WTO dispute resolution, but customary rules of interpretation of public international law do apply. The concept of interpretation needs some clarification. Interpretation is defined as 'The process of determining what something, esp. the law or a legal document, means'.[58] The interpretative process tries to extract the pertinent meaning from a number of possible meanings the terms used in a treaty can have. It may not go beyond the scope of the possible meanings of the words.[59] This limit of treaty interpretation is reinforced by the prohibition for panels to add to or diminish the rights and obligations under WTO law. Furthermore, the interpretation of WTO law by a panel is only binding on the parties to the case— under Article IX:2 of the WTO Agreement only the Ministerial Conference and the General Council can issue authoritative interpretations.[60]

The reference to 'customary rules of interpretation of public international law' in Article 3.2 of the DSU opens two routes to taking non-WTO law into account when interpreting WTO law. The first of these is the 'presumption against conflict',[61] according to which treaties have to be interpreted so as to avoid a conflict

---

[52] Bartels (n 1 above) 507–508.   [53] Pauwelyn (n 1 above) 561.

[54] Pauwelyn (n 1 above) 564–565.

[55] E Canal-Forgues, 'Sur l'Interprétation Dans le Droit de l'OMC' (2001) RGDIP 5, 7 ff; Trachtman (n 1 above) 343.

[56] 'Apply' is taken to mean more than the mere use of the law for interpretative purposes.

[57] Böckenförde (n 1 above) 983.   [58] BA Garner, *Black's Law Dictionary* (7th edn, 2000).

[59] Böckenförde (n 1 above) 983 f; MG Bloche, 'WTO Deference to National Health Policy: Toward an Interpretative Principle' (2002) 5 JIEL 825, 843 (arguing that health has emerged as an interpretive principle in WTO law).   [60] Böckenförde (n 1 above) 993.

[61] *Indonesia—Certain Measures Affecting the Automobile Industry*, WT/DS54/R, WT/DS55/R, WT/DS59/R, WT/DS64/R, para 14.28 (1998); *India—Measures Affecting the Automotive Sector*,

between them. Although traditionally applied to treaties, there is nothing inherent in the rule that prevents it from being applied to avoid conflicts of WTO Agreements with rules of customary international law or with general principles of law. The fact that there is no hierarchy between customary rules, general principles, and treaty law strongly supports such an interpretation of the rule.

The other, more comprehensive, route via which non-WTO law can be taken into account when interpreting WTO law is Articles 31 and 32 of the Vienna Convention on the Law of Treaties (Vienna Convention), which are universally acknowledged as customary rules of interpretation of public international law[62] and consistently referred to by the Appellate Body.[63] Article 31(1) of the Vienna Convention states that a treaty shall be interpreted in good faith in accordance with the ordinary meaning to be given to the terms of the treaty in their context and in the light of its object and purpose. Paragraph 2 enumerates which documents made in connection with the conclusion of the treaty are part of the context and paragraph 3 lists three more types of rules that shall be taken into account 'together with the context': subsequent agreements between the parties regarding the interpretation of the treaty or the application of its provisions (a), subsequent practice in the application of the treaty establishing the agreement of the parties regarding its interpretation (b), and 'any relevant rules of international law applicable in the relations between the parties' (c). It is Article 31(3)(c) of the Vienna Convention that opens the door to non-WTO law and thus to human rights law. The reference to 'rules' means that all sources of international law can be taken into account under this provision.[64] As Marceau has pointed out, this interpretative rule advances coherence in international law.[65] It encompasses the presumption against conflict, as other rules will be taken into account in the interpretation of a treaty, thus leading to interpretations that avoid conflict.[66]

It remains to be seen which provisions on the right to access to medicine could be referred to under the Vienna Convention for the interpretation of the TRIPS

WT/DS146/R, WT/DS175/R, para 7.58, footnote 332 (2001); *Argentina—Safeguard Measures on Imports of Footwear*, WT/DS121/R, para 8.68 (1999) (citing the presumption, its holding was overruled on another ground); *Canada—Term of Patent Protection*, WT/DS170/R, para 6.45 (2000).

[62] Marceau, *Human Rights* (n 3 above) 779; Böckenförde (n 1 above) 994; Cameron and Gray (n 40 above) 254; Canal-Forgues (n 55 above) 7–8.

[63] *Japan—Taxes on Alcoholic Beverages*, WT/DS8/AB/R, WT/DS10/AB/R, WT/DS11/AB/R, 10 (1996); *United States—Final Countervailing Duty Determination with Respect to Certain Softwood Lumber from Canada*, WT/DS257/AB/R, para 58, footnote 42 (2004). The provisions are also referred to by the United States, which is not a party to the Convention. *United States—Final Dumping Determination on Softwood Lumber from Canada*, WT/DS264/AB/R, para 107 (2004).

[64] *European Communities—Measures Affecting the Approval and Marketing of Biotech Products*, WT/DS291/R, para 7.67 (2006) (*EC—Biotech*).   [65] Marceau (n 1 above) 127.

[66] In practice the approach will not differ substantially from the approach suggested by Bartels: a WTO panel will rule in favour of the complaining party if that party has a claim based on WTO law. If it does not have such a claim, the party will lose. The application of non-WTO law would now either merely confirm this ruling, in which case it is irrelevant, or it would change the ruling, in which case Bartels suggests that the 'conflict rules' kick in and WTO law prevails, thus reinstating the result that was achieved in the first place. Marceau, *Human Rights* (n 3 above) 777.

Agreement. Article 31(1)(c) of the Vienna Convention imposes two conditions that international law rules have to fulfil for the provision to apply. First of all they have to be 'relevant', ie they have to have 'significant and demonstrable bearing on the matter at hand'.[67] This means that the rule of international law has to be applicable to the facts of the case at hand.[68] As chapter 3 has shown, the right to access to medicine is relevant for grants of pharmaceutical patents.

Furthermore the rule has to be 'applicable in the relations between the parties'. Views on the interpretation of these terms diverge. Some authors interpret the term 'relations between the parties' broadly and admit the relevance of a rule of international law as context even if merely one party is bound by it on the grounds of effects of the rule in the inter-state relations with another state.[69] The precise implications of this view are unclear. It seems to imply that in a dispute settlement case concerning the TRIPS Agreement both the general international and the treaty-based rights to access to medicine can be taken into account if one party to the proceeding is bound by it. Palmeter and Mavroidis suggest another reading of the requirement. They take the term 'the parties' to mean the parties to the dispute, so that both parties to the dispute before a WTO panel would have to be bound by the right to access to medicine for the right to be relevant in the interpretation of the TRIPS Agreement.[70] Both of these approaches are not convincing. First of all, they focus on dispute settlement, although Article 2(1)(g) of the Vienna Convention indicates that 'party' means 'a State which has consented to be bound by the treaty and for which the treaty is in force'—and not party to the dispute settlement proceeding.[71] Also, both of these approaches would result in different interpretations of the same WTO provision *inter partes*. This would not be of great concern within the GATT Agreement as it is of the bilateral type. However, the TRIPS Agreement as an integral agreement is adverse to *inter se* modifications and it would be equally adverse to *inter se* interpretation.[72]

Two other approaches to interpreting the 'between the parties' prong seem preferable. The first of them argues that the reference to 'all the parties' in Article 31(2)(a) of the Vienna Convention and to 'one or more parties' in Article 31(2)(b) can only mean that the term 'the parties' used in Article 31(3)(c) implies more than one, but less than all the parties.[73] It therefore demands that the international law rule binds at least a large number of the WTO Members. The rights to access to

[67] FC Mish *et al* (eds), *Merriam-Webster's Collegiate Dictionary* (10th edn, 1998).

[68] Böckenförde also suggests the criterion of wide membership for relevancy, but the criterion of pertinent subject matter is more in accord with the plain meaning of the words and the fact that the provision's second condition targets required membership. Böckenförde (n 1 above) 995–996; Marceau, *Call for Coherence* (n 3 above) 123–124.   [69] Böckenförde (n 1 above) 997.

[70] Palmeter and Mavroidis (n 1 above) 411. Neumann (n 3 above) 387 interprets parties to mean parties to dispute settlement insofar as multilateral treaties of the bilateral type are concerned.

[71] Böckenförde (n 1 above) 996–997.

[72] This is not to deny that interpretation in a dispute settlement proceeding is technically only binding on the parties to the proceeding.

[73] Marceau, *Call for Coherence* (n 3 above) 124–125; Böckenförde (n 1 above) 996.

medicine under the ICCPR, the ICESCR and general international law all fulfil this requirement[74] and could therefore be taken into account in the interpretation of the TRIPS Agreement in any dispute. Some authors, however, read the term 'the parties' to mean all the parties to the treaty. They argue that any other approach would fall short of the principle of *pacta tertiis*, as it would make an agreement relevant for the interpretation of the WTO Agreements even where a WTO Member is not a member to this other agreement.[75] This is also the approach taken by the Panel in *EC—Biotech*, although the Panel at the end seems to be undecided whether the term has to be read as 'the parties to the dispute'.[76] Pursuant to this approach only the right to access to medicine under general international law is relevant in the interpretation of the TRIPS Agreement. The approach is commonly criticized as it excludes almost all treaties from being taken account of and would therefore foster a further fragmentation of public international law. It is highly unlikely for any major treaty to have the exact same membership as the WTO Agreements. Indeed, as Marceau has pointed out, the more the membership of the WTO grows, the more unlikely it will become for any other treaty to have the same membership.[77] Also, the principle of *pacta tertiis* lends but little support to the latter view. Interpretation is a process that a panel has to undertake by necessity. It *has* to choose between different possible interpretations of a term, even where the object and purpose of the treaty and the context do not lead to any definite conclusion. In those situations, citing an agreement enjoying wide support will endow the tribunal's decision with more legitimacy than selecting one of the possible interpretations without further argument. In fact, in many cases international tribunals will even seize 'soft law' for this purpose. Nevertheless, as both Marceau and Böckenförde have pointed out, none of these two approaches should be dismissed. Article 31(3)(c) demands that panels take the rules of international law 'into account', allowing for some flexibility. The more WTO Members are bound by the international law rule, the more persuasive it will be for the panel. Thus the right to access to medicine under general international law, which binds both the WTO and its Members, will be taken to be more persuasive than the right under the ICCPR or the ICESCR.

c Interpretation in Light of the Object and Purpose

Chapter 2 demonstrated that public health interests have to be taken into account in the interpretation of the TRIPS Agreement as part of its object and purpose.

---

[74] For a comparison of the memberships of the WTO Agreement and the ICCPR/ICESCR see chapter 3 and the Annex.

[75] M Lennard, 'Navigating by the Stars: Interpreting the WTO Agreements' (2002) 5 JIEL 17, 36–37.

[76] *EC—Biotech*, WT/DS291/R, paras 7.70 ff (2006) (the Panel achieves a similar result to the one supported here by taking treaties into account under Art 31(1) of the Vienna Convention even where not all Members are parties to the treaties, paras 7.92 ff).

[77] Marceau, *Call for Coherence* (n 3 above) 124; Böckenförde (n 1 above) 996.

The right to access to medicine as an interpretative aid lends specificity to the vague terminology of public health and focuses the attention on the individual, namely the availability and accessibility of medication to the individual.[78] Also, the additional interpretative guideline connects the interpretation of the TRIPS Agreement to the wider body of public international law and efforts undertaken in other fora, namely the Committee for Economic, Social and Cultural Rights, that has put an increasing amount of work into establishing concrete benchmarks for the compliance with economic, social, and cultural rights such as the right to health. Not only does this connection simplify to some extent the interpretative tasks that panels are faced with, it also enables an interpretation of the TRIPS Agreement that takes account of recent developments.

At the same time a cautious note should be added. Given US resistance to economic, social, and cultural rights, any ruling explicitly referring to such rights, even if only as an interpretative aid, is likely to meet severe criticism from the United States. A likely solution for a panel to this problem is to take inspiration from work going on in human rights fora, but to justify its interpretation explicitly only with a reference to the object and purpose of the TRIPS Agreement.

5 Jurisprudence on Non-WTO Law in WTO Dispute Settlement

Dispute settlement practice has discussed the applicability of non-WTO law on several occasions and generally confirmed the suggested approach. It is helpful to consider the practice with respect to non-WTO treaties and general international law separately.

A Treaties

Under the old GATT regime the *US—Tuna II* Panel rejected the arguments the parties had made under environmental and trade treaties other than the GATT, stating that 'these treaties were not relevant as a primary means of interpretation of the text of the General Agreement'.[79] Under the WTO, however, the situation concerning non-WTO treaty law changed. In *US—Gasoline* the Appellate Body famously stated that Article 3.2 of the DSU reflects 'a measure of recognition that the *General Agreement* is not to be read in clinical isolation from public international law'.[80]

The Appellate Body report in *EC—Computer Equipment* is indicative of the approach the Appellate Body pursues. In the report the Appellate Body criticizes a

---

[78] Similar: M Hussain, 'World Trade Organisation and the Right to Health: An Overview' (2003) 43 Indian J Int'l L 279, 296–297.

[79] *United States—Restrictions on Imports of Tuna II*, DS29/R (not adopted), para 5.19 *et seq* (1994) (*US—Tuna II*). For further practice of the GATT regime on the issue see Neumann (n 3 above) 358–359.   [80] *US—Gasoline*, WT/DS2/AB/R, 17 (1996) (emphasis in original).

panel for not considering the International Convention on the Harmonized Commodity Description and Coding System, its Explanatory Notes and the decisions taken by the Harmonized System Committee of the WCO as context under the Vienna Convention in interpreting a tariff schedule of the European Communities.[81] Even though the Appellate Body failed to mention the precise subparagraph of Article 31 of the Vienna Convention under which it acted, it showed that it would use treaties and other international documents for the interpretation of covered agreements, even where not all WTO Members are parties to the treaty in question.[82] The Appellate Body soon had the opportunity to reconsider the *US—Tuna II* holding in the light of this new attitude. In *US—Shrimp* the Appellate Body stated that the meaning of the terms in the GATT is not static and went on to interpret 'natural resources' in Article XX(g) of the GATT by drawing inspiration from numerous international documents, among them the UNCLOS and the Convention on Biological Diversity.[83] Furthermore it used the Convention on International Trade in Endangered Species of Wild Fauna and Flora (CITES) in the interpretation of the term 'exhaustible' under Article XX(g).[84] Similarly, in *EC—Bananas* the Appellate Body referred to the Lomé Convention to interpret a waiver granted under a WTO covered agreement, namely under the WTO Agreement. The case also shows that waivers and other WTO decisions on covered agreements will be considered as part of the applicable law.[85] The Appellate Body justified its use of non-WTO law as follows:

We note that since the GATT CONTRACTING PARTIES incorporated a reference to the Lomé Convention into the Lomé waiver, the meaning of the Lomé Convention became a GATT/WTO issue at least to that extent. Thus, we have no alternative but to examine the provisions of the Lomé Convention ourselves in so far as it is necessary to interpret the Lomé waiver.[86]

The Panel in *EC—Biotech* extensively discussed the relevance of non-WTO law to the interpretation of the WTO Agreements. Relying both on Article 31(3)(c) and 31(1) of the Vienna Convention it concluded that conventions may be relied on in the interpretation of WTO Agreements even where one or more disputing parties are not parties to them, as that mere fact 'does not necessarily mean that a

---

[81] *European Communities—Customs Classification of Certain Computer Equipment*, WT/DS62/ AB/R, WT/DS67/AB/R, WT/DS/68/AB/R, paras 89 ff (*EC—Computer Equipment*).

[82] The parties to the International Convention on the Harmonized Commodity Description and Coding System as well as the date of entry into force of the Convention for the parties are listed in World Customs Organization, *Position Regarding Contracting Parties (on 1 July 2006)*, NG0095E1 (25 July 2006).

[83] *United States—Import Prohibition of Certain Shrimp and Shrimp Products*, WT/DS58/AB/R, para 130 (1998) (*US—Shrimp*).   [84] *US—Shrimp*, WT/DS58/AB/R, para 132 (1998).

[85] See also *European Communities—Export Subsidies on Sugar. Complaint by Thailand*, WT/DS283/R para 7.219 (2004).

[86] *European Communities—Regime for the Importation, Sale and Distribution of Bananas*, WT/DS27/ AB/R, para 167 (1997) (*EC—Bananas*).

convention cannot shed light on the meaning and scope of a treaty term to be interpreted'.[87]

Case law thus clearly confirms that non-WTO treaties will be used as aids in the interpretation of the covered agreements.

Böckenförde argues that WTO jurisprudence goes one step further and regards any legal document as applicable law that is negotiated under a mandate granted in a covered agreement. Thus, in *Argentina—Footwear* Argentina tried to justify an *ad valorem* tax it imposed on imports with its obligations under an agreement with the International Monetary Fund (IMF). The Appellate Body held that there is nothing in the relevant documents about the relationship between the IMF and the WTO that modifies Argentina's obligations under the relevant GATT provision. It justifies its examination of these documents and the apparent implication that those documents could prevail over GATT obligations if they explicitly so provide by pointing out that they were negotiated under the WTO's mandate to cooperate with the IMF under Article III:5 of the WTO Agreement.[88] Whether the Appellate Body would really allow a non-WTO treaty to prevail over the covered agreements on this basis, however, is questionable in the light of the Appellate Body Report in *EC—Poultry*. In that case the European Communities and Brazil had come to sign Agreed Minutes (the 'Oilseeds Agreement') in negotiations under Article XXVIII of the GATT before the entry into force of the WTO Agreements. The Appellate Body discussed the relationship between the European tariff schedule and the Oilseeds Agreement and rejected an application of general international law principles on conflict of treaties. Rather, it held that only the schedule is part of the covered agreements. Consequently it is the schedule that contains the relevant obligations—the Appellate Body considered the Oilseeds Agreement merely as useful in the interpretation of the schedule under Article 32 of the Vienna Convention.[89] The WTO adjudicating bodies will, of course, apply non-WTO treaties as applicable law where the covered Agreements explicitly refer to such Agreements, eg in Article XV:9(a) of the GATT.[90]

Other commentators have found support for their position that panels can apply all international law in the Appellate Body's frequent references to the non-retroactivity of treaties, both as a general principle of international law and as a treaty norm under Article 28 of the Vienna Convention.[91] However, these cases

---

[87] *EC—Biotech*, WT/DS291/R, paras 7.94 (2006). The Panel distinguishes conventions to which all WTO Members are parties, which have to be taken into account under Art 31(3)(c) of the Vienna Convention and other conventions which may be taken into account under Art 31(1) of the Vienna Convention.

[88] *Argentina—Measures Affecting Imports of Footwear, Textiles, Apparel and Other Items*, WT/DS56/AB/R, paras 64 ff (1998) (*Argentina—Footwear*).

[89] *European Communities—Measures Affecting the Importation of Certain Poultry Products*, WT/DS69/AB/R, paras 77 ff (1998) (*EC—Poultry*).

[90] *Dominican Republic—Measures Affecting the Importation and Internal Sale of Cigarettes*, WT/DS302/R, paras 7.150 ff (2004).

[91] *Brazil—Measures Affecting Desiccated Coconut*, WT/DS22/AB/R, p 15 (1997) (although the parties arguably included Art 28 of the Vienna Convention in this case under the non-standard terms

lend no support to such a position. As the Appellate Body indicated in *EC—Sardines*, it regards the rule as an 'interpretation principle' and thus uses the norm in the interpretation of the covered agreements to determine their applicability *ratione temporis*.[92] The situation would be different if it could be shown that panels have referred to general international law rules on conflicts between norms to allow non-WTO law to override WTO law. However, in the few cases that those rules, eg Article 30 of the Vienna Convention, were mentioned they were either not applied at all or, in one case, applied only to let WTO law override a non-WTO agreement.[93] Even this recourse to Article 30 is superfluous and misleading, however, given the unequivocal ruling of the Appellate Body in *EC—Poultry*:

In our view, it is not necessary to have recourse to either Article 59.1 or Article 30.3 of the Vienna Convention, because the text of the WTO Agreement and the legal arrangements governing the transition from the GATT 1947 to the WTO resolve the issue of the relationship between Schedule LXXX and the Oilseeds Agreement in this case. Schedule LXXX is (...) an integral part of the GATT 1994. As such, it forms part of the multilateral obligations under the WTO Agreement. The Oilseeds Agreement, in contrast, is a bilateral agreement negotiated by the European Communities and Brazil (...). *As such, the Oilseeds Agreement is not a 'covered agreement'* within the meaning of Articles 1 and 2 of the DSU.[94]

B *General International Law*

WTO dispute settlement has made more frequent use of general international law than it has of non-WTO treaty law. It is appropriate to distinguish between rules of interpretation and other rules.

Article 3.2 of the DSU mandates the application of customary rules of interpretation of public international law. The Appellate Body has generally taken this statement to refer to Articles 31, 32 of the Vienna Convention. But the Appellate Body has applied other rules of interpretation, such as Article 28 of the Vienna

---

of reference that include the document *Brazil—Measures Affecting Desiccated Coconut. Communication from Brazil*, WT/DS22/3 (1996) explicitly addressing the question of the applicable rules *ratione temporis*); *EC Measures Concerning Meat and Meat Products*, WT/DS26/AB/R, WT/DS48/AB/R, para 128 (1998); *Canada—Term of Patent Protection*, WT/DS170AB/R, paras 71 ff (2000); *European Communities—Trade Description of Sardines*, WT/DS231/AB/R, para 200 (2002) (*EC—Sardines*); see also *Canada—Measures Affecting the Export of Civilian Aircraft*, WT/DS70/R para 9.42 (1999).

[92] *EC—Sardines*, WT/DS231/AB/R, para 200 (2002).
[93] *EC—Measures Concerning Meat and Meat Products (Hormones)—Recourse to Arbitration by the European Communities under Article 22.6 of the DSU*, WT/DS26/ARB, para 51 (1999). Critical Neumann (n 3 above) 350. The rules on conflicts are mentioned in *United States—Section 110(5) of the US Copyright Act*, WT/DS160/R, para 6.41 (2000); *Japan—Measures Affecting Consumer Photographic Film and Paper*, WT/DS44/R, para 10.65 (1998); see also *EC—Imposition of Anti-Dumping Duties on Imports of Cotton Yarn from Brazil*, ADP/137, paras 540 f (1995).
[94] *EC—Poultry*, WT/DS69/AB/R, para 79 (1998), emphasis added.

Convention,[95] the principle of effectiveness (*ut res magis valeat quam pereat*),[96] that of *in dubio mitius*,[97] or the principle of good faith.[98]

Where the Appellate Body has referred to other rules of general international law, it has generally used them in the interpretation of the covered agreements or to confirm an interpretation of the covered agreements, much like it uses non-WTO treaty law.[99] Thus, in *EC—Bananas* the Appellate Body first held that a requirement of legal interest was not contained in the DSU to then state that such a requirement could also not be deduced from general international law and to finally examine the question under Article XXIII of the GATT.[100] In *EC—Hormones* the Appellate Body discussed the precautionary principle under the heading '[t]he Relevance of the Precautionary Principle in the Interpretation of the *SPS Agreement*' and even though it refused to rule on the status of the principle, it held that the 'principle does not, by itself, and without a clear textual directive to that effect, relieve a panel from the duty of applying the normal (ie customary international law) principles of treaty interpretation in reading the provisions of the *SPS Agreement*'.[101] The *EC—Biotech* Panel Report contains a similar discussion.[102]

Several cases can be cited for the proposition that the Appellate Body goes a step further and applies general international law when it comes to procedural questions on which the DSU is silent. Thus, the case law recognizes the principle of estoppel.[103] The best-known example for this position is the Appellate Body's

---

[95] N 91 above.

[96] *US—Gasoline*, WT/DS2/AB/R (1996); *Canada—Measures Affecting the Importation of Milk and the Exportation of Dairy Products*, WT/DS103/AB/R, WT/DS113/AB/R, para 133 (1999); *Korea—Definitive Safeguard Measure on Imports of Certain Dairy Products*, WT/DS98/AB/R, para 80 (1999); *EC—Asbestos*, WT/DS135/AB/R, para 115 (2001). In *Brazil—Export Financing Programme for Aircraft. Recourse to Arbitration By Brazil under Article 22.6 of the DSU and Article 4.11 of the SCM Agreement*, WT/DS46/ARB, paras 3.6 ff (2000) arbitrators have pointedly not applied Art 60 of the Vienna Convention to a bilateral agreement.

[97] *EC Measures Concerning Meat and Meat Products (Hormones)*, WT/DS26/AB/R, WT/DS48/AB/R, para 165 (1998) (*EC—Hormones*); *Argentina—Safeguard Measures on Imports of Footwear*, WT/DS121/R, para 7.8 (1999); *United States—Safeguard Measures on Imports of Fresh, Chilled or Frozen Lamb Meat from New Zealand and Australia*, WT/DS177/R, WT/DS178/R, para 7.16 footnote 59 (2000); *United States—Anti-Dumping Act of 1916*, WT/DS136/R, para 6.87 (2000).

[98] *United States—Tax Treatment for 'Foreign Sales Corporations'*, WT/DS108/AB/R, para 166 (2000); *European Communities—Conditions for the Granting of Tariff Preferences to Developing Countries*, WT/DS246/AB/R, para 117 (2004); *United States—Anti-Dumping Measures on Certain Hot-Rolled Steel Products from Japan*, WT/DS184/AB/R, para 101 (2001).

[99] *United States—Transitional Safeguard Measure on Combed Cotton Yarn from Pakistan*, WT/DS192/AB/R, para 120 (2001); *United States—Definitive Safeguard Measures on Imports of Circular Welded Carbon Quality Line Pipe from Korea*, WT/DS202/AB/R, para 259 (2002).

[100] *European Communities—Regime for the Importation, Sale and Distribution of Bananas*, WT/DS27/AB/R, paras 132 ff (1997) (*EC—Bananas*). Pauwelyn alleges that the Appellate Body would have fallen back on a general international law rule requiring a legal interest. Given the reliance of the Appellate Body on WTO rules, however, this seems rather unlikely. Pauwelyn (n 17 above) 208.

[101] *EC—Hormones*, WT/DS26/AB/R, WT/DS48/AB/R, para 124 (emphasis in original).

[102] *EC—Biotech*, WT/DS291/R, paras 7.76 ff (2006).

[103] *Mexico—Anti-Dumping Investigation of High Fructose Corn Syrup (HFCS) from the United States. Recourse to Article 21.5 of the DSU by the United States*, WT/DS132/AB/RW, para 50 (2001);

holding on the question of burden of proof. In *US—Shirts and Blouses* the Appellate Body determined that 'the burden of proof rests upon the party (...) who asserts the affirmative of a particular claim or defence'.[104] The justification it cites for this holding is that this rule is generally accepted both by international tribunals and national courts.[105] It then goes on to show that other panels have handled the issue of burden of proof in a similar manner.

The furthest-reaching statement on the applicability of general international law favours the application of general international law also outside the area of procedure. It stems from the Panel in *Korea—Government Procurement*, that held:

> We take note that Article 3.2 of the DSU requires that we seek within the context of a particular dispute to clarify the existing provisions of the WTO Agreements in accordance with customary rules of interpretation of public international law. However, the relationship of the WTO Agreements to customary international law is broader than this. Customary international law applies generally to the economic relations between the WTO Members. Such international law applies to the extent that the WTO treaty agreements do not 'contract out' from it. To put it another way, to the extent there is no conflict or inconsistency, or an expression in a covered WTO agreement that implies differently, we are of the view that the customary rules of international law apply to the WTO treaties and to the process of treaty formation under the WTO.[106]

However, it is unlikely that panels will follow this precedent and apply the whole *corpus* of general international law in WTO dispute settlement. In *US—Shirts and Blouses* the Appellate Body arguably had no choice but to apply general international law as it intrinsically had to rule on the procedural questions involved and the DSU was silent on the issue. The same cannot be said of matters of substance, namely claims under the WTO Agreements, on which WTO law cannot be silent. The Panel statement in *Korea—Government Procurement* overstepped the boundaries of the Appellate Body's habitual, far more cautious, approach examined above.[107] It is more likely that panels will continue to use general international law merely in the interpretation of the covered agreements and concerning procedural questions. Practice thus confirms the interpretation of the pertinent articles of the DSU, according to which international law merely serves as an aid to the interpretation of the covered agreements—with the small caveat of the application of general international law in procedural questions on which the DSU is silent.

Guatemala—Definitive Anti-Dumping Measures on Grey Portland Cement from Mexico, WT/DS156/R, paras 8.23 f (2000); Neumann (n 3 above) 353.

[104] *United States—Measure Affecting Imports of Woven Wool Shirts and Blouses from India*, WT/DS33/AB/R, p 14 (1997) (*US—Shirts and Blouses*). M Hilf, *Freiheit des Welthandels contra Umweltschutz?*, NVwZ 2000, 481, 488.

[105] Böckenförde argues that the Appellate Body determined the rule by interpreting Art 6 of the Agreement on Textiles and Clothing (ATC), but there is virtually no interpretation of the provision in the Report. Böckenförde (n 1 above) 990.

[106] *Korea—Government Procurement* (n 26 above) para 7.96 (footnotes omitted).

[107] But see J Cazala, 'L'Invocation de l'Estoppel dans le Cadre de la Procédure de Règlement des Différends de l'Organisation Mondiale du Commerce' (2003) RGDIP, 885, 887.

6 Access to Medicine as *jus cogens* within WTO Dispute Settlement?

Given that human rights thus may only be used in the interpretation of the covered agreements, a WTO Member cannot rely on these rights in the defence against a claim of violation of WTO law absent a basis for this defence in the covered agreements. The situation is different, however, where the human right has attained the status of *jus cogens*. Such rules cannot be contracted out of—indeed, under the Vienna Convention they void any agreement that attempts to do so. This hierarchically superior position would allow a defence against the claim of a violation of WTO law even within WTO dispute settlement. What remains to be discussed is whether the right to access to medicine has attained such a position. It is hard not to feel sympathy with the proposition that it has: does access to medicine not have to prevail over economic interests, particularly where the life of millions is at stake? But the question oversimplifies the issues involved. The doctrine of *jus cogens* is a relatively young one and is still awaiting its first serious test case. Commonly, only a mere handful of principles are cited as examples of the doctrine, such as the prohibition of genocide. All of these are widely accepted and of comparatively long standing. The same cannot be said for access to medicine: the reluctance of the United States to recognize economic, social, and cultural rights is indicative of the problems the right faces and while this reluctance might have subsided sufficiently in the area of access to medicine in health emergencies to recognize such a right as customary, it is not sufficient to raise it immediately to the status of *jus cogens*.[108]

II TRIPS Agreement Flexibilities in the Light of Human Rights

The TRIPS Agreement allows Members to take measures that limit the rights of patent holders, commonly known as 'TRIPS flexibilities'. Chapter 4 demonstrated that a weakening of patent rights can be of significant importance to make medicine accessible. This section will give a thorough overview of the flexibilities,[109] highlighting where the right to access to medicine can be used as an argument in the interpretation of the flexibilities. It will discuss the question of parallel imports, 'limited exceptions' to patents as provided for by Article 30 of the TRIPS Agreement, compulsory licenses (particularly as part of local working requirements) as they are currently regulated by the TRIPS Agreement, ie before the amendment, which has not yet come into force, and patent revocation according to Article 32

---

[108] P Cullet, 'Patents and Medicines: The Relationship between TRIPS and the Human Right to Health' (2003) 79 Int'l Affairs 130, 158–159. *Contra*, arguing with the human rights provisions in the UN Charter, Hussain (n 78 above) 312.

[109] An in-depth overview can also be found in Peter Rott, *Patentrecht und Sozialpolitik unter dem TRIPS-Abkommen* (2002).

of the TRIPS Agreement. Article 40 of the TRIPS Agreement, which allows measures to control anti-competitive practices in contractual licences, harking back to the principle in Article 8.2 of the TRIPS Agreement, will not be discussed, as that would enlarge the scope of the study significantly and the patent exceptions are not subsidiary to these anti-trust measures.[110] The section will show that while the interpretative approach presented above is of some assistance, it suffers from the fundamental weakness that the right to access to medicine is just one argument among several in the interpretation of the flexibilities. It falls short of providing developing country Members that intend to take measures to safeguard access to medicine with any security that they will not be dragged into WTO dispute settlement or exposed to pressure by developed country Members to adopt more stringent standards required under a different interpretation of the TRIPS Agreement.[111] These risks serve as significant disincentives for making use of the flexibilities.

1 Parallel Imports

Chapter 2 already introduced the first sale doctrine, also known as the doctrine of exhaustion. Where a patented product is placed on the market by the patent holder or with its consent, the patent holder has exhausted its patent rights and the buyer of the product is free to resell the product as it wishes.[112] The doctrine balances the interests of the patent holder and those of the buyer, who obtains full property of the product.[113] While it is uncontested in the national context, it is highly contested where the patented product has been placed on a foreign market by the patent holder or with its consent. The debate is not just about the details, such as the meaning of 'consent',[114] but about the permissibility of this concept of 'international exhaustion' itself. The question can succinctly be stated as follows: does the TRIPS Agreement provide that a patent holder can prevent the importation of a product where the product has been placed on a foreign market by the

---

[110] This seems to be implied by R Kampf, 'Patents versus Patients?' (2002) 40 Archiv des Völkerrechts 90, 102. However, there is nothing in the Agreement that would require such a subsidiarity.

[111] Such pressure has become commonplace, usually initiated by the pharmaceutical industry serving as a watchdog. E Ghanotakis, 'How the U.S. Interpretation of Flexibilities Inherent in TRIPS Affects Access to Medicines for Developing Countries' (2004) 7 J World Intell Prop 563 (discussing pressure on Argentina, South Africa, and Guatemala).

[112] Dogmatically, the limitation of the right is construed either as an implied licence, an interpretation of the statutes on patent violations, or it is derived from the functions of intellectual property rights. W Nauta, 'Ausnahmen vom Erschöpfungsgrundsatz im Markenrecht' (2004) GRUR Int 994, 995–996.

[113] HC Jehoram, 'International Exhaustion versus Importation Right: A Murky Area of Intellectual Property Law' (1996) GRUR Int 280.

[114] L Rubini, 'Is the Siege of Fortress Europe Really Over? The Exhaustion of Trademarks in the EC, Competition and International Trade' (2002) 29 Legal Issues of Economic Integration 205 ff. One highly important 'detail' is whether the sale under a compulsory licence may trigger exhaustion. FM Abbott, 'Compulsory Licensing for Public Health Needs: The TRIPS Agenda at the WTO after the Doha Declaration on Public Health' Quaker United Nations Office—Geneva Occasional Paper 9 (2002) 52–53.

patent holder itself or with its consent (parallel import)? The WTO organs have now conclusively established that Members are free to establish the system of international exhaustion they consider appropriate—a decision that will be discussed later on. This part will describe the debate before the decision and illustrate that the right to access to medicine could have served as an argument in the debate, but is not dispositive.

While the inquiry is focused on patent law, it must be noted that patented pharmaceuticals are sold under trademarks and that the importer of the pharmaceuticals will have to comply both with trademark and patent laws. While the different rationales of these two intellectual property rights seemingly justify a different treatment of the question of international exhaustion,[115] the fact that in practice an importer will have to comply with both laws favours an identical solution to the question of international exhaustion for both rights.

The admissibility *vel non* of parallel imports is an important factor for the pricing strategy of producers, as has already been mentioned in chapter 4. If parallel imports are not admissible, the patent holder can separate markets—it can sell products at low prices where the market would not pay for high ones and at high prices where the market allows for such prices. Where parallel imports are admissible, importers would make use of such price discrimination and buy the product in low-price markets to resell them in high price-markets, the low price would leak into the high-price market. Consequently, the patent holder might raise the price in the low-price market to prevent parallel imports.

Taking account of the skewed income distribution in many developing countries the Commission on Intellectual Property Rights concluded that the most beneficial policy for developing countries is to adopt a rule of international exhaustion, allowing them to purchase drugs at the lowest price at which the manufacturer offers them anywhere in the world. Developed countries, however, should not allow parallel imports in the pharmaceutical area from developing countries. This enables companies to price-discriminate and sell their products at low prices in the developing world without the price leaking into the developed world.[116] However, parallel imports will not lower prices below the level at which a manufacturer is willing to sell the drugs.

Despite the seemingly clear language of the TRIPS Agreement on exhaustion of intellectual property rights, commentators could not agree on the legality of a

---

[115] AJ Stack, 'TRIPS, Patent Exhaustion and Parallel Imports' (1998) 4 J World Intell Prop 657, 658.
[116] Commission on Intellectual Property Rights, *Integrating Intellectual Property Rights and Development Policy* (2002) 41–42; FM Scherer and J Watal, 'The Economics of TRIPS Options for Access to Medicines' in B Granville (ed), *The Economics of Essential Medicines* (2002) 32, 49; KE Maskus and M Ganslandt, 'Parallel Trade in Pharmaceutical Products: Implications for Procuring Medicines for Poor Countries' in B Granville (ed), *The Economics of Essential Medicines* (2002) 57, 79. For some areas of technology developing countries might profit from a policy of international exhaustion in developed countries, because such a policy would allow the export of products produced by the patent holder or under licence in developing countries to developed countries. FM Abbott, 'First Report (Final) to the Committee on International Trade Law of the International Law Association on the Subject of Parallel Importation' (1998) 1 JIEL 607, 612 ff.

principle of international exhaustion under the TRIPS Agreement.[117] Article 6 of the TRIPS Agreement, which explicitly covers the exhaustion of intellectual property rights, provides that:

[f]or the purposes of dispute settlement under this Agreement, subject to the provisions of Articles 3 and 4 nothing in this Agreement shall be used to address the issue of the exhaustion of intellectual property rights.

A No International Exhaustion

Arguing that Article 28.1 of the TRIPS Agreement grants patent holders the exclusive right to prevent third parties from importing the product even if they placed the product on the foreign market themselves and that national patents are independent of each other,[118] some authors consider the TRIPS Agreement as prohibiting the adoption of a system of international exhaustion.[119] For these authors, Article 6 of the TRIPS Agreement, which is also referenced in a footnote to Article 28.1 of the TRIPS Agreement, is a mere procedural rule for 'the purposes of dispute settlement under this Agreement'. It prevents Members from challenging a Member's regime of international exhaustion before the dispute resolution mechanism, but it does not legalize such a regime.[120] Not surprisingly, this view has apparently been adopted by the pharmaceutical industry when it challenged South Africa's Medicines and Related Substances Control Act.[121]

B Mandatory International Exhaustion

A second group of commentators claim that under WTO law Members are obligated to adopt a regime of international exhaustion of patent rights. They deduce this solution from Article III:4 of the GATT and Article XI of the GATT, which prohibit quantitative restrictions and internal laws granting less favourable treatment to imported products compared to like domestic products. A ban on parallel imports, however, would establish a non-tariff trade barrier incompatible with those provisions and not excused under Article XX(d) of the GATT, as it is not necessary to secure compliance with patent laws.[122] Under a similar reasoning the European Court of Justice prohibited EU member states' banning parallel imports originating

---

[117] C Freytag, *Parallelimporte nach EG- und WTO-Recht. Patente und Marken versus Handelsfreiheit*, (2001) 210 ff.

[118] The principle of territoriality and the independence of a patent granted in one country from a patent granted in another country are contained in Art 4*bis* of the Paris Convention, applicable via Art 2.1 of the TRIPS Agreement.

[119] J Straus, 'Implications of the TRIPs Agreement in the Field of Patent Law' in F-K Beier and G Schricker (eds), *From GATT to TRIPs—The Agreement on Trade-Related Aspects of Intellectual Property Rights* (1997) 160, 191 ff.

[120] HE Bale, Jr, 'The Conflicts Between Parallel Trade and Product Access and Innovation: The Case of Pharmaceuticals' (1998) 1 JIEL 637, 638. [121] See chapter 1.

[122] S Rinnert, *Parallelimporte und TRIPs*, Mitteilungen der deutschen Patentanwälte (2001) 403, 407 ff; C Herrmann, 'TRIPS, Patentschutz für Medikamente und staatliche Gesundheitspolitik: Hinreichende Flexibilität?' (2002) EuZW 37, 41.

within the European Communities under Articles 30, 36 (now Articles 28, 30) of the EC Treaty.[123]

C The Choice is Left to Members

Most commentators[124] and some courts,[125] see Article 6 of the TRIPS Agreement as an 'agreement to disagree', leaving each WTO Member free to decide for itself whether to follow the principle of international exhaustion or not. Article 28 of the TRIPS Agreement does not prohibit such a system, as it refers to Article 6 in a foot-note. Nor do the principles of territoriality and independence imply that acts hap-pening abroad may not be taken into account in the application of national patent law—as is evident, for example, in establishing novelty.[126] The position is further buttressed by subsequent state practice with some Members, including both developing country Members such as Thailand and Indonesia,[127] and devel-oped country Members such as Switzerland[128] and Japan,[129] having adopted inter-national exhaustion and others following a rule of national exhaustion only.[130] The

---

[123] European Court of Justice, Case C-16/74 *Centrafarm BV v Winthrop BV* [1974] ECR 01183 (31 October 1974); European Court of Justice, Cases C-267/95, C-268/95 *Merck & Co Inc v Primecrown Ltd* [1996] ECR I-06285 (5 December 1996); European Court of Justice, Case C-9/93 *IHT Internationale Heiztechnik GmbH v Ideal-Standard GmbH* [1994] ECR I-02789 (22 June 1994); European Court of Justice, Case C-10/89 *SA CNL-Sucal NV v HAG GF AG* [1990] ECR I-03711 (17 October 1990).

[124] Kampf (n 110 above) 115 f; K Gamharter, *Access to Affordable Medicines. Developing Responses under the TRIPS Agreement and EC Law* (2004) 42–43; MCEJ Bronckers, 'The Exhaustion of Patent Rights under WTO Law' in MCEJ Bronckers (ed), *A Cross-Section of WTO Law* (2003) 157, 184; HC Jehoram, 'Prohibition of Parallel Imports Through Intellectual Property Rights' (1999) 30 IIC 495, 508; C Heath, 'Parallel Imports and International Trade' (1997) 28 IIC 623, 628 ff; FM Abbott, 'The TRIPS-Legality of Measures Taken to Address Public Health Crises: A Synopsis' (2001) 7 Widener L Symp J 71, 78–79; MM Slotboom, 'The Exhaustion of Intellectual Property Rights. Different Approaches in EC and WTO Law' (2003) 6 J World Intell Prop 421, 433; S Sołtysiński, 'International Exhaustion of Intellectual Property Rights under TRIPs, the EC Law and the Europe Agreements' (1996) GRUR Int 316, 318–319; CM Correa, *Intellectual Property Rights, the WTO, and Developing Countries. The TRIPS Agreement and Policy Options* (2000) 83; Freytag (n 117 above) 231, 235–236, 248; AW White, 'Sunglasses: A Benefit to Health' (1999) 21 EIPR 176, 179; JH Barton, 'Issues Posed by a World Patent System' (2004) 7 JIEL 341, 351.

[125] EFTA Court, *Mag Instrument Inc. v California Trading Company Norway, Ulsteen*, Case E-2/97 (3 December 1997); Bundesgericht (Switzerland), *Kodak SA v Jumbo-Markt AG*, 31 IIC 1018, 1022 (2000); note also BGH 32 IIC 685, 688 (2001).

[126] J Busche in J Busche and P-T Stoll (eds), *TRIPS* (2007) Art 2, para 10.

[127] N Gallus, 'The Mystery of Pharmaceutical Parallel Trade and Developing Countries' (2004) 7 J World Intell Prop 169, 176.

[128] Concerning trademarks and copyrights, not patents: Bundesgericht (Switzerland), *Kodak SA v Jumbo-Markt AG*, 31 IIC 1018, 1024, 1033 (2000); Bundesgericht (Switzerland), *Chanel SA*, 31 IIC 337 (2000).

[129] According to the court, a patent holder can prevent exhaustion by giving notice to subsequent purchasers of an import ban. T Hays, 'BBS Kraftfahrzeugtechnik AG v Rcimex Japan KK; JAP Auto Products KK. Japan Opens the Door to Parallel Imports of Patented Goods' (2001) 2 Melb J Int'l L 191.

[130] ICTSD and UNCTAD, *Resource Book on TRIPS and Development* (2002) pt 1, 103–104. The United States have repeatedly discussed whether to allow parallel imports of patented medicine from Canada, but so far have not reached a clear stance. S Ghosh, 'Pills, Patents, and Power: State Creation of Gray Markets as a Limit on Patent Rights' (2001) 53 Fla L Rev 789, 793–794, 807 ff.

European Union and the *Organisation Africaine de la Propriété Intellectuelle* (OAPI) occupy a peculiar position in the debate as they apply a system of regional exhaustion.[131] The history of Article 6 of the TRIPS Agreement, too, confirms an agreement to disagree: whereas the US delegation favoured a rule of national exhaustion only, many developing countries wanted to adopt a rule of international exhaustion. The parties could solely admit their failure to reach agreement.[132]

The right to access to medicine supports the position of leaving WTO Members to choose the right approach for themselves. Only this approach allows developing country Members to opt for international exhaustion and developed country Members to only apply national exhaustion. While this additional argument is helpful for advocates, its fundamental flaw is apparent: it is not dispositive. A Member that regards Article 28.1 of the TRIPS Agreement as conclusively establishing the patent holder's right to prohibit parallel imports will hardly be swayed by the additional argument and might still exert pressure on a Member wishing to adopt a rule of international exhaustion.

2 Limited Exceptions

The second TRIPS flexibility is provided for in Article 30 of the TRIPS Agreement which states that:

Members may provide limited exceptions to the exclusive rights conferred by a patent, provided that such exceptions do not unreasonably conflict with a normal exploitation of the patent and do not unreasonably prejudice the legitimate interests of the patent owner, taking account of the legitimate interests of third parties.

The provision allows for exceptions to the rights of a granted patent.[133] As the heading of Article 31 of the TRIPS Agreement ('Other Use Without Authorization of the Right Holder') and its footnote ('"Other use" refers to use other than that allowed under Article 30') indicate, the exceptions of Article 30 apply without authorization of the patent holder. Accordingly, they can limit the effects of a patent monopoly and hence lower the prices of the product to some extent. The precise

---

[131] An intellectual property rights holder exhausts its rights for the whole European Economic Area if the product is placed on the market within this Area by itself or with its consent, but not if it is placed on the market outside of the Area. Article 7 of the First Council Directive (EE) 89/104 of 21 December 1988 to Approximate the Laws of the Member States Relating to Trade Marks, European Court of Justice, Case C-355/96 *Silhouette International Schmied GmbH & Co. KG v Hartlauer Handelsgesellschaft mbH* [1998] ECR I-04799 (16 July 1998); European Court of Justice, Case C-173/98 *Sebago Inc v G-B Unic SA* [1999] ECR I-04103 (1 July 1999); M Hann, '*Silhouette v Hartlauer*—Fortress Europe?' (1998) 1 J World Intell Prop 809; J Pagenberg, 'The Exhaustion Principle and "Silhouette" Case' (1999) 30 IIC 19; M Meulenbelt, 'Parallel Imports of Medicinal Products—A New Balance?' (1998) 1 J World Intell Prop 525; C Heath, 'Parallel Imports of Patented Pharmaceuticals from the New EU Accession States' (2004) 35 IIC 776. For OAPI: T Kongolo, 'The New OAPI Agreement as Revised in February 1999. Complying with TRIPs' (2000) 3 J World Intell Prop 717, 720.   [132] F Höhne in J Busche and P-T Stoll (eds), *TRIPs* (2007) Art 6, para 4.
[133] ICTSD and UNCTAD (n 130 above) pt 2.5, 94.

scope of the permissible exceptions is hard to gauge as the wording of the provision is notoriously vague.[134] It is this vague wording that would provide an apt entry point for the right to access to medicine. However, the Panel in *Canada—Patent Protection of Pharmaceutical Products* (*Canada—Patent*)[135] failed to take the right into account in its interpretation of the provision, even though it did consider the objectives of the TRIPS Agreement, ie Articles 7, 8 of the TRIPS Agreement.[136] At issue in the case were two provisions of the Canadian Patent Act: the first was a Bolar exemption,[137] allowing competitors of the patent holder to take the necessary action during the patent term to obtain approval for marketing their product in Canada or abroad, so they could start selling the product immediately upon the expiration of the patent term. The second was a stockpiling exception, allowing competitors who invoked the Bolar exemption to manufacture and stockpile the patented goods during a period of six months before the expiration of the patent, so that they had a sufficient amount of goods on stock when they could start marketing the product.[138] The Panel held that Article 30 establishes three criteria that a measure must meet to qualify for the exception: (i) it must be 'limited', (ii) it must not 'unreasonably conflict with a normal exploitation of the patent', and (iii) it must not 'unreasonably prejudice the legitimate interests of the patent owner, taking account of the legitimate interests of third parties'. Each of the three terms must be presumed to mean something different to avoid redundancy.[139]

A Limited

The Panel adopted a very narrow definition of the term 'limited', arguing that 'exception' already implies a limited derogation which is narrowed even further by the word 'limited'. The limited character is determined by reference to the limitation of the exclusive rights granted under Article 28 of the TRIPS Agreement rather than by the economic impact of the exception, which is examined under the other conditions of Article 30 of the TRIPS Agreement.[140] The Panel concluded that the stockpiling exception was not limited, as it allowed competitors to 'make' and 'use' the patented product during the last six months of the patent term without imposing any limitation on the production of goods. The Bolar exemption, on the other hand, was limited, as it only allowed very few acts of making and using the patented product, namely those necessary for the regulatory approval process.[141]

Howse has rightly criticized the panel's holding as unduly narrow. The panel's reliance on the narrow scope of exceptions is in direct contradiction both to a statement by the Appellate Body that the mere characterization as an exception

---

[134] J Straus, 'Bedeutung des TRIPS für das Patentrecht' (1996) GRUR Int 179, 199.
[135] WT/DS114/R (2000). See *United States—Section 110 (5) of the US Copyright Act*, WT/DS160/R (2000) on the similar Art 13 of the TRIPS Agreement in the area of copyrights.
[136] *Canada—Patent* (n 135 above) paras 7.23 ff; see chapter 2.   [137] See chapter 2.
[138] *Canada—Patent* (n 135 above) paras 7.2 ff.
[139] *Canada—Patent* (n 135 above) paras 7.20 ff.
[140] *Canada—Patent* (n 135 above) paras 7.27 ff.
[141] *Canada—Patent* (n 135 above) paras 7.34 ff.

does not in and of itself justify a narrower interpretation of a provision[142] and to the principle of *in dubio mitius*.[143] The Panel should have departed from the dictionary definition of 'limited' as 'confined within limits'[144] and, taking account of both Articles 7, 8 of the TRIPS Agreement and the right to access to medicine, allowed exceptions that are narrowly tailored to achieve the purposes laid down in Articles 7 and 8.[145]

B Conflict with Normal Exploitation

The measure also must not unreasonably conflict with a normal exploitation of the patent. 'Exploitation' refers to the commercial activity of the patent owner to extract economic value from the patent. The term 'normal' could relate to normative standards or empirical findings. The Panel held the term to include both notions.[146] At its core, the 'normal exploitation' consists of the right to exclude competition during the patent term. The Panel went further and considered a period of market exclusivity after the expiration of the patent term to be part of the normal exploitation, as competitors need some time to build an inventory before they can enter the market.[147] In contrast, it considered the additional period of market exclusivity gained because of a regulatory approval process not to be part of the normal exploitation of the patent, so that a Bolar exemption does not conflict with the normal exploitation.[148]

The Panel's holding on the 'normal exploitation' prong is surprisingly one-sided, including only considerations on the side of the patent holder for the definition of what is 'normal'. Including access to medicine in its considerations it could well have held the exploitation after the expiration of the patent term not to be normal and hence allowed the stockpiling of medicine.[149] The one-sided holding can be compensated by a proper interpretation of 'unreasonably', for even measures in conflict with a normal exploitation are permissible if they do not unreasonably conflict with that exploitation. The dictionary defines 'unreasonable' as 'exceeding the bounds of reason or moderation'.[150] In determining whether a measure exceeds these bounds the right to access to medicine must be taken into account.

C Prejudice Legitimate Interests

Finally, the measure may not 'unreasonably prejudice the legitimate interests of the patent owner, taking account of the legitimate interests of third parties'. Rejecting

---

[142] *EC Measures Concerning Meat and Meat Products (Hormones)*, WT/DS26/AB/R, WT/DS48/AB/R, 38 (1998) (*EC—Hormones*).
[143] R Howse, 'The Canadian Generic Medicines Panel. A Dangerous Precedent in Dangerous Times' (2000) 3 J World Intell Prop 493, 496 ff.   [144] Mish *et al* (eds) (n 67 above).
[145] Howse (n 143 above) 496 ff; ICTSD and UNCTAD (n 130 above) pt 2.5, 97.
[146] *Canada—Patent* (n 135 above) para 7.54.
[147] *Canada—Patent* (n 135 above) para 7.56.
[148] *Canada—Patent* (n 135 above) para 7.57.
[149] Howse (n 143 above) 498 ff; ICTSD and UNCTAD (n 130 above) pt 2.5, 98–99; C Dommen, 'Raising Human Rights Concerns in the World Trade Organization: Actors, Processes and Possible Strategies' (2002) 24 Hum Rts Q 1, 27.   [150] Mish *et al* (eds) (n 67 above).

the European Communities' claim that 'legitimate interests' are legal interests the Panel ultimately considered 'legitimate' to play on the moral and ethical rather than legal field.[151] Peculiarly, the Panel seems to be of the view that with this argument it can brush aside the patent holder's interests under Article 27 of the TRIPS Agreement, which would imply that a legal interest cannot be legitimate. The Panel then considered the interest of the patent holder in obtaining a compensation for the time it lost in obtaining administrative approval, particularly where the competitor does not lose any such time. It concluded that these interests were not so compelling or widely recognized as to be 'legitimate' interests.[152]

The Panel's reasoning is not convincing. Its exclusive focus on the interests of the patent holder and its inquiry whether these interests are compelling, absent any basis for such a requirement, seem to indicate that it will let the rights holder's interests prevail where these are compelling.[153] The open-ended character of 'legitimate' should have opened the discussion to other values, such as access to medicine and the considerations of Articles 7, 8 of the TRIPS Agreement.[154] In a next step, a panel would have to establish whether the legitimate interests of the patent holder have been 'unreasonably prejudiced', taking account of legitimate interests of third parties, of which access to medicine indubitably is one.[155]

D *Article 27 of the TRIPS Agreement and Its Scope*

The most contested part of the holding of *Canada—Patent* concerns the rule of non-discrimination contained in Article 27.1 of the TRIPS Agreement. It states that 'patents shall be available and patent rights enjoyable without discrimination as to the place of invention, the field of technology and whether products are imported or locally produced'. Canada had argued that the non-discrimination rule itself was subject to the exception of Article 30 of the TRIPS Agreement and it could thus establish separate rules for the field of pharmaceuticals. The Panel, however, held otherwise and considered the rule of non-discrimination to apply to measures taken under Articles 30 and 31 of the TRIPS Agreement. It reasoned that the non-discrimination rule does not just cover the grant, but also the enjoyment of patent rights and that there is no indication that it does not apply to Articles 30 and 31. The *travaux préparatoires* show that the non-discrimination rule was adopted to prevent automatic compulsory licences on pharmaceuticals and it hence must be applicable to Article 31—and therefore also to Article 30, which is closely linked to Article 31.[156]

---

[151] *Canada—Patent* (n 135 above) para 7.68 ff.

[152] *Canada—Patent* (n 135 above) para 7.82.   [153] Howse (n 143 above) 501 ff.

[154] It also opens the discussion up to the question of whether the patent holder's rights are legitimate. This can be questionable where a drug was developed almost exclusively by the government. PL Wojahn, 'A Conflict of Rights: Intellectual Property Under TRIPS, the Right to Health and AIDS Drugs' (2001–2002) 6 UCLA J Int'l L & Foreign Aff 463, 488.

[155] P Rott, 'TRIPS-Abkommen, Menschenrechte, Sozialpolitik und Entwicklungsländer' (2003) GRUR Int 103, 116; Rott (n 109 above) 262 ff.

[156] *Canada—Patent* (n 135 above) paras 7.88 ff; PT Stoll and K Raible, 'Schutz geistigen Eigentums und das TRIPS-Abkommen' in H-J Prieß, GM Berrisch and C Pitschas (eds), *WTO-Handbuch* (2003) 565, 593.

Commentators have treated this reasoning less than kindly.[157] Exceptions generally apply to the obligations they are meant to except from and anything to the contrary must be contained in the rule, ie in Article 27 of the TRIPS Agreement, and not the other way around.[158] Other exceptions in the WTO Agreements also except from all obligations, eg Article XX of the GATT without further ado justifies a breach of both obligations under Articles I and III of the GATT. Recourse to the *travaux préparatoires* is premature, as according to Article 32 of the Vienna Convention the negotiation history only serves as a subsidiary source of treaty interpretation.

Yet, the Panel did not forbid all discrimination as to the field of technology: as discussed in chapter 2, the Panel distinguished permissible differential treatment and impermissible discrimination. This holding allows Members to react to problems that arise only in specific areas of technology. The right to health provides Members with an argument that health concerns and accessibility of medicine require special regulation in the area of pharmaceuticals.[159] However, it provides for very little legal certainty in this respect, as it is unclear to what extent Members may provide for differential treatment.

E Examples of Measures under Article 30 of the TRIPS Agreement

Because of the vagueness of Article 30 of the TRIPS Agreement, it is helpful to illustrate its scope by some of the exceptions commonly cited as permissible under it. The most common such provision certainly is the Bolar exemption. Other permissible exceptions are the preparations of drugs by pharmacies to fill single prescriptions,[160] the prior use exception,[161] and the experimental use exception, which exempts experimental uses from patent infringement and allows science to progress despite the fact that a technology is patented.[162] Private non-commercial

---

[157] FM Abbott, 'The TRIPS Agreement, Access to Medicines and the WTO Doha Ministerial Conference' Quaker United Nations Office Occasional Paper 7 (2001) 22–23 (also published as FM Abbott, 'The TRIPS Agreement, Access to Medicines and the WTO Doha Ministerial Conference' (2002) 5 J World Intell Prop 15 and FM Abbott, 'The TRIPS Agreement, Access to Medicines and the WTO Doha Ministerial Conference' Florida State University College of Law Public Law and Legal Theory Working Paper No 36 (2001)); D Shanker, 'The Vienna Convention on the Law of Treaties, the Dispute Settlement System of the WTO and the Doha Declaration on the TRIPS Agreement' (2002) 36 JWT 721, 745.

[158] Howse (n 143 above) 506; Kampf alleges that Art 30 of the TRIPS Agreement spells out that it is an exception to Art 28 of the TRIPS Agreement and fails to do so with respect to Art 27 of the TRIPS Agreement. However, there is nothing in Art 30 of the TRIPS Agreement that would restrict its effect to Art 28 of the TRIPS Agreement. Kampf (n 110 above) 106.

[159] K Stegemann and B Pzderka, 'The TRIPS Agreement as an Alliance for Knowledge Production. The Funding of Pharmaceutical Innovation' (2003) 6 J World Intell Prop 529, 541.

[160] G Velásquez and P Boulet, 'Globalization and Access to Drugs: Implications of the WTO/TRIPS Agreement' in WHO (ed), *Globalization and Access to Drugs. Perspectives on the WTO/TRIPS Agreement* (2nd edn, 1999) 1, 33.   [161] Rott (n 109 above) 272–273.

[162] The exception was first mentioned by Justice Story in *Whittemore v Cutter* 29 F Cas 1120, 1121 (CCD Mass, 1813). On the exception in Germany W von Meibom and J Pitz, 'Experimental Use, Patent Infringement—A Transatlantic Review from the German Perspective in Regard to the Decision of the German Supreme Court in *Ortho v Merckle, "Clinical Trial II"*' (1998) 1 J World

use by individuals—mainly the import of patented drugs from other Members, can also be legalized under Article 30 of the TRIPS Agreement.[163]

However, the narrow interpretation of the provision by the *Canada—Patent* Panel would not permit an exception under Article 30 that could meaningfully enhance access to medicine in the developing world, such as governmental non-commercial use—permitting the government to produce the medicine and to provide it to large parts of the population.[164]

3 Compulsory Licences

A more likely candidate for lowering drug prices below the original manufac-turer's price are compulsory licences, ie licences granted by the government without the consent of the patent holder, permitting someone else (or the govern-ment itself, which is then called 'government use')[165] to produce the patented product or use the process and thus creating competition. Such a licence is directed to a single, identified patent and benefits an identified authorized party.[166] It can serve three goals: (1) safeguarding the supply of the domestic market with a patented product; (2) promoting competition by creating domestic competitors; or (3) promoting a domestic industry.[167]

Compulsory licences were one of the most contentious topics during the negotiations of the TRIPS Agreement. Developing countries were in favour of giving governments broad powers to grant compulsory licences and could sup-port their view with the former practice of Canada and the United Kingdom to grant compulsory licences on pharmaceuticals automatically or near automat-ically.[168] Developed countries took a restrictive approach with the United States initially proposing a near-total ban on such licences.[169] Ultimately, the two sides

---

Intell Prop 633 and BGH 28 IIC 103 ('Klinische Versuche') (1997); for Japan Tokyo High Court 30 IIC 454 (1999). SF Ferman, 'Argentina: The New Patent Law and the Agreement on Trade Related Aspects of Intellectual Property Right (TRIPS)' (2001) 8 Sw J L & Trade Am 157, 169; RS Eisenberg, 'Patents and the Progress of Science: Exclusive Rights and Experimental Use' (1989) 56 U Chi L Rev 1017.

  [163] Rott (n 109 above) 269–270. See Art 60 of the TRIPS Agreement.

  [164] Rott (n 109 above) 270 ff, 273 ff; PJ Hammer, 'Differential Pricing of Essential AIDS Drugs: Markets, Politics and Public Health' (2002) 5 JIEL 883, 911. *Contra*, suggesting a programme for dis-tributing AIDS drugs under a public health licence AM Curti, 'The WTO Dispute Settlement Understanding: An Unlikely Weapon in the Fight Against AIDS' (2001) 27 Am J L & Medicine, 469.

  [165] Strictly speaking, government use and compulsory licensing are different legal constructions. However, as the TRIPS Agreement deals with both in one provision without a general distinction, the presentation will follow the example.

  [166] WTO, *TRIPS and Pharmaceutical Patents. Fact Sheet*, 4 (2006); ICTSD and UNCTAD (n 130 above) pt 2.5, 122; C Ridder, *Die Bedeutung von Zwangslizenzen im Rahmen des TRIPS-Abkommens* (2004) 54 ff.   [167] Rott (n 109 above) 276.

  [168] F-K Beier, 'Exclusive Rights, Statutory Licenses and Compulsory Licenses in Patent and Utility Model Law' (1999) 30 IIC 251, 259–260.

  [169] F Höhne in J Busche and P-T Stoll (eds), *TRIPs* (2007) Art 31, para 3.

compromised on the wording contained in Article 31 of the TRIPS Agreement that covers:

other use [than that permitted by Article 30 of the TRIPS Agreement] of the subject matter of a patent without the authorization of the right holder, including use by the government or third parties authorized by the government.

Hence, where a measure fails to be justified under Article 30 of TRIPS Agreement, it has to be examined under Article 31.[170] This is the case with compulsory licences.[171] This section will examine the law of compulsory licences as it still is in force at the time of writing. The amendment to the TRIPS Agreement already decided by the General Council will be described below.

The majority of patent laws in Western industrialized countries contain provisions on the grant of compulsory licences.[172] The United States, too, makes use of compulsory licences to promote the availability of technology, albeit in a limited manner:[173] statutes permit compulsory licences for inventions relating to atomic energy,[174] and air pollution control.[175] In addition, courts have granted compulsory licences in antitrust cases.[176] Commentators mentioning the limited use of compulsory licences in the United States often fail to mention that government use by the United States is far more expansive.[177]

Even though they are no panacea for the lack of access to medicine,[178] compulsory licences are a valuable tool in promoting such access. They are not only indispensable when a patent holder refuses to supply a market at all, often the mere

---

[170] *Contra* D Gervais, *The TRIPS Agreement. Drafting History and Analysis* (2nd edn, 2003) Art 30, para 2.293 who regards Art 31 of the TRIPS Agreement as the more specialized rule. However, the wording suggests that Art 30 of the TRIPS Agreement has to be examined first.

[171] WTO (n 166 above); SM Ford, 'Compulsory Licensing Provisions Under the TRIPs Agreement: Balancing Pills and Patents' (2000) 15 Am U Int'l L Rev 941, 949; Herrmann (n 122 above) 39; Ridder (n 166 above) 68.

[172] According to Correa overall 96 countries allow for compulsory licences. CM Correa, 'Patent Rights' in CM Correa and AA Yusuf, *Intellectual Property and International Trade: The TRIPs Agreement* (1998) 189, 208. Nevertheless, in many Western countries such grants are rare occurrences. For example, see the *Bundesgerichtshof's* demands imposed on a sufficient public interest to justify a compulsory licence in BGH 28 IIC 242 (1997).

[173] JA Yosick, 'Compulsory Patent Licensing for Efficient Use of Inventions' (2001) 2001 U Ill L Rev 1275, 1278–1279.   [174] 42 USC § 2183 (Atomic Energy Act).

[175] 42 USC § 7608 (Clean Air Act).   [176] Beier (n 168 above) 264.

[177] The legal construction of government use is complex: the doctrine of sovereign immunity insulates the US government from lawsuits unless it consents to such suits. It has done so where a patented invention 'is used or manufactured by or for the United States without license of the owner thereof or lawful right to use or manufacture the same'. In such cases the patent holder can sue the United States in the US Claims Court for the recovery of 'his reasonable and entire compensation'. 28 USC § 1498(a). Hence, where a patent is violated by the US government or one of its contractors, an injunction is not available, merely a suit for compensation. DM Schlitz and RJ McGrath, 'Patent Infringement Claims against the United States Government' (2000) 9 Fed Circuit BJ 351, 353; RJ McGrath, 'The Unauthorized Use of Patents by the United States Government or its Contractors' (1991) 18 AIPLA QJ 349, 352; DR Cahoy, 'Treating the Legal Side Effects of CIPRO®: A Reevelution of Compensation Rules for Government Takings of Patent Rights' (2002) 40 Am Bus LJ 125.

[178] Kampf (n 110 above) 102; G Curci and M Vittori, 'Improving Access to Life-Saving Patented Drugs. Between Compulsory Licensing and Differential Pricing' (2004) 7 J World Intell Prop 739, 754.

threat by a government to grant a compulsory licence, even the mere existence of a governmental power to grant such a licence, will coerce the patent holder into reducing the price,[179] as demonstrated by the example of *Cipro* described in chapter 1. Consequently, the Commission on Intellectual Property Rights advised developing countries to make use of compulsory licensing to the extent allowed under the TRIPS Agreement.[180]

A Grounds for Granting Compulsory Licences

The TRIPS Agreement does not contain any explicit limitations for the grounds on which a compulsory licence may be granted.[181] Some authors argue, nevertheless, that compulsory licences may only be granted in cases of abuse of the patent, deducing this requirement from Article 5A(2) of the Paris Convention, applicable via Article 2.1 of the TRIPS Agreement, which permits Members to grant compulsory licences to 'prevent the abuses which might result from the exercise of the exclusive rights conferred by the patent'.[182] Others consider Article 8.1 of the TRIPS Agreement to limit the grounds of compulsory licences, requiring Members to demonstrate that the grant of a compulsory licence is necessary in the light of the public interest.[183]

The majority are of the view that Members are at liberty to determine the grounds for which compulsory licences are granted, so that compulsory licences for pharmaceutical patents could be granted for a number of reasons.[184] As the German *Bundesgerichtshof* states, Article 5A(2) of the Paris Convention clarifies that countries may impose compulsory licences for abuses, particularly for failure to work a patent. It does not prohibit the grant of compulsory licences on other grounds, eg in the public interest.[185] Article 8 of the TRIPS Agreement does not purport to limit the freedom of Members to take measures, its purpose is on the

---

[179] Beier (n 168 above) 260; Ridder (n 166 above) 65 f; C May, 'Why IPRs are a Global Political Issue' (2003) 25 EIPR 1, 4–5; Brazil's 2005 threat to impose a compulsory licence succeeded in making the producer sell the drug at issue at reduced prices. T Benson, 'Brazil and U.S. Maker Reach Deal on AIDS Drug' *NY Times* (9 July 2005).

[180] Commission on Intellectual Property Rights (n 116 above) 44.

[181] For semi-conductors, however, note Art 31(c) of the TRIPS Agreement.

[182] Straus (n 134 above) 199; Kampf (n 110 above) 103; Abbott (n 124 above) 74. RP Rozek and RL Rainey, 'Broad-Based Compulsory Licensing of Pharmaceutical Technologies. Unsound Public Policy' (2001) 4 J World Intell Prop 459, 468 list the grounds of compulsory licences mentioned in Art 31 of the TRIPS Agreement as the only permissible grounds. There is nothing in the wording of the provision that justifies such a restriction.

[183] ER Gold and DK Lam, 'Balancing Trade in Patents—Public Non-Commercial Use and Compulsory Licensing' (2003) 6 J World Intell Prop 5, 22–23; Herrmann (n 122 above) 39.

[184] T Cottier, 'TRIPS, the Doha Declaration and Public Health' (2003) 6 J World Intell Prop 385, 386; Gervais (n 170 above) Art 31, para 2.305; P Champ and A Attaran, 'Patent Rights and Local Working Under the WTO TRIPS Agreement: An Analysis of the U.S.-Brazil Patent Dispute' (2002) 27 Yale J Int'l L 365, 384; A Staehelin, *Das TRIPs-Abkommen. Immaterialgüterrecht im Licht der globalisierten Handelspolitik* (2nd edn, 1999) 151; M Blakeney, *Trade Related Aspects of Intellectual Property Rights: A Concise Guide to the TRIPS Agreement* (1996) para 8.22.

[185] BGH 28 IIC 242, 246 (1997); WIPO, *Introduction to Intellectual Property. Theory and Practice*, paras 7.173 ff (1997); Rott (n 109 above) 280.

contrary to clarify that the TRIPS Agreement is not supposed to prevent Members from taking certain measures. To impose a necessity test on Members for all measures in the public interest would go against both the wording and the spirit of the provision.

The majority view is consistent with the right to access to medicine. Chapter 4 demonstrated that the price level is not just raised by the abuse of patents, but by the mere normal exploitation of patent rights. Compulsory licences can lower the prices and hence improve access to medicine where problems arise.

a Local Working Requirements and Article 27 of the TRIPS Agreement

While there is no enumeration of permissible grounds for the grant of compulsory licences, the non-discrimination rule of Article 27.1 of the TRIPS Agreement is argued, by some, to be applicable to compulsory licences and ban grounds that would discriminate as to the place of invention, the field of technology, and as to whether products are imported or locally produced. The application of the rule would first of all limit, but not totally eliminate, a country's ability to create technology-specific rules, eg for pharmaceutical patents. Secondly, it would prohibit so-called 'local working requirements'. This concept demands some explanation.

'Failure to work' a patent is a commonly discussed ground for the grant of a compulsory licence. Members clearly may grant a compulsory licence if the patent holder fails to bring the patented product to the market, a situation that raises particular concern where essential drugs are concerned. Article 5A(2) of the Paris Convention states in this respect that:

[e]ach country of the Union shall have the right to take legislative measures providing for the grant of compulsory licenses to prevent the abuses which might result from the exercise of the exclusive rights conferred by the patent, for example, failure to work.[186]

According to paragraph 4 of the same article, such a licence may not be applied for 'before the expiration of a period of four years from the date of filing of the patent application or three years from the date of the grant of the patent, whichever period expires last'. The patent holder can justify its inaction with legitimate reasons—such as the inability to commence working the patent due to the requirement of obtaining administrative approval.[187] A local working requirement goes further and provides for the grant of a compulsory licence for failure to work the patent *locally*, ie it requires the patent holder to manufacture the patented good in the country of the patent grant rather than to merely import it. Local working requirements used to be a feature of many national patent laws[188] and hark back to the historical function of patents to ensure the introduction of knowledge in the territory of the patent grant.[189] Nowadays, they are of particular

---

[186] The wording of the provision indicates that failure to work is an example of an abuse of the patent rights—hence, a separate showing of abuse is not required. Rott (n 109 above) 291.
[187] Rott (n 109 above) 291.   [188] Champ and Attaran (n 184 above) 366.
[189] See chapter 2.

interest to developing countries, as these often cannot ensure the introduction of
know-how in their territory by the disclosure requirement alone, but instead need
the patent holder to transfer technology by producing in the country. Local working requirements provide an incentive for such local production by threatening to
impose a compulsory licence. As Article 27.1 of the TRIPS Agreement states that
patent rights shall be enjoyable without discrimination as to whether products are
imported or locally produced, its application in the field of compulsory licences
would impose that any working requirement can be fulfilled entirely by
imports[190] and thus render local working requirements illegal.

The permissibility of local working requirements under the TRIPS Agreement
was raised in dispute settlement in 2000, when the Brazilian Patent Act establishing such a requirement[191] was the subject of a request for the establishment of a
WTO panel by the United States.[192] However, the dispute was resolved by a
mutually agreed solution. Commentators who oppose the permissibility of such
requirements have strong arguments on their side. The *Canada—Patent* Panel
held Article 27.1 of the TRIPS Agreement to apply to measures under Article 31
of the TRIPS Agreement.[193] The applicability of the non-discrimination rule is
also supported by Article 70.6 of the TRIPS Agreement, which grandfathers
compulsory licences already granted by Members with respect to both Article 31
and non-discrimination as to field of technology (Article 27.1 of the TRIPS
Agreement), thus implying that Article 27.1 applies to compulsory licences.

Other commentators strongly reject the application of the non-discrimination
rule to compulsory licences. In practice, such an application would lead to the
curious result that a patent law allowing the grant of compulsory licences for failure to work locally would be in violation of the TRIPS Agreement, whereas a
much broader law allowing for the grant of a compulsory licence on any ground
would be permissible.[194] Preferably, Article 31 and Article 30 of the TRIPS
Agreement have to be regarded as exceptions to the rules of Article 27 of the
TRIPS Agreement and therefore as not subject to the non-discrimination rule
imposed therein.[195] Article 5A(2) of the Paris Convention, which explicitly allows
compulsory licences for 'failure to work', also supports this position: the provision

---

[190] Straus (n 134 above) 200; Rott (n 109 above) 292; Kampf (n 110 above) 103; JJ Gorlin, *An Analysis of the Pharmaceutical-Related Provisions of the WTO TRIPS (Intellectual Property) Agreement* (1999) 22.

[191] Article 68(1) Lei da Propriedade Industrial N 9.279 de 14 de Maio de 1996, effective 15 May 1997. Brazil is not the only country providing for a local working requirement. Similar requirements exist, eg in the patent laws of Egypt, Morocco, and Tunisia. T Kongolo, 'Compulsory Licence Issues in African Arab Countries' (2004) 7 J World Intell Prop 185, 192, 195, 198.

[192] *Brazil—Measures Affecting Patent Protection. Request for the Establishment of a Panel by the United States*, WT/DS199/3 (2001).

[193] *Canada—Patent* (n 135 above) paras 7.88 ff; Stoll and Raible (n 156 above) 594.

[194] Champ and Attaran (n 184 above) 392; Gorlin (n 190 above) 22 (explicitly accepting this consequence).

[195] Champ and Attaran (n 184 above) 367. For a discussion of the scope of Art 27.1 of the TRIPS Agreement see the section on Art 30 of the TRIPS Agreement in this chapter above.

strengthened the rights of patent holders, as, before, many countries had provided for the forfeiture of a patent if it was not worked locally. Now, states could only provide for compulsory licences. States Parties remained free to define 'failure to work', but normally working is understood to mean working the patent industrially, ie by manufacturing the product rather than by importation or sale.[196] The object of technology transfer[197] also supports the permissibility of local working requirements, although local working of inventions does not make economic sense in Members the internal market of which is too small to provide the required economies of scale to support a domestic manufacturing base.

The right to access to medicine can again be used to support the permissibility of more flexibility. In developing countries with a sufficiently large domestic market forcing companies to work pharmaceutical patents locally would improve the manufacturing base for essential pharmaceuticals and thus their accessibility. However, again access to medicine is only one argument amongst several.

b Commonly Suggested Grounds

Even though the grounds for the grant of compulsory licences are not limited, it is helpful to give some examples of commonly discussed grounds. Article 31 of the TRIPS Agreement itself mentions a number of grounds: national emergencies or other circumstances of extreme urgency, public non-commercial use, refusal to deal (lit b of the Article), the grant as a remedy for a practice determined after judicial or administrative process to be anti-competitive (lit c, k),[198] or where a patent cannot be exploited without infringing another patent (so-called 'dependent patents', lit l).[199] Other common grounds are the public interest in the patented invention,[200] an insufficient supply of the patented product, new diseases, or the refusal of the patent holder to either work or license the patent.[201] All of these grounds are also relevant in the field of pharmaceutical patents. Additionally, Members can

[196] GHC Bodenhausen, *Guide to the Application of the Paris Convention for the Protection of Industrial Property As Revised at Stockholm in 1967* (1968) 71; WIPO (n 185 above) para 7.156; M Halewood, 'Regulating Patent Holder: Local Working Requirements and Compulsory Licenses at International Law' (1997) 35 Osgoode Hall L J 243, 267.

[197] Preamble and Art 7, 66.2 of the TRIPS Agreement.

[198] This provision provides an opportunity for NGOs to promote the accessibility of drugs by commencing competition proceedings. JM Berger, 'Litigation Strategies to Gain Access to Treatment for HIV/AIDS: The Case of South Africa's Treatment Action Campaign' (2001–2002) 20 Wis Int'l L J 595, 607.

[199] These are subject to additional conditions contained in Art 31 (l) of the TRIPS Agreement that are outside the scope of this study.

[200] This is the case in German patent law (§ 24 (1) No 2 PatentG). Under German law, the grant of a compulsory licence can be warranted not only in the case of abuse of a patent, but also for social or medicinal reasons. R Kraßer, *Patentrecht* (5th edn, 2004) 857 ff, 861 ff.

[201] WHO, *Network for Monitoring the Impact of Globalization and TRIPS on Access to Medicines*, Health Economics and Drugs EDM Series No 11, 18 (2002); Correa (n 172 above) 213.

explicitly provide for compulsory licensing on public health grounds—permitting the grant of compulsory licences, eg where a medicine plays an essential role in health policy.[202]

B Procedure of the Grant

While not limiting the grounds for the grant of compulsory licences, the TRIPS Agreement attaches several explicit conditions to such a grant.[203]

a Authorization on Individual Merits

The first of these is that the 'authorization of such use [of the subject matter of a patent without the authorization of the right holder] shall be considered on its individual merits'.[204] Before the grant of a compulsory licence, the individual case has to be considered; hence automatic compulsory licences for all pharmaceuticals are not permissible.[205]

The wording of the provision does, however, allow some flexibility for constructing a compulsory licensing system, an interpretation that is, again, supported by the right to access to medicine. Thus, a law establishing a presumption in favour of the grant of a compulsory licence in the public interest for essential drugs is permissible if the authority granting the licence still has to consider each case individually.[206] Also, the provision permits the commencement of compulsory licensing procedures both by competitors and *ex officio*. The latter procedure has the advantage that competitors do not have to go through costly and lengthy proceedings. It was used in Thailand between 1992 and 1999, where a body examined the availability of patented pharmaceuticals on the Thai market and—where necessary—granted compulsory licences.[207]

b Prior Negotiations

Furthermore, the proposed beneficiary of the compulsory licence has to have made 'efforts to obtain authorization from the right holder on reasonable commercial terms and conditions' before the grant of the licence and these efforts have to have failed 'within a reasonable period of time'.[208]

---

[202] Velásquez and Boulet (n 160 above) 35. Eg France, Egypt, Morocco, and Tunisia provide for such grounds (Arts 613–16 Code de la Propriété Intellectuelle, Kongolo (n 191 above) 190, 193, 195, 197).

[203] The TRIPS Agreement's general provisions on procedure in Arts 42 ff, 62 are outside the scope of the study and will not be discussed.   [204] Article 31(a) of the TRIPS Agreement.

[205] Ridder (n 166 above) 90.

[206] ICTSD and UNCTAD (n 130 above) pt 2.5, 129, regarding the consideration of individual merits after the grant of the licence as sufficient in reliance on the US rules on government use. That interpretation, however, clearly contradicts the TRIPS Agreement, implying that the US rules on government use are in violation of the Agreement.

[207] Rott (n 109 above) 282 f; K Timmermans and T Hutadjulu, *The TRIPS Agreement and Pharmaceuticals. Report of an ASEAN Workshop on the TRIPs Agreement and its Impact on Pharmaceuticals. Jakarta 2–4 May 2000* (2000) 36.   [208] Article 31(b) of the TRIPS Agreement.

aa The Requirement of Prior Negotiations   The terms of this requirement, in particular the definition of 'reasonable commercial terms and conditions', are deliberately vague, allowing the circumstances of the case in question to be taken into account. Reasonable terms for licensing vary from industry to industry and from invention to invention,[209] as does the length of the 'reasonable period of time'. The reasonability requirement also provides an entry point for the right to access to medicine: where a patent holder delays negotiations to prevent the grant of a compulsory licence the 'reasonable period' has ended, where the conditions imposed are unduly cumbersome, they are unreasonable.

bb Waiver of the Requirement   A Member may waive the requirement of prior negotiations (i) in the case of a national emergency or other circumstances of extreme urgency (instead, the right holder only need to be notified 'as soon as reasonably practicable'), (ii) in the case of public non-commercial use (with a notification obligation only in certain cases),[210] (iii) where the use is permitted to remedy a practice determined after judicial or administrative process to be anti-competitive.[211] Thus, in these three cases a 'fast track procedure' is established. All three exceptions are relevant for pharmaceuticals. Particularly the first two deserve some explanation.

While the fast-track procedure for national emergencies or other circumstances of extreme urgency at a first glance seems to be custom-made for access to medicine, arguments can go either way:[212] the term 'emergency' implies both a situation with possibly grave consequences and the need for a quick reaction, 'extreme urgency' also refers to situations requiring a speedy reaction. The effect of the provision, namely the waiver of the negotiation requirement, implies that the situation has to be such that there is no time for negotiations with the patent holder. Given that some commentators want the provision to be read narrowly,[213] it could be argued that the provision was not introduced for longer-term problems, such as pandemics. However, it is unclear why the provision needs to be read narrowly. The general principles of interpretation apply. Access to medicine supports a broad interpretation, according to which grave diseases constitute circumstances of extreme urgency, as they require a rapid reaction. Hence, a Member in such a situation can make use of the fast track procedure—irrespective of the fact that it could theoretically have acquired the patented products from the patent holder.[214] Nevertheless, the provision is not very attractive for Members in

[209] Relevant factors are listed in ICTSD and UNCTAD (n 130 above) pt 2.5, 130 f; Gervais (n 170 above) Art 31, para 2.306; Ridder (n 166 above) 91–92.
[210] Article 31(b) of the TRIPS Agreement.   [211] Article 31(k) of the TRIPS Agreement.
[212] On the uncertainty concerning the provision see Kampf (n 110 above) 106.
[213] Rott (n 109 above) 289. However, Rott does not state that diseases are not an emergency; S Bartelt, 'Compulsory Licenses Pursuant to TRIPS Article 31 in the Light of the Doha Declaration on the TRIPS Agreement and Public Health' (2003) 6 J World Intell Prop 283, 295.
[214] With a different line of argument Herrmann (n 122 above) 40.

such a situation, as they are reluctant to label their situation one of emergency because of the effect that would inevitably have on likely investors and tourists.

The 'public non-commercial use' fast-track procedure is potentially broader and more attractive for developing countries.[215] It refers to use of the patented invention (by making, selling, etc) either by a government entity or a private contractor of a government entity.[216] At least one commentator has taken a broader view and considers any use for the public benefit as public use.[217] The term 'non-commercial' implies that the use is taking place outside of commerce, ie not for profit.[218] A narrow reading of this condition would imply that nobody involved in the use may act for the purpose of making a profit. Such a reading would prevent private companies from being involved in public non-commercial use—and thereby ultimately render the provision useless, as governments commonly need to rely on contractors to make use of the invention. A better reading focuses on the intended public use, which has to be non-commercial.[219] Thus, where a government contracts with a private company to manufacture patented pharmaceuticals that the government then distributes for free (or without profit), the use is non-commercial.[220] The right to access to medicine supports this more permissive interpretation. Again, however, some Members may take a different view as to the interpretation of 'public non-commercial use' and a Member relying on the suggested interpretation risks litigation.

c Adequate Remuneration

Where a compulsory licence is granted, the right holder has to be paid 'adequate remuneration in the circumstances of each case, taking into account the economic value of the authorization'.[221] Where the licence is granted to remedy a practice determined after judicial or administrative process to be anti-competitive, the need to correct anti-competitive practices may be taken into account in determining the amount of remuneration.

[215] J Love, *Compulsory Licensing: Models For State Practice in Developing Countries, Access to Medicine and Compliance with the WTO TRIPS Accord, Prepared for the United Nations Development Programme* (2001) at para 2, at <http://www.cptech.org/ip/health/cl/recommendedstatepractice. html>. In these cases Members need not provide for injunctive relieve, but may limit the remedies available to payment of remuneration under Art 31(h) of the TRIPS Agreement. Article 44.2 of the TRIPS Agreement.

[216] A restrictive interpretation allowing only the use by a government entity itself would essentially reduce the provision to naught, because few governments have the capacity to manufacture patented products themselves. Rott (n 109 above) 293 f; Correa (n 172 above) 212.

[217] ICTSD and UNCTAD (n 130 above) pt 2.5, 132.

[218] ICTSD and UNCTAD (n 130 above) pt 2.5, 132. Gold and Lam have suggested that the provision also limits the possible areas of use, extending certainly to public health and national defence, possibly to nutrition, environmental protection, and the promotion of the public interest in sectors of vital importance to Members' socio-economic and technological developments. Gold and Lam (n 183 above) 25. There is nothing in the wording to suggest such a limitation.

[219] Correa (n 172 above) 212.   [220] Velásquez and Boulet (n 160 above) 35.

[221] Article 31(h) of the TRIPS Agreement. The remuneration also has to be paid in the case of public non-commercial use.

If access to medicine is to be promoted by compulsory licences, ie if the price of the drug is to be lowered, the issue of remuneration is particularly thorny. Any benefit would be nullified if the company manufacturing under a compulsory licence has to pay too high a remuneration.[222] The key question is: which level of remuneration is adequate? The dictionary defines 'adequate' as 'sufficient for a specific requirement'; 'barely sufficient or satisfactory'; 'lawfully and reasonably sufficient'.[223] According to the provision, each case has to be considered on its own merits, taking the value of the authorization into account. But the 'value of the authorization' is difficult to establish. Habitual royalties for licences in the relevant market and for the relevant field of invention can provide some orientation, even though these, too, are often contested. Pharmaceutical Research and Manufacturers of America (PhRMA), the group representing the US innovative pharmaceutical industry, in 2000 stated that 5 per cent was the average US royalty rate for pharmaceuticals.[224] The German *Richtlinien für die Vergütung von Arbeitnehmererfindungen im Privaten Dienst*[225] consider a royalty of 2–10 per cent of net sales[226] as habitual in the pharmaceutical industry. In contrast, a 1995 study of licensing agreements in Germany cited a royalty of 5–15 per cent of net sales for pharmaceuticals.[227] Given that the royalty rate depends heavily on the specifics of each case, such general figures are of rather limited value—all the more so where the patent is not on the final product, but on an intermediary one. They are further discredited by the fact that many voluntary licences are granted within the same enterprise and used (or abused) to transfer profits in between countries.[228] Finally, it has to be born in mind that Article 31(d) of the TRIPS Agreement requires compulsory licences to be non-exclusive, which further reduces the value of such a licence.

But the value of the authorization is not the only factor in establishing 'adequate' remuneration, as 'full' compensation is not owed under the TRIPS Agreement.[229] The adequacy of the remuneration depends on a number of factors including both interests of the patent holder and interests of the public as well as the economic circumstances of the country granting the licence.[230] Canadian

---

[222] Scherer and Watal (n 116 above) 36; A Subramanian, 'The AIDS Crisis, Differential Pricing of Drugs, and the TRIPS Agreement. Two Proposals' (2001) 4 J World Intell Prop 323, 331.

[223] Mish *et al* (eds) (n 67 above).   [224] Love (n 215 above) para 39.

[225] Guidelines for the compensation for workers' inventions in the private sector (translation by the author).

[226] The guidelines contain several rules on what figure the royalty rate refers to. E Reimer *et al*, *Das Recht der Arbeitnehmererfindung* (7th edn, 2000) 285 ff, 296 ff.

[227] M Groß, 'Aktuelle Lizenzgebühren in Patentlizenz-, Know-how- und Computerprogrammlizenz-Verträgen' (1995) BB 885, 891.   [228] ICTSD and UNCTAD (n 130 above) pt 2.5, 137.

[229] Timmermans and Hutadjulu (n 207 above) 32; Ridder (n 166 above) 103. A US proposal to grant 'full' compensation was not adopted. F Höhne in J Busche and P-T Stoll (eds), *TRIPs* (2007) Art 31, para 3.

[230] ICTSD and UNCTAD (n 130 above) pt 2.5, 137; S Vastano Vaughan, 'Compulsory Licensing of Pharmaceuticals under TRIPS: What Standard of Compensation?' (2001) 25 Hastings Int'l & Comp L Rev 87, 100 ff; Gervais (n 170 above) Art 31, para 2.306; Ridder (n 166 above) 104–105.

practice for compulsory licences of pharmaceutical patents regarded a 4 per cent royalty of the sale price as adequate.[231]

The right to access to medicine is an important consideration in the determination of adequate remuneration. Thus, a developing country reacting to a public health crisis can determine a relatively low, in special cases even symbolic,[232] rate of remuneration to be adequate. The consideration is illustrated by the compulsory licence granted by Zambia in September 2004, the first compulsory licence on a medicine granted by an African country.[233] The licence was granted to a Zambian company for the local production of a triple-combination AIDS drug (lamivudine, stavudine, and nevirapine) after the patent holders could not reach an agreement to produce such a drug. Considering the fact that the final price of the product should be as low as possible, Zambia fixed the royalties at a level not exceeding 2.5 per cent of the total turnover of the product at the end of each financial year.[234] A compulsory licence granted one month later by Indonesia on nevirapine and lamivudine fixed the royalty at a mere 0.5 per cent of the net selling value of the drugs.[235]

d Review of the Decisions
Members have to provide for the possibility of judicial review or other independent review by a distinct higher authority in the Member of both the legal validity of any decision relating to the authorization of use under Article 31 of the TRIPS Agreement and any decision relating to the remuneration provided in respect of such use according to Article 31(i) and (j) of the TRIPS Agreement.

C Scope of the Rights under Compulsory Licences
A compulsory licence allows the 'use' of the subject matter of a patent. The term 'use' in Article 31 of the TRIPS Agreement differs from the one in Article 28 of the TRIPS Agreement. It refers to any of the acts that a patent holder normally can exclude a third party from. Thus, for products, it refers to making, using, offering for sale, selling, or importing, for these purposes, the product.[236]

Pursuant to the principle of territoriality the effect of a compulsory licence is limited to the territory in which it is granted. Thus, a compulsory licence for the manufacture of a drug granted by state X to company C allows C to manufacture

---

[231] Subramanian (n 222 above) 331; Love (n 215 above) para 5.
[232] Ridder (n 166 above) 106.   [233] Love (n 215 above) para 6.
[234] Republic of Zambia Ministry of Commerce, Trade and Industry, *Compulsory License No CL 01/2004*, MCT1/104/1/1c (21 September 2004).
[235] Decree 83 of 2004 of the President of the Republic of Indonesia, *Regarding Exploitation of Patent by the Government on Anti Retroviral Drugs* (5 October 2004) (translation by O Valverde Mordt, IP-Health, 6 December 2004). Brazil regarded a 3% royalty as adequate in its recent threat to break Abbott's patent on the AIDS drug Kaletra. The threat succeeded in making Abbott agree to price reductions. T Benson, 'Brazil to Copy AIDS Drug Made by Abbott' *NY Times* (25 June 2005); T Benson, 'Brazil and U.S. Maker Reach Deal on AIDS Drug' *NY Times* (9 July 2005).
[236] Article 28.1(a) of the TRIPS Agreement.

the drug solely within the territory of X and nowhere else.[237] If there are no manufacturing capacities in the country granting the licence and the beneficiary does not establish such capacities, it can only work the licence by importing the patented product from a third country—whether it was produced there by the patent holder or not.[238] It is the patent situation in that third country that regulates who may manufacture the product. I will come back to the situation of countries without manufacturing capacities below.

a Limited by the Purpose

The TRIPS Agreement obliges Members to limit the scope and duration of a compulsory licence to the purpose for which the licence was granted.[239] Where the circumstances leading to the grant have ceased to exist and are unlikely to recur, the compulsory licence has to be terminated,[240] with the caveat that the legitimate interests of the beneficiary of the licence must be adequately protected. The caveat is important to bear in mind, as the beneficiary of a licence has to make investments before it can work the licence and it would be difficult to find a beneficiary willing to do so if the licence is liable to be terminated at any given moment.[241]

b Non-exclusive, Non-assignable

Compulsory licences have to be non-exclusive,[242] allowing the patent holder to continue to use and license the patent, and non-assignable, except with that part of the enterprise or goodwill which uses the licence.[243]

c Territoriality

A further limitation of the permissible scope of compulsory licences is contained in Article 31(f), which provides that 'any such use shall be authorized predominantly for the supply of the domestic market of the Member authorizing such use'. The provision is applicable unless the licence has been granted to remedy a practice determined after judicial or administrative process to be anti-competitive.[244] Its consequences are dramatic and have caused heated debates. An amendment that is not yet in force modifies these consequences. It will be described below.

---

[237] Kampf (n 110 above) 107; Herrmann (n 122 above) 40.

[238] FM Abbott, 'WTO TRIPS Agreement and Its Implications for Access to Medicines in Developing Countries' UK Commission on Intellectual Property Rights Study Paper 2a (2002) 13, 18; C Otero García-Castrillón, 'An Approach to the WTO Ministerial Declaration on the TRIPS Agreement and Public Health' (2002) 5 JIEL 212, 217; Cottier (n 184 above) 386.

[239] Article 31(c) of the TRIPS Agreement.

[240] The competent authority must have the power to review, upon motivated request, whether the circumstances still exist. Article 31(g) of the TRIPS Agreement; see also Art 31(k) sentence 3 of the TRIPS Agreement.   [241] Ridder (n 166 above) 101–102.

[242] Article 31(d) of the TRIPS Agreement.

[243] Article 31(e) of the TRIPS Agreement; Ridder (n 166 above) 97 f.

[244] Article 31(k) of the TRIPS Agreement.

aa Interpretation of the Provision   The word 'predominantly' can be read in three ways. Firstly, it could imply that more than 50 per cent of the use has to take place for the supply of the domestic market.[245] Secondly, it could mean that the domestic market has to be the single most important market for the beneficiary. Such a reading would allow the 'predominant' part of the supply reserved for the domestic market to be well below 50 per cent if the beneficiary exports to several Members.[246] Thirdly, the word 'predominantly' could be interpreted to refer to the intent of the Member granting the compulsory licence rather than to the predominant part of the production.[247]

Again, the right to access to medicine can be used as an argument for the most permissive interpretation, which is the reference to the Member's intent. A company will only be willing to manufacture under a compulsory licence if the market it can supply is sufficiently large. The production solely for the supply of the internal market of a small Member is often inefficient. To be efficient a manufacturer would need to manufacture more products and to export the surplus production. The first two interpretations significantly restrict the possibility of such exports. However, Members can, again, not safely rely on this interpretation, as it is unclear whether a panel would follow this argument.

bb Options for Members Lacking Pharmaceutical Manufacturing Capacity   The implications of the provision for Members lacking pharmaceutical manufacturing capacities are severe—and such manufacturing capacity is available in very few Members.[248] The beneficiary of a compulsory licence in such a Member can either set up manufacturing capacities upon the grant of the licence—a rather unlikely event given that the relevant markets are often not sufficiently large to support such an industry—or it has to work the licence by importing drugs from third Members.[249] To be able to import cheap generics the beneficiary has to find a market where such generics are available, ie where the drug is produced and not under patent.[250] However, with the expiration of the TRIPS Agreement

---

[245] Kampf (n 110 above) 108.

[246] HP Hestermeyer, 'Flexible Entscheidungsfindung in der WTO. Die Rechtsnatur der neuen WTO Beschlüsse über TRIPS und Zugang zu Medikamenten' (2004) GRUR Int 194, 198; Abbott (n 114 above) 26.

[247] Rott (n 109 above) 285; Staehelin (n 184 above) 152; *Contra* Ridder (n 166 above) 99–100.

[248] An excellent, but somewhat outdated (1992), overview of manufacturing capacities is CM Correa, *Implications of the Doha Declaration on the TRIPS Agreement and Public Health*, WHO Health Economics and Drugs EDM Series No 12, 49 ff (2002). The table lists ten countries as having a 'Sophisticated Pharmaceutical Industry and Research Base', 17 countries as having 'Innovative Capabilities' (among these India and China), 14 Countries as possessing 'Reproductive Capabilities' for both active ingredients and finished products (among them Brazil, Bolivia, and Cuba), 89 countries as having reproductive capabilities for finished products from imported ingredients only and 60 countries as having no pharmaceutical industry. Hence, according to the table, 149 countries rely on imported ingredients produced by 41 countries. Another source for data is Council for TRIPS, *Available Information on Manufacturing Capacity for Medicines*, IP/C/W/345 (24 May 2002). See chapters 1 and 4.   [249] See this chapter above; Kampf (n 110 above) 107.

[250] Bartelt (n 213 above) 296.

transition period on 1 January 2005[251] all developing country WTO Members with manufacturing capacities have to provide for patent protection.[252] Companies will be able to obtain patents on new drugs in all manufacturing Members and hence, for the duration of the patent term, the importing Member cannot find an exporting market—at least within the WTO—where the new drug is available off-patent.[253]

The only way to still obtain generics for such a Member is to find an exporting Member that exempts the drug from patent protection for export. Some scholars argue that a patent law exception allowing the manufacture of a drug solely for export is permissible under Article 30 of the TRIPS Agreement.[254] However, the *Canada—Patent* Panel's unduly narrow interpretation of Article 30 stands in the way of such an interpretation. The other way out is to find an exporting Member willing to grant a compulsory licence authorizing the production of the drug. Even at a first glance the solution is far from elegant: first of all, it puts the importing Member at the mercy of the exporting one. Secondly, the exporting Member will have to adapt its patent rules to allow the grant of a compulsory licence in such cases. Thirdly, the solution is administratively cumbersome. Thus, for example, the exporting Member might have to engage in prior negotiations with the patent holder according to Article 31(b) of the TRIPS Agreement even where the importing Member can waive this requirement because of an emergency.[255]

Most significantly, however, Article 31(f) prohibits this approach. The exporting Member may only export a non-predominant part of the production under the compulsory licence. The grant of a compulsory licence solely to assist an importing Member is not permitted. Scholars have proposed several arguments to avoid this outcome, such as allowing the manufacture of a drug in one country on the basis of a compulsory licence granted by another country if the production is solely for the supply of that second country;[256] or allowing the manufacture for

---

[251] See chapter 2.

[252] The President of India, one of the most significant developing country producers of generics, promulgated the Patents (Amendment) Ordinance 2004 (Ord No 7 of 2004), to abide by the deadline. In March 2005 the Patent (Amendment) Bill 2005 was passed. DG McNeil, Jr, 'India Alters Law on Drug Patents' *NY Times* (24 March 2005).

[253] Abbott (n 157 above) 10 ff. Cottier argues that the problem does not exist, as a right holder preventing a generic manufacturer from exporting engages in anti-competitive behaviour and Art 31(f) of the TRIPS Agreement does not apply in such a case according to Art 31(k). That assessment is erroneous as a patent holder's insistence on compliance with Art 31(f) is well within its rights under the TRIPS Agreement and could therefore not be deemed anti-competitive behaviour. Also, Cottier's interpretation would render Art 31(f) moot, as it would automatically become non-applicable whenever someone tries to rely on it. Cottier (n 184 above) 386–387. Shanker argues that patents do not grant an exclusive right for manufacturing solely for export and deduces this from the experimental use exception. However, the manufacture for export does not fall under this exception and is a manufacturing act within the territory of the patent grant and hence within the scope of the patent rights. D Shanker, 'The Paragraph 6 Solution of the Doha Public Health Declaration and Export under the TRIPS Agreement' (2004) 7 J World Intell Prop 365 ff.

[254] Eg KM Gopakumar, 'The WTO Deal on Cheap Drugs. A Critique' (2004) 7 J World Intell Prop 99, 102–103.   [255] Kampf (n 110 above) 109; *contra* Abbott (n 238 above) 19–20.

[256] Rott (n 109 above) 285–286; with a suggestion for pharmaceutical production export zones Abbott (n 238 above) 21.

export as a limited exception under Article 30.[257] But these arguments strained the language of the Agreement and were unlikely to be upheld in dispute settlement—even taking the right to access to medicine into account.

D Conclusion as to Compulsory Licences

This section has demonstrated that much about the interpretation of Article 31 of the TRIPS Agreement remains in doubt[258] and while the right to access to medicine is a useful argument to support a broader, more flexible interpretation, it is merely one argument amongst several. It remains uncertain to what extent it would carry the day in a dispute settlement proceeding.

Faced with the uncertainty about the interpretation of the intricate requirements imposed by Article 31 of the TRIPS Agreement and the pressure exerted by developed countries to not impose compulsory licences for pharmaceuticals, developing countries have largely foregone imposing such licences to alleviate health concerns.[259] Indeed, in the wake of the TRIPS Agreement many countries have limited the provisions on compulsory licensing in their laws.[260]

4 Revocation of Patents

A yet harsher measure than the imposition of a compulsory licence is the complete revocation of a patent. Many national patent laws provide for such revocation or forfeiture of a patent if the maintenance fees are not paid timely[261] or if the conditions for the grant of a patent were not fulfilled at the time of the grant.[262] The revocation of a patent could theoretically also be used to lower prices by allowing competition and thereby enhance access to medicine. The TRIPS Agreement language on revocation is sparse. Article 32 of the TRIPS Agreement merely states 'An opportunity for judicial review of any decision to revoke or forfeit a patent shall be available'. The provision is silent as to the grounds of any such revocation or forfeiture. The limits of the provision are entirely unclear. In a statement to the Committee on Trade and Environment India has advanced the view that the provision gives wide latitude to Members, allowing the revocation of patents on any grounds.[263] The United States considers that interpretation to be in conflict

---

[257] Abbott (n 238 above) 24.

[258] Gervais (n 170 above) Art 31, para 2.305; MM Nerozzi, 'The Battle Over Life-Saving Pharmaceuticals: Are Developing Countries Being "TRIPped" by Developed Countries?' (2002) 47 Villanova L R 605, 613, 615 ff; Ford (n 171 above) 961.

[259] Other reasons for the lack of recourse to compulsory licensing by developing countries include the lack of an administrative infrastructure to grant such licences, the lack of manufacturing capacities, concern about foreign investors, and a preference for reaching agreement with patent holders. Commission on Intellectual Property Rights (n 116 above) 42; Abbott (n 114 above) 25.

[260] Apart from Canada, Halewood lists New Zealand, China, India, and Mexico. Halewood (n 196 above) 245.   [261] For the limits of this ground see Art 5*bis* of the Paris Convention.

[262] ICTSD and UNCTAD (n 130 above) pt 2.5, 87.

[263] Committee on Trade and Environment, *Cluster on Market Access. Item 8: The Relationship of the TRIPS Agreement to the Development, Access and Transfer of Environmentally-Sound Technologies*

with the context of the provision, namely Articles 27, 28, 29, 33 of the TRIPS Agreement. The revocation of patents without cause reduces the obligation to grant patents (and thereby the patent provisions in the TRIPS Agreement) to naught. In particular, it makes no sense to carefully impose conditions on the grant of compulsory licences if the patent can be revoked entirely at will. Accordingly, the United States has argued that patents may only be revoked where they should never have been granted in the first place.[264]

The *travaux préparatoires* show that Members could not agree on a position during the negotiations. Whereas India suggested that revocation should be permissible where the patent 'is being used in a manner prejudicial to the public interest'[265] the United States wanted to permit revocation only where the invention was not patentable.[266] The heavily bracketed Chairman's draft dated 23 July 1990 reflects the disagreement:

A patent [may not be revoked or forfeited [merely] on grounds [of non-working] stipulated in 5A.2 above] [may only be revoked on grounds that it fails to meet the requirements of 1.1 and 1.3 above].[267]

Article 5A(3) of the Paris Convention indicates that a proper interpretation of Article 32 of the TRIPS Agreement occupies a middle ground between the two positions. The Paris Convention explicitly allows forfeiture of a patent in cases of abuse in which the abuse cannot be prevented by the grant of a compulsory licence, provided that two years have expired from the grant of the first compulsory licence before a proceeding for forfeiture or revocation is commenced.[268] There is no indication that the TRIPS Agreement prohibits this ground for revocation, or that it prohibits the revocation of a patent in case of non-payment of maintenance fees.

The right to access to medicine favours allowing the revocation of a patent in case of its abuse where the abuse cannot be remedied by a compulsory licence. It is highly unlikely that a panel would uphold a revocation provision that goes beyond that standard (with the exception of the revocation for non-payment of maintenance fees or for lack of patentability), as that would threaten to render

and Products *(EST&PS). Input from India*, WT/CTE/W/66, para 15 (29 September 1997); ICTSD/UNCTAD (n 130 above) pt 2.5, 87; Correa (n 172 above) 216; Gervais (n 170 above) Art 31, para 2.312.

[264] Council for TRIPS, *Remarks on Revocation of Patents and the TRIPS Agreement by the United States of America*, IP/C/W/32 (6 August 1996).

[265] Negotiating Group on Trade-Related Aspects of Intellectual Property Rights, including Trade in Counterfeit Goods, *Synoptic Table Setting out Existing International Standards and Proposed Standards and Principles. Prepared by the Secretariat*, MTN.GNG/NG11/W/32/Rev.1, at VI (5) (29 September 1989).

[266] Negotiating Group on Trade-Related Aspects of Intellectual Property Rights, including Trade in Counterfeit Goods, *Draft Agreement on the Trade-Related Aspects of Intellectual Property Rights. Communication from the United States*, MTN.GNG/NG11/W/70, pt 2, Art 24(2) (11 May 1990).

[267] Negotiating Group on Trade-Related Aspects of Intellectual Property Rights, including Trade in Counterfeit Goods, *Status of Work in the Negotiating Group. Chairman's Report to the GNG*, MTN.GNG/NG11/W/76, pt III Section 5 para 6A.1 (23 July 1990).

[268] Article 5A(3) of the Paris Convention; Straus (n 119 above) 208; Bodenhausen (n 196 above) 70.

the patent provisions of the TRIPS Agreement pointless.[269] Again, however, access to medicine is only one argument and a country permitting the revocation of patents on grounds other than the non-payment of maintenance fees and the lack of patentability risks being pressured to change its laws.

5 Conclusion

To sum up, many provisions in the TRIPS Agreement can be interpreted liberally to advance access to medicine. The human right is a helpful argument favouring such flexibilities of the TRIPS Agreement, but there are other arguments in favour of more restrictive readings and it is unclear which position would ultimately prevail. The ensuing legal insecurity[270] prevents the flexibilities, which could provide for more balance in the TRIPS Agreement, from being fully effective. Many developing country Members are reluctant to make use of the flexibilities, as their actions would incur strong criticism by developed country Members and could result in a WTO dispute settlement proceeding with uncertain outcome. In contrast to the European Communities and the United States developing country Members are in no position to engage in such a 'trade war'. Hence, solutions with a smaller litigation risk, such as price control schemes, pooled procurement schemes,[271] and donation programmes[272] have often been preferred.

III WTO Decisions to Remedy Insufficiencies

Beginning with the South African pharmaceutical trial,[273] pressure for remedying the deficiencies of the TRIPS Agreement in the area of access to medicine began to rise and ultimately could no longer be ignored by the WTO, which, in 2001, adopted the so-called Doha Declaration, in 2003, as a follow-up, the Decision of 30 August 2003 and finally, in December 2005, a decision to amend the TRIPS Agreement.

This section will describe and evaluate the three decisions (1)–(3). It is not just the content of the decisions that is of interest, but also their legal status (4). In the case of the first two decisions the WTO showed considerable flexibility in

---

[269] Stoll and Raible (n 156 above) 598; Rott (n 109 above) 295 would allow a revocation where it is based on the behaviour of the patent holder or where the invention was not patentable.

[270] The importance of legal security for developing countries has been emphasized by Subramanian (n 122 above) 327; R Islam, 'The Generic Drug Deal of the WTO from Doha to Cancun. A Peripheral Response to a Perennial Conundrum' (2004) 7 J World Intell Prop 675, 677 and the sources cited n 258 above. On the deficiencies of the TRIPS Agreement before the Doha Declaration see Abbott (n 157 above).

[271] P Marc, 'Compulsory Licensing and the South African Medicine Act of 1997: Violation or Compliance of the Trade Related Aspects of Intellectual Property Rights Agreement?' (2001) 21 NYL Sch J Int'l & Comp L 109, 120.

[272] Wojahn (n 154 above) 489; Nerozzi (n 258 above) 619. Developed countries also apply price controls and other measures. Stegemann and Pzderka (n 159 above) 547 ff.   [273] See chapter 1.

handling its decision-making procedures, which is highly significant as an approach to accommodating the right to access to medicine in the WTO order.

1 The Doha Declaration

In the months and years after the South African drug trial the issue of the TRIPS Agreement and access to medicine was discussed in diverse fora, building up pressure for the WTO to take up the issue or lose the initiative as both human rights bodies and the WHO took the stage.[274] In 1999, the issue reached the WTO. While it was not yet on the agenda during the Seattle Ministerial Conference, it was at Seattle that President Clinton chose to announce the reversal of US policy with respect to intellectual property and access to medicine.[275] But the Seattle Ministerial became known for another reason. Growing public discontent with a world trading order often perceived as illegitimate and secretive sent 20,000 protestors into the streets. Power relationships also began to change as developing country Members had strengthened their negotiation position. Ultimately, the attempt to commence a new WTO negotiation round failed[276] and developed country Members realized they needed to compromise with developing country Members to start a new negotiation round.

A Negotiating History

Against this background Zimbabwe, at the time chair of the Council for TRIPS, suggested a special session of that Council on the TRIPS Agreement and access to medicine. Welcoming the special session, the WTO's Director-General at that time, Moore, described the task to be tackled as follows:

[The TRIPS Agreement] strikes a carefully-negotiated balance between providing intellectual property protection—which is essential if new medicines and treatments are to be developed—and allowing countries the flexibility to ensure that treatments reach the world's poorest and most vulnerable people.

  Countries must feel secure that they can use this flexibility. The work started today in the TRIPS Council should reinforce that security.[277]

---

[274] See chapter 3.
[275] See chapter 1. A chronology of events leading up to the Doha Declaration can be found in E 't Hoen, 'TRIPS, Pharmaceutical Patents, and Access to Essential Medicines: A Long Way From Seattle to Doha' (2002) 3 Chicago J Int'l L 27 ff and H Sun, 'The Road to Doha and Beyond: Some Reflections on the TRIPS Agreement and Public Health' (2004) 15 EJIL 123, 127 ff. At the beginning of the discussion it was far from clear whether modifications to the *status quo* could be achieved. S Salazar, *Intellectual Property and the Right to Health*, in WIPO (ed), *Intellectual Property and Human Rights. A Panel Discussion to commemorate the 50th Anniversary of the Universal Declaration of Human Rights. Geneva, November 9, 1998* (1999) 65.
[276] G Horlick, 'The Speedbump at Seattle' (2000) 3 JIEL 167; DC Esty, 'An Environmental Perspective on Seattle' (2000) 3 JIEL 176; EH Preeg, 'The South Rises in Seattle' (2000) 3 JIEL 183. On the question of the legitimacy of the WTO see M Krajewski, *Verfassungsperspektiven und Legitimation des Rechts der Welthandelsorganisation* (2001) 217 ff.
[277] M Moore, *Moore: Countries Must Feel Secure that They Can Use TRIPS' Flexibility*, at <http://www.wto.org/english/news_e/news01_e/dg_trips_medicines_010620_e.htm> (2001).

The session took place in June 2001. Both the European Communities[278] and the African Group along with 16 other developing countries[279] had prepared papers for it. It was followed up by another full day of discussion in September focusing on the provisions of the TRIPS Agreement on objectives and principles, compulsory licences, and parallel imports.[280] At the second meeting, two opposing drafts for a ministerial declaration were presented. One had been submitted by the African Group and 19 other developing countries,[281] the other by Australia, Canada, Japan, Switzerland, and the United States.[282] The former draft aimed at letting health concerns take precedence over intellectual property rights: '[n]othing in the TRIPS Agreement shall prevent Members from taking measures to protect public health.' In contrast, the latter draft emphasized the importance of patents for the creation of new drugs.[283] The discussion was contentious, but Members reached agreement on a Declaration during the Doha Ministerial Conference.[284] One of the catalysts fostering agreement was the *Cipro* episode recounted in chapter 1, which compromised the developed Members, negotiating position:[285] after letters containing anthrax had surfaced in the United States, neither the United States nor Canada had wasted much time before threatening to break the patent on *Cipro*, at the time the only available drug against anthrax.

B Content of the Decision

The Doha Declaration on the TRIPS Agreement and Public Health (hereinafter 'Doha Declaration')[286] was adopted by the Ministerial Conference on 14 November 2001 in a consensus decision. The first three paragraphs of the decision are introductory. After developed country Members had initially attempted to

---

[278] Council for TRIPS, *The Relationship between the Provisions of the TRIPS Agreement and Access to Medicines. Communication from the European Communities and their Member States*, IP/C/W/280 (12 June 2001). On the background of the paper: P Vandoren, 'Médicaments sans Frontières? Clarification of the Relationship between TRIPS and Public Health Resulting from the WTO Doha Ministerial Declaration' (2002) 5 J World Intell Prop 5, 6; Kampf (n 110 above) 92–93.

[279] Council for TRIPS, *TRIPS and Public Health. Submission by the Africa Group, Barbados, Bolivia, Brazil, Dominican Republic, Ecuador, Honduras, India, Indonesia, Jamaica, Pakistan, Paraguay, Philippines, Peru, Sri Lanka, Thailand and Venezuela*, IP/C/W/296 (19 June 2001).

[280] Vandoren (n 278 above) 6.

[281] Council for TRIPS, *Draft Ministerial Declaration. Proposal by the African Group, Bangladesh, Barbados, Bolivia, Brazil, Cuba, Dominican Republic, Ecuador, Haiti, Honduras, India, Indonesia, Jamaica, Pakistan, Paraguay, Philippines, Peru, Sri Lanka, Thailand and Venezuela*, IP/C/W/312 (4 October 2001).

[282] Council for TRIPS, *Draft Ministerial Declaration. Contribution from Australia, Canada, Japan, Switzerland and the United States*, IP/C/W/313 (4 October 2001).

[283] Vandoren (n 278 above) 7.

[284] 't Hoen (n 275 above) 39. During the discussions the European Union tried to act as an honest broker. Vandoren (n 278 above) 12; Kampf (n 110 above) 93; B Faracik, 'The Right to Health and Right to Intellectual Property in the EU. Analysis of the Internal and External Policies' Master Thesis (Lund), (2002) 66–67; sceptical: 't Hoen (n 275 above) 40.

[285] M Perez Pugatch, *The International Political Economy of Intellectual Property Rights* (2004) 218; Kampf (n 110 above) 111.

[286] Ministerial Conference, *Doha Declaration on the TRIPS Agreement and Public Health*, WT/MIN(01)/DEC/W/2 (14 November 2001).

limit the declaration to pandemics and access to medicines[287] Members in the final text 'recognize the gravity of the public health problems afflicting many developing and least-developed countries, especially those resulting from HIV/AIDS, tuberculosis, malaria and other epidemics',[288] thus making the declaration applicable to all of public health and mentioning specific pandemics only by way of illustration.[289] The TRIPS Agreement needs to be 'part of the wider national and international action to address these problems'.[290] While Members again stress that intellectual property protection is necessary for developing new medicines, they recognize for the first time 'the concerns about its effects on prices'.[291] This finding is essential, as it reflects the acknowledgement that intellectual property can, indeed, be an impediment to access to medicine.

One of the most controversial provisions follows in paragraph 4. The provision reflects a compromise between the developing Members' hope for a statement giving preference to health concerns over intellectual property rights, akin to deleting the last part of the sentence in Article 8.1 of the TRIPS Agreement and resembling the solution found in Article XX of the GATT,[292] and developed Members' position that the TRIPS Agreement should not be departed from as it advances rather than impedes public health.[293] Its wording runs as follows:

We agree that the TRIPS Agreement does not and should not prevent members from taking measures to protect public health. Accordingly, while reiterating our commitment to the TRIPS Agreement, we affirm that the Agreement can and should be interpreted and implemented in a manner supportive of WTO members' right to protect public health and, in particular, to promote access to medicines for all.

In this connection, we reaffirm the right of WTO members to use, to the full, the provisions in the TRIPS Agreement, which provide flexibility for this purpose.

While the second part of the paragraph—the reaffirmation of Members' right to use the TRIPS flexibilities to the full—clearly does not depart from the TRIPS Agreement the evaluation is somewhat more complex with respect to the first part of the paragraph. Falling short of allowing health concerns to override TRIPS Agreement obligations[294] the provision offers the interpretative guideline that the Agreement should be interpreted to support Members' action to promote access to medicines for all. Technically, this is a mere reiteration of what the first part of this chapter has already shown to be the law, namely that the right to access to medicine has to be taken into account when interpreting the TRIPS Agreement. However, the argument gains force through the provision. It obtains a special rank among the numerous possible and contradictory arguments in the interpretation of the Agreement, as the Agreement now 'should' be interpreted to support a

---

[287] Kampf (n 110 above) 99; 't Hoen (n 275 above) 42; JT Gathii, 'The Legal Status of the Doha Declaration on TRIPS and Public Health under the Vienna Convention on the Law of Treaties' (2002) 15 Harvard J L & Tech 291, 297.   [288] Paragraph 1 of the Doha Declaration.
[289] Correa (n 248 above) 5.   [290] Paragraph 2 of the Doha Declaration.
[291] Paragraph 3 of the Doha Declaration.   [292] See chapter 2.
[293] Correa (n 248 above) 9; 't Hoen (n 275 above) 40.   [294] *Contra* Correa (n 248 above) 11.

Member's right to protect public health. Members concur that the Agreement should also be implemented that way.

The *chapeau* of paragraph 5 of the Doha Declaration announces substantive interpretations of the flexibilities of the TRIPS Agreement in its subparagraphs and simultaneously reaffirms Members' commitment to the TRIPS Agreement, thus continuing the complex balancing act between accommodating developing Members' concerns and developed Members' reluctance to change the TRIPS Agreement. Subparagraph (a) reiterates that in applying the customary rules of interpretation of public international law, the TRIPS Agreement has to be read 'in the light of the object and purpose of the Agreement as expressed, in particular, in its objectives and principles' and thus does not add anything new. The fact that the subparagraph was even included in the Declaration indicates the state of uncertainty that developing Members are in, faced with the persistent pressure of developed Members for stronger intellectual property protection. The same can be said of the reaffirmation of the commitment of developed Members to provide incentives for technology transfer to least-developed country (LDC) Members in paragraph 7 of the Doha Declaration—an obligation that is already contained in Article 66.2 of the TRIPS Agreement.[295] Subparagraphs (b), (c) and (d), however, clarify a number of interpretative questions that were the subject of heated debates. Thus, Members' right to grant compulsory licences and their freedom to determine the grounds for such grants is explicitly enshrined in the Doha Declaration.[296] Subparagraph (c) clarifies the terms 'national emergency or other circumstances of extreme urgency' used in Article 31(b) of the TRIPS Agreement: it is left to Members to determine what constitutes a national emergency or other circumstances of extreme urgency, but it is clarified that public health crises, including epidemics, can represent such circumstances.[297] Finally, subparagraph (d) settles the extremely contentious question of the international exhaustion of intellectual property rights. It explicitly provides that the effect of the relevant TRIPS Agreement provisions is to leave Members free to establish their own regime of exhaustion or non-exhaustion 'without challenge', subject to Articles 3 and 4 of the TRIPS Agreement. While the term 'without challenge' is an awkward reminder of the words '[f]or the purposes of dispute settlement under this Agreement' in Article 6 of the TRIPS Agreement, the provision in the Doha

---

[295] Paragraph 7 of the Doha Declaration. The obligation is now monitored by a state reporting mechanism. Ministerial Conference, *Implementation-related Issues and Concerns, Decision of 14 November 2001*, WT/MIN(01)/17, para 11.2 (20 November 2001); Council for TRIPS, *Implementation of Article 66.2 of the TRIPS Agreement. Decision of the Council for TRIPS*, IP/C/28 (20 February 2003); Council for TRIPS, *Report on the Implementation of Article 66.2 of the TRIPS Agreement*, IP/C/W/412 (10 November 2003) and addenda, Council for TRIPS, *Report on the Implementation of Article 66.2 of the TRIPS Agreement*, IP/C/W/431 (16 November 2004) and addenda.

[296] Paragraph 5(b) of the Doha Declaration.

[297] The discretion of Members concerning the determination of a state of emergency has been suggested to imply that the complainant would bear the burden of proof that an emergency does not exist. Correa (n 248 above) 17; 't Hoen (n 275 above) 41.

Declaration clearly does not allow any challenge to a regime of international exhaustion and therefore permits it as legal.[298]

The Doha Declaration finally acknowledges that some important tasks remain. The most significant of these is the issue that WTO Members with insufficient or no manufacturing capacity in the pharmaceutical sector cannot make effective use of compulsory licences.[299] Rather than proposing a solution to the intricate problem, paragraph 6 of the Doha Declaration instructs the Council for TRIPS to find an 'expeditious solution' to it and report to the General Council before the end of 2002. The solution that has been passed will be discussed below.

Furthermore, the Doha Declaration instructs the Council for TRIPS to extend the transition period for implementing and applying Sections 5 and 7 of Part II and enforcing rights provided for under these sections of the TRIPS Agreement for LDC Members with respect to pharmaceutical products for a further ten years until 1 January 2016.[300] The extension was granted on 1 July 2002 on the initiative of the Doha Declaration, not, as Article 66.1 of the TRIPS Agreement provides, upon a request by a LDC Member.[301]

Negotiators failed to consider that LDCs would still have had to provide 'exclusive marketing rights' under Article 70.9 of the TRIPS Agreement, putting the effectiveness of the transition period at risk.[302] However, the oversight was corrected by the grant of a waiver by the General Council on 12 July 2002 of the obligations under Article 70.9 for LDC Members for pharmaceutical products during the transition period.[303] Nevertheless, the extension of the transition period will have a limited effect. Firstly, because of the practical consideration mentioned in chapter 2 that to control the global market of a product the inventor only needs to obtain patents in all countries with manufacturing capacity—and thus generally not in LDCs. Secondly, because most LDCs already grant pharmaceutical patents.[304]

---

[298] Correa (n 248 above) 17.

[299] See above. The problem exists for Members without manufacturing capacity whether they themselves provide for patent protection or not. 't Hoen (n 275 above) 44.

[300] Paragraph 7 of the Doha Declaration. See Art 66.1 of the TRIPS Agreement. The extension is without prejudice to the right of LDCs to seek a further extension of the transition period.

[301] Council for TRIPS, *Extension of the Transition Period under Article 66.1 of the TRIPS Agreement for Least-Developed Country Members for Certain Obligations with Respect to Pharmaceutical Products*, IP/C/25 (1 July 2002). The extension is granted 'with respect to pharmaceutical products'. The wording does not imply that it only applies to product patents—rather, it applies to all patents that effectively control pharmaceutical products, ie also process patents. Correa (n 248 above) 36. In November 2005 WTO Members extended the TRIPS transition period for LDC Members until 1 July 2013. Council for TRIPS, *Extension of the Transition Period under Article 66.1 for Least-Developed Country Members*, IP/C/40 (30 November 2005).

[302] 't Hoen (n 275 above) 41; Abbott (n 114 above) 11.

[303] Council for TRIPS, *Least-Developed Country Members—Obligations under Article 70.9 of the TRIPS Agreement with Respect to Pharmaceutical Products. Draft Waiver*, IP/C/W/359 (28 June 2002), General Council, *Least-Developed Country Members—Obligations under Article 70.9 of the TRIPS Agreement with Respect to Pharmaceutical Products, Decision of 8 July 2002*, WT/L/478 (12 July 2002).

[304] Out of 30 African LDCs only two, Angola and Eritrea, did not grant pharmaceutical patents in 2002, and Eritrea is not a WTO Member. Correa (n 248 above) 36–37.

C Evaluation

WTO Members and scholars have generally hailed the Doha Declaration as a breakthrough in the conflict between the TRIPS Agreement and public health.[305] Only few scholars—along with some voices from the pharmaceutical industry—took a critical stance, regarding the Doha Declaration as a threat to vital incentives for research and development.[306]

In reality, as demonstrated, the Doha Declaration mostly reiterates the state of the law.[307] It does not clarify the role of access to medicine within the WTO system. In particular, it does not establish an automatic superiority of the right over TRIPS Agreement obligations.[308] However, the Doha Declaration has to be credited with clarifying some of the uncertainty in the interpretation of the TRIPS Agreement, most importantly the question of the permissibility of international exhaustion. It also significantly strengthens an argument based on the right to access to medicine by its paragraph 4, which has potential effects on all questions of interpretation, eg the 'adequacy' of remuneration for compulsory licences.[309] Nevertheless, much of the insecurity in the interpretation of the TRIPS Agreement remains.

2 The Decision of 30 August 2003

The Doha Declaration set out the mandate for the next problem to be tackled: finding a way for Members lacking manufacturing capacity for pharmaceutical products to make use of compulsory licensing. Paragraph 6 of the Doha Declaration reads:

We recognize that WTO members with insufficient or no manufacturing capacities in the pharmaceutical sector could face difficulties in making effective use of compulsory licensing under the TRIPS Agreement. We instruct the Council for TRIPS to find an expeditious solution to this problem and to report to the General Council before the end of 2002.

---

[305] 't Hoen (n 275 above) 28; T Kongolo, 'TRIPS, the Doha Declaration and Public Health' (2003) 6 J World Intell Prop 373, 378; Gamharter (n 124 above) 156.

[306] AO Sykes, 'TRIPs, Pharmaceuticals, Developing Countries and the Doha "Solution"' John M. Olin Law & Economics Working Paper No 140 (2nd Series), University of Chicago Law School (2002) 22.

[307] E Noehrenberg, 'TRIPS, the Doha Declaration and Public Health' (2003) 6 J World Intell Prop 379; Kampf (n 110 above) 125; Herrmann (n 122 above) 42; O Lippert, 'A Market Perspective on Recent Developments in the TRIPS and Essential Medicines Debate' in B Granville (ed), *The Economics of Essential Medicines* (2002) 3, 18–19; P Vandoren and JC Van Eeckhaute, 'The WTO Decision on Paragraph 6 of the Doha Declaration on the TRIPS Agreement and Public Health—Making It Work' (2003) 6 J World Intell Prop 779, 780. Kampf (n 110 above) 103 refers to the Doha Declaration as providing 'comfort language' to developing countries. *Contra* Sykes (n 306 above) 11.

[308] Kampf (n 110 above) 98; *contra* Ghanotakis (n 111 above) 579.

[309] Herrmann (n 122 above) 42.

A Negotiating History

The Council for TRIPS put the issue on the agenda for its meeting on 5–7 March 2002,[310] in preparation of which the European Communities submitted a 'concept paper'.[311] Within a few months, further communications were received from Kenya,[312] the European Communities,[313] the United Arab Emirates,[314] Brazil,[315] and the United States,[316] and lively discussions were held at the Council for TRIPS Meeting on 25–27 June 2002.[317] Scholars and NGOs followed the process with intense interest and made valuable contributions to the debate. They feared the adoption of a mechanism that would not offer generic manufacturers a sufficient incentive to produce under a compulsory licence for export.[318] By the time of the Council for TRIPS meeting in September 2002[319] four main proposals for a solution had emerged:

(1) An amendment of Article 31(f) of the TRIPS Agreement to allow compulsory licences for the manufacture of a pharmaceutical product for export. A Member without manufacturing capacity could then ask another Member to grant a compulsory licence and export the pharmaceutical product. The importing Member could then import the product—if necessary under its own compulsory licence.[320]

(2) A waiver of the limitation on exports imposed by Article 31(f) of the TRIPS Agreement.

[310] Council for TRIPS, *Minutes of Meeting. Held in the Centre William Rappard on 5–7 March 2002*, IP/C/M/35, para 64 ff (22 March 2002).

[311] Council for TRIPS, *Concept Paper Relating to Paragraph 6 of the Doha Declaration on the TRIPS Agreement and Public Health. Communication from the European Communities and their member States*, IP/C/W/339 (4 March 2002). Later, another paper was circulated by the United States. Council for TRIPS, *Paragraph 6 of the Doha Declaration on the TRIPS Agreement and Public Health. Communication from the United States*, IP/C/W/340 (14 March 2002).

[312] Council for TRIPS, *Proposal on Paragraph 6 of the Doha Declaration on the TRIPS Agreement and Public Health. Joint Communication from the African Group in the WTO*, IP/C/W/351 (24 June 2002).

[313] Council for TRIPS, *Paragraph 6 of the Doha Declaration on the TRIPS Agreement and Public Health. Communication from the European Communities and their member States*, IP/C/W/352 (20 June 2002).

[314] Council for TRIPS, *Paragraph 6 of the Doha Declaration of (sic) the TRIPS Agreement and Public Health. Communication from the United Arab Emirates*, IP/C/W/354 (24 June 2002).

[315] Council for TRIPS, *Paragraph 6 of the Ministerial Declaration on the TRIPS Agreement and Public Health*, IP/C/W/355 (24 June 2002).

[316] Council for TRIPS, *Paragraph 6 of the Doha Declaration on the TRIPS Agreement and Public Health*, IP/C/W/358 (9 July 2002).

[317] Council for TRIPS, *Minutes of Meeting. Held in the Centre William Rappard on 25–27 June 2002*, IP/C/M/36, paras 1 ff (18 July 2002).

[318] Correa (n 248 above) 32–33; Commission on Intellectual Property Rights (n 116 above) 48.

[319] Council for TRIPS, *Minutes of Meeting. Held in the Centre William Rappard on 17–19 September 2002*, IP/C/M/37 (11 October 2002).

[320] An even broader proposal was to allow the recognition of a compulsory licence granted by the importing Member to the exporting Member provided that all the drugs produced under the licence are actually exported. Abbott (n 114 above) 30 ff.

(3) An authoritative interpretation stating that Article 30 of the TRIPS Agreement allows the production solely for export in certain cases.

(4) A moratorium on dispute settlement, committing Members not to challenge the production of pharmaceutical products for export if such production takes place under the circumstances described in paragraph 6 of the Doha Declaration.[321]

In the negotiations, two further issues beyond the mere mechanism of the solution proved to be controversial. Firstly, developed Members insisted on the establishment of safeguards to prevent products produced under the solution from being diverted back to the exporting markets.[322] The point was well-taken, as pharmaceuticals offered at a discount or donated to developing countries had, time and again, resurfaced in developed countries' markets.[323]

It was the second issue, the scope of the solution, which emerged as the most controversial one. A dispute about the eligibility of Members to profit from the solution was to be expected, given the vagueness of the term 'members with insufficient or no manufacturing capacities in the pharmaceutical sector'.[324] Another issue of debate was the diseases to which the solution could be applied[325] and this issue rapidly developed into a deal breaker. Starting with its first submission, the United States hinted at its wish to limit the solution to certain diseases, namely those 'referred to in the Declaration, such as HIV/AIDS, malaria, tuberculosis and other epidemics'[326]—taking the language from paragraph 1 of the Doha Declaration. Developing country Members strongly opposed such a limitation, pointing out that paragraph 1 of the Doha Declaration referred to 'public health problems' afflicting developing and least-developed countries, 'especially' epidemics.

---

[321] A Attaran, 'The Doha Declaration on the TRIPS Agreement and Public Health, Access to Pharmaceuticals, and Options Under WTO Law' (2002) 12 Fordham Intell Prop Media & Ent L J 859, 871 ff suggested a similar solution, a rule of non-justiciability. The Secretariat compiled a comprehensive document from the discussions and proposed solutions: Council for TRIPS, *Proposals on Paragraph 6 of the Doha Declaration on the TRIPS Agreement and Public Health: Thematic Compilation*, IP/C/W/363 (11 July 2002). The merits of the solutions have been discussed extensively, eg by Correa (n 248 above) 25 ff; Abbott (n 114 above) 33 ff; Kampf (n 110 above) 108 ff; Commission on Intellectual Property Rights (n 116 above) 46 ff; JHJ Bourgeois and TJ Burns, 'Implementing Paragraph 6 of the Doha Declaration on TRIPS and Public Health. The Waiver Solution' (2002) 6 J World Intell Prop 835, 842 ff; N Zürcher Fausch, 'Die Problematik der Nutzung von Zwangslizenzen durch Staaten ohne eigene Pharmaindustrie: Zur instrumentellen Umsetzung von Art. 6 der Erklärung zum TRIPs und zum öffentlichen Gesundheitswesen' (2002) 57 Aussenwirtschaft 495, 505 ff.

[322] Correa (n 248 above) 30; Kampf (n 110 above) 109–110; Cottier (n 184 above) 387; Council for TRIPS, *Proposals* (n 321 above) 10.

[323] Bartelt (n 213 above) 297; Noehrenberg (n 307 above) 379 ff.

[324] Council for TRIPS, *Proposals* (n 321 above) 5 ff. Attaran criticizes the wording of para 6 of the Doha Declaration as it allows its application to countries like Liechtenstein and Luxembourg. Attaran (n 321 above) 863. There was also some debate about the eligibility of exporting Members and the products to be covered. Council for TRIPS, *Proposals* (n 321 above) 4.

[325] Council for TRIPS, *Proposals* (n 321 above) 4.

[326] Council for TRIPS, *Paragraph 6 of the Doha Declaration on the TRIPS Agreement and Public Health. Communication from the United States*, IP/C/W/340 (14 March 2002).

Accordingly, they insisted on coverage of all areas of public health.[327] The two positions reflect the different extent to which countries participating in the debate are bound by the right to access to medicine.[328]

The conflict escalated in December 2002 when the United States was the sole WTO Member to reject a draft decision written by the then Chairman of the Council for TRIPS, Motta,[329] causing the negotiations to come to a standstill and the deadline set by the Doha Declaration for finding a solution to be missed. The United States declared a moratorium on dispute settlement for Members exporting patented pharmaceuticals in violation of Article 31(f) of the TRIPS Agreement to middle or low-income Members facing grave infectious epidemics and having no or insufficient manufacturing capacity.[330] It was not until 30 August 2003 that Members finally agreed on a solution. The tiebreaker was a statement by the Chairman of the General Council. The General Council took note of that statement and, in the light of it,[331] adopted the Decision of 30 August 2003,[332] which was based on the Motta draft.

B Content of the Decision

The Decision of 30 August 2003 is highly complex. It contains three waivers and a number of additional provisions. For better comprehension, its scope as to products and Members will be discussed first, then the three waivers will be described, after which the additional safeguards against trade diversion will be discussed. Finally, some more technical provisions deserve to be noted. The adoption of the Decision 'in the light of' the Chairman's statement begs the question which legal connection exists between the two texts. Suffice it to say for the moment that, as an agreement relating to the decision which was made between all the parties in connection with the conclusion of the decision, the statement is part of the context of the Decision for the purposes of interpretation pursuant to Article 31(2)(a) of the Vienna Convention. The issue will be discussed in-depth below, along with the legal status of the Decision.

---

[327] Eg Council for TRIPS, *Elements of a Paragraph 6 Solution. Communication from Kenya, the Coordinator of the African Group*, IP/C/W/389, paras 2 f (14 November 2002). The head of the South African Permanent Mission to the WTO commented that 'the U.S. Delegation could not obtain a mandate from PhRMA to join the consensus'. F Ismail, 'The Doha Declaration on TRIPS and Public Health and the Negotiations in the WTO on Paragraph 6. Why PhRMA Needs to Join the Consensus!' (2003) 6 J World Intell Prop 393, 398.   [328] See chapter 3.

[329] Council for TRIPS, *Minutes of Meeting. Held in the Centre William Rappard on 25–27 and 29 November, and 20 December 2002*, IP/C/M/38, para 34 (5 February 2003).

[330] Council for TRIPS, *Moratorium to Address Needs of Developing and Least-Developed Members with no or Insufficient Manufacturing Capacities in the Pharmaceutical Sector*, IP/C/W/396 (14 January 2003).

[331] General Council, *Minutes of Meeting. Held in the Centre William Rappard on 25, 26 and 30 August 2003*, WT/GC/M/82, paras 29 ff (13 November 2003).

[332] General Council, *Implementation of Paragraph 6 of the Doha Declaration on the TRIPS Agreement and Public Health. Decision of 30 August 2003*, WT/L/540 (2 September 2003). On the negotiating history: Vandoren and Van Eeckhaute (n 307 above) 780–781; C Herrmann, *Historischer Wendepunkt für den internationalen Patentschutz? Der internationale Patentschutz für Medikamente*

a Product Scope of the Decision

The Decision applies to 'pharmaceutical products', which paragraph 1(a) of the Decision defines as 'any patented product, or product manufactured through a patented process, of the pharmaceutical sector needed to address the public health problems as recognized in paragraph 1 of the Declaration'. The reference to the scope of the Doha Declaration implies that the United States did not prevail with its attempt to limit the mechanism to specific diseases.[333] Like the Doha Declaration, the Decision applies to all 'public health problems' in developing and least-developed countries—with a non-exhaustive illustration reading 'especially those resulting from HIV/AIDS, tuberculosis, malaria and other epidemics'.[334] Both active ingredients necessary for the manufacture and diagnostic kits needed for the use of products of the pharmaceutical sector are explicitly included in the scope of the decision. Vaccines, although not explicitly mentioned, are products of the pharmaceutical sector and therefore also included.[335]

b Country Scope

Any Member may become an exporting Member under the decision.[336] 'Eligible importing Members' are all LDC Members and any other Member establishing that it has insufficient or no pharmaceutical manufacturing capacities for the product and making a notification to the Council for TRIPS of its intention to use the system as an importer. The notification need not be approved by the Council for TRIPS.[337]

An importing Member that is not a LDC[338] has to establish that it has insufficient or no manufacturing capacities in the pharmaceutical sector for the product(s) in question.[339] The establishment of a lack of manufacturing capacities is within the sole responsibility of each Member itself.[340] The Member merely makes a notification to the Council for TRIPS confirming that it has established

---

nach der Ausnahmeregelung der WTO für Exportzwangslizenzen vom 30. August 2003, ZEuS 2003, 589, 598 ff; Zürcher Fausch (n 321 above) 501 ff; YA Vawda, 'From Doha to Cancun: The Quest to Increase Access to Medicines under WTO Rules' (2003) 19 SAJHR 679, 681 ff; M Blakeney, 'TRIPS After the Doha Ministerial Declaration' in C Antons, M Blakeney and C Heath (eds), *Intellectual Property Harmonisation within ASEAN and APEC* (2004) 11, 25 ff.

333 M Slonina, 'Durchbruch im Spannungsverhältnis TRIPS and Health: Die WTO-Entscheidung zu Exporten unter Zwangslizenzen' (2003) Beiträge zum Transnationalen Wirtschaftsrecht 20, 8; Herrmann (n 332 above) 604. 334 Paragraph 1 of the Doha Declaration.

335 Vandoren and Van Eeckhaute (n 307 above) 784. *Contra* the representative of Cuba. General Council, *Minutes of Meeting. Held in the Centre William Rappard on 25, 26 and 30 August 2003*, WT/GC/M/82, para 39 (13 November 2003).

336 Paragraph 1(b) of the Decision of 30 August 2003.

337 Paragraph 1(b), footnote 2 of the Decision of 30 August 2003. The notification may also contain limitations, eg to the case of a national emergency.

338 LDCs are deemed to have insufficient or no manufacturing capacities in the pharmaceutical sector according to the Annex of the Decision of 30 August 2003.

339 Paragraph 2(a)(ii) of the Decision of 30 August 2003.

340 Vandoren and Van Eeckhaute (n 307 above) 785.

that it has insufficient or no manufacturing capacities. A footnote clearly states that the notification 'does not need to be approved by a WTO body' to use the system of the Decision.[341] While the Dispute Settlement Body can examine whether a Member abided by the Decision, it has to give due deference to the determination by the Member.[342] The language indicates that the determination of manufacturing capacity is made on a product-by-product basis, so that a Member that can produce antibiotics is not necessarily deemed to have the capacity to produce antiretrovirals.[343] Apart from that, the Decision remains unclear on the definition of lacking manufacturing capacities. The Annex merely states that Members can either establish that they have no manufacturing capacity in the pharmaceutical sector or that, excluding any capacity owned or controlled by the patent holder, they have insufficient capacities for meeting their needs. When the capacity has become sufficient to meet the needs, they can no longer benefit from the system.[344]

Some 33 developed country Members[345] have declared that they would not use the system as importing Members and 11 other Members have stated that they would only do so in case of a national emergency or other circumstances of extreme urgency.[346]

c Waiver of Article 31(f) of the TRIPS Agreement

Members ultimately decided against an approach based on Article 30 of the TRIPS Agreement[347] and adopted a mechanism based on compulsory licensing, ie a modification of Article 31(f) of the TRIPS Agreement. The Decision waives the obligation to grant a compulsory licence 'predominantly for the supply of the domestic market' under Article 31(f) insofar as necessary for the production of a pharmaceutical product or pharmaceutical products and the export to an eligible importing Member or several such Members. To benefit from the waiver, several conditions have to be fulfilled.

---

[341] Paragraph 2(a)(ii) of the Decision of 30 August 2003.

[342] According to para 10 of the Decision of 30 August 2003 Members shall not challenge measures taken in conformity with the waivers under Art XXIII:1(b), (c) of the GATT 1994.

[343] Vandoren and Van Eeckhaute (n 307 above) 785.

[344] Annex, Decision of 30 August 2003.

[345] The ten EU accession countries have to be added to the list of 23 countries in footnote 3 of the Decision. Blakeney (n 332 above) 27; Slonina (n 333 above) 9.

[346] Chinese Taipei, Hong Kong, Israel, Korea, Kuwait, Macao, Mexico, Qatar, Singapore, Turkey, and the United Arab Emirates. Blakeney (n 332 above) 27; Slonina (n 333 above) 9.

[347] However, the decision cannot be taken as a subsequent agreement between the parties regarding the interpretation of the treaty or the application of its provisions (Art 31(3)(a) of the Vienna Convention) that would in future bar an interpretation of Art 30 of the TRIPS Agreement allowing the production solely for export. Such an agreement on the interpretation of Art 30 did not exist. Many Members were in favour of a broad interpretation of Art 30. Gopakumar (n 254 above) 103.

aa Notification by Importing Member The importing Member has to make a notification to the Council for TRIPS containing the following elements:[348]

- the names and expected quantities of the product(s) needed, which will be published on the WTO website;
- the confirmation that the eligible importing Member (other than an LDC) has established that it has insufficient or no manufacturing capacities in the pharmaceutical sector for the product(s) in question;
- the confirmation that it has granted or intends to grant a compulsory licence if the product is patented in its territory.

Where the product is not patented in the importing Member, the mechanism also applies, but a compulsory licence by the importing Member is, of course, not necessary. The notification does not need to be approved by any WTO body.[349]

bb Conditions of Compulsory Licence Granted by Exporting Member The compulsory licence granted by the exporting Member has to contain several conditions:[350]

(1) Only the quantity of the drug necessary to meet the needs of the importing Member(s) may be manufactured under the licence and the entirety of the production has to be exported to the notifying importing Member(s). The plural used in the provision indicates that the licence can be granted for the pooled needs of several importing Members. Of course, the exporting Member can simultaneously grant a compulsory licence for its own needs.[351]

(2) The 'products produced under the licence shall be clearly identified as having been produced under the system set out in th[e] Decision through specific labelling or marking. Suppliers should distinguish such products through special packaging and/or special colouring/shaping of the products themselves, provided that such distinction is feasible and does not have a significant impact on price'. The Chairman's statement clarifies that this requirement does not only apply to formulated pharmaceuticals, but also active ingredients and finished products using such ingredients. The provision is one of the key elements in preventing trade diversion or the abuse of the system. It makes the re-export of the finished products from the importing Member much more difficult, as

---

[348] Paragraph 2(a) of the Decision of 30 August 2003.

[349] Gopakumar argues that the 'involvement' of the WTO in the grant of the compulsory licence establishes obligations that go beyond the TRIPS Agreement. As far as the notification requirement is concerned, this charge is incorrect. The waiver merely gives Members an additional option: they can now grant licences in violation of Art 31(f) of the TRIPS Agreement, in which case they have to comply with the mechanism of the Decision of 30 August 2003. This additional option does not add to the obligations under the TRIPS Agreement, as Members can continue to grant standard, TRIPS-compliant compulsory licences as before without having to comply with the notification requirements. The same cannot be said of the safeguard provisions (see below). Gopakumar (n 254 above) 108–109.   [350] Paragraph 2(b) of the Decision of 30 August 2003.

[351] Vandoren and Van Eeckhaute (n 307 above) 787.

the products can be identified as having been produced under the mechanism. Members can either directly impose the type of identification required in the compulsory licence or they can merely require identification and leave it to the manufacturer to decide on the most appropriate type of identification. As an illustration of labelling measures that may be used the Chairman's statement contains 'Best Practices' guidelines with a number of examples that companies have used so far to prevent trade diversion. Importantly, no such measures are necessary where they are either not feasible or would have a significant impact on the price. The latter is the case where changes to the pharmaceutical itself are in question (eg colouring) that would require new studies to obtain regulatory approval.[352]

(3) Before shipment begins, the licensee has to post the quantities supplied to each destination and the distinguishing feature of the product(s) either on its own website or on a website maintained by the WTO Secretariat.

cc Notification by Exporting Member   The exporting Member has to notify the Council for TRIPS of the grant of the licence, including the conditions attached to it.[353] Again, the notification need not by approved by a WTO body.

d Waiver of Article 31(f) of the TRIPS Agreement within Regional Trade Agreements

A Member that is also a member of a regional grouping can benefit from a different waiver of Article 31(f) of the TRIPS Agreement that is contained in paragraph 6(i) of the Decision. The provision was drafted with African regional groupings in mind and facilitates the use of compulsory licences for them.[354] Where at least half of the current membership of a regional trade agreement are LDCs and a developing country or LDC Member of that grouping has produced or imported a pharmaceutical product under a compulsory licence, its obligations under Article 31(f) are waived to the extent necessary to enable the Member to export the product to the markets of the other developing or LDC Members of the regional trade agreement that share the health problem in question.[355] As patents remain territorial, an importing Member would still have to grant a compulsory licence, however. The additional administrative hassle could be avoided by the grant of regional patents—which should be promoted according to paragraph 6(ii) of the Decision.

---

[352] Vandoren and Van Eeckhaute (n 307 above) 788. A similar labelling requirement is contained in Council Regulation (EC) 953/2003 of 26 May 2003 to Avoid Trade Diversion into the European Union of Certain Key Medicines [2003] OJ L135/5 (3 June 2003).

[353] For details on the notification see para 2(c) of the Decision of 30 August 2003.

[354] Vandoren and Van Eeckhaute (n 307 above) 790.

[355] For details see para 6(i) of the Decision of 30 August 2003. Contrary to the statement by Herrmann (n 332 above) 606, the fact that the territorial nature of the patent rights is not put into question by the provision does not imply that the importing Member has to comply with para 2(a) of the Decision: the wording of the Decision indicates that paras 6 and 2 provide for separate and independent waivers of Art 31(f) of the TRIPS Agreement, each with its own conditions attached.

e Waiver of Article 31(h) of the TRIPS Agreement

The peculiar construction that a compulsory licence granted by one Member is merely used to manufacture products for export and that the products are ultimately put to use in another Member raises the question how to determine the 'adequate remuneration' due. Paragraph 3 of the Decision solves that problem. Under the Decision, the remuneration has to be paid in the exporting Member, but the relevant 'economic value' is the value of the use to the importing Member. Where the product was also under patent in the importing Member, so that it had to grant a compulsory licence, too, its obligation to provide for adequate remuneration under Article 31(h) of the TRIPS Agreement is waived.

f Further Safeguards against Trade Diversion

At the urging of developed Members, safeguards against trade diversion and a possible abuse of the system were provided for. Thus, according to paragraph 4 of the Decision, eligible importing Members, including developing countries and LDCs, shall take 'reasonable measures within their means, proportionate to their administrative capacities and to the risk of trade diversion to prevent re-exportation of the products that have actually been imported into their territories under the system'. Where necessary, developing country and LDC Members can obtain the technical and financial assistance of developed Members for this purpose. The provision takes due account of the lack of financial and administrative capacities in many Members and thereby allows Members without the capacity to take safeguard measures to make use of the mechanism.

Paragraph 5 of the Decision goes much further and obliges all Members to ensure the availability of effective legal means (using the means already required to be available under the TRIPS Agreement) to prevent the importation into and sale in their territories of products produced under the mechanism and diverted to their markets.

The Chairman's statement reiterates that the system should not be abused. In the statement Members recognize that the system 'should be used in good faith to protect public health and (...) not be an instrument to pursue industrial or commercial policy objectives'. Some critics voiced fears that these terms could be held to imply that under the mechanism the generic industry may not work for profit.[356] But the Chairman's statement neither can nor wants to introduce such a limitation to the Decision, particularly as such a limitation would vitiate the whole purpose of the Decision, because the system clearly involves the grant of compulsory licences to generic drug manufacturers that work on a for-profit basis. Also, the promotion of technology transfer and capacity building in the pharmaceutical sector is explicitly within the purview of the Decision and Members are encouraged to use the system to promote this objective.[357] However, the Chairman's statement indicates that the Decision is meant to alleviate health problems and

---

[356] Gopakumar (n 254 above) 107.
[357] For details see para 7 of the Decision of 30 August 2003. Gamharter (n 124 above) 232.

Members may not use the Decision solely for the purpose of supporting their industry and absent such health problems.

g Technicalities

On the more technical side, the Decision provides that the Council of TRIPS reviews the functioning of the system annually with a view to ensuring its effective operation, this review being 'deemed to fulfil the review requirement' of Article IX:4 of the WTO Agreement.[358] Paragraph 11 of the Decision determines that the Decision 'including the waivers granted in it' terminates 'for each Member on the date on which an amendment to the TRIPS Agreement replacing its provisions takes effect for that Member'.[359] Both of these provisions are highly significant for the analysis of the legal status of the Decision, which will be discussed in detail below. The amendment to the TRIPS Agreement mentioned in paragraph 11 of the Decision has been decided on, but is not yet in force. It will be treated below.

C Implementation

The mechanism relies on exporting Members' granting compulsory licences for production for export. The mere existence of a WTO Decision *allowing* Members to grant such licences does not suffice for the mechanism to be operational. Before exporting Members can actually grant compulsory licences for production for export at the request of importing Members, they have to amend their internal patent laws to provide for such licences. Chapter 4 pointed out that amending patent laws to that effect is a way to comply with a state's obligation to cooperate towards the achievement of access to medicine. Limited progress has been made concerning the amendments of internal patent laws. Canada,[360] China,[361] the European Communities,[362] India,[363] the Netherlands,[364]

---

[358] Paragraph 8 of the Decision of 30 August 2003.

[359] Paragraph 11 of the Decision of 30 August 2003.

[360] An Act to Amend the Patent Act and the Food and Drugs Act (The Jean Chrétien Pledge to Africa), Statutes of Canada 2004, Chapter 23, Bill C-9 (The Bill received Royal Assent on 14 May 2004).

[361] State Intellectual Property Office Order No 37 (in effect as of 1 January 2006). An unofficial translation is available at <http://www.cptech.org/ip/health/cl/china-order37.html>.

[362] Regulation (EC) 816/2006 of the European Parliament and of the Council of 17 May 2006 on Compulsory Licensing of Patents Relating to the Manufacture of Pharmaceutical Products for Export to Countries with Public Health Problems.

[363] The provisions are contained in the Indian Patent Act passed in 2005. Attempts to introduce the relevant provisions were made before, namely with § 49 The Patents (Amendment) Bill, 2003 (Bill No 92 of 2003). M Singh Nair, *India Moving Towards a TRIPS Compliant Patent Regime— Implications for the Pharmaceutical Industry*, at <http://www.mondaq.com/i_article.asp_Q_articleid_E_27499> (2004); S Mukherjee, *The Journey of Indian Patent Law towards TRIPS Compliance*, IIC 2004, 125, 148.

[364] Policy rules on issuing compulsory licences pursuant to WTO Decision WT/L/540 on the implementation of para 6 of the Doha Declaration on the TRIPS Agreement and public health, under s 57(1) of the Kingdom Act on Patents of 1995 (unofficial English translation), de Staatscourant, 21 December 2004.

Norway,[365] and South Korea[366] have passed the relevant amendments to their patent legislation.[367]

D Evaluation

Members greeted the adoption of the Decision with praise: Brazil, India, and South Africa agreed that it would contribute to making pharmaceuticals more accessible and help to solve the problem of fulfilling the needs of countries with insufficient pharmaceutical manufacturing capacities.[368] On behalf of the African Group, the representative of Morocco spoke of a 'historic moment'.[369] Developed countries, such as the United States and the European Communities, too, voiced their contentment.[370] The representative of the Holy See, speaking as an observer, gave a moral stamp of approval, calling the Decision a 'historic turning point and a decisive sign showing the world that trade could open itself to the needs of humanity and respond to the broadest well-being of the individual'.[371]

But the enthusiasm was not universal. Some argued that the mechanism would not be viable, as its intricate legal and institutional requirements would prevent Members from using it effectively.[372] Others wrote that only time could tell whether the solution would really be effective and that every stakeholder would have to make efforts towards making the solution work.[373]

After more than three years into the existence of the mechanism, the designated WTO website[374] still shows no notifications of importing Members wishing to make use of the system. Several reasons explain this at first sight astonishing fact, given the hard fight needed to reach the Decision. First of all, importers will import Indian generics without the necessity to have recourse to the cumbersome mechanism as long as these are available, and the transition period for India to grant pharmaceutical patents only ran out in 2005. Secondly, importing Members had to wait for the implementation of the Decision in exporting Members' national legislation and the implementation took some time. The European

---

[365] Council for TRIPS, *Implementation of Paragraph 6 of the Doha Declaration on the TRIPS Agreement and Public Health. Norway*, IP/C/W/427 (17 September 2004).

[366] As of 1 December 2005 the South Korean Patent Act contains the relevant provisions. A translation is available at <http://lists.essential.org/pipermail/ip-health/2005-November/008728.html>.

[367] The different internal proposals up to May 2004 are discussed in J Hepburn, *Implementing the Paragraph 6 Decision and Doha Declaration: Solving Practical Problems to Make the System Work*, Quaker United Nations Office (2004) 12 ff.

[368] General Council, *Minutes of Meeting. Held in the Centre William Rappard on 25, 26 and 30 August 2003*, WT/GC/M/82 (13 November 2003) paras 40 ff, 50 ff, 44.   [369] Ibid para 36.

[370] Ibid paras 81, 83.

[371] Ibid para 87. For a positive evaluation see also F Morri, 'Patentes y medicamentos: la batalla de los países en desarrollo' (2004) Revista de Estudios Internacionales 123, 135 ff.

[372] Gopakumar (n 254 above) 112–113. There are also doubts whether developed Members will grant compulsory licences for export given their strong pharmaceutical manufacturing lobby. Islam (n 270 above) 683 ff.

[373] Vawda (n 332 above) 689; Vandoren and Van Eeckhaute (n 307 above) 792; Gamharter (n 124 above) 242.

[374] <http://www.wto.org/english/tratop_e/trips_e/public_health_notif_import_e.htm>.

Communities, for example, did not implement the Decision into their internal laws until May 2006. Thirdly, importing Members face intricate legal problems in using the mechanism and have to be familiar not only with WTO law and their own internal patent laws, but also with the (different) implementations of the Decision in national patent laws of potential exporting Members, expertise that is often lacking in developing Members. Fourthly, as the exporting Member has to pay the 'adequate remuneration' but the importing Member enjoys the benefit of the compulsory licence, there is at least a disincentive to grant licences for export. Ultimately, the Decision simply cannot restore what Members without manufacturing capacity lost when the large developing country Members with manufacturing capacity were obliged to begin granting pharmaceutical product patents in January 2005. Before that date, generic manufacturers automatically began operating in countries like Brazil and India, which have a sufficiently large number of customers. Importing Members could simply approach these manufacturers, which could then boost their production at minimum cost. Now, manufacturers will often have to decide whether to start manufacturing the product at all on the basis of the request of importing Members—and it will commonly be uneconomic for them to do so for the sake of supplying the drugs to just one or two of those often small importing markets.[375] The Decision has therefore not solved this aspect of the conflict between the TRIPS Agreement and access to medicine.

3 Amendment of the TRIPS Agreement

The Decision set up an arduous follow-up task. According to paragraph 11 of the Decision '[t]he TRIPS Council shall initiate by the end of 2003 work on the preparation of [an] amendment [to the TRIPS Agreement] with a view to its adoption within six months, on the understanding that the amendment will be based, where appropriate, on this Decision (...)'.

A Negotiating History

The TRIPS Council commenced work on the amendment during its meeting on 18 November 2003.[376] Members largely agreed that their task was to faithfully transform the Decision into an amendment, an exercise that, in the words of an EC submission, 'should remain essentially technical'.[377] However, the first informal consultations of the Chairman of the TRIPS Council showed that the supposedly simple technical exercise turned out to be divisive. During these discussions and later debates there was no agreement either about the form or the content of

---

[375] N Mathiason, 'Drugs deal "not viable"' *Mail and Guardian* (31 August 2003).

[376] Council for TRIPS, *Minutes of Meeting. Held in the Centre William Rappard on 18 November 2003*, IP/C/M/42, paras 134 ff (4 February 2004).

[377] Council for TRIPS, *Implementation of the General Council Decision on Paragraph 6 of the Doha Declaration on the TRIPS Agreement and Public Health. Communication from the European Communities*, IP/C/W/416 (21 November 2003).

the amendment. As to the form, some Members favoured a footnote to Article 31 of the TRIPS Agreement, others—regarding a footnote as an attempt to both downplay the importance of the Decision and to upgrade the legal status of the Chairman's statement—argued for a full incorporation in the TRIPS Agreement.[378] As to the content, Members could not agree on how to proceed with the Chairman's statement that had proven the tiebreaker for the Decision of 30 August 2003. Some delegations, like Switzerland and the United States, considered the statement essential in reaching the Decision and therefore wanted it reflected in the amendment.[379] Others, like Argentina and Brazil, argued against an inclusion, stating that such an inclusion would give the statement greater legal status in relation to the amendment than it had in relation to the Decision. [380]

Emphasizing that the Decision of 30 August 2003 continued in force, Members moved their deadline to reach agreement to the end of March 2005.[381] But even that deadline became impossible to meet and had to be moved[382] after a substantive proposal for an amendment submitted in November 2004 by Nigeria on behalf of the African Group[383] met with substantial criticism. The proposal eliminated a number of provisions in the Decision that, according to the African Group, were redundant in the context of an amendment.[384] Other Members, such as Switzerland and the United States, considered the approach to re-open the discussions held before the Decision of 30 August 2003 and rejected it. The representative of the United States emphasized its desire to not abandon any part of the Decision, regarding the Chairman's statement as part of the deal: 'What might seem like surplusage to some delegations was essential to others.'[385] Members remained divided on these issues until shortly before the Sixth WTO Ministerial Conference held in Hong Kong in December 2005.[386] After holding consultations

---

[378] Council for TRIPS, *Minutes of Meeting. Held in the Centre William Rappard on 8 March 2004*, IP/C/M/43, para 86 (7 May 2004).

[379] Council for TRIPS, *Minutes of Meeting. Held in the Centre William Rappard on 16 June 2004*, IP/C/M/44, paras 96, 123 (19 July 2004).

[380] Council for TRIPS (n 378 above) para 84; Council for TRIPS (n 379 above) paras 77 ff; Council for TRIPS, *Minutes of Meeting. Held in the Centre William Rappard on 25–26 October, 29 November and 6 December 2005*, IP/C/M/49, para 177 (31 January 2006).

[381] Council for TRIPS (n 379 above) para 71.

[382] Council for TRIPS, *Minutes of Meeting. Held in the Centre William Rappard on 8–9 and 31 March 2005*, IP/C/M/47, para 217 (3 June 2005).

[383] Council for TRIPS, *Implementation of Paragraph 11 of the 30 August 2003 Decision. Communication from Nigeria on behalf of the African Group*, IP/C/W/437 (10 December 2004).

[384] Council for TRIPS, *Legal Arguments to Support the African Group Proposal on the Implementation of Paragraph 11 of the 30 August 2003 Decision. Communication from Rwanda on behalf of the African Group*, IP/C/W/440, paras 9 ff (1 March 2005); Council for TRIPS, *Minutes of Meeting. Held in the Centre William Rappard on 1–2 December 2004*, IP/C/M/46, para 106 (11 January 2005).

[385] Council for TRIPS, *Minutes* (n 384 above) para 117. See also Council for TRIPS, *Comments on Implementation of the 30 August 2003 Agreement (Solution) on the TRIPS Agreement and Public Health. Communication from the United States*, IP/C/W/444, para 8 (18 March 2005).

[386] Council for TRIPS, *Minutes of Meeting. Held in the Centre William Rappard on 25–26 and 28 October, 29 November and 6 December 2005*, IP/C/M/49, para 204 (31 January 2006).

with delegations, the Chairman reached Members' agreement on a proposal for a decision on an amendment to the TRIPS Agreement a mere week before the Hong Kong Ministerial. Members also agreed on the text of two statements to be made by the Chairman of the General Council prior to the adoption of the proposal by the General Council.[387] The first statement relates to non-violation complaints. The second one is entirely identical to the Chairman's statement for the Decision of 30 August 2003, apart from the changes required by the fact that the decision is an amendment, because of EU enlargement, and because of the renumbering of provisions in the amendment. In the light of this statement and reaffirming Members' statements after the adoption of the Decision of 30 August 2003 the General Council adopted the draft Decision.[388] As an amendment of a multilateral WTO Agreement altering the rights and obligations of Members the decision takes effect for the Members that have accepted it upon acceptance by two thirds of the Members according to Article X:3 of the WTO Agreement. Members set themselves a deadline of 1 December 2007 to reach the two thirds threshold. The deadline may be extended. By December 2006, three countries had accepted the amendment.

B Content of the Decision

The amendment of the TRIPS Agreement follows the wording of the Decision of 30 August 2003. As the content of the amendment is identical with that of the Decision, this section sets out the structure of the amendment in comparison to that of the Decision. It should also be pointed out again that the Chairman's statement, too—whatever its legal value—is identical with that made before the adoption of the Decision of 30 August 2003.

The amendment inserts an Article 31*bis* after Article 31 of the TRIPS Agreement and an Annex after Article 73 of the TRIPS Agreement. Article 31*bis*.1 of the TRIPS Agreement exempts Members from complying with Article 31(f) of the TRIPS Agreement when granting a compulsory licence to the extent necessary for the production of a pharmaceutical product or pharmaceutical products and the export to an eligible importing Member or several such Members. The conditions for this exemption that were contained in paragraph 2 of the Decision of 30 August 2003—notification by the importing Member, conditions to be imposed in the compulsory licence issued by the exporting Member, notification by the exporting Member—are contained in paragraph 2 of the Annex to the TRIPS Agreement. Article 31*bis*.2 of the TRIPS Agreement treats the obligation to pay 'adequate remuneration' pursuant to Article 31(h) and transposes the waiver of Article 31(h) contained in paragraph 3 of the Decision of 30 August 2003. Article 31*bis*.3 of the TRIPS Agreement transposes the waiver of Article 31(f) within regional trade

---

[387] Ibid para 214.

[388] General Council, *Minutes of Meeting Held in the Centre William Rappard on 1, 2 and 6 December 2005*, WT/GC/M/100, paras 31 ff (27 March 2006); General Council, *Amendment of the TRIPS Agreement. Decision of 6 December 2005*, WT/L/641 (8 December 2005).

agreements that is contained in paragraph 6(i) of the Decision of 30 August 2003. The obligation of Members not to resort to non-violation complaints against measures taken in conformity with the mechanism contained in paragraph 10 of the Decision of 30 August 2003 is to be found in Article 31*bis*.4 of the TRIPS Agreement. Paragraph 9 of the Decision of 30 August 2003 stating that the Decision is without prejudice to the existing rights under the TRIPS Agreement other than Article 31(f) and (h) of the TRIPS Agreement will become Article 31*bis*.5. Paragraph 1 of the Annex to the TRIPS Agreement contains the definitions of paragraph 1 of the Decision of 30 August 2003. Paragraphs 3 and 4 of the Annex to the TRIPS Agreement contain the safeguards against trade diversion contained in paragraphs 4 and 5 of the Decision of 30 August 2003. The promotion of regional patents laid down in paragraph 6 (ii) of the Decision of 30 August 2003 will become paragraph 5 of the Annex to the TRIPS Agreement, that of technology transfer[389] paragraph 6 of the Annex to the TRIPS Agreement. The annual review created by paragraph 8 of the Decision of 30 August 2003 will be maintained,[390] but no longer has to function as a fulfilment of the review requirement of Article IX:4 of the WTO Agreement. Finally, the section on the Assessment of Manufacturing Capacities in the Pharmaceutical Sector put down in the Annex of the Decision of 30 August 2003 will become the Appendix to the Annex to the TRIPS Agreement. Paragraph 11 of the Decision of 30 August 2003, which provided for the termination of the waiver did not have to be transformed into an amendment. The footnotes contained in the Decision have been maintained in the amendment—except for the changes required by EU enlargement.

C Evaluation

The Ministerial Conference welcomed the Decision to amend the TRIPS Agreement on 18 December 2005.[391] The innovative pharmaceutical industry, too, voiced its contentment with the agreement.[392] NGOs, on the other hand, rejected the amendment: they regarded it as too cumbersome and failing to see the economic realities of the production of generics.[393]

As the TRIPS amendment does not differ from the Decision of 30 August 2003, the evaluation of the amendment is not very different, either. The amendment does not restore what Members without manufacturing capacity lost when the LDC Members with manufacturing capacity started to be obliged to grant

---

[389] Paragraph 7 of the Decision of 30 August 2003.

[390] Paragraph 7 of the Annex to the TRIPS Agreement.

[391] Ministerial Conference, *Doha Work Programme. Ministerial Declaration. Adopted on 18 December 2005*, WT/MIN(05)/DEC, para 40 (22 December 2005).

[392] PhRMA, 'PhRMA Welcomes TRIPS and Public Health Agreement' Press Release (6 December 2005); IFPMA, 'TRIPS Amendment Permanently Resolves Export Compulsory License Issue' Press Release (6 December 2005).

[393] Médecins Sans Frontières, 'Amendment to WTO TRIPS Agreement Makes Access to Affordable Medicines Even More Bleak' Press Release (6 December 2006); CPTech, 'Statement of CPTech on TRIPS Amendment' Press Release (6 December 2005).

patents. It does not solve the patent-related problems of access to medicines for Members without manufacturing capacity.

4 The Legal Status of the Decisions: Flexibility in Decision-Making

It is not just the substance of the decisions that is of interest, but also the procedure by which they were passed. In the case of the first two decisions, WTO organs showed considerable disregard for their formal rules of decision-making.[394] I will argue that both of these decisions are, nevertheless, valid and legally binding and that the disregard for decision-making procedures evinces that another type of flexibility is emerging, namely that, where human rights law is in conflict with WTO law, the WTO will apply its decision-making powers in a flexible manner.

A Background: Decision-Making in the WTO

The validity of the decisions must be examined under the decision-making procedures of the WTO Agreement, to which the TRIPS Agreement is subject as Annex 1C of the WTO Agreement, unless where the TRIPS Agreement provides otherwise.[395]

Decisions are taken by the different bodies of the WTO. Of particular importance is the Ministerial Conference as the WTO's highest organ. It is composed of representatives of all Members, commonly the ministers for trade or economic affairs, and meets at least once every two years.[396] The General Council, composed of representatives of all Members, usually diplomats or other officials, conducts the functions of the Ministerial Conference in the intervals between its meetings[397] and acts as Dispute Settlement Body and Trade Policy Review Body.[398] Furthermore, there are the three specialized Councils overseeing the major Multilateral Trade Agreements, the Council for Trade in Goods, the Council for Trade in Services, and the Council for Trade-Related Aspects of Intellectual Property Rights (Council for TRIPS), which operate under the general guidance of the General Council.[399] Finally, the WTO Agreement provides for Committees, subsidiary bodies, and bodies provided for under the Plurilateral Trade Agreements.[400]

---

[394] HP Hestermeyer, 'Flexible Entscheidungsfindung in der WTO. Die Rechtsnatur der neuen WTO Beschlüsse über TRIPS und Zugang zu Medikamenten' (2004) GRUR Int 194.

[395] Eg Art 71.2 of the TRIPS Agreement with respect to amendments adjusting the Agreement to a higher level of intellectual property protection achieved, and in force, in other multilateral agreements and accepted under those agreements by all WTO Members.

[396] Article IV:1 of the WTO Agreement.   [397] Article IV:2 of the WTO Agreement.

[398] Article IV:3, 4 of the WTO Agreement.   [399] Article IV:5 of the WTO Agreement.

[400] Article IV:6–8 of the WTO Agreement. W Weiß and C Herrmann, *Welthandelsrecht* (2003) 89.

Several decision-making procedures exist under the WTO Agreement. As a general rule, the Agreement continues the practice of decision-making by consensus followed under GATT 1947.[401] According to this practice the body concerned shall be deemed to have rendered a decision if no Member present at the meeting formally objects to the proposed decision.[402] Hence, absence of Members does not preclude a decision from being made. Where consensus cannot be reached, decisions can be taken by a majority of the votes cast. Votes are cast according to the principle one Member—one vote.[403] Abstentions do not count as votes cast.[404]

Article IX:2 of the WTO Agreement contains special rules for authoritative interpretations of the Multilateral Trade Agreements. It is not the Dispute Settlement Body that is competent to render such interpretations, but exclusively the Ministerial Conference and the General Council. For interpretations of the TRIPS Agreement these bodies exercise their authority on the basis of a recommendation by the Council for TRIPS. To decide on an authoritative interpretation, the Ministerial Conference or General Council first tries to reach a consensus.[405] Where a consensus decision cannot be arrived at, the decision is taken by a three-fourths majority of the Members.[406] The interpretation of an Agreement has to be distinguished from its amendment: Article IX:2 of the WTO Agreement explicitly provides that the amendment provisions in Article X shall not be undermined by the application of the provision on interpretation. However, the line separating interpretation and amendment is blurry, particularly as in international law an evolutionary approach to interpretation is well-established, with the ICJ acknowledging that 'an international instrument has to be interpreted and applied within the framework of the entire legal system prevailing at the time of the interpretation'.[407]

---

[401] Article IX:1 of the WTO Agreement. On GATT practice see JH Jackson, *World Trade and the Law of GATT* (1969).

[402] Fn 1 to Art IX:1 of the WTO Agreement.

[403] Article IX:1 of the WTO Agreement. Despite its wording the article does not limit the one-Member one-vote principle to the Ministerial Conference and the General Council. The awkward wording results from the fact that not all Members need to be represented in the specialized Councils and Committees. Weiß and Herrmann (n 400 above) 93. The Council for TRIPS takes decisions by consensus only. If consensus cannot be reached, the matter is referred to the General Council. Rule 33, Council for TRIPS, *Rules of Procedure for Meetings of the Council for TRIPS*, IP/C/1 (28 September 1995). [404] Weiß and Herrmann (n 400 above) 93.

[405] The practice of consensus decisions is based on Art IX1 of the WTO Agreement. Weiß and Herrmann (n 400 above) 94 fn 46; R Wolfrum, 'Das internationale Recht für den Austausch von Waren und Dienstleistungen' in R Schmidt (ed), *Öffentliches Wirtschaftsrecht* (1996) 535, 566; P Picone and A Ligustro, *Diritto dell'Organizzazione mondiale del Commercio* (2002) 61 ff.

[406] Article IX:2 of the WTO Agreement.

[407] *Legal Consequences for States of the Continued Presence of South Africa in Namibia (South West Africa) notwithstanding Security Council Resolution 276 (1970)*, Advisory Opinion, ICJ Reports 1971, 16, 31 (21 June 1971); Separate Opinion Weeramatry, *Gabčíkovo-Nagymaros Project (Hungary/Slovakia)*, Judgment, ICJ Reports 1997, 7, 113 (25 September 1997); but see Separate Opinion Bejaoui, ibid 123.

In exceptional circumstances it is also possible to waive obligations under the Multilateral Agreements. Article IX:3 of the WTO Agreement contains the rules on such waivers. With respect to the TRIPS Agreement, a request to waive an obligation under the Agreement must be submitted to the Council for TRIPS for consideration. Within 90 days the Council submits a report to the Ministerial Conference, which again strives to reach a consensus.[408] If a consensus cannot be obtained, the decision can be taken by three-fourths of the Members, but a decision to grant a waiver in respect of an obligation subject to a transition period that the requesting Member has not performed by the end of the period can be taken only by consensus.[409] The decision has to state the exceptional circumstances justifying it, the terms and conditions governing the application of the waiver, and the date on which the waiver terminates.[410] If the waiver is granted for more than one year, it has to be reviewed annually by the Ministerial Conference.[411] Waivers, too, have to be distinguished from amendments. The propensity to abuse waivers as a convenient mechanism to circumvent amendment procedures has already been noted by commentators under the GATT 1947.[412]

Finally, amendments to the Multilateral Trade Agreements can be proposed to the Ministerial Conference by any Member, amendments to the TRIPS Agreement can also be proposed by the Council for TRIPS. The Ministerial Conference decides by consensus or, in case consensus cannot be reached within 90 days, by a two-thirds majority of the Members to submit the amendment to the Members.[413] To take effect the amendment has to be accepted by the Members if it does not fall under Article 71.2 of the TRIPS Agreement.[414] The requirements for an amendment's taking effect vary according to the character of the amended provision. An amendment to Article 4 of the TRIPS Agreement requires acceptance by all Members;[415] an amendment to the TRIPS Agreement altering rights and obligations of the Members takes effect for the Members that have accepted it upon acceptance by two thirds of the Members[416] and an amendment to the TRIPS Agreement that does not alter the rights and obligations of the Members takes effect for all Members upon acceptance by two-thirds of the Members.[417]

---

[408] Article IX:3(b) of the WTO Agreement; the applicability of the consensus procedure of Art IX:1 of the WTO Agreement to this case has been affirmed by General Council, *Decision-making Procedures under Articles IX and XII of the WTO Agreement*, WT/L/93 (24 November 1995). Understanding in Respect of Waivers of Obligations under the General Agreement on Tariffs and Trade 1994, 33 ILM 1163.   [409] Fn to Art IX:3 of the WTO Agreement.

[410] Article IX:4 of the WTO Agreement. On the 'exceptional circumstances' required see D Marinberg, 'GATT/WTO Waivers: "Exceptional Circumstances" as Applied to the Lomé Waiver' (2001) 19 BU Int'l L J 129.

[411] Article IX:4 of the WTO Agreement. Understanding in Respect of Waivers of Obligations under the GATT 1994.

[412] JH Jackson, *The World Trade Organization—Constitution and Jurisprudence* (1998) 44; Weiß and Herrmann (n 400 above) 95.   [413] Article X:1 of the WTO Agreement.

[414] Article X:6 of the WTO Agreement.   [415] Article X:2 of the WTO Agreement.

[416] Article X:3 of the WTO Agreement.

[417] Article X:4 of the WTO Agreement. Weiß and Herrmann (n 400 above) 98 ff; P-T Stoll and F Schorkopf, *WTO—Welthandelsordnung und Welthandelsrecht* (2002) 21–22.

B The Doha Declaration

The legal status of the Doha Declaration has been widely discussed. Some authors have suggested that the Declaration is devoid of any legal value and in particular that it does not constitute an authoritative interpretation pursuant to Article IX:2 of the WTO Agreement.[418] The view goes back to a comment by United States Trade Representative (USTR) Zoellick, who called the Doha Declaration a 'landmark political declaration'.[419] The word 'declaration' in the title of the document is commonly used to support this view. The document could have been entitled 'decision', clearly placing it within the ambit of the WTO's decision-making machinery. A mere 'declaration', however, is not a legally binding document.[420] Furthermore, the document does not invoke Article IX:2 of the WTO Agreement, the relevant provision for an authoritative interpretation. Such an invocation of the legal basis for a decision is common in WTO law.[421] What is more, the document

---

[418] Kampf (n 110 above) 95; Sykes (n 306 above) 9; JJ Schott, 'Comment on the Doha Ministerial' (2002) 5 JIEL 191, 194–195. Less clear on the legal status, but in favour of weak legal effects of the declaration: GN Horlick, 'Over the Bump in Doha?' (2002) 5 JIEL 195, 199–200 ('Arguably that Declaration creates an atmosphere which would lead a panel or the Appellate Body to be less likely to find WTO inconsistencies in developing countries' use of existing compulsory licensing (…)'). The pharmaceutical industry, too, seems to regard the declaration as political. *Pharmaindustrie kritisiert WTO-Einigung zum Patentschutz*, Handelsblatt, 15 November 2001.

[419] USTR, *USTR Zoellick Says World Has Chosen Path of Hope, Openness, Development and Growth* (2001).

[420] S Charnovitz, 'The Legal Status of the Doha Declaration' (2002) 5 JIEL 207, 208. The view is supported by the fact that the very same Ministerial Conference passed decisions entitled as such: Ministerial Conference, *Implementation-related Issues and Concerns, Decision of 14 November 2001*, WT/MIN(01)/17 (20 November 2001). Correa (n 248 above) argues that the declaration is a Ministerial decision with legal effects, but at the same time asserts that the document has 'no specific legal status' in the WTO framework, only effects similar to those of an authoritative interpretation.

[421] Examples concern both waivers under Art IX:3 of the WTO Agreement and other decisions. See, eg, the prolongation of waivers under GATT 1947 using wordings such as 'The General Council, acting pursuant to the provision of Article IX of the WTO Agreement', *Pakistan—Establishment of a New Schedule XV. Extension of Time-Limit. Decision of 15 November 1995*, WT/L/102 (24 November 1995); *Carribean Basin Economic Recovery Act*, WT/L/102 (24 November 1995); *Trinidad and Tobago—Establishment of a New Schedule LXVII*, WT/L/121 (16 January 1996); *Zambia— Renegotiation of Schedule LXXVIII*, WT/L/123 (16 January 1996); *Malawi—Renegotiation of Schedule LVIII*, WT/L/131 (16 February 1996); a similar clause is used in new waivers: *Introduction of Harmonized System Changes into WTO Schedules of Tariff Concessions on 1 January 1996. Decision of 13 December 1995*, WT/L/124 (16 January 1996); *Hungary—Agreement on Agriculture*, WT/L/238 (29 October 1997); *Preferential Tariff Treatment for Least-Developed Countries*, WT/L/304 (17 June 1999); *Peru—Agreement on Implementation of Article VII of the General Agreement on Tariffs and Trade 1994*, WT/L/307 (23 July 1999), similarly invoking Art IX of the WTO Agreement: *European Communities—The ACP-EC Partnership Agreement*, WT/MIN(01)/15 (14 November 2001); *Least-Developed Country Members—Obligations under Article 70.9 of the TRIPS Agreement with Respect to Pharmaceutical Products*, WT/L/478 (12 July 2002). For invocations by the Ministerial Conference see *Implementation-related Issues and Concerns, Decision of 14 November 2001*, WT/MIN(01)/17 (20 November 2001). There are, however, no examples explicitly invoking Art IX:2 of the WTO Agreement. The EC requested an authoritative interpretation pursuant to Art IX:2 in General Council, *Request for an Authoritative Interpretation Pursuant to Article IX:2 of the Marrakesh Agreement Establishing the World Trade Organization*, WT/GC/W133 (25 January 1999), but the interpretation was not passed. Nevertheless, a WTO Committee stated that '[t]here certainly are precedents that

was not passed in accordance with the procedures for an authoritative interpretation. Whereas Article IX:2 of the WTO Agreement requires a recommendation by the Council for TRIPS, the Doha Declaration was not passed pursuant to such a recommendation.[422] Some also find fault in the fact that the Doha Declaration was passed by consensus, not necessarily fulfilling the three-fourths majority of Article IX:2.[423] For proponents of this view all of these details indicate that Members consciously decided not to adopt an authoritative interpretation and therefore the document cannot be endowed with the legal value of such an interpretation, at most it could be used as a supplementary means of interpretation.[424]

Most authors, however, regard the Doha Declaration as binding on Members. The plain meaning of the text ('We agree')[425] already supports its characterization as a binding agreement.[426] Procedurally, the Declaration was passed by a consensus—confirming its importance and Members' commitment and making it unrealistic to not regard it as binding.[427] The use of the term 'declaration' is irrelevant—the Doha Ministerial Declaration, too, is entitled 'declaration', even though it contains decisions.[428] Furthermore, it is unconvincing to argue that Members consciously decided not to adopt a binding decision. Members reached the consensus after much debate and it can be assumed that they wanted that consensus to be binding.[429]

But even though this group of authors agrees on the binding character of the Declaration, they differ with respect to its precise legal status: some regard it as an authoritative interpretation according to Article IX:2 of the WTO Agreement.[430] Others agree that the Declaration is a decision within the WTO system, but regard

could be characterized as Article IX:2 "interpretations"' (Committee on Budget, Finance and Administration, *Biennial Budgeting in the WTO*, WT/BFA/W/104 (16 July 2003)).

[422] Kampf (n 110 above) 97; FM Abbott, 'The Doha Declaration on the TRIPS Agreement and Public Health: Lighting a Dark Corner at the WTO' (2002) 5 JIEL 469, 492.

[423] Weiß and Herrmann (n 400 above) 418.

[424] Abbott (n 157 above) 33 f (written before the Doha Ministerial). The use of the Declaration as a supplementary means of interpretation could be based on Art 32 of the Vienna Convention, which allows the use of such means either to confirm the meaning, arrived at by treaty interpretation according to Art 31 of the Vienna Convention, or when such an interpretation leaves the meaning ambiguous or obscure or leads to a manifestly absurd or unreasonable result. García-Castrillón (n 238 above) 212.

[425] Paragraph 4 of the Doha Declaration.

[426] Abbott (n 422 above) 491. The press chose a similar wording: H Cooper and G Winestock, 'Poor Nations Win Gains in Global Trade Deal, as U.S. Compromises' *Wall Street Journal* (15 November 2001); H Cooper and G Winestock, 'How Activists Outmanoeuvred Drug Makers in WTO Deal' *Wall Street Journal Europe* (15 November 2001); 'Startschuss für neue Welthandelsrunde in Katar—Die Europäische Union schraubt ihre Forderungen herunter' *Handelsblatt*, (15 November 2001) ('Übereinkunft').   [427] Charnovitz (n 420 above) 209.

[428] Ministerial Conference, *Ministerial Declaration*, WT/MIN(01)/DEC/1 para 11 (20 November 2001); Charnovitz (n 420 above) 209.   [429] Charnovitz (n 420 above) 210.

[430] Weiß and Herrmann (n 400 above) 418; Herrmann (n 122 above) 42; Shanker (n 157 above) 722. Characterizing the content of the Declaration as interpretative: J Straus, 'Patentschutz durch TRIPS-Abkommen—Ausnahmeregelungen und–praktiken und ihre Bedeutung, insbesondere hinsichtlich pharmazeutischer Produkte' in Stiftung Gesellschaft für Rechtspolitik and Institut für Rechtspolitik (eds), *Bitburger Gespräche. Jahrbuch 2003* (2003) 117, 126 ff.

Article IX:1 as its legal basis and take the decision into account for interpretative purposes as a subsequent agreement between the parties regarding the interpretation of the treaty.[431] A third group considers the Declaration as a decision taken outside of the WTO setting. They argue that under general international law the parties, as the masters of the organization, are not bound by any procedural requirement in the treaty establishing the organization.[432] Hence, they are free to modify the WTO Agreements both explicitly (by consensus)[433] or implicitly.

In the end, the only tenable solution is to regard the Doha Declaration as an authoritative interpretation pursuant to Article IX:2. Nobody questions that content-wise the Declaration is an interpretation of the TRIPS Agreement, and many of the arguments advanced against characterizing the Declaration as such an interpretation are not convincing. First of all, the title 'declaration' and the absence of an invocation of Article IX:2 are largely irrelevant given that there is no legal duty to entitle an authoritative interpretation as such or to invoke the legal basis for the decision. Also, there is no WTO practice as to invoking Article IX:2 that would indicate otherwise.[434] Finally, the requirement of a three-fourths majority only has to be fulfilled if a consensus decision according to Article IX:1 cannot be reached.[435] Hence, the only aspect in which the procedure prescribed by Article IX:2 was not followed is the requirement of a recommendation of the Council for TRIPS. This defect can be overcome. While I disagree with the suggestion that the recommendation could be replaced by a thorough discussion in the Council[436]— after all, it is the agreement of the Members of the specialized body and not the mere discussion of the topic that is required—I do not consider the procedural defect to suffice for denying the Declaration the legal status of an authoritative interpretation. As Members are even entitled to change the treaty by mere agreement,[437] there can be no doubt that they can disregard a procedural requirement in decision-making. Rather than regarding the decision as binding, but outside the ambit of the WTO, it is systematically more coherent to place the Declaration within the WTO system. Hence, it is most convincing to regard the Declaration as a binding authoritative interpretation. The procedural defect has to be regarded

[431] Article 31(3)(a) of the Vienna Convention. Abbott (n 422 above) 491; Correa (n 248 above) (albeit not applying Art IX:1 of the WTO Agreement); referring to Art 31(3)(b) of the Vienna Convention: Gamharter (n 124 above) 157; *contra* Charnovitz (n 420 above) 210 (invoking Art III:2, IV:1 of the WTO Agreement, but also favouring an application of Art 31(3)(a) of the Vienna Convention).

[432] Pauwelyn (n 17 above) 47; R Bernhardt, 'Völkerrechtliche und verfassungsrechtliche Aspekte konkludenter Vertragsänderungen' in H-W Andt *et al* (eds), *Völkerrecht und deutsches Recht. FS Walter Rudolf* (2001) 15, 16–17; I Seidl-Hohenveldern and G Loibl, *Das Recht der Internationalen Organisationen einschließlich der Supranationalen Gemeinschaften* (7th edn, 2000) 234–235; HF Köck and P Fischer, *Das Recht der Internationalen Organisationen* (3rd edn, 1997) 602; R Bernhardt, *Die Auslegung völkerrechtlicher Verträge* (1963) 126 ff.

[433] Note that the meaning 'consensus' in this context differs from the meaning of consensus decision within the WTO context.   [434] N 421 above.

[435] Weiß and Herrmann (n 400 above) 94 fn 46.

[436] Weiß and Herrmann (n 400 above) 42.   [437] N 432 above.

as irrelevant.[438] This view is in line with general international law, as bodies of other international organizations, such as the Security Council, have also at times departed from procedural rules by subsequent practice of member states.[439] Later state practice confirms that Members regard themselves as bound by the Declaration. Thus, the United States has explicitly adapted its trade policy to the Declaration.[440]

C The Decision of 30 August 2003

The consensus decision of the General Council of 30 August 2003 on the implementation of paragraph 6 of the Doha Declaration also poses serious problems with respect to the decision-making machinery of the WTO. The Decision could constitute a waiver pursuant to Article IX:3 of the WTO Agreement or an amendment pursuant to Article X of the WTO Agreement.

At first glance, much favours a classification of the Decision as a waiver. It explicitly invokes Articles IX:1, 3 and 4 of the WTO Agreement as its legal basis, it explicitly waives Article 31(f) of the TRIPS Agreement obligations for the exporting Member and (where applicable) Article 31(h) of the TRIPS Agreement obligations for the importing Member. Finally, the document was passed as a consensus decision, in accordance with the voting procedure.[441]

But there are doubts about such a classification. If these doubts were to prevail, the Decision would have to be regarded as an amendment of the TRIPS Agreement adopted in fragrant violation of the applicable procedure under Article X of the WTO Agreement, resulting either in it having been adopted *ultra vires* and being void *ab initio*, or in it constituting an agreement of the Members outside of the WTO Agreement changing the TRIPS Agreement. The wording of the Decision already indicates that there is more to it than a simple waiver when it states: '[t]his Decision, including the waivers granted in it'.[442] Its content nurtures the doubts about its classification as a waiver. The Decision does not just waive obligations, in its paragraph 5 it also imposes obligations on other Members relating to the prevention of trade diversion of generics into third countries. This new obligation is not a condition that has to be fulfilled by a Member wishing to make use of the waiver—it is imposed on every Member independent of its benefiting from the waiver and is hence entirely outside of the scope of waivers under Article IX:3 of the WTO Agreement. A final and most obvious sign that this waiver in reality is something different is the way the Decision constructs the termination date.

---

[438] Committee on Budget, Finance and Administration, *Biennial Budgeting in the WTO*, WT/BFA/W/104 (16 July 2003).

[439] T Bruha, 'Security Council' in R Wolfrum and C Philipp (eds), *United Nations: Law, Policies and Practice, Volume 2* (1995) 1147, 1152.

[440] § 2102 (b) (4) (C) of the Bipartisan Trade Promotion Authority Act of 2002, Pub L 107–210, 116 Stat 993 (6 August 2002).

[441] The document is classified as a waiver by Slonina (n 333 above) 7.

[442] Paragraph 10 of the Decision of 30 August 2003.

The fact that the Decision remains in effect until it is replaced by an amendment indicates that it functions as an amendment.

Nevertheless, I consider the Decision to be a waiver, even if some doubts persist. Most of the issues raised can be resolved. I will start with doubts pertaining to the content of the waiver, proceed to procedural question and then cover the formal content requirements of Article IX:4 of the WTO Agreement.

First of all, the fact that the Decision contains new obligations is put into perspective by paragraph 9 of the Decision of 30 August 2003 stating that it is 'without prejudice to the rights, obligations and flexibilities that Members have under the provisions of the TRIPS Agreement other than paragraphs (f) and (h) of Article 31'. Also, the obligation of Members to prevent trade diversion is accompanied by the statement 'using the means already required to be available under the TRIPS Agreement'. Both of these clauses suggest that no new obligations are imposed. Some doubt remains in this respect, because the explicit creation of a new obligation can hardly be mitigated by adding such a savings clause.

Concerning procedure, Article IX:3 of the WTO Agreement puts down that in exceptional circumstances[443] a waiver 'of an obligation imposed on a Member' can be passed, with the request for a waiver initially being submitted to the Council for TRIPS and the Council submitting a report to the Ministerial Conference. The Decision of 30 August 2003 was passed without such a request and waives the obligation under Article 31(f) of the TRIPS Agreement of not just one Member, but of any exporting Member which decides to make use of the waiver.[444] However, there are precedents for such liberal use of the waiver provisions, so that this departure from the rules is only a further step in a history of widening flexibility in the application of the norm. In at least one case the request for a waiver was inferred from a Council's determination that the waiver was needed.[445] Waivers for several Members have been granted at several occasions.[446] It thus seems warranted to regard the present waiver as a small and permissible further step towards a more flexible use of waivers. Finally, some irritation was caused by the fact that the Ministerial Conference in Cancun, which planned to explicitly approve of the waiver,[447] failed and hence did not adopt the waiver.[448] The irritation stems from Article IX:3 of the WTO Agreement, which states that the Ministerial Conference may decide on a waiver. Here, the Decision was taken by

---

[443] The history of the provision indicates that the circumstances have to be so exceptional as to only exist for one Member. Marinberg (n 410 above) 135. However, the *travaux préparatoires* are of limited value in the interpretation of provisions of public international law.

[444] Where applicable, the obligation of importing Members under Art 31(h) of the TRIPS Agreement is also waived.

[445] Council for TRIPS, *Paragraph 6 of the Doha Declaration on the TRIPS Agreement and Public Health: Information on Waivers*, IP/C/W/387, para 8 (24 October 2002).

[446] Ibid paras 16 ff.

[447] *Draft Cancún Ministerial Text*, para 3, at <http://www.wto.org/english/thewto_e/minist_e/min03_e/draft_decl_e.htm> (24 August 2003).

[448] Ministerial Conference, *Ministerial Statement*, WT/MIN(03)/20 (23 September 2003).

the General Council. However, Article IV:2 of the WTO Agreement determines that the General Council conducts the functions of the Ministerial Conference in between its meetings. Hence, the General Council could pass the waiver and it is irrelevant that the Ministerial Conference did not approve of it.

Another troubling aspect of the waiver is its treatment of the requirements imposed by Article IX:4 of the WTO Agreement. The annual review by the Ministerial Conference, which serves to examine whether the conditions of the waiver were complied with and whether it is still necessary, was not only delegated to the Council for TRIPS (with a duty to report to the General Council), but also constructed as a review of effectivity aiming at fine-tuning the Decision 'with a view to ensuring its effective operation'.[449] This review is simply 'deemed' to fulfil the requirement of Article IX:4. While it is beyond doubt that the General Council may exercise the functions of the Ministerial Conference in-between meetings, it is doubtful whether these functions can be delegated to the Council for TRIPS given its possibly different composition. However, it must be taken into account that the Council for TRIPS acts under the guidance of the General Council and that the Council for TRIPS shall 'report' annually on the operation of the system to the General Council—and for this reason it seems appropriate to accept the delegation.

The most problematic provision of the waiver, however, is its termination date. The requirement to name such a date stresses the temporary character of waivers as a reaction to exceptional circumstances.[450] While it has been common practice to extend waivers, they may not be granted without a termination date. To allow a waiver to continue in effect until its provisions are replaced by an amendment is a blatant indication that the waiver is used in place of an amendment. Such a circumvention of amendment procedures by waivers can claim some tradition within the GATT 1947[451] and has rightly been criticized by Jackson,[452] but there has been no WTO precedent before the Decision. It seems that the only example of a liberal use of the termination date requirement before was a waiver granted in 2000 extending a pre-existing waiver 'until the entry into force' of the EU-Morocco Association Agreement.[453] But a closer look reveals that the termination date in that case was clear. The European Communities had requested a waiver valid 'until 1 March 2000, date of the entry into force' of the EU-Morocco

---

[449] Paragraph 8 of the Decision of 30 August 2003.

[450] Marinberg (n 410 above) 140–141. This is not supposed to imply that the exceptional circumstances have to be very limited in time—waivers have often been granted, eg to account for special, long-standing relationships between countries. *United States—Former Trust Territory of the Pacific Islands*, WT/L/183 (18 October 1996).

[451] Eg *Waiver Granted to the United States in Connection with Import Restrictions Imposed under Section 22 of the United States Agricultural Adjustment Act (of 1933), as Amended*, BISD 3S/32 (5 March 1955). Less problematic: *Generalized System of Preferences*, BISD 18S/24 (25 June 1971).

[452] JH Jackson, *The World Trading System. Law and Policy of International Economic Relations*, (2nd edn, 1997) 55–56, 63.

[453] General Council, *EC/France—Trading Arrangements with Morocco*, WT/L/361 (19 July 2000).

Association Agreement.[454] At the time the waiver was granted that agreement had already entered into force—and the waiver thus concerned past obligations.

The decisive argument for accepting the waiver as such is that it is a consensus decision of the Members. In light of their authority to change the treaties implicitly there can be no doubt about the legal status of the Decision, all the more so given Members' enthusiastic reception of it.[455] While the Decision of 30 August 2003 has to be accepted as a valid waiver, it must be noted that the WTO was willing to treat its own decision-making procedures with the utmost flexibility.[456]

With the legal status of the Decision itself clarified, I now turn to the status of the General Council Chairman's statement. A footnote in the Decision pointing to the statement seemed to indicate that the statement is a textual part of the Decision. But the footnote was only an editorial comment of the Secretariat and not part of the original decision.[457] It was severely criticized by some Members[458] and now carries the disclaimer 'Secretariat note for information purposes only and without prejudice to Members' legal rights and obligations'.[459] The only link between the two documents is the drafting history of the Decision, as indicated by the minutes of the General Council: 'The Chairman then proposed that the General Council take note of the statements and, in the light of the Chairman's Statement he had just read out, adopt the draft Decision (...)'.[460] Scholars and Members do not agree on the legal status of the statement. At times it has been called legally irrelevant and only of interest as a source of further state practice.[461] Others regard it as relevant in the context of Articles 31 and 32 of the Vienna Convention.[462]

While the former view underestimates the legal impact of the statement, the latter is too vague, as Articles 31 and 32 of the Vienna Convention differ significantly in the legal effect they assign to documents. Legally, Chairmen's statements accepted without dissent are commonly cited as an example of the application of Article 31(2)(a) of the Vienna Convention.[463] Some Members later argued that this should not be the case here, as the statement was 'unilateral' and did not reflect an 'agreement' between the parties.[464] However, the General Council explicitly agreed to the adoption of the Decision in the light of the Chairman's statement.[465] Hence, the statement is an agreement relating to the treaty made

[454] Council for Trade in Goods, *EC/France—Trading Arrangements with Morocco. Request for an Extension of the Waiver*, G/L/357 (22 March 2000).   [455] N 368 above ff.

[456] Herrmann (n 332 above) 603; Gamharter (n 124 above) 242 ff (basing the decision on Art IX:1 of the WTO Agreement).   [457] E-mail statement by the WTO Secretariat.

[458] Council for TRIPS (n 382 above) para 187.

[459] <http://www.wto.org/english/tratop_e/trips_e/implem_para6_e.htm>.

[460] General Council, *Minutes of Meeting. Held in the Centre William Rappard on 25, 26 and 30 August 2003*, WT/GC/M/82, para 30 (13 November 2003).

[461] C Herrmann, 'Viagra für den Welthandel oder historischer Wendepunkt für den internationalen Patentschutz' (2003) EuZW 673.   [462] Slonina (n 333 above) 14.

[463] A Aust, *Modern Treaty Law and Practice* (2000) 189–190.

[464] Representative of Argentina. Council for TRIPS (n 379 above) para 82.

[465] General Council (n 460 above) paras 30–31.

between all the parties in connection with the conclusion of the treaty pursuant to Article 31(2)(a) of the Vienna Convention and thus constitutes context for the purpose of the interpretation of the Decision.

D The Amendment of the TRIPS Agreement

The amendment of the TRIPS Agreement raises no genuine additional questions. Its passage followed the procedure set down in Article X:1 of the WTO Agreement. The amendment was proposed by the Council for TRIPS and passed by a consensus decision by the General Council in exercise of the functions of the Ministerial Conference in the interval between meetings. Its entry into force is, as stated correctly by the Decision containing the amendment, subject to the rules of Article X:3 of the WTO Agreement.

Like the Decision of 30 August 2003 the amendment raises the question of the status of the statement of the Chairman of the General Council. The Decision to amend the TRIPS Agreement itself neither mentions, nor refers to the Chairman's statement. The connection between the decision to amend the Agreement and the Chairman's statement shows in the minutes that read: '[t]he Chairman then proposed that the General Council take note of the statements and, in the light of the Chairman's Statement just read out, adopt the draft Decision contained in document IP/C/41. The General Council so agreed.'[466] Again, following the same line of argument as with respect to the Decision of 30 August 2003, the Chairman's statement constitutes an agreement relating to the treaty made between all the parties in connection with the conclusion of the treaty pursuant to Article 31(2)(a) of the Vienna Convention. It therefore constitutes context for the purpose of the interpretation of the amendment.

5 Conclusion

As seen in this section, the WTO reacted to the public pressure brought to bear on it and its Members: the publicity of the South African AIDS trial, the gravity of the AIDS crisis, the imminent expiration of the transition period all played a part in convincing Members that they had no choice but to tackle the conflict between the TRIPS Agreement and access to medicine. While the decisions that were passed, including the amendment to the TRIPS Agreement, certainly present a step forward, they do not solve the conflict. Uncertainty about the flexibilities of the TRIPS Agreement still prevails.

The decisions also added another type of flexibility to the Agreement. Both the Doha Declaration and the Decision of 30 August 2003 were reached with significant bending and twisting of the WTO decision-making procedures, indicating that Members will apply procedural rules flexibly where a conflict between WTO law and human rights law arises.

---

[466] General Council, *Minutes* (n 388 above) paras 31–32 (emphasis and para numbering deleted).

Nevertheless, the conflict between international patent law put down in the TRIPS Agreement and access to medicine remains unresolved, as generic versions of new drugs will disappear from world markets. The next section will consider options available for improving the situation.

IV Towards Solving the Conflict

There are a number of possibilities as to how the tension between the TRIPS Agreement and access to medicines—at the core a conflict between WTO and human rights law—can be eased. Many of them have already been passed upon in the course of the discussion.

1 Possible Solutions

First of all, the WTO Agreements could be amended to accommodate human rights. Such an amendment could take the form of a WTO human rights treaty or it could include the ICCPR and the ICESCR by reference. Much like in national systems, human rights provisions could be endowed with a superior status, allowing them to prevail over traditional WTO law in case of a conflict.

Full integration of human rights law would imply that the human rights provisions could be enforced by WTO dispute settlement. However, that proposition is politically impossible to achieve, as developing country Members fear that industrialized country Members would use human rights provisions to justify trade sanctions against them, invoking as a human rights violation what they regard as their comparative advantage: cheap labour.[467] The same political opposition also prevents endowing the human rights regime with a stronger enforcement mechanism which would counterbalance the strength of the WTO regime in the 'factual hierarchy' of regimes.

A less ambitious amendment would be the creation of an exception allowing Members to break TRIPS obligations to protect human rights. However, the negotiations of the Doha Declaration show that this option, too, is politically unfeasible. Some developed Members unequivocally opposed any attempt to include a provision that would let the interests of public health simply prevail over the obligation to provide for patent protection.[468]

A third option is to provide for institutional linkages between the WTO and human rights related bodies and organizations, which would allow cross-influences between the two regimes.[469] So far, such institutional cooperation is

---

[467] See this chapter above.   [468] See this chapter above.
[469] Petersmann (n 3 above) 246; in-depth on this approach to coordinate treaty regimes: N Matz, *Wege zur Koordinierung völkerrechtlicher Verträge. Völkervertragsrechtliche und institutionelle Ansätze* (2005) 365 ff.

generally limited to reciprocal information, participation of other organizations at Ministerial Conferences as observers,[470] and informal cooperation, as illustrated by the joined WHO/WTO workshop on differential pricing.[471] There is little hope that linkages can be created that give human rights-related organizations any influence on WTO governance. Developing countries' fear that the International Labour Organization would be one of the first candidates for such cross-regime governance, leading to a similar result as enforceable human rights provisions, is too great to make this option politically feasible. The current 'soft' networking approach at regime coordination[472] is of great benefit, as it enhances mutual understanding within the different regimes, but it does not provide the human rights regime with the necessary clout to produce any substantial change. Article 13.1 of the DSU could arguably play a major role in allowing a more substantial institutional linkage.[473] The provision permits a WTO panel to seek 'information and technical advice from any (...) body which it deems appropriate'.[474] In the matter of TRIPS and access to medicines a WTO panel could, via this provision, seek information from the WHO or the Committee on Economic, Social and Cultural Rights on the effects of patents on public health or the right to health.

This power of panels already alludes to what I consider the most likely route for the importation of human rights law into WTO law: WTO jurisprudence. It is well worth remembering that in the European Union, regarded by many as a beacon for human rights protection, human rights were imported via the judiciary, too. The treaties of the European Communities did not provide for human rights protection. It was the European Court of Justice (ECJ) that began to apply fundamental rights as general principles of law, drawing inspiration from member states' constitutions and international treaties on which the member states collaborated.[475] WTO panels could follow the example and apply human rights provisions as part of general international law, which—as discussed in chapter 3—includes access to medicines. But even though the parallel is tempting, there are important differences stemming from the different characteristics of the organizations: the 'ever closer Union' on the one hand, with member states that show large

---

[470] Article V of the WTO Agreement allows such cooperative arrangements between the WTO and other organizations. T Flory and N Ligneul, 'Commerce International, Droits de l'Homme, Mondialisation: Les Droits de l'Homme et l'Organisation Mondiale du Commerce' in L'Institut International des Droits de l'Homme (ed), *Commerce Mondial et Protection des Droits de l'Homme* (2001) 179, 183.

[471] WHO and WTO, *Report of the Workshop on Differential Pricing and Financing of Essential Drugs, 8–11 April 2001, Høsbjør, Norway* (2001).

[472] In-depth: A-M Slaughter, *A New World Order* (2004).   [473] Pauwelyn (n 1 above) 118 ff.

[474] Note Art 13.2 of the DSU, allowing panels to request advisory opinions from experts with respect to factual scientific or technical issues.

[475] HG Schermes, *The Protection of Human Rights in the European Community. Referat im Rahmen der Vortragsreihe 'Europäisches Wirtschaftsrecht nach Maastricht'. Bonn, 22. November 1993* (1994); NA Neuwahl, 'The Treaty on European Union: A Step forward in the Protection of Human Rights?' in NA Neuwahl and A Rosas (eds), *The European Union and Human Rights* (1995) 1; J Kühling, 'Grundrechte' in A von Bogdandy (ed), *Europäisches Verfassungsrecht. Theoretische und dogmatische Grundzüge* (2003) 583.

commonalities even in their heterogeneity and in which member states' courts threatened to reverse the unification process if the ECJ would not protect human rights effectively; the specialized trade body without any integrational goal on the other hand, with a diverse membership and Members actively opposed to an integration of human rights.[476] The differences require a WTO panel to find a strong basis in the wording of the WTO Agreements for the import of human rights considerations. Chapter 2 introduced one provision of the TRIPS Agreement that fulfils this requirement: the security exception of Article 73 of the TRIPS Agreement. Relying on a modern, broad definition of security that includes large-scale threats to human rights, a WTO panel can invoke the provision to allow Members facing public health crises including India and Brazil to refuse the grant of patents for drugs to treat pandemics altogether. Such a holding would ensure that generics to treat pandemics remain available—even if the medicine is still under patent protection in the developed world.

2 Challenges Ahead: FTAs and BITs

But even if such a solution were to be adopted immediately, the next challenges in the conflict between patent law and access to medicines have long materialized and threaten the very flexibilities that have so fervently been fought for. In response to developing country Members' more effective cooperation within the WTO and their corresponding gain in negotiating power,[477] developed countries, in particular the United States, shifted negotiations to bilateral and regional fora.[478]

As a consequence, a web of international obligations in the patent field is developing that has a triple effect. Firstly, it often obligates developing countries to not make use of the flexibilities of the TRIPS Agreement. Secondly, it commonly imposes minimum patent standards that go well beyond the standards put down in the TRIPS Agreement (referred to as 'TRIPS-plus'). Thirdly, its intricate structure involving multiple treaties with slightly different provisions adds to the pro-patent argumentative ammunition of developed countries, discouraging developing countries from using any of the flexibilities to avoid challenges and pressure—even where technically they might be allowed to use the flexibilities. The more and more tightly woven web consists mainly of two elements: free trade agreements (FTAs) and bilateral investment treaties (BITs).

A Free Trade Agreements

In recent years a growing number of FTAs have been signed, commonly between one of the great trading powers and its trading partners.[479] The multiplication of

---

[476] Hilf and Oeter in Hilf and Oeter (eds) (n 3 above) 707.
[477] FM Abbott, 'The WTO Medicines Decision: World Pharmaceutical Trade and the Protection of Public Health' (2005) 99 AJIL 317, 344.   [478] Ibid 349.
[479] In 2006 Correa stated that since 2001 the United States had initiated 11 bilateral and regional free trade agreements with 23 countries. CM Correa, 'Implications of Bilateral Free Trade Agreements on Access to Medicines' (2006) 84 Bulletin of the WHO 399.

FTAs is not limited to the bilateral level, but also takes place on a regional level. Suffice it to mention that in the American context with respect to the United States the Dominican Republic-Central America Free Trade Agreement (CAFTA-DR) has joined the North American Free Trade Agreement (NAFTA). The giant Free Trade Area of the Americas is still being negotiated.

The United States particularly strives to include intellectual property rights in its FTAs. The content of the Agreements varies widely, from merely reiterating TRIPS provisions to explicitly limiting TRIPS flexibilities or imposing additional obligations: eg some FTAs require patent term extension for the factual curtailment of the patent term as a result of the marketing approval process of pharmaceuticals,[480] some the grant of 'new use' patents,[481] others ban parallel imports,[482] limit the grounds for the grant of compulsory licences,[483] or require more extensive protection of test data.[484] Even where these agreements simply repeat TRIPS language, they can limit a country's TRIPS Agreement flexibilities, as the FTAs are interpreted independently of the TRIPS Agreement. Also, decisions taken by the WTO in the context of the TRIPS Agreement, such as the Doha Declaration, the Decision of 30 August 2003 and the amendment to the TRIPS Agreement are not binding with respect to the FTAs.

The situation is not resolved by side letters and understandings to the FTAs explicitly addressing access to medicines:[485] not all FTAs include such side letters, they commonly do not override the explicit language of the FTA and their terms at times differ from those used in the WTO documents.[486] It is not just the flexibilities already achieved that are at risk, but also the ability to further change and develop the TRIPS Agreement system—at least to the extent that standards are to be weakened. A possible solution to the conundrum would be the inclusion of a clause in the FTAs that goes beyond the non-derogation clauses that

---

[480] Eg US-Chile FTA, Art 17.10.2 (a); CAFTA-DR, Art 15.9.6 (b).

[481] Eg US-Morocco FTA, Art 15.9.2; US-Australia FTA, Art 17.9.1.

[482] Eg US-Morocco FTA, Art 15.9.4; US-Australia FTA, Art 17.9.4.

[483] Eg US-Jordan FTA, Art 4.20.

[484] Eg US-Bahrain FTA, Art 14.9.1 (a); CAFTA-DR, Art 15.10.1 (a). In-depth on the threats created by FTAs: Correa (n 479 above); C Fink and P Reichenmiller, *Tightening TRIPS: The Intellectual Property Provisions of Recent US Free Trade Agreements*, World Bank Trade Note No 20 (2005); Generic Pharmaceutical Association, *Access to Affordable Medicines: A Comparison of Provisions of the TRIPS Agreements and Selected Bilateral Trade Agreements*, at <http://www.cptech.org/ip/health/trade/>; PH Kang and CS Stone, 'IP, Trade and U.S./Singapore Relations. Significant Intellectual Property Provisions of the 2003 U.S.-Singapore Free Trade Agreement' (2003) 6 J World Intell Prop 721, 724; P Roffe, 'Bilateral Agreements and a TRIPS-plus World: the Chile-USA Free Trade Agreement' Quaker International Affairs Programme TRIPS Issues Paper 4 (2004); FM Abbott, 'The Doha Declaration on the TRIPS Agreement and Public Health and the Contradictory Trend in Bilateral and Regional Free Trade Agreements' Quaker United Nations Office Occasional Paper 14 (2004); Abbott (n 477 above) 349 ff; Ghanotakis (n 111 above) 580 ff.

[485] Eg CAFTA, *Understanding regarding Certain Public Health Measures* (5 August 2004); US-Morocco FTA *Side Letter on Public Health*; *Understanding between Canada and the United States regarding the implementation of the Decision of the WTO General Council of August 30, 2003 and NAFTA* (16 July 2004).   [486] Abbott (n 477 above) 352.

have been used so far[487] and lets the TRIPS Agreement provisions, including all future developments of that Agreement and of WTO jurisprudence, override the FTA provisions.

B Bilateral Investment Treaties

BITs constitute a threat to the TRIPS Agreement flexibilities that has not yet been sufficiently recognized. Typically signed between a developing and a developed country, these treaties govern the treatment of foreign investment, amongst others protecting it against expropriation.[488] The first BIT was adopted in 1959. The number of BITs increased dramatically in the 1990s and until 2004 over 2,300 BITs had been concluded.[489]

Already the first BIT signed in 1959 between Germany and Pakistan explicitly regarded patents as within the scope of the term 'investment'.[490] Nowadays, countries, among them the United States[491] and Germany,[492] habitually include intellectual property in their BITs as a form of protected investment. Consequently, patents can be protected by the standards set up in BITs, with effects such as that the grant of a compulsory licence could be subject to the BIT as an expropriation.[493]

The potential for conflicts with the TRIPS Agreement could be reduced by an appropriate interpretation of the term 'intellectual property' in BITs. The term must be read as a reference to the intellectual property rights defined in the TRIPS Agreement, so that the grant of TRIPS-compliant compulsory licences or the use of any other TRIPS Agreement flexibility is inherent in the right itself and not an expropriation. However, BITs commonly provide for the possibility of dispute

[487] Eg US-Chile FTA, Art 17.1.5: 'Nothing in this Chapter concerning intellectual property rights shall derogate from the obligations and rights of one Party with respect to the other by virtue of the TRIPS Agreement (...).'

[488] AT Guzman, 'Why LDCs Sign Treaties that Hurt Them: Explaining the Popularity of Bilateral Investment Treaties' (1998) 38 Va J Int'l L 639, 641–642.

[489] UNCTAD, *Bilateral Investment Treaties 1959–1999*, 1 (2000); TR Braun, 'Investment Protection under WTO-Law—New Developments in the Aftermath of Cancún' (2004) Beiträge zum Transnationalen Wirtschaftsrecht 28, 5.

[490] Article 8(1)(a) of the Treaty for the Promotion and Protection of Investments. Pakistan and Federal Republic of Germany, available in the UNCTAD BITs database.

[491] Eg Treaty Between the United States of America and the People's Republic of Bangladesh Concerning the Reciprocal Encouragement and Protection of Investment; Treaty between the Government of the United States of America and the Government of the Republic of Honduras Concerning the Encouragement and Reciprocal Protection of Investment.

[492] Eg Treaty between the Federal Republic of Germany and the Democratic Socialist Republic of Sri Lanka concerning the Promotion and Reciprocal Protection of Investments; Vertrag zwischen der Bundesrepublik Deutschland und der Republik Honduras über die Förderung und den gegenseitigen Schutz von Kapitalanlagen; Agreement between the Federal Republic of Germany and the People's Republic of Bangladesh concerning the Promotion and Reciprocal Protection of Investments.

[493] D Gervais and V Nicholas-Gervais, 'Intellectual Property in the Multilateral Agreement on Investment. Lessons to be Learned' (1999) 2 J World Intell Prop 267, 270. For the discussion of other possible 'TRIPS-Plus' aspects from a developing world perspective see, eg ET Biadgleng, 'IP Rights Under Investment Agreements: the TRIPS-plus Implications for Enforcement and Protection of Public Interest' South Centre Research Paper No 8 (2006).

settlement between the investor and the host state,[494] so that there is a substantial risk that some of the arbitrators fail to adequately take the TRIPS Agreement into account. The United States must be credited with having updated its draft US Model BIT to exclude TRIPS-compliant compulsory licences from its scope[495] and it can only be hoped that other countries will follow that move and that old BITs will be amended,[496] or, even better, that the TRIPS Agreement, including its future developments, is explicitly given precedence over the BIT.

C Conclusion

The challenges that lie ahead prove those who considered the conflict between access to medicines and intellectual property law solved wrong. To some extent it is there to stay, as we constantly evaluate and re-evaluate the balance between the two conflicting rights. However, this study shows that the next step must be to give human rights law a larger role in the WTO system.[497] States have affirmed and reaffirmed their commitment to these rights on numerous occasions. It is time to live up to those commitments. It will be up to judges—namely the members of the WTO Appellate Body—to courageously hold Members to their legal obligations.

---

[494] A number of *fora* can be used by the parties, eg the International Centre for Settlement of Investment Disputes, domestic courts, the International Chamber of Commerce, the United Nations Commission on International Trade Law, *ad hoc* arbitration. A Reinisch, '2.2 Selecting the Appropriate Forum' in UNCTAD (ed), *Course on Dispute Settlement. International Centre for Settlement of Investment Disputes* (2003) 5.

[495] Article 6(5) of the 2004 Model BIT, at <http://www.ustr.gov/assets/Trade_Sectors/Investment/Model_BIT/asset_upload_file847_6897.pdf>.

[496] Finally, a growing number of regional patent conventions (besides the better-known EPC) impose substantive patent law obligations on their states parties and contribute to the impenetrable web of patent law obligations. However, they also constitute a laudable development towards regional patents. C Heath, 'Intellectual Property Rights in Asia—An Overview' (1997) 28 ICC 303; MA Richardt, 'A New Instrument of International Patent Cooperation: The Eurasian Patent Convention' (1997) 28 IIC 466; ES Nwauche, 'An Evaluation of the African Regional Intellectual Property Rights Systems' (2003) 6 J World Intell Prop 101.

[497] Cf Flory and Ligneul (n 470 above) 180.

Summary of Arguments

This chapter is intended to enable the reader to get a quick overview of the theses advanced in the book. It does not and cannot replace reading the book. As it does not repeat the arguments made to arrive at the theses, the reader is encouraged to refer back to the relevant chapter where he or she is interested in the facts and arguments supporting the theses.

Chapter 1—Background of the Debate

1. The events surrounding HIV/AIDS medication served as a catalyst for the debate about the effects of the TRIPS Agreement on access to medicine. Despite the fact that much of the research for the first AIDS drug AZT was conducted by publicly funded institutions, a private corporation obtained patents in many countries for the use of AZT in the treatment of AIDS. Initially, it priced the drug at $10,000 for a yearly supply for one patient. With the introduction of generic (off-patent) medication produced in India the price of HIV/AIDS drugs fell significantly and in 2006 a yearly supply of a three-drug combination pill, the current standard of treatment, was priced at $150 per person. Modern AIDS drug treatment can be administered adequately in countries with an extremely poor infrastructure and gives HIV patients the hope of living through a normal life span. Despite the price discrepancy between the patented and the generic drugs both the pharmaceutical industry with its 1998 lawsuit in South Africa and developed countries, in particular the United States, have exerted pressure on developing countries to provide for stringent patent protection for pharmaceuticals.

2. With 38.6 million people living with HIV in 2005 and 80 per cent of those in clinical need of antiretroviral treatment not receiving such treatment, HIV/AIDS remains an unresolved health crisis on an unprecedented scale.

3. However, HIV/AIDS is not the only example of the conflict between patents and access to medicine. When anthrax letters were sent to important personalities in the United States in October 2001 both the United States and Canada threatened to break Bayer's patents on *Cipro* to negotiate a significant price reduction. Concerns have also been voiced, eg with respect to the patent on Roche's *Tamiflu*, the WHO-recommended treatment for bird flu.

4. The supply of cheap generics for drugs under patent in the developed world depended on a mere handful of developing countries in which the medication was not patented and which have the technological capacity to manufacture drugs, above all India, but also Brazil, Argentina, Thailand, South Africa, and Cuba.

Chapter 2—Patent Law

5. Historically, patents were granted by rulers at their discretion to introduce new arts into their realm, whether by importation or by invention. To ensure the importation of knowledge, rulers commonly required the invention to be practised and at times to be taught to locals.

6. Today, patents are justified by several rationales: natural law, the contract theory, the reward theory, the incentive theory, and the prospect theory. However, the natural law rationale has been discredited. The most widely favoured rationale for patents is that they allow the inventor to recoup research and development costs and thereby provide an incentive for investment in research (incentive theory).

7. Many countries, including developed countries such as Germany, Japan, Switzerland, Italy, and Norway, have excluded pharmaceutical products from patentability until well into the second half of the 20th Century for fear of detrimental effects on public health.

8. The international patent regime under the Paris Convention and the Patent Corporation Treaty did not harmonize national patent laws, one of the defects industrialized countries, whose corporations own most patents worldwide, criticized. Using a mixture of unilateral pressure, compromises in other trade fields and their large negotiating power in the GATT setting, developed countries managed to negotiate stronger international patent standards within the WTO against developing countries' opposition: the TRIPS Agreement.

9. Despite recent criticism of the TRIPS Agreement culminating in a claim of invalidity the Agreement is valid and, in particular, not void for duress even assuming that such a ground of invalidity of a treaty is admitted.

10. The interpretation of the TRIPS Agreement has to take account of access to medicine as a public health concern, mentioned as an object and purpose of the agreement.

11. Many provisions of the TRIPS Agreement remain vague. According to the principle *in dubio mitius* and the interpretation of the agreement with a view to public health concerns Members enjoy considerable latitude in the implementation of those provisions. Examples of the latitude that Members possess when defining the conditions for patentability under national law are: a wide definition of discoveries (which are exempted from patentability), not granting new use patents, more or less stringent standards of novelty, inventive step, and industrial applicability.

12. Despite the TRIPS Agreement's prohibition of discrimination as to the field of technology in Article 27.1 of the TRIPS Agreement, bona fide exceptions to deal with problems that exist only in certain product areas are permissible under WTO jurisprudence, also in the area of pharmaceuticals. This fact is illustrated by technology-specific patent laws in the pharmaceutical field reacting to the effects of the drug approval process.

13. However, according to Article 27 of the TRIPS Agreement Members are under a clear obligation to grant pharmaceutical product and process patents. Article 27.2-3(a) of the TRIPS Agreement cannot be read to exempt pharmaceuticals from patent protection. Articles 7, 8.1 of the TRIPS Agreement do not contain exceptions to the obligations of the TRIPS Agreement. The TRIPS Agreement also includes stringent standards for the rights conferred by a patent.

14. A Member suffering from a grave pandemic could try to exclude pharmaceuticals necessary to fight the pandemic from patent protection under the security exception

contained in Article 73 of the TRIPS Agreement. However, such action involves a high risk of losing in litigation, as it relies on an expansive interpretation of 'security', which is only emerging and far from settled in international law.

15. LDC Members benefit from a transition period until 1 January 2016 with respect to pharmaceutical products and until 1 July 2013 with respect to most other TRIPS Agreement obligations. However, these Members rarely have the capacity to manufacture drugs.

16. The transition period that allowed many developing country Members including India and Brazil to not grant product patent protection for pharmaceuticals expired on 1 January 2005. With the expiration of the transition period these Members, the only sources for generics still under patent in developed countries, now have to provide for pharmaceutical product patents. Hence, manufacturers will now be able to obtain product patents for new medicines and prevent the manufacture of generics in all Members having the relevant production capacity for the duration of the patent term.

17. While Members thus, in principle, have to grant patent protection for pharmaceuticals, the TRIPS Agreement also provides for flexibilities. These are discussed in chapter 5 after analyzing how and if human rights have to be taken into account in their interpretation. They need not be discussed here, as under the definition of 'conflict' used in the book and discussed below, the general obligation to grant pharmaceutical patents is sufficient to create a 'conflict' between the TRIPS Agreement and the human rights provision on access to medicine described in the next chapter.

Chapter 3—Access to Medicine as a Human Right

18. Due to the ideological rift between Western and socialist countries, there are two major universal human rights Covenants, one protecting civil and political rights (the ICCPR) and one economic, social, and cultural rights (the ICESCR). Both have been ratified by approximately 85 per cent of the WTO Members, and thus not the whole WTO membership—eg the United States has not ratified the ICESCR.

19. Even though international economic, social, and cultural rights are not enforced through judicial proceedings, they are justiciable in the sense that they are inherently amenable to be applied by judicial bodies, albeit in the application of the rights courts should give some deference to political bodies. These are often better situated to analyze the different factors involved in the progressive implementation of the rights. The theoretic distinction between civil and political rights on the one hand and economic, social, and cultural rights on the other hand cannot be maintained. The justiciability of economic, social, and cultural rights is demonstrated by the jurisprudence of the South African Constitutional Court and has been confirmed by the ICJ.

20. International human rights law is binding on states and not on private corporations. However, states are under a duty to protect individuals from violations of their rights by private parties. As a non-signatory the WTO is not bound by human rights treaties. However, it is bound by human rights that are part of general international law except where the WTO Agreements contradict human rights standards that are not *juris cogentis*.

21. Access to medicine is protected as a minimum core obligation under the right to health contained in Article 12 of the ICESCR, further strengthened by the right to

enjoy the benefits of scientific progress contained in Article 15(1)(b) of the ICESCR. The right covers essential drugs as defined by the WHO. Components of the right are the availability of medicine in sufficient quantity, the accessibility of that medication to everybody including the economic accessibility of the medication, the acceptability of the treatment with respect to the culture and ethics of the individual and an appropriate quality of the medicine. States have to achieve the right progressively, but are under an immediate obligation to take steps to the maximum of their available resources to respect, protect and fulfil the right. Non-compliance with access to medicine as a minimum core obligation is a prima facie violation of the ICESCR. To justify its non-compliance a state must demonstrate that every effort has been made to use all resources that are at its disposition in an effort to satisfy, as a matter of priority, this minimum obligation.

22. States can fulfil the right to access to medicine by establishing a comprehensive health care system and funding the drugs for their citizens. As developing countries do not have the resources for such a system, they have to protect the right by preventing private parties from pricing drugs excessively. They can do so by enforcing their competition laws and adjusting their patent legislation accordingly, both of which do not require significant state resources.

23. The WHO Constitution does not create a legally binding right to health. It merely mentions the right in its preamble.

24. The ICCPR protects access to life-saving medicine as part of the right to life contained in Article 6 of the ICCPR. States have an immediate duty to respect and ensure the right, which includes a duty to protect individuals against violations of the right by the state and by private parties—resembling the duties contained in the ICESCR.

25. The UDHR is not a binding contractual document, nor can it be construed as an authoritative interpretation of the human rights provisions of the UN Charter.

26. The right to life and/or to health is also protected by numerous other international conventions, albeit in a more limited manner (*ratione materiae* or *ratione loci*).

27. Access to life-saving medicines in the face of national health emergencies, particularly pandemics is protected as customary international law and a general principle and thus binding on all states. State practice shows that the United States, while persistently objecting to a right to health with a larger scope, does not object to this limited rule.

Chapter 4—Conflict between Patents and Access to Medicine

28. Patents move pricing behaviour from that in a competitive, unregulated market, in which pharmaceuticals would be priced at marginal cost, towards monopoly pricing, thereby raising the price level and reducing the quantity sold. This gives the pharmaceutical innovator the possibility to recoup research and development costs, estimated at between $115m and $802m per drug.

29. Patents will also raise the price level in developing countries. If these markets are strictly separated from developed markets, patentees will set a monopoly price for each market separately, which will commonly (but not necessarily) be lower in developing countries

than in developed countries, but which will still be higher than marginal cost. If the markets are not separated and the price can leak from one market into another, eg because of parallel imports, patentees will try to limit the supply for the lower-price market or set a unitary price for both markets.

30. The fact that corporations do not patent pharmaceuticals in all developing country markets where patents are available does not indicate that patents are not an obstacle to access to medicine, as an innovator need only obtain patents in countries with the capacity to manufacture drugs to monopolize the world market.

31. Patents are far from the only hurdle in providing access to medicine. To wit, other hurdles such as setting up a basic infrastructure are significantly more costly. However, even though other impediments to greater access are even bigger, patents can still constitute an impediment to access to medicines.

32. As developing countries cannot afford to pay the monopoly rent caused by patent protection while still providing the same level of access to medicine, the obligation to grant pharmaceutical patents interferes with access to medicine in those countries.

33. This interference is not justified by Article 15 of the ICESCR, Article 27(2) of the UDHR protecting the right of authors to benefit from the protection of the moral and material interest resulting from scientific productions, including the interests of inventors. The human rights protection is granted for the livelihood of the inventor and neither encompasses the profits necessary as an incentive for research and development, nor benefits legal entities like pharmaceutical companies. Also, Article 15 of the ICESCR balances public access to the invention and the protection of the inventor's interests, a balance that falls on the side of access to the invention where other human rights provisions are put at risk by the protection of the inventor's interests.

34. The interference is not justified by the incentive function of patents, either. That approach at justification argues that patents provide an indispensable incentive for research and development so that without them the relevant medicine never would have been invented. Legally, it justifies an interference with access to today's medicine with the protection of access to tomorrow's medicine. Patents in developed countries are necessary as an incentive for research. However, patents in developing countries' markets do not contribute in an economically significant manner to research costs on global diseases and are not a sufficient incentive for research on diseases prevalent in the developing world. They are also not a sufficient incentive for the local, developing world industry. The local pharmaceutical industry rarely has the capacity for research and where it does it prefers, much as the industry in the developed world, to do research for diseases that also concern developed countries because of the larger economic opportunities those markets offer. Patents in the developing world do prevent prices in the developed world from dropping, particularly by eliminating the possibility to compare prices with the price of generics. However, this function cannot justify an interference with access to medicine in the developing world. Hence, pharmaceutical patents in the developing world are an impediment to access to medicine without causing any adequate benefit. As they interfere with access to medicine without justification, they violate the right.

35. Under the UN Charter and the ICESCR states have a duty to cooperate to achieve the right to access to medicine to the extent they are bound by it. Hence, states may not interfere with access in other states, must prevent third parties from violating the right in other states, and must help other states fulfil the right depending on the availability

of resources. While this does not impose a concrete obligation to give a certain amount of development aid, it obliges developed states to enable their pharmaceutical industry to produce generics for export to developing countries without manufacturing capacity.

36. The TRIPS Agreement is in conflict with access to medicine regardless of the breadth of the 'flexibilities' granted in the Agreement. As patents in developing country Members unjustifiably interfere with access to medicine, developing country Members could only escape the verdict of violating their human rights obligations by making use of the TRIPS Agreement flexibilities (assuming they are sufficiently broad). This changes a permission to use an exception into an obligation, which—under a proper definition of 'conflict'—is a conflict between the two regimes.

37. The conflict between the TRIPS Agreement and access to medicine—in substance a conflict between the world trade and the human rights regimes—is a consequence of the structure of international law, in which states regulate different issue areas independently, at times endowing areas with adjudicative mechanisms (the 'fragmentation of international law').

38. The conflict is particularly intricate as, to the extent that it concerns a conflict between treaties, it involves multilateral treaties with only partly identical membership. However, the two regimes are not fundamentally opposed (*Systemkonflikt*), it is merely norms from the two regimes that come into conflict.

39. Under the traditional international law of coexistence such a conflict would have been resolved by disassembling the multilateral treaties into bilateral relations and using the concept of *inter se* modifications. With the increasing need for states to cooperate to achieve community goals, concepts of hierarchy, including *erga omnes* norms and *jus cogens*, have been introduced and the bilateral mode of resolving conflicts is often no longer appropriate.

40. A true hierarchy in international law is, however, prevented both by the fact that the concept of *jus cogens* still awaits its first real test and by the existence of sectorally organized regimes. These latter regimes are at times endowed with an adjudication and enforcement system, often with limited jurisdiction and empowered to apply only a limited set of norms or give preference to a certain set of norms. These adjudicatory systems can come into conflict by applying the same law differently or by applying different laws and imposing contradictory rulings on a state. In the latter case, a *factual hierarchy* of regimes arises, which is independent of the normative hierarchy. States will tend to abide by the rules of the regime with the strongest enforcement mechanism—even if the rules enforced by this mechanism are inferior to the conflicting rules under general international law.

41. The two regimes involved in the conflict that is the subject of this study are diverse in nature. The WTO regime is second to none in the factual hierarchy due to its effective enforcement mechanism, whereas the human rights regime has a rather weak enforcement mechanism. On the other hand, human rights law is regarded to be higher in what could be called the moral appeal than WTO law.

42. While the GATT takes account of the possibility of regime conflict in its Article XX, exempting certain measures from GATT compliance and thereby giving preference also to some human rights considerations, the TRIPS Agreement fails to do so.

43. With more and more international norms resembling national legislation (such as the TRIPS Agreement), it seems only natural to grant a superior, constitutional function

to human rights norms. However, international law currently does not accommodate such a function. This fact is apparent where human rights law is in conflict with WTO law, as states will tend to abide by the rulings of WTO dispute settlement organs due to the superior factual hierarchy of the WTO regime. Hence, the vital question is how human rights can be accommodated within the WTO system.

Chapter 5—Access to Medicine as a Human Right in the WTO Order

44. Scholars have discussed five different approaches as to how human rights law can be applied in WTO dispute settlement: not at all (conceiving the WTO as a self-contained regime), merely for the interpretation of WTO covered agreements, to the extent there is no conflict with WTO rules, along with WTO rules and general international law rules on conflict of norms, or on a par with WTO rules so that human rights law could be enforced by WTO dispute settlement proceedings.

45. The notion of the WTO as a self-contained regime outside international law is based on a misperceived conception of self-contained regimes and is at odds with the plain wording of the WTO Agreements.

46. The WTO dispute settlement system cannot be used to enforce human rights law, as it only has jurisdiction for violations of covered agreements. Neither could human rights provisions be enforced under the heading of 'non-violation complaints', which is an exceptional procedure and not meant to import the whole body of international law for enforcement under WTO dispute settlement. While the WTO Agreements could be changed to allow the enforcement of human rights provisions, such a change is unlikely to happen given that states have consistently refused to strengthen enforcement mechanisms for international human rights law.

47. Article 7.1 of the DSU limits the applicable law in WTO dispute settlement to the covered agreements. However, human rights law plays a role in the interpretation of the covered agreements. Article 3.2 of the DSU prescribes the application of customary rules of interpretation of public international law. Hence, pursuant to Article 31(3)(c) of the Vienna Convention human rights law must be taken into account together with the context for interpreting the covered agreements.

48. The right to access to medicine under the ICESCR, ICCPR, and general international law can all be taken into account in the interpretation of the TRIPS Agreement. However, the right under general international law, though more limited in its scope, is more persuasive than the other two as it is binding on all WTO Members that are states.

49. The use of the right to access to medicine as an interpretative aid resembles the interpretation of the TRIPS Agreement in light of its object and purpose. However, it is more specific than the latter and connects the interpretation to efforts undertaken in fora such as the Committee on Economic, Social and Cultural Rights.

50. WTO jurisprudence confirms that both non-WTO treaties and general international law can be used as an aid for interpreting the covered agreements, but that they are not part of the applicable law.

51. Because of these findings and because access to medicine is not *juris cogentis*, a WTO Member cannot rely on the right to access to medicine as a defence against a claim of violation of WTO law absent a basis for the defence in the covered agreements.

52. Access to medicine serves as an argument for a broad interpretation of the flexibilities of the TRIPS Agreement. However, access to medicine is only one argument amongst several and is not necessarily dispositive. Hence, developing country Members relying on the argument are not sheltered from pressure by other Members or the risk of losing in litigation if another argument is found to be more convincing. This prevents the flexibilities of the TRIPS Agreement from being fully effective. The following paragraphs describe the TRIPS Agreement flexibilities and their interpretation before the WTO decisions in the area of public health.

53. Access to medicine supports an interpretation of the TRIPS Agreement that leaves Members at liberty as to the regime of international exhaustion they want to adopt. Nevertheless, some commentators regarded a regime of international exhaustion as mandatory, some others as prohibited.

54. With respect to limited exceptions under Article 30 of the TRIPS Agreement access to medicine mitigates in favour of a broad interpretation. In particular, access to medicine has to be taken into account in defining 'normal' exploitation and 'legitimate' interests and Article 30 of the TRIPS Agreement has to be read as an exception to the rule of non-discrimination in Article 27 of the TRIPS Agreement. The *Canada—Patent* Panel failed to do so.

55. Compulsory licences are an important tool for safeguarding access to medicine and access to medicine has to be taken into account in the interpretation of Article 31 of the TRIPS Agreement, favouring free choice of grounds for compulsory licences, the reading of Article 31 as an exception to Article 27 non-discrimination (allowing local working requirements), and lowering the level of 'adequate remuneration' where a compulsory licence is granted to safeguard access to medicine. However, again it is merely one argument among many and fails to provide legal security for Members wishing to make full use of the flexibilities. Even a human-rights friendly interpretation does not provide a solution for Members without manufacturing capacities for pharmaceuticals. From January 2005 onwards they can no longer simply import new generic medicines from other developing country Members, if necessary under a compulsory licence granted by the importing Member, as those other developing country Members have to grant patents. Members without manufacturing capacity now have to rely on compulsory licences granted by exporting Members to obtain generic medicines. But the grant of a compulsory licence for exports is restricted under Article 31(f) of the TRIPS Agreement, an amendment to which has been decided on but is not yet in force.

56. Access to medicine favours allowing the revocation of patents under Article 32 of the TRIPS Agreement in case of abuse of the patent where the abuse cannot be remedied by a compulsory licence. Nevertheless, some Members consider the revocation of patents to be permissible only where the invention was not patentable or patent office fees are not paid.

57. The WTO has issued three decisions on TRIPS and public health to remedy the situation. The first of these, the Doha Declaration, even though mostly reiterating the state of the law, clarified some of the uncertainty involved in the interpretation of the flexibilities, such as permitting each Member to choose its own regime of international exhaustion. While falling short of clarifying the role of access to medicine within the WTO system, it strengthens an argument based on the right by its paragraph 4. Nevertheless, much of the insecurity in the interpretation of the TRIPS Agreement remains.

58. After much discussion and attempts by the United States to limit the scope of the decision to epidemics, Members agreed on the Decision of 30 August 2003, a waiver of Article 31(f) of the TRIPS Agreement under multiple conditions (such as special labelling/colouring of the drugs) for Members granting a compulsory licence for the manufacture of drugs for export to Members lacking pharmaceutical manufacturing capacities. The Decision applies to all public health problems afflicting developing and least-developed countries. Where the importing Member has to grant a compulsory licence to allow the importation of the generics, its obligation under Article 31(h) of the TRIPS Agreement is waived. The consensus Decision also imposes safeguards, such as obliging all Members to ensure the availability of legal means to prevent the diversion of drugs produced under the mechanism into their territory. The Decision was adopted in the light of a Chairman's statement recognizing that the system should be used in good faith to protect public health and not be an instrument for industrial or commercial policy objectives. To be put into effect the Decision requires exporting Members to amend their legislation to allow compulsory licences for manufacture for export. States are obliged to pass such amendments under their obligation to cooperate for the achievement of access to medicine. Some states have now passed the relevant amendments. However, the Decision is unlikely to restore to Members without manufacturing capacity the advantages of the situation before 2005. Before that date, large generic manufacturers in India started operations for many drugs already because of the Indian market and Members could then simply buy the generic drugs from them. Now, generic manufacturers will often have to decide whether to incur the investment necessary to start producing a new generic drug on the sole request of a compulsory licence by a small, poor, importing Member. Apart from HIV/AIDS drugs, where manufacturers might automatically assume follow-up requests from other Members, the necessary economies of scale are unlikely to be reached under the Decision. Also, delays caused by the intricate legal mechanism are inevitable.

59. In December 2005 Members passed an amendment to the TRIPS Agreement. The amendment will come into force for Members that have accepted it upon acceptance by two-thirds of the Members. It transforms the entire Decision of 30 August 2003 into a permanent amendment, using identical wording wherever possible. The exceptions to Article 31(f) and (h) of the TRIPS Agreement will be contained in a new Article 31*bis* of the TRIPS Agreement, with details and definitions contained in an Annex to the TRIPS Agreement. The Chairman's statement for the Decision of 30 August 2003 was remade with respect to the amendment. As the content of the amendment is identical to that of the Decision of 30 August 2003, the amendment will not bring any further benefits besides the permanency of the mechanism.

60. Even though the Doha Declaration was not passed according to the procedure prescribed by Article IX:2 of the Marrakesh Agreement and suffers from some other minor formal defects, it constitutes an authoritative interpretation under that provision.

61. The Decision of 30 August 2003 has to be classified as a waiver under Article IX of the Marrakesh Agreement, even though it disregards many of the requirements imposed by that provision, such as the termination date, and also provides for new obligations for Members. The Chairman's statement constitutes an agreement relating to the Decision made between all the parties in connection with the conclusion of the

Decision pursuant to Article 31(2)(a) of the Vienna Convention and thus constitutes context for the purpose of the interpretation of the Decision.

62. The amendment of the TRIPS Agreement follows the rules put down in Article X of the WTO Agreement. The Chairman's statement constitutes context for the purpose of the interpretation. The amendment is not yet in force.

63. Both the Doha Declaration and the Decision of 30 August 2003 were reached with significant bending and twisting of the WTO decision-making procedures, indicating that Members will apply procedural rules flexibly where a conflict between WTO law and human rights law arises.

64. A solution to the conflict between the TRIPS Agreement and access to medicine can only be achieved by giving human rights law a stronger status within the WTO system. While hopes for a treaty amendment in this respect—be it a WTO human rights treaty, the creation of a human rights exception within the TRIPS Agreement, or stronger cooperation with human rights bodies—are unrealistic given the political opposition to such suggestions, it is high time for WTO jurisprudence to courageously step in and start using human rights law, at least to the extent it constitutes customary international law, in the interpretation of the WTO Agreements. To pre-empt political resistance against such a move, the Appellate Body can base the import of human rights law in the conflict between the TRIPS Agreement and access to medicine on a broad, modern definition of 'security', holding large-scale threats to human rights to be a threat to security and allowing Members facing public health crises to refuse the grant of patents for medicines to treat pandemics altogether under Article 73 of the TRIPS Agreement.

65. Beyond the TRIPS Agreement, free trade agreements and bilateral investment treaties impose new international obligations with respect to patent law that threaten the flexibilities of the TRIPS Agreement that have so fervently been fought for. To protect the TRIPS Agreement flexibilities and to uphold the ability of the WTO to further fine-tune the obligations, it is essential to ensure the superiority of the TRIPS Agreement and its flexibilities as well as of present and future WTO decisions and panel and Appellate Body reports over such treaties.

States and their Membership in Relevant Organizations and Agreements

Country	UN	WTO	WHO	WIPO	ICESCR	ICCPR
Afghanistan	1946	Observer	X	X	1983	1983
Albania	1955	2000	X	X	1991	1991
Algeria	1962	Observer	X	X	1989	1989
Andorra	1993	Observer	X	X		signed
Angola	1976	1996	X	X	1992	1992
Antigua and Barbuda	1981	1995	X	X		
Argentina	1945	1995	X	X	1986	1986
Armenia	1992	2003	X	X	1993	1993
Australia	1945	1995	X	X	1975	1980
Austria	1955	1995	X	X	1978	1978
Azerbaijan	1992	Observer	X	X	1992	1992
Bahamas	1973	Observer	X	X		
Bahrain	1971	1995	X	X		
Bangladesh	1974	1995	X	X	1998	2000
Barbados	1966	1995	X	X	1973	1973
Belarus	1945	Observer	X	X	1973	1973
Belgium	1945	1995	X	X	1983	1983
Belize	1981	1995	X	X	signed	1996
Benin	1960	1996	X	X	1992	1992
Bhutan	1971	Observer	X	X		
Bolivia	1945	1995	X	X	1982	1982
Bosnia and Herzegovina	1992	Observer	X	X	1993	1993
Botswana	1966	1995	X	X		2000
Brazil	1945	1995	X	X	1992	1992
Brunei Darussalam	1984	1995	X	X		
Bulgaria	1955	1996	X	X	1970	1970
Burkina Faso	1960	1995	X	X	1999	1999
Burundi	1962	1995	X	X	1990	1990
Cambodia	1955	2004	X	X	1992	1992
Cameroon	1960	1995	X	X	1984	1984
Canada	1945	1995	X	X	1976	1976
Cape Verde	1975	Observer	X	X	1993	1993
Central African Republic	1960	1995	X	X	1981	1981
Chad	1960	1996	X	X	1995	1995
Chile	1945	1995	X	X	1972	1972
China	1945	2001	X	X	2001	signed
Colombia	1945	1995	X	X	1969	1969
Comoros	1975		X	X		

(cont.)

Country	UN	WTO	WHO	WIPO	ICESCR	ICCPR
Congo	1960	1997	X	X	1983	1983
Cook Islands			X			
Costa Rica	1945	1995	X	X	1968	1968
Croatia	1992	2000	X	X	1992	1992
Cuba	1945	1995	X	X		
Cyprus	1960	1995	X	X	1969	1969
Czech Republic	1993	1995	X	X	1993	1993
Côte d'Ivoire	1960	1995	X	X	1992	1992
Democratic People's Republic of Korea	1991		X	X	1981	1981
Democratic Republic of the Congo	1960	1997	X	X	1976	1976
Denmark	1945	1995	X	X	1972	1972
Djibouti	1977	1995	X	X	2002	2002
Dominica	1978	1995	X	X	1993	1993
Dominican Republic	1945	1995	X	X	1978	1978
Ecuador	1945	1996	X	X	1969	1969
Egypt	1945	1995	X	X	1982	1982
El Salvador	1945	1995	X	X	1979	1979
Equatorial Guinea	1968	Observer	X	X	1987	1987
Eritrea	1993		X	X	2001	2002
Estonia	1991	1999	X	X	1991	1991
Ethiopia	1945	Observer	X	X	1993	1993
Fiji	1970	1996	X	X		
Finland	1955	1995	X	X	1975	1975
France	1945	1995	X	X	1980	1980
Gabon	1960	1995	X	X	1983	1983
Gambia	1965	1996	X	X	1978	1979
Georgia	1992	2000	X	X	1994	1994
Germany	1973	1995	X	X	1973	1973
Ghana	1957	1995	X	X	2000	2000
Greece	1945	1995	X	X	1985	1997
Grenada	1974	1996	X	X	1991	1991
Guatemala	1945	1995	X	X	1988	1992
Guinea	1958	1995	X	X	1978	1978
Guinea-Bissau	1974	1995	X	X	1992	signed
Guyana	1966	1995	X	X	1977	1977
Haiti	1945	1996	X	X		1991
Holy See		Observer		X		
Honduras	1945	1995	X	X	1981	1997
Hungary	1955	1995	X	X	1974	1974
Iceland	1946	1995	X	X	1979	1979
India	1945	1995	X	X	1979	1979
Indonesia	1950	1995	X	X	2006	2006
Iran (Islamic Republic of)	1945	Observer	X	X	1975	1975
Iraq	1945	Observer	X	X	1971	1971
Ireland	1955	1995	X	X	1989	1989
Israel	1949	1995	X	X	1991	1991
Italy	1955	1995	X	X	1978	1978

(*cont.*)

Country	UN	WTO	WHO	WIPO	ICESCR	ICCPR
Jamaica	1962	1995	X	X	1975	1975
Japan	1956	1995	X	X	1979	1979
Jordan	1955	2000	X	X	1975	1975
Kazakhstan	1992	Observer	X	X	2006	2006
Kenya	1963	1995	X	X	1972	1972
Kiribati	1999		X			
Kuwait	1963	1995	X	X	1996	1996
Kyrgyzstan	1992	1998	X	X	1994	1994
Lao People's Democratic Republic	1955	Observer	X	X	signed	signed
Latvia	1991	1999	X	X	1992	1992
Lebanon	1945	Observer	X	X	1972	1972
Lesotho	1966	1995	X	X	1992	1992
Liberia	1945		X	X	2004	2004
Libyan Arab Jamahiriya	1955	Observer	X	X	1970	1970
Liechtenstein	1990	1995		X	1998	1998
Lithuania	1991	2001	X	X	1991	1991
Luxembourg	1945	1995	X	X	1983	1983
Madagascar	1960	1995	X	X	1971	1971
Malawi	1964	1995	X	X	1993	1993
Malaysia	1957	1995	X	X		
Maldives	1965	1995	X	X	2006	2006
Mali	1960	1995	X	X	1974	1974
Malta	1964	1995	X	X	1990	1990
Marshall Islands	1991		X			
Mauritania	1961	1995	X	X	2004	2004
Mauritius	1968	1995	X	X	1973	1973
Mexico	1945	1995	X	X	1981	1981
Micronesia (Federated States of)	1991		X			
Monaco	1993		X	X	1997	1997
Mongolia	1961	1997	X	X	1974	1974
Morocco	1956	1995	X	X	1979	1979
Mozambique	1975	1995	X	X		1993
Myanmar	1948	1995	X	X		
Namibia	1990	1995	X	X	1994	1994
Nauru	1999		X			signed
Nepal	1955	2004	X	X	1991	1991
Netherlands	1945	1995	X	X	1978	1978
New Zealand	1945	1995	X	X	1978	1978
Nicaragua	1945	1995	X	X	1980	1980
Niger	1960	1996	X	X	1986	1986
Nigeria	1960	1995	X	X	1993	1993
Niue			X			
Norway	1945	1995	X	X	1972	1972
Oman	1971	2000	X	X		
Pakistan	1947	1995	X	X	Signed	
Palau	1994		X			
Panama	1945	1997	X	X	1977	1977
Papua New Guinea	1975	1996	X	X		
Paraguay	1945	1995	X	X	1992	1992

(*cont.*)

Country	UN	WTO	WHO	WIPO	ICESCR	ICCPR
Peru	1945	1995	X	X	1978	1978
Philippines	1945	1995	X	X	1974	1986
Poland	1945	1995	X	X	1977	1977
Portugal	1955	1995	X	X	1978	1978
Qatar	1971	1996	X	X		
Republic of Korea	1991	1995	X	X	1990	1990
Republic of Moldova	1992	2001	X	X	1993	1993
Romania	1955	1995	X	X	1974	1974
Russian Federation	1945	Observer	X	X	1973	1973
Rwanda	1962	1996	X	X	1975	1975
Saint Kitts and Nevis	1983	1996	X	X		
Saint Lucia	1979	1995	X	X		
Saint Vincent and the Grenadines	1980	1995	X	X	1981	1981
Samoa	1976	Observer	X	X		
San Marino	1992		X	X	1985	1985
Sao Tome and Principe	1975	Observer	X	X	signed	signed
Saudi Arabia	1945	2005	X	X		
Senegal	1960	1995	X	X	1978	1978
Serbia and Montenegro (in 2006 Serbia and Montenegro became two independent members of the UN, both of them with WTO observer status and WHO members)	2000	Observer	X	X	2001	2001
Seychelles	1976	Observer	X	X	1992	1992
Sierra Leone	1961	1995	X	X	1996	1996
Singapore	1965	1995	X	X		
Slovakia	1993	1995	X	X	1993	1993
Slovenia	1992	1995	X	X	1992	1992
Solomon Islands	1978	1996	X		1982	
Somalia	1960		X	X	1990	1990
South Africa	1945	1995	X	X	signed	1998
Spain	1955	1995	X	X	1977	1977
Sri Lanka	1955	1995	X	X	1980	1980
Sudan	1956	Observer	X	X	1986	1986
Suriname	1975	1995	X	X	1976	1976
Swaziland	1968	1995	X	X	2004	2004
Sweden	1946	1995	X	X	1971	1971
Switzerland	2002	1995	X	X	1992	1992
Syrian Arab Republic	1945		X	X	1969	1969
Tajikistan	1992	Observer	X	X	1999	1999
Thailand	1946	1995	X	X	1999	1996
The former Yuguslav Republic of Macedonia	1993	2003	X	X	1994	1994
Timor-Leste	2002		X		2003	2003
Togo	1960	1995	X	X	1984	1984
Tonga	1999	Observer	X	X		
Trinidad and Tobago	1962	1995	X	X	1978	1978
Tunisia	1956	1995	X	X	1969	1969

(*cont.*)

Country	UN	WTO	WHO	WIPO	ICESCR	ICCPR
Turkey	1945	1995	X	X	2003	2003
Turkmenistan	1992		X	X	1997	1997
Tuvalu	2000		X			
Uganda	1962	1995	X	X	1987	1995
Ukraine	1945	Observer	X	X	1973	1973
United Arab Emirates	1971	1996	X	X		
United Kingdom	1945	1995	X	X	1976	1976
United Republic of Tanzania	1961	1995	X	X	1976	1976
United States of America	1945	1995	X	X	signed	1992
Uruguay	1945	1995	X	X	1970	1970
Uzbekistan	1992	Observer	X	X	1995	1995
Vanuatu	1981	Observer	X			
Venezuela	1945	1995	X	X	1978	1978
Vietnam	1977	Observer	X	X	1982	1982
Yemen	1947	Observer	X	X	1987	1987
Zambia	1964	1995	X	X	1984	1984
Zimbabwe	1980	1995	X	X	1991	1991

The year indicates the year of accession/ratification.
'X' indicates that the country is a member of the WHO/WIPO.

Sources

UN: UN, List of Member States, at <http://www.un.org/Overview/unmember.html> (last updated 3 July 2006)

WTO: WTO, Members and Observers, at <http://www.wto.int/english/thewto_e/ whatis_e/tif_e/org6_e.htm> (last updated 11 December 2005)
    Note: the European Communities, and Hong Kong, Macau, and Chinese Taipei are also listed as WTO members

WHO: WHO, Countries, at <http://www.who.int/country/en/>

WIPO: WIPO, Member States, at <http://www.wipo.int/members/en/>

ICESCR/ICCPR: Office of the UN High Commissioner for Human Rights, Status of Ratifications of the Principal International Human Rights Treaties As of 9 June 2004, at <http://www.unhchr.ch/pdf/report.pdf> (9 June 2004); International Covenant on Economic, Social and Cultural Rights at <http://www.ohchr.org/english/countries/ ratification/3.htm> (last updated 19 September 2006); International Covenant on Civil and Political Rights at <http://www.ohchr.org/english/countries/ratification/4.htm> (last updated 19 September 2006)

WTO Disputes on the TRIPS Agreement

	Dispute	Request for Consultations	Date of Receipt of the Request for Consultation	IP Area	Resolution	Date
IP/D/1	Japan—Measures Concerning Sound Recordings	US WT/DS28/1	09.02.96	Copyright	Mutually Agreed Solution WT/DS28/4	24.01.97
IP/D/2	*Pakistan—Patent Protection for Pharmaceutical and Agricultural Chemical Products*	US WT/DS36/1	30.04.96	Patents	Mutually Agreed Solution WT/DS36/4	07.03.97
IP/D/3	*Portugal—Patent Protection under the Industrial Property Act*	US WT/DS37/1	30.04.96	Patents	Mutually Agreed Solution WT/DS37/2 and Corr1	15.10.96
IP/D/4	Japan—Measures Concerning Sound Recordings	EC WT/DS42/1	28.05.96	Copyright	Mutually Agreed Solution WT/DS42/4	7.11.97
IP/D/5	*India—Patent Protection for Pharmaceutical and Agricultural Chemical Products*	US WT/DS50/1 US WT/DS50/11	02.07.96	Patents	Appellate Body Report WT/DS50/AB/R	19.12.97
IP/D/6	Indonesia—Certain Measures Affecting the Automobile Industry	US WT/DS59/1	08.10.96	Trademarks	Panel Report WT/DS54/R WT/DS55/R WT/DS59/R WT/DS64/R and Corr 2	02.07.98
IP/D/7	*India—Patent Protection for Pharmaceutical and Agricultural Chemical Products*	EC WT/DS79/1	28.04.97	Patents	Panel Report WT/DS79/R	24.08.98

Ref	Title	Party	Date	Subject	Status	Date
IP/D/8	Ireland—Measures Affecting the Grant of Copyright and Neighbouring Rights	US WT/DS82/1	14.05.97	Copyright / Enforcement	Mutually Agreed Solution WT/DS82/3	06.11.00
IP/D/9	Denmark—Measures Affecting the Enforcement of Intellectual Property Rights	US WT/DS83/1	14.05.97	Enforcement	Mutually Agreed Solution WT/DS83/2	13.06.01
IP/D/10	Sweden—Measures Affecting the Enforcement of Intellectual Property Rights	US WT/DS86/1	28.05.97	Enforcement	Mutually Agreed Solution WT/DS86/2	02.12.98
IP/D/11	*Canada—Patent Protection of Pharmaceutical Products*	EC WT/DS114/1	19.12.97	Patents	Panel Report WT/DS114/R	17.03.00
IP/D/12	European Communities—Measures Affecting the Grant of Copyright and Neighbouring Rights	US WT/DS115/1	06.01.98	Copyright / Enforcement	Mutually Agreed Solution WT/DS115/3	06.11.00
IP/D/13	European Communities—Enforcement of Intellectual Property Rights for Motion Pictures and Television Programmes	US WT/DS124/1	30.04.98	Enforcement	Mutually Agreed Solution WT/DS124/2	20.03.01
IP/D/14	Greece—Enforcement of Intellectual Property Rights for Motion Pictures and Television Programmes	US WT/DS125/1	04.05.98	Enforcement	Mutually Agreed Solution WT/DS125/2	20.03.01
IP/D/15	*European Communities—Patent Protection for Pharmaceutical and Agricultural Chemical Products*	Canada WT/DS153/1	02.12.98	Patents	Pending consultations	
IP/D/16	United States—Section 110(5) of US Copyright Act	EC WT/DS160/1	26.01.99	Copyright	Panel Report WT/DS160/R	15.06.00
IP/D/17	*Canada—Term of Patent Protection*	US WT/DS170/1	06.05.99	Patents	Appellate Body Report WT/DS170/AB/R	18.09.00
IP/D/18	*Argentina—Patent Protection for Pharmaceuticals and Test Data Protection for Agricultural Chemicals*	US WT/DS171/1	06.05.99	Patents / Industrial Designs	Mutually Agreed Solution WT/DS171/3	31.05.02

Dispute	Request for Consultations	Date of Receipt of the Request for Consultation	IP Area	Resolution	Date
IP/D/19	European Communities—Protection of Trademarks and Geographical Indications for Agricultural Products and Foodstuffs	US WT/DS174/1 and WT/DS174/1/Add.1	01.06.99 04.04.03	Trademarks / Geographical Indications	Panel Report WT/DS174/R	20.04.05
IP/D/20	United States—Section 211 Omnibus Appropriations Act of 1998	EC WT/DS176/1	08.07.99	Trademarks / Enforcement	Appellate Body Report WT/DS176/AB/R	02.01.02
IP/D/21	United States—Section 337 of the Tariff Act of 1930 and Amendments thereto	EC WT/DS186/1	12.01.00	Enforcement	Pending consultations	
IP/D/22	*Argentina—Certain Measures on the Protection of Patents and Test Data*	US WT/DS196/1	30.05.00	Patents / Test data / Enforcement	Mutually Agreed Solution WT/DS196/4	31.05.02
IP/D/23	*Brazil—Measures Affecting Patent Protection*	US WT/DS199/1	30.05.00	Patents	Mutually Agreed Solution WT/DS199/4	05.07.01
IP/D/24	*United States—US Patents Code*	Brazil WT/DS224/1	31.01.01	Patents	Pending consultations	
IP/D/25	European Communities—Protection of Trademarks and Geographical Indications for Agricultural Products and Foodstuffs	Australia WT/DS290/1	17.04.03	Trademarks / Geographical Indications	Panel Report WT/DS290/R	20.04.05

The names of cases relevant to patent law are shown in bold italics.
The IP dispute numbers of pending cases are shown in bold italics.

Sources

Update of WTO Dispute Settlement Cases, WT/DS/OV/21 (30 June 2004)
Update of WTO Dispute Settlement Cases, WT/DS/OV/23 (7 April 2005)
Update of WTO Dispute Settlement Cases, WT/DS/OV/24 (15 June 2005)
Update of WTO Dispute Settlement Cases, WT/DS/OV/27 (9 June 2006)

Dispute Settlement Body, *Annual Report (2003) Addendum. Overview of the States of Play of WTO Disputes*, WT/DSB/35/Add.1 (5 December 2003)

The identification of the IP area has been taken from Dara Williams, 'Developing TRIPS Jurisprudence. The First Six Years and Beyond' (2001) 4 J World Intell Prop 177

Bibliography

't Hoen, E, 'The Responsibility of Research Universities to Promote Access to Essential Medicines' (2003) 3 Yale J Health Pol'y, L & Ethics 293

——, 'TRIPS, Pharmaceutical Patents, and Access to Essential Medicines: A Long Way From Seattle to Doha' (2002) 3 Chicago J Int'l L 27

—— and Moon, S, 'Pills and Pocketbooks: Equity Pricing of Essential Medicines in Developing Countries' WHO-WTO Workshop on Differential Pricing and Financing of Essential Drugs (2001)

Abbott, FM, 'Commentary: The International Intellectual Property Order Enters the 21st Century' (1996) 29 Vand J Transnat'l L 471

——, 'Compulsory Licensing for Public Health Needs: The TRIPS Agenda at the WTO after the Doha Declaration on Public Health' Quaker United Nations Office—Geneva Occasional Paper 9 (2002)

——, 'First Report (Final) to the Committee on International Trade Law of the International Law Association on the Subject of Parallel Importation' (1998) 1 JIEL 607

——, 'Protecting First World Assets in the Third World: Intellectual Property Negotiations in the GATT Multilateral Framework' (1989) 22 Vand J of Transnat'l L 689

——, 'The Doha Declaration on the TRIPS Agreement and Public Health: Lighting a Dark Corner at the WTO' (2002) 5 JIEL 469

——, 'The Doha Declaration on the TRIPS Agreement and Public Health and the Contradictory Trend in Bilateral and Regional Free Trade Agreements' Quaker United Nations Office Occasional Paper (2004)

——, 'The Enduring Enigma of TRIPS: A Challenge for the World Economic System' (1998) 1 JIEL 497

——, 'The TRIPS Agreement, Access to Medicines and the WTO Doha Ministerial Conference' Quaker United Nations Office Occasional Paper 7 (2001) (also published as (2002) 5 J World Intell Prop 15 and Florida State University College of Law Public Law and Legal Theory Working Paper No 36 (2001))

——, 'The TRIPS-Legality of Measures Taken to Address Public Health Crises: A Synposis' (2001) 7 Widener L Symp J 71

——, 'The WTO Medicines Decision: World Pharmaceutical Trade and the Protection of Public Health' (2005) 99 AJIL 317

——, 'WTO TRIPS Agreement and Its Implications for Access to Medicines in Developing Countries' UK Commission on Intellectual Property Rights Study Paper 2a (2002)

——, Cottier, T, and Gurry, F (eds), *The International Intellectual Property System: Commentary and Materials. Pt One* (1999)

——, Cottier, T, and Gurry, F (eds), *The International Intellectual Property System: Commentary and Materials. Pt Two* (1999)

Abi-Saab, G, 'Cours Général de Droit International Public' (1987—VII) 207 RdC 9

——, 'Éloge du "Droit Assourdi". Quelques Réflexions sur le Rôle de la *Soft Law* en Droit International Contemportain' in *Nouveaux Itinéraires en Droit. Hommage à François Rigaux* (1993) 59

——, 'Fragmentation or Unification: Some Concluding Remarks' (1998–1999) 31 NYUJ Int'l L & Pol 919

——, 'La Coutume dans Tous ses États ou le Dilemme du Développement du Droit International Général dans un Monde Éclaté' in Batiffol, HC *et al* (eds), *Le Droit International à l'Heure de sa Codification. Études en l'Honneur de Roberto Ago. I* (1987) 53

Acconci, P, 'L'Accesso ai Farmaci Essenziali. Dall'Accordo TRIPS alla Dichiarazione della Quarta Conferenza Ministeriale OMC di Doha' (2001) 4 La Communitá Internazionale 637

Ackerman, B, *We the People. 1 Foundations* (1991)

Ackermann, TG, 'Diso'ordre'ly Loopholes: TRIPS Patent Protection, GATT and the ECJ' (1997) 32 Tex Int'l L J 489

ACT UP, *ACT UP Capsule History 1989*, at <http://www.actupny.org/documents/cron-89.html>

Addo, K, 'The Correlation Between Labour Standards and International Trade. Which Way Forward?' (2002) 36 JWT 285

Addo, MK, 'Justiciability Re-examined' in Beddard, R and Hill, DM (eds), *Economic, Social and Cultural Rights. Progress and Achievement* (1992) 93

Ago, R, *Sixth Report on State Responsibility*, YBILC, II (1977) 3

Akehurst, M, 'Custom as a Source of International Law' (1974–1975) 47 BYIL 1

——, 'The Hierarchy of the Sources of International Law' (1974–1975) 47 BYIL 273

Alexander, BC, 'Lack of Access to HIV/AIDS Drugs in Developing Countries: Is There a Violation of the International Human Rights (sic) to Health?' (2001) 8/3 Hum Rts Brief 12

Alexy, R, *Theorie der Grundrechte* (1994)

Alfredsson, G and Tomaševski, K (eds), *A Thematic Guide to Documents on Health and Human Rights. Global and Regional Standards Adopted by Intergovernmental Organizations, International Non-Governmental Organizations and Professional Associations* (1998)

Allen, NR, 'When Does the Clock Begin Ticking? Interaction of the Hatch-Waxman Act 180-Day Generic Abbreviated New Drug Application and Food and Drug Administration Modernization Act Pediatric Exclusivity Provisions—A Significant Issue in Eli Lilly & Co. v. Barr Laboratories, Inc.' (2002) 30 AIPLA QJ 1

Alliance for Health Reform, *Covering Health Issues: A Sourcebook for Journalists* (2006)

Alston, P, *Draft Optional Protocol Providing for the Consideration of Communications*, UN Doc E/C.12/1994/12 (1994)

——, 'Economic and Social Rights' (1994) 26 Stud Transnat'l Legal Pol'y 137

——, 'Out of the Abyss: The Challenges of Confronting the New UN Committee on Economic, Social and Cultural Rights' (1987) 9 Hum Rts Q 331

——, 'Resisting the Merger and Acquisition of Human Rights by Trade Law: A Reply to Petersmann' (2002) 13 EJIL 815

——, 'U.S. Ratification of the Covenant on Economic, Social and Cultural Rights: The Need for an Entirely New Strategy' (1990) 84 AJIL 365

Alston, P and Quinn, G, 'The Nature and Scope of States Parties' Obligations under the International Covenant on Economic, Social and Cultural Rights' (1987) 9 Hum Rts Q 156

Amerasinghe, CF, *Principles of the Institutional Law of International Organizations* (1996)

American Law Institute, *Restatement of the Law Third. The Foreign Relations Law of the United States. Volume 2* (1987)

Amnesty International, *Amnesty International Report 2003* (2003)

Andresen, DR, 'US Active in Helping Poorer Nations Tackle Health Crises' *IP-Health* (27 January 2003)

Annacker, C, *Die Durchsetzung von erga omnes Verpflichtungen vor dem Internationalen Gerichtshof* (1994)

Annan, K, *In Larger Freedom: Towards Development, Security and Human Rights for All. Report of the Secretary-General*, UN Doc A/59/2005 (2005)

——, 'Secretary-General Proposes Global Compact on Human Rights, Labour, Environment, in Address to World Economic Forum in Davos' UN Press Release SG/SM/6881 (1 February 1999)

Annas, GJ, 'The Right to Health and the Nevirapine Case in South Africa' (2003) 348 New Eng J Med 750

Anonymous, 'Africa vows to step up investment in R&D' (2004) 2 A World of Science 8

Anzilotti, D, *Corso di Diritto Internazionale (Ad uso degli studenti dell'Università di Roma), Volume Primo: Introduzione—Teorie Generali* (3rd edn, 1928)

Aoki, K, 'Weeds, Seeds & Deeds: Recent Skirmishes in the Seed Wars' (2003) 11 Cardozo J Int'l & Comp L 247

Arambulo, K, 'Drafting an Optional Protocol to the International Covenant on Economic, Social and Cultural Rights: Can an Ideal Become Reality' (1996) 2 UC Davis J Int'l L & Pol'y 111

——, *Strengthening the Supervision of the International Covenant on Economic, Social and Cultural Rights. Theoretical and Procedural Aspects* (1999)

Arangio-Ruiz, G, 'The ICJ Statute, the Charter and Forms of Legality Review of Security Council Decisions' in Vohrah, LC *et al* (eds), *Man's Inhumanity to Man. Essays on International Law in Honour of Antonio Cassese* (2003) 41

——, 'The Normative Role of the General Assembly of the United Nations and the Declaration of Principles of Friendly Relations' (1972—III) 137 RdC 419

Arno, PS and Davis, MH, 'Why Don't We Enforce Existing Drug Price Controls? The Unrecognized and Unenforced Reasonable Pricing Requirements Imposed upon Patents Deriving in Whole or in Part from Federally Funded Research' (2001) 75 Tul L Rev 631

Arno, PS and Feiden, KL, *Against the Odds. The Story of AIDS Drug Development, Politics and Profits* (1992)

Attaran, A, 'The Doha Declaration on the TRIPS Agreement and Public Health, Access to Pharmaceuticals, and Options Under WTO Law' (2002) 12 Fordham Intell Prop Media & Ent L J 859

—— and Gillespie-White, L, 'Do Patents for Antiretroviral Drugs Constrain Access to AIDS Treatment in Africa?' (2001) 286 JAMA 1886

Aust, A, *Modern Treaty Law and Practice* (2000)

Aventis, *2002 Annual Report* (2002)

Bacchus, J, 'The Bicycle Club: Affirming the American Interest in the Future of the WTO' in Bacchus, J, *Trade and Freedom* (2004) 329

——, ' "Woulda, Coulda, Shoulda": The Consolations of WTO Dispute Settlement' in Bacchus J, *Trade and Freedom* (2004) 361

Bagwell, K, Mavroidis, PC and Staiger, RW, 'It's a Question of Market Access' (2002) 96 AJIL 56

Bail, C, 'Das Profil einer neuen Welthandelsordnung: Was bringt die Uruguay Runde?— Teil 2' (1990) EuZW 465

Bale, HE, Jr, 'Consumption and Trade in Off-Patented Medicines' CMH Working Paper Series Paper No WG4: 3 (2001)

——, 'The Conflicts Between Parallel Trade and Product Access and Innovation: The Case of Pharmaceuticals' (1998) 1 JIEL 637

——, 'Patents, Patients and Developing Countries: Access, Innovation and The Political Dimensions of Trade Policy' in Granville, B (ed), *The Economics of Essential Medicines* (2002) 100

Banerji, S, 'The Indian Intellectual Property Rights Regime and the TRIPs Agreement' in Long, C (ed), *Intellectual Property Rights in Emerging Markets* (2000) 47

Banner, DW, 'An Unanticipated, Nonobvious, Enabling Portion of the Constitution: The Patent Provision—The Best Mode' (1987) 69 J Pat & Trademark Off Soc'y 631

Barnes, DM, 'AIDS Case Dismissed on Legal Technicality' (1986) 233 Science 414

——, 'AIDS patent dispute settled' (1987) 236 Science 17

Barr, B, 'Protecting National Sovereignty in an Era of International Meddling: An Increasingly Difficult Task' (2002) 29 Harv J on Legis 299

Barre-Sinoussi, F *et al*, 'Isolation of a T-Lymphotropic Retrovirus from a Patient at Risk for Acquired Immune Deficiency Syndrome (AIDS)' (1983) 220 Science 868

Barrett, M, *Intellectual Property* (3rd edn, 1999–2000)

——, *Intellectual Property. Patents, Trademarks & Copyrights* (2000)

Bartels, L, 'Applicable Law in WTO Dispute Settlement Proceedings' (2001) 35 JWT 499

Bartelt, S, 'Compulsory Licenses Persuant to TRIPS Article 31 in the Light of the Doha Declaration on the TRIPS Agreement and Public Health' (2003) 6 J World Intell Prop 283

Barton, JH, 'Differentiated Pricing of Patented Products' CMH Working Paper Series, Paper No WG4: 2 (2001)

——, 'Issues Posed by a World Patent System' (2004) 7 JIEL 341

——, 'The Human Genome Patent Applications' (1993) 354 PLI/Pat 681

Bass, NA, 'Implications of the TRIPS Agreement for Developing Countries: Pharmaceutical Patent Laws in Brazil and South Africa in the 21st Century' (2002) 34 The Geo Wash Int'l L Rev 191

Baxter, RR, 'Multilateral Treaties as Evidence of Customary International Law' (1968) 41 BYIL 275

——, 'Treaties and Custom' (1970—I) 129 RdC 27

Bayer, *Bayer to Supply Government by Year-End with 100 Million Tablets for $95 Million* (24 October 2001), at <http://lists.essential.org/pipermail/ip-health/2001-October/002261.html>

Bedjaoui, M, 'Du Contrôle de Légalité des Actes du Conseil de Sécurité' in *Nouveaux Itinéraires en Droit. Hommage à François Rigaux* (1993) 69

Beers, DO, *Generic and Innovator Drugs. A Guide to FDA Approval Requirements* (5th edn, 1999)

Beers, DO, *Generic and Innovator Drugs. A Guide to FDA Approval Requirements. 2003 Supplement* (5th edn, 2003)

Behrman, G, *The Invisible People. How the US Has Slept through the Global AIDS Pandemic, the Greatest Humanitarian Catstrophe of Our Time* (2004)

Beier, F-K, 'Exclusive Rights, Statutory Licenses and Compulsory Licenses in Patent and Utility Model Law' (1999) 30 IIC 251

Beigbeder, Y, *The World Health Organization* (1998)

Bello, J, 'The WTO Dispute Settlement Understanding: Less Is More' (1996) 90 AJIL 416

Berger, JM, 'Litigation Strategies to Gain Access to Treatment for HIV/AIDS: The Case of South Africa's Treatment Action Campaign' (2001–2002) 20 Wis Int'l L J 595

Berger, KP, *The Creeping Codification of the Lex Mercatoria* (1999)

Berkenfeld, E, 'Das älteste Patentgesetz der Welt' (1949) GRUR 139

Bernhardt, R, *Die Auslegung völkerrechtlicher Verträge* (1963)

——, 'Evolutive Treaty Interpretation, Especially of the European Convention on Human Rights' (1999) 42 GYIL 11

——, 'Thoughts on the interpretation of human-rights treaties' in Matscher, F and Petzold, H (eds), *Protecting Human Rights: The European Dimension, Studies in honor of Gérard J. Wiarda* (1988) 65

——, 'Völkerrechtliche und verfassungsrechtliche Aspekte konkludenter Vertragsänderungen' in Andt, H-W *et al* (eds), *Völkerrecht und deutsches Recht. FS Walter Rudolf* (2001) 15

Bhagwati, J, *In Defense of Globalization* (2004)

Biadgleng, ET, 'IP Rights Under Investment Agreements: the TRIPS-plus Implications for Enforcement and Protection of Public Interest' South Centre Research Paper No 8 (2006)

Biehler, G, 'Individuelle Sanktionen der Vereinten Nationen und Grundrechte' (2003) 41 AVR 169

Billib, RA, *Die allgemeinen Rechtsgrundsätze gemäß Art. 38 I c des Statuts des Internationalen Gerichtshofes—Versuch einer Deutung* (1972)

Blackstone, W, *Commentaries on the Laws of England. Book the Second* (4th edn, 1770)

Blakeney, M, *Trade Related Aspects of Intellectual Property Rights: A Concise Guide to the TRIPS Agreement* (1996)

——, 'TRIPS After the Doha Ministerial Declaration' in Antons, C, Blakeney, M and Heath, C (eds), *Intellectual Property Harmonisation within ASEAN and APEC* (2004) 11

Bleckmann, A, *Staatsrecht II—Die Grundrechte* (4th edn, 1997)

——, *Völkerrecht* (2001)

——, 'Zur Feststellung und Auslegung von Völkergewohnheitsrecht' (1977) 37 ZaöRV 504

——, 'Zur originären Entstehung gewohnheitsrechtlicher Menschenrechtsnormen' in Klein, E (ed), *Menschenrechtsschutz durch Gewohnheitsrecht. Kolloquium. 26.–28. September 2002. Potsdam* (2003) 29

——, 'Zur Verbindlichkeit des allgemeinen Völkerrechts für internationale Organisationen' (1977) 37 ZaöRV 107

Bledsoe, RL and Boczek, BA, *The International Law Dictionary* (1987)

Bloche, MG, 'WTO Deference to National Health Policy: Toward an Interpretative Principle' (2002) 5 JIEL 825

Bluntschli, JC, *Das moderne Völkerrecht der civilisirten Staten als Rechtsbuch dargestellt* (2nd edn, 1872)

Blüthner, A, *Welthandel und Menschenrechte in der Arbeit* (2004)

Böckenförde, M, 'Zwischen Sein und Wollen—Über den Einfluss umweltvölkerrechtlicher Verträge im Rahmen eines WTO-Streitbeilegungsverfahrens' (2003) 63 ZaöRV 971

Bodenhausen, GHC, *Guide to the Application of the Paris Convention for the Protection of Industrial Property As Revised at Stockholm in 1967* (1968)

Bodewig, T, 'Aktuelle Informationen, Internationales—Tagung der Leitenden Organe der WIPO; PVÜ-Revision; Harmonisierung des Patentrechts; GATT' (1988) GRUR Int 81

Bodin, J, *Sechs Bücher über den Staat. Buch I-III* (trans Bernd Wimmer 1981)

Bohrer, RA and Prince, JT, 'A Tale of Two Proteins: The FDA's Uncertain Interpretation of the Orphan Drug Act' (1999) 12 Harv J L & Tech 365

Bombach, KM, 'Can South Africa Fight AIDS? Reconciling the South African Medicines and Related Substances Act with the TRIPS Agreement' (2001) 19 BU Int'l L J 273

Bossuyt, MJ, *Guide to the 'Travaux Préparatoires' of the International Covenant on Civil and Political Rights* (1987)

——, 'La Distinction Juridique entre les Droits Civils et Politiques et les Droits Économiques, Sociaux et Culturels' (1975) Revue des Droits de l'Homme, Human Rights Journal 783

Bothe, M, *Das völkerrechtliche Verbot des Einsatzes chemischer und bakteriologischer Waffen. Kritische Würdigung und Dokumentation der Rechtsgrundlagen* (1973)

——, 'Le Droit de la Guerre et les Nations Unies. A Propos des Incidents Armés au Congo' (1967) 5 Etudes et Travaux de l'Institut Universitaire de Hautes Etudes Internationales 135

——, 'Les concepts fondamentaux du droit à la santé: Le point de vue juridique' in Dupuy, R-J (ed), *Le droit à la santé en tant que droit de l'homme. The Right to Health as a Human Right* (1979) RdC 1978 Colloque 14

Boulet, P, Perriens, J and Renaud-Théry, F, *Patent Situation of HIV/AIDS-related Drugs in 80 Countries*, UNAIDS/WHO (2000)

Bourgeois, JHJ and Burns, TJ, 'Implementing Paragraph 6 of the Doha Declaration on TRIPS and Public Health. The Waiver Solution' (2002) 6 J World Intell Prop 835

Boval, B, 'L'Accord sur les Droits de Propriété Intellectuelle quit Touchent au Commerce (ADPIC ou TRIPS)' in Société Française pour le Droit International (ed), *La Réorganisation Mondiale des Échanges. Colloque de Nice* (1996) 131

Bozicevic, K, 'Patenting DNA-Obviousness Rejections' (1992) 74 J Pat & Trademark, Off Soc'y 750

Branstetter, LG, 'Do Stronger Patents Induce More Local Innovation?' (2004) 7 JIEL 359

Braun, TR, 'Investment Protection under WTO-Law—New Developments in the Aftermath of Cancún' (2004) Beiträge zum Transnationalen Wirtschaftsrecht 28

Breslow, LH, 'The Best Pharmaceuticals for Children Act of 2002: The Rise of the Voluntary Incentive Structure and Congressional Refusal to Require Pediatric Testing' (2003) 40 Harv J on Legis 133

Bronckers, MCEJ, 'The Exhaustion of Patent Rights under WTO Law' in Bronckers, MCEJ (ed), *A Cross-Section of WTO Law* (2003) 157

——, 'The Impact of TRIPS: Intellectual Property Protection in Developing Countries' in Bronckers, MCEJ, *A Cross-Section of WTO Law* (2000) 185

Brownlie, I, *Principles of Public International Law* (6th edn, 2003)

Bruha, T, 'Security Council' in Wolfrum, R and Philipp, C (eds), *United Nations: Law, Policies and Practice, Volume 2* (1995) 1147

Buck, P, *Geistiges Eigentum und Völkerrecht* (1994)

Buckingham, DE, 'A Recipe for Change: Towards an Integrated Approach to Food under International Law' (1994) 6 Pace Int'l L Rev 285

Buergenthal, T, *International Human Rights in a Nutshell* (2nd edn, 1995)

——, 'International Human Rights Law and Institutions: Accomplishments and Prospects' (1988) 63 Wash L Rev 1

——, 'To Respect and to Ensure: State Obligations and Permissible Derogations' in Henkin, L (ed), *The International Bill of Rights. The Covenant on Civil and Political Rights* (1981) 72

Bundesregierung, *Denkschrift zum Internationalen Pakt über wirtschaftliche, soziale und kulturelle Rechte vom 19. Dezember 1966*, BT-Drucks. 7/658, 18 (1973)

Burk, DL and Lemley, MA, 'Is Patent Law Technology-Specific?' (2002) 17 Berkeley Tech LJ 1155

Busche, J and Stoll, P-T (eds), *TRIPs* (2007)

Byers, M, 'Conceptualising the Relationship between Jus Cogens and Erga Omens Rules' (1997) 66 Nordic J Int'l L 211

——, *Custom, Power and the Power of Rules. International Relations and Customary International Law* (1999)

Byström, M and Einarsson, P, *TRIPS—vad betyder WTOs patentavtal för de fattiga ländernas människor och miljö?*, Diakonia Forum Syd Svenska Naturskyddsföreningen (2002)

Cahier, P, 'Les Caractéristiques de la Nullité en Droit International et Tout Particulièrement dans la Convention de Vienne de 1969 sur le Droit des Traités' (1972) 76 RGDIP 645

Cahoy, DR, 'Treating the Legal Side Effects of CIPRO®: A Reeveluation of Compensation Rules for Governement Takings of Patent Rights' (2002) 40 Am Bus LJ 125

Cameron, J and Gray, KR, 'Principles of International Law in the WTO Dispute Settlement Body' (2001) 50 ICLQ 248

Canadian Drug Manufacturers Association, 'Bill C-91: An Act to Amend the Patent Act. Position Paper' in Canadian Drug Manufacturers Association (ed), *Preliminary Submissions of the Canadian Drug Manufacturers Association Regarding Intellectual Property Rights in the Dunkel Draft Tabled on December 21, 1991 in the General Agreement on Tariffs and Trade ('Gatt') Negotiations* (1993)

Canal-Forgues, E, 'Sur l'Interprétation Dans le Droit de l'OMC' (2001) RGDIP 5

Canelias, PS, *Patent Practice Handbook* (looseleaf, last updated 2002)

Capotorti, F, 'Interferenze fra la Convenzione Europea dei Diritti dell'Uomo ed Altri Accordi, e Loro Reflessi negli Ordinamenti Interni' in Instituto di Diritto Internazionale e Straniero della Università di Milano (ed), *Comunicazioni e Studi. Volume Dodicesimo* (1966) 115

Carstensen, PC, 'Concentration and the Destruction of Competition in Agricultural Markets: The Case for Change in Public Policy' (2000) Wis L Rev 531

Carter, BE and Trimble, PR, *International Law* (3rd edn, 1999)

Cass, DZ, 'The "Constitutionalization" of International Trade Law: Judicial Norm-Generation as the Engine of Constitutional Development in International Trade' (2001) 12 EJIL 39

Cassese, A, *International Law in a Divided World* (1986)

Caves, RE, Whinston, MD and Hurwitz, MA, 'Patent Expiration, Entry, and Competition in the U.S. Pharmaceutical Industry' Brookings Papers on Economic Activity. Micro-economics (1991) 1

Cazala, J, 'L'Invocation de l'Estoppel dans le Cadre de la Procédure de Règlement des Différends de l'Organisation Mondiale du Commerce' (2003) RGDIP 885

Centers for Disease Control, 'Update on acquired immune deficiency syndrome (AIDS)' (1982) 31 Morbidity and Mortality Weekly Rep 507

Central Intelligence Agency, *The World Factbook 2004* (2004)

Challú, P, 'The Consequences of Pharmaceutical Product Patenting' (1991) 15–2 World Competition 65

Champ, P and Attaran, A, 'Patent Rights and Local Working Under the WTO TRIPS Agreement: An Analysis of the U.S.-Brazil Patent Dispute' (2002) 27 Yale J Int'l L 365

Chapman, AR, 'Approaching Intellectual Property as a Human Right: Obligations Related to Article 15 (1) (c)' in UNESCO (ed), 35 *Copyright Bulletin Approaching Intellectual Property as a Human Right* (2001) 4

——, 'Conceptualizing the Right to Health: A Violations Approach' (1998) 65 Tenn L Rev 389

——, 'Monitoring Women's Right to Health under the International Covenant on Economic, Social and Cultural Rights' (1994–1995) 44 Am U L Rev 1157

Charney, JI, 'Is International Law Threatened by Multiple International Tribunals?' (1998) 271 RdC 101

Charnovitz, S, 'The Legal Status of the Doha Declaration' (2002) 5 JIEL 207

——, 'Trade Measures and the Design of International Regimes' in Charnovitz, S (ed), *Trade Law and Global Governance* (2002) 27

——, 'Triangulating the World Trade Organization' (2002) 96 AJIL 28

Chaudhuri, S, Goldberg, PK, and Jia, P, 'The Effects of Extending Intellectual Property Rights Protection to Developing Countries: A Case Study of the Indian Pharmaceutical Market' NBER Working Paper 10159 (2003)

Chen, L-c, 'Protection of Persons (Natural and Juridical)' (1989) 14 Yale J Int'l L 542

Cheng, B, *General Principles of Law as Applied by International Courts and Tribunals* (1953)

——, 'Some Remarks on the Constituent Element(s) of General (or So-called Customary) International Law' in Anghie, A and Sturgess, G (eds), *Legal Visions of the 21st Century: Essays in Honour of Judge Christopher Weeramantry* (1998) 377

——, 'United Nations Resolutions on Outer Space: "Instant" International Customary Law?' (1965) 5 Indian J Int'l L 23

Cheves Aguilar, N and Araya Pochet, C (eds), *Constitución Política Comentada de Costa Rica* (2001)

Chirwa, DM, '*Minister of Health and Others v. Treatment Action Campaign and Others*: Its Implications for the Combat against HIV/AIDS and the Protection of Economic, Social and Cultural Rights in Africa' (2003) 9 E Afr J Peace & Hum Rts 174

——, 'The Right to Health in International Law: Its Implications for the Obligations of State and Non-State Actors in Ensuring Access to Essential Medicine' (2003) 19 SAJHR 541

Chisum, DS, *Chisum on Patents. A Treatise on the Law of Patentability, Validity and Infringement. Volume 1* (looseleaf, last updated 2003)

——, 'Remarks of Professor Donald S. Chisum' (1989) 22 Vand J Transnat'l L 341

Churchill, RR and Khaliq, U, 'The Collective Complaints System of the European Social Charter: An Effective Mechanism for Ensuring Compliance with Economic and Social Rights?' (2004) 15 EJIL 417

Churchill, RR and Scott, J, 'The MOX Plant Litigation: The First Half-Life' (2004) 53 ICLQ 643

Clapham, A, *Human Rights in the Private Sphere* (1993)

Clinton, WJ, 'Remarks at a World Trade Organization Luncheon in Seattle, December 1, 1999' in Office of the Federal Register National Archives and Records Administration (ed), *Public Papers of the Presidents of the United States. William J. Clinton. 1999 (in Two Books). Book II—July 1 to December 31, 1999* (2001) 2189

Coate, RA, *Global Issue Regimes* (1982)

Cohen, J, 'HHS: Gallo Guilty of Misconduct' (1993) 259 Science 168

——, 'Pasteur Wants More HIV Blood Test Royalties' (1992) 255 Science 792

——, 'US-French Patent Dispute Heads for a Showdown' (1994) 265 Science 23

——, and Marshall, E, 'NIH-Pasteur: A Final Rapprochement?' (1994) 265 Science 313

Combacau, J and Sur, S, *Droit International Public* (5th edn, 2001)

Commission on Intellectual Property Rights, Innovation and Public Health, *Public Health. Innovation and Intellectual Property Rights* (2006)

——, *Integrating Intellectual Property Rights and Development Policy* (2002)

Commission on Macroeconomics and Health, *Macroeconomics and Health: Investing in Health for Economic Development* (2001)

Committee on Intellectual Property Rights in the Knowledge-Based Economy, National Research Council, *A Patent System for the 21st Century* (2004)

Conforti, B, *Diritto Internazionale* (5th edn, 1997)

Consumer and Corporate Affairs Canada, *Compulsory Licensing of Pharmaceuticals. A Review of Section 41 of the Patent Act* (1983)

Coomans, F, 'Clarifying the Core Elements of the Right to Education' in Coomans, F and Hoof, F van (eds), *The Right to Complain about Economic, Social and Cultural Rights* (1995) 11

Cooper, I, 'Patent Problems for Chemical Researchers—the Utility Requirement After *Brenner v Manson*' (1976) 18 IDEA 23

Copelon, R, 'The Indivisible Framework of International Human Rights: A Source of Social Justice in the U.S.' (1998) 3 NY City L Rev 59

Cornish, WR, *Intellectual Property: Patents, Copyright, Trademarks and Allied Rights* (1981)

Correa, CM, *Acuerdo TRIPs* (1996)

——, 'Implementing National Public Health Policies in the Framework of WTO Agreements' (2000) 34 JWT 89

——, 'Implementing the TRIPS Agreement in the Patents Field—Options for Developing Countries' (1998) 1 J World Intell Prop 75

——, 'Implications of Bilateral Free Trade Agreements on Access to Medicines' (2006) 84 Bulletin of the WHO 399

——, 'Implications of the Doha Declaration on the TRIPS Agreement and Public Health' WHO Health Economics and Drugs EDM Series No 12 (2002)

——, *Integrating Public Health Concerns into Patent Legislation in Developing Countries* (2000)

——, *Intellectual Property Rights and Foreign Direct Investment* (1993) UN Doc ST/CTC/SER.A/24

——, *Intellectual Property Rights, the WTO, and Developing Countries. The TRIPS Agreement and Policy Options* (2000)

——, 'Patent Rights' in Correa, CM and Yusuf, AA (eds), *Intellectual Property and International Trade: The TRIPs Agreement* (1998) 189

——, *Protection of Data Submitted for the Registration of Pharmaceuticals: Implementing the Standards of the TRIPS Agreement* (2002)

——, 'Some Assumptions on Patent Law and Pharmaceutical R&D' Quaker United Nations Office—Geneva—Occasional Paper 6 (2001)

Corriente Cordoba, JA, *Valoración jurídica de los preámbulos de los tratados internacionales* (1973)

Cottier, T, 'The Prospects for Intellectual Property in GATT' (1991) 28 Common Market Law Review 383

——, 'TRIPS, the Doha Declaration and Public Health' (2003) 6 J World Intell Prop 385

Couhin, C, *La Propriété Industrielle, Artistique & Littéraire. Tome Premier* (1894)

Coxe, T, 'Draft of the Report on the Subject of Manufactures' in Syrett, HC (ed), *The Papers of Alexander Hamilton, vol. X. December 1791–January 1792* (1966) 15

Cptech, *Appendix B. Time-line of Disputes over Compulsory Licensing and Parallel Importation in South Africa*, at <http://www.cptech.org/ip/health/sa/sa-timeline.txt>

—— (ed), *Health Care and Intellectual Property*, at <http://www.cptech.org/ip/health>

Crampes, C, 'La Recherche et la Protection des Innovations dans le Secteur Pharmaceutique' (2000) RIDE 125

Cranston, M, *What are Human Rights?* (1973)

Craven, MCR, *The International Covenant on Economic, Social and Cultural Rights. A Perspective on its Development* (1995)

Crawford, J, *The International Law Commission's Articles on State Responsibility. Introduction, Text and Commentaries* (2002)

Crespi, RS, 'IPRs Under Siege: First Impressions of the Report of the Commission on Intellectual Property Rights' (2003) 25 EIPR 242

Cullet, P, 'Patents and Medicines: The Relationship between TRIPS and the Human Right to Health' (2003) 79 Int'l Affairs 130

Curci, G and Vittori, M, 'Improving Access to Life-Saving Patented Drugs. Between Compulsory Licensing and Differential Pricing' (2004) 7 J World Intell Prop 739

Currie, DP, 'Positive und negative Grundrechte' (1986) 111 AÖR 230

Curti, AM, 'The WTO Dispute Settlement Understanding: An Unlikely Weapon in the Fight Against AIDS' (2001) 27 Am J L & Medicine 469

Curzon, G and Curzon, V, 'GATT: Traders' Club' in Cox, RW and Jacobson, HK (eds), *The Anatomy of Influence, Decision Making in International Organization* (1973) 298

Czapliński, W and Danilenko, G, 'Conflict of Norms in International Law' (1990) 21 NYIL 3

D'Adesky, A-C, *Moving Mountains. The Race to Treat Global AIDS* (2004)

D'Amato, A, 'Human Rights as Norms of Customary International Law' in D'Amato, A (ed), *International Law: Prospect and Process* (1987) 123

——, *The Concept of Custom in International Law* (1971)

——, 'Trashing Customary International Law' (1987) 81 AJIL 101

Daillier, P and Pellet, A, *Droit International Public. Nguyen Quoc Dinh* (6th edn, 1999)

Damrosch, LF, 'Obligations of Cooperation in the International Protection of Human Rights' in Delbrück, J (ed), *International Law of Cooperation and State Sovereignty. Proceedings of an International Symposium of the Kiel Walther-Schücking-Institute of International Law May 23–26, 2001* (2002) 15

Danilenko, GM, *Law-Making in the International Community* (1993)

Danzon, PM, 'Differential Pricing for Pharmaceuticals: Reconciling Access, R & D and Patents' CMH Working Paper Series, Paper No WG2: 10 (2001)

—— and Towse, A, *Differential Pricing for Pharmaceuticals: Reconciling Access, R & D and Patents* (2003)

De, D, *The Constitution of India. Volume I Articles 1–104* (2002)

de Frouville, O, *L'Intagibilité des Droits de L'Homme en Droit International. Regime Conventionnel des Droits de l'Homme et Droits des Traités* (2004)

de Hoogh, A, *Obligations Erga Omnes and International Crimes. A Theoretical Inquiry into the Implementation and Enforcement of the International Responsibility of States* (1996)

de Pauw, LG, Bickford, CB, and Hauptman, LS (eds), *Documentary History of the First Federal Congress of the United States of America. March 4, 1789–March 3, 1791. Volume III. House of Representatives Journal* (1977)

de Vattel, E, *Le Droit des Gens, ou Principes de la Loi Naturelle, Appliquée à la Conduite et aux Affaires des Nations et des Souverains* (1839)

de Velasco Vallejo, MD, *Las Organizaciones Internacionales* (12th edn, 2002)

de Visscher, C, *Théories et Réalités en Droit International Public* (3rd edn, 1960)

de Waart, PJIM, 'Quality of Life at the Mercy of WTO Panels: GATT's Article XX and Empty Shell?' in Weiss, F, Denters, E and de Waart, P (eds), *International Economic Law with a Human Face* (1998) 109

de Wet, E, *The Chapter VII Powers of the United Nations Security Council* (2004)

Deardorff, AV, 'Welfare Effects of Global Patent Protection' (1992) 59 Economica 35

—— and ——, *Völkerrecht. Begründet von Georg Dahm. Band I/1 Die Grundlagen. Die Völkerrechtssubjekte* (2nd edn, 1989)

—— and ——, *Völkerrecht. Begründet von Georg Dahm. Band I/2 Der Staat und andere Völkerrechtssubjekte; Räume unter internationaler Verwaltung* (2nd edn, 2002)

Delbrück, J and Wolfrum, R, *Völkerrecht. Begründet von Georg Dahm. Band I/3 Die Formen des völkerrechtlichen Handelns; Die inhaltliche Ordnung der internationalen Gemeinschaft* (2nd edn, 2002)

Deller, AW, *Deller's Walker on Patents. Volume One* (2nd edn, 1964)

Delmas-Marty, M, *Trois Défis pour un Droit Mondial* (1998)

Demaret, P and B, J-F and García Jiménez, G (eds), *Regionalism and Multilateralism after the Uruguay Round. Convergence, Divergence and Interaction* (1997)

Denicolò, V and Franzoni, LA, 'The Contract Theory of Patents' (2004) 23 Int'l Rev L & Econ 365

Dennis, MJ and Stewart, DP, 'Justiciability of Economic, Social, and Cultural Rights: Should There Be an International Complaints Mechanism to Adjudicate the Rights to Food, Water, Housing, and Health?' (2004) 98 AJIL 462

Department of Health and Human Services, *HHS, Bayer Agree to Cipro Purchase*, (24 October 2001), at <http://www.cptech.org/ip/health/cl/cipro/dhhs10242001.html>

Department of Trade and Industry, *Joint Understanding betweeen the Governments of South Africa and the United States of America*, at <http://www.polity.org.za/html/govdocs/pr/1999/pr0917b.html?rebookmark=1> (17 September 1999)

Dickinson, EH, 'FDA's Role in Making Exclusivity Determinations' (1999) 54 Food & Drug LJ 195

Dijk, P van and Hoof, GJH van, *Theory and Practice of the European Convention on Human Rights* (3rd edn, 1998)

Dijk, P van and Sideri, S (eds), *Multilateralism versus Regionalism: Trade Issues after the Uruguay Round* (1996)

DiMasi, JA, *Price Trends for Prescription Pharmaceuticals: 1995–1999*, Tufts Center for the Study of Drug Development (2000)

——, Hansen, RW, and Grabowski, HG, 'The Price of Innovation: New Estimates of Drug Development Costs' (2003) 22 J Health Econ 151

—— *et al*, 'Cost of Innovation in the Pharmaceutical Industry' (1991) J Health Econ 107

Dinstein, Y, 'The Right to Life, Physical Integrity and Liberty' in Henkin, L (ed), *The International Bill of Rights. The Covenant on Civil and Political Rights* (1981) 119

Dinwoodie, GB, Hennesey, WO and Perlmutter, S, *International Intellectual Property Law and Policy* (2001)

Döbert, R, van den Daele, W, and Seiler, A, 'Access to Essential Medicines—Rationality and Consensus in the Conflict Over Intellectual Property Rights' WZB discussion papers No SP IV 2003-108 (2003)

Doehring, K, *Die undifferenzierte Berufung auf Menschenrechte*, in Beyerlin, U (ed), *Festschrift für Rudolf Bernhardt* (1995) 355

——, 'Gewohnheitsrechtsbildung aus Menschenrechtsverträgen' in Klein, E (ed), *Menschenrechtsschutz durch Gewohnheitsrecht. Kolloquium. 26.–28. September 2002. Potsdam* (2003) 84

——, *Völkerrecht* (2nd edn, 2004)

Doherty, J *et al*, 'Health Care Financing and Expenditure' in Ijumba, P (ed), *South African Health Review 2002* (2003) 13

Dommen, C, 'Raising Human Rights Concerns in the World Trade Organization: Actors, Processes and Possible Strategies' (2002) 24 Hum Rts Q 1

Donzel, L, *Commentaire de la Convention Internationale Signée à Paris le 20 Mars 1883 pour la Protection de la Propriété Industrielle* (1891)

Doutrelepont, C, 'Das droit moral in der Europäischen Union' (1997) GRUR Int 293

Drahos, P, 'Developing Countries and International Intellectual Property Standard-Setting' UK Commission on Intellectual Property Rights Study Paper 8

——, 'The Universality of Intellectual Property Rights: Origins and Development' in World Intellectual Property Organization (ed), *Intellectual Property and Human Rights. A Panel Discussion to commemorate the 50th Anniversary of the Universal Declaration of Human Rights. Geneva, November 9, 1998* (1999) 13

Dreier, H, 'Kontexte des Grundgesetzes' (1999) DVBl 667

Dreier, T, 'TRIPS und die Durchsetzung von Rechten des geistigen Eigentums' (1996) GRUR Int 205

Drews, J, *In Quest of Tomorrow's Medicines. An Eminent Scientist Talks About the Pharmaceutical Industry, Biotechnology, and the Future of Drug Research* (trans David Kramer, 1999)

Dröge, C, *Positive Verpflichtungen der Staaten in der Europäischen Menschenrechtskonvention* (2003)

Drzewicki, K, 'The Right to Work and Rights in Work' in Eide, A, Krause, C and Rosas, A (eds), *Economic, Social and Cultural Rights. A Textbook* (2nd edn, 2001) 223

Dumoulin, J, 'Les Brevets et le Prix des Médicaments' (2000) RIDE 45

Dunbar, MM, 'Shaking up the Status Quo: How AIDS Activists Have Challenged Drug Development and Approval Procedures' (1991) 46 Food Drug Cosm L J 673

Dupuy, P-M, *Droit international public* (5th edn, 2000)

——, 'L'Unité de l'Ordre Juridique International. Cours Général de Droit International Public' (2002) 297 RdC 9

——, 'Reviewing the Difficulties of Codification: On Ago's Classification of Obligations of Means and Obligations of Result in Relation to State Responsibility' (1999) 10 EJIL 317

——, 'The Constitutional Dimension of the Charter of the United Nations Revisited' (1997) 1 Max Planck UNYB 1

——, 'The Danger of Fragmentation or Unification of the International Legal System and the International Court of Justice' (1998–1999) 31 NYU J Int'l L & Pol 791

——, 'The Duty to Protect and to Ensure Human Rights under the International Covenant on Civil and Political Rights—Comment on the Paper by Eckart Klein' in Klein, E (ed), *The Duty to Protect and to Ensure Human Rights. Colloquium Potsdam, 1–3 July 1999* (2000) 391

——, 'The Place and Role of Unilateralism in Contemporary International Law' (2000) 11 EJIL 19

Dupuy, R-J, 'Communauté Internationale et Disparités de Développement' (1979—IV) 165 RdC 21

——, 'Coutume Sage et Coutume Sauvage' in Ago, R *et al* (eds), *La Communauté Internationale. Mélanges Offerts à Charles Rousseau* (1974) 75

—— (ed), 'Résumé des débats—Summing up' in Dupuy, R-J (ed), *Le droit à la santé en tant que droit de l'homme. The Right to Health as a Human Right* (1979) RdC 1978 Colloque 124, 130 ff

Durham, AL, *Patent Law Essentials. A Concise Guide* (1999)

Dutton, HI, *The Patent System and Inventive Activity During the Industrial Revolution 1750–1852* (1984)

Duvergier, JB (ed), *Collection Complète des Lois, Decrets, Ordannances, Reglements et Avis du Conseil D'État. Tome Deuxième* (1834)

Edel, E, *Der Vertrag zwischen Ramses II. von Ägypten und Hattušili III. von Hatti* (1997)

Edmunds, L, *The Law and Practice of Letters Patent for Inventions with the Patents Acts and Rules Annotated, and the International Convention, a Full Collection of Statutes, Forms and Precedents, and an Outline of Foreign and Colonial Patent Laws* (1890)

Eggers, B and Mackenzie, R, 'The Cartagena Protocol on Biosafety' (2000) 3 JIEL 525

Eggert, PH, 'Uses, New Uses and Chemical Patents—A Proposal' (1969) 51 J Pat Off Soc'y 768

Ehlermann, C-D, 'Six Years on the Bench of the "World Trade Court". Some Personal Experiences as Member of the Appellate Body of the World Trade Organization' in Ortino, F and Petersmann, E-U, *The WTO Dispute Settlement System 1995–2003* (2004) 499

Eide, A, *The New International Economic Order and the Promotion of Human Rights. Report on the Right to Adequate Food as a Human Right*, UN Doc E/CN.4/Sub.2/1987/23 (1987)

—— and Rosas, A, 'Economic, Social and Cultural Rights: A Universal Challenge' in Eide, A, Krause, C and Rosas, A (eds), *Economic, Social and Cultural Rights. A Textbook* (2nd edn, 2001)

—— *et al* (eds), *The Universal Declaration of Human Rights: A Commentary* (1992)

Eisenberg, RS, 'Patenting the Human Genome' (1990) 39 Emory LJ 721

——, 'Patents and the Progress of Science: Exclusive Rights and Experimental Use' (1989) 56 U Chi L Rev 1017

——, 'Re-Examining the Role of Patents in Appropriating the Value of DNA Sequences' (2000) 49 Emory LJ 783

—— and Merges, RP, 'Opinion Letter as to the Patentability of Certain Inventions Associated with the Indentification of Partial cDNA Sequences' (1995) 23 AIPLA QJ 1

Eissen, M-A, 'The European Convention on Human Rights and the Duties of the Individual' (1962) 32 Nordisk Tidsskrift for International Ret 230

Eli Lilly & Co, *Developing Innovation. Annual Report 2002* (2002)

Elliott, R, *TRIPS and Rights: International Human Rights Law, Access to Medicines and the Interpretation of the WTO Agreement on Trade-Related Aspects of Intellectual Property Rights, Canadian HIV/AIDS Legal Network & AIDS Law Project, South Africa* (2001)

Ellison, SF *et al*, 'Characteristics of Demand for Pharmaceutical Products: An Examination of four Cephalosporins' (1997) 28 RAND J of Econ 426

Empell, H-M, *Die Staatengemeinschaftsnormen und ihre Durchsetzung. Die Pflichten erga omnes im geltenden Völkerrecht* (2003)

Engelberg, AB, 'Special Patent Provisions for Pharmaceuticals: Have they Outlived their Usefulness? A Political, Legislative and Legal History of U.S. Law and Observations for the Future' (1999) 39 IDEA 389

Epstein, MA, *Epstein on Intellectual Property* (looseleaf, last updated 2003)

Ernst & Young, *Health Care Systems and Health Market Reform in the G20 Countries* (2003)

——, *Pharmaceutical Industry R&D Costs: Key Findings about the Public Citizen Report* (2001)

Esty, DC, 'An Environmental Perspective on Seattle' (2000) 3 JIEL 176

European Federation of Pharmaceutical Industries and Associations, *Partnerships for the Developing World (Summary of Industry Contributions)* (2002)

——, *Local Production: Protectionism, Technology Transfer or Improved Access?*, at <http://www.efpia.org/4_pos/access/localprod.pdf>

European Generic Medicines Association, 'Tangled Patent Linkages Reduce Pharmaceutical Innovation. 6,730 patents for 27 pharmaceutical inventions' EGA Press Release, at <http://www.EGAgenerics.com/pr-2004-07-01.htm> (1 July 2004)

European Patent Office, Japanese Patent Office, and United States Patent and Trademark Office, *Trilateral Project B3b. Comparative Study on Biotechnology Patent Practices* (2000)

Evans, G and Newnham, J, *Dictionary of International Relations* (1998)

Falke, D, 'Vertragskonkurrenz und Vertragskonflikt im Recht der WTO: Erste Erfahrungen der Rechtsprechung 1995–1999' (2000) 3 ZeuS 307

Fanara, E, *Gestione di affari e arrichimento senza causa nel diritto internazionale* (1966)

Faracik, B, 'The Right to Health and Right to Intellectual Property in the EU. Analysis of the Internal and External Policies' Master Thesis (Lund) (2002)

Fassbender, B, 'The United Nations Charter as Constitution of the International Community' (1998) 36 Colum J Transnat'l L 529

Fastenrath, U, 'Relative Normativity in International Law' (1993) 4 EJIL 305

Fawcett, JES, *The Application of the European Convention on Human Rights* (2nd edn, 1987)

Federal Trade Commission, *Generic Drug Entry Prior to Patent Expiration: An FTC Study* (2002)

——, *The Proper Balance of Competition and Patent Law and Policy* (2003)

Fedtke, J, 'Das Recht auf Leben und Gesundheit, Patentschutz und das Verfahren des High Court of South Africa zur Verfassungsmäßigkeit des südafrikanischen Medicines and Related Substances Control Amendment Act' (2001) 34 VRÜ 489

Feist, C, *Kündigung, Rücktritt und Suspendierung von mulitlateralen Verträgen* (2001)

Ferman, SF, 'Argentina: The New Patent Law and the Agreement on Trade Related Aspects of Intellectual Property Right (TRIPS)' (2001) 8 Sw J L & Trade Am 157

Feuer, G, 'L'Uruguay Round, les Pays en Développement et le Droit International du Développement' (1994) 40 AFDI 758

Fidler, DP, *International Law and Public Health: Materials on and Analysis of Global Health Jurisprudence* (2000)

Fikentscher, W, *Wirtschaftsrecht. Band I Weltwirtschaftsrecht Europäisches Wirtschaftsrecht* (1983)

Fink, C, 'How Stronger Patent Protection in India Might Affect the Behavior of Transnational Pharmaceutical Industries' World Bank Working Paper No 2352 (2000)

—— and Reichenmiller, P, 'Tightening TRIPS: The Intellectual Property Provisions of Recent US Free Trade Agreements' World Bank Trade Note No 20 (2005)

Fiscal and Financial Branch of the Department of Economic and Social Affairs, *The Role of Patents in the Transfer of Technology to Developing Countries. Report of the Secretary-General*, UN Doc E/3861/Rev.1 (1964)

Fischer-Lescano, A and Teubner, G, 'Regime-Collisions: The Vain Search for Legal Unity in the Fragmentation of Global Law' (2004) 25 Michigan J Int'l L 999

Fischl, MA *et al*, 'The Efficacy of Azidothymidine (AZT) in the Treatment of Patients with AIDS and AIDS-Related Complex' (1987) 317 New Eng J Med 185

Fitzmaurice, GG, 'Third Report on the Law of Treaties', in YBILC, II (1958) 20, 44

Fitzmaurice, M, 'Current Legal Development. OSPAR Tribunal' (2003) 18 The International Journal of Marine and Costal Law 541

Fleischer-Black, M, 'The Cipro Dilemma—In the Anthrax Crisis, Tommy Thomspon Distorted Patent Law to Save Public Health. Good Move?' *The American Lawyer* (January 2002)

Flory, T and Ligneul, N, 'Commerce International, Droits de l'Homme, Mondialisation: Les Droits de l'Homme et l'Organisation Mondiale du Commerce' in L'Institut International des Droits de l'Homme (ed), *Commerce Mondial et Protection des Droits de l'Homme* (2001) 179

Floyd, K and Gilks, C, *Cost and Financing Aspects of Providing Anti-retroviral Therapy: A Background Paper*, Worldbank (1998)

Food and Drug Administration, *Electronic Orange Book. Approved Drug Products with Therapeutic Equivalence Evaluations*, at <http://www.fda.gov/cder/ob/default.htm> (last updated September 2004)

Ford, SM, 'Compulsory Licensing Provisions Under the TRIPs Agreement: Balancing Pills and Patents' (2000) 15 Am U Int'l L Rev 941

Forlati, S, 'Azioni Dinanzi alla Corte Internazionale di Giustizia Rispetto a Violazioni di Obblighi Erga Omnes' (2001) 84 Rivista di Diritto Internazionale 69

Forsythe, DP, 'Socioeconomic Human Rights: The United Nations, the United States, and Beyond' (1982) 4 Hum Rts Q 433

Fowler, DJ and Gordon, MJ, *The Effect of Public Policy Initiatives on Drug Prices in Canada, 10 Canadian Public Policy—Analyse de Politiques* (1984) 64

Foyer, J, 'Problèmes Internationaux Contemporains des Brevets d'Invention' (1981–II) 171 RdC 341

Freytag, C *Parallelimporte nach EG- und WTO-Recht. Patente und Marken versus Handelsfreiheit* (2001)

Friedmann, W, *The Changing Structure of International Law* (1964)

Froomkin, AM, 'ICANN 2.0: Meet the New Boss' (2003) 36 Loy LA L Rev 1087

Frowein, JA, 'jus cogens' in Bernhardt, R (ed), *Encyclopedia of Public International Law, III, 1* (1997) 65

——, 'Konstitutionalisierung des Völkerrechts' in Deutsche Gesellschaft für Völkerrecht (ed), *Völkerrecht und Internationales Privatrecht in einem sich globalisierenden internationalen System—Auswirkungen der Entstaatlichung transnationaler Rechtsbeziehungen* (2000) 427

——, 'Obligations Erga Omnes' in Bernhardt, R (ed), *Encyclopedia of Public International Law, III* (1997) 2, 757

——, 'Reactions by not Directly Affected States to Breaches of Public International Law' (1994—IV) 248 RdC 345

—— and Peukert, W (eds), *Europäische MenschenRechtsKonvention. EMRK-Kommentar* (2nd edn, 1996)

Gadbaw, RM, 'Intellectual Property and International Trade: Merger or Marriage of Convenience?' (1989) 22 Vand J Transnat'l L 223

Gaja, G, '*Jus Cogens* beyond the Vienna Convention' (1981) 172 RdC 271

——, 'Obligations *Erga Omens*, International Crimes and *Jus Cogens*: A Tentative Analysis of Three Related Concepts' in Weiler, JHH, Cassese, A and Spinedi, M (eds), *International Crimes of States. A Critical Analysis of the ILC's Draft Article 19 on State Responsibility* (1989) 151

Gallagher, P, *Guide to the WTO and Developing Countries* (2000)

Gallus, N, 'The Mystery of Pharmaceutical Parallel Trade and Developing Countries' (2004) 7 J World Intell Prop 169

Gambardella, A, Orsenigo, L and Pammolli, F, 'Global Competitiveness in Pharmaceuticals. A European Perspective' (2001) European Commission Enterprise Papers No 1—2001

Gamharter, K, *Access to Affordable Medicines. Developing Responses under the TRIPS Agreement and EC Law* (2004)

Gammie, B, 'Human Rights Implications of the Export of Banned Pesticides' (1994) 25 Seton Hall L Rev 558

Garcia, FJ, 'The Global Market and Human Rights: Trading Away the Human Rights Principle' (1999) 25 Brook J Int'l L 51

——, 'The *Salmon* Case: Evolution of Balancing Mechniams for Non-Trade Values in WTO' (2003) Boston College Law School Public Law and Legal Theory Research Paper No 19

Garcia, FJ, 'Trade Linkage Phenomenon: Pointing the Way to the Trade Law and Global Social Policy of the 21st Century, The Symposium on Linkage as Phenomenon: An Interdisciplinary Approach: Introduction' (1998) 19 U Pa J Int'l Econ L 201

García-Amador, FV, 'Calvo Doctrine, Calvo Clause' in Bernhardt, R (ed), *Encyclopedia of Public International Law, I* (1992) 521

Garner, BA, *Black's Law Dictionary* (7th edn, 2000)

Gathii, JT, 'Construing Intellectual Property Rights and Competition Policy Consistently with Facilitating Access to Affordable AIDS Drugs to Low-end Consumers' (2001) 53 Fla L Rev 727

——, 'Rights, Patents, Markets and the Global AIDS Pandemic' (2002) 14 Fla J Int'l L 261

——, 'The Legal Status of the Doha Declaration on TRIPS and Public Health under the Vienna Convention on the Law of Treaties' (2002) 15 Harv J L & Tech 291

Gattini, A, 'A Return Ticket to "Communitarisme" Please' (2002) 13 EJIL 1181

Geffen, N, 'Pharmaceutical Patents, Human Rights and the HIV/AIDS Epidemic' (2001) TAC discussion document

Geisel, VN, *Das TRIPS-Übereinkommen in der WTO-Rechtsordnung. Eine Untersuchung zum Spannungsverhältnis zwischen dem Schutz von geistigen Eigentumsrechten und der WTO-Zielsetzung der Handelsliberalisierung* (2003)

Generic Pharmaceutical Association, *Access to Affordable Medicines: A Comparison of Provisions of the TRIPS Agreements and Selected Bilateral Trade Agreements*, at <http://www.cptech.org/ip/health/trade/>

Geny, F, *Méthode d'Interprétation et Sources on Droit Privé Positif. Essai Critique. Tome Premier* (2nd edn, 1919)

Gervais, D, *The TRIPS Agreement: Drafting History and Analysis* (2nd edn, 2003)

—— and Nicholas-Gervais, V, 'Intellectual Property in the Multilateral Agreement on Investment. Lessons to be Learned' (1999) 2 J World Intell Prop 267

Getlan, M, 'TRIPs and the Future of Section 301: A Comparative Study in Trade Dispute Resolution' (1995) 34 Colum J Transnat'l L 173

Ghanotakis, E, 'How the US Interpretation of Flexibilities Inherent in TRIPS Affects Access to Medicines for Developing Countries' (2004) 7 J World Intell Prop 563

Ghosh, S, 'Pills, Patents, and Power: State Creation of Gray Markets as a Limit on Patent Rights' (2001) 53 Fla L Rev 789 (also published as (2002) 14 Fla J Int'l L 217)

Giegerich, T, *Privatwirkung der Grundrechte in den USA* (1992)

Gilbert, M, *History of the Twentieth Century* 212 (2001)

Gilbert, R and Shapiro, C, 'Optimal Patent Length and Breadth' (1990) 21 RAND J of Econ 502

Gill, TD, *Rosenne's The World Court. What It Is and How It Works* (6th edn, 2003)

GlaxoSmithKline, *The Impact of Medicines. Annual Report 2002* (2002)

Glick, LA, 'Section 337 of the Tariff Act of 1930 (Unfair Trade Practices and Methods of Competition in Importation of Products into the United States)' in Ince, WK and Glick, LA (eds), *Manual for the Practice of U.S. International Trade Law* (2001) 1

Gold, ER and Lam, DK, 'Balancing Trade in Patents—Public Non-Commercial Use and Compulsory Licensing' (2003) 6 J World Intell Prop 5

Goldberg, R, 'Pharmaceutical Price Controls: Saving Money Today or Lives Tomorrow' (1993) IPI Policy Report No 123

Gomes Canotilho, JJ and Moreira, V, *Constituição da República Portuguesa Anotada* (3rd edn, 1993)

Gómez Robledo, A, '*Le ius cogens* International: Sa Genèse, sa Nature, ses Fonctions' (1981—III) 172 RdC 9

Goodman, R and Jinks, D, 'Measuring the Effects of Human Rights Treaties' (2003) 14 EJIL 171

Goozner, M, *The $800 Million Pill: The Truth Behind the Cost of New Drugs* (2004)

Gopakumar, KM, 'The WTO Deal on Cheap Drugs. A Critique' (2004) 7 J World Intell Prop 99

Gordon, RI, 'Facilitating the Transnational Exchange of Scientific Information: Institut Pasteur v United States' (1988) 6 BU Int'l LJ 179

Gorlin, JJ, *An Analysis of the Pharmaceutical-Related Provisions of the WTO TRIPS (Intellectual Property) Agreement* (1999)

——, 'Encouragement of New Clinical Drug Development: The Role of Data Exclusivity' (2000) IFPMA 5

Gormley, WP, 'The Right to Life and the Rule of Non-Derogability: Peremptory Norms of *jus cogens*' in Ramcharan, BG (ed), *The Right to Life in International Law* (1985) 120

Gostin, LO and Lazzarini, Z, *Human Rights and Public Health in the AIDS Pandemic* (1997)

Grabenwarter, C, *Europäische Menschenrechtskonvention* (2003)

Grace, C, *Equitable Pricing of Newer Essential Medicines for Developing Countries: Evidence for the Potential of Different Mechanisms* (2003)

Graf zu Dohna, B, *Die Grundprinzipien des Völkerrechts über die freundschaftlichen Beziehungen und die Zusammenarbeit zwischen den Staaten* (1973)

Grassmuck, V, *Freie Software. Zwischen Privat- und Gemeineigentum* (2002)

Green, M, *Drafting History of the Article 15(1)(c) of the International Covenant on Economic, Social and Cultural Rights* UN Doc E/C.12/2000/15 (2000)

Grewe, WG, *The Epochs of International Law* (trans Michael Byers 2000)

Grisel, E, 'Les droits sociaux' (1973) 92 Zeitschrift für Schweizerisches Recht, Neue Folge 1

Grmek, MD, *History of AIDS. Emergence and Origin of a Modern Pandemic* (Maulitz, RC and Duffin, J trans 1990)

Groß, M, 'Aktuelle Lizenzgebühren in Patentlizenz-, Know-how- und Computerprogrammlizenz-Verträgen' (1995) BB 885

Grotius, H, *De iure belli ac pacis* (1646)

Guggenheim, P, 'Les deux Éléments de la Coutume en Droit International' in *La Technique et les Principes du Droit Public. Études en l'Honneur de Georges Scelle. Tome Premier* (1950) 275

Guillaume, G, 'The Future of International Judicial Institutions' (1995) 44 ICLQ 848

Gupta, A, *Patent Rights for Pharmaceuticals: TRIPS and the Right to Health at Crossroads*, at <http://users.ox.ac.uk/~edip/gupta.pdf>

Guzman, AT 'Why LDCs Sign Treaties that Hurt Them: Explaining the Popularity of Bilateral Investment Treaties' (1998) 38 Va J Int'l L 639

Haas, EB, 'Why Collaborate? Issue-Linkage and International Regimes' (1980) 32 World Politics 357

Hahn, M, *Die einstige Aussetzung von GATT-Verpflichtungen als Repressalie* (1996)

Hailbronner, K, 'Der Staat und der Einzelne als Völkerrechtssubjekte' in Graf Vitzthum, W (ed), *Völkerrecht* (2nd edn, 2001) 161

Halewood, M, 'Regulating Patent Holder: Local Working Requirements and Compulsory Licenses at International Law' (1997) 35 Osgoode Hall L J 243

Hamilton, A, 'Report on the Subject of Manufactures' in Syrett, HC (ed), *The Papers of Alexander Hamilton, vol. X. December 1791–January 1792* (1966) 230

Hammer, PJ, 'Differential Pricing of Essential AIDS Drugs: Markets, Politics and Public Health' (2002) 5 JIEL 883

Hann, M, '*Silhouette v Hartlauer*—Fortress Europe?' (1998) 1 J World Intell Prop 809

Hannikainen, L, *Peremptory Norms (jus cogens) in International Law* (1988)

Hare, I, '*Minister of Health v. Treatment Action Campaign:* The South African AIDS Pandemic and the Constitutional Right to Healthcare' (2002) 5 EHRLR 624

Harvard Law School Human Rights Program (ed), *Economic and Social Rights and the Right to Health. An Interdisciplinary Discussion Held at Harvard Law School in September, 1993* (1995)

Hathaway, OA, 'Do Human Rights Treaties Make a Difference?' (2002) 111 Yale LJ 1935

——, 'Testing Conventional Wisdom' (2003) 14 EJIL 185

Hays, T, 'BBS Kraftfahrzeugtechnik AG v Rcimex Japan KK; JAP Auto Products KK. Japan Opens the Door to Parallel Imports of Patented Goods' (2001) 2 Melb J Int'l L 191

Heath, C, 'Bedeutet TRIPS wirklich eine Schlechterstellung von Entwicklungsländern?' (1996) GRUR Int 1169

——, 'Industrial Property Protection in Vietnam' (1999) 30 IIC 419

——, 'Intellectual Property Rights in Asia—An Overview' (1997) 28 IIC 303

——, C, 'Parallel Imports and International Trade' (1997) 28 IIC 623

——, C, 'Parallel Imports of Patented Pharmaceuticals from the New EU Accession States' (2004) 35 IIC 776

Helfer, LR, 'Adjudicating Copyright Claims under the TRIPS Agreement: The Case for a European Human Rights Analogy' (1998) 39 Harv Int'l L J 357

——, 'Human Rights and Intellectual Property' (2004) 22 Netherlands Q of Hum Rts 167

Heller, MA and Eisenberg, RS, 'Can Patents Deter Innovation? The Anticommons in Biomedical Research' (1998) 280 Science 698

Henkin, L, *The Age of Rights* (1990)

Hepburn, J, 'Implementing the Paragraph 6 Decision and Doha Declaration: Solving Practical Problems to Make the System Work' (2004) Quaker United Nations Office

Herdegen, MJ, 'The "Constitutionalization" of the UN Security System' (1994) 27 Vand J Transnat'l L 135

Herrmann, C, 'Historischer Wendepunkt für den internationalen Patentschutz? Der internationale Patentschutz für Medikamente nach der Ausnahmeregelung der WTO für Exportzwangslizenzen vom 30. August 2003' (2003) ZEuS 589

——, 'TRIPS, Patentschutz für Medikamente und staatliche Gesundheitspolitik: Hinreichende Flexibilität?' (2002) EuZW 37

——, 'Viagra für den Welthandel oder historischer Wendepunkt für den internationalen Patentschutz (2003) EuZW 673

Hestermeyer, HP, 'Access to Medication as a Human Right' (2005) 8 Max Planck Yearbook for United Nations Law 101

——, 'African Union replaces Organization of African Unity' (2002) 3 German Law Journal 8

——, 'Flexible Entscheidungsfindung in der WTO. Die Rechtsnatur der neuen WTO Beschlüsse über TRIPS und Zugang zu Medikamenten' (2004) GRUR Int 194

——, 'The Language of Trade Linkage. Lessons for the Singapore Issues Learned from TRIPS' in A Steinmann, F Höhne and P-T Stoll (eds), *Die WTO vor neuen Herausforderungen* (2005) 139

Higgins, R, 'Derogations under Human Rights Treaties' (1976–1977) 48 BYIL 281

High-level Panel on Threats, Challenges and Change, *A More Secure World: Our Shared Responsibilty* (2004)

Hilf, M, 'Freiheit des Welthandels contra Umweltschutz?' (2000) NVwZ 481

—— and Oeter, S (eds), *WTO-Recht. Rechtsordnung des Welthandels* (2005)

Hillgenberg, H, 'A Fresh Look at Soft Law' (1999) 10 EJIL 499

Holcombe, AN, *Human Rights in the Modern World* (1948)

Holmes, OW, 'The Path of the Law' (1996–1997) 110 Harv L Rev 991

Holmes, S and Sunstein, CR, *The Cost of Rights. Why Liberty Depends on Taxes* (2000)

Hope, KR, 'Africa's HIV/AIDS Crisis in a Development Context' (2001) 15 International Relations 15

Horlick, GN, 'Over the Bump in Doha?' (2002) 5 JIEL 195

——, 'The Speedbump at Seattle' (2000) 3 JIEL 167

Horwitz, JP, Chua, J, and Noel, M, 'The Monomesylates of 1-(2'-Deoxy-β-D-lyxofuranosyl) thymine' (1964) 29 J Org Chem 2076

Howse, R, 'From Politics to Technocracy—and Back Again: The Fate of the Multilateral Trading Regime' (2002) 96 AJIL 94

——, 'Human Rights in the WTO: Whose Rights, What Humanity? Comment on Petersmann' (2002) 13 EJIL 651

——, 'The Canadian Generic Medicines Panel. A Dangerous Precedent in Dangerous Times' (2000) 3 J World Intell Prop 493

——, 'The Most Dangerous Branch? WTO Appellate Body Jurisprudence on the Nature and Limits of the Judicial Power' in Cottier, T and Mavroidis, PC (eds), *The Role of the Judge in International Trade Regulation. Experience and Lessons for the WTO* (2003) 11

—— and Mutua, M, *Protecting Human Rights in a Global Economy. Challenges for the World Trade Organization* (2000)

—— and Nicolaidis, K, 'Legitimacy through "Higher Law"? Why Constitutionalizing the WTO Is a Step too Far' in Cottier, T and Mavroidis, PC (eds), *The Role of the Judge in International Trade Regulation. Experience and Lessons for the WTO* (2003) 307

Hubley, J, *The AIDS Handbook. A Guide to the Prevention of AIDS and HIV* (3rd edn, 2002)

Hubmann, H and Götting, H-P, *Gewerblicher Rechtsschutz* (7th edn, 2002)

Hudec, RE, *Enforcing International Trade Law. The Evolution of the Modern GATT Legal System* (1993)

——, 'GATT or GABB? The Future Design of the General Agreement on Tariffs and Trade' in Hudec, RE, *Essays on the Nature of International Trade Law* (1999) 77

——, 'Remarks of Professor Robert Hudec' (1989) 22 Vand J Transnat'l L 321

——, *The GATT Legal System and World Trade Diplomacy* (1990)

Hudec, RE, 'The Gatt Legal System: A Diplomat's Jurisprudence' in Hudec, RE (ed), *Essays on the Nature of International Trade Law* (1999) 17

——, 'The Relationship of International Environmental Law to International Economic Law' in Morrison, FL and Wolfrum, R (eds), *International, Regional and National Environmental Law* (2000) 133

Humphrey, JP, 'The Universal Declaration of Human Rights: Its History, Impact and Juridical Character' in Ramcharan, BG (ed), *Human Rights: Thirty Years After the Universal Declaration* (1979) 21

Hunt, P, *Economic, Social and Cultural Rights. The Right of Everyone to the Enjoyment of the Highest Attainable Standards of Physical and Mental Health. Report of the Special Rapporteur, Paul Hunt, Submitted in Accordance with Commission Resolution 2002/31,* E/CN.4/2003/58 (13 February 2003)

Hussain, M, 'World Trade Organisation and the Right to Health: An Overview' (2003) 43 Indian J Int'l L 279

Hymes, KB *et al*, 'Kaposi's sarcoma in homosexual men: A report of eight cases' (1981) 2 Lancet 598

ICTSD and UNCTAD, *Resource Book on TRIPS and Development* (2002)

International Federation of Pharmaceutical Manufacturers Associations, *Building Healthier Societies Through Partnership* (2004)

——, *Research & Development*, at <http://www.ifpma.org/Issues/issues_research.aspx> (2004)

International Intellectual Property Institute, *Patent Protection and Access to HIV/AIDS Pharmaceuticals in Sub-Saharan Africa* (2000)

Ipsen, K (ed), *Völkerrecht* (4th edn, 1999)

Isensee, J, 'Verfassung ohne soziale Grundrechte. Ein Wesenszug des Grundgesetzes' (1980) 19 Der Staat 367

Islam, R, 'The Generic Drug Deal of the WTO from Doha to Cancun. A Peripheral Response to a Perennial Conundrum' (2004) 7 J World Intell Prop 675

Ismail, F, 'The Doha Declaration on TRIPS and Public Health and the Negotiations in the WTO on Paragraph 6. Why PhRMA Needs to Join the Consensus!' (2003) 6 J World Intell Prop 393

Iyer, VRK, 'A Prolegomenon' in Keayla, BK, *Conquest by Patents. TRIPs Agreement on Patent Laws: Impact on Pharmaceuticals and Health for All* (1999) 1

Jack, W and Lanjouw, JO, *Financing Pharmaceutical Innovation: When Should Poor Countries Contribute?* (2003)

Jackson, JH, 'Fragmentation or Unification among International Institutions: The World Trade Organization' (1998–1999) 31 NYU J Int'l L & Pol 823

——, 'International Economic Law: Jurisprudence and Contours' (1999) 93 ASIL Proceedings 98

——, 'Remarks of Professor John H. Jackson' (1989) 22 Vand J Transnat'l L 343

——, *Restructuring the GATT System* (1990)

——, 'Sovereigty-Modern: A New Approach to an Outdated Concept' (2003) 97 AJIL 782

——, *The World Trade Organization—Constitution and Jurisprudence* (1998)

——, *The World Trading System. Law and Policy of International Economic Relations* (2nd edn, 1997)

——, *World Trade and the Law of GATT* (1969)

Jamar, SD, 'The International Human Right to Health' (1994) 22 SUL Rev 1

Jarass, HD and Pieroth, B, *Grundgesetz für die Bundesrepublik Deutschland. Kommentar* (7th edn, 2004)

Jefferson, T, 'Letter to James Madison (July 31, 1788)' in Boyd, JP (ed), *The Papers of Thomas Jefferson. Volume 13. March to 7 October 1788* (1956) 440

——, 'Letter to Jeudy de L'Hommande (Aug 9, 1787)' in Boyd, JP (ed), *The Papers of Thomas Jefferson. Volume 12. 7 August 1787 to 31 March 1788* (1955) 11

Jehoram, HC, 'International Exhaustion versus Importation Right: a Murky Area of Intellectual Property Law' (1996) GRUR Int 280

——, 'Prohibition of Parallel Imports Through Intellectual Property Rights' (1999) 30 IIC 495

Jekewitz, J, 'The Implementation of the Basel Convention in German National Environmental Law as an Example for the Use of the Economic Mechanisms' in Wolfrum, R (ed), *Enforcing Environmental Standards: Economic Mechanisms as Viable Means?* (1996) 395

Jenks, W, 'The Conflict of Law-Making Treaties' (1953) 30 BYIL 401

Jennings, R, 'Nullity and Effectiveness in International Law' in Jennings, R (ed), *Cambridge Essays in International Law. Essays in Honour of Lord McNair* (1965) 64

——, 'Treaties as "Legislation"' in Abi-Saab, G (ed), *Collected Writings of Sir Robert Jennings. Volume 2* (1998) 719

—— and Watts, A, *Oppenheim's International Law. Volume I Peace. Introduction and Part 1* (9th edn, 1992)

Joseph, S, 'Pharmaceutical Corporations and Access to Drugs: The "Fourth Wave" of Corporate Human Rights Scrutiny' (2003) 25 Hum Rts Q 425

Kabaalioğlu, HA, 'The Obligations to "Respect" and to "Ensure" the Right to Life' in Ramcharan, BG (ed), *The Right to Life in International Law* (1985) 160

Kadelbach, S, *Allgemeines Verwaltungsrecht unter europäischem Einfluß* (1999)

——, *Zwingendes Völkerrecht* (1992)

Kaiser, K, *Geistiges Eigentum und Gemeinschaftsrecht. Die Verteilung der Kompetenzen und ihr Einfluss auf die Durchsetzbarkeit der völkerrechtlichen Verträge* (2004)

Kalanje, CM, 'Intellectual Property, Foreign Direct Investment and the Least-Developed Countries. A Perspective' (2002) 5 J World Intell Prop 119

Kammerhofer, J, 'Uncertainty in the Formal Sources of International Law: Customary International Law and Some of its Problems' (2004) 15 EJIL 523

Kampf, R, 'Patents versus Patients?' (2002) 40 AVR 90

Kang, PH and Stone, CS, 'IP, Trade and U.S./Singapore Relations. Significant Intellectual Property Provisions of the 2003 U.S.-Singapore Free Trade Agreement' (2003) 6 J World Intell Prop 721

Kaplan, WA *et al*, *Is Local Production of Pharmaceuticals a Way to Improve Pharmaceutical Access in Developing and Transitional Countries? Setting a Research Agenda (Draft)*, Boston University School of Public Health (2003)

Karl, W, 'Treaties, Conflict Between' in Bernhardt, R (ed), *Encyclopedia of Public International Law, IV, 2* (2000) 935

Katzenberger, P and Kur, A, 'TRIPs and Intellectual Property' in Beier, F-K and Schricker, G (eds), *From GATT to TRIPs—The Agreement on Trade-Related Aspects of Intellectual Property Rights* (1996) 1

Kearns, AP, 'The Right to Food Exists via Customary International Law' (1998) 22 Suffolk Transnat'l L Rev 223

Kelsen, H, *General Theory of Norms* (trans Hartney, M 1991)

Kelsen, H, *Principles of International Law* (1952)

——, *Reine Rechtslehre. Einleitung in die rechtswissenschaftliche Problematik* (1934)

——, 'Théorie du Droit International Coutumier' (1939) 1 Revue Internationale de la Théorie du Droit. Nouvelle Série 253

Kennedy, D, 'The International Human Rights Movement: Part of the Problem?' (2002) 15 Harv Hum Rts J 101

Keohane, RO, 'The Demand for International Regimes' (1982) 36 International Organization 325

—— and Nye, JS, *Power and Interdependence* (2nd edn, 1989)

Kesan, JP, 'Private Internet Governance' (2003) 35 Loy U Chi L J 87

Kettler, HE, 'Using Intellectual Property Regimes to Meet Global Health R&D Needs' (2002) 5 J World Intell Prop 655

—— and Collins, C, 'Using Innovative Action to Meet Global Health Needs through Existing Intellectual Property Regimes' UK Commission on Intellectual Property Rights Study Paper 2b

—— and Modi, R, 'Building Local Research and Development Capacity for the Prevention and Cure of Neglected Diseases: The Case of India' (2001) 79 Bulletin of the World Health Organization 742

Khan, BZ, 'Intellectual Property and Economic Development: Lessons from American and European History' Commission on Intellectual Property Rights Study Paper 1a (2002)

Kingsbury, B, 'Is the Proliferation of International Courts and Tribunals a Systematic Problem?' (1999) 31 NYU J Int'l L & Politics 679

Kinney, ED, 'The International Human Right to Health: What Does this Mean for Our Nation and World?' (2001) 34 Ind L Rev 1457

Kiss, A, 'The Role of the Universal Declaration of Human Rights in the Development of International Law' (1988) Bull of Hum Rts Special Issue. Fortieth Anniversary of the Universal Declaration of Human Rights 47

——, Shelton, D, and Ishibashi, K, *Economic Globalization and Compliance with International Environmental Agreements* (2003)

Kitch, EW, 'Patents: Monopolies or Property Rights?' (1986) 8 Res in L & Econ 31

——, 'The Nature and Function of the Patent System' (1977) 20 JL & Econ 265

Klabbers, J, *An Introduction to International Institutional Law* (2002)

Klein, E, 'Bedeutung des Gewohnheitsrechts für den Menschenrechtsschutz' in Klein, E (ed), *Menschenrechtsschutz durch Gewohnheitsrecht. Kolloquium 26.–28. September 2002 Potsdam* (2003) 11

——, 'International Régimes' in Bernhardt, R (ed), *Encyclopedia of Public International Law, II, 2* (1995) 1354

——, 'The Duty to Protect and to Ensure Human Rights Under the Internatioanl Covenant on Civil and Political Rights' in Klein, E (ed), *The Duty to Protect and to Ensure Human Rights. Colloquium. Potsdam, 1–3 July 1999* (2000) 296

Klein, F, 'Vertragskonkurrenz' in Schlochauer, H-J (ed), *Wörterbuch des Völkerrechts. Begründet von Professor Dr. Karl Strupp* (2nd edn, 1962) 555

Klemperer, P, 'How Broad Should the Scope of Patent Protection Be?' (1990) 21 RAND J of Econ 113

Koch, IE, 'Social Rights as Components in the Civil Right to Personal Liberty: Another Step Forward in the Integrated Human Rights Approach?' (2002) 20 Netherlands Q of Hum Rts 29

Köck, HF and Fischer, P, *Das Recht der Internationalen Organisationen* (3rd edn, 1997)

Kohler-Koch, B, 'Zur Empirie und Theorie internationaler Regime' in Kohler-Koch, B (ed), *Regime in den internationalen Beziehungen* (1989) 17

Kokott, J, *Beweislastverteilung und Prognoseentscheidungen bei der Inanspruchnahme von Grund- und Menschenrechten* (1993)

Kommers, DP, *The Constitutional Jurisprudence of the Federal Republic of Germany* (2nd edn, 1997)

Kongolo, T, 'Compulsory Licence Issues in African Arab Countries' (2004) 7 J World Intell Prop 185

——, 'Public Interest *versus* the Pharmaceutical Industry's Monopoly in South Africa' (2001) 4 J World Intell Prop 605

——, 'The New OAPI Agreement as Revised in February 1999. Complying with TRIPS' (2000) 3 J World Intell Prop 717

——, 'TRIPS, the Doha Declaration and Public Health' (2003) 6 J World Intell Prop 373

Kontou, N, *The Termination and Revision of Treaties in the Light of New Customary International Law* (1994)

Koshy, S, 'The Effect of TRIPs on Indian Patent Law: A Pharmaceutical Industry Perspective' (1995) 1 BUJ Sci & Tech L 4

Koskenniemi, M, *Fragmentation of International Law: Difficulties Arising from the Diversification and Expansion of International Law*, ILC(LVI)/SG/FIL/CRD.1/Add.1 (4 May 2004).

——, *Fragmentation of International Law: Difficulties Arising from the Diversification and Expansion of International Law. Report of the Study Group of the International Law Commission*, UN Doc A/CN.4/L.682 (13 April 2006)

——, *From Apology to Utopia. The Structure of International Legal Argument* (1989)

——, 'The Pull of the Mainstream' (1990) 88 Mich L Rev 1946

—— and Leino, P, 'Fragmentation of International Law? Postmodern Anxieties' (2002) 15 LJIL 553

Krajewski, M, *Verfassungsperspektiven und Legitimation des Rechts der Welthandelsorganisation* (2001)

Krasner, SD, *Sovereignty. Organized Hypocrisy* (1999)

——, 'Structural Causes and Regime Consequences: Regimes as Intervening Variables' (1982) 36 International Organization 185

Kraßer, R, *Patentrecht* (5th edn, 2004)

Kreibich, S, *Das TRIPs-Abkommen in der Gemeinschaftsordnung. Aspekte der Kompetenzverteilung zwischen WTO, Europäischer Gemeinschaft und ihren Mitgliedstaaten* (2002)

Kremer, M, 'Creating Markets for New Vaccines. Part I: Rationale' (2001) 1 Innovation Policy and the Economy 35

——, 'Creating Markets for New Vaccines: Part II: Design Issues' (2001) 1 Innovation Policy and the Economy 73

Krenzler, HG, 'Die Nachkriegsentwicklung des Welthandelssystems—von der Havanna-Charta zur WTO' in Prieß, H-J, Berrisch, G and Pitschas, C (eds), *WTO-Handbuch* (2003) 1

Kretschmer, F, 'Aktuelle Informationen. Internationales—GATT und gewerblicher Rechtsschutz' (1988) GRUR Int 186

Krisch, N, 'More Equal than the Rest? Hierarchy, Equality and US Predominance in International Law' in Byers, M and Nolte, G (eds), *United States Hegemony and the Foundations of International Law* (2003) 135

Kronstein, H and Till, I, 'A Reevaluation of the International Patent Convention' in Dinwoodie, GB, Hennesey, WO and Perlmutter, S (eds) *International Intellectual Property Law and Policy* (2001) 378

Krueger, P and Mommsen, T (eds), *Corpus Iuris Civilis. Volumen Primum. Institutiones Digesta* (7th edn, 1895)

Kühling, J, 'Grundrechte' in von Bogdandy, A (ed), *Europäisches Verfassungsrecht. Theoretische und dogmatische Grundzüge* (2003) 583

Kumar, N, 'Intellectual Property Rights, Technology and Economic Development: Experiences of Asian Countries' Commission on Intellectual Property Rights Study Paper 1b (2002)

Kunz-Hallstein, HP, 'The United States Proposal for a GATT Agreement on Intellectual Property and the Paris Convention for the Protection of Industrial Property' (1989) 22 Vand J Transnat'l L 265

Kuyper, PJ, 'The Law of GATT as a Special Field of International Law. Ignorance, further Refinement or Self-contained System of International Law?' (1994) 25 NYIL 227

Lal Das, B, *The World Trade Organisation. A Guide to the Framework for International Trade* (1999)

Lanjouw, JO and Cockburn, IM, 'New Pills for Poor People? Empirical Evidence after GATT' (2001) 29 World Development 265

Lapointe, S, 'L'Histoire des brevets' (2000) 12 Les Cahiers de Propriété Intellectuelle 633

Larenz, K and Canaris, C-W, *Methodenlehre der Rechtswissenschaft* (3rd edn, 1995)

Lauterpacht, H, *International Law and Human Rights* (1950)

——, *International Law. A Treatise. By L. Oppenheim. Vol. I.—Peace* (8th edn, 1955)

——, 'Règles Générales du Droit de la Paix' (1937—IV) 82 RdC 99

——, 'Report on the Law of Treaties' in YBILC, II (1953) 90

Law and Treatment Access United of the AIDS Law Project and Treatment Action Campaign (eds), *The Price of Life. Hazel Tau and Others vs GlaxoSmithKline and Boehringer Ingelheim: A Report on the Excessive Pricing Complaint to South Africa's Competition Commission* (2003)

Leebron, DW, 'Linkages' (2002) 96 AJIL 5

Leibenstein, H, 'Allocative Efficiency vs. "X-Efficiency"' (1966) 56 Am Econ Rev 392

Lennard, M, 'Navigating By the Stars: Interpreting the WTO Agreements' (2002) 5 JIEL 17

Lenz, C and Kieser, T, 'Schutz vor Milzbrandangriffen durch Angriffe auf den Patentschutz?' (2002) NJW 401

Lessig, L, *The Future of Ideas. The Fate of the Commons in a Connected World* (2001)

Letsas, G, 'The Truth in Autonomoous Concepts: How to Interpret the ECHR' (2004) 15 EJIL 279

Levitt, GM, Czaban, JN, and Paterson, AS, 'Human Drug Regulation' in Adams, DG, Cooper, RM, and Kahan, JS (eds), *Fundamentals of Law and Regulation. Volume II. An In-depth Look at Therapeutic Products* (1997)

Lichtenberg, FR and Philipson, TJ, 'The Dual Effects of Intellectual Property Regulations: Within- and Between- Patent Competition in the US Pharmaceuticals Industry' NBER Working Paper 9303 (2002)

Light, DW and Lexchin, J, 'Will Lower Drug Prices Jeopardize Drug Research? A Policy Fact Sheet' (2004) Am J of Bioethics 4(1), W3

Lim, H, 'Trade and Human Rights. What's at Issue?' (2001) 35 JWT 275

Lincoln, A, 'Second Lecture on Discoveries and Inventions (Feb. 11, 1859)' in Basler, RP, Pratt, MD, Dunlap, LA (eds), *The Collected Works of Abraham Lincoln. Volume III*, 356 (1953)

Lippert, O, 'A Market Perspective on Recent Developments in the TRIPS and Essential Medicines Debate' in Granville, B (ed), *The Economics of Essential Medicines* (2002) 3

List, F, *Das Nationale System der politischen Ökonomie* (1841)

Locke, J, 'An Essay Concerning the True Original Extent and End of Civil Government' in Hutchins, RM (ed), *Great Books of the Western World. 35 Locke Berkeley Hume* (1952) 25

López Guerra, L *et al*, *Derecho Constitucional. Volumen I* (3rd edn, 1997)

Love, J, *Compulsory Licensing: Models for State Practice in Developing Countries, Access to Medicine and Compliance with the WTO TRIPS Accord*, Prepared for the United Nations Development Programme, at <http://www.cptech.org/ip/health/cl/recommended-statepractice.html> (2001)

—— and Palmedo, M, *Cost of Human Use Clinical Trials: Surprising Evidence from the US Orphan Drug Act*

Lovell, MC, 'Second Thoughts: Do the FDA's Responses to a Fatal Drug Trial and the AIDS Activist Community's Doubts about Early Access to Drugs Hint at a Shift in Basic FDA Policy?' (1996) 51 Food & Drug L J 273

Lowenfeld, AF, *International Economic Law* (2002)

Lu, ZJ and Comanor, WS, 'Strategic Pricing of New Pharmaceuticals' (1998) 80 Rev of Econ & Statistics 108

Lucas-Schloetter, A, 'Die Rechtsnatur des Droit Moral' (2002) GRUR Int 809

Luhmann, N, *Einführung in die Systemtheorie* (2nd edn, 2004)

Lyons, S, 'The African Court on Human and Peoples' Rights' (2006) 10 ASIL Insight 24

Lyons, SR, 'The New United Nations Human Rights Council' (2006) 10 ASIL Insight 7

Machlup, F, *An Economic Review of the Patent System, Study of the Subcommittee on Patents, Trademarks, and Copyrights of the Committee on the Judiciary, United States Senate, Eighty-Fifth Congress, Second Session* (1958)

MacLead, C, *Inventing the Industrial Revolution. The English Patent System, 1660–1800* (1988)

Madison, J, 'The Federalist No. 43' in Hamilton, A, Jay, J, and Madison, J, *The Federalist. A Commentary on the Constitution of the United States* (1888)

Makgoba, MW, 'HIV/AIDS: The Peril of Pseudoscience' (2000) 288 Science 1171

Malanczuk, P, 'Globalization and the Future Role of Sovereign States' in Weiss, F, Denters, E, and de Waart, P, *International Economic Law with a Human Face* (1998) 45

Mandich, G, 'Venetian Patents (1450–1550)' (trans Prager, FD 1948) 30 J Pat & Trademark Off Soc'y 166

Mangoldt, H v, Klein, F, and Starck, C (eds), *Das Bonner Grundgesetz. Kommentar. Band 1: Präambel, Artikel 1 bis 19* (4th edn, 1999)

Marc, P, 'Compulsory Licensing and the South African Medicine Act of 1997: Violation or Compliance of the Trade Related Aspects of Intellectual Property Rights Agreement?' (2001) 21 NYL Sch J Int'l & Comp L 109

Marceau, G, 'A Call for Coherence in International Law. Praises for the Prohibition Against "Clinical Isolation" in WTO Dispute Settlement' (1999) 33 JWT 87

Marceau, G, 'Conflict of Norms and Conflicts of Jurisdiction. The Relationship between the WTO Agreements and MEAs and other Treaties' (2001) 35 JWT 1081

——, 'Conflicts of Norms and Conflicts of Jurisdictions' (2001) 35 JWT 1081

——, 'WTO Dispute Settlement and Human Rights' (2002) 13 EJIL 753

Maresca, A, *Il diritto dei trattati. La convenzione codificatrice di Vienna del 23 Maggio 1969* (1971)

Marinberg, D, 'GATT/WTO Waivers: "Exceptional Circumstances" as Applied to the Lomé Waiver' (2001) 19 BU Int'l L J 129

Marschik, A, *Subsysteme im Völkerrecht. Ist die Europäische Union ein 'Self-Contained Regime'?* (1997)

Marx, JL, 'Aids Virus Has New Name—Perhaps' (1986) 232 Science 699

Maskus, KE, 'Ensuring Access to Essential Medicines: Some Economic Considerations' (2001–2002) 20 Wis Int L Rev 563

——, *Intellectual Property Rights in the Global Economy* (2000)

—— and Ganslandt, M, 'Parallel Trade in Pharmaceutical Products: Implications for Procuring Medicines for Poor Countries' in Granville, B (ed), *The Economics of Essential Medicines* (2002) 57

—— and Reichman, JH, 'The Globalization of Private Knowledge Goods and the Privatization of Global Public Goods' (2004) 7 JIEL 279

Matscher, F, 'Menschenrechte in Europa: Gedanken zur Weiterentwicklung des Grundrechtsschutzes in Europa' in Schuhmacher, W (ed), *Perspektiven des europäischen Rechts* (1994) 305

Matthews, D, *Globalising Intellectual Property Rights. The TRIPs Agreement* (2002)

Matz, N *Wege zur Koordinierung völkerrechtlicher Verträge. Völkervertragsrechtliche und institutionelle Ansätze* (2005)

Maunz, T *et al* (eds), *Grundgesetz. Kommentar. Band II Art. 12–20* (looseleaf, last updated February 2003)

Max Planck Institute for Foreign and International Patent, Copyright and Competition Law, 'Comment of the Max Planck Institute' in *Economic, Social and Cultural Rights. Intellectual Property Rights and Human Rights. Report of the Secretary General*, UN Doc E/CN.4/Sub.2/2001/12 (14 June 2001)

May, C, 'Why IPRs are a Global Political Issue' (2003) 25 EIPR 1

McCrudden, C and Davies, A, 'A Perspective on Trade and Labor Rights' (2000) 3 JIEL 43

McDougal, MS, Lasswell, HD, and Chen, L-c, *Human Rights and World Public Order. The Basic Policies of an International Law of Human Dignity* (1980) 273

McGrath, RJ, 'The Unauthorized Use of Patents by the United States Government or its Contractors' (1991) 18 AIPLA QJ 349

McNair, *The Law of Treaties* (1961)

McRae, DM, 'The Contribution of International Trade Law to the Development of International Law' (1996) 260 RdC 99

——, 'The WTO in International Law: Tradition Continued or New Frontier?' (2000) 3 JIEL 27

McWhinney, E, 'The Concept of Co-operation' in Bedjaoui, M (ed), *International Law: Achievement and Prospects* (1991) 425

Médecins Sans Frontières (ed), *AccessNews* (February 2002)

Mendelson, MH, 'The Formation of Customary International Law' (1998) 272 RdC 155

Meng, W, 'GATT and Intellectual Property Rights—The International Law Framework' in Sacerdoti, G (ed), *Liberalization of Services and Intellectual Property in the Uruguay Round of GATT. Proceedings of the Conference on 'The Uruguay Round of GATT and the Improvement of the Legal Framework of Trade in Services', Bergamo, 21.-23. September 1989* (1990) 57

Menghistu, F, 'The Satisfaction of Survival Requirements', in Ramcharan, BG (ed), *The Right to Life in International Law* (1985) 63

Merck & Co, Inc, *Annual Report 2002* (2002)

Merges, RP and Duffy, JF, *Patent Law and Policy: Cases and Materials* (3rd edn, 2002)

——, Menell, PS and Lemley, MA, *Intellectual Property in the New Technology Age* (1997)

Meron, T, *Human Rights and Humanitarian Norms as Customary Law* (1991)

Meshbesher, TM, 'The Role of History in Comparative Patent Law' (1996) 78 J Pat & Trademark Off Soc'y 594

Meulenbelt, M, 'Parallel Imports of Medicinal Products—A New Balance?' (1998) 1 J World Intell Prop 525

Meyer, WH and Stefanova, B, 'Human Rights, the UN Global Compact, and Global Governance' (2001) 34 Cornell Int'l L J 501

Mill, JS, 'Principles of Political Economy with Some of Their Applications to Social Philosophy' in *Collected Works of John Stuart Mill. Volume III* (1965)

Miller, AR and Davis, MH, *Intellectual Property in a Nutshell. Patents, Trademarks, and Copyright* (3rd edn, 2000)

Milne, C-P, 'Exploring the Frontiers of Law and Science: FDAMA's Pediatric Studies Incentive' (2002) 57 Food & Drug LJ 491

Mish, FC *et al* (eds), *Merriam-Webster's Collegiate Dictionary* (10th edn, 1998)

Mogollón-Rojas, ID, 'The New Andean Pact Decision No. 486 on the Common Industrial Rights Regime. Complying with TRIPS Regulations' (2001) 4 J World Intell Prop 549

Mohnhaupt, H, 'Die Unendlichkeit des Privilegienbegriffs' in Dölemeyer, B and Mohnhaupt, H (eds), *Das Privileg im europäischen Vergleich. Bd. 1* (1997) 1

Monshipouri, M, Welch, Jr, CE, and Kennedy, ET, 'Multinational Corporations and the Ethics of Global Responsibility: Problems and Possibilities' (2003) 25 Hum Rts Q 965

Montaguti, E and Lugard, M, 'The GATT 1994 and other Annex 1A Agreements: Four Different Relationships?' (2000) 3 JIEL 473

Montgomery, J, 'Recognising a Right to Health' in Beddard, R and Hill, DM (eds), *Economic, Social and Cultural Rights. Progress and Achievement* (1992) 184

Moore, M, *Moore: Countries Must Feel Secure that They Can Use TRIPS' Flexibility*, at <http://www.wto.org/english/news_e/news01_e/dg_trips_medicines_010620_e.htm> (2001)

Morelli, G, 'Aspetti Processuali della Invalidità dei Trattati' (1974) 57 Rivista di Diritto Internazionale 5

Morri, F, 'Patentes y medicamentos: la batalla de los países en desarrollo' (2004) Revista de Estudios Internacionales 123

Morrison, WM, *China—U.S. Trade Issues*, CRS Issue Brief for Congress, at <http://fpc.state.gov/documents/organization/21120.pdf> (last updated 16 May 2003)

Moser, B, *Die Europäische Menschenrechtskonvention und das bürgerliche Recht. Zum Problem der Drittwirkung von Grundrechten* (1972)

Mosler, H, 'General Principles of Law' in Bernhardt, R (ed), *Encyclopedia of Public International Law, II* (1995) 511

Mossoff, A, 'Rethinking the Development of Patents: An Intellectual History, 1550–1800' (2001) 52 Hastings LJ 1255

Moynihan, R and Smith, R, 'Too much medicine? Almost certainly' (2002) 324 British Medical Journal 859

Muennich, FE, 'Les Brevets Pharmaceutiques et L'Accès Aux Médicaments' (2000) RIDE 71

Mukherjee, S, 'The Journey of Indian Patent Law towards TRIPS Compliance' (2004) IIC 125

Müller, JP, 'Soziale Grundrechte in der Verfassung?' (1973) 92 Zeitschrift für Schweizerisches Recht, Neue Folge 687

Nagan, WP, 'International Intellectual Property, Access to Health Care, and Human Rights: South Africa v United States' (2002) 14 Fla J Int'l L 155

National Institute for Health Care Management Research and Education Foundation, *Changing Patterns of Pharmaceutical Innovation* (2002)

Nauta, W, 'Ausnahmen vom Erschöpfungsgrundsatz im Markenrecht' (2004) GRUR Int 994

Nerozzi, MM, 'The Battle Over Life-Saving Pharmaceuticals: Are Developing Countries Being "TRIPped" by Developed Countries?' (2002) 47 Villanova L R 605

Neuhold, H, 'Die Pflicht zur Zusammenarbeit zwischen den Staaten: Moralisches Postulat oder völkerrechtliche Norm?' in Miehsler, H *et al* (eds), *Ius Humanitatis. Festschrift zum 90. Geburtstag von Alfred Verdross* (1980) 575

Neumann, J, *Die Koordination des WTO-Rechts mit anderen völkerrechtlichen Ordnungen. Konflikte des materiellen Rechts und Konkurrenzen der Streitbeilegung* (2001)

Neuwahl, NA, 'The Treaty on European Union: A Step forward in the Protection of Human Rights?' in Neuwahl, NA and Rosas, A (eds), *The European Union and Human Rights* (1995) 1

Nicholson, W, *Microeconomic Theory. Basic Principles and Extensions* (7th edn, 1998)

Nicoloudis, EP, *La Nullité de jus cogens et le Developpement Contemporain du Droit International Public* (1974)

Nielsen, HK, *The World Health Organisation. Implementing the Right to Health* (2nd edn, 2001)

Noehrenberg, E, 'TRIPS, the Doha Declaration and Public Health' (2003) 6 J World Intell Prop 379

Noll, A, 'International Telecommunication Union' in Bernhardt, R (ed), *Encyclopedia of Public International Law, II, 2* (1995) 1379

Nordhaus, WD, *Invention, Growth, and Welfare. A Theoretical Treatment of Technological Change* (1969)

Norman, C, 'FDA Approves Pasteur's AIDS Test Kit' (1986) 213 Science 1063

——, 'Patent Dispute Divides AIDS Researchers. The War on AIDS, Part 2' (1985) 230 Science 640

Nowak, JE and Rotunda, RD, *Constitutional Law* (5th edn, 1995)

Nowak, M, *Introduction to the International Human Rights Regime* (2003)

——, 'The Right to Education' in Eide, A, Krause, C and Rosas, A (eds), *Economic, Social and Cultural Rights. A Textbook*, (2nd edn, 2001) 245

——, *U.N. Covenant on Civil and Political Rights. CCPR Commentary* (1993)

Nozick, R, *Anarchy, State, and Utopia* (1974)

Nwauche, ES, 'An Evaluation of the African Regional Intellectual Property Rights Systems' (2003) 6 J World Intell Prop 101

O'Boyle, M, 'The development of the Right to Life' in Björgvinsson, DÞ *et al* (eds), *Afmælisrit Þór Vilhjálmsson. Sjötugur. 9. Júní 2000* (2000) 65

Ochoa, TT and Rose, M, 'The Anti-Monopoly Origins of the Patent and Copyright Clause' (2002) 84 J Pat & Trademark Off Soc'y 909

Odman, NA, 'Using TRIPS to Make the Innovation Process Work' (2000) 3 J World Intell Prop 343

Oellers-Frahm, K, 'Comment: The erga omnes Applicability of Human Rights' (1992) 30 AVR 28

——, 'Die Entscheidung des IGH im Fall LaGrand—Eine Stärkung der internationalen Gerichtsbarkeit und der Rolle ds Individuums im Völkerrecht' (2001) EuGRZ 265

Oeter, S, 'International Law and General Systems Theory' (2001) 44 GYIL 72

Office of Technology Assessment, *Patent-Term Extension and the Pharmaceutical Industry* (1981)

——, US Congress, *Pharmaceutical R&D: Costs, Risks and Rewards* (1993)

Office of the High Representative for the Least Developed Countries, Landlocked Developing Countries and Small Island Developing States, *The Criteria for the Identification of the LDCs*, at <http://www.un.org/special-rep/ohrlls/ldc/ldc%20criteria.htm>

Office of the United States Global AIDS Coordinator (ed), *The President's Emergency Plan for AIDS Relief, US Five-Year Global HIV/AIDS Strategy* (2004)

Oloka-Onyango, J and Udagama, D, *Economic Social and Cultural Rights. Globalization and its Impact on the Full Enjoyment of Human Rights*, UN Doc E/CN.4/Sub.2/2001/10 (2001)

—— and ——, *The Realization of Economic, Social and Cultural Rights. Globalization and its Impact on the Full Enjoyment of Human Rights*, UN Doc E/CN.4/Sub.2/2000/13 (2000)

Oppenheim, L, *International Law. A Treatise. Vol. I. Peace* (2nd edn, 1912)

Opsahl, T, 'The Right to Life' in Macdonald, RSJ, Matscher, F, and Petzold, H (eds), *The European System for the Protection of Human Rights* (1993) 207

O'Reilly, JT, *Food and Drug Administration. Volume One* (2nd edn, looseleaf, last updated 2002)

Organization for Economic Co-operation and Development (ed), *The OECD Guidelines for Multinational Enterprises. Revision 2000* (2000)

Örücü, E, 'The Core of Rights and Freedoms: The Limit of Limits' in Campbell, T *et al* (eds), *Human Rights: From Rhetoric to Reality* (1986) 37

Ostergard, RL, Jr, 'Intellectual Property: A Universal Human Rights?' (1999) 21 Hum Rts Q 156

——, 'The Political Economy of the South Africa—United States Patent Dispute' (1999) 2 J World Intell Prop 875

Ostertag, W *et al*, *Induction of Endogenous Virus and of Thymidine Kinase by Bromodeoxy-uridine in Cell Cultures Transformed by Friend Virus* (1974) 71 Proc Nat Acad Sci USA 4980

Otero García-Castrillón, C, 'An Approach to the WTO Ministerial Declaration on the TRIPS Agreement and Public Health' (2002) 5 JIEL 212

Otten, A, 'Les Brevets Couvrant les Produits Pharmaceutiques et l'Accord sur Les Adpic' (2000) RIDE 161

Otten, A and Wagner, H, 'Compliance with TRIPS: The Emerging World View' in Abbott, F, Cottier, T and Gurry, F (eds), *The International Intellectual Property System. Commentary and Materials Part One* (1999) 697

Oxfam, 'TRIPS and Public Health. The next battle' Oxfam Briefing Paper 15 (2002)

Pacón, AM, 'What Will TRIPs Do for Developing Countries?' in Beier, F-K and Schricker, G (eds), *From GATT to TRIPs—The Agreement on Trade-Related Aspects of Intellectual Property Rights* (1996) 329

Pagenberg, J, 'The Exhaustion Principle and "Silhouette" Case' (1999) 30 IIC 19

Palmeter, D, 'National Sovereignty and the World Trade Organization' (1999) 2 J World Intell Prop 88

—— and Mavroidis, PC, 'The WTO Legal System: Sources of Law' (1998) 92 AJIL 398

Panel on Clinical Practices for Treatment of HIV Infection, *Guidelines for the Use of Antiretroviral Agents in HIV-1-Infected Adults and Adolescents* (2004)

Papa, MI, *I Rapporti Tra La Corte Internazionale di Giustizia e il Consiglio di Sicurezza* (2006)

Park, RS, 'The International Drug Industry: What the Future Holds for South Africa's HIV/AIDS Patients' (2002) 11 Minn J Global Trade 125

Paulson, C, 'Compliance with Final Judgments of the International Court of Justice Since 1987' (2004) 98 AJIL 434

Paulus, AL, *Die internationale Gemeinschaft im Völkerrecht. Eine Untersuchung zur Entwicklung des Völkerrechts im Zeitalter der Globalisierung* (2001)

Pauwelyn, J, *Conflict of Norms in Public International Law. How WTO Law Relates to other Rules of International Law* (2003)

——, 'Cross-agreement Complaints before the Appellate Body: A Case Study of the EC-Asbestos Dispute' (2002) 1 World Trade Review 63

——, 'Does the WTO Stand for "Deference to" or "Interference with" National Health Authorities When Applying the Agreement on Sanitary and Phytosanitary Measures (SPS Agreement)?' in Cottier, T and Mavroidis, PC (eds), *The Role of the Judge in International Trade Regulation. Experience and Lessons for the WTO* (2003) 175

——, 'The Nature of WTO Obligations' Jean Monnet Working Paper No 1/02 (2002)

——, 'The Role of Public International Law in the WTO: How Far Can We Go?' (2001) 95 AJIL 535

Pechota, V, 'The Development of the Covenant on Civil and Political Rights' in Henkin, L (ed), *The International Bill of Rights. The Covenant on Civil and Political Rights* (1981) 32

Pellet, A, *Droits de l'Hommisme et Droit international,* Droits fondamentaux 1 (2001)

Penrose, ET, *The Economics of the International Patent System* (1951)

Perez, A, 'The Implementation of the GATT/WTO TRIPS Agreement in Venezuela. An Overview in 1998' (1998) 1 J World Intell Prop 747

Perez Pugatch, M, *The International Political Economy of Intellectual Property Rights* (2004)

Perloff, JM, *Microeconomics* (1999)

Petersmann, E-, '"Entwicklungsvölkerrecht", "Droit International Du Développement", "International Economic Development Law": Mythos oder Wirklichkeit' (1974) 17 GYIL 145

Petersmann, E-U, 'Challenges to the Legitimacy and Efficiency of the World Trading System: Democratic Governance and Competition Culture in the WTO' (2004) 7 JIEL 585

——, *Constitutional Functions and Constitutional Problems of International Economic Law* (1991)

——, 'From "Negative" to "Positive" Integration in the WTO: Time for "Mainstreaming Human Rights" into WTO Law?' (2000) 37 Common Market Law Review 1363

——, 'From the Hobbesian International Law of Coexistance to Modern Integration Law: The WTO Dispute Settlement System' (1998) 1 JIEL 175

——, 'Human Rights and International Economic Law in the 21st Century. The Need to Clarify their Interrelationships' (2001) 4 JIEL 3

——, 'Human Rights and the Law of the World Trade Organization' (2003) 37 JWT 241

——, 'The WTO Constitution and Human Rights' (2000) 3 JIEL 19

——, 'Time for a United Nations "Global Compact" for Integrating Human Rights into the Law of Worldwide Organizations: Lessons from European Integration' (2002) 13 JIEL 621

Pharmaceutical Research and Manufacturers Association, *NIHCM's Report on Pharmaceutical Innovation: Fact vs. Fiction, a preliminary report* (2002)

Picket, JP *et al* (eds), *The American Heritage Dictionary of the English Language* (4th edn, 2000)

Picone, P, 'Interventi delle Nazioni Unite e Obblighi Erga Omnes' in Picone, P (ed), *Interventi delle Nazioni Unite e Diritto Internazionale* (1995) 517

——, 'Nazioni Unite e Obblighi "erga omnes"' (1993) 48 La Communitá internazionale 709

——, 'Obblighi Reciproci ed Obblighi erga omnes degli Stati nel Campo della Protezione Internazionale dell'Ambiente Marino dall'Inquinamento' in Starace, V (ed), *Diritto Internazionale e Protezione dell'Ambiente Marino* (1983) 15

—— and Ligustro, A, *Diritto dell'Organizzazione Mondiale del Commercio* (2002)

Pieroth, B and Schlink, B, *Grundrechte. Staatsrecht II* (11th edn, 1995)

Pindyck, RS and Rubinfeld, DL, *Microeconomics* (5th edn, 2001)

Pinto, M, 'Fragmentation or Unification among International Institutions: Human Rights Tribunals' (1998–1999) 31 NYU J Int'l L & Pol 833

Pires de Carvalho, N, *The TRIPS Regime of Patent Rights* (2002)

Plaisant, M, *Traité de Droit Conventionnel International concernant la Propriété Industrielle* (1949)

Plaisant, R, 'Les Brevets Spéciaux de Médicaments' (1961) I JCP 1616

Plasseraud, Y and Savignon, F, *L'Etat et l'Invention. Histoire des Brevets* (1986)

Pohlmann, H, 'Neue Materialien zur Frühentwicklung des deutschen Erfinderschutzes im 16. Jahrhundert' (1960) GRUR 272

——, 'The Inventor's Right in Early German Law. Materials of the Time from 1531 to 1700' (1961) 43 J Pat & Trademark Off Soc'y 121 (trans Prager, FD)

Pollaud-Dulian, F, *Droit de la Propriété industrielle* (1999)

Pontecorvo, CM, 'Interdependence between Global Environmental Regimes: The Kyoto Protocol on Climate Change and Forest Protection' (1999) 59 ZaöRV 709

Pouillet, E, *Traité Théorique et Pratique des Brevets d'Invention et de la Contrefaçon* (3rd edn, 1889)

Powell-Bullock, E, 'Gaming the Hatch-Waxman System: How Pioneer Drug Makers Exploit the Law to Maintain Monopoly Power in the Prescription Drug Market' (2002) 29 J Legis 21

Prager, FD, 'A History of Intellectual Property from 1545 to 1787' (1944) 26 J Pat & Trademark Off Soc'y 711

——, 'Brunelleschi's Patent' (1946) 28 J Pat & Trademark Off Soc'y 109

Preeg, EH, 'The South Rises in Seattle' (2000) 3 JIEL 183

Primo Braga, CA, 'The Economics of Intellectual Property Rights and the GATT: A View From the South' (1989) 22 Vand J Transnat'l L 243

—— and Fink, C, 'Reforming Intellectual Property Rights Regimes: Challenges for Developing Countries' (1998) 1 JIEL 537

——, ——, and Paz Sepulveda, C, *Intellectual Property Rights and Economic Development*, World Bank Discussion Paper No 412 (2000)

Przetacznik, F, 'The Right to Life as a Basic Human Right' (1976) Revue des Droits de l'Homme, Human Rights Journal 585

Public Citizen (ed), *Rx R&D Myths: The Case Against the Drug Industry's R&D 'Score Card'* (2001)

Qureshi, AH, 'International Trade and Human Rights from the Perspective of the WTO' in Weiss, F, Denters, E, and de Waart, P (eds), *International Economic Law with a Human Face* (1998) 159

Rabbow, M, 'From Awareness to Behavioural Change—Challenges in HIV/AIDS Control in Southern Africa/Namibia' (2001) 36 afrika spectrum 17

Rafiquzzaman, M, 'The Optimal Patent Term under Uncertainty' (1987) 5 Int'l J of Indus Org 233

Ragazzi, M, *The Concept of International Obligations* Erga Omnes (1997)

Rahn, G, 'Die Bedeutung des gewerblichen Rechtsschutzes für die wirtschaftliche Entwicklung: Die japanischen Erfahrungen' (1982) GRUR Int 577

Rai, AK and Eisenberg, RS, 'Bayh-Dole Reform and the Progress of Biomedicine' (2003) 66-SPG Law & Contemp Probs 289

Ramcharan, BG, 'The Concept and Dimensions of the Right to Life' in Ramcharan, BG (ed), *The Right to Life in International Law* (1985) 1

——, 'The Right to Life' (1983) 30 NILR 297

Rao, PK, *The World Trade Organization and the Environment* (2000)

Ratner, SR, 'Corporations and Human Rights: A Theory of Legal Responsibility' (2001) 111 Yale L J 443

Rau, M, 'Comment: The Swordfish Case: Law of the Sea v. Trade' (2002) 62 ZaöRV 37

Redelbach, A, 'Protection of the Right to Life by Law and by other Means' in Ramcharan, BG (ed), *The Right to Life in International Law* (1985) 182

Regnault, T, *De la Législation et de la Jurisprudence concernant les Brevets d'Invention, et Perfectionnement et d'Importation* (1825)

Reichman, JH, 'From Free Riders to Fair Followers: Global Competition under the TRIPS Agreement' (1996–1997) 29 NYU J Int'l L & Pol 11

——, 'Intellectual Property in International Trade: Opportunities and Risks of a GATT Connection' (1989) 22 Vand J Transnat'l L 747

Reimer, E *et al*, *Das Recht der Arbeitnehmererfindung* (7th edn, 2000)

Reinbothe, J, 'Der Schutz des Urheberrechts und der Leistungsschutzrechte im Abkommensentwurf GATT/TRIPs' (1992) GRUR Int 707

Reindel, F, *Auslegung menschenrechtlicher Verträge am Beispiel der Spruchpraxis des UN-Menschenrechtsausschusses, des Europäischen und des Interamerikanischen Gerichtshofs für Menschenrechte* (1995)

Reinisch, A, '2.2 Selecting the Appropriate Forum' in UNCTAD (ed), *Course on Dispute Settlement. International Centre for Settlement of Investment Disputes* (2003)

Richardt, MA, 'A New Instrument of International Patent Cooperation: The Eurasian Patent Convention' (1997) 28 IIC 466

Ridder, C, *Die Bedeutung von Zwangslizenzen im Rahmen des TRIPS-Abkommens* (2004)

Riedel, E, 'Menschenrechte der dritten Dimension' in Riedel, E, *Die Universalität der Menschenrechte. Philosophische Grundlagen Nationale Gewährleistungen Internationale Garantien* (2003) 329

——, 'New Bearings to the State Reporting Procedure: Practical Ways to Operationalize Economic, Social and Cultural Rights—The Example of the Right to Health' in von Schorlemer, S (ed), *Praxishandbuch UNO. Die Vereinten Nationen im Lichte globaler Herausforderungen* (2003) 345

——, *Verhandlungslösungen im Rahmen des Sozialpakts der Vereinten Nationen*, Arbeitspapiere—Mannheimer Zentrum für Europäische Sozialforschung Nr 28 (2000)

Rin-laures, L-H and Janofsky, D, 'Recent Development Concerning the Orphan Drug Act' (1991) 4 Harv J L & Tech 269

Rinnert, S, 'Parallelimporte und TRIPs' (2001) Mitteilungen der deutschen Patentanwälte 403

Riphagen, W, 'Fifth Report on the Content, Forms and Degrees of International Responsibility (Part 2 of the Draft Articles)' in YBILC, II (1984) Part 1, 1

Robinson, N, *The Universal Declaration of Human Rights* (1958)

Roche, *Annual Report 2002* (2002)

——, *Factsheet Tamiflu* (2006)

Rodley, NS, 'Can Armed Opposition Groups Violate Human Rights?' in Mahoney, K and Mahoney, P (eds), *Human Rights in the Twenty-first Century. A Global Challenge* (1993) 297

Roessler, F, 'Foreword' in Hudec, RE (ed), *Essays on the Nature of International Trade Law* (1999) 10

Roffe, P, 'Bilateral Agreements and a TRIPS-plus World: the Chile-USA Free Trade Agreement' Quaker International Affairs Programme TRIPS Issues Paper (2004)

Roscam Abbing, HD, *International Organizations in Europe and the Right to Health Care* (1979)

Rosenne, S, 'The Perplexities of Modern International Law. General Course on Public International Law' (2001) 291 RdC 9

Rosenstock, J, *The Law of Chemical and Pharmaceutical Invention* (2nd edn, looseleaf, 2003)

Rosenstock, R, 'The Declaration of Principles of International Law concerning Friendly Relations: A Survey' (1971) 65 AJIL 713

Rott, P, *Patentrecht und Sozialpolitik unter dem TRIPS-Abkommen* (2002)

——, 'TRIPS-Abkommen, Menschenrechte, Sozialpolitik und Entwicklungsländer' (2003) GRUR Int 103

Roubier, P, *Le Droit de la Propriété Industrielle. Partie Générale I.—Les Droits Privatifs (Histoire et nature juridique, régime intérieur et international). II.—Les Actions en Justice (Action en contrefaçon et action en concurrence déloyale)* (1952)

Roucounas, E, 'Engagements Parallèles et Contradictoires' (1987—VI) 206 RdC 9

Rousseau, C, 'De la Compatibilité des Normes Juridiques Contradictoires dans l'Ordre International' (1932) 39 RGDIP 133

——, *Droit International Public. Tome I: Introduction et Sources* (1970)

Rozek, RP, 'The Effects of Compulsory Licensing on Innovation and Access to Health Care' (2000) 3 J World Intell Prop 889

—— and Berkowitz, R, 'The Effects of Patent Protection on the Prices of Pharmaceutical Products—Is Intellectual Property Protection Raising the Drug Bill in Developing Countries?' (1998) 2 J World Intell Prop 179

—— and Rainey, RL, 'Broad-Based Compulsory Licensing of Pharmaceutical Technologies. Unsound Public Policy' (2001) 4 J World Intell Prop 459

—— and Tully, N, 'The TRIPS Agreement and Access to Health Care' (1999) 2 J World Intell Prop 813

Rubini, L, 'Is the Siege of Fortress Europe Really Over? The Exhaustion of Trademarks in the EC, Competition and International Trade' (2002) 29 Legal Issues of Economic Integration 205

Ruiz, M, *The Andean Community's New Industrial Property Regime: Creating Synergies between the CBD and Intellectual Property Rights*, Bridges November–December 2000, 11

Sachs, JD, 'A New Global Effort to Control Malaria' (2002) 298 Science 122

——, 'Financing Global Public Goods: Approaches to Health' in Kaul, I, Le Goulven, K, and Schnupf, M (eds), *Global Public Goods Financing: New Tools for New Challenges. A Policy Dialogue* (2002)

Sachs, M, *Verfassungsrecht II. Grundrechte* (2000)

Sadat-Akhavi, SA, *Methods of Resolving Conflicts between Treaties* (2003)

Šahović, M, 'Codification des Principes du Droit International des Relations Amicales et de la Coopération entre les États' (1972—III) 137 RdC 243

Saint-Paul, G, 'To What Extent Should Less-Developed Countries Enforce Intellectual Property?' CEPR Discussion Paper No 4713 (2004)

Salazar, S, 'Intellectual Property and the Right to Health' in World Intellectual Property Organization (ed), *Intellectual Property and Human Rights. A Panel Discussion to commemorate the 50th Anniversary of the Universal Declaration of Human Rights. Geneva, November 9, 1998* (1999) 65

Scalabrino-Spadea, M, 'Le Droit à la Santé. Inventaire de Normes et Principes de Droit International' in Institut International d'Études des Droits de l'Homme (ed), *Le Médecin face aux Droits de l'Homme*, (1990) 95

Scelle, G, *Manuel de Droit International Public* (1948)

Schachter, O, 'International Law in Theory and Practice. General Course in Public International Law' (1982—V) 178 RdC 9

Schäfers, A and Schennen, D, 'Der erste Teil der Diplomatischen Konferenz zum Abschluß eines Vertrages zur Harmonisierung des Patentrechts' (1991) GRUR Int

Scherer, FM, 'Le Système des Brevets et l'Innovation dans le Domaine Pharmaceutique' (2000) RIDE 109

——, 'The Economic Effects of Compulsory Patent Licensing' in Towse, R and Holzhauer, R (eds), *The Economics of Intellectual Property Volume II. Patents* (2002) 315

——, *The Patent System and Innovation in Pharmaceuticals* (1998)

—— and Watal, J, 'Post-Trips Options for Access to Patented Medicines in Developing Countries' CMH Working Paper Series, Paper No WG4:1 (2001)

—— and ——, 'The Economics of TRIPS Options for Access to Medicines' in Granville, B (ed), *The Economics of Essential Medicines* (2002) 32

—— and Weisburst, S, 'Economic Effects of Strengthening Pharmaceutical Patent Protection in Italy' (1995) IIC 1009

Schermers, HG, 'The Legal Bases of International Organization Action' in Dupuy, R-J (ed), *A Handbook on International Organizations* (2nd edn, 1998) 401

——, *The Protection of Human Rights in the European Community. Referat im Rahmen der Vortragsreihe 'Europäisches Wirtschaftsrecht nach Maastricht'. Bonn, 22. November 1993* (1994)

—— and Blokker, NM, *International Institutional Law. Unity within Diversity* (3rd edn, 1995)

Scheuner, U, 'Conflict of Treaty Provisions with a Peremptory Norm of General International Law' (1969) 29 ZaöRV 28

Schiff, E, *Industrialization without National Patents* (1971)

Schiuma, D, 'TRIPS and Exclusion of Software "as Such" from Patentability' (2000) 31 IIC 36

Schlitz, DM and McGrath, RJ, 'Patent Infringement Claims Against the United States Government' (2000) 9 Fed Circuit BJ 351

Schloemann, HL and Ohlhoff, S, '"Constitutionalization" and Dispute Settlement in the WTO: National Security as an Issue of Competence' (1999) 93 AJIL 424

Schmidt-Szalewski, J and Pierre, J-L, *Droit de la Propriété Industrielle* (1996)

Schott, JJ, 'Comment on the Doha Ministerial' (2002) 5 JIEL 191

Schricker, G, 'Problems of Convention Priority for Patent Applications' in Abbott, F, Cottier, T and Gurry, F (eds), *The International Intellectual Property System. Commentary and Materials Part One* (1999) 678

Schroeter, K and Poschenrieder, R, *Der Ausübungszwang in der Patentgesetzgebung aller Länder* (looseleaf 2 volumes, 1934 *et seq*)

Schütz, R, *Solidarität im Wirtschaftsvölkerrecht* (1994)

Schwartz, HF, *Patent Law and Practice* (3rd edn, 2001)

Schwartz, P and Randall, D, *An Abrupt Climate Change Scenario and Its Implications for United States National Security* (2003)

Schwarzenberger, G, 'The Principles and Standards of International Economic Law' (1966—I) 117 RdC 1

Schwelb, E, 'Some Aspects of International jus cogens as Formulated by the International Law Commission' (1967) 61 AJIL 946

Sciso, E, *Gli Accordi Internazionali Confliggenti* (1986)

Scobbie, I, 'International Organizations and International Relations' in Dupuy, R-J (ed), *A Handbook on International Organizations* (2nd edn, 1998) 831

Scott, C, 'The Interdependence and Permeability of Human Rights Norms: Towards a Partial Fusion of the International Covenants on Human Rights' (1989) 27 Osgoode Hall L J 769

Scuffi, M, 'Die Erfindungen auf dem Pharmasektor—Stand der Mailänder und Turiner Rechtsprechung' (1991) GRUR Int 481

Seibert-Fohr, A, 'Die Deliktshaftung von Unternehmen für die Beteiligung an im Ausland begangenen Völkerrechtsverletzungen. Anmerkungen zum Urteil Doe I v. Unocal Corp. des US Court of Appeal (9th Circuit)' (2003) 63 ZaöRV 195

Seidl-Hohenveldern, I, *International Economic Law* (3rd edn, 1999)

—— and Loibl, G, *Das Recht der Internationalen Organisationen einschließlich der Supranationalen Gemeinschaften* (7th edn, 2000)

Sell, SK, 'Industry Strategies for Intellectual Property and Trade: The Quest for TRIPS, and Post-TRIPS Strategies' (2002) 10 Cardozo J Int'l & Comp L 79

Sell, SK, *Private Power, Public Law. The Globalization of Intellectual Property Rights* (2003)

Sepúlveda, M, *The Nature of the Obligations under the International Covenant on Economic, Social and Cultural Rights* (2003)

Shah, SB, 'Illuminating the Possible in the Developing World: Guaranteeing the Human Right to Health in India' (1999) 32 Vand J Transnat L 435

Shahabuddeen, M, 'Consistency in Holdings by International Tribunals' in Ando, N *et al* (eds), *Liber Amicorum Judge Shigeru Oda. Volume 1* (2002) 633

Shanker, D, 'India, the Pharmaceutical Industry and the Validity of TRIPS' (2002) 5 J World Intell Prop 315

——, 'Legitimacy and the TRIPS Agreement' (2003) 6 J World Intell Prop 155

——, 'The Paragraph 6 Solution of the Doha Public Health Declaration and Export under the TRIPS Agreement' (2004) 7 J World Intell Prop 365

——, 'The Vienna Convention on the Law of Treaties, the Dispute Settlement System of the WTO and the Doha Declaration on the TRIPS Agreement' (2002) 36 JWT 721

Shany, Y, *The Competing Jurisdictions of International Courts and Tribunals* (2003)

Shapiro, HS, 'Section 301 of the Trade Act of 1974' in Ince, WK and Glick, LA (eds), *Manual for the Practice of U.S. International Trade Law* (2001) 1275

Shue, H, *Basic Rights: Subsistence, Affluence & U.S. Foreign Policy* (1980)

Shulman, S, *Unlocking the Sky. Glenn Hammond Curtiss and the Race to Invent the Airplane* (2002)

Siebeck, WE *et al*, 'Strengthening Protection of Intellectual Property in Developing Countries: A Survey of the Literature' (1990) World Bank Discussion Paper No 112

Simma, B, *Das Reziprozitätselement im Zustandekommen völkerrechtlicher Verträge* (1972)

——, *Das Reziprozitätselement in der Entstehung des Völkergewohnheitsrecht* (1970)

——, 'Der Schutz wirtschaftlicher und sozialer Rechte durch die Vereinten Nationen' in Vassilouni, S (ed), *Aspects of the Protection of Individual and Social Rights* (1995) 75

——, 'Die Erzeugung ungeschriebenen Völkerrechts: Allgemeine Verunsicherung— klärende Beiträge Karl Zemaneks' in Ginther, K *et al* (eds), *Völkerrecht zwischen normativem Anspruch und politischer Realität. Festschrift für Karl Zemanek zum 65. Geburtstag* (1994) 95

——, 'From Bilateralism to Community Interest in International Law' (1994—VI) 250 RdC 217

——, 'Self-contained Regimes' (1985) 16 NYIL 111

—— (ed), *The Charter of the United Nations. A Commentary. Volume I* (2nd edn, 2002)

——, 'The Implementation of the International Covenant on Economic, Social and Cultural Rights' in Matscher, F (ed), *Die Durchsetzung wirtschaftlicher und sozialer Grundrechte* (1991) 75

—— and Alston, P, 'The Sources of Human Rights Law: Custom, Jus Cogens, and General Principles' (1992) 12 Australian Y B Int'l L 82

—— and Paulus, AL, 'The "International Community": Facing the Challenge of Globalization' (1998) 9 JIEL 266

—— and von Bennigsen, S, 'Wirtschaftliche, soziale und kulturelle Rechte im Völkerrecht' in Baur, JF, Hopt, KJ and Mailänder, KP (eds), *Festschrift für Ernst Steindorff zum 70. Geburtstag am 13. März 1990* (1990) 1477

—— *et al* (eds), *The Charter of the United Nations. A Commentary. Volume II* (2nd edn, 2002)

Singer, PW, *Corporate Warriors. The Rise of the Privatized Military Industry* (2004)

Singh Nair, M, *India Moving Towards a TRIPS Compliant Patent Regime—Implications for the Pharmaceutical Industry*, at <http://www.mondaq.com/i_article.asp_Q_articleid_E_27499> (2004)

Skaggs, NT and Carlson, JL, *Microeconomics. Individual Choice and Its Consequences* (2nd edn, 1996)

Slaughter, A-M, *A New World Order* (2004)

——, 'An International Relations Approach' (2001) 95 AJIL 25

——, 'International Law and International Relations' (2000—I) 285 RdC 9

Slonina, M, *Durchbruch im Spannungsverhältnis TRIPS and Health: Die WTO-Entscheidung zu Exporten unter Zwangslizenzen*, Beiträge zum Transnationalen Wirtschaftsrecht 20 (2003)

Slotboom, MM, 'The Exhaustion of Intellectual Property Rights, Different Approaches in EC and WTO Law' (2003) 6 J World Intell Prop 421

Smith, A, *An Inquiry into the Nature and Causes of the Wealth of Nations* (11th edn, 1805)

Smith, RKM, *Textbook on International Human Rights* (2003)

Sohn, LB, ' "Generally Accepted" International Rules' (1986) 61 Wash L Rev 1073

——, 'The Human Rights Law of the Charter' (1977) 12 Tex Int'l L J 129

——, 'The New International Law: Protection of the Rights of Individuals Rather than States' (1982–1983) 32 Am U L Rev 1

Soltysiński, S, 'International Exhaustion of Intellectual Property Rights under TRIPs, the EC Law and the Europe Agreements' (1996) GRUR Int 316

Spence, M, 'Which Intellectual Property Rights are Trade-Related?' in Francioni, F (ed), *Environment, Human Rights and International Trade* (2001) 263

Spielmann, D, *L'Effet Potentiel de la Convention Européenne des Droits de l'Homme entre Personnes Privées* (1995)

Ssenyonjo, M, 'Justiciability of Economic and Social Rights in Africa: General Overview, Evaluation and Prospects' (2003) 9 E Afr J Peace & Hum Rts 1

Stack, AJ, 'TRIPS, Patent Exhaustion and Parallel Imports' (1998) 4 J World Intell Prop 657

Staehelin, A, *Das TRIPs-Abkommen. Immateralgüterrechte im Licht der globalisierten Handelspolitik* (2nd edn, 1999)

Stanton, J, 'Comment: Lesson for the United States from Foreign Price Controls on Pharmaceuticals' (2000) 16 Conn J Int'l L 149

Starck, D, *Die Rechtmäßigkeit von UNO-Wirtschaftssanktionen in Anbetracht ihrer Auswirkungen auf die Zivilbevölkerung. Grenzen der Kompetenzen des Sicherheitsrats am Beispiel der Maßnahmen gegen den Irak und die Bundesrepublik Jugoslawien* (2000)

Stegemann, K and Pzderka, B, 'The TRIPS Agreement as an Alliance for Knowledge Production. The Funding of Pharmaceutical Innovation' (2003) 6 J World Intell Prop 529

Steinberg, RH, 'In the Shadow of Law or Power? Consensus-Based Bargaining and Outcomes in the GATT/WTO' (2002) 56 Int'l Org 339

——, 'Judicial Lawmaking at the WTO: Discursive, Constitutional, and Political Constraints' (2004) 98 AJIL 247

Steiner, HJ and Alston, P, *International Human Rights in Context. Law, Politics, Morals* (1996)

Stengel, D, 'Intellectual Property in Philosophy' (2004) 90 ARSP 20

Stiglitz, J, *Globalization and Its Discontents* (2002)

Stoll, P-T, 'Die WTO: Neue Welthandelsorganisation, neue Welthandelsordnung. Ergebnisse der Uruguay-Runde des GATT' (1994) 54 ZaöRV 241

——, *Technologietransfer. Internationalisierungs- und Nationalisierungstendenzen. Die Gestaltung zwischenstaatlicher Wirtschaftsbeziehungen, privater Verfügungsrechte und Transaktionen durch die Vereinten Nationen, die UNCTAD, die WIPO und die Uruguay-Runde des GATT* (1994)

—— and Raible, K, 'Schutz geistigen Eigentums und das TRIPS-Abkommen' in Prieß, H-J, Berrisch, GM, and Pitschas, C (eds), *WTO-Handbuch* (2003) 565

—— and Schorkopf, F, *WTO—Welthandelsordnung und Welthandelsrecht* (2002)

—— and ——, *WTO. World Economic Order, World Trade Law* (2006)

—— and Vöneky, S, 'The Swordfish Case: Law of the Sea v. Trade' (2002) 62 ZaöRV 21

Stolleis, M, *Geschichte des öffentlichen Rechts in Deutschland. Erster Band, Reichspublizistik und Policeywissenschaft 1600–1800* (1988)

Stone, CD, 'Common but Differentiated Responsibilities in International Law' (2004) 98 AJIL 276

Story, J, *Commentaries on the Constitution of the United States with a Preliminary Review of the Constitutional History of the Colonies and States, Before the Adoption of the Constitution. Volume II* (3rd edn, 1858)

Straus, J, 'Bedeutung des TRIPS für das Patentrecht' (1996) GRUR Int 179

——, 'Implications of the TRIPs Agreement in the Field of Patent Law' in Beier, F-K and Schricker, G (eds), *From GATT to TRIPs—The Agreement on Trade-Related Aspects of Intellectual Property Rights* (1996) 160

——, *Patentschutz durch das TRIPS-Abkommen.—Ausnahmeregelungen und –praktiken und ihre Bedeutung, insbesondere hinsichtlich pharmazeutischer Produkte—*, in Stiftung Gesellschaft für Rechtspolitik/Institut für Rechtspolitik (eds), *Bitburger Gespräche. Jahrbuch 2003* (2003) 117

Stringham, E, *Patents and Gebrauchmuster in International Law*, in Dinwoodie, GB, Hennesey, WO, and Perlmutter, S (eds), *International Intellectual Property Law and Policy* (2001) 376

Struchio, JL and Colatrella, BD, 'Successful Public-Private Partnerships in Global Health: Lessons from the MECTIZAN Donation Program' in Granville, B (ed), *The Economics of Essential Medicines* (2002) 255

Study Group of the ILC, *Fragmentation of International Law: Difficulties Arising from the Diversification and Expansion of International Law. Report of the Study Group of the International Law Commission*, UN Doc A/CN.4/L.702 (18 July 2006)

Subramanian, A, 'The AIDS Crisis, Differential Pricing of Drugs, and the TRIPS Agreement. Two Proposals' (2001) 4 J World Intell Prop 323

Sun, H, 'The Road to Doha and Beyond: Some Reflections on the TRIPS Agreement and Public Health' (2004) 15 EJIL 123

Sutherland, P et al, *The Future of the WTO. Addressing Institutional Challenges in the New Millennium* (2004)

Sykes, AO, 'International Trade and Human Rights: An Economic Perspective' (2003) John M Olin Law & Economics Working Paper No 188 (2nd series)

——, 'The Persistent Puzzles of Safeguards: Lessons from the Steel Dispute' (2004) 7 JIEL 523

——, 'TRIPs, Pharmaceuticals, Developing Countries, and the Doha "Solution"' John M. Olin Law & Economics Working Paper No 140 (2002) (2nd series) (also published at (2002) 3 Chicago J Int'l L 47)

Szabo, I, 'Fondements historiques et développement des droits de l'homme' in Vasak, K (ed), *Les dimensions internationales des droits de l'homme. Manuel destiné à l'enseignement des droits de l'homme dans les universités* (1978) 11

Sze, S, *The Origins of the World Health Organization. A Personal Memoir 1945–1948* (1982)

Templeman, S, 'Intellectual Property' (1998) 1 JIEL 603

Teubner, G, '"Global Bukowina": Legal Pluralism in the World Society' in Teubner, G (ed), *Global Law without a State* (1996) 3

The Global Alliance for TB Drug Development, *Exective Summary for the Economics of TB Drug Development* (2001), at <http://www.tballiance.org/downloads/publications/TBA_Economics_Report_Exec.pdf>

Thompson, D (ed), *The Concise Oxford Dictionary of Current English* (9th edn, 1995)

Thorpe, P, 'Study on the Implementation of the TRIPS Agreement by Developing Countries' UK Commission on Intellectual Property Rights Study Paper 7

Timmermans, K and Hutadjulu, T, *The TRIPS Agreement and Pharmaceuticals, Report of an ASEAN Workshop on the TRIPs Agreement and its Impact on Pharmaceuticals. Jakarta, 2–4 May 2000* (2000)

Tinbergen, J, *International Economic Integration* (2nd edn, 1956)

Ting Goh, A and Olivier, J, 'Free Trade and Protection of Intellectual Property Rights: Can We Have One Without the Other' CEPR Discussion Paper No 3127 (2002)

Toebes, BCA, *The Right to Health as a Human Right in International Law* (1999)

Tomandl, T, *Der Einbau sozialer Grundrechte in das positive Recht* (1967)

Tomuschat, C, 'Die Bundesrepublik Deutschland und die Menschenrechtspakte der Vereinten Nationen' (1978) 26 Vereinte Nationen 1

——, 'Die Charta der wirtschaftlichen Rechte und Pflichten der Staaten. Zur Gestaltungskraft von Deklarationen der UN-Generalversammlung' (1976) 36 ZaöRV 445

——, 'Die internationale Gemeinschaft' (1995) 33 AVR 1

——, 'International Law: Ensuring the Survival of Mankind on the Eve of a New Century. General Course on Public International Law' (1999) 281 RdC 9

——, 'International Standards and Cultural Diversity' (1985) Bulletin of Human Rights. Special Issue. Human Rights Day 24

——, 'Obligations Arising for States without or against Their Will' (1993–IV) 241 RdC 209

Torres, MA, 'The Human Right to Health, National Courts, and Access to HIV/AIDS Treatment: A Case Study from Venezuela' (2002) 3 Chicago J Int'l L 105

Trachtman, JP, 'Institutional Linkage: Transcending "Trade and ..."' (2002) 96 AJIL 77

——, 'The Domain of WTO Dispute Resolution' (1999) 40 Harv Int'l L J 333

——, 'Trade and ... Problems, Cost-Benefit Analysis and Subsidiarity' (1998) 9 EJIL 32

Trebilcock, MJ and Howse, R, *The Regulation of International Trade* (2nd edn, 1999)

Treviranus, H-D, 'Preamble' in Bernhardt, R (ed), *Encyclopedia of Public International Law, III* (1997) 1097

Triepel, H, *Völkerrecht und Landesrecht* (1899)

Türk, D, *The Realization of Economic, Social and Cultural Rights*, UN Doc E/CN.4/ Sub.2/1992/16 (1992)

UK Patent Office, *Manual of Patent Practice* (5th edn, 2003)

UNAIDS, *2004 Report on the Global AIDS Epidemic* (2004)

——, *2006 Report on the Global AIDS Epidemic* (2006)

——, *Report on the Global HIV/AIDS Epidemic 2002* (2002)

——, *Uniting the World Against AIDS*, at <http://www.unaids.org/en/AboutUNAIDS/ default.asp>

UNCTAD, *Bilateral Investment Treaties 1959–1999* (2000)

UNDP, *Human Development Report 1999* (1999)

United Nations High Commissioner for Human Rights, *Economic, Social and Cultural Rights. The Impact of the Agreement on Trade-Related Aspects of Intellectual Property Rights on Human Rights. Report of the High Commissioner*, UN Doc E/CN.4/Sub.2/2001/13 (2001)

——, *Economic, Social and Cultural Rights. Globalization and its impact on the full enjoyment of human rights*, UN Doc E/CN.4/2002/54 (2002)

United States Department of State, *The United Nations Conference on International Organization. San Francisco, California April 25 to June 26, 1945. Selected Documents* (1946)

United States Global AIDS Coordinator, *The President's Emergency Plan for AIDS Relief, U.S. Five-Year Global HIV/AIDS Strategy* (2004)

United States Patent and Trademark Office, *Utility Examination Guidelines*, 66 Fed Reg1092 (2001)

United States Trade Representative, *2001 Special 301 Report* (2001)

——, *2002 Special 301 Report* (2002)

——, *2003 Special 301 Report* (2003)

——, *2004 Special 301 Report* (2004)

——, *Mission of the USTR*, at <http://www.ustr.gov/Who_We_Are/Mission_of_the_ USTR.html>

——, *USTR Zoellick Says World Has Chosen Path of Hope, Openness, Development and Growth* (2001)

University of California, *Technology Transfer Program. 2002 Annual Report* (2002)

Vaisrub, S, 'The Magic of a Name' (1980) 243 JAMA 1931

van Aaken, A, 'Rational Choice' in *der Rechtswissenschaft. Zum Stellenwert der ökonomischen Theorie im Recht* (2003)

van Boven, TC, 'Les Critères de Distinction des Droits de l'Homme' in Vasak, K (ed), *Les Dimensions Internationales des Droits de l'Homme* (1978) 45

van Hoof, F, 'Explanatory Note on the Utrecht Draft Optional Protocol' in Coomans, F and van Hoof, F (eds), *The Right to Complain about Economic, Social and Cultural Rights* (1995) 147

van Hoof, GJH, *Rethinking the Sources of International Law* (1983)

——, 'The Legal Nature of Economic, Social and Cultural Rights: a Rebuttal of Some Traditional Views' in Alston, P and Tomaševski, K (eds), *The Right to Food* (1984) 97

Vandoren, P, 'Médicaments sans Frontières? Clarification of the Relationship between TRIPS and Public Health Resulting from the WTO Doha Ministerial Declaration' (2002) 5 J World Intell Prop 5

—— and Van Eeckhaute, JC, 'The WTO Decision on Paragraph 6 of the Doha Declaration on the TRIPS Agreement and Public Health—Making It Work' (2003) 6 J World Intell Prop 779

Vasak, K, 'A 30-year Struggle. The Sustained Efforts to Give Force of Law to the Universal Declaration of Human Rights' *The UNESCO Courier* (November 1977) 29

Vastano Vaughan, S, 'Compulsory Licensing of Pharmaceuticals under TRIPS: What Standard of Compensation?' (2001) 25 Hastings Int'l & Comp L Rev 87

Vawda, YA, 'From Doha to Cancun: The Quest to Increase Access to Medicines under WTO Rules' (2003) 19 SAJHR 679

Velásquez, G, 'Médicaments Essentiels et Mondialisation' (2000) RIDE 37

—— and Boulet, P, 'Globalization and Access to Drugs: Implications of the WTO/TRIPS Agreement' in World Health Organization (ed), *Globalization and Access to Drugs. Perspectives on the WTO/TRIPS Agreement* (2nd edn, 1999) 1

Verband der Automobilindustrie, *Auto Jahresbericht 2004* (2004)

Verband Forschender Arzneimittelhersteller eV, *Statistics 2004. Die Arzneimittelindustrie in Deutschland* (2004)

Verdirame, G, 'The Definition of Developing Countries under GATT and other International Law' (1996) 39 GYIL 164

Verdross, A, *Völkerrecht* (2nd edn, 1950)

—— and Simma, B, *Universelles Völkerrecht. Theorie und Praxis* (3rd edn, 1984)

Verhoeven, J, 'Les activités normatives et quasi normatives—élaboration, adoption coordination' in Dupuy, R-J (ed), *Manuel sur les organisations internationales* (2nd edn, 1998) 413

Vierdag, EW, 'Comments on the Utrecht and Committee Draft Optional Protocols' in Coomans, F and van Hoof, F (eds), *The Right to Complain about Economic, Social and Cultural Rights* (1995) 199

——, 'The Legal Nature of the Rights Granted by the International Covenant on Economic, Social and Cultural Rights' (1978) 9 NYIL 69

——, 'The Time of the "Conclusion" of a Multilateral Treaty: Article 30 of the Vienna Convention on the Law of Treaties and Related Provisions' (1988) 59 BYIL 75

Vierheilig, M, *Die rechtliche Einordnung der von der Weltgesundheitsorganisation beschlossenen regulations* (1984)

Vierheilig-Langlotz, M, 'WHO—World Health Organization' in Wolfrum, R and Philipp, C (eds), *United Nations: Law, Policies and Practice. New, Revised English Edition. Volume 2* (1995) 1425

Villiger, ME, *Customary International Law and Treaties* (1985)

——, *Handbuch der Europäischen Menschenrechtskonvention* (EMRK) (2nd edn, 1999)

Vitanyi, B, 'Les positions doctrinales concernant le sens de la notion de "principes généraux de droit reconnus par les nations civilisées"' (1982) 86 RGDIP 48

Volken, P, *Konventionskonflikte im internationalen Privatrecht* (1977)

von Böventer, E, *et al, Einführung in die Mikroökonomie* (7th edn, 1991)

von Hahn, A, *Traditionelles Wissen indigener und lokaler Gemeinschaften zwischen geistigen Eigentumsrechten und der* public domain (2004)

von Hase, AM, 'The Application and Interpretation of the Agreement on Trade-Related Aspects of Intellectual Property Rights' in Correa, CM and Yusuf, AA (eds), *Intellectual Property and International Trade: The TRIPs Agreement* (1998) 93

von Jhering, R, *Der Zweck im Recht. Erster Band* (4th edn, 1904)

von Meibom, W and Pitz, J, 'Experimental Use, Patent Infringement—A Transatlantic Review from the German Perspective in Regard to the Decision of the German Supreme Court in *Ortho v Merckle*, "Clinical Trial II"' (1998) 1 J World Intell Prop 633

von Münch, I and Kunig, P (eds), *Grundgesetz-Kommentar. Band 1 (Präambel bis Art. 20)* (4th edn, 1992)

von Pufendorf, S, *Über die Pflicht des Menschen und des Bürgers nach dem Gesetz der Natur* (trans Luig, K 1994)

Vukmir, M, 'The Roots of Anglo-American Intellectual Property Law in Roman Law' (1992) 32 IDEA 123

Wai, R, 'Countering, Branding, Dealing: Using Economic and Social Rights in and around the International Trade Regime' (2003) 14 EJIL 35

Waldock, H, 'General Course on Public International Law' (1962—II) 106 RdC 5

Wal-Mart, *Annual Report 2002* (2002)

Walter, C, 'Constitutionizing (Inter)national Governance—Possibilities for and Limits to the Development of an International Constitutional Law' (2001) 44 GYIL 170

——, 'Die Europäische Menschenrechtskonvention als Konstitutionalisierungsprozeß' (1999) 59 ZaöRV 961

——, 'Grundrechtsschutz gegen Hoheitsakte internationaler Organisationen' (2004) 129 AÖR 39

Walterscheid, EC, 'Defining the Patent and Copyright Term: Term Limits and the Intellectual Property Clause' (2000) 7 J Intell Prop L 315

——, 'The Early Evolution of the United States Patent Law: Antecedents (Pt 1)' (1994) 76 J Pat & Trademark Off Soc'y 697

——, 'The Early Evolution of the United States Patent Law: Antecedents (Pt 2)' (1994) 76 J Pat & Trademark Off Soc'y 849

——, 'The Early Evolution of the United States Patent Law: Antecedents (Pt 3)' (1995) 77 J Pat & Trademark Off Soc'y 771

——, 'The Early Evolution of the United States Patent Law: Antecedents (5 Pt I)' (1996) 78 J Pat & Trademark Off Soc'y 615

——, 'The Early Evolution of the United States Patent Law: Antecedents (Pt 4)' (1996) 78 J Pat & Trademark Off Soc'y 77

——, 'To Promote the Progress of Science and Useful Arts: The Background and Origin of the Intellectual Property Clause of the United States Constitution' (1994) 2 J Intell Prop L 1

——, *To Promote the Progress of Useful Arts: American Patent Law and Administration, 1798–1836* (1998) 121

Watts, A, 'The International Court and the Continuing Customary International Law of Treaties' in Ando, N, McWhinney, E, and Wolfrum, R (eds), *Liber Amicorum Judge Shigeru Oda. Volume I* (2002) 251

Weber, A, *Menschenrechte. Texte und Fallpraxis* (2004)

Weil, P, 'Le Droit International Économique Mythe ou Réalité?' in Société Française pour le Droit International (ed), *Aspects du Droit International Économique. Élaboration—Controle—Sanction. Colloque d'Orléans 25–27 Mai 1971* (1972) 1

——, 'Towards Relative Normativity in International Law' (1983) 77 AJIL 413

Weisburd, AM, 'Customary International Law: The Problem of Treaties' (1988) 21 Vand J Transnat'l L 1

Weiß, W and Herrmann, C, *Welthandelsrecht* (2003)

Weissbrodt, D and Schoff, K, 'Human Rights Approach to Intellectual Property Protection: The Genesis and Application of Sub-Commission Resolution 2000/7' (2003) 5 MIPR 1

—— and ——, 'The Sub-Commission's Initiative on Human Rights and Intellectual Property' (2004) 22 Netherlands Q of Hum Rts 181

Weissmann, R, 'A Long, Strange TRIPS: The Pharmaceutical Industry Drive to Harmonize Global Intellectual Property Rules, and the Remaining WTO Legal Alternatives Available to Third World Countries' (1996) 17 U Pa J Int'l Econ L 1069

Wellens, K, *Remedies against International Organisations* (2002)

Wendland, W, *La Propriété Intellectuelle et les Droits de l'Homme*, UN Doc E/CN.12/2000/19 (2000)

Werner, J, 'The TRIPS Agreement under the Scrutiny of the WTO Dispute Settlement System—The Case of Patent Protection for Pharmaceutical and Agricultural Chemical Products in India' (1998) 1 J World Intell Prop 309

White, AW, 'Sunglasses: A Benefit to Health?' (1999) 21 EIPR 176

Wiesbrock, K, *Internationaler Schutz der Menschenrechte vor Verletzungen durch Private* (1999)

Wilcox, C, *A Charter for World Trade* (1949)

Wilting, WH, *Vertragskonkurrenz im Völkerrecht* (1996)

Winkler, M, *Kollision verfassungsrechtlicher Schutznormen. Zur Dogmatik der 'verfassungsimmanenten Grundrechtsschranken'* (2000)

Witzstrock, H, *Der polizeiliche Todesschuß* (2001)

Wojahn, PL, 'A Conflict of Rights: Intellectual Property Under TIRPS, the Right to Health and AIDS Drugs' (2001–2002) 6 UCLA J Int'l L & Foreign Aff 463

Wojcik, ME, 'On the Sudden Loss of a Human Rights Activist: A Tribute to Dr Jonathan Mann's Use of International Human Rights Law in the Global Battle against AIDS' (1998) 32 J Marshall L Rev 129

Wolffgang, H-M and Feuerhake, W, 'Core Labour Standards in World Trade Law. The Necessity for Incorporation of Core Labour Standards in the World Trade Organization' (2002) 36 JWT 883

Wolfke, K, *Custom in Present International Law* (2nd edn, 1993)

Wolfrum, R, 'Comment on Chapters 10 and 11' in Byers, M and Nolte, G (eds), *United States Hegemony and the Foundations of International Law* (2003) 356

——, 'Coordination among Multilateral Agreement through Treaty Provisions' in Stoll, P-T and Berger, B (eds), *International Governance for Environment and Sustainable Development. Goettingen Workshop 10–11 December 2001, Germany* (2001) 19

——, *Das Internationale Recht für den Austausch von Waren und Dienstleistungen*, in Schmidt, R (ed), *Öffentliches Wirtschaftsrecht* (1996) 535

——, *Die Internationalisierung staatsfreier Räume. Die Entwicklung einer internationalen Verwaltung für Antarktis, Weltraum, Hohe See und Meeresboden* (1984)

——, *Enforcing Environmental Standards: Economic Mechanisms as a Viable Means?* (1996)

——, 'Entwicklung des Völkerrechts von einem Koordinations- zu einem Kooperationsrecht' in Müller-Graff, P-C and Roth, H (eds), *Recht und Rechtswissenschaft. Signaturen und Herausforderungen zum Jahrtausendbeginn. Ringvorlesung der Juristischen Fakultät der Ruprecht-Karls-Universität Heidelberg* (2000) 421

Wolfrum, R, 'International Convention on the Elimination of All Forms of Racial Discrimination' in Klein, E (ed), *The Monitoring System of Human Rights Treaty Obligations* (1998) 49

——, 'International Law of Cooperation' in Bernhardt, R (ed), *Encyclopedia of Public International Law, II, 2* (1995) 1242

——, 'Konkurrierende Zuständigkeiten internationaler Streitentscheidungsinstanzen: Notwendigkeit für Lösungsmöglichkeiten und deren Grenzen' in Ando, N *et al* (eds), *Liber Amicorum Judge Shigeru Oda. Volume 1* (2002) 651

——, 'Le Régime de l'Antarctique et les États Tiers' in *La Mer et Son Droit. Mélanges Offerts à Laurent Lucchini et Jean-Pierre Quéneudeuc* (2003) 695

——, 'Purposes and Principles of International Environmental Law' (1990) 33 GYIL 308

——, 'The Progressive Development of Human Rights: A Critical Appraisal of Recent UN Efforts' in Jekewitz, J *et al* (eds), *Des Menschen Recht zwischen Freiheit und Verantwortung, Festschrift für Karl Josef Partsch zum 75. Geburtstag* (1989) 67 ff

——, 'The Protection of Indigenous Peoples in International Law' (1999) 59 ZaöRV 369

——, 'Verfassungsrechtliche Fragen der Zweitanmeldung von Arzneimitteln, Pflanzenbehandlungsmitteln und Chemikalien—Zugleich ein Beitrag zum Schutz technischer Innovationen' (1986) GRUR Int 512

——, Stoll, P-T and Franck, S, *Die Gewährleistung freier Forschung an und mit Genen und das Interesse an der wirtschaftlichen Nutzung ihrere Ergebnisse* (2002)

Woloshin, S *et al*, 'Direct-to-Consumer Advertisements for Prescription Drugs: What Are Americans Being Sold?' (2001) 358 Lancet 1141

World Bank, *Total GDP 2002, World Development Indicators database*

World Customs Organization, *Position Regarding Contracting Parties (on 1 July 2006)*, NG0095E1 (15 July 2006)

World Health Organization, *3 by 5 Progress Report. December 2003 through June 2004* (2004)

——, *Avian influenza ('bird flu')—Fact sheet*, at <http://www.who .int/mediacentre/fact-sheets/avian_influenza/en/index.html> (2006)

——, *Essential Medicines. WHO Model List* (14th edn, 2005)

——, *Globalization, TRIPS and access to pharmaceuticals*, WHO Policy Perspectives on Medicines, No 3 (March 2001)

——, 'Investing in Health Investing in Development. Paper Prepared by WHO for the UN Conference on Financing for Development Mexico, March 2002' (2002)

——, *Network for Monitoring the Impact of Globalization and TRIPS on Access to Medicines. Meeting Report, 19–21 February 2001 Chulalongkorn University Bangkok, Thailand* (2002)

——, *Network for Monitoring the Impact of Globalization and TRIPS on Access to Medicines*, Health Economics and Drugs EDM Series No 11 (2002)

——, *Procurement, Quality and Sourcing Project: Access to HIV/AIDS Drugs and Diagnostics of Acceptable Quality. Suppliers Whose HIV-Related Products Have Been Found Acceptable, in Principle, for Procurement by UN Agencies* (15th edn, 2004)

——, *Scaling up Antiretroviral Therapy in Resource-limited Settings: Treatment Guidelines for a Public Health Approach. 2003 Revision* (2003)

——, *The First Ten Years of the World Health Organization* (1958)

——, *WHO Rapid Advice Guidelines on Pharmacological Management of Humans Infected with Avian Influenza A (H5N1) Virus* (2006)

——, *WHO-WTO Workshop on Differential Pricing and Financing of Essential Drugs, Høsbjør, 2001* (2001)

—— and World Trade Organization, 'Report of the Workshop on Differential Pricing and Financing of Essential Drugs, 8–11 April 2001, Høsbjør, Norway (2001) (also published as 'Differential Pricing and the Financing of Essential Drugs' in Granville, B (ed), *The Economics of Essential Medicines* (2002) 209

—— and ——, *WTO Agreements & Public Health. A Joint Study by the WHO and the WTO Secretariat* (2002)

World Intellectual Property Organization (ed), *Intellectual Property and Human Rights. A Panel Discussion to commemorate the 50th Anniversary of the Universal Declaration of Human Rights. Geneva, November 9, 1998* (1999)

——, 'Basic Facts about the Patent Cooperation Treaty' in Abbott, F, Cottier, T, and Gurry, F (eds), *The International Intellectual Property System. Commentary and Materials Part Two* (1999) 1433

——, *General Information*, at <http://www.wipo .int/aboutwipo/en/gib.htm#P29_4637>

——, 'International Protection of Industrial Property Paris Convention for the Protection of Industrial Property (1883)' in Abbott, F, Cottier, T, and Gurry, F (eds), *The International Intellectual Property System. Commentary and Materials Part One* (1999) 647

——, *Introduction to Intellectual Property. Theory and Practice* (1997)

World Trade Organization, *TRIPS and Pharmaceutical Patents. Fact Sheet* (2006)

——, *Understanding the WTO: Developing Countries. Overview*, at <http://www.wto.org/english/thewto_e/whatis_e/tif_e/dev1_e.htm>

——, *Understanding the WTO: The Organization. Least-developed countries*, at <http://www.wto.org/english/thewto_e/whatis_e/tif_e/ org7_e.htm>

World Trade Organization Secretariat, *Guide to the Uruguay Round Agreements* (1999)

Wußing, H (ed), *Geschichte der Naturwissenschaft* (1987)

Yakemtchouk, R, *La Bonne Foi dans la Conduite Internationale des États* (2002)

Yamin, AE, 'Not just a Tragedy: Access to Medications as a Right under International Law' (2003) 21 BU Int'l L J 325

Yarchoan, R *et al*, 'Administration of 3'-Azido-3'Deoxythymidine, an Inhibitor of HTLV-III/LAV Replication, to Patients with AIDS or AIDS-Related Complex' (1986) 1 Lancet 575

Yosick, JA, 'Compulsory Patent Licensing for Efficient Use of Inventions' (2001) U Ill L Rev 1275

You, P, *Le préambule des traités internationaux* (1941)

Yusuf, AA, 'TRIPs: Background, Principles and General Provisions' in Correa, CM and Yusuf, AA (eds), *Intellectual Property and International Trade: The TRIPs Agreement* (1998) 3

Zacher, MW, 'Global Epidemiological Surveillance. International Cooperation to Monitor Infectious Diseases' in Kaul, I, Grunberg, I, and Stern, MA (eds), *Global Public Goods. International Cooperation in the 21st Century* (1999) 266

Zanghì, C, *La Protezione Internazionale dei Diritti dell'Uomo* (2002)

Zeiler, TW, *Free Trade Free World. The Advent of GATT* (1999)

Ziegler, K-H, *Völkerrechtsgeschichte* (1994)

Zoellick, RB, 'Letter to Trade Ministers dated December 27, 2002' in InsideHealthPolicy. com, (17 January 2003)

——, 'Statement of Robert B. Zoellick, U.S. Trade Representative before the Committee on Ways and Means of the House of Representatives' (2003) IP-Health, 26 February 2003

Zuleeg, M, 'Vertragskonkurrenz im Völkerrecht. Teil I: Verträge zwischen souveränen Staaten' (1977) 20 GYIL 246

Zumbansen, P, 'Die vergangene Zukunft des Völkerrechts' (2001) 34 Kritische Justiz 46

Zürcher Fausch, N, 'Die Problematik der Nutzung von Zwangslizenzen durch Staaten ohne eigene Pharmaindustrie: Zur instrumentellen Umsetzung von Art. 6 der Erklärung zum TRIPs und zum öffentlichen Gesundheitswesen' (2002) 57 Aussenwirtschaft 495

Newspaper Articles, Press Releases

L Altman, 'Rare Cancer Seen in 41 Homosexuals' *NY Times* (3 July 1981)

M Chase, 'Wellcome Unit Cuts Price of AIDS Drug 20%' *Wall Street Journal* (15 December 1987)

L Garrett, 'French First to Isolate HIV' *Newsday* (12 July 1994)

E Chen, 'U.S. Admits French Role in HIV Test Kit' *Los Angeles Times* (12 July 1994)

S Greenhouse, 'Nike Shoe Plant in Vietnam is Called Unsafe for Workers' *NYTimes* (8 November 1997)

JH Cushman Jr, 'Nike Pledges to End Child Labor and Increase Safety' *NY Times* (13 May 1998)

'Accessions Update: China and Others in the Pipeline' 3 *Bridges Weekly Trade News Digest* 37 (20 September 1999)

JD Sachs, 'A Global Fund for the Fight Against AIDS' *Washington Post* (7 April 2001)

M Peterson and R Pear, 'Anthrax Fears Send Demand for a Drug Far Beyond Output' *NY Times* (16 October 2001)

'Angst vor Milzbrand bringt Schub für Bayer-Produkt' *Handelsblatt* (17 October 2001)

'Milzbrand legt Repräsentantenhaus zum Teil lahm' *Handelsblatt* (18 October 2001)

S Vedantam and T Chea, 'Drug Firm Plays Defense in Anthrax Scare' *Washington Post* (20 October 2001)

E Clark, 'America's Anthrax Patent Dilemma' *BBC* (23 October 2001) at <http://news.bbc. co.uk/1/hi/business/1613410.stm>

S Vedantam and DL Brown, 'U.S. Seeks Price Cut from Cipro Maker' *Washington Post* (24 October 2001)

K Bradsher and EL Andrews, 'U.S. Says Bayer Will Cut Cost of its Anthrax Drug' *NY Times* (24 October 2001)

'Pharmaindustrie kritisiert WTO-Einigung zum Patentschutz' *Handelsblatt* (15 November 2001)

'Startschuss für neue Welthandelsrunde in Katar—Die Europäische Union schraubt ihre Forderungen herunter' *Handelsblatt* (15 November 2001)

H Cooper and G Winestock, 'Poor Nations Win Gains in Global Trade Deal, as U.S. Compromises' *Wall Street Journal* (15 November 2001)

H Cooper and G Winestock, 'How Activists Outmaneuvered Drug Makers in WTO Deal' *Wall Street Journal Europe* (15 November 2001)

V Sridhar, 'Perilous Patent' *Frontline* (24 November 2001)

R Guyonnet, 'Alerte en Asie' *Jeune Afrique/L'Intelligent* (25 December 2001)

AF Holmer, 'Innovation Is Key Mission' *USA Today* (31 May 2002)

'Government raised the Glivec Price' *IP-Health* (21 January 2003)

'Korea: Rejection of Glivec Compulsory License' *IP-Health* (10 March 2003)

X Lei, 'China: Sars and the Politics of Silence. SARS is Making a Change' 50 *World Press Review* (July 2003)

N Mathiason, 'Drugs deal "not viable"', *Mail and Guardian* (31 August 2003)

C Cookson and G Dyer, 'A Drugs Deal for the World's Poorest: Now the Fight over Patents and Cheap Medicine is in Middle-Income Countries' *Financial Times* (2 September 2003)

A Meldrum, 'Call for "dishonest" Mbeki to apologise for Aids gaffe' *The Observer* (28 September 2003)

S Vedantam, 'AIDS Plan Would Cut Drug Costs for Poor. WHO Would Provide 3-in-1 Pill to Nations' *Washington Post* (25 October 2003)

'Novartis Receives EMR for Glivec' *Express Pharma Pulse* (12 November 2003)

'Natco to Challenge Grant of Exclusive Rights to Novartis Cancer Drug' *The Hindu Business Line* (13 November 2003)

A Park, 'China's Secret Plague' *Time Magazine* (15 December 2003)

J Datta, 'Exclusive Marketing Rights—Novartis Gest Stay against 6 Firms' *The Hindu Business Line* (25 January 2004)

S Lueck, 'White House Gets Pressure on AIDS Plan—Activists, Drug Firms Duel Over Use of Funds For Generic Combination Drugs in Africa' *Wall Street Journal* (25 March 2004)

'Botswana Conference Sparks Debate on Generics' *Bridges Weekly Trade Digest* (ed) (31 March 2004)

S Boseley, 'Clinton's Aids Deal Snubs Bush Plan' *The Guardian* (7 April 2004)

S Lueck, 'White House Aims To Answer Critics Of Its AIDS Fight' *Wall Street Journal* (29 April 2004)

D Jehl and K Zernike, 'Greater Urgency on Prison Interrogation Led to Use of Untrained Workers' *NY Times* (28 May 2004)

LK Altman and DG McNeil Jr, 'U.N. Agency Drops 2 Drugs for AIDS Care Worldwide' *NY Times* (16 June 2004)

DG McNeil Jr, 'Study Finds Generic AIDS Drug Effective' *NY Times* (2 July 2004)

J Love, 'CIPLA 3 in 1 ARV patent' *IP-Health* (5 July 2004)

A Kazmin, 'Thailand's Cheap Aids Drugs Revive Patients' Hope' *Financial Times* (9 July 2004)

'Thailand Eyes Generic Versions of Two AIDS Drugs' *Reuters* (10 July 2004)

'Generic AIDS Pill Gets Patent in Africa' *Reuters* (13 July 2004)

D Sontag, 'Early Tests for U.S. in Its Global Fight on AIDS' *NY Times* (14 July 2004)

M Santora, 'City Sues Drug Companies, Claiming Medicaid Fraud' *NY Times* (6 August 2004)

'China verabschiedet erstes Aids-Gesetz' *FAZ* (30 August 2004)

M Wagner, 'Intellectual property bill risks US censure' *Jerusalem Post* (9 September 2004)

DG McNeil, Jr, 'A Path to Cheaper AIDS Drugs for Poor Nations' *NY Times* (26 January 2005)

DG McNeil, Jr, 'India Alters Law on Drug Patents' *NY Times* (24 March 2005)

T Benson, 'Brazil to Copy AIDS Drug Made by Abbott' *NY Times* (25 June 2005)

T Benson, 'Brazil and U.S. Maker Reach Deal on AIDS Drug' *NY Times* (9 July 2005)

Aids Healthcare Foundation, 'Glaxo Loses Patent on First AIDS Drug, AZT; AHF Blasts Glaxo's & Drug Industry's Greed' Press Release (17 September 2005)

P Prada, 'Brazil Near Deal with Abbott for Price Cut on AIDS Drug' *NY Times* (5 October 2005)

'Avian Influenza. In a Flap' *The Economist* (20 October 2005)

CPTech 'Statement of CPTech on TRIPS Amendment' Press Release (6 December 2005)

IFPMA 'TRIPS Amendment Permanently Resolves Export Compulsory License Issue' Press Release (6 December 2005)

Médecins Sans Frontières, 'Amendment to WTO TRIPS Agreement Makes Access to Affordable Medicines Even More Bleak' Press Release (6 December 2006)

PhRMA 'PhRMA Welcomes TRIPS and Public Health Agreement' Press Release (6 December 2005)

USTR, 'United States Welcomes Negotiations Leading to Positive Outcome on Enhancing Access to Medicines' Press Release (6 December 2005)

'Tamiflu Maker Roche Agrees on Generics' *Reuters* (8 December 2005)

DG McNeil Jr, 'Clinton in Deal to Cut AIDS Treatment Costs' *NY Times* (12 January 2006)

M Binyon, 'Indian Hero's New Mission: To Bring Cheap Drug for Bird Flu to Millions' *The Times* (6 March 2006)

'Top Industries' *Fortune* (17 April 2006)

'WIPO Development Agenda Meeting Breaks Down over Chair's Text' 10 *Bridges Weekly Trade News Digest* 24 (5 July 2006)

A Pollack, 'New Medicine for AIDS Is One Pill, Once a Day' *NY Times* (9 July 2006)

Index

Note that references to laws and treaties are listed in the Table of Laws and Treaties.
Page references in bold are the key pages for the topic.

Abbreviated New Drug Application 6, **62–3**
access to medicine
  facts 11–14, 18, 51, 56, 102–21, 124, 127,
    130–2, 135, 142–52, 158–69, 175–6,
    179–80, 193, 207, 229, 239–40, 242,
    244–6, 248, 253, 255–8, 271, 276, 286,
    288, 290; *see also* AIDS, access to medicine
  right to 78–9, 86, 95; **102–66**, 167–9,
    175–6, 179–80, 193, 207–8, 220–3,
    229–30, 234–42, 244–7, 249, 251, 253–6,
    258, 261, 264, 270, 272, 286–9, 292
activisim, *see* civil society
African Commission on Human and Peoples'
  Rights 93, 117
African Court on Human and Peoples'
  Rights 93
African Regional Industrial Property
  Organization 19, 36
AIDS (Acquired Immunodeficiency Syndrome)
  2–11, 14–15, 18, 59, 99, 104–6, 108,
  110–12, 118, 129–32, 148, 150, 156,
  239, 249, 258, 263, 265, 286
  access to medicine 8–11, 14–15, 18,
    111–12, 118, 129–32
  activisim, *see* civil society
  AZT (azidothymidine) **3–6**, 8, 165
  drug pricing 5–6, 10, 12, 111–12, 129–30,
    165, 249; *see also* pricing
  generic drugs, *see* medicine, generics
  medicine 3–5, 8–11, 14–15, 18, 104–5,
    111–12, 118, 129–32, 239, 249; *see also*
    AIDS, access to medicine; AZT;
    nevirapine
  nevirapine 8, 104, 111–12, 249
  patents on drugs, *see* patents, AIDS
    medicine
  patents on test kit, *see* patents, AIDS test kit
  treatment 8–11, 105
  UNAIDS 7, 9, 130
Andean Community 55, 65
anthrax **16–17**, 241, 257
antiretrovirals, *see* AIDS, medicine
approval process for medicine, *see* medicine,
  approval
Argentina 10, 56, 63, 71
avian flu, *see* bird flu
AZT, *see* AIDS, AZT

Bilateral Investment Treaties (BITs), 289, **291–2**
bilateral treaties 34, 168, 171, 179, 183–5,
  189, 213, 226–7, 289
bird flu 15–16
Bolar exemption 61–2, 235–6, 238
Brazil 10–11, 40–1, 48, 55, 71, 75, 132,
  147–8, 214, 225–6, 241, 243, 249, 251,
  262, 271–3, 289
  AIDS programme 10, 132, 148, 249
  patent legislation 10–11, 40–1, 55, 132,
    147, 214, 243
  producer of generic medicine 10–11, 71,
    251, 272
Bretton Woods 42
bulk purchasing, *see* pooled procurement
burden of proof 47, 68, 111, 228, 259

Canada 29, 40, 47, 63–4, 69, 147–8, 161, 233,
  235, 239, 248–9, 253, 257, 270
Cipro, *see* anthrax
civil and political rights 80, **81–3**, 88
  89–94, 115–19
civil society 5, 6, 9, 14, 48, 76, 106, 124, 128,
  131, 137, 142, 192, 204, 244, 255–6,
  262, 275, 286
clinical studies, *see* medicine, approval
coercion, *see* duress
commercial use 62–3
Commission on Human Rights, *see* UN,
  Commission on Human Rights
Committee on Economic, Social and Cultural
  Rights, *see* UN, Committee on Economic,
  Social and Cultural Rights
community 51, 86, 96, 116, 127, 182, 185,
  186–7, 188–93, 199
comparative advantage 41, 287
competition law 110, 112, 230, 240, 244,
  246–7, 250, 252
compliance 45, 49, 126–7, 167, 199–200,
  205, 208, 223; *see also* international law,
  enforcement; human rights, enforcement
compulsory licences 12–13, 16, 20, 29, 35, 37,
  47, 76, 148, 169, 229–30, 237, **239–53**,
  254, 257, 259, **260–76**, 279, 282, 290–2
  adequate remuneration 12, 20, 246, **247–9**,
    261, 269, 272, 274, 282
  automatic 237, 239, 245

compulsory licences (*cont.*):
  conditions of grant **245–53**
  ex officio **245**
  export 252, 262–3, 265–6, 268–70, 272, 274, 282
  grounds **241–5**, 259, 290
  national laws 240, 242–5, 248–9, 252–3, 270–2
  non-exclusive 248, **250**
  notification to the Council for TRIPS 265–6, **267–8**, 271, 274
  prior negotiations **245–7**, 252
  review **249**
  rights granted **249–53**
  supply of domestic market **250–3**, 266, 268, 274, 282
  trade diversion 263–4, 267, **269–70**, 275, 282–3
concessions 42, 45–7, 49, 197, 199, 214
  suspension of, *see* trade sanctions
conflict of norms / regimes 18, 101, 137, **169–206**, 208–10, 213, 217–29, 287–8, 291
  terminology 170, **174–81**
constitutionalization 80, **192–4**, 204, 206, 289
copyright 30, 48, 84, 153–5
corporations 37–9, 44, 48, 69, 72, 78–9, 84, 94–9, 106, 109–12, 130, 136, 138–51, 154–66, 171–2, 181, 230–2, 239–52, 260–2, 264, 267–9, 272, 275, 279; *see also* individuals in international law; obligation to protect
  human rights obligations 79, **94–9**
  research, *see* research
customary international law 79, 85, 100–1, 115, 120, 121, **122–34**, 171, 183–4, 186, 190, 192–4, 219–20, 226–9, 259
  and treaties **122–3**, 193–4, 219–20, 226–8
  contracting out of, *see* general international law, contracting out of
  opinio juris, *see* opinio juris
  persistent objector 121–2, 132–3, 171
  state practice, *see* state practice

Decision of 30 August 2003 255, **261–72**, 273–6, **282–6**, 290
developed countries 36, 37–9, 41, 44–8, 54, 71, 73, 109–10, 146–7, 149, 151, 162–3, 165, 168, 181, 215, 230–1, 233–4, 239, 253, 255–9, 263, 266, 269, 271, 279, 287, 289, 291
developing countries 36, 37–9, 44–50, 55, 60, 70, **71–2**, 73–6, 78, 101, 109, 111, 132, 136–8, 146–52, **161–6**, 168–9, 176, 180, 215, 230–1, 233–4, 239, 241, 243–4, 247, 249, 252–3, 255–60, 263, 265–6, 268–9, 272, 275–6, 287–9, 291

capacity to manufacture medicine, *see* medicine, capacity to manufacture
health infrastructure, *see* health infrastructure
development and patents 27, 29, 38–9, 50, 75–6, 78, **158–66**, 169, 239
differential pricing, *see* pricing, differential pricing
discoveries, *see* invention
discrimination as to field of technology / place of invention, *see* TRIPS Agreement, non-discrimination
discriminatory pricing, *see* pricing, differential pricing
disease 58, 76, 83–4, 102–4, 107, 129–32, 134, 136, 142, 146, 159–66, 244, 246, 258–9, 263–5, 289; *see also* AIDS; anthrax; bird flu; health
dispute resolution, *see* international courts and tribunals; GATT, dispute resolution; WTO, dispute settlement
Doha Declaration 255, **256–61**, 263–5, 276, **279–82**, 286–7, 290
Draft Norms on the Responsibilities of Transnational Corporations and Other Business Enterprises with Regard to Human Rights 99
drug companies, *see* corporations
  charity 9, 112, 151, 255, 263
  collaboration with public sector 5–6
  human rights obligations, *see* corporations, human rights obligations
  litigation 13–14, 232
  lobbying 13, 40, 55, 142, 165, 230, 248, 264, 271
  research, *see* research
  pricing, *see* pricing
  profits 5, 16, 69, 109, 143, 145, **159**, 160, 161, 163, 269
drugs, *see* medicine
duress 49

economic duress, *see* duress
economic, social and cultural rights 79, **81–3**, 86–8, **89–94**, 102–16, 119, 128, 132, 223, 229
  budgetary implications 89–90, 92, 103, 106–8, 110–12, 130–1, 138, 151, 165, 168
  control of reasonableness 92, 108, 111–12
  justiciability 79, 82, **86–94**
  justification of non-compliance 107–8, **110–12**
  minimum core obligations 92, 106–7, 110–11, 169
  programmatic 88, 90, 107–8, 110–11, 130
  progressive realization 82, 91, 102–3, 107–8, 110, 112, 130, 223

emergency 59, 116, 129, 131–2, 134, 136, 151–2, 229, 244, **246**, 249, 252, **259**, 266, 289
England, *see* United Kingdom
epidemics, *see* disease
erga omnes (partes) obligations / integral treaties 83, 179, 182, **187–90**, 191, 194, 197–9, 205, 221
essential medicines, *see* medicine, essential medicines
estoppel 227
European Commission of Human Rights 117, 158
European Communities 11, 13, 39, 44, 47, 62–4, 102, 161, 195, 212, 224–6, 232–4, 237, 255, 257, 262, 270–2, 274–5, 279, 284, 288–9
European Court of Human Rights 90, 138, 194
European Patent Office 19, 36, 65, 181
European Union, *see* European Communities
exclusive marketing rights 73–4, 150, **260**; *see also* TRIPS Agreement, mailbox system
exhaustion 68, 230; *see also* international exhaustion; parallel imports

first sale doctrine, *see* exhaustion
foreign direct investment 38–9, **162–3**, 247, 251, 253, **291–2**
fragmentation of international law **170–2**, 176, 182, 186, **194–7**, 205, 209–11, 215–17, 220, 222–3
France 2–3, 25–6, 28, 30, 147, 191
free trade 27, 34, 41–2, 46, 198–9
    agreements **289–91**; *see also* Andean Community; European Communities; GATT; MERCOSUR; regionalism; WTO

GATT
    as an institution 41–3, 211
    dispute resolution 42, **211**
    intellectual property 43–8
    Protocol of Provisional Application 42
    sanctions, *see* trade sanctions
    Tokyo Round 43
    Uruguay Round **44–8**, 199, 213
General Comments, role of 91–2, 156
general international law 94, 97, 100–1, 121–35, 179–80, 182, 187, 190, 193, 195–6, 208, 210, 216, 218, 221–2, 225, **226–8**, 281–2, 288; *see also* customary international law; general principles of law
    contracting out of 100–1, 192, 194, 212, 216, 228–9

general principles of law 79, 121, **134–5**, 171, 220, 225, 288
Generalized System of Preferences 13, 39, 71
generics, *see* medicine, generics
Germany 3, 6, 27, 29, 32, 54, 57, 65, 97–8, 118, 135, 147, 152, 155, 187, 191, 211, 240–1, 248, 291
Global Fund to Fight AIDS, Tuberculosis and Malaria 9
globalization 77–8, 185
government use **239–40**, 245, 247; *see also* compulsory licences

health 8–9, 14, 47–8, 51, 53, 56–9, 76, 81, **83–4**, 99, 101, 103–12, **113**, 114, 116–21, 129–31, 136, 145, 151, 162, 165, 169, 201–3, 207, 219, 222–3, 229, 239, 244, 249, 253, 257–9, 261, 263–5, 268–70, 287–9
    infrastructure 8–9, 103–5, 109–12, 116–19, 129–31, 136, 145, 151, 165
    insurance 109–11, 136, 145
    right to 13, 78–9, 83–4, 91, 93–5, **102–15**, 127, 130–2, 157–8, 167, 169, 207, 223, 238, 288
    services, *see* health, infrastructure
hierarchy in international law 134, 158, 170, **182–97**, **203–6**, 208, 215, 220, 229, 287; *see also* jus cogens
    factual 182, **196–7**, **199–200**, 205–6, 287
HIV (Human Immunodeficiency Virus), *see* AIDS
human rights
    access to medicine, *see* access to medicine, right to
    civil and political rights, *see* civil and political rights
    conflict with world trade / patent regime 137, **169–206**, 207–30, 234–42, 244–7, 249, 251, 253–76, 286–9, 292; *see also* WTO, human rights obligations; WTO, human rights in WTO dispute settlement
    corporations, *see* corporations, human rights obligations
    economic, social and cultural rights, *see* economic, social and cultural rights
    enforcement 87–8, 90, 126, 203, **205**, **213–15**, 287–8
    European Communities **288–9**
    generations of 82
    implementation 89, 107–10, 118, 122, 124, 127, 131, 205; *see also* economic, social and cultural rights, progressive realization
    indirect effect on private parties 98–9, 109–10; *see also* individuals in international law; obligation to protect

human rights (*cont.*):
  individual communication procedure 87,
    115, 203
  indivisibility 82, 90, 93
  intellectual property as human right, *see*
    inventor, moral and material interests
  interference 109, 137, **138**, 147, 149,
    151–66, 168–9
  international organizations, *see* international
    organizations, human rights obligations
  inventor's moral and material interests, *see*
    inventor, moral and material interests
  justiciability, *see* economic, social and cultural
    rights, justiciability
  justification of interference 119, 138, 144,
    152–66, 169; *see also* economic, social and
    cultural rights, justification of non-
    compliance
  life, *see* life, right to
  mittelbare Drittwirkung, *see* human rights,
    indirect effect on private parties
  obligation to fulfil, *see* obligation to fulfil
  obligation to protect, *see* obligation to protect
  obligation to respect, *see* obligation to respect
  positive obligations 82, 86, 89–90, 117–18,
    128, 138; *see also* obligation to fulfil;
    obligation to protect
  regional human rights treaties 94, 121, 158,
    171; *see also* African Commission on
    Human and Peoples' Rights, African
    Court on Human and Peoples' Rights;
    European Commission of Human Rights;
    European Court of Human Rights; Inter-
    American Commission on Human Rights;
    Inter-American Court of Human Rights
  reporting procedure 87
  right to health, *see* health, right to
  treaty interpretation 79, **85–6**, 91–2, 96, 98,
    105, 108, 116, 120, 122, 158, 204; *see also*
    interpretation; treaties, interpretation
  WTO, *see* WTO, human rights obligations;
    WTO, human rights in WTO dispute
    settlement

imports 10, 19, 21–5, 39, 43, 48, 59, 68,
    109–10, 146–7, 230–4, 237, 242–4,
    249–52, 262, 265, 268–9, 271; *see also*
    parallel imports
in dubio mitius, *see* interpretation, in dubio
    mitius
India 8, 10, 16, 48, 56, 71, 73–5, 117–18,
    147, 149, 163, 251–4, 270–2, 289
  patent legislation 10, 73, 147, 252–3, 270
  producer of generic medicine 8, 10, 16, 71,
    251, 271–2
individuals in international law 79–81, 88,
    94–9, 109, 118, 155, 198, 203, 206, 214,

    223, 271; *see also* Draft Norms on the
    Responsibilities of Transnational
    Corporations and Other Business
    Enterprises with Regard to Human Rights;
    OECD Guidelines for Multination
    Enterprises; obligation to protect; UN,
    Global Compact
industrial property, *see* intellectual property
Industrial Revolution 25, 81
industrialization 27
industry, *see* corporations
integral treaties, *see* erga omnes (partes)
    obligations / integral treaties
intellectual property 14, 20, 35, 38–40, 43–8,
    50–2, 55, 58, 68, 84–5, 132, 149, 153–5,
    158, 164, 173–4, 198, 214, 230, 256–9,
    290–1; *see also* copyright; patents;
    trademarks
  human right, *see* inventor, moral and material
    interests
Inter-American Commission on Human Rights
    105
Inter-American Court of Human Rights 117
International Bank for Reconstruction and
    Development 42
International Bill of Human Rights 83, 124–5,
    126–7, 204; *see also* human rights
International Court of Justice (ICJ) 37, 93,
    120, 122–3, 187–9, 191, 194, 211, 215,
    277
international courts and tribunals 88, 92, 123,
    128, **171–2**, 174, **194–7**, 208, 213, 215,
    222, 228, 291–2; *see also* International
    Court of Justice; GATT, dispute
    resolution; WTO, dispute settlement
  applicable law 194–7, 208, 213, **215–17**;
    see also WTO, applicable law
  jurisdiction 194, 196, 213, 215; *see also*
    WTO jurisdiction
international exhaustion, *see* parallel imports
International Labour Organization 288
international law, enforcement 37, 88, 124,
    183, **188–9**, 194, 196–7, 199–200, 203,
    207–8, 210, 213–14; *see also* human
    rights, enforcement; international courts
    and tribunals
international law, structure **170–3**, **182–97**,
    204–6, 217, 289
international law of coexistence **182–5**
international law of cooperation 86, 119, 129,
    137, **166–9**, **185–93**, 270
International Monetary Fund (IMF) 41–2,
    225
international organizations 100–2, 168, 171,
    174, 281–2, 285, 287–8; *see also* African
    Regional Industrial Property
    Organization; Andean Community;

European Communities; GATT; International Bank for Reconstruction and Development; International Monetary Fund; International Trade Organization; League of Nations; Organisation Africaine de la Propriété Intellectuelle; UN; WHO; WIPO; World Bank; WTO
  human rights obligations **99–102**
international patent 36
international patent law, *see* patents
international relations 134, **172–3**
  regime theory, *see* regime
International Sanitary Conventions 83
international trade 33, **41–8**, 50, 173, 180, 186, 197, 200–1, 214, 256, 282; *see also* Andean Community; European Communities; GATT; MERCOSUR; WTO
International Trade Organization 42
interpretation, *see* treaties, interpretation; human rights, treaty interpretation; TRIPS Agreement, interpretation
  effective 175, 177, 217–18, 227, 252, 254–5, 269
  evolutive 86, 218, 224, 277
  good faith 50, 85, 91–2, 134, 227, 269
  in dubio mitius 53, 65, 86, 227, 235–6
  presumption against conflict 178–9, 184, 219–20
invention 6, **54–5**, 56, 64–8, 73, 75, 156, 244, 246–7, 254
inventor 6, 19, 21, 23, 25, 30, 31, 33–5, 51, 78, 141–2, 153, **154–5**, 156–8, 181, 260
  moral and material interests 30, 34, 78–9, 84–6, **153–8**, 198
Italy 29, 159
ius cogens, *see* jus cogens

jus cogens 48, 101–2, 116, 182, 187, 188, **190–2**, 193–4, 198, 205, 208–9, 212, 217, 229
justiciability, *see* economic, social and cultural rights, justiciability

knowledge-based economy 36, 45

labels, *see* medicine, labelling
League of Nations 84
least-developed countries (LDC), *see* developing countries
lex posterior 184–7, 189
lex specialis 122, 184
life, right to 78, 93, 95–6, 99, 104, 111, **115–19**, 127–9, 134, 152, 170
local working requirement, *see* working requirement

marginal cost 141
  pricing, *see* pricing, differential pricing
medicine
  access to, *see* access to medicine
  advertising 160
  approval 4, 6, **60–4**, 69, 74, 105–6, 146, 235–7, 242, 268, 290
  capacity to manufacture 10, 71–3, 75, 150, 166, 169, 244, 250, **251–3**, **260–76**
  drug security 60–4, 105–6, 109, 112, 130
  essential medicines 59, 75, **106–7**, 108–12, 136, 150, 160, 242, 245
  generics 6, 8–11, 57, 61–2, 69, 71, 75, 106, 110, 145–6, 148–9, 151, 164–6, 169, 251–2, 262, 269, 271–2, 275, 282, 287, 289
  labelling 61, **267–8**
  life-saving medicines 115–19, 128–31, 134–6
  orphan drugs, *see* orphan drugs
  patentability 28–9, 37, 40, **54–7**, 59, 70, 72–6, 138, 175, 208, 221, 251–2, 260, 272, 289; *see also* patents, patentable subject matter
  price controls 145, 149, 255
  pricing, *see* pricing; patents, effects of grant
research, *see* research, *see also* research, cost of resistances 8–9
MERCOSUR 195, 215
minimum core obligations, *see* economic, social and cultural rights, minimum core obligations
monopoly 23, 60, 138, **142–6**, 147, 166; *see also* patents, monopoly
morality 124, 134, 166, 190–1, 193, 203, 237, 271
most-favoured nation treatment 42, 52, 198

national emergency, *see* emergency
national security, *see* security
national treatment 35, 42, 52, 232
Netherlands 27
networks 287–8
nevirapine, *see* AIDS, nevirapine
New Drug Application 61–3
Non-governmental Organizations (NGOs), *see* civil society

obligation to fulfil 90, 108, **110**, 118, 130, 136, 168
obligation to protect 82, 90, 99, 108, **109–10**, 116, 118, 130, 136, 168
obligation to respect 90, **108–9**, 116, 118, 130, 136, 168
OECD Guidelines for Multination Enterprises 99
opinio juris 122, 124–5, **133–4**

ordre public 56
Organisation Africaine de la Propriété
Intellectuelle 19, 36, 234
orphan drugs 4, **63**, 162, 164–5

pacta tertiis 123, 125, 179, 183, 193, 222
paediatric tests 63
panels, *see also* GATT, dispute resolution;
WTO, dispute settlement
GATT 42, 201, 223
WTO 45, 73, 176–8, 199–200, 210,
212–15, **216**, 217–19, 221–2,
224–8, 235–7, 243, 251–2, 254,
279, 288–9
parallel imports 12–13, 68, 146–7, 165, 169,
229, **230–4**, 257, **259**, 261, 290
patents, *see also* TRIPS Agreement
abuse 23, 32, 35, 51, 69–70, 241–2, 244,
254
AIDS medicine 3–6, 8–9, 11
AIDS test kit 3
assignment 67, 78, 154
blocking patents, *see* patents, dependent
patents
Bolar exemption, *see* Bolar exemption
claims 19–20, 66, 69
compulsory licence, *see* compulsory
licences
damages, *see* patents, remedies
dependent patents 64, 244
disclosure 19, 24, 31, 53, 65, **67**, 156, 243
discoveries, *see* invention
DNA 55, 66–7, 181
doctrine of equivalents 20
effects of grant, particularly on prices 20, 23,
28, 38, 56–7, 70–2, 75, 78–9, 103,
109–10, 112, 137, **138–52**, **157–66**, 234,
237, 242, 257–8, 276, 288; *see also*
patents, monopoly; pricing
enforcement 68–70, 72, 232
examination 19, 28, 69–70, 159
experimental use 238, 252
first-to-file v. first-to-invent 19
harmonization of patent laws 35–7, 51–2,
176, 198; *see also* TRIPS Agreement
history **20–8**, 75
human right, *see* inventor, moral and material
interests
incentive theory, *see* patents, purpose
industrial application 19, 53, **66–7**, 181
infringement 20, 38, 62, 65, 69; *see also*
patents, remedies
injunctive relief, *see* patents, remedies
invention, *see* invention
inventive step 19, 53, 55, **66**
licence 67, 150, 164, 230, 244, 248
limited exceptions 229, 234–9

limits on 13, 20, 51, 203, 229–87; *see also*
compulsory licences; parallel imports;
working requirement; TRIPS Agreement,
flexibilities
manufacture for export 252–3, 263–4,
266
minimum standards 37, 46, 52–3, 67, 75–6,
169, 176, 289
monopoly 22, 68, 72, 138, 142, **144–6**,
163, 166, 234, 236; *see also* patents,
effects of grant; monopoly
national patent law 19–28, 49–53, 75, 78,
109, 112, 132, 163, 169, 233, 240,
242–3, 253, 270–2; *see also* compulsory
licences, national laws
natural law rationale, *see* patents,
purpose
non-commercial use 238–9, 244, **246–7**
non-obviousness, *see* patents, inventive step
novelty 19, 25, 34, 53, **65–6**, 181, 233
opposition proceedings 70
parallel imports, *see* parallel imports
patentable subject matter 19, 27–9, 37, 47,
53–64, 76, 203; *see also* medicine,
patentability
prior use exception 238
priority 35, 73–4
process patents 19–20, 28, 54–5, **64–5**,
67–8, 75, 150, 239, 260, 265
product patents 19–20, 28, 53–5, **64–5**,
67–8, 70, 73–5, 150, 159, 181, 239, 260,
265
prospect theory, *see* patents, purpose
purification 54–5
purpose 18, 21–3, 25, **29–33**, 34, 38, 50,
67, 75, 78, 84–5, 137–8, 141–2, 144,
147, 157, **158–66**, 242, 256–8, 261
rationale, *see* patents, purpose
remedies 20, 57, **68–9**, 240, 247
revocation 23, 26, 34–5, 174, 229–30, 244,
253–5
rights conferred 19, 59, **67–70**, 75, 142,
232, 234–8, 241–2, 249, 252; *see also*
patents, effects of grant
term 20, 22, 24, 26, 30, 37, 47, 61–2, **69**,
75, **159**, 163, 235–6, 252, 290
territoriality 18, 35, 38, 232–3, **249–53**,
268
TRIPS Agreement, *see* TRIPS Agreement
use patents 4, 61, **64–5**, 69, 150, 290
utility, *see* patents, industrial application
pharmaceutical industry, *see* corporations
pharmaceuticals, *see* medicine
piracy 38
pooled procurement 145, 255
preambles 96, 113–14
precautionary principle 227

pricing
  differential pricing 130, 146–7, 231, 263, 288
  discriminatory pricing, *see* pricing, differential pricing
  equitable pricing, *see* pricing, differential pricing
  marginal pricing 141, 146
  medicine 12, 18, 29, 56–7, 79, 94–5, 105–6, 109–12, 130, 136–7, **138–52**, 159, 165, 231, 234, 239–42, 248, 253, 267–8; *see also* AIDS, drug pricing
  monopoly pricing, 142–7, 166
  price controls, *see* medicine, price controls
  Ramsey pricing, *see* pricing, differential pricing
  reference pricing 147, 165
private sector, *see* corporations
  research, *see* research
privatization 94, 109
privileges 21–2, 28
proliferation of international courts and tribunals, *see* international courts and tribunals
property 18, 20, 25, 29–30, 34, 38, 84, 154–5, 158, 174, 291; *see also* patents, purpose
  human right, *see* inventor, moral and material interests
proportionality 152
protectionism 41, 186, 215; *see also* trade barriers
public sector research, *see* research

reasonableness, *see* economic, social and cultural rights, control of reasonableness
regime 101, 137, **172–206**, 210–13, 287–8
  conflict, *see* conflict of norms / regimes
  factual hierarchy, *see* hierarchy in international law, factual
  self-contained, *see* self-contained regimes
regionalism 36, 171, 215, 268, 274–5, **289–91**, 292; *see also* African Regional Industrial Property Organization; Andean Community; European Communities; MERCOSUR; Organisation Africaine de la Propriété Intellectuelle
regulatory review, *see* medicine, approval
research 2–6, 32–3, 75, 78–9, 106–7, 130, 137–8, 141–2, 146, 156–7, **159–66**, 181, 238, 257–8, 261
  cost of 5, 31–2, 37, 78, 106, 130, 141, **142**, 146, 157, 159–66
reverse engineering 30
right to access to medicine, *see* access to medicine, right to
right to health, *see* health, right to
right to intellectual property, *see* inventor, moral and material interests

right to life, *see* life, right to

sanctions, *see* trade sanctions
scientific progress, right to enjoyment 112, 119, 156, 158
security 7, 16, **58–9**, 75, 174, 185–6, 201, 203, **289**
self-contained regimes 208–9, **210–12**
soft law 114–15, 120, 123, 125–6, 134, **171**, 202, 222
sources of international law 79, 102, 136, 179, 184, 215, 220
South Africa 7–9, 71, 92, 94, 102, 104, 107, 111–12, 131, 148, 150–1, 232, 255–6, 264, 271, 286
  Medicines Act **11–15**, 232, 255–6, 286
sovereignty 80, 86, 135, **182**, 183–5, 211, 240
state practice 50, 64, 66, 86, 92, 97, 103, 106–7, 114, 120, 122, **123–32**, 133, 155–6, 220, 233, 281–5, 288
state responsibility 107, 182, 188, 190–1, 194, 211–12; *see also* self-contained regimes
Sub-Saharan Africa 7, 15, 95, 132
subjects of international law 79–80, 95–6, 100, 170, 174–5, 182, 203
suspension of concessions, *see* concessions; trade sanctions

Tamiflu, *see* bird flu
tariffs 42, 109, 151, 175, 224–5
taxes 42, 225
technology transfer 11, 21–4, 38–9, 50, 58, 73, 101, 242, 244, 259, 269, 275
test data exclusivity 62, 71–2, 290
Thailand 9–11, 71, 233, 245
trade barriers 43, 45–6, 50–1, 55, 201, 232; *see also* protectionism
trade in goods 42, 44–6; *see also* international trade
trade sanctions 40, 42, 45, 49, 173, 197, 199–200, 205, 214, 287
trademarks 34, 154, 231
traditional knowledge 85, **181**
travaux préparatoires 86, 98, 156, 237–8, 254, 283, 285–6; *see also* treaties, interpretation
treaties
  and customary international law, *see* customary international law, and treaties
  interpretation 37, **50, 85**, 92, 96, 113, 120, 122, 175, 179, 184, 202, 204–6, 208, 211–12, 217–18, **219–29**, 238, 264, 276, 280–1, 286, 290–1; *see also* human rights, treaty interpretation; interpretation; TRIPS Agreement, interpretation
  invalidity 49
  modification 114, 122, 179–80, 189, 198, 221, 266, 281–2, 285

TRIPS Agreement
  amendment 229, 240, 250, 255, 259, 262,
    270, **272–6, 278,** 282–4, 286, 290–1
  conflict with human rights, *see* human rights,
    conflict with world trade / patent regime
  effects, *see* patents, effects of grant
  flexibilities 18, 49, 53, 58, 168–9, 176, 203,
    207, **229–87,** 289–92; *see also* compulsory
    licences; parallel imports; patents, limited
    exceptions; patents, revocation
  history 18, 43–8, 76; *see also* TRIPS
    Agreement, international patent law
    before TRIPS
  implementation 99, 259–60, 270–1
  integral or bilateral obligations **198,** 221
  international patent law before TRIPS **34–9,**
    55, 70; see *also* TRIPS Agreement, history
  interpretation **49–51,** 52–75, 207, **220–9,**
    230–57, **258–61,** 262–87, 290; *see also*
    treaties, interpretation; WTO,
    authoritative interpretation of WTO
    Agreements
  mailbox system 56, **73–4,** 260; *see also*
    exclusive marketing rights
  non-discrimination 53, **59–60,** 63–4,
    237–8, 242–4
  object and purpose 49, **50–1,** 58–9, 65, 101,
    207, 222–3, 235, 244, 256–7, 259
  patents, *see* patents
  test data exclusivity, *see* test data exclusivity
  transition period 56, **70–5,** 251–2, **260,**
    271–2, 278, 286; *see also* TRIPS
    Agreement, mailbox system
  TRIPS-plus 207, 267, **289–92**
  validity 48–9

UN (United Nations) 35, 72, 80–1, 84, 100,
    119–20, 125–6, 129, 193
  Commission on Human Rights 77, 81
  Committee on Economic, Social and
    Cultural Rights 77, 85, **87,** 91–2, 103,
    106–7, 110, 155–7, 168–9, 181,
    223, 288
  Economic and Social Council (ECOSOC)
    77, 81, 87
  General Assembly 77, 81, 119–20, 123,
    129–30, 132, 167
  Global Compact 99
  High Commissioner for Human Rights
    77–8
  Human Rights Committee 87, 116, 118–19
  Human Rights Council 77
  Secretary-General 14, 99
  Special Rapporteurs on Globalization 77–8
  specialized agency 100; *see also* International
    Monetary Fund; WHO; WIPO; World
    Bank

Sub-Commission on the Promotion and
    Protection of Human Rights 14, 77, 99,
    180
UNAIDS, *see* AIDS, UNAIDS
unilateral measures **39–41,** 49, 214,
    230, 285
United Kingdom 4, 21, 23–5, 29, 65, 135,
    147–8, 239
  Commission on Intellectual Property Rights
    164, 231, 241
United States of America 11, 13–17, 34,
    39–40, 41, 43–4, 46, 48, 56, 60–4, 69, 71,
    97–8, 102, 105–6, 128–32, 147–9, 151,
    155, 159, 161, 192–3, 211, 214, 220,
    223, 229, 233–4, 239, 243, 253–7,
    262–5, 271, 273, 279, 282, 289–92
  Congress 5, 14, 24–5, 32, 42, 160
  Food and Drug Administration (FDA) 4, 8,
    61–3, 105–6, 161; *see also* medicine,
    approval
  Hatch-Waxman 61–2
  patent legislation 54, 59–67, 240,
    245, 248
  President 42, 132, 256
  Trade Representative (USTR) 40, 279

WHO (World Health Organization) 8–10, 14,
    15, 76–7, 84, 103, 106–8, **112–14,**
    130–1, 148, 150, 164, 256, 288
  Commission on Intellectual Property Rights,
    Innovation and Public Health 77, 164
  Commission on Macroeconomics and
    Health 164
WIPO (World Intellectual Property
    Organization) 14, 35, 39, 41, 44–5, 47,
    200
work, right to 93
working requirement 20, 23, 26, 34–5, 47, 59,
    229, **242–4**
World Bank 71
world trade, *see* international trade
World War II 41, 80, 84, 185–6, 191
WTO (World Trade Organization)
  amendment of WTO Agreements 218–19,
    274, 277, **278,** 282–4, 287; *see also* TRIPS
    Agreement, amendment
  Appellate Body 45, 69, 73, 177–8,
    199–202, 207, 212, 218, 220, 223–8,
    235–6, 279, 292
  applicable law 208–10, 212, 213, **215–29**
  authoritative interpretation of WTO
    Agreements 218–19, 263, **277,** 279–82
  chairman's statement 264, 267–70, 273–4,
    285–6
  conflict with other regimes **200–3;** *see also*
    human rights, conflict with world trade /
    patent regime; WTO, human rights

obligations; WTO, human rights in WTO
dispute settlement
Council for TRIPS 72–3, 256, 260–5,
267–8, 270, 272–4, **276**, 277–8, 280–1,
283–4, 286
decision-making/decisions 207, 231, 240,
255–75, **276–8**, **279–87**, 290
dispute settlement 44–5, 47, 99, 195,
197, **199–200**, 203, 205–10,
212–30, 232, 243, 247, 251,
253–5, 259–60, 263–4, 266, 277,
287–8, 291
General Council 219, 240, 260–1, 264,
274, **276**, 277, 284–6
history 44–8
human rights in WTO dispute settlement
79, 99, 182, 196–7, 202–3, 206, **207–29**,
287–9, 292
human rights obligations 79, 94, **100–2**,
167, 180, 202–4, 287–9, 292; *see also*
international organizations, human rights
obligations

integral or bilateral obligations **197–9**; *see
also* TRIPS Agreement, integral or bilateral
obligations
interpretation 208–9, 216–17, **219–29**,
276–7, 280–1; *see also* treaties,
interpretation; TRIPS Agreement,
interpretation; WTO, authoritative
interpretation of WTO Agreements
jurisdiction 208, 210, **212–15**, 219, 287
Ministerial Conference 219, 256–7, 273–5,
276, 277–80, 283–4, 286, 288
moratorium on dispute settlement 263–4
non-violation complaints 42, **213–14**,
274–5
non-WTO law in WTO dispute settlement
207–29; *see also* WTO, human rights in
WTO dispute settlement
panels, *see* panels, WTO
sanctions, *see* trade sanctions
TRIPS Agreement, *see* TRIPS Agreement
waiver 218, 224, 260, 262, 264, **266–9**,
274–5, **278**, 279, 282–5